CRITICAL SURVEY
OF
SHORT FICTION

Fourth Edition

CRITICAL SURVEY
OF
SHORT FICTION
Fourth Edition

Volume 2
American Writers

Charles D'Ambrosio - Washington Irving

Editor
Charles E. May
California State University, Long Beach

SALEM PRESS
Ipswich, Massachusetts   Hackensack, New Jersey

Copyright © 1981, 1987, 1993, 2001, 2012, Salem Press, A Division of EBSCO Publishing, Inc.

Some of the essays in this work, which have been updated, originally appeared in the following Salem Press publications, *Critical Survey of Short Fiction* (1981); *Critical Survey of Short Fiction, Supplement* (1987); *Critical Survey of Short Fiction: Revised Edition*, (1993; preceding volumes edited by Frank N. Magill); *Critical Survey of Short Fiction Second Revised Edition* (2001; edited by Charles E. May).

The paper used in these volumes conforms to the American National Standard for Permanence of Paper for Printed Library Materials, X39.48-1992 (R1997).

LIBRARY OF CONGRESS CATALOGING-IN-PUBLICATION DATA

Critical survey of short fiction / editor, Charles E. May. -- 4th ed.
     p. cm.

Includes bibliographical references and index.
ISBN 978-1-58765-789-4 (set : alk. paper) -- ISBN 978-1-58765-790-0 (set, american : alk. paper) --
ISBN 978-1-58765-791-7 (vol. 1, american : alk. paper) -- ISBN 978-1-58765-792-4 (vol. 2, american : alk. paper) --
ISBN 978-1-58765-793-1 (vol. 3, american : alk. paper) -- ISBN 978-1-58765-794-8 (vol. 4, american : alk. paper) --
ISBN 978-1-58765-795-5 (set, british : alk. paper) -- ISBN 978-1-58765-796-2 (vol. 1, british : alk. paper) --
ISBN 978-1-58765-797-9 (vol. 2, british : alk. paper) -- ISBN 978-1-58765-798-6 (european : alk. paper) --
ISBN 978-1-58765-799-3 (world : alk. paper) -- ISBN 978-1-58765-800-6 (topical essays : alk. paper) --
ISBN 978-1-58765-803-7 (cumulative index : alk. paper)

1. Short story. 2. Short story--Bio-bibliography. I. May, Charles E. (Charles Edward), 1941-
PN3321.C7 2011
809.3'1--dc23

2011026000

First Printing

PRINTED IN THE UNITED STATES OF AMERICA

CONTENTS

Contributors vii
Key to Pronunciation xxi
D'Ambrosio, Charles 475
Danticat, Edwidge 478
Davenport, Guy 483
Davies, Peter Ho 494
Davis, Lydia 497
Delany, Samuel R. 501
Derleth, August 507
Díaz, Junot 513
Dick, Philip K. 516
Disch, Thomas M. 522
Divakaruni, Chitra Banerjee 526
Dixon, Stephen 531
Doctorow, E. L. 534
Doerr, Anthony 538
Doerr, Harriet 541
Dorris, Michael 545
Douglas, Ellen 550
Dreiser, Theodore 554
Dubus, Andre 559
Ducornet, Rikki 565
Dunbar, Paul Laurence 569
Dybek, Stuart 573
Earley, Tony 578
Eisenberg, Deborah 582
Elkin, Stanley 586
Elliott, George P. 591
Ellison, Harlan 597
Ellison, Ralph 604
Englander, Nathan 609
Erdrich, Louise 612
Evenson, Brian 617
Everett, Percival 621
Farrell, James T. 626
Faulkner, William 632
Fitzgerald, F. Scott 640
Ford, Richard 648

Fox, Paula 654
Franklin, Benjamin 658
Freeman, Mary E. Wilkins 664
Freudenberger, Nell 671
Friedman, Bruce Jay 675
Gaines, Ernest J. 681
Gaitskill, Mary 687
Gardner, John 691
Garland, Hamlin 698
Garrett, George 704
Gass, William H. 710
Gates, David 715
Gautreaux, Tim 719
Gay, William 723
Gilchrist, Ellen 727
Gilman, Charlotte Perkins 735
Glasgow, Ellen 739
Godwin, Gail 745
Gold, Herbert 749
Gordon, Caroline 753
Gordon, Mary 759
Goyen, William 763
Grau, Shirley Ann 767
Greenberg, Joanne 773
Grisham, John 778
Gurganus, Allan 782
Hagy, Alyson 787
Hale, Nancy 791
Hall, Lawrence Sargent 796
Hall, Martha Lacy 799
Hammett, Dashiell 803
Hannah, Barry 807
Hansen, Ron 812
Harjo, Joy 816
Harris, Joel Chandler 820
Harrison, Jim 826
Harte, Bret 833
Haslett, Adam 840

Hawthorne, Nathaniel 843

Heinlein, Robert A. 852

Helprin, Mark 858

Hemingway, Ernest 866

Hempel, Amy 875

Henríquez, Cristina 879

Henry, O. 882

Highsmith, Patricia 887

Himes, Chester 894

Hoch, Edward D. 900

Homes, A. M. 908

Houston, Pam 912

Howells, William Dean 915

Hughes, Langston 920

Humphrey, William 926

Hurston, Zora Neale 932

Irving, Washington 939

CONTRIBUTORS

Randy L. Abbott
University of Evansville

Michael Adams
CUNY Graduate Center

Patrick Adcock
Henderson State University

Thomas P. Adler
Purdue University

A. Owen Aldridge
University of Illinois

Charmaine Allmon-Mosby
Western Kentucky University

Emily Alward
College of Southern Nevada

Andrew J. Angyal
Elon University

Jacob M. Appel
The Mount Sinai Medical School

Gerald S. Argetsinger
Rochester Institute of Technology

Karen L. Arnold
Columbia, Maryland

Marilyn Arnold
Brigham Young University

Leonard R. N. Ashley
Brooklyn College, City University of New York

Bryan Aubrey
Fairfield, Iowa

Stephen Aubrey
Brooklyn College

Edmund August
McKendree College

Jane L. Ball
Wilberforce University

David Barratt
Montreat College

Melissa E. Barth
Appalachian State University

Martha Bayless
University of Oregon

Alvin K. Benson
Utah Valley University

Stephen Benz
Barry University

Margaret Boe Birns
New York University

Nicholas Birns
Eugene Lang College, The New School

Elizabeth Blakesley
Washington State University Libraries

Richard Bleiler
University of Connecticut

Lynn Z. Bloom
University of Connecticut

Julia B. Boken
Indiana University, Southeast

Jo-Ellen Lipman Boon
Buena Park, California

William Boyle
University of Mississippi

Virginia Brackett
Park University

Harold Branam
Savannah State University

Gerhard Brand
California State University, Los Angeles

Alan Brown
Livingston University

Mary Hanford Bruce
Monmouth College

Carl Brucker
Arkansas Tech University

John C. Buchanan
Original Contributor

Stefan Buchenberger
Kanagawa University

Louis J. Budd
Original Contributor

Rebecca R. Butler
Dalton College

Susan Butterworth
Salem State College

Edmund J. Campion
University of Tennessee, Knoxville

Larry A. Carlson
Original Contributor

Amee Carmines
Hampton University

Thomas Gregory Carpenter
Lipscomb University

John Carr
Original Contributor

Warren J. Carson
University of South Carolina, Spartanburg

Mary LeDonne Cassidy
South Carolina State University

Thomas J. Cassidy
South Carolina State University

Hal Charles
Eastern Kentucky University

C. L. Chua
California State University, Fresno

David W. Cole
University of Wisconsin Colleges

Laurie Coleman
Original Contributor

Richard Hauer Costa
Texas A&M University

Ailsa Cox
Edge Hill University

Lisa-Anne Culp
Nuclear Regulatory Commission

Heidi K. Czerwiec
Univeristy of North Dakota

Dolores A. D'Angelo
American University

Anita Price Davis
Converse College

Frank Day
Clemson University

Danielle A. DeFoe
Sierra College

Bill Delaney
San Diego, California

Joan DelFattore
University of Delaware

Kathryn Zabelle Derounian
University of Arkansas-Little Rock

Joseph Dewey
University of Pittsburgh

Marcia B. Dinneen
Bridgewater State University

Thomas Du Bose
Louisiana State University-Shreveport

Stefan Dziemianowicz
Bloomfield, New Jersey

Wilton Eckley
Colorado School of Mines

K Edgington
Towson University

Robert P. Ellis
Northborough Historical Society

Sonia Erlich
Lesley University

Thomas L. Erskine
Salisbury University

Christopher Estep
Original Contributor

Walter Evans
Augusta College

Jack Ewing
Boise, Idaho

Kevin Eyster
Madonna University

Nettie Farris
University of Louisville

Howard Faulkner
Original Contributor

James Feast
Baruch College

Thomas R. Feller
Nashville, Tennessee

John W. Fiero
*University of Louisiana
at Lafayette*

Edward Fiorelli
St. John's University

Rebecca Hendrick Flannagan
Rrancis Marion University

James K. Folsom
Original Contributor

Ben Forkner
Original Contributor

Joseph Francavilla
Columbus State University

Timothy C. Frazer
Western Illinois University

Kathy Ruth Frazier
Original Contributor

Tom Frazier
Cumberland College

Rachel E. Frier
Rockville, Maryland

Terri Frongia
Santa Rosa Junior College

Miriam Fuchs
University of Hawaii-Manoa

Jean C. Fulton
Landmark College

Louis Gallo
Radford University

Ann Davison Garbett
Averett University

Marshall Bruce Gentry
Georgia College & State University

Jill B. Gidmark
University of Minnesota

M. Carmen Gomez-Galisteo
*Esne-Universidad Camilo
Jose Cela*

Linda S. Gordon
Worcester State College

Julian Grajewski
Tuscon, Arizona

Charles A. Gramlich
Xavier University of Louisiana

James L. Green
Arizona State University

Glenda I. Griffin
Sam Houston State University

John L. Grigsby
*Appalachian Research & Defense
Fund of Kentucky, Inc.*

William E. Grim
Ohio University

Elsie Galbreath Haley
Metropolitan State College of Denver

David Mike Hamilton
Original Contributor

Katherine Hanley
*St. Bernard's School of Theology
and Ministry*

Michele Hardy
Prince George's Community College

Betsy Harfst
Kishwaukee College

Alan C. Haslam
Sierra College

CJ Hauser
Brooklyn College

Peter B. Heller
Manhattan College

Terry Heller
Coe College

Diane Andrews Henningfeld
Adrian College

DeWitt Henry
Emerson College

Cheryl Herr
Original Contributor

Allen Hibbard
Middle Tennessee State University

Cynthia Packard Hill
University of Massachusetts at Amherst

Jane Hill
Original Contributor

Nika Hoffman
Crossroads School for Arts & Sciences

William Hoffman
Fort Myers, Florida

Hal Holladay
Simon's Rock College of Bard

Kimberley M. Holloway
King College

Gregory D. Horn
Southwest Virginia Commmunity College

Sylvia Huete
Original Contributor

Edward Huffstetler
Bridgewater College

Theodore C. Humphrey
California State Polytechnic University, Pomona

Robert Jacobs
Central Washington University

Shakuntala Jayaswal
University of New Haven

Clarence O. Johnson
Joplin, Missouri

Eunice Pedersen Johnston
North Dakota State University

Theresa Kanoza
Lincoln Land Community College

William P. Keen
Washington & Jefferson College

Fiona Kelleghan
South Miami, Florida

Cassandra Kircher
Elon College

Paula Kopacz
Eastern Kentucky University

Uma Kukathas
Seattle, Washingtom

Rebecca Kuzins
Pasadena, California

Marvin Lachman
Santa Fe, New Mexico

Thomas D. Lane
Original Contributor

John Lang
Emory & Henry College

Carlota Larrea
Pennsylvania State University

Donald F. Larsson
Mankato State University

William Laskowski
Jamestown College

Norman Lavers
Arkansas State University

David Layton
*University of California,
Santa Barbar*

Allen Learst
Oklahome State University

James Ward Lee
University of North Texas

Katy L. Leedy
Marquette University

Leon Lewis
Appalachian State University

Elizabeth Johnston Lipscomb
*Randolph-Macon
Women's College*

Douglas Long
Pasadena, California

Michael Loudon
Eastern Illinois University

Robert M. Luscher
*University of Nebraska
at Kearney*

Carol J. Luther
*Pellissippi State Community
College*

R. C. Lutz
CII Group

Laurie Lykken
Century College

Andrew F. Macdonald
Loyola University

Joanne McCarthy
Tacoma Washington

Richard D. McGhee
Arkansas State University

S. Thomas Mack
University of South Carolina-Aiken

Victoria E. McLure
Texas Tech University

Robert J. McNutt
*University of Tennessee
at Chattanooga*

Bryant Mangum
Original Contributor

Barry Mann
Alliance Theatre

Mary E. Markland
Argosy University

Patricia Marks
Valdosta State College

Wythe Marschall
Brooklyn College

Karen M. Cleveland Marwick
*Hemel Hempstead,
Hertfordshire, England*

Charles E. May
*California State University,
Long Beach*

Laurence W. Mazzeno
Alvernia College

Patrick Meanor
SUNY College at Oneonta

Martha Meek
Original Contributor

Ann A. Merrill
Emory University

Robert W. Millett
Original Contributor

Christian H. Moe
*Southern Illinois University at
Carbondale*

Robert A. Morace
Daemen College

Christina Murphy
Original Contributor

Earl Paulus Murphy
Harris-Stowe State College

John M. Muste
Ohio State University

Donna B. Nalley
South University

Keith Neilson
California State University, Fullerton

Allen Shepherd
Original Contributor

Nancy E. Sherrod
Georgia Southern University

Thelma J. Shinn
Arizona State University

R. Baird Shuman
University of Illinois at Urbana-Champaign

Paul Siegrist
Fort Hays State University

Charles L. P. Silet
Iowa State University

Karin A. Silet
University of Wisconsin-Madison

Genevieve Slomski
New Britain, Connecticut

Roger Smith
Portland, Oregon

Ira Smolensky
Monmouth College

Katherine Snipes
Spokane, Washington

Sandra Whipple Spanier
Original Contributor

Brian Stableford
Reading, United Kingdom

John Stark
Original Contributor

Joshua Stein
Los Medanos College

Karen F. Stein
University of Rhode Island

Judith L. Steininger
Milwaukee School of Engineering

Ingo R. Stoehr
Kilgore College

Louise M. Stone
Bloomsburg University

William B. Stone
Chicago, Illinois

Theresa L. Stowell
Adrian College

Gerald H. Strauss
Bloomsburg University

Ryan D. Stryffeler
Western Nevada College

W. J. Stuckey
Purdue University

Catherine Swanson
Austin, Texas

Philip A. Tapley
Louisiana College

Terry Theodore
University of North Carolina at Wilmington

Maxine S. Theodoulou
The Union Institute

David J. Thieneman
Original Contributor

Lou Thompson
Texas Woman's University

Michael Trussler
University of Regina

Richard Tuerk
Texas A&M University-Commerce

Scott Vander Ploeg
Madisonville Community College

Dennis Vannatta
University of Arkansas at Little Rock

Jaquelyn W. Walsh
McNeese State University

Shawncey Webb
Taylor University

James Michael Welsh
Salisbury State University

James Whitlark
Texas Tech University

Barbara Wiedemann
Auburn University at Montgomery

COMPLETE LIST OF CONTENTS

American Volume 1

Publisher's Note vii

Contributors x

Complete List of Contents xix

Key to Pronunciation xxv

Abbott, Lee K. 1

Adams, Alice 5

Agee, James 10

Aiken, Conrad 14

Aldrich, Thomas Bailey 19

Alexie, Sherman 23

Algren, Nelson 28

Allen, Woody 31

Allison, Dorothy 37

Almond, Steve 41

Anderson, Sherwood 45

Angelou, Maya 52

Apple, Max 55

Asimov, Isaac 60

Auchincloss, Louis 67

Baldwin, James 77

Bambara, Toni Cade 83

Bank, Melissa 87

Banks, Russell 91

Banner, Keith 97

Baraka, Amiri 101

Barrett, Andrea 106

Barth, John 110

Barthelme, Donald 118

Barthelme, Frederick 126

Bass, Rick 130

Bausch, Richard 135

Baxter, Charles 140

Beattie, Ann 144

Bell, Madison Smartt 153

Bellow, Saul 157

Bender, Aimee 164

Benedict, Pinckney 168

Benét, Stephen Vincent 171

Berriault, Gina 177

Berry, Wendell 180

Betts, Doris 185

Bierce, Ambrose 190

Bloom, Amy 196

Bontemps, Arna 200

Boswell, Robert 204

Bowles, Jane 206

Bowles, Paul 212

Boyle, Kay 219

Boyle, T. Coraghessan 227

Bradbury, Ray 235

Brady, Catherine 246

Brautigan, Richard 250

Braverman, Kate 257

Brockmeier, Kevin 261

Brodkey, Harold 265

Brown, Jason 270

Brown, Larry 274

Broyard, Bliss 277

Buck, Pearl S. 281

Burke, James Lee 287

Busch, Frederick 291

Butler, Robert Olen 295

Byers, Michael 300

Bynum, Sarah Shun-Lien 303

Cable, George Washington 308

Cain, James M. 314

Caldwell, Erskine 318

Calisher, Hortense 323

Canin, Ethan 329

Caponegro, Mary 333

Capote, Truman 337

Card, Orson Scott 342

Carlson, Ron 349

Carr, John Dickson 353

Carver, Raymond 358

Cassill, R. V. 367

Cather, Willa 371
Chabon, Michael...............................377
Chandler, Raymond 384
Chang, Lan Samantha 390
Chaon, Dan 394
Chappell, Fred...................................398
Cheever, John....................................403
Cherry, Kelly 412
Chesnutt, Charles Waddell 416

Chopin, Kate 423
Cisneros, Sandra 428
Clark, Walter Van Tilburg 435
Connell, Evan S. 440
Conroy, Frank 446
Coover, Robert 450
Cozzens, James Gould 457
Crane, Stephen 462
Crone, Moira......................................471

American Volume 2

Contributors vii
Key to Pronunciation xxi
D'Ambrosio, Charles 475
Danticat, Edwidge...............................478
Davenport, Guy...................................483
Davies, Peter Ho 494
Davis, Lydia 497
Delany, Samuel R................................501
Derleth, August 507
Díaz, Junot 513
Dick, Philip K. 516
Disch, Thomas M. 522
Divakaruni, Chitra Banerjee 526
Dixon, Stephen....................................531
Doctorow, E. L. 534
Doerr, Anthony....................................538
Doerr, Harriet 541
Dorris, Michael 545
Douglas, Ellen.....................................550
Dreiser, Theodore 554
Dubus, Andre 559
Ducornet, Rikki 565
Dunbar, Paul Laurence.........................569
Dybek, Stuart 573
Earley, Tony 578
Eisenberg, Deborah..............................582
Elkin, Stanley 586
Elliott, George P. 591
Ellison, Harlan 597
Ellison, Ralph......................................604
Englander, Nathan................................609
Erdrich, Louise 612

Evenson, Brian....................................617
Everett, Percival 621
Farrell, James T. 626
Faulkner, William................................632
Fitzgerald, F. Scott 640
Ford, Richard 648
Fox, Paula 654
Franklin, Benjamin 658
Freeman, Mary E. Wilkins 664
Freudenberger, Nell..............................671
Friedman, Bruce Jay 675
Gaines, Ernest J. 681
Gaitskill, Mary 687
Gardner, John 691
Garland, Hamlin...................................698
Garrett, George 704
Gass, William H. 710
Gates, David..715
Gautreaux, Tim 719
Gay, William 723
Gilchrist, Ellen 727
Gilman, Charlotte Perkins.....................735
Glasgow, Ellen 739
Godwin, Gail.......................................745
Gold, Herbert 749
Gordon, Caroline 753
Gordon, Mary......................................759
Goyen, William....................................763
Grau, Shirley Ann 767
Greenberg, Joanne...............................773
Grisham, John 778
Gurganus, Allan 782

Hagy, Alyson 787
Hale, Nancy 791
Hall, Lawrence Sargent 796
Hall, Martha Lacy 799
Hammett, Dashiell 803
Hannah, Barry 807
Hansen, Ron 812
Harjo, Joy 816
Harris, Joel Chandler 820
Harrison, Jim 826
Harte, Bret 833
Haslett, Adam 840
Hawthorne, Nathaniel 843
Heinlein, Robert A. 852
Helprin, Mark 858

Hemingway, Ernest 866
Hempel, Amy 875
Henríquez, Cristina 879
Henry, O. 882
Highsmith, Patricia 887
Himes, Chester 894
Hoch, Edward D. 900
Homes, A. M. 908
Houston, Pam 912
Howells, William Dean 915
Hughes, Langston 920
Humphrey, William 926
Hurston, Zora Neale 932
Irving, Washington 939

American Volume 3

Contributors vii
Key to Pronunciation xxi
Jackson, Shirley 947
James, Henry 953
Jewett, Sarah Orne 962
Johnson, Adam 968
Johnson, Charles 972
Johnson, Denis 977
Johnston, Bret Anthony 982
Jones, Edward P. 986
Jones, Thom 990
Kaplan, David Michael 994
Keillor, Garrison 997
Kincaid, Jamaica 1004
King, Stephen 1010
Kingsolver, Barbara 1019
Kingston, Maxine Hong 1023
Knowles, John 1027
Lahiri, Jhumpa 1033
Lardner, Ring 1038
Leavitt, David 1042
Lee, Andrea 1050
Leegant, Joan 1054
Le Guin, Ursula K. 1058
Lennon, J. Robert 1065
Lethem, Jonathan 1069
L'Heureux, John 1074

Li, Yiyun 1078
London, Jack 1082
Longstreet, Augustus Baldwin 1087
Lopez, Barry 1092
Lordan, Beth 1096
Lott, Bret 1100
Lovecraft, H. P. 1103
Major, Clarence 1110
Malamud, Bernard 1114
Marshall, Paule 1122
Mason, Bobbie Ann 1128
McCarthy, Mary 1135
McCorkle, Jill 1141
McCullers, Carson 1145
McGuane, Thomas 1152
McKnight, Reginald 1156
McPherson, James Alan 1160
Means, David 1165
Meloy, Maile 1169
Melville, Herman 1173
Michaels, Leonard 1180
Miller, Sue 1183
Millhauser, Steven 1187
Minot, Susan 1192
Moody, Rick 1196
Moore, Lorrie 1200
Morris, Wright 1204

Mosley, Walter 1210
Nabokov, Vladimir 1215
Nelson, Antonya 1223
Norman, Gurney 1227
Norris, Frank 1231
Nugent, Beth 1237
Oates, Joyce Carol 1241
O'Brien, Tim 1252
O'Connor, Flannery 1256
Offutt, Chris 1265
O'Hara, John 1269
Olsen, Tillie 1275
Orringer, Julie 1280
Ortiz Cofer, Judith 1284
Ozick, Cynthia 1288
Packer, ZZ 1295
Paine, Tom 1299
Paley, Grace 1302
Pancake, Breece D'J 1308
Parker, Dorothy 1312
Pearlman, Edith 1316
Peck, Dale 1320
Perabo, Susan 1324
Perelman, S. J. 1327

Petry, Ann 1332
Phillips, Jayne Anne 1339
Plath, Sylvia 1343
Poe, Edgar Allan 1347
Pollock, Donald Ray 1356
Porter, Katherine Anne 1360
Powell, Padgett 1368
Powers, J. F. 1372
Price, Reynolds 1376
Prose, Francine 1383
Proulx, E. Annie 1387
Purdy, James 1393
Pynchon, Thomas 1401
Queen, Ellery 1408
Rash, Ron 1415
Reid, Elwood 1419
Richard, Mark 1422
Rivera, Tomás 1426
Roberts, Elizabeth Madox 1430
Robinson, Roxana 1433
Robison, Mary 1437
Roth, Philip 1445
Russo, Richard 1451

American Volume 4

Contributors vii
Key to Pronunciation xxi
Salinger, J. D. 1455
Salter, James 1462
Saroyan, William 1466
Saunders, George 1471
Sayles, John 1475
Schwartz, Delmore 1479
Schwartz, Lynne Sharon 1484
Shacochis, Bob 1488
Shaw, Irwin 1491
Shepard, Sam 1495
Silko, Leslie Marmon 1499
Silver, Marisa 1507
Simms, William Gilmore 1510
Simpson, Helen 1517
Simpson, Mona 1521
Slavin, Julia 1525

Smiley, Jane 1528
Smith, Lee 1535
Sontag, Susan 1541
Spencer, Elizabeth 1545
Stafford, Jean 1551
Steele, Wilbur Daniel 1556
Stegner, Wallace 1559
Stein, Gertrude 1564
Steinbeck, John 1573
Stern, Richard G. 1579
Still, James 1585
Stockton, Frank R. 1589
Stone, Robert 1593
Straight, Susan 1597
Strout, Elizabeth 1602
Stuart, Jesse 1606
Sturgeon, Theodore 1612
Tallent, Elizabeth 1618

Tan, Amy 1621
Targan, Barry 1625
Taylor, Peter 1629
Thompson, Jean 1635
Thurber, James 1637
Tilghman, Christopher 1642
Toomer, Jean 1646
Tower, Wells 1652
Twain, Mark 1656
Tyler, Anne 1662
Updike, John 1668
Viramontes, Helena María 1680
Vizenor, Gerald R. 1683
Vonnegut, Kurt 1688
Walbert, Kate 1697
Walker, Alice 1701
Wallace, David Foster 1711
Warren, Robert Penn 1715
Waters, Mary Yukari 1721
Weidman, Jerome 1725
Welty, Eudora 1729
Wescott, Glenway 1737

West, Jessamyn 1743
Wharton, Edith 1748
White, E. B. 1755
Wideman, John Edgar 1759
Wiggins, Marianne 1767
Williams, Joy 1771
Williams, Tennessee 1776
Williams, William Carlos 1783
Woiwode, Larry 1788
Wolfe, Thomas 1793
Wolff, Tobias 1799
Wright, Richard 1805
Yoon, Paul 1811
Terms and Techniques 1817
Bibliography 1831
Guide to Online Resources 1858
Timeline 1862
Major Awards 1867
Chronological List of Writers 1933
Categorical Index 1941
Subject Index 1960

KEY TO PRONUNCIATION

To help users of the *Critical Survey of Short Fiction* pronounce unfamiliar names of profiled writers correctly, phonetic spellings using the character symbols listed below appear in parentheses immediately after the first mention of the writer's name in the narrative text. Stressed syllables are indicated in capital letters, and syllables are separated by hyphens.

VOWEL SOUNDS
Symbol: Spelled (Pronounced)

a: answer (AN-suhr), laugh (laf), sample (SAM-puhl), that (that)

ah: father (FAH-thur), hospital (HAHS-pih-tuhl)

aw: awful (AW-fuhl), caught (kawt)

ay: blaze (blayz), fade (fayd), waiter (WAYT-ur), weigh (way)

eh: bed (behd), head (hehd), said (sehd)

ee: believe (bee-LEEV), cedar (SEE-dur), leader (LEED-ur), liter (LEE-tur)

ew: boot (bewt), lose (lewz)

i: buy (bi), height (hit), lie (li), surprise (sur-PRIZ)

ih: bitter (BIH-tur), pill (pihl)

o: cotton (KO-tuhn), hot (hot)

oh: below (bee-LOH), coat (koht), note (noht), wholesome (HOHL-suhm)

oo: good (good), look (look)

ow: couch (kowch), how (how)

oy: boy (boy), coin (koyn)

uh: about (uh-BOWT), butter (BUH-tuhr), enough (ee-NUHF), other (UH-thur)

CONSONANT SOUNDS
Symbol: Spelled (Pronounced)

ch: beach (beech), chimp (chihmp)

g: beg (behg), disguise (dihs-GIZ), get (geht)

j: digit (DIH-juht), edge (ehj), jet (jeht)

k: cat (kat), kitten (KIH-tuhn), hex (hehks)

s: cellar (SEHL-ur), save (sayv), scent (sehnt)

sh: champagne (sham-PAYN), issue (IH-shew), shop (shop)

ur: birth (burth), disturb (dihs-TURB), earth (urth), letter (LEH-tur)

y: useful (YEWS-fuhl), young (yuhng)

z: business (BIHZ-nehs), zest (zehst)

zh: vision (VIH-zhuhn)

CRITICAL SURVEY
OF
SHORT FICTION

Fourth Edition

D

CHARLES D'AMBROSIO

Born: Seattle, Washington; 1958

PRINCIPAL SHORT FICTION
The Point, 1995
The Dead Fish Museum, 2006

OTHER LITERARY FORMS

Charles D'Ambrosio (dam-BROH-see-oh) published a collection of essays entitled *Orphans* in 2004, which included essays on his brother's suicide, Mary Kay Letourneau (a teacher who had an affair with her student), whaling rights for the Makahs in Alaska, and life in a Russian orphanage.

ACHIEVEMENTS

Charles D'Ambrosio received a Humanities Fellowship from the University of Chicago for work on a Ph.D. in English, a National Endowment for the Arts grant, a James Michener Fellowship, a Whiting Writers Award in 2006, a U.S.A. Rasmuson Fellowship in 2007, and a Lannan Foundation Fellowship in 2008. He has won a Pushcart Prize, the Aga Khan Fiction Prize, and the Henfield/Trans-Atlantic Review Award, and he has been a finalist for the PEN/Hemingway Award and the National Magazine Award. His story "The Point" was chosen for *Best American Short Stories* in 1991; "Screenwriter" appeared in *Best American Short Stories* in 2004; and "The High Divide" was selected for *The O. Henry Prize Stories* in 2005. His collection *The Point* was a *New York Times* Notable Book for 1995. His book of stories *The Dead Fish Museum* won the Washington State Book Award for fiction in 2007 and also was a finalist for the PEN/Faulkner Award.

BIOGRAPHY

Charles D'Ambrosio was born and raised in a family of seven children in Seattle, Washington. His father taught business finance at the University of Washington, where D'Ambrosio began his college education. He then transferred to Oberlin College in Ohio, from which he received a B.A. degree in 1982. He was a Humanities Fellow at the University of Chicago, where he worked toward a Ph.D. in English, but he became disillusioned that, in graduate school, literature was treated as a kind of business and dropped out of the program. He did construction work in New York and wrote journalistic pieces. He said at this time he began to read not as an academic but as a writer--to see how sentences worked and how writers tried to get emotion into prose. He began writing fiction and applied to the Iowa Writers' Workshop at the University of Iowa, from which he received an M.F.A. in 1991. Since then he has been a visiting faculty member at Iowa and has taught at the Tin House Summer Writers Workshop and the Warren Wilson M.F.A. program for writers. D'Ambrosio has been the William Kittredge Visiting Writer at the University of Montana in Missoula. He settled in Portland, Oregon.

ANALYSIS

Charles D'Ambrosio has said many times in interviews that short stories are like a song, and that he works a long time to get the sound just right. Until he does get the sentence-by-sentence sound right, he cannot go forward in the story; the sound contains a substantial part of the narrative. He has argued that short stories, like songs, have an associated feel: Readers can return to stories they have read many times and get the same kind of feeling they get from listening to an oldies song with which they are very familiar but love to hear over and over again. In a great short story, D'Ambrosio has suggested, just as in a great song, one almost does not need the lyrics. In his short stories, he feels the lives of his characters experience a sort of desperation, and he longs for those lives to come together.

"THE POINT"

This story is told from the point of view of Kurt, a precocious thirteen-year-old boy who found his father's body in the family car after the father shot himself in the head. Since that time, his mother has taken to throwing wild drunken parties, largely for women friends who struggle with unhappy lives and relationships. The boy's job, since he turned ten years old, has been to escort the most drunken of the women at the party home, for which he usually receives a few dollars. "I guess it's better than a paper route," he says laconically. He knows all the gossip of his mother's friends, their falling fortunes and marital discords. However, he has developed a priestly sense of his position, keeping everything he hears to himself.

When he tries to get Mrs. Gurney, a thirty-six year-old woman whose husband does not love her, up the beach to her home, she drunkenly takes off her blouse and bra and half-heartedly tries to seduce him. She feels sorry for herself, cries, and threatens to commit suicide, but finally allows the boy to get her home and in bed. When Kurt returns home, the party is in its final

Charles D'Ambrosio (Writer Pictures/Edouard Smekens via AP Images)

stages, and he sits on a swing in the yard and thinks about his father, who earned a Silver Star and a Purple Heart while serving as a medic in Vietnam. He reads a long letter his father sent his mother, which Kurt has stolen from a box under her bed. "The Point" ends with a long paragraph describing Kurt's discovery of his father, who blew half his face away with a shotgun. Coming at the end of what has been a comic struggle with a drunken woman, the graphic description of the still-quivering body of his dying father comes as a shock that makes the reader reflect back on the boy's trauma and how he has been forced to take on a caretaker role of his mother and her drunken friends.

"HER REAL NAME"

A former sailor named Jones takes up with an unnamed eighteen-year-old girl at a service station in Illinois, and they drive west together, spending his discharge money. At one point, Jones sees the girl without her wig and discovers that she has incurable cancer. Although the girl fears he will send her home to her fundamentalist stepfather, who believes the rapture of Judgment Day is near at hand, Jones sympathetically becomes bound to her and her needs.

Jones gets the young woman to a doctor, an alcoholic named McKillop, who has lost his medical license for prescribing drugs for himself. The doctor knows the girl is dying but gives them morphine and sends them to see another doctor just outside of Seattle. The girl becomes weaker, her limbs growing skeletal and fleshless, as she gradually seems to disappear. Her death hardly is mentioned. In the final section of the story, Jones takes her to the coast of Washington, through the Makah Indian Reservation. He finds a small boat and takes her body out into the shipping lanes. In a formal, ritualized fashion, Jones lets slip into the sea the sleeping bag with the girl's body. What makes D'Ambrosio a great short-story writer is his sympathy for the frailty of the self, his respect for the delicacy of story structure, and his reverence for the precision of language. The conclusion of "Her Real Name" is a poetic burial song for a young woman who has, at the end of her life, finally found someone who loves her.

THE DEAD FISH MUSEUM

D'Ambrosio's contributor's notes in *Best Short Stories* and *The O. Henry Prize Stories*, where three of the stories in his second collection have appeared, reveal his respect for his characters and the integrity of his work. He describes how he struggled with sympathy for the two drifters in "The Scheme of Things," how "Screenwriter" developed slowly over the years from his experience with several wounded people, and how the sentences of "The High Divide" finally became "healthy and true" only after 116 drafts. The fish in the title of the collection, which refers to a refrigerator, is suggestive of Christ, faith, and miracles, D'Ambrosio has said. Telling an interviewer he was obsessed with questions of faith and doubt during the writing of the stories in *The Fish Museum*, D'Ambrosio said he intended the word "museum" to suggest the current sense of the "God is dead" world.

Two stories-- "The High Divide" and "Drummond and Son"--are about the delicate division between fathers and sons. The first one is about two boys trying to come to terms with the inexplicability of fathers, and the second one is about a man trying to care for a son suffering from a neurological disorder brought on by the drugs he takes for schizophrenia. D'Ambrosio has said that it took twelve years to write "The High Divide," because it originally was "animated by hatred," and hatred does not have a shape. When he changed the story and made it more loving, it began to take on its present form. In his comments on the story in the 2005 *O. Henry Prize Stories* collection, D'Ambrosio argues that anger is endless, and the "deepest urge of love is toward completion."

D'Ambrosio said that he particularly likes "Drummond and Son"--in which the central character spends a day with his twenty-five-year-old schizophrenic son, as they wait for a social worker to come to evaluate the young man--because of its traditional structure. While many of the stories in *The Dead Fish Museum* test narrative boundaries, D'Ambrosio is fond of this story because it is straightforward. The complexity of the story, according to D'Ambrosio, lies in the language and images. He got the idea for the story when he walked into a typewriter repair shop in Seattle one day and saw a whole wall full of refurbished machines filled with blank pieces of paper, which waved back and forth when he opened the door. At that moment, he felt that the imagery of the machines and the paper--a writer's nightmare--might work in a story.

D'Ambrosio has said that each of the stories in this collection was constructed to lead up to a moment when love could be presented without sentimentality or irony. Rigorously unsentimental, yet absolutely heart wrenching in their consummately controlled language, D'Ambrosio's stories have the ability to leave the reader stunned with love and marveling at the concluding images of echoes reverberating out of darkness and reflections staring back out of mist.

"Screenwriter" is a combination of the comic coping language of a skilled writer suffering in a psychiatric ward with suicidal obsessions and frighteningly beautiful images of a ballerina who burns herself. From the first time she ignites her paper gown and seems to levitate, phoenixlike, in flames to the final excruciating assault she makes on her body with a cigarette, the screenwriter narrator is unable to take his eyes off her. When he tells her he would like to crawl into her mouth and die, she says her mouth is full of dead boys and blows him a communal kiss that elevates the moment out of space and time.

The title story is about a man energized by his desire to kill himself. Supervising carpentry on the filming of a pornographic film in the desert, he becomes involved with his Hispanic crew and the film's female star, all of whom save him, at least for a time. The title comes from a Spanish woman's inability to pronounce "refrigerator," calling it instead "the dead fish museum." It is a sardonic name for a book filled with painfully alive characters.

The final story, "The Bone Game," is about a young man, who, while looking for a place to scatter his grandfather's ashes, ends up on a reservation playing a guessing game with an Indian woman by the shores of a salmon graveyard, littered with the bodies of the dead and dying, all of whom have failed in their primal quest to return to their origin. D'Ambrosio is a great short-story writer because he compellingly confronts the inexplicable mysteries of what it means to be a human being--mysteries that cannot be solved, only gaped at with awe--and because he honestly struggles with the way language tries to capture those mysteries.

OTHER MAJOR WORKS
NONFICTION: *Orphans*, 2004

BIBLIOGRAPHY

Donahue, Peter. "The Point." *Studies in Short Fiction* 33 (Summer, 1996): 430-432. Donahue discusses the importance of context in the story "The Point" and the surrealistic effect of the story "Her Real Name." He addresses D'Ambrosio's understanding of adolescence and the efforts of young adults to get by and the complications that drinking creates for his characters.

Knezovich, Stephen, and Pete Sheehy. "A Conversation with Charles D'Ambrosio." *Willow Springs* (Spring, 2007): 80-99. D'Ambrosio talks about several stories in *The Dead Fish Museum*. He discusses how he spends a great deal of time trying to get the right sound--a kind of music he hears in his head that he wants to match on the page. Form is the central problem of the short story, how to capture density in a limited space. D'Ambrosio also addresses the issue of the West and its influence on his work.

O'Rourke, Megan. "The Man's Guide to Hunting and Fishing." *The New York Times Book Review*, May 21, 2006, p. 10. O'Rourke says that D'Ambrosio's tight control sometimes contrasts effectively with his subject matter, particularly when his stories deal with schizophrenia. However, sometimes the writer keeps his work under too tight a wrap in favor of measured prose or the clipped, hypermasculine style of much American realism since Ernest Hemingway.

Charles E. May

EDWIDGE DANTICAT

Born: Port-au-Prince, Haiti; January 19, 1969

PRINCIPAL SHORT FICTION

Krik? Krak!, 1995
The Dew Breaker, 2004
"Reading Lessons," 2005
"Ghosts," 2008

OTHER LITERARY FORMS

Edwidge Danticat (ehd-WEEZH DAN-tih-ka) has published a range of long fiction and nonfiction texts. Her novels include *The Farming of Bones* (1998). Her nonfiction works include *Brother, I'm Dying* (2007), part novelistic memoir and part social criticism, and *After the Dance: A Walk Through Carnival in Jacmel, Haiti* (2002), part memoir and part travel book. She has written novels for young readers, such as *Anacaona, Golden Flower, Haiti* (2005) and *Behind the Mountains* (2002). She also has edited collections of works, notably *The Butterfly's Way: Voices from the Haitian Dyaspora in the United States* (2001).

ACHIEVEMENTS

Since her early success with engaging stories that often take on serious issues, Edwidge Danticat has emerged as one of the most powerful voices for Haiti, advocating in her fiction, nonfiction, and speeches for Haitians who live in their impoverished homeland and those who live in diaspora in the United States and elsewhere.

Danticat started writing at a young age, and her work won critical acclaim and wide public interest early. For example, *Breath, Eyes, Memories* (1994), her first book publication, won the 1996 Best Young American Novelists award by *Granta* and was selected for Oprah's Book Club in May, 1998. Her collection of short stories, *Krik? Krak!,* was a finalist for the 1996 National Book Award. She was awarded the 1999 National Book Award for her novel *The Farming of Bones* (1998). She won several prizes for *Brother, I'm Dying,* and she received the 2009 MacArthur Foundation "genius" grant.

BIOGRAPHY

Edwidge Danticat is a good example of an author whose personal experiences and literary work interweave in obvious ways. Born in Haiti in 1969, she was two years old when her father André immigrated to the United States and four years old when her mother Rose followed him. While her father and mother worked in New York as a cabdriver and textile worker, respectively, Danticat (and her brother) stayed behind in Haiti with her aunt and uncle until she was twelve years old. Her frequent trips to Haiti and her childhood there give Danticat direct access to one of the two major subject matters for her writing: life in Haiti.

In 1981, her parents brought Danticat to live with them in a heavily Haitian American neighborhood in Brooklyn, New York. This experience provides the second major subject matter for Danticat's writing: life in the immigrant diaspora. Having been taught French in school in Haiti and having spoken Kreyol at her aunt and uncle's house, Danticat had to adjust not only to a new home and school but also to a new language and culture. While she felt the challenges keenly, she also was provided with opportunities to rise to these challenges. For example, an African American history class, which she attended with fellow immigrants at Clara Barton High School in Brooklyn, provided her with a feeling of how literature can help to work through one's experiences. Having started to write at nine in Haiti, in the United States she soon turned to English for writing, a source of healing for her, and for publishing.

After high school, Danticat first received a bachelor's degree in French literature from Barnard College in 1990 and then in 1993 a master's degree in fine arts (in creative writing) from Brown University. The reworking of her migration story into fiction flowed into her master's thesis, "My Turn in the Fire," which she turned into her first book publication, *Breath, Eyes, Memory*. Danticat taught creative writing at New York University and at the University of Miami. Her husband owns a translation business, and they have a daughter.

ANALYSIS

Edwidge Danticat's writing is marked by a realism whose eloquent style may be called "luminous," shining with clarity and shedding light on the harsh and unsettling realities of Haitian life at home and in exile. Most of her stories deal with trauma of some sort: death

Edwidge Danticat (AP Photo/Wilfredo Lee)

or life at risk, either literally (in "Children of the Sea," the refugees in the boat all drown) or figuratively (in "Caroline's Wedding," the mother tries to hold on to tradition as she fears the loss of her Haitian cultural identity in her new life in the United States).

Danticat's stories may also be called "haunting" and "transformative." Danticat claims that it is impossible for her to write happy stories; instead, she faces disturbing realities until her way of storytelling has made these realities more bearable. This infuses the stories with a sense of hope, to the extent that even the most melancholy tale does not let readers down emotionally but rather leaves them with a feeling of empowerment.

Experiences that resonate with Danticat's life are the general themes of her texts. In addition to the two main subject matters of life in Haiti and the immigrant experience, sexuality and gender issues are central themes. Moreover, history beyond the author's own lifetime plays a role, stretching into Haiti's past, which Danticat has researched. These themes place her writing in the context of postcolonialism and feminism. She pays close attention to the mother-daughter bond; however, she also examines the role of fathers and father figures with sympathy (in her own father's and uncle's stories in *Brother, I'm Dying*) and with critical distance (in *The Dew Breaker*).

Images and minor themes are also extremely important because they add to the particular texture of Danticat's stories. Death, butterflies, and flying are often pointed out as recurring images. The landscape itself is symbolic: The Haitian capital city of Port-au-Prince often stands for the threat of political violence, while the relative safety of the countryside evokes Eden. Other themes include the radio, magic, food, and education. In a country with a 70 percent illiteracy rate, the radio plays an immeasurable role in everyday life. In some stories, such as "Children of the Sea" and "Ghosts," the radio is also the location where young people seek to effect social change and where the government tries to assert its control. Magic, often linked to Voodoo practices, shows up as superstition; for example, the imprisoned women in "Nineteen Thirty-Seven" are described as victims of oppression, while it is clear that they are believed to be witches by the prison guards. The mother in "Caroline's Wedding" believes that her "strong bone soup" will cure everything, combining the themes of magic and food. Food is important as sustenance and as communal experience. In "Caroline's Wedding," the daughter's Bahamian fiancé fails to win over his future mother-in-law because he does not serve the right (that is, Haitian) food. Education is valued highly both in the life of immigrants, who try to learn their new language and culture (as in "The Funeral Singer"), and in the life of the poor in Haiti, who try to escape their dire situation and whose poverty forces them, after nightfall, to study under streetlights (as in "A Wall of Fire Rising").

KRIK? KRAK!

Danticat clearly wants her audience to understand the meaning of the title; she explains it on three separate occasions in the collection. The sequence of the question "Krik?" and the answer "Krak!" is the formulaic interaction that establishes a sense of community between the traditional storyteller and her audience: The question of whether the audience is ready to listen to the story is answered with an expression of the willingness to listen to the story. By extension, it may be speculated that Danticat wishes to involve her audience more directly and actively by entering into such a communal realm of oral storytelling.

The nine stories of this collection form a short-story cycle in which each story is self-contained and, at the same time, relates to the other stories, not only with Danticat's two major subject matters (oppressed life in Haiti and immigration) but also with other connections. This way, the meaning of each individual story is as important as the incredibly rich cohesion among all stories.

The collection's fifth story, "Between the Pool and the Gardenias," literally occupies the central position. Marie has had several miscarriages but is desperate to be a mother. When she finds an abandoned baby girl, she pretends that this baby is hers, although it is already dead. After hiding the dead baby, she is found out and suspected of having killed the baby. In two short passages, this story also casts a net of possible connections over several stories.

Marie names the baby Rose--the name of Danticat's mother--and also remembers all the names she wanted to give her own babies. Five of these six names are also the names of characters in other stories: Josephine is a woman who accepts her mother's legacy with the help of an older woman, Jacqueline, in "Nineteen Thirty-Seven"; Hermine is the name of an aunt who is briefly mentioned in "New York Day Women"; Marie Magdalène is the dead mother's name that the daughter decides to assume--to assert her own identity in accepting her mother's death in childbirth--in the beautiful story "The Missing Peace"; Célianne is a young mother who commits suicide in "Children of the Sea." These meanings appear fluid because there is no certainty that these suggested identities hold; nevertheless, they evoke a haunting and underlying sense of human connection. In the same way, it is no coincidence that these are all names of women. Danticat's storytelling often explores female traditions; in the collection's "Epilogue," she speaks of "nam[ing] each braid after those 999 women who were boiling in your blood." Evoking the names of a few of these 999 women, Marie's story emerges in the sense of a text and texture that, like a "braid," is woven to provide cohesion.

Other female names in Marie's story suggest family relations that are also part of the narrative relationship. Eveline, the sixth name in Marie's list, is identified within the same story as the name of Marie's great-grandmother. In addition, Marie names Défilé as her grandmother, whom Josephine in "Nineteen Thirty-Seven" refers to as great-great-great-grandmother; however, the short description of Défilé's death in prison and with a shaved head suggests that the name of Josephine's unnamed mother is also Défilé. This connection seems a strong probability because of the specific details, which still refer to a common fate of prisoners suspected to be witches. The circumstances of Marie's godmother Lili, however, are so specific that the identity with the mother and wife in "A Wall of Fire Rising" seems beyond doubt. In "A Wall of Fire Rising," Lili's husband Guy jumps to his death from a hot-air balloon, in a desperate act of claiming agency in a life without prospects, counteracted by the high-spirited revolutionary speeches the young son is rehearsing for a school play.

Varying the tale of star-crossed lovers, "Children of the Sea" is the collection's first story, which consists of alternating passages: a young man's letters written in his notebook and a young woman's thoughts addressed to the young man. However, they are never able to share these passages. The young man is on a boat with other refugees. As their situation at sea becomes more dire, with the boat drawing water, Célianne, a female refugee who had been raped by several soldiers, gives birth to a stillborn daughter and, after a while, throws the baby into the sea and jumps after her. They become the titular children of the sea, who the man fears will soon be coming after him. Indeed, the story ends with the young woman fearing that the capsized boat she heard about on the radio is the one her lover was on. This is a harrowing story that gains even more political depth as the story reveals that the young man had to flee Haiti because he had a radio show that was critical of the government. The young woman writes from the relative safety of Ville Rose, a village in the countryside, to where the father made the family flee.

"Nineteen Thirty-Seven" is a brilliant story that has a horrific background and at the same time an uplifting ending. The background is the massacre of 1937, when General Rafael Trujillo, the dictator of the Dominican Republic, had the Haitians who lived in his country murdered (a historical event that Danticat also explores in her novel *The Farming of Bones*). The story weaves together fear of superstition and female self-determination. Josephine was born on the night of the massacre. For many years, the mother journeys with her daughter to commemorate the massacre at the river. Years later, her mother suffers a fate endured by many women in a society "ruled" by a dictator and by superstition. Denounced by others for having caused the death of a loved one, these women are imprisoned for being witches, who were also believed to be able to fly. With the help of Jacqueline, an older woman, Josephine is able to deal with her mother's death in prison and to realize that her mother once did fly--that is, she possessed the exceptional will to make it across the border river to give birth to Josephine.

The fourth story, "Night Women," and the eighth story, "New York Day Women," mirror each other. In the first story, the mother is a prostitute in Haiti and worries about her young son's well-being, hoping he will be asleep when her clients arrive; in the other, a daughter in New York happens to spy on her mother's daytime activity (caring for a young boy in the park while his mother is jogging). Both stories reveal the bond and the gap, which may be heightened by the immigrant experience, between the generations when the next generation develops its own identity. Both stories also show that Danticat's characters are often types--for example, "night women" or "day women--but enriched as an exemplar of a type with specific, individual traits.

THE DEW BREAKER

This book is usually referred to as a "novel-in-stories," and as such it is reviewed with longer fiction. However, the case could be made that it is a short-story cycle: Stories from the book are anthologized individually, and "The Dew Breaker" received The Story Prize in 2005. In either case, the genre designation clearly points to a certain hybridity. Some stories only loosely fit into the book's framework; in contrast, other stories are so closely related that, while each can be read on its own, each informs the others and thus adds layers of deeper meaning. This is particularly clear with the two stories that bookend the work.

In the first of the nine stories, "The Book of the Dead," the adult daughter Ka finds out that her beloved father was not a prisoner in Haiti but, on the contrary, a torturer--or "dew breaker"--for the infamous Tonton Macoutes, the militia of the François Duvalier regime. Leading a new life as a barber and landlord in New York, the father cannot shake his past and finally confesses the truth to his daughter while they are on a trip to Florida to deliver a sculpture she made of him. Afraid that someone might recognize his true identity, he destroys the sculpture and feels the need to explain himself to his daughter.

The book never resolves the conflicts resulting from this confession, because the following stories deal with events the precede the trip to Florida. Some stories depict episodes in the lives of Eric, Dany, and Michel, the three tenants in the former dew breaker's house. The story of Dany is the only one that relates to the activities of the former dew breaker because Dany believes he has recognized the killer of his parents in his landlord. Dany travels to Haiti to ask his aunt for advice; however, she dies during his visit--perhaps so that Dany can come to terms with his parents' violent deaths by witnessing a peaceful death.

The last story, "The Dew Breaker," relates the events that led the dew breaker to start a new life. After he botches his mission in 1967, he kills a brave priest after the latter attacked and scarred him. Leaving the compound, the dew breaker runs into a half-crazed woman he does not know. This woman is Anne, the priest's half-sister; she takes care of the dew breaker, leaves with him to live in New York, and has a daughter with him.

These stories are woven together by the incredible trauma of politically motivated violence. The collection casts a much wider net than the dew breaker's family and his renters. In "The Bridal Seamstress," the retiring seamstress is haunted by her belief that her torturer--who may or may not be the dew breaker who has become a barber--is still after her, living in empty houses to better spy on her. In "The Book of Miracles," Anne, who is very religious, takes her family to a Christmas Eve Mass. During the service, her daughter believes that she recognizes a fugitive Haitian war criminal. Anne assures Ka that it is a different man, but Anne also understands the ironic situation that her own husband is such a war criminal--one of many.

"READING LESSONS" AND "GHOSTS"

It has been estimated that more than twenty-five periodicals have published Danticat's short stories. For literature, *The New Yorker* is one of the most important weekly magazines in wide circulation (and one of the most accessible ones because of its online archive). Printed in *The New Yorker*, "Reading Lessons" deals with the immigrant experience in the United States, and "Ghosts" is set Haiti.

"Reading Lessons" is about a few lessons that life teaches Danielle, a teacher, as she tries to cope with the behavior of her regular students and some of their Haitian immigrant mothers, to whom she has just started to teach English. "Ghosts" is a gripping story about Pascal Dorien, a young man who has an idea for a radio program in which his neighborhood's gang members, who are "called chimès--chimeras, or ghosts," would be given a voice. His project never materializes; instead, one of the ghosts gives Pascal a harrowing reality check in what life is like for them when Pascal is unexpectedly arrested and later, just as suddenly, released.

OTHER MAJOR WORKS

LONG FICTION: *The Farming of Bones*, 1998;.

NONFICTION: *After the Dance: A Walk Through Carnival in Jacmel, Haiti*, 2002; *Brother, I'm Dying*, 2007.

CHILDREN'S LITERATURE: *Breath, Eyes, Memory*, 1994; *Behind the Mountains*, 2002; *Anacaona, Golden Flower, Haiti*, 2005.

EDITED TEXTS: *The Butterfly's Way: Voices from the Haitian Dyaspora in the United States*, 2001; *The Beacon Best of 2000: Great Writing by Men and Women of All Colors and Cultures*, 2001.

BIBLIOGRAPHY

Danticat, Edwidge. "The Dangerous Job of Edwidge Danticat: An Interview." Interview by Renee H. Shea. *Callaloo* 19, no. 2 (1996): 382-389. Danticat discusses her attraction to the theme of the relationship between mothers and daughters.

_____. "My Turn in the Fire: A Conversation with Edwidge Danticat." Interview by Sandy Alexandre and Ravi Y. Howard. *Journal of Caribbean Literatures* 4, no. 3 (2007): 161-174. Danticat talks about her reading and her writing process.

Davis, Ricio G. "Oral Narrative as Short Story Cycle: Forging Community in Edwidge Danticat's *Krik? Krak!*" *Melus* 26, no. 2 (2001): 65-81. How the short-story cycle became important to the development of ethnic literature, with a focus on Danticat's work.

Munro, Martin, ed. *Edwidge Danticat: A Reader's Guide*. Charlottesville: University of Virginia Press, 2010. Contains essays by leading scholars on the work of Danticat.

Walcott-Hackshaw, Elizabeth. "Home Is Where the Heart Is: Danticat's Landscapes of Return." *Small Axe: A Caribbean Journal of Criticism* 27 (October, 2008): 71-82. Discusses Danticat's use of home in her works, which can be Haiti or the United States.

Wucker, Michele. "Edwidge Danticat: A Voice for the Voiceless." *Americas* 52, no. 3 (2000): 40-45. Contains biographical information about Danticat and explores how her works show the human spirit under duress.

Ingo R. Stoehr

GUY DAVENPORT

Born: Anderson, South Carolina; November 23, 1927
Died: Lexington, Kentucky; January 4, 2005

PRINCIPAL SHORT FICTION

Tatlin!, 1974
Da Vinci's Bicycle: Ten Stories, 1979
Eclogues: Eight Stories, 1981
Apples and Pears, and Other Stories, 1984
The Jules Verne Steam Balloon, 1987
The Drummer of the Eleventh North Devonshire Fusiliers, 1990
A Table of Green Fields: Ten Stories, 1993
The Cardiff Team: Ten Stories, 1996
Twelve Stories, 1997
The Death of Picasso: New and Selected Writing, 2003
Wo es war, soll ich werden, 2004

OTHER LITERARY FORMS

Guy Davenport occupies a rare position in American letters, being renowned in many diverse areas. He was one of contemporary American literature's most complex short-story writers and one of its most influential literary critics, translators, and classical scholars. He published more than seventy stories in several collections. In the first four collections, he supplied his own distinctive black-and-white illustrations. He also published a collection of poems and translations, *Thasos and Ohio: Poems and Translations* (1986), and an early volume of poems, *Flowers and Leaves* (1966).

Besides his collections of short fiction and poetry, Davenport published highly acclaimed translations of Heraclitus, Diogenes, and the poets Sappho and Archilochus. He also published a number of critically praised nonfiction works: *The Geography of the Imagination* (1981), *Every Force Evolves a Form* (1987), *The Hunter Gracchus, and Other Papers on Literature and Art* (1996), and *Objects on a Table: Harmonious Disarray in Art and Literature* (1998). These volumes contain essays that cover such challenging thinkers as James Joyce, Ezra Pound, Charles Olson, Ludwig Wittgenstein, and the late work of Samuel Beckett, to mention but a few. He also edited a selection of writings on Swiss naturalist Louis Agassiz.

ACHIEVEMENTS

Among Guy Davenport's honors are a Blumenthal-Leviton Prize (1967), a Kentucky Research Award (1976), a University of Kentucky Arts and Sciences Distinguished Professor citation (1977), a Morton Dauwen Zabel Award (1981), American Book Award nominations (1981 and 1982), a National Book Critics Circle Award nomination (1982), a University of Kentucky Alumni Distinguished Professor citation (1983), a Thomas Carter Award for literary criticism (1987), and a MacArthur Foundation Fellowship (1990).

BIOGRAPHY

Guy Mattison Davenport, Jr., was born on November 23, 1927, in Anderson, South Carolina, to Guy Mattison, an express agent, and Marie Fant. Guy Davenport earned a B.A. from Duke University in 1948. He then attended the University of Oxford, Merton College, on a Rhodes Scholarship, receiving a B.Litt. in 1950, writing his first thesis at Oxford on James Joyce. After spending two years in the military (1950-1952), he taught for several years at Washington University in St. Louis. After finishing his Ph.D. in 1961 at Harvard University, where he studied classical literature and wrote a dissertation on Ezra Pound, he taught at Haverford College in Philadelphia until 1963. He then accepted a position in the English Department at the University of Kentucky, where he taught until 1992. Davenport died January 4, 2005, of cancer at the University of Kentucky Cancer Center.

ANALYSIS

First and foremost, Guy Davenport was a practicing modernist in a postmodernist literary world. In much of his fiction, he employs standard modernist techniques, still called "experimental" by conservative critics. By using methods usually associated with the visual art of collage, he juxtaposes images of the past with the present, hoping to demonstrate the persistent efficacious energies of the archaic and how they can still be used to redeem humankind from the relentless onslaught of mechanization. These energies reside in the human imagination as it intersects and interacts with the local environment, in much the same way that Ezra Pound, one of Davenport's major influences, and William Carlos Williams present the fragmentation that takes place when human beings are separated from their geographical, cultural, and spiritual origins. Davenport called his literary techniques, especially in his more experimental stories, "assemblages of history and necessary fiction," thus combining Wallace Stevens's notion of a "supreme fiction" with Pound's and Williams's reliance on a historical tradition grounded in a specific geographical location. He once stated that "my stories are lessons in history."

Much of Davenport's fiction is obsessed with an attempt to regenerate an Edenic innocence that "civilization" has destroyed by its incessant rationality. The "Fall" into experience, time, and knowledge is the major subject matter of most of his fiction. His greatest work was the trilogy detailing the highly intellectual and erotic adventures of Adriaan van Hovendaal, a Dutch philosopher, and his attempt to create a utopian community based on the teachings of the French philosopher Charles Fourier. The work of Fourier can be read as a virtual blueprint of this trilogy, which consists of the bulk of *Apples and Pears, and Other Stories*, most of *The Jules Verne Steam Balloon*, and the longest story in *The Drummer of the Eleventh North Devonshire Fusiliers* (which can also be called a novella), *Wo es war, soll ich werden*. A number of other stories, while not containing the identical characters as does the trilogy, treat the theme of the damage done to the instinctual life by so-called civilization and its persistent need to thwart the human desire for affection. The "apples and pears" Davenport frequently mentions in his fiction constitute a fractal motif, which establishes his extreme allusiveness, for such trees are what Odysseus returns to at the end of his epic wandering. These orchards also echo the purity of the Garden of Eden, in which healthy human desires are permitted full prelapsarian expression.

Davenport's earliest short stories appeared in his first collection, entitled *Tatlin!* He readily admitted that he was forty-three years old when he first began writing short stories and unashamedly labeled his writing "primitive and contrived." His stories are much closer to the openly inventive fictions of the ancient Roman writer Lucius Apuleius, the medieval tales of Sir Thomas Malory, and the sensual celebrations of François Rabelais. Davenport also listed those writers who have had the greatest influence on him as a fiction writer: James Joyce, Franz Kafka, Eudora Welty, and Gustave Flaubert. Davenport identified other artists, not necessarily writers, who helped form his creative sensibilities. His admiration for the techniques of ideogram, used in the poetry of Pound, Williams, and Olson, along with the enormous range of their poetic projects, entered the highly original imagination of Davenport. He attributed, as an important influence on his unique way of envisioning reality, the architectonic arrangement of images of the experimental filmmaker Stan Brakhage. Davenport also adopted a number of Brakhage's methods for fiction making, specifically the replacement of narrative and documentation with a series of images that formulate a structure of their own as they emerge. As Davenport stated: "I trust the image; my business is to get it onto the page." As example of such is one of the ten "stories" in *The Cardiff Team*, a quarter-page prose image reminiscent of haiku, entitled "Veranda Hung with Wisteria."

Davenport's fiction cannot be deciphered according to standard literary techniques, such as plot, character, theme, and setting. There is rarely a clearly outlined plot in which a protagonist journeys somewhere, confronts overwhelming difficulties, and, by overcoming them, learns something new about his or her inner self. Readers stand a much better chance of understanding Davenport's works if readers stop trying to analyze them as conventional short stories. Davenport wanted his readers to experience the creative process along with him, much in the way one tours a museum of modern art accompanied by an all-knowing guide, who points out important structural elements in what looks chaotic on first viewing. Davenport was a declared modernist and must be examined with the same methods that would apply to Max Ernst, Pablo Picasso, Georges Braque, or Paul Klee: collage and montage. What the viewer brings to collage and montage is the ability to detect multilayered structures in terms of juxtaposition and parataxis-- that is, the way certain similar elements begin to formulate parallels and play off each other, to create new combinations and, therefore, new forms.

"THE AEROPLANES AT BRESCIA"

Davenport's story "The Aeroplanes at Brescia" illustrates clearly the way he uses montage and juxtaposition to engender fictive possibilities that create information and entertainment. What becomes compelling about the story is not its narrative structure but rather the process of its creation. Watching the way that Davenport permits his imagination to work on certain facts about a famous air show that took place in Brescia in 1909, featuring archaic flying machines, takes precedence over the actual event. The subject matter of the story is not what happened at that air show but, more important, who saw it and what they wrote about it. Davenport is much more interested in versions of what happened because that is how he envisions history. What he finds fascinating, and the account on which he bases his fiction, is the version that Kafka described in a newspaper article that he wrote about the event and that subsequently became his first published writing. Davenport places next to it (the literal meaning of "parataxis") a version of the same event by Kafka's biographer, Max Brod, who was there with Kafka. Other important people also were present, such as opera composer Giacomo Puccini and writer Gabriele D'Annunzio, and Davenport offers his version of what he imagined they observed, which becomes as plausible as that of Kafka and of Brod. There is also some conjecture that the linguistic philosopher Wittgenstein may have been there since he had been obsessed with flight and flying machines from his early youth. The author therefore includes what Wittgenstein might have seen as an alternate possibility that adds to the richness of multiple fictive possibilities of a single event in 1909. Other critics have labeled these literary techniques "fictive approximations of reality" that rest on "as-if" propositions about history rather than so-called objective documentation.

"TATLIN!"

Davenport, a painterly writer, envisions a page as a picture or a texture of images and uses pictures as integral parts of the text. In the stories "Tatlin!" and "Robot," he uses drawings that he did to illustrate important elements, in these cases images of both Vladimir Ilich Lenin and Joseph Stalin as iconographic presences, and abstract sculptures that Tatlin created and that Davenport copied from fading photographs. In the charming narrative called "Robot," telling of the serendipitous discovery of the Caves of Lascaux by French teenage boys in 1941 and the awesome entry of the great French anthropologist priest-scholar Abbé Henri Breuil into the caves, Davenport uses his drawings of the images found in the cave. While his drawings replicate those magnificent prehistorical images, they also become an additional text, another version of the historical event and, therefore, form a collage rather than a flat, linear report of an important discovery. By fabricating layers of perception, paratactically, he creates multiple perspectives that resemble Pablo Picasso's cubist vision. Since Robot is the name of the dog that leads the boys to the caves while chasing a rabbit, the reader gets a dog's-eye view of the event, a version as significant as the human, since the title of the story is "Robot."

"THE DAWN IN EREWHON"

The most important story in the collection *Tatlin!* is the concluding one, entitled "The Dawn in Erewhon," which takes up exactly half of the entire book. Davenport expands enormously the range of his allusions, rivaling Pound at his densest in the *Cantos LII-LXXI* (1940) and Olson at his most allusive in *The Maximus Poems* (1960). Davenport admits to evoking the names of ninety-three historical personages in the story "The Aeroplanes at Brescia" alone. In "The Dawn in Erewhon," the allusions and perspectives accelerate prodigiously. While an omniscient voice narrates most of the story, a few pages are taken from the notebooks of the Dutch philosopher Adriaan van Hovendaal, whom Davenport thinks he saw in Amsterdam fifteen years earlier, although no biography or notebooks are known to exist. The title evolved from Samuel Butler's satiric, pastoral utopia called *Erewhon* (1872), an anagram of "nowhere."

Davenport's "The Dawn in Erewhon" is his version of an Edenic pastoral utopia modeled on Butler's *Erewhon* to the extent that they both criticize the damage that modern civilization does to the life of instinct. Butler's satire attacks the Victorian fear of sexuality and Christianity's persistent condemnation of the body, while traditionally favoring the needs of the intellect over those of the body. Consistent with Davenport's recurrent theme, that of the fall from a childhood innocence into the experience of self-consciousness, he attempts in this story to regenerate an Edenic, childlike vision through which experience can be redeemed on both spiritual and physical levels. The intellectual genius of van Hovendaal is always put to the service of the desires of the body; his life is the opposite of the overly cerebral thinker lost in the life-denying abstractions of philosophical inquiry. Though Davenport documents in spectacular detail the cognitive sources of van Hovendaal's intellectual background by using a Joycean stream-of-consciousness technique of juxtaposing hundreds of quotations, in at least six languages, running through his mind, he demonstrates in much greater detail the endless sexual activities that vivify his affective life and transform it into form of ecstatic consciousness, which are multiplied many times over with each succeeding chapter.

The major characters Bruno and Kaatje, who reappear in many later works, first appear in "The Dawn in Erewhon." They revel in each other's and Adriaan's company. They also enjoy each other sexually in couples and trios without guilt or jealousy. They have become the first group that Davenport consciously forms into a unit, best described by the French sociological philosopher Charles Fourier as "Little Hordes," whose primary duty is to fulfill their instinctual desires for pleasure. Much of the action throughout "The Dawn in Erewhon" consists of camping trips to idyllic forests, elaborate assignment of duties in establishing campsites, careful division of labor, and a strict parceling out of time spent alone doing whatever each wishes. The day concludes with multiple sexual activities in which everyone must be satisfied. All erotic exercises, while delineated in the most specific sexual language, are presented as elaborate rituals of innocence and childlike joy. Since control and aggression, elements that prevent healthy sexual expression, have been removed from this little but highly structured society, Davenport's fictions become rituals of regenerative innocence.

Certain standard literary and philosophical dichotomies, such as the Dionysian versus the Apollonian, or the mind-body struggle, and other typical Freudian battlefields that produce neurosis and anxiety, are notably absent from Davenport's fiction. Fourier, who predated Sigmund Freud by a hundred years, proposed that people could be truly happy if they were permitted to construct lives that would cooperate with the instincts rather than denigrating and deploring them. Fourier has been called the only true philosopher of happiness. Indeed, he wrote twelve volumes in which he outlined exactly how such a society might come about. All of Davenport's major fictions, from "The Dawn in Erewhon" to *Wo es war, soll ich werden,* can be read as philosophical parables, illustrating the possibility of regenerating innocent happiness when characters live according to their deepest instinctual desires but only, however, within highly structured Fourierist parameters. Though the white-hot sexual rhetoric may appear to promote sexual anarchy, nothing could be further from the author's intention. Sex is healthy only if it is practiced in a healthy society; there is no possibility that a "sexual outlaw" would ever be permitted within Davenport's Fourierist society.

What Davenport has accomplished within much of his utopian fiction is to exclude any figure that even slightly resembles the typical hero--that is, a charismatic male who by the force of his individuality and aggressive power becomes the director and, in essence, owner of a specific locale and group. Adriaan van Hovendaal is respected by the younger and indefatigably sexual Bruno and Kaatje not because of his ability to control situations but rather because he permits himself to participate in their passionate attraction, a key concept in Fourier. They also see him as an intellectual whose mind and body work in consonance and as one whose intuition and perception have led him back to a primal imagination that understands the continuity of life and death. He, first and last, lives a life of balance and harmony. Most important, however, is that the society created by the mutual trust, love, and care among Adriaan, Bruno, and Kaatje demonstrates the concept of harmony by embodying it. As long as they are assisting one another in enjoying the desires of the body, they are helping to enact what Fourier called "Sessions of the Court of Love," which will eventually regenerate a new Eden or the Fourierist "New Amorous World."

DA VINCI'S BICYCLE

Davenport's next collection of stories is *Da Vinci's Bicycle.* Four of these stories deal with classical Greek and Roman locations and characters, though "Ithaka" details an awkward meeting with Pound and his mistress, Olga Rudge, in Rapallo, Italy. In the story "The Antiquities of Elis," the place, Elis, site of the ancient Olympic Games, becomes the principal character, while ancient voices supply historical information to the reader. In "The Invention of Photography in Toledo," Davenport plays with a quasi-surrealist montage, juxtaposing the glorious Toledo of Spain with its American counterpart, Toledo, Ohio. The most effective and humorous piece in the collection, however, is the first story, called "The Richard Nixon Freischutz Rag," in which Davenport juxtaposes the oracular utterings of Chairman Mao Tse-tung with the documented banality of Richard Nixon's responses on his visit to China in 1972.

The most important assemblage in this collection is "Au Tombeau de Charles Fourier" (at the tomb of Charles Fourier), a French expression which also means paying homage to a great person. There are thirty chapters, or cantos, composed of nine paragraphs, or stanzas, each, and each paragraph is made up of four lines. The exceptions are the tenth section, which is two lines, and the thirtieth paragraph, which consists of two paragraphs: the first containing the usual four lines while the second contains three. The scene of the meditation on the tomb of Fourier in the famous cemetery of Montmartre is an example of a meditation on ruins, one of the literary forms in which Davenport has maintained an interest throughout his career. Among Davenport's most famous literary essays is his brilliant explication of Olson's densely constructed poem "The Kingfishers." Davenport found Olson's "The Kingfishers," along with Percy Bysshe Shelley's "Ozymandias" and John Keats's "Ode on a Grecian Urn," to be involved in the same poetic process--that is, an observer laments the destructive ravages that time has on all material objects, even those of great religious or political significance. The point that Davenport is making, along with Shelley, Keats, and Olson, is that, even though time has destroyed the physical body of Fourier and the others, the body of their work, the essence of their aesthetic beliefs, still exists and affects people to this very day.

The principal message that runs throughout this dense and complicated assemblage is that reality comes into existence only through words and the ability of the poet or priest or shaman to construct worlds through the efficacy of verbal power. Davenport celebrates other linguistic saints in the story, such as Gertrude Stein, whose presence at the beginning and the end of the work establishes the verbal as the iconographic medium through which other saints become visible. The hero to whom Davenport compares Fourier is the great Dogon metaphysician and wise man Ogotemmêli. After the French anthropologist Marcel Griaule spent fifteen years, off and on, with the West African Dogon tribe, the elders decided to trust him with the deep information concerning the cosmology on which their reality was built. The blind Ogotemmêli invited Griaule to sit with him for thirty-three days, during which he revealed to him, in massive detail and from memory (since Dogon society had no written language), the Dogon cosmology. As Davenport puts it: "He teaches him the structure and meaning of the world." The entire Dogon cosmological structure is based on the model of a loom, in which all things are stitched together to create a harmonious world, very much in the way Fourier stitched together an equally coherent utopian society, which he called the "New Harmonious World." The book that Griaule published subsequently influenced another contemporary American writer, Robert Kelly, who is often compared to Davenport not only because of the erudite scholarship embedded in his work but also because of his long poem "The Loom" (1975), which is also built on Dogon cosmology.

The point that Davenport wants to make is that the spiritual realities that these great cosmological geniuses proposed are not really dead, because their words exist and are felt today. Language is key in that it alone escapes the ravages of time and it alone preserves the numinous power of the sacred. In paying homage to Fourier, Davenport also pays homage to the other priests of the word, modernists such as Beckett, Joyce, and Picasso, whose high modernism evolved from their recognition of the persistent recurrence of the energies of the archaic, which reestablishes a sense of order in the world.

ECLOGUES

Davenport's third collection of short fiction, *Eclogues*, continues his interest in, and exploration of, ancient and modern Edenic narratives. The title of the collection comes from a literary form used by many classical Greek and Roman poets, such as Vergil and Theocritus, and is synonymous with the term "pastoral." Important practitioners of the form in English literature were Edmund Spenser, William Shakespeare, Christopher Marlowe, John Milton, Shelley, and Matthew Arnold. Davenport, being a classical scholar, wants to expand the application of the term to include lives lived under ideal conditions. The ideal that Davenport pursues evolves from the word's etymological root: idyll. His models are the *Idylls* (c. 270 b.c.e.; English translation, 1684) of Theocritus, the Greek poet and inventor of the pastoral form in which he presents the happy rustic lives of shepherds and farmers in Sicily. The Greek root of the word means "form" or "picture," which applies accurately to Davenport's precise drawings of the idealized figures of adolescent boys throughout the text.

Two stories stand out as further elaborations of Davenport's parables of innocence. "The Death of Picasso" consists of thirty-nine excerpts from the notebooks of the major character from the "The Dawn in Erewhon," van Hovendaal. A new and even more precociously sexual teenager named Sander appears; he becomes a kind of ephebe, or student, of van Hovendaal. They exchange information and insights focused on the death of Picasso and the mutual meditations they share on Picasso's significance as an artistic synthesizer of the ancient and the modern world, which resulted in modernism, a movement that Picasso virtually invented. By pursuing art's chaotic boundaries, Picasso rediscovered the archaic imagination, which then enabled him to ground his aesthetic energies in an unbounded primordial source. His work removed any residual negative implications that the word "primitivism" may have previously acquired. Indeed, modernism finds its order in the pre-Socratic, process-oriented imagination of Heraclitus rather than the life-denying categories of Aristotelian abstractions. Though the story records the death of Picasso, it also dramatizes his revolutionary restoration of the archaic to its proper place in what Davenport calls the "history of attention."

In one of the shorter stories in *Eclogues*, called "Mesoroposthonippidon," Davenport narrates humorous anecdotes about the ancient Greek philosopher Diogenes, who spent his life disarming people of high rank with the simplicity of his life. Because he had no possessions, he felt perfectly free to speak his mind to anyone, including Plato and Alexander the Great, whom he chided for blocking his sunlight. Five of the eight stories in this collection deal with classical settings and characters, with the purpose of pointing out their relevance to modern times.

The longest and most complex story in the collection is the pastoral romance entitled "On Some Lines of Virgil." The piece is carefully structured, consisting of 135 sections of five stanzas or paragraphs each; every stanza is four lines long. The allusion to Vergil immediately alerts the reader to the possibility that the narrative may reveal Davenport's habitual theme of the regeneration of an Edenic or, in this case, Arcadian community. Indeed, Vergil's *Georgics* (c. 37-29 b.c.e.; English translation, 1589) and *Eclogues* (43-37 b.c.e.; also known as *Bucolics*; English translation, 1575) were presentations of such idealized settings.

In this romance, the setting is Bordeaux, an ancient, southwestern French city and the birthplace of such famous painters and writers as Rosa Bonheur, Odilon Redon, François Mauriac, Charles de Montesquieu, and, most important, Michel Eyquem de Montaigne. The painter Francisco de Goya, though not native to Bordeaux, painted some of his greatest works there. Davenport is careful to point out that Bonheur's *The Horse Fair* and Goya's *The Bulls of Bordeaux* are unconscious continuations of the horses and bulls found in the Caves of Lascaux, another example of how the modern imagination is grounded in the archaic. Tullio, the professorial scholar, exhorts his little horde of four that true history, which is the history of attention, consists of developing the ability to detect these patterns and that his deepest desire is "to write a history of the imagination in our time. . . . All these need to be reseen [in the light of the archaic]. The new modifies everything before, and even finds a tradition for the first time." Davenport's aesthetic theory resembles T. S. Eliot's classic statement in "Tradition and the Individual Talent" but lacks the Calvinist undertones that would not permit Eliot to use the word "imagination."

The Little Horde in this highly erotic Arcadia consists of four French teenagers: Jonquille, Jolivet, Michel, and the barely adolescent Victor. In the midst of their frequent erotic games, they travel to one of the ancient caves near Bordeaux, taking with them the young, legless Marc Aurel but accompanied by Tullio, a mature and responsible married adult. Davenport, though giving his adolescents full sexual freedom, positions an older scholar nearby to place their orgies in some sort of context. Tullio, the shepherd in this eclogue and whose name obviously derives from Marcus Tullius Cicero (known throughout the ancient world as "Tully"), serves as their intellectual guide and helps them understand the nature of their friendship, much in the same way that Cicero wrote the definitive essays on friendship (*Laelius de amicitia*, 44 b.c.e.) and old age (*Cato maior de senectute*, 44 b.c.e.), which became handbooks on Stoic philosophy. Again, youth and friendship are better understood if they are viewed against the background of old age, just as the prelogical tableaux in the caves of Lascaux become subtextual foundations of the great works of Picasso, Klee, and Goya.

APPLES AND PEARS, AND OTHER STORIES

There can be little doubt that Davenport's fourth collection of stories, *Apples and Pears, and Other Stories*, is his masterpiece. The 233-page novella *Apples and Pears* constitutes a fine work of fiction. This novella revels in its richness, diversity, and brilliance and demonstrates the enormous scope of his intellectual terrain. The style recalls James Joyce's *Ulysses* (1922) at its most lucid; its four parts are firmly grounded in Davenport's most successful use of Fourier's utopian vision.

The three stories preceding *Apples and Pears* are also some of Davenport's most convincing fictions. All three are journeys of one kind or another. "The Bowmen of Shu" is constructed out of the battlefield diaries of the sculptor Henri Gaudier-Brzeska, while "Fifty-seven Views of Fujiyama" paratactically narrates the seventeenth century poet Matsuo Bashō's mountain journey alongside a modern couple's camping trip in New Hampshire. One of the most delightful and humorous stories in all Davenport's work is "The Chair," which finds Kafka accompanying the Rebbe of Belz on a tour of the Czechoslovakian spa at Marienbad in 1916.

In the novella *Apples and Pears*, Davenport uses the same techniques that he used in "The Death of Picasso" and "The Dawn in Erewhon"--that is, notebooks, diaries, and memoirs. The major consciousness throughout most of the text is the same Dutch philosopher and essayist in Butler's *Erewhon*, van Hovendaal. New members swell the Fourierist "horde" into eight participants, including van Hovendaal. There are characters from previous works, Sander, Bruno, and Kaatje, and new adolescents, Jan, Hans, Saartje, and Sander's sister, Grietje.

The work is also structured along rather firm Fourierist lines, in that it contains four major sections that follow his four-part structure of an ideal society, which he called "The Harmony of the Four Movements"; Fourier divides them into categories of the social, the animal, the organic, and the material. The four chapters of Davenport's work generally follow that scheme but not necessarily in that order. Van Hovendaal labels the first section "An Erewhonian Sketchbook" and uses a Napoleonic rather than a Gregorian calendar, calling the months Messidor (July), Thermidor (August), and Fructidor (September). The changes of the names of the months signified the arrival of the New Harmonious World, which was expected to follow the French Revolution.

Davenport translates the major line from Fourier's twelve-volume work that summarizes his entire philosophy of social happiness: "The series distributes the harmonies. The attractions are proportionate to our destinies." The series, to Fourier and Davenport, are groups that operate democratically and are drawn together by mutual attractions. As long as each member of the group is permitted to act on his mutually passional attraction toward others, an order and balance is established, and harmony reigns. These harmonious conjunctions take place continuously throughout *Apples and Pears*, as the group, gently directed by van Hovendaal, combine in every conceivable sexual coupling. Most important, however, is that this work becomes Davenport's "history of affection."

THE JULES VERNE STEAM BALLOON

The fifth volume is a collection of nine short stories entitled *The Jules Verne Steam Balloon*. Four of the nine stories are connected within the collection, since some of the same characters appear in all four, and some of those characters were participants in the novella *Apples and Pears*. The setting has moved from the Netherlands to Denmark, but youthful beauty and charm dictate the action. "The Meadow," "The Bicycle Rider," "The Jules Verne Steam Balloon," and the concluding story, "The Ringdove Sign," are all parables of innocence involving basically the same Fourierist ritual camping trips to idyllic forests, where the participants enjoy one another's bodies in clean, childlike sexual celebration. New adolescents join the "little horde," such as Pascal, Hugo, Franklin, Mariana, Kim, and Anders, but the project remains the same--that is, the more sexually comfortable enable those fearful of letting go to become more relaxed in their bodies. Only in "The Bicycle Rider" does a negative presence enter the highly organized promiscuity of the group. One of the most attractive and strongest of the young men has become addicted to drugs and has fallen into the condition of not being able to focus on life around him; most important, he has become incapable of any sexual response. Since the dynamics of the community are predicated on the passional attraction among the members of the group, he becomes the outcast and eventually dies.

THE DRUMMER OF THE ELEVENTH NORTH DEVONSHIRE FUSILIERS

The sixth volume of short fiction, which contains four stories and a novella, is entitled *The Drummer of the Eleventh North Devonshire Fusiliers*. While "Colin Maillard" and "Badger" both deal with the early passional attraction between preadolescent boys, the novella *Wo es war, soll ich werden* continues the activities of the expanding Fourierist group. Davenport also makes major philosophical and critical statements that help the reader understand some of his theoretical background. Davenport's style is so packed with multiphasic allusions, Joycean puns and conundrums, and phenomenological scene-shifting that an occasional glance at his sources and influences usually helps. He does inform his reader that *Wo es war, soll ich werden* is the conclusion of a trilogy that also includes *Apples and Pears* and *The Jules Verne Steam Balloon*.

The activity remains the same, as do some of the characters, but a deeper philosophical note enters both the dialogue and the general discussion of the group. A superb Joycean, Davenport describes for the reader some of his own literary methods through a character named Allen in the story "Badger." He first explains the fall that takes place when one enters adolescence: "What you see, you know, Allen said, you own. You take it in. Everything's an essence . . . at twelve you understand everything. Afterward, you have to give it up and specialize." He then further elucidates:

> The film of essences, one photon thick, is continuous. Everything apprehended is in the continuum of this film. So all correspondences, the relation of information to other information, are first of all differences. Colors, shapes, textures.

If a reader of Davenport applies these "ways" of reading and observing to Davenport's work, a number of confusing elements might become clear.

Hugo explains that the title of the novella *Wo es war, soll ich werden* is a phrase from Freud. Jacques Lacan, the eminent French psychoanalyst, said that the phrase contains "pre-Socratic eloquence." Hugo translates it as "where it was, there must I begin to be," and Holger then sees it as another proof that "genius is a disease: Mann's paradox," with Thomas Mann's great *Der Tod in Venedig* (1912; *Death in Venice*, 1925) and *Doktor Faustus* (1947; *Doctor Faustus*, 1948) being notable examples of German Romantic agony. Hugo quickly points out Freud's meaning: "No no, Hugo said. Freud meant that a wound, healing, can command the organism's whole attention, and thus becomes the beginning of a larger health." Hugo's explication summarizes Davenport's entire fictive enterprise in that all of his Fourierest parables of innocence attempt to move the joyfully "erotic" away from the German Romantic death wish. western civilization need not end in apocalyptic self-immolation.

THE CARDIFF TEAM

In crafting *The Cardiff Team* collection, Davenport relies on many of the props he used in previous works. The first story in the collection places Kafka in a nudist colony. Whereas Davenport used Stein in *Da Vinci's Bicycle*, in "Boys Smell Like Oranges" he evokes the presence of two perambulatory philosophers: Professor Lucien Levy-Bruhl and Pastor Maurice Leenhardt. These older men, on walking through the Bois de Boulogne, encounter the lawn-strewn bodies of a team of footballers. Two of these later remark that the old men were either shocked or infatuated by their adolescent forms, and the boys constitute part of yet another "Little Horde" of sexual utopians. In the last work of the collection, "The Cardiff Team," they also arrive at the same philosophical speculation the philosophers had been discussing in the Bois--the power of language to enact religion, as witnessed by the New Caledonians in their reverence for math multiplication tables, a litany of which concludes the story. This story clarifies an opposition of friendship, in its imagination-driven pan-sexual diversity ("what's in books and the world and feeling great in my pants were cooperative"), to tyranny and war and all manner of oppression.

Davenport reveres Fourier for the same reasons that André Breton, the founder of Surrealism, honored him with an ode. All three men attempt to regenerate forms of prelapsarian innocence that envision the world with a childlike sense of the marvelous and celebrate life in all of its ecstatic physicality. The purpose of the sexual exercises, as opposed to the spiritual exercises of Saint Ignatius of Loyola, for example, is to recuperate the endless capacities of the imagination, with pleasure as the primary motivating force; to eradicate the life-denying abstractions of logical positivism; and to celebrate again and again the renaissance of the archaic.

THE DEATH OF PICASSO

Published in 2003, Davenport's tenth collection of stories and essays includes two previously uncollected stories, "The Owl of Minerva" and "The Playing Field." These stories explore the relationship between new characters in the author's canon, the Danes Magnus and Mikkel Rasmussen. Reminiscent of van Hovendaal ("The Death of Picasso") and Hugo ("The Jules Verne Steam Balloon") and their role as mentors for younger male acolytes, Magnus befriends the orphan Mikkel, taking him into his living quarters, enabling the youngster to become an unofficial student at Oak Hill School, where Magnus teaches, and even giving Mikkel his last name. Once others at the school become privy to their living conditions, including sharing a bed, Magnus and Mikkel decide to leave to begin their lives together anew. Both stories partake of classical allusions, historical references, biblical and scientific language, and Davenport's use of modernist narrative technique, the most prominent being fractured nonchronological story lines, a preference for dramatic scene over summary, and intertextuality.

"The Owl of Minerva" opens with Magnus and Mikkel, grown older, after they have departed Oak Hill. Both are officers fulfilling different assignments in the Danish military. Magnus also is a professor of geology at the Niels Bohr Institute, and Mikkel is married to a Scotswoman, Susanna. They have two adolescent sons, Adam and Henry, who adore their "Onkel Magnus." The story shifts to a scene in which Mikkel, in his official uniform as a major, revisits Oak Hill. He meets with the school's retired director, Colonel Rask, who never knew what happened to Mikkel and Magnus. The story concludes with Mikkel's son Adam on a scout's camping trip. Adam and his friend Sholto have located an abandoned house that becomes their temporary haven to pursue their fascination with each other.

"The Playing Field" moves from Magnus and Mikkel's budding relationship at Oak Hill School to Mikkel's visit to the school as Major Rasmussen. By happenstance, Mikkel is introduced by Rask to his namesake, the student Mikkel Havemand, whose father Marcus was a former student in love with Mikkel and was deeply hurt by his departure with Magnus. After showering with the major at the school's locker room, the younger Mikkel informs him that where he and Magnus once lived, a "long room over the stables," is where "a young couple . . . now" lives "with a baby." The couple is Hugo and his girlfriend Mariana, with their infant son, Barnabas.

While readers might speculate that Magnus and Mikkel and Adam and Sholto represent new cycles of characters that Davenport planned on developing more fully, it is clear that they embody qualities inherent in other major characters from previous stories that celebrate the human body unabashedly and embrace an ethos dedicated to knowledge and the imagination. Similar in form, technique, and subject matter to the classical and modernist writers he studied and understood, Davenport has yet to receive the extensive critical attention his canon deserves.

OTHER MAJOR WORKS

POETRY: *Flowers and Leaves*, 1966; *Thasos and Ohio: Poems and Translations*, 1986.

NONFICTION: *Pennant Key-Indexed Study Guide to Homer's "Iliad,"* 1967; *Pennant Key-Indexed Study Guide to Homer's "Odyssey,"* 1967; *The Geography of the Imagination*, 1981; *Every Force Evolves a Form*, 1987; *A Balthus Notebook*, 1989; *Charles Burchfield's Seasons*, 1994; *The Hunter Gracchus, and Other Papers on Literature and Art*, 1996; *The Geography of the Imagination: Forty Essays*, 1997; *Objects on a Table: Harmonious Disarray in Art and Literature*, 1998; *Guy Davenport and James Laughlin: Selected Letters*, 2007 (W. C. Bamberger, editor).

TRANSLATIONS: *Poems and Fragments*, 1965 (of Sappho); *Herakleitos and Diogenes*, 1979; *Archilochos, Sappho, Alkman: Three Lyric Poets of the Late Greek Bronze Age*, 1980; *Anakreon*, 1991; *Seven Greeks*, 1995; *The Logia of Yeshua: The Sayings of Jesus*, 1996 (with Benjamin Urrutia).

EDITED TEXTS: *The Intelligence of Louis Agassiz: A Specimen Book of Scientific Writings*, 1963; *Selected Stories*, 1993 (of O. Henry).

BIBLIOGRAPHY

Arias-Misson, Alain. "Erotic Ear, Amoral Eye." *Chicago Review* 35 (Spring, 1986): 66-71. Arias-Misson proposes that *Apples and Pears* constitutes Davenport's mythmaking as an alternative to the demythologizing that most contemporary fiction exemplifies. He genuinely wants his storytelling to aspire to the condition of myth and, as such, revivify the reader's sense of the world as a physically satisfying place.

Bawer, Bruce. "The Stories of Guy Davenport's Fiction à la Fourier." *The New Criterion* 3 (December, 1984): 8-14. One of the most intelligent and perceptive analyses of Davenport's work. Bawer labels Davenport a foursquare modernist and a devout Poundian. Bawer admires greatly Davenport's enormously esoteric imagination but is worried about where the affectionate stops and the merely sexual begins. He praises Davenport for reminding readers of their humanity and the importance of affection.

Blake, Nancy. "'An Exact Precession': Leonardo, Gertrude, and Guy Davenport's *Da Vinci's Bicycle*." In *Critical Angles: European Views of Contemporary Literature*, edited by Marc Chénetier. Carbondale: southern Illinois University Press, 1986. Blake suggests that Davenport can be best understood if one views his work as rendering homage to his predecessors and, thus, renewing their vital force and the reader's.

Cozy, David. "Guy Davenport." *Review of Contemporary Fiction* 25, no. 3 (Fall 2005): 42-85. An accessible, balanced, and worthwhile introduction to Davenport and his writing.

Crane, Joan St. C. *Guy Davenport: A Descriptive Bibliography, 1947-1995*. Haverford, Pa.: Green Shade, 1996. A good source for the student of Davenport.

Davenport, Guy. *Fifty Drawings*. New York: Dim Gray Bar Press, 1996. A collection of the writer's drawings.

_____. *The Hunter Gracchus: And Other Papers on Literature and Art*. Washington, D.C.: Counterpoint, 1996. This collection of essays written by Davenport during the 1980's and 1990's on a variety of literary and cultural subjects reflects the extensive reading and erudition so evident in his short fiction.

Furlani, André. *Guy Davenport: Postmodern and After*. Evanston, Ill.: Northwestern University Press, 2007. Furlani offers the first book-length study of Davenport and his creative and critical writings. His book is a much needed addition to the study of this complex and challenging writer and artist.

Jarman, Mark. "The Hunter Davenport." *Hudson Review* 50, no. 2 (Summer, 1997): 333. Discusses Davenport's adherence to modernist techniques despite his postmodernist milieu. He focuses on nineteenth and twentieth century subjects, drawing comparisons between past events and present occurrences.

Klinkowitz, Jerome. Review of *Apple and Pears, and Other Stories. The Review of Contemporary Fiction* (Spring, 1986): 216-218. Klinkowitz proposes that *Apples and Pears* is not only Davenport's strongest work but also the work in which he pulls all his influences together, from Wallace Stevens's necessary fictions to Pound's reverence of the archaic. Davenport keeps philosophy, sexuality, and history in an ideal balance. A genuinely helpful and intelligent essay.

Madden, David W. "Stories Told in Collage." *San Francisco Chronicle*, January 9, 1994, p. 4. A review of Davenport's collection of stories *A Table of Green Fields* by a well-known short-story writer, critic, and novelist; claims that the stories recall Ernest Hemingway and Sherwood Anderson but have most in common with Raymond Carver; argues that many of the stories are difficult postmodern experiments in themes of the illusion of time and the relationship between artists and their models.

Olsen, Lance. "A Guidebook to the Last Modernist: Davenport on Davenport and *Da Vinci's Bicycle*." *Journal of Narrative Technique* 16 (Spring, 1986): 148-161. A brilliant and insightful essay written on Davenport, even though it covers only *Da Vinci's Bicycle*. Olsen traces the origin of Davenport's modernism in the "renaissance of the archaic" and places him alongside classic modernists such as Joyce, Eliot, and Pound. Davenport is the last modernist because he still believes in the omnipotence of language and its ability to humanize an increasingly dehumanizing world.

Patrick Meanor; Scott Vander Ploeg
Updated by Kevin Eyster

PETER HO DAVIES

Born: Coventry, England; August 30, 1966

PRINCIPAL SHORT FICTION

The Ugliest House in the World, 1997 (includes *A Union*)
Equal Love, 2000

OTHER LITERARY FORMS

Peter Ho Davies published his first novel, *The Welsh Girl*, in 2007.

ACHIEVEMENTS

Peter Ho Davies' work was selected for *The Best American Short Stories* in 1995, 1996, and 2001. He won an O. Henry Award in 1998 and the PEN/Malamud Award in 2008. A recipient of fellowships from the National Endowment for the Arts, the Guggenheim Foundation, and the Fine Arts Work Center in Provincetown, Massachusetts, he has also been awarded the John Llewelyn Rhys and PEN/Macmillan Prizes in the United Kingdom and the H. L. Davis Oregon Book Award in the United States. In 2003, *Granta* magazine named him among its twenty Best of Young British Novelists. *The Welsh Girl* was long-listed for the Man Booker Prize in 2007 and short-listed for a British Book Award in 2008.

BIOGRAPHY

Peter Ho Davies was born in Coventry, England, on August 30, 1966, to a Welsh father and a Chinese mother. In 1987, he earned a B.S. in physics and in the history of philosophy and science from the University of Manchester, England. In 1989, he received a B.A. in English from Cambridge University. In 1992, he moved to the United States, where he received an M.A. in creative writing from Boston University in 1993. His first published story was "The Ugliest House in the World," which appeared in *The Antioch Review* in 1995. Subsequent stories appeared in magazines, including *The Atlantic Monthly*, *Harper's*, *The Paris Review*, *Ploughshares*, and *Story*.

Davies was a lecturer at Emory University from 1996 to 1997, and he became assistant professor in the creative writing program at the University of Oregon in 1997. In 1999, he took up a similar position at the University of Michigan at Ann Arbor. He married Lynne Anne Raugley in 1994.

ANALYSIS

Peter Ho Davies' first collection, *The Ugliest House in the World*, is notable for the variety of times and places in which the stories are set. "The Ugliest House in the World" and *A Union* take place in Wales, in different time periods. "Buoyancy"--about a man's obsession with diving to the bottom of an old mining pool--and "The Silver Screen"--about a group of Malayan communists who fight the British--are set in Southeast Asia. "Relief" takes place in South Africa. among veterans of Rourke's Drift, which was where British troops defeated the Zulus. Other stories take place in Patagonia and England.

In such a wide-ranging collection, many themes emerge. Some stories are shaped by tragedy, such as the death of a child or a suicide. Deception, both of self and others, underlies "Coventry," as well as "I Don't Know, What Do You Think?" Happy endings are rare; optimism, where it occurs, is hard won and never absolute. Occasionally there is humor, especially in the hilarious "The Silver Screen," which also has its moments of horror, cruelty, and betrayal.

The dominant theme of Davies' second collection, *Equal Love*, is family relationships, particularly, as Davies put it, "the relationships between grown children and aging parents." "Today Is Sunday" explores the antagonistic but affectionate relationship between a man and his father as they visit the father's senile mother. In "Cakes for Baby," a couple decide to support the wife's divorced mother financially, even though it may postpone their having children. In "Brave Girl," a young girl has to cope with the separation of her parents; "On the Terraces" shows a mother and her elder son facing the death of a younger son from acquired immunodeficiency syndrome (AIDS), although they are never able to comprehend his homosexuality.

The tone of Davies' stories is often detached, tending to the unemotional. His writing is crisp and lucid, and the images are precisely observed. The stories are quietly compassionate; Davies is reluctant to judge human foibles, preferring instead to delineate the complexity, the inconclusiveness of life, with its painful defeats and occasional small victories.

"THE UGLIEST HOUSE IN THE WORLD"

Guilt and social resentments surface when a young physician visits his Welsh father, who has retired to a village in North Wales after forty years in England. The purpose of the son's visit is to attend the funeral of Gareth, a neighborhood boy who was killed when a stone gatepost on the father's property fell on him.

At the funeral, local people accuse the father of negligence, a charge that adds to his feelings of guilt. Underlying the hostility is the feeling that the father is an outsider, even though he was born in the village. The next day, Welsh nationalist slogans are daubed on the father's house. The son, however, believes no one was to blame for the boy's death, and he appears to understand neither the local resentments nor the depth of his father's feelings. The latter are revealed when, in the emotional climax of the story, the father goes to great lengths to catch a fish that he had promised to Gareth and presents it to the boy's mother instead.

In an ironic conclusion, the son whitewashes his father's cottage. When he has finished, it shines brightly in the morning sun. The reader suspects that the feelings of guilt that the tragic incident has caused, and the social strife it has aroused, will not be so easily healed.

A UNION

This novella about a strike at a Welsh quarry in 1899 explores the themes of shame and responsibility. To whom is a man responsible when he goes on strike--his fellow workers or his wife and family?

Davies explores this theme in the subtly drawn tensions that surface in the marriage of Thomas and Catrin Jones. The tension is apparent on the day the strike begins, when they take delivery of a grandfather clock for which they had been saving. Catrin has set her heart on the clock, and Thomas pretends that it is still all right for her to have it. The irony is that the clock is too big to fit in their small parlor, and Thomas must saw it down to make room for it.

As the strike drags on, tensions between husband and wife become apparent in the wife's offhand remarks that convey her resentment. There are hints that Catrin has become pregnant, but since the couple earlier agreed they could not afford a third child, neither mentions it. After some months, the union money runs out and workers begin to straggle back to the quarry; Thomas clings to his pride until he gazes on his newborn baby, after which he, too, returns to work. In a nice irony, Catrin expresses her new pride in him. The episode parallels and contrasts the incident with the clock, which also, like the baby, was more than the couple could afford. This time, however, the newcomer, a living thing not an inanimate object, produces reconciliation rather than conflict.

In addition to the light it shines on the different attitudes of the men and the women to the strike, the story presents a sympathetic portrait of the striking quarrymen in their bitter struggle with the ruthless quarry owners. It also has humor concerning the fanatical, bald clergyman Price, who urges the strikers on and is the only character who gains from the dispute. As his power and influence increase, he develops a full head of hair and a black beard. As the strike collapses, he falls into the quarry and is killed. There is little mourning; it is time for a new beginning.

"THE HULL CASE"

In this calmly told story, a harmonious marriage is gradually destroyed by a couple's differing responses to an unidentified-flying-object (UFO) sighting. The story takes place in the early 1960's in New Hampshire. An African American man, Henry Hull, and his white wife Helen are being interviewed about their strange experience by an Air Force colonel.

Through flashbacks, the difficulties the interracial couple has had to endure in white New England are made clear. Henry is constantly reminded that he has transgressed a social code: People stare as the couple enter a diner, and a motel, pretending to be full, turns them away. Helen dismisses such slights as imaginary, and although Henry feels them keenly, he does not become embittered, and the marriage thrives. How ironic it is, then, that a successful interracial marriage should founder at the intrusion of a supposed encounter with aliens.

During the interview with the colonel, Henry is embarrassed; he does not expect to be believed (another incident that reveals the black man's perspective). Helen claims to remember being abducted by aliens who performed experiments on her; Henry has no memory of this and resents the way she insists on mentioning it. Helen believes the aliens have taken one of her eggs; she remembers being shown strange children. Henry suspects the dreams may be unconscious compensations for the fact that Helen has miscarried twice. This conflict suggests that it is Helen's anxiety about her inability to produce children that may be at the heart of the chasm that opens between the couple, even though ostensibly the cause is their disagreement over the UFO. The fact that Henry finally, under hypnosis, recalls being abducted does nothing to improve the marriage. The final image, of Henry dreaming that he sees his wife levitating from the bed surrounded by a blue light, is an ample metaphor for their estrangement: She is apart from him now, the dream seems to say, unreachable, alien.

"Small World"

Wilson, a married man in early middle age, returns to Boston alone on a business trip, near where he grew up. He thinks back to when he was fifteen and his parents divorced. He remembers the guilt he felt when his father told him that he and his wife realized they did not love each other at the time Wilson was born, since the love they felt for the baby was so much more real and intense. Wilson concluded he was to blame for their divorce. The guilt has dominated his life. Pointedly, he is referred to only by his family name, Wilson--he cannot escape his family past.

Wilson encounters Joyce, his high school sweetheart, prompting reminiscences of how, in his confusion, he had "adopted" her parents as surrogates, which made him feel guilty yet again for "cheating" on his own parents. Then Joyce informs him that her own parents are now divorcing. Like the young Wilson, she too feels guilt.

Davies weaves many variations and crosscurrents into this finely wrought story about parental love and the long shadow cast by parents' relations with their children. The effect is like a complex dance in which love and trust are lost but then recovered, if only precariously, as the children seek their own life and loves. The fact that Wilson's wife is pregnant with their first child is a telling detail; the cycle of interlocking family destinies is about to spring up again. Although Wilson betrays his wife by making love to Joyce, the story ends on an optimistic note. Somehow his act of adultery rekindles his love for his wife, a sign of the many detours, none of them predictable, that love may take on its meandering course through human life.

Other major work

LONG FICTION: *The Welsh Girl*, 2007.

Bibliography

Carey, Jacqueline. "Ties That Bind." *The New York Times*, March 19, 2000, p. 7-11. A review of *Equal Love* that praises Davies for his depiction of the burdens of family ties.

Eder, Richard. "'Equal Love': When Children Become Parents of Their Parents." Review of *Equal Love*, by Peter Ho Davies. *The New York Times*, February 2, 2000, p. E9. Eder comments that Davies writes with considerable skill but sometimes at the expense of "conveyed feeling." Not all the stories are successful; the best are on the wild side, including "The Next Life" and "The Hull Case." Eder argues that the latter story is the most "moving and suggestive" story in the collection.

Egan, Jennifer. "Through the Prison Camp Fence." Review of *The Welsh Girl* by Peter Ho Davies. *The New York Times Book Review*, February 18, 2007 p. 10. A generally favorable review of Davies's first novel. Although Egan says she sometimes "missed the tangy snap of his short fiction," she praises Davies's creation of an "absorbing world," and states that his achievement in the novel "is significant, like good social history."

Fernandez, Jay A. "The Ugliest House in the World." *The Washington Post*, January 4, 1998, p. X08. Says Davies is another example of the "mishmash" of global experiences. Calls the title story a flawless rendering of the effects of guilt.

Hensher, Philip. "Arts and Books Feature." *The Daily Telegraph*, February 19, 2000, p. 5. In this interview, Davies talks about how it felt to publish his first book, how he reacts to reviews, and the difficulty he has keeping from being distracted while writing.

Kirkus Reviews. Review of *The Ugliest House in the World*, by Peter Ho Davies (July 15, 1997). This review finds the collection "ingenious, moving, and exasperating in turn." The reviewer praises Davies' insightful view of human nature and his skill in plotting, especially in the title story. Also singled out for praise are Davies' originality and his affection for his characters in *A Union*. "Relief" and "Safe" are found to be the weaker stories.

Mullan, John. "My New Found Land." *London Guardian*, April 1, 2000, p. 9. A discussion of *Equal Love* that situates Davies' fiction within the genre of the short story, arguing that the form gives him ranges of experiment.

Reynolds, Susan Salter. "Equal Love." Review of *Equal Love*, by Peter Ho Davies. *Los Angeles Times*, February 6, 2000, p. 11. Brief review that selects "The Hull Case" as one of the best stories in the collection and in general praises the "dignified precision" with which Davies describes the inner lives of his characters.

Steinberg, Sybil S. Review of *Equal Love*, by Peter Ho Davies. *Publishers Weekly* 246, no. 47 (November 22, 1999): 41. Maintains that Davies' stories use "resonant, precise images to pave the way to intimate truths." Steinberg also praises Davies' craftsmanship, complexity, and his "compassionate voice."

_____. Review of *The Ugliest House in the World*, by Peter Ho Davies. *Publishers Weekly* 244, no. 33 (August 11, 1997): 384. Davies' first collection is hailed for its "spare style, taut prose and arresting images," the only weak point being the "melodramatic" *A Union*.

Bryan Aubrey

LYDIA DAVIS

Born: Northampton, Massachusetts; 1947

PRINCIPAL SHORT FICTION

The Thirteenth Woman, and Other Stories, 1976
Sketches for a Life of Wassilly, 1981
Story, and Other Stories, 1983
Break It Down, 1986
Almost No Memory, 1997
Samuel Johnson Is Indignant, 2001
Varieties of Disturbance, 2007
The Collected Stories of Lydia Davis, 2009

OTHER LITERARY FORMS

Lydia Davis has published one novel, *The End of the Story* (1995). Largely earning her living as a translator of French fiction and nonfiction, she is best known for her translations of Maurice Blanchot. In addition, she has translated the work of numerous authors, including Marcel Proust and Gustave Flaubert, in addition to biographies of Alexis de Tocqueville and Marie Curie.

ACHIEVEMENTS

Lydia Davis is known for her unique style of minimalist fiction, which borders on prose poetry and contains elements of nonfiction. Her collection of short stories *Break It Down* earned her the Whiting Award in

1988 and also was a finalist for the Hemingway Foundation/PEN Award. Her story "St. Martin" appeared in *The Best American Short Stories, 1997.* She earned a MacArthur Fellowship in 2003. *Varieties of Disturbance* was a finalist for the National Book Award in 2007. In addition, she earned a Guggenheim Fellowship (1997) and a Lannan Literary Award (1998). Also respected for her work as a translator, Davis received the French-American Foundation translation award in 1993 and was named Chevalier of the Order of Arts and Letters. In 2003, Davis translated *Du côté de chez Swann* (1913; *Swann's Way*, 1922), the first volume of Marcel Proust's *À la recherche du temps perdu* (1913-1927; *Remembrance of Things Past*, 1922-1931, 1981) for Penguin Classics and also wrote the notes on translation for the series. In addition, she is known for her translations of Maurice Blanchot and has earned grants from the National Endowment for the Arts for fiction translation.

BIOGRAPHY

Lydia Davis was born in 1947 in Northampton, Massachusetts. Her father, Robert Gorham Davis, was a professor of English at Smith College and the editor of the classic anthology of short stories *Ten Modern Masters* (1953). Her mother, Hope Hale Davis, taught at the Radcliffe Institute. Both of Lydia Davis's parents published fiction in *The New Yorker*. Her mother published a collection of short fiction, *Dark Way to the Plaza* (1945). In 1954, her father took a sabbatical and the family traveled to Austria, so Davis learned to read and write German in the second grade. In 1957, her father accepted a position at Columbia University, and the family moved to New York City. Although she knew early on in her life that she would become a writer, Davis first immersed herself in music, playing both the piano and the violin.

Davis majored in English at Barnard College. While in college, she took a writing workshop led by Grace Paley and met Paul Auster, whom she married in 1974. Davis and Auster traveled to Europe. Settling in France, they began working as translators. Davis's early translations were collaborations with Auster. The couple had a son, Daniel, in 1977 and divorced in the early 1980's. Davis later married the artist Alan Cote, with

whom she had a son, Theo. In 2002, Davis began teaching creative writing at the University of Albany.

ANALYSIS

Noted for its brevity, the short fiction of Lydia Davis is unmistakably unique. Many of her stories are less than two pages, some only one page, some merely one paragraph. Dialogue is noticeably absent. Often the protagonist is unnamed and identified with simply a pronoun. The narrative point of view tends to be microscopic and obsessively focused on solving a problem. Davis has aligned herself with no artistic school or political group. In interviews, she has identified her literary influences as Franz Kafka and Samuel Beckett.

BREAK IT DOWN

Break It Down begins with "Story," which opens with a woman returning from work to find a message on her answering machine: "I return home from work and there is a message from him: that he is not coming, that he is busy. He will call again." The man who left the message does not, in fact, call back; thus, the narrative unfolds as the narrator attempts to interpret the message and the motives behind it. Interpretation is complicated by the narrator's former relationship with her ex-husband. The plot involves a series of communications--telephone, written, and in person--and these communications serve to complicate the problem rather than solve it. Finally, the man says, "You don't understand, do you?" After a break of white space, the narrator states: "I try to figure it out." The rest of "Story" reads much like the discussion section of a scientific research report, as the narrator attempts to form a conclusion; instead, she arrives at new series of questions.

In "Story," the narrator questions where she stands in a current relationship with a man, while in "A Few Things Wrong with Me," the narrator questions why a man ended a romantic relationship with her. The story begins: "He said there were things about me that he hadn't liked from the very beginning." Similar to "Story," this communication occurs over the telephone, and although the narrator finds this admission initially disturbing, she eventually reasons: "But if I try to be logical, I have to think that after all there may be a few things wrong with me. Then the problem is to figure out what these things are." Interestingly, the narrator does not ask the man to reveal these things; she prefers to speculate on possibilities as she reviews events in the relationship. The story ends by acknowledging its central question as an unsolvable problem: "a useless question, really, since I'm not the one who can answer it and anyone else who tries will come up with a different answer though of course all the answers together may add up to the right one, if there is such a thing as a right answer to a question like that."

ALMOST NO MEMORY

"The Thirteenth Woman," in *Almost No Memory*, exemplifies Davis's shortest fiction. This story consists of one paragraph. The opening sentence is in passive voice: "In a town of twelve women there was a thirteenth." The rest of the story is composed of a series of negations that define the thirteenth woman of this unspecified town. Similarly, "The Center of the Story," in the form of a story within a story, is about a woman who has written a story that lacks a center. The reader is told that the story is about religion and is not easy to write. The story and the writing of the story become problems for the protagonist to solve. The reader is provided many concrete details from the story and details regarding the woman's reasoning in the writing process. A character in the story commits blasphemy and reflects that blasphemy indicates a belief in God. The problem shifts from the writing of the story to the storyteller's own religious beliefs, then back to the writing of the story. In the end, the problem remains unsolvable: "There may be no center . . . or . . . there is a center but the center is empty . . . in the same way that the man was sick but not dying, the hurricane approached but did not strike, and she had a religious calm but no faith."

Like "The Thirteenth Woman," "Foucault and Pencil" consists of a single paragraph. Though told in first person, the first-person pronoun does not occur within the story, as the attention is strongly focused on the telling rather than the teller. The narrative is extremely telescopic. The plot unfolds as a series of actions. The narrator begins reading Foucault ("with pencil in hand") while in the waiting room of a counselor's office, then proceeds to the counseling session, where she "sat with counselor discussing situation

Lydia Davis (AP Photo/MacArthur Foundation)

fraught with conflict." The narrator leaves the session, travels on the subway while again reading Foucault, where she conflates the argument in question with the idea of travel and the reading of Foucault. Again, the main subject is interpretation; in this specific instance, interpretation of Foucault and interpretation of the conflict under discussion with the counselor. The narrator obsessively differentiates what is understood with what is not understood; generally, concrete nouns are understood while abstract nouns are not. By the end of the story, the narrator comes to no ultimate conclusion.

SAMUEL JOHNSON IS INDIGNANT

"New Year's Resolution," included in *Samuel Johnson Is Indignant,* continues the concepts of negation and absence as exemplified in "The Thirteenth Woman" and "The Center of the Story." Again, this story consists of a single paragraph. This story begins: "I ask my friend Bob what his New Year's resolutions are," to which the narrator (who has "been studying . . . Zen again") receives typical answers. The narrator, like typical Davis narrators, takes several days to think about her own resolutions: "My

New Year's Resolution is to see myself as nothing," for this narrator has been diligently studying: "a medal or a rotten tomato, it's all the same, says the book I have been reading." Again, the problem proves insurmountable, and the narrator decides: "So what I think at this point is that I'm aiming too high, that maybe nothing is too much, to begin with. Maybe for now I should just try, each day, to be a little less than I usually am."

"Letter to a Funeral Parlor" exemplifies both Davis's attention to language and her subtle sense of humor. This story, as suggested by its title, is in epistolary form. Typical of Davis's style, the letter lacks a specific recipient: Both the funeral parlor and the addressee are unnamed. The letter focuses on the offensive use of the invented word "cremains" in reference to the ashes of the letter writer's father. The letter writer, who is also unnamed, first announces the problem of misinterpretation: "At first we did not even know what he meant. Then when we realized, we were frankly upset." The letter writer concludes by suggesting a more typical term: "You could very well continue to employ the term *ashes*. We are used to it from the Bible, and are even comforted by it. We would not misunderstand."

VARIETIES OF DISTURBANCE

The later work of Davis seems more attuned to aging parents and death. Similar to "Letter to a Funeral Parlor," "Grammar Questions," from *Varieties of Disturbance*, focuses on the use of language in connection to death. This very short story begins with a series of questions concerning the appropriate use of verbs in connection to the narrator's dying father: "If someone asks me, 'Where does he live?' can I say, 'He lives in Vernon Hall' Or should I say, 'He is dying in Vernon Hall'?" The narrator shifts to concerns of pronoun usage: "Is he, once he is dead, still 'he,' and if so, for how long is he still 'he'?" Continuing on this speculative path, the narrator questions the use of the possessive noun after the body of her father is cremated: "When I later visit the graveyard, will I point and say, 'My father is buried there,' or will I say, 'My father's ashes are buried there'? But the ashes will not belong to my father, he will not own them." The story ends with the question of active verbs and whether or not the father is actively dying:

In the phrase, "he is dying," the words *he is* with the present participle suggest that he is actively doing something. But he is not actively dying . . . "is not eating" sounds more correct for him than "is dying" because of the negative. "Is not" seems correct for him, at the moment anyway, because he looks as though he is refusing something, because he is frowning.

OTHER MAJOR WORKS

LONG FICTION: *The End of the Story*, 1995.

TRANSLATIONS: *Madness of the Day*, 1981 (of Maurice Blanchot); *Marie Curie: A Life*, 1986 (of Françoise Giroud); *Tocqueville: A Biography*, 1988 (of André Jardin, with Robert Hemenway); *Aerea in the Forests of Manhattan*, 1992 (of Emmanuel Hocquard); *Scraps: Rules of the Game II*, 1992 (of Michel Leiris); *Helene*, 1995 (of Pierre Jean Jouve); *The Station Hill Blanchot Reader: Fiction and Literary Essays*, 1999 (of Maurice Blanchot); *Swann's Way*, 2003 (of Marcel Proust); *Madame Bovary*, 2010 (of Gustave Flaubert).

BIBLIOGRAPHY

Cohen, Josh. "No Matter: Aesthetic Theory and the Self-Annihilating Artwork." In *Literature and Philosophy: A Guide to Contemporary Debates*, edited by David Rudrum. New York: Palgrave MacMillan, 2006. Focusing on two stories from *Almost No Memory*-- "The Thirteenth Woman" and "The Center of the Story"--Cohen examines the aesthetic paradox of defining presence through its absence.

_____. "Reflexive Incomprehension: On Lydia Davis." *Textual Practice* 24, no. 3 (2010): 501-516. A psychoanalytical interpretation of the title story of *Break It Down* and Davis's novel *The End of the Story*.

Lee, Sue-Im. "Motion in Stasis: Impossible Community in Fictions of Lydia Davis and Lynne Tillman." In *A Body of Individuals: The Paradox of Community in Contemporary Fiction*. Columbus: Ohio State University Press, 2009. Focusing on stories from *Break It Down* and *Almost No Memory*, Lee explores the ambivalent response of the protagonists in the fiction of Davis to the paradox of community.

McCaffery, Larry. "Deliberately, Terribly Neutral: An Interview with Lydia Davis." In *Some Other Frequency: Interviews with Innovative American Authors*. Philadelphia: University of Pennsylvania Press, 1996. This interview with Davis places her fiction within the context of her work as a translator.

Knight, Christopher J. "An Interview with Lydia Davis." *Contemporary Literature* 40, no. 4 (1999): 525-551. This lengthy interview touches on the in-

fluence of Davis's parents and contains some biographical information.

Perloff, Marjorie. "Fiction as Language Game: The Hermeneutic Parables of Lydia Davis and Maxine Chernoff." In *Breaking the Sequence: Women's Experimental Fiction*, edited by Ellen G. Friedman and Miriam Fuchs. Princeton, N.J.: Princeton University Press, 1989. Examines the use of language in the minimalist fiction of Davis and the problem of interpretation.

Nettie Farris

SAMUEL R. DELANY

Born: Harlem, New York; April 1, 1942
Also known as: Chip Delany

PRINCIPAL SHORT FICTION

"The Star Pit," 1966

"Aye, and Gomorrah," 1967

We, in Some Strange Power's Employ, Move on a Rigorous Line, 1968 (novella; also known as *Lines of Power*)

"Time Considered as a Helix of Semiprecious Stones," 1969

Driftglass: Ten Tales of Speculative Fiction, 1971 (revised and expanded, 2003, as *Aye, and Gomorrah*)

"Prismatica," 1977

Tales of Nevèrÿon, 1979

Distant Stars, 1981

Atlantis: Three Tales, 1995

OTHER LITERARY FORMS

Samuel R. Delany has produced more than twenty novels, including *Hogg* (1993), *They Fly at Çiron* (1993), *The Mad Man* (1994), and *Dark Reflections* (2007), and a relatively small body of highly acclaimed short fiction. He has worked primarily in science fiction and fantasy, but all his fiction is known for its

intricate literary qualities. His work has been translated into many languages and is internationally renowned. Delany's memoirs, especially *The Motion of Light in Water: Sex and Science Fiction Writing in the East Village, 1957-1965* (1988), provide insight into his formative writing years. His nonfiction works include *Shorter Views: Queer Thoughts and the Politics of the Paraliterary* (1999) and *Times Square Red, Times Square Blue* (1999).

ACHIEVEMENTS

Throughout Samuel R. Delany's career, his work has been recognized as far above the level of "pulp" science fiction. Many of his novels and short stories have been nominated for Nebula or Hugo awards, including *The Ballad of Beta-2* (nominated in 1965), "The Star Pit" (1966), "Driftglass" (1971), *Nova* (1968), *Dhalgren* (1975), *Triton* (1976), and "Prismatica" (1977). *The Einstein Intersection* and "Aye, and Gomorrah" won Nebula Awards in 1967, and "Time Considered as a Helix of Semiprecious Stones" won this award in 1969; that year, "Time Considered as a Helix of Semiprecious Stones" also received a Hugo Award. In 1980, Delany was honored with an American Book Award nomination for his *Tales of Nevèrÿon*, and he was given the Science Fiction Research Association's Pilgrim Award in 1985. *The Motion of Light in Water* was awarded a Hugo Award for Nonfiction in 1989, and in 1996 Delany received the

Lambda Literary Award in Science Fiction and Fantasy for *Altantis: Three Tales*. In 1993, Delany received the William Whitehead Memorial Award for a Lifetime Contribution to Gay and Lesbian Literature. Delany was inducted into the Science Fiction Hall of Fame in 2002.

BIOGRAPHY

Samuel Ray Delany, Jr., was born April 1, 1942, into a middle-class, professional family (two uncles were well-known judges in New York City) in the Harlem neighborhood of New York City. His father, Samuel Ray Delany, Sr., was a funeral director, and his mother, Margaret Carey Delaney (née Boyd), was a clerk in a local library. At summer camp one year, he chose the nickname "Chip" for himself and has been called that ever since.

Delany's early education took place at Dalton, an exclusive, primarily white school on the East Side of New York City. He then attended the Bronx High School of Science, where the average intelligence

Samuel R. Delany (MCT /Landov)

quotient of the students was 140. Although his scores in most subjects were excellent (particularly in math), Delaney's school career was often made more difficult by what would much later be diagnosed as dyslexia. His parents had forced him to become right-handed, and, partially as a result, Delany had immense difficulty with spelling, with a particular propensity for writing words backward. A broken and jumbled mishmash of misspellings, his writing was opaque even to him once he had forgotten the intended meaning of the words. His parents always encouraged him to write, however, because they had been told by a tutor that if Delany wrote as much as possible his spelling would have to improve. His mother read to him constantly, and his father even read aloud Mark Twain's *The Adventures of Huckleberry Finn* (1884), chapter by chapter.

On August 24, 1961, Delany married Marilyn Hacker. A first pregnancy for Marilyn ended in a miscarriage in 1961, but in 1974 the couple had a daughter, Iva Alyxander. Delany and Hacker were divorced in 1980, after an unconventional marriage about which he wrote in *The Motion of Light in Water*.

Delany attended City College in New York City (now City University of New York) in 1960 and again from 1962 to 1963, but he dropped out to finish *Babel-17* (1966). Despite his lack of a formal degree, Delany has held several prestigious academic posts. He was Butler Professor of English at State University of New York at Buffalo, in 1975, and senior fellow at the Center for Twentieth Century Studies at the University of Wisconsin, Milwaukee, in 1977. He also held the posts of senior fellow at the Society for the Humanities at Cornell University, in 1987, and professor of comparative literature at the University of Massachusetts, Amherst, in 1988. In 1995, Delaney was a visiting writer at the universities of Minnesota and Idaho, and in 1997 he was a visiting professor at Michigan State University. Since January, 2001, he has been a professor of English and creative writing at Temple University in Philadelphia, where he is the director of the graduate creative writing program in the College of Liberal Arts.

ANALYSIS

In *The Motion of Light in Water*, Delany spoke of himself as: "A black man. A gay man. A writer." Though these three truths do not "explain" Delany's life, they are the primary roots from which his writings have sprung. Delany's work often features marginalized characters, people outside society's mainstream, such as slaves or those who have been biologically modified (through tattooing or piercing, for example).

Delany himself--in his lifestyle, chosen profession, and chosen genre--is outside the American mainstream. However, he has found a way, through writing, to express and empower himself. This has not been easy, and many of the characters in his early short stories, whose tales were often narrated in first person, were as full of longing--or more so--at the end of the story as at the beginning. In Delany's later stories, particularly in *Tales of Nevèrÿon*, the characters often do find a place and a purpose for themselves.

Delany's first published novels, while grand in scope and rich with allusion, metaphor, and lyricism, still fit easily within science fiction's traditions. In 1975, however, Delany changed everyone's perspective of him with *Dhalgren* (1975), his longest book at more than eight hundred pages and his best-known and most controversial work. *Dhalgren* has been Delany's most commercially successful work, but despite being nominated for a Nebula Award, most of the book's critical acclaim has come from outside the science-fiction community. In fact, many within that community, both fans and other writers, disliked the book, perhaps because it met few of the expectations that had been established within science fiction.

Some fans and critics hailed *Triton* as a return to science fiction, but a careful reading of the book will show the same underlying complex of ideas at work. With *The Mad Man*, Delany departed completely from science fiction and moved into realism with a tale of murder, New York, and homosexuality in the age of acquired immunodeficiency syndrome (AIDS).

"AYE, AND GOMORRAH"

Though Delany is primarily known for his novels, his short stories form a critical body of work that must be considered. One of his best-known stories is "Aye, and Gomorrah," which was written in September,

1966, while Delany was at the Milford Science Fiction Writers Conference in Connecticut. It was immediately bought by Harlan Ellison for an influential anthology called *Dangerous Visions*, published in 1967. It was the story that, as Delany himself noted, helped him to make the transition from "an unknown to a known entity."

This very brief story takes place mainly in Istanbul, Turkey, but its setting is clearly secondary to its subject: the neutering of people who work in space and those who, because of a syndrome called free-fall-sexual-displacement complex, worship them sexually. The former, known as spacers, are attracted to the latter, called frelks, only for the money that the frelks will give them to perform acts that are not specified in the story but that have clearly sexual undertones. The androgynous nature of the frelks prevents any real sexual relationship.

While on the spacer equivalent of "shore leave," the young protagonist of "Aye, and Gomorrah" meets a Turkish girl, who wants to seduce the spacer but does not have the money necessary to bribe him. She is open about her obsession with spacers, although she does not like being a frelk--she believes that she is a "pervert" in the sense that a "pervert substitutes something unattainable for 'normal' love: the homosexual, a mirror, the fetishist, a shoe or a watch or a girdle."

The idea of being a sexual outcast is a frequent theme in Delany's work, perhaps stemming from his coming to terms with his homosexuality. In *Triton*, for example, the main character, Bron, undergoes a sex change, ostensibly to be able to understand women better, but instead becomes even more confused about his (or her) own sexuality. "Aye, and Gomorrah" focuses on the retarded sexuality of the spacers and the futile sexual longings of the frelks. In "The Tale of the Small Sarg," the character of Gorgik, a former slave who has become "civilized," reveals that he cannot function sexually unless either he or his partner is wearing some physical sign of ownership, such as a slave collar.

Delany often applies a light touch to these issues in his stories. In "Aye, and Gomorrah," the young spacer is constantly being corrected because of his tendency to assign the wrong gender of the word "frelk" in different languages. "*Une* frelk," he is told by a Frenchman, and he learns from a Latina that it is *frelko* in Spanish.

WE, IN SOME STRANGE POWER'S EMPLOY, MOVE ON A RIGOROUS LINE

We, in Some Strange Power's Employ, Move on a Rigorous Line tells the story of a power-cable layer, or "line demon," who is promoted to "line devil" and faces his first tough decisions while in command. The power company group stumbles across a band of "angels" who live up on a cliff with their "pteracycles," which seem to be flying motorcycles. Bringing power to this wild gang is seen by its members as a challenge to their lifestyle, but the power company must abide by the law, which states that power must be made available to each individual.

The irony of the story lies in its conclusion. Having defeated the head angel's attempt to drive them off, the power company employees go up to the gang's retreat, called High Haven. On finding that it has been deserted by the angels, however, the head devil decides that: "If there's nobody living up here, there's no reason to run power up here--by law." In essence, the power workers have destroyed what they set out to help with their civilizing gift of electricity. The story's narrator, at least, regrets it.

"TIME CONSIDERED AS A HELIX OF SEMIPRECIOUS STONES"

"Time Considered as a Helix of Semiprecious Stones," which was written in Milford in July, 1968, and published in 1969, also presents a mocking approach to modern society. The main character, who changes his identity almost with each page, comments, often bitingly (in parentheses within the text) on the world as it passes by: "A very tanned, very blond man . . . came down the rocks (artificial) between the ferns (real) growing along the stream (real water; phony current)." Later, he notes that "automation has become the upper crust's way of flaunting the labor surplus."

The subject of the story is the behavior of a criminal once it has been predicted that he will commit a specific crime. Interwoven with this theme is that of the Singers, who are "people who look at things, then go and tell people what they've seen. What makes them Singers is their ability to make people listen." One Singer, a youth named Hawk, is a familiar Delany

character all the way down to his deeply bitten fingernails. Unable to love in a "normal" way, he prefers pain to pleasure, much to the protagonist's dismay. The protagonist, meanwhile, characterizes his own aberration, the "will" to steal, as "an impulse toward the absurd and the tasteless . . . ," but it is a *want*, a *need*--like the need for love--and it cannot be forever denied.

"DRIFTGLASS"

"Driftglass" bears some similarity to "Aye, and Gomorrah," particularly in its description of adolescents sent off for surgical alteration so they can perform certain tasks better. In this case, however, the youths, rather than having body parts removed, have them added. Marine work for the Aquatic Corp. requires "a week of operations [to] make an amphibious creature that can exist for a month on either side of the sea's foam-fraught surface." The resulting "amphimen," a term that includes females, lay huge power cables to run oil wells and chemical distillation plants and to provide for herds of whales, as well as to supply underwater farms and mines.

The main character, however, has had his life ruined in an undersea volcanic accident. Living his lonely life on a Brazilian beach, Cal Svenson hunts for what he calls driftglass in the surf--unlikely treasures in the form of Coca-Cola bottles and discarded glass pounded by the sea into objets d'art. Cal has no regrets about his choice of career; in fact, he persuades his friend to allow his children (Cal's godchildren) to go into service with "the Corp" and be made into "amphimen."

TALES OF NEVÈRŸON

Not all Delany's stories are science-fiction tales set in the future. For example, the loosely related stories found in the *Tales of Nevèrÿon* collection are set in a mythical past. These stories owe much to the genre of swashbuckling fantasy fiction called sword-and-sorcery, though they depart as radically from the conventions of that genre as *Dhalgren* does from science fiction.

Sword-and-sorcery is, itself, a marginalized literature. It has received little respect from mainstream critics, even those willing to admit, grudgingly, that science fiction has something to offer. However, in the hands of some writers (Robert E. Howard, Fritz Leiber, Karl Edward Wagner), sword-and-sorcery has achieved notable commercial success and generated enough small press scholarship to deserve broader critical consideration.

Delany is, according to James Sallis in *Ash of Stars: On the Writing of Samuel R. Delany* (1996), "the man who would intellectualize" sword-and-sorcery. Certainly, Delany's *Nevèrÿon* stories have contributed two things to the genre. First, while sword-and-sorcery must develop a historical "feel," most writers achieve this with descriptions of walled cities, ruins, and sword fights. The focus is on large-scale, dramatic events--war being a favorite. A common criticism here is that readers seldom see how armies are fed or how cities survive in the absence of an economy other than trade.

Delany's *Nevèrÿon* stories, in contrast, develop a sense of history by focusing on exactly those details that other writers neglect. In "The Tale of Gorgik," the first *Nevèrÿon* story, the reader learns of docks and warehouses, of sailors and slaves. The main trade item described is not jewels or exotic furs but little rubber balls.

"The Tale of Old Venn" shows readers the ship builders and fishing boats. The astrolabe's invention is part of the story's background, and the development of an early writing system leads one character, Norema, to thoughts on origins and philosophy.

Although sword-and-sorcery works are generally set at a time when cultures are moving from barter to monetary economies and from rural to urban societies, most writers use these facts only to force characters into motion. Delany makes the change to a monetary economy a major focus of such stories as "The Tale of Potters and Dragons," where attempts to control the rubber ball trade and the change from three-legged to four-legged pots are important plot developments. Is it coincidence that one character is named Madam Keyne (reminiscent of John Maynard Keynes, the economist)?

Delany's second contribution to sword-and-sorcery is his far greater emphasis on character than on the plot and action that drive most work in the genre. In fact, there is little plot at all in the *Nevèrÿon* stories. There are certainly no larger-than-life characters. Gorgik, who appears in most of the tales and is the closest Delany comes to a barbarian warrior, is, in fact, a

"civilized" man and has the psychological scars to prove it. Only "The Tale of Dragons and Dreamers" has much fighting, and it is not an imprisoned Gorgik who does it; rather it is Small Sarg, a youth, who handles the killing.

Many characters in the *Nevèrÿon* stories are women, but not in the usual roles of princess, harlot, or woman warrior (the only woman warrior is named Raven). Instead, women are merchants, inventors, and fishers. There is a part-time prostitute whose story is told in "The Tale of Rumor and Desire"; this is Clodon, a man.

OTHER MAJOR WORKS

LONG FICTION: *The Jewels of Aptor*, 1962; *Captives of the Flame*, 1963 (revised 1968, as *Out of the Dead City*); *The Towers of Toron*, 1964; *City of a Thousand Suns*, 1965; *The Ballad of Beta-2*, 1965; *Babel-17*, 1966; *Empire Star*, 1966; *The Einstein Intersection*, 1967; *Nova*, 1968; *The Fall of the Towers*, 1970 (includes revised versions of *Out of the Dead City*, *The Towers of Toron*, and *City of a Thousand Suns*); *The Tides of Lust*, 1973 (also known as *Equinox*); *Dhalgren*, 1975; *Triton*, 1976 (also known as *Trouble on Triton*); *Empire*, 1978; *Neveryóna: Or, The Tale of Signs and Cities*, 1983; *Stars in My Pocket Like Grains of Sand*, 1984; *Flight from Nevèrÿon*, 1985; *The Bridge of Lost Desire*, 1987 (also known as *Return to Nevèrÿon*); *Hogg*, 1993; *They Fly at Çiron*, 1993; *The Mad Man*, 1994; *Phallos*, 2004 (novella); *Dark Reflections*, 2007.

NONFICTION: *The Jewel-Hinged Jaw: Notes on the Language of Science Fiction*, 1977, rev. ed. 2009; *The American Shore: Meditations on a Tale of Science Fiction by Thomas M. Disch*, 1978; *Heavenly Breakfast: An Essay on the Winter of Love*, 1979; *Starboard Wine: More Notes on the Language of Science Fiction*, 1984; *The Straits of Messina*, 1987; *The Motion of Light in Water: Sex and Science-Fiction Writing in the East Village, 1957-1965*, 1988 (memoir); *Silent Interviews*, 1994; *Longer Views*, 1996; *Bread and Wine: An Erotic Tale of New York City, an Autobiographical Account*, 1998; *Shorter Views: Queer Thoughts and the Politics of the Paraliterary*, 1999; *Times Square Red, Times Square Blue*, 1999; *Nineteen Eighty-Four: Selected Letters*, 2000; *About Writing: Seven Essays, Four*

Letters, and Five Interviews, 2005; *Conversations with Samuel R. Delany*, 2009 (Carl Freedman, editor).

EDITED TEXT: *Quark: A Quarterly of Speculative Fiction*, 1970-1971 (with Marilyn Hacker).

BIBLIOGRAPHY

Barbour, Douglas. *Worlds Out of Words: The SF Novels of Samuel R. Delany*. London: Bran's Head Books, 1979. This fairly early critique of Delany's novels gives a brief biography of Delany and a general discussion of his works before concentrating on different aspects, such as cultural, literary, and mythological allusions and some individual works. Includes notes and primary bibliography.

DeGraw, Sharon. *The Subject of Race in American Science Fiction*. New York: Routledge, 2007. Examines the work of Edgar Rice Burroughs, George S. Schuyler, and Delany to chart the changing depiction of racial identity in American science fiction.

Delany, Samuel R. *Conversations with Samuel R. Delany*. Edited by Carl Freedman. Jackson: University Press of Mississippi, 2009. Collection of interviews with Delany that were conducted from 1980 to 2007.

Dery, Mark. "Black to the Future: Interviews with Samuel R. Delany, Greg Tate, and Tricia Rose." *The South Atlantic Quarterly* 92 (Fall, 1993): 735-778. Examines why so few African Americans write science fiction, since it is a genre in which encounters with the Other are central; discusses these matters with Delany and others.

Fox, Robert Elliot. *Conscientious Sorcerers: The Black Postmodernist Fiction of LeRoi Jones/Amiri Baraka, Ishmael Reed, and Samuel R. Delany*. New York: Greenwood Press, 1987. Fox's text is useful for comparing and contrasting Delany's writing with that of his contemporaries in black fiction. Despite the gulf between their genres, Fox manages to find some similarity in the styles and subjects of these writers. Contains bibliographical information and an index.

Kelso, Sylvia. "'Across Never': Postmodern Theory and Narrative Praxis in Samuel R. Delany's *Nevèrÿon* Cycle." *Science-Fiction Studies* 24 (July, 1997): 289-301. Argues that Derridean theory supplies the "Symbolic Order" of the blurred margins and centerless structure of Delany's *Nevèrÿon* cycle and that Michel Foucault's use of sadomasochistic experience is mirrored in the cycle's "homoerotic Imaginary."

McEvoy, Seth. *Samuel R. Delany*. New York: Frederick Ungar, 1984. Much of the information in this text comes from personal interviews that McEvoy conducted with Delany. The book covers biographical information and interpretation of individual works, including short fiction, as well as long fiction. Complemented by notes to the chapters and an index.

Reid-Pharr, Robert F. "Disseminating Heterotopia." *African American Review* 28 (Fall, 1994): 347-357. Discusses how Delany confronts traditional ideas of proper identity and community politics, deconstructing lines between black and white communities and homosexual and heterosexual communities.

Review of Contemporary Fiction 16 (Fall, 1996). Special issue on Delany with essays on his novels and his science-fiction theory and criticism. Features an essay on his tales and an interview with Delany in which he discusses his theory of science fiction and his ideas about science fiction as a genre and a way of reading.

Sallis, James, ed. *Ash of Stars: On the Writing of Samuel R. Delany*. Jackson: University Press of Mississippi, 1996. An excellent source for information on Delany's life and work. Includes a bibliography and an index.

Slusser, George Edgar. *The Delany Intersection: Samuel R. Delany Considered as a Writer of Semi-Precious Words*. San Bernardino, Calif.: Borgo Press, 1977. Sets out the structuralist interpretation of Delany's works, using his literary criticism essays to judge his own writing. Also traces the evolution of Delany's work from heroic epics to psychological fiction and beyond. Includes brief biographical and bibliographical notes.

Tucker, Jeffrey Allen. *A Sense of Wonder: Samuel R. Delany, Race, Identity, and Difference*. Middletown, Conn.: Wesleyan University Press, 2004. A sophisticated analysis of Delany's work within the framework of postmodernism. Includes bibliography and index.

Weedman, Jane. *Samuel R. Delany*. Mercer Island, Wash.: Starmont House, 1982. Weedman discusses a wide range of subjects, including influences on Delany's writing, biographical events, stylistic and critical concepts, and Delany's development as a writer. A detailed chronology can be found at the beginning of the book, and annotated primary and secondary bibliographies have been included at its end. Also contains an index.

Jo-Ellen Lipman Boon
Updated by Charles A. Gramlich

AUGUST DERLETH

Born: Sauk City, Wisconsin; February 24, 1909
Died: Sauk City, Wisconsin; July 4, 1971
Also known as: Will Garth, Romily Devon, Stephen Grendon, Eldon Heath, Tally Mason, Kenyon Holmes, Simon West, Michael West

PRINCIPAL SHORT FICTION

Place of Hawks, 1935
Consider Your Verdict: Ten Coroner's Cases for You to Solve, 1937 (as Tally Mason)
Any Day Now, 1938
Country Growth, 1940
Someone in the Dark, 1941
In re, Sherlock Holmes: The Adventures of Solar Pons, 1945 (also known as *The Adventures of Solar Pons,* 1975)
Something Near, 1945
Not Long for This World, 1948
Sac Prairie People, 1948
The Memoirs of Solar Pons, 1951
Three Problems for Solar Pons, 1952
The House of Moonlight, 1953
The Survivor and Others, 1957 (with H. P. Lovecraft)
The Mask of Cthulhu, 1958
The Return of Solar Pons, 1958
The Reminiscences of Solar Pons, 1961
Wisconsin in Their Bones, 1961
Lonesome Places, 1962
Mr. George and Other Odd Persons, 1963 (also known as *When Graveyards Yawn*)

The Adventure of the Orient Express, 1965
The Casebook of Solar Pons, 1965
Praed Street Papers, 1965
Colonel Markesan and Less Pleasant People, 1966 (with Mark Schorer)
The Adventure of the Unique Dickensians, 1968
Mr. Fairlie's Final Journey, 1968
A Praed Street Dossier, 1968
The Shadow Out of Time, and Other Tales of Horror, 1968 (with H. P. Lovecraft)
A House Above Cuzco, 1969
The Chronicles of Solar Pons, 1973
The Watchers Out of Time and Others, 1974 (with H. P. Lovecraft)
Harrigan's File, 1975
Dwellers in Darkness, 1976
Aunt May Strikes Again!, 1996
Shane's Girls, 1997
The Final Adventures of Solar Pons, 1998
The Quest for Cthulhu, 2000

OTHER LITERARY FORMS

A tremendously prolific writer, August Derleth (dehr-LEHTH) produced an amazing number of novels, poems, and essays, in addition to short fiction. Included among these are mystery and horror tales, children's books, and histories. He wrote a series of novels, nonfiction, and poetry called the Sac Prairie Saga; five books in his Wisconsin Saga; ten novels in the Judge Peck mystery series (1934-1953); biographies of Henry David Thoreau, Ralph Waldo Emerson, Zona Gale, and H. P. Lovecraft; and a memoir of Sinclair Lewis, Sherwood Anderson, and Edgar Lee Masters. In addition, he wrote about and collected comic books, edited many anthologies of science fiction, and made several studies of homicide.

ACHIEVEMENTS

Although Derleth was certainly one of the most versatile and prolific American writers of the twentieth century, he is also relatively unknown, and little has been written about him and his work. He became a professional writer while in his teens and received a John Simon Guggenheim Memorial Foundation Fellowship in 1938. Among the honors he received were the Award of Merit given by the State Historical Society (for children's books based on Wisconsin's history) in 1954, the Scholastic Award in 1958, the Midland Authors Award (for poetry) in 1965, the Ann Radcliffe Award in 1967, and the Best Nonfiction Award from the Council for Wisconsin Writers for *Return to Walden West* (1970) in 1971. His greatest literary achievement may well be his Sac Prairie Saga.

In the area of short fiction, his contributions are most notable in mystery-detective fiction and horror stories. As editor and publisher, he is credited with preserving and bringing to the reading public the tales of the major horror fiction writer H. P. Lovecraft. His major contribution to mystery-detective fiction is his Solar Pons series (1945-1973), which kept alive the spirit and style of Sir Sir Arthur Conan Doyle's work after he had ceased writing new adventures.

BIOGRAPHY

Born in Sauk City, Wisconsin, on February 24, 1909, August William Derleth was the son of William Julius and Rose Louise Volk Derleth. He attended St. Aloysius School and Sauk City High School and received his B.A. from the University of Wisconsin at Madison in 1930. His career in writing began early, when he sold his first story, "Bat's Belfry," at age fifteen, and his interest in horror stories continued throughout his life. Some of his later tales are written on themes reminiscent of Lovecraft, whose work Derleth admired.

During his youth, Derleth also enjoyed Doyle's Sherlock Holmes stories. After writing to Doyle to ask if he would write any more adventures and receiving no promise that he would do so, Derleth decided to

continue the tradition himself. Thus, in 1928, while still a student, he created the Solar Pons character, patterned after Doyle's legendary detective, Sherlock Holmes. His story "The Adventures of the Black Narcissus" appeared in *Dragnet* magazine in February, 1929. With this success, he quickly wrote new adventures. Unfortunately, the 1929 stock market crash wiped out *Dragnet*, and these stories remained unpublished until years later.

Derleth worked as an editor of *Mystic Magazine* for Fawcett Publications in Minneapolis in 1930-1931, leaving when the magazine was discontinued to edit *The Midwesterner* in Madison. In 1933, he contracted with the publishers Loring and Mussey for a series of mystery novels, and in 1934 the first Judge Peck novel, *Murder Stalks the Wakely Family*, was published.

In 1939, Derleth bought property near Sauk City, where he built his home, "Place of Hawks." From 1939 to 1943 he was a lecturer in American regional literature at the University of Wisconsin. With David Wandrei, he founded Arkham House Publishers in 1939. As owner and cofounder from 1939 to 1971, he made some of his greatest contributions, including the preservation of Lovecraft's fiction in book form after the original collections went out of print in the late 1940's and 1950's.

After his early successes, Derleth never achieved much national recognition. After the late 1930's and early 1940's, his work was no longer reviewed in the major publications. Since he wrote quickly and rarely revised his work, he has been criticized for failing to develop and polish his craft. Indeed, much of his writing was done for magazines and commercial books in an attempt to supplement his income, but even his "serious" work, such as his Sac Prairie Saga, seemed to flow easily and was not critically revised.

In 1941, he was appointed literary editor of the Madison *Capital-Times*, and he remained at this job for most of the rest of his life. He married Sandra Winters in 1953, and they had two children. They were divorced in 1959. From 1960 to 1963, he edited the poetry magazine *Hawk and Whippoorwill*, and from 1967 to 1971, he edited and published *The Arkham Collector*. He died in Sauk City, Wisconsin, on July 4, 1971, after a heart attack.

ANALYSIS

Although it has been said that the "true and most original Derleth" is not to be found in his fiction, August Derleth's short stories have also won him admirers. His horror stories, many in the tradition of H. P. Lovecraft, have appeared in magazines for popular reading. His most skilled work in the area of short fiction, however, is probably his Solar Pons series. Clearly undertaken as an imitation, these stories recall for Sherlock Holmes fans the wonderful adventures of Baker Street, with Solar Pons as the new master detective. Each of these stories is constructed along a line of deductive reasoning that is very Holmesian in character. The three examples that follow will serve to illustrate Derleth's skill in creating adventures of this type.

"THE ADVENTURE OF THE RUDBERG NUMBERS"

"The Adventure of the Rudberg Numbers" is an ingenious speculation on the invention of the atomic bomb as a tangential result of one of Solar Pons's elegant solutions to a crime. The story is related by Pons's Dr. Watson-like associate, Parker, who is the detective's foil. Bancroft Pons, a high official in the Foreign Office and brother to the detective, introduces the plot. A young woman with defective eyesight named Lillian Pargeter has consulted him, by mistake, about the abduction of her brother, a thirty-five-year-old physicist employed by the government in research. A double has been substituted in his place who goes to his office at the regular times. Lillian detects the substitution only by the calluses on his right hand. The imposter is able to mimic her brother's gait, speech, and appearance but not his left-handedness.

Pons consults his reference book on physics and studies the scientist's papers assiduously. After an entire night's concentration he concludes that the formulae are Rudberg numbers, which refer to the radiation of heat and light, and he speculates that Pargeter has discovered the law of the fissionability of the atom. Pons puts together the information he has gotten from Lillian, who says that her and her brother's social lives are quite constricted because her brother insists on boring everyone with his theories, since no one at work takes him seriously, with the fact that one of the people whom Pargeter had recently expatiated to is a close associate of the German ambassador, who is a friend of an espionage agent, von Grafenstein.

Pons summons Alfred Peake, who is head of a gang of boys, the Praed Street Irregulars, who will do anything for a guinea. Pons gives them money to buy Halloween costumes and instructs them to storm into Grafenstein's house as if they were trick-or-treating. They are to search through the mansion until they find the scientist, and Pons gives them a photograph so they will recognize him. Just as he suspected, the physicist's face has been bandaged and he has been confined to bed. The twenty boys manage to get him to the waiting limousine. Pargeter is sent to America, and his double is charged with giving information to foreign agents and put under detention pending trial. Subsequent events prove that the Americans were not as skeptical as the British about Pargeter's radical theories. Not only is the plotline of this story elegantly maneuvered, with an extraordinary amount of highly technical information used in its solution, but also the minor characters, such as the landlady and the boys in the street gang, are amusingly handled. Everything falls perfectly into place, like a masterly chess game without a single wasted move.

"THE ADVENTURE OF THE REMARKABLE WORM"

"The Adventure of the Remarkable Worm" turns on a cryptic postcard and an etymological specimen. It begins on a summer afternoon in the 1930's as a heavy woman in a housedress and a shawl with a florid face and a provincial accent enters, quite agitated. Her employer is an expatriate American of Spanish background named Idomeno Persano, who lives alone, collects insects, and is always ready to give the neighborhood children a shilling for an interesting bug to add to his collection. A month ago he received a postcard that frightened him so intensely that he has not since left the house. On the front of the card was a sketch of a fat man running away from a dog. That very day he had gotten a worm, mailed inside a matchbox. He became paralyzed as he inspected it; his last words were "the dog."

As Pons and Parker arrive with the cleaning woman, they see immediately that Persano, seated in front of a horrible caterpillar in a small box, is dead. Scattered on the table are etymology books in which, apparently, he had been attempting to identify the insect. Pons finds the discarded wrapping and notes that the return address does not coincide with the postmark. The caterpillar is furry and has four horns; from the head uncoils a slender, threadlike tongue; it has four rows of centipede feet; and it is four inches long and two inches wide, with double antennae. Pons deduces that it has been artificially assembled: The head is a sphinx moth, the torso is a centipede, one set of antennae are from a Luna moth, the other from a katydid. He squeezes it with a tweezers and fangs spurting venom shoot forth from the horns. He has noted the gash with a swollen area around it on the victim's finger and deduces that he had been poisoned. Pons excuses himself and returns at midnight to announce that he has found the murderer: "a short, dark-skinned man" who is named Angelo Perro, which is Spanish for *dog*.

Parker is totally bewildered, so Pons shows him a clipping from a Chicago paper announcing that on June 29, Angelo Perro was paroled from the U.S. Penitentiary at Leavenworth; he was convicted in 1914 for transporting and delivering narcotics and served eleven years. Evidence against him had been furnished by a former member of his gang named "Big Id" Persano, who had been given a suspended sentence in return for his assistance in obtaining the conviction. The postcard had been the announcement that "the little dog" was now free to chase the fat man, and Persano had been corpulent. Pons congratulates his own neat solution in the concluding sentence: "an ingenious little puzzle, Parker, however elementary in final analysis."

"THE ADVENTURE OF THE CAMBERWELL BEAUTY"

"The Adventure of the Camberwell Beauty" is about the disappearance of the lovely ward of a millionaire, an ancient Chinese man who lives underground, through dusty, cobwebbed corridors and sliding passages in a slum neighborhood of London. Set on a May evening in the early 1930's, shortly after Parker's marriage, the solution takes Pons only a single day. Karah, the beautiful girl who has been abducted, is supposed to have been taken by Baron Corvus, who has one wooden leg. Three sets of footprints at the foot of Corvus's boat landing are shown to Pons. Pons notices that both the peg-legged prints and the woman's high-heeled prints are uneven, deeper on one side than

the other. He puts this fact together with the fact that Peters, the Chinese man's servant, limps. It does not take him long to establish the fact that Peters and Karah met at Oxford, that Peters's leg was wounded in the war, that their marriage has been opposed by his employer, that Peters himself has hidden his fiancé on a boat and taken her shoes with which to make the fake footprints, and that they plan to elope. Pons helps the lovers make their getaway and then reports back to his Chinese client, who says contentedly, "So I shall lose both of them. They should be happy with each other."

Derleth creates likable characters with credible motivations; even his villains are not totally unsympathetic. Pons is modeled on Sherlock Holmes down to the last detail, even to his violin-playing and the deerstalker hat. Derleth's public was apparently as insatiable as Sir Arthur Conan Doyle's; he said in his foreword to *Three Problems for Solar Pons* that his detective "managed to attract a solid core of followers; it is for these devotees of the Sacred Writings that this little book is offered in, as it were, the last bow of the Sherlock Holmes of Praed Street." He went on, however, at his public's insistence, to write a number of other detective novels featuring Pons, who took several more "last bows."

OTHER MAJOR WORKS

LONG FICTION: *The Man on All Fours*, 1934; *Murder Stalks the Wakely Family*, 1934 (also known as *Death Stalks the Wakely Family*); *Sign of Fear*, 1935; *Three Who Died*, 1935; *Still Is the Summer Night*, 1937; *Wind over Wisconsin*, 1938; *Restless Is the River*, 1939; *Sentence Deferred*, 1939; *Bright Journey*, 1940; *The Narracong Riddle*, 1940; *Evening in Spring*, 1941; *Sweet Genevieve*, 1942; *The Seven Who Waited*, 1943; *Shadow of Night*, 1943; *The Lurker at the Threshold*, 1945 (with H. P. Lovecraft); *Mischief in the Lane*, 1944; *No Future for Luana*, 1945; *The Shield of the Valiant*, 1945; *Death by Design*, 1953; *Fell Purpose*, 1953; *The House on the Mound*, 1958; *The Hills Stand Watch*, 1960; *The Trail of Cthulhu*, 1962; *The Shadow in the Glass*, 1963; *The Wind Leans West*, 1969; *The Wind in the Cedars*, 1997.

POETRY: *To Remember*, 1933; *Hawk on the Wind*, 1938; *Elegy: On a Flake of Snow*, 1939; *Man Track*

Here, 1939; *Here on a Darkling Plain*, 1940; *Wind in the Elms*, 1941; *Rind of Earth*, 1942; *And You, Thoreau!*, 1944; *Selected Poems*, 1944; *The Edge of Night*, 1945; *Habitant of Dusk: A Garland for Cassandra*, 1946; *Rendezvous in a Landscape*, 1952; *Psyche*, 1953; *Country Poems*, 1956; *Elegy: On the Umbral Moon*, 1957; *West of Morning*, 1960; *This Wound*, 1962; *Country Places*, 1965; *The Only Place We Live*, 1966; *By Owl Light*, 1967; *Collected Poems, 1937-1967*, 1967; *Caitlin*, 1969; *The Landscape of the Heart*, 1970; *Last Light*, 1971; *Love Letters to Caitlin*, 1971; *In a Quiet Graveyard*, 1997.

NONFICTION: *The Heritage of Sauk City*, 1931; *Atmosphere of Houses*, 1939; *Still Small Voice: The Biography of Zona Gale*, 1940; *Village Year: A Sac Prairie Journal*, 1941; *Wisconsin Regional Literature*, 1941 (revised 1942); *The Wisconsin: River of a Thousand Isles*, 1942; *H. P. L.: A Memoir*, 1945; *Writing Fiction*, 1946; *Village Daybook: A Sac Prairie Journal*, 1947; *Sauk County: A Centennial History*, 1948; *The Milwaukee Road: Its First Hundred Years*, 1948; *Wisconsin Earth: A Sac Prairie Sampler*, 1948; *Arkham House: The First Twenty Years: 1939-1959*, 1959; *Some Notes on H. P. Lovecraft*, 1959; *Walden West*, 1961; *Concord Rebel: A Life of Henry D. Thoreau*, 1962; *Countryman's Journal*, 1963; *Three Literary Men: A Memoir of Sinclair Lewis, Sherwood Anderson, Edgar Lee Masters*, 1963; *Wisconsin Country: A Sac Prairie Journal*, 1965; *Vincennes: Portal to the West*, 1968; *Walden Pond: Homage to Thoreau*, 1968; *Wisconsin Murders*, 1968; *The Wisconsin Valley*, 1969; *Emerson, Our Contemporary*, 1970; *Return to Walden West*, 1970; *Thirty Years of Arkham House: A History and a Bibliography, 1939-1969*, 1970; *Country Matters*, 1996.

CHILDREN'S LITERATURE: *Oliver, the Wayward Owl*, 1945; *A Boy's Way: Poems*, 1947; *It's a Boy's World: Poems*, 1948; *The Captive Island*, 1952; *The Country of the Hawk*, 1952; *Empire of Fur: Trading in the Lake Superior Region*, 1953; *Land of Gray Gold: Lead Mining in Wisconsin*, 1954; *Father Marquette and the Great Rivers*, 1955; *Land of Sky-Blue Waters*, 1955; *St. Ignatius and the Company of Jesus*, 1956; *Columbus and the New World*, 1957; *The Moon Tenders*, 1958; *The Mill Creek Irregulars*, 1959; *Wilbur, the Trusting*

Whippoorwill, 1959; *The Pinkertons Ride Again*, 1960; *The Ghost of Black Hawk Island*, 1961; *Sweet Land of Michigan*, 1962; *The Tent Show Summer*, 1963; *Forest Orphans*, 1964 (also known as *Mr. Conservation*, 1971); *The Irregulars Strike Again*, 1964; *The House by the River*, 1965; *The Watcher on the Heights*, 1966; *Wisconsin*, 1967; *The Beast in Holger's Woods*, 1968; *The Prince Goes West*, 1968; *The Three Straw Men*, 1970.

EDITED TEXTS: *Poetry Out of Wisconsin*, 1937; *Sleep No More: Twenty Masterpieces of Horror for the Connoisseur*, 1944; *Who Knocks? Twenty Masterpieces of the Spectral for the Connoisseur*, 1946; *Dark of the Moon: Poems of Fantasy and the Macabre*, 1947; *The Night Side: Masterpieces of the Strange and Terrible*, 1947; *The Sleeping and the Dead*, 1947; *Strange Ports of Call: Twenty Masterpieces of Science Fiction*, 1948; *The Other Side of the Moon*, 1949; *Beyond Time and Space: A Compendium of Science Fiction Through the Ages*, 1950; *Far Boundaries: Twenty Science-Fiction Stories*, 1951; *The Outer Reaches: Favorite Science-Fiction Tales Chosen by Their Authors*, 1951; *Beachheads in Space: Stories on a Theme in Science-Fiction*, 1952; *Night's Yawning Peal: A Ghostly Company*, 1952; *Worlds of Tomorrow: Science Fiction with a Difference*, 1953; *Portals of Tomorrow: The Best of Science Fiction and Other Fantasy*, 1954; *Time to Come: Science Fiction Stories of Tomorrow*, 1954; *Fire and Sleet and Candlelight: New Poems of the Macabre*, 1961; *Dark Mind, Dark Heart*, 1962; *When Evil Wakes: A New Anthology of the Macabre*, 1963; *Over the Edge*, 1964; *Wisconsin Harvest*, 1966; *Travellers by Night*, 1967; *New Poetry Out of Wisconsin*, 1969; *Dark Things*, 1971; *The Angler's Companion*, 1997.

EDITED TEXTS (WORKS OF H. P. LOVECRAFT): *The Outsider and Others*, 1939; *Beyond the Wall of Sleep*, 1943; *Marginalia*, 1944; *Supernatural Horror in Literature*, 1945; *The Best Supernatural Stories of H. P. Lovecraft*, 1945; *The Haunter of the Dark, and Other Tales of Horror*, 1951; *The Survivor and Others*, 1957; *The Shuttered Room, and Other Pieces*, 1959; *Collected Poems*, 1960; *Dreams and Fancies*, 1962; *Autobiography: Some Notes on a Nonentity*, 1963; *The Dunwich Horror, and Others: The Best Supernatural Stories of H. P. Lovecraft*, 1963; *At the Mountains of*

Madness, and Other Novels, 1964; *Dagon, and Other Macabre Tales*, 1965; *H. P. Lovecraft Selected Letters 1911-1924*, 1965; *The Dark Brotherhood, and Other Pieces*, 1966; *H. P. Lovecraft Selected Letters 1925-1929*, 1968; *The Shadow Out of Time, and Other Tales of Horror*, 1968; *Tales of the Cthulhu Mythos*, 1969; *The Tomb, and Other Tales*, 1969; *The Horror in the Museum, and Other Revisions*, 1970; *H. P. Lovecraft Selected Letters, 1929-1931*, 1971; *Something About Cats, and Other Pieces*, 1971.

MISCELLANEOUS: *Wisconsin Earth: A Sac Prairie Sampler*, 1948; *The Praed Street Papers*, 1965; *Buster Brown*, 1974 (with Richard Felton Outcault); *The Katzenjammer Kids*, 1974 (with Rudolph Dirks); *The Only Place We Live*, 1976.

BIBLIOGRAPHY

Bishop, Zealia. "A Wisconsin Balzac: A Profile of August Derleth." In *The Curse of Yig*. Sauk City, Wis.: Arkham House, 1953. One of the few articles of any length on Derleth's life and career.

Blei, Norbert. "August Derleth: Storyteller of Sac Prairie." *Chicago Tribune Magazine*, August 15, 1971. An informative and interesting article based on an interview with Derleth that offers a good short study of the man and his work.

Grant, Kenneth B. "August (William) Derleth." In *The Authors*. Vol. 1 in *Dictionary of Midwestern Literature*. Bloomington: Indiana University Press, 2001. A brief biographical and critical overview.

Grobe Litersky, Dorothy M. *Derleth: Hawk . . . and Dove*. Aurora, Colo.: National Writers Press, 1997. The first major, book-length, comprehensive critical study of Derleth's life and works.

Liebow, Ely M., ed. *August Harvest*. New York: Magico Magazine, 1994. Features essays dealing with Derleth's work in all genres.

Muckian, Michael, and Dan Benson. "One of the State's Great Writers Is Nearly Forgotten." *Milwaukee Journal Sentinel Magazine*, August 13, 1995, p. 8. A biographical sketch, accompanied by an account of the efforts by Derleth's children and admirers to reissue his work and create new interest in him. Includes an interview with Derleth's son, who talks about his father's death wish in the last years of his life.

Ross, Dale H. "August Derleth." In *Critical Survey of Mystery and Detective Fiction*, edited by Carl Rollyson. Rev. ed. Pasadena, Calif.: Salem Press, 2008. An overview of Derleth's mystery and detective fiction, discussing his contribution to the genre and analyzing the short stories that feature Solar Pons, Derleth's major mystery character.

Schultz, David E., and Scott Connors, eds. *Selected Letters of Clark Ashton Smith*. Sauk City, Wisc.: Arkham House, 2003. Derleth is among the most prolific correspondents in this collection of Smith's letters, and this is an excellent source for an informal glimpse of the author in his own words.

Starrett, Vincent. Introduction to *The Adventures of Solar Pons*. London: Robson Books, 1975. A short introduction to Derleth and his character Solar Pons. Since so little is available on Derleth, students who wish additional information on the Solar Pons series could also consult introductions in these collections: *The Reminiscences of Solar Pons* (an introduction by Anthony Boucher and "A Chronology of Solar Pons" by Robert Patrick), and *The Return of Solar Pons* (introduction by Edgar W. Smith).

Stephens, Jim. Introduction to *An August Derleth Reader*. Madison, Wis.: Prairie Oak Press, 1992. A solid biographical and critical overview of Derleth and his works.

Wilson, Alison W. *August Derleth: A Bibliography*. Metuchen, N.J.: Scarecrow Press, 1983. The best full-length source available for information on the life and works of Derleth and an indispensable volume for sorting through his amazing literary production. Contains a preface, an introduction, and a chronology, including interesting details on Derleth's activities and literary reputation. Lists and briefly explains all of his works, divided into "Fantasy World" and "Sac Prairie and the Real World." Contains a helpful index by title.

Zell, Fran. "August Derleth's Gus Elker Stories in One Volume." *Milwaukee Journal Sentinel Cue*, November 10, 1996, p. 13. A review of *Country Matters*, arguing that the Gus Elker stories are formulaic and predictable, but that they have preserved a bucolic world and way of life prior to television.

Ruth Rosenberg
Updated by Susan L. Piepke

JUNOT DÍAZ

Born: Santo Domingo, Dominican Republic; December 31, 1968

PRINCIPAL SHORT FICTION

Drown, 1996
"The Sun, the Moon, the Stars," 1998
"Otravida, Otravez," 1999
"Nilda," 1999
"Alma," 2007
"The Pura Principle," 2010

OTHER LITERARY FORMS

The first novel of Junot Díaz (JEW-noh DEE-az), *The Brief Wondrous Life of Oscar Wao*, created a literary sensation when it was published in 2007 to breathless literary reviews, and it won the National Book Critics Circle Award for Best Novel of 2007, followed by the Pulitzer Prize. In addition, Díaz has published nonfiction; his essay "He'll Take El Alto," which appeared in *Gourmet* magazine in September, 2007, won the M. L. K. Fisher Distinguished Writing Award of the James Beard Foundation. He also edited *The Beacon Best of 2001: Great Writing by Women and Men of All Colors and Cultures*.

ACHIEVEMENTS

Junot Díaz is among the most important contemporary Dominican American writers, along with Julia Alvarez (*How the Garcia Girls Lost Their Accents*, 1991) and one of a growing number of American writers whose roots lie in the Caribbean, such as Edwidge Danticat from Haiti, Judith Ortiz Cofer from Puerto Rico, Michelle Cliff from Jamaica, Jamaica Kincaid from Antigua, and Cuban American Oscar Hijuelos. In addition, Díaz has had four stories selected for the annual *Best American Short Stories*, in 1996, 1997, 1999, and 2010, and "Wildwood"--a chapter from *The Brief Wondrous Life of Oscar Wao*--was named one of the PEN/O. Henry Prize Stories in 2009. Díaz won a Guggenheim Fellowship in 1999, a PEN/Malamud Award in 2002, and the Rome Prize from the American Academy of Arts and Letters in 2007. Few writers have garnered as many prizes so early in their career, for both short and long fiction, and the awards acknowledge Díaz's unique ethnic voice and his continuing contribution to American literature.

BIOGRAPHY

Junot Díaz was born in the Villa Juana section of Santo Domingo, the third in a family of five children, and for most of his childhood Díaz lived in the Dominican Republic with his mother and grandmother, because his father was working in the United States. Díaz immigrated to New Jersey in 1974, where he was reunited with his father, although the father would abandon the family a few years later. Díaz earned a B.A. degree from Rutgers in 1992, where he majored in English. After college he worked as an editorial assistant at Rutgers University Press, and in 1995 he gained his M.F.A. in creative writing at Cornell University in Ithaca, New York, where he wrote many of the stories he would later publish. The same year *The New Yorker* published his first story (later collected in *Drown*), "How to Date a Browngirl, Blackgirl, Whitegirl, or Halfie." *The New Yorker* has published a dozen of his stories and listed him among the top twenty writers for the twenty-first century. His fiction also has appeared in *Story* magazine and *The Paris Review*, among other journals. He began teaching creative writing at the Massachusetts Institute of Technology

(MIT) in Cambridge, where he also edited the *Boston Review*, and he has given readings of his fiction at venues across the country. Díaz also is active in the Dominican American community and is a founding member of the Voices of Our Nations Writing Workshop, which focuses on writers of color.

ANALYSIS

Junot Díaz's stories take place in the Dominican Republic, in the metropolitan New York area, or in both. Nearly all are narrated by a young male ("Yunior"), who, like Díaz himself, grew up in the Dominican Republic and then migrated to New Jersey. Unlike Díaz, the narrator is often a drug dealer holding one of a series of dead-end jobs. Many are coming-of-age stories about a young Dominican in a troubled family that the father will eventually abandon. Stories often describe escapes, characters crossing borders (or failing to cross) into another life. What is noticeable about almost all of the stories is the sureness of the narrative voice, its humor, and its spare but dazzling style. Few readers have encountered a streetwise narrator who slips so easily between English and Spanish and describes sex, drugs, and violence with such apparent casualness.

DROWN

Four of the ten stories in Díaz's first short-story collection take place in the Dominican Republic, and all the stories make reference to the island where most of the characters started their lives. All but one of the stories ("No Face") have Yunior as the narrator, starting out in the Dominican Republic as a nine-year-old and moving up to his late teens, when he lives and works in New Jersey. The opening story in the collection, "Ysrael," describes Yunior and his older brother, Rafa, being sent away for the summer from their Santo Domingo barrio into the country, where they seek out a boy who, as a baby, had had his face eaten off by a pig. They tear off the hand-sewn mask to see the boy's disfigured face ("No Face" tells Ysrael's life and hopes for reconstructive surgery from his own point of view). All the stories contain violence and sexual language and acts and all deal, in one way or another, with troubled families. The last story in the collection, "Negocios," tells of the father getting to "Nueva York," working

hard, marrying a second wife, and having another child. At the end of the story, years later, the narrator goes to meet the wife and hears her story of how the father abandoned them as well, to return to the Dominican Republic for his first family. Yunior as the older narrator steals, deals drugs, or works at jobs with little future. In "Edison, New Jersey," the narrator and his partner Wayne work delivering pool tables, and in an expensive home in suburban Bedminster they meet a Dominican immigrant, who gets the narrator to abandon Wayne and drive her to the Dominican section of Washington Heights in New York City. In the title story the narrator is thinking back on his urban New Jersey childhood and his best friend, Beto, when they shoplifted and hung out at the community swimming pool. Beto, as a young adult, has come back to the neighborhood from college, and he is gay. It is a coming-of-age story, but in the end readers realize that Beto has escaped his no-win street life and the narrator is stuck there in his homophobia. Many of the stories deal with sexual relationships, which are often violent, abusive, and meaningless, and almost all define the limits of gender and racial identities and roles. Yunior also sees events in his world in terms of class structure; the only full-time commuter in his poor neighborhood, he observes wryly in the title story, is the drug dealer who drives into the city to sell his wares. The stories are also infused with a stark, ironic humor: the furniture in the Bronx apartment of the uncle and aunt who have just arrived from the island is "furnished in Contemporary Dominican Tacky" ("Fiesta"). If you're trying to score, he advises readers in "How to Date a Browngirl, Blackgirl, Whitegirl, or Halfie," hide the government cheese in the refrigerator. In your favor, "pollutants have made Jersey sunsets one of the wonders of the world."

"THE SUN, THE MOON, THE STARS"

This 1998 *New Yorker* story typifies Díaz's post-*Drown* concerns. An older Yunior has cheated on his Cuban American girlfriend, Magdalena, with a woman in the office where he works, but after a difficult reconciliation Yunior and Magda take a vacation they had planned earlier back to Santo Domingo. (The 2007 story "Alma" tells a similar story of Yunior's infidelity.) Magda soon gets bored with Yunior's hometown and family, and they leave for a resort on the beach, where Magda demands time alone. That night Yunior meets two men at the hotel bar, who drive him into the country and lower him into a cave they claim is the birthplace of the nation and where Yunior has an epiphany that his relationship with Magda is over. The story shows Yunior as weak and unfaithful, but it also highlights the kind of tensions or binary oppositions Díaz's fiction often uncovers, such as the contrast between the girlfriend he claims he loves and the woman he uses to cheat on Magda. There is also the pull between the Dominican Republic, to which Yunior loves to return, and the New Jersey, where they live now. (His swim trunks--unlike the sexy bikini Magda wears on the beach--read "Sandy Hook Forever!") There is, importantly, the class opposition Yunior recognizes on the island, between the poverty of the ghetto he grew up in and the lavish luxury of the resort, where the rich probably come "to relax after a month of oppressing the masses."

"OTRAVIDA, OTRAVEZ"

The story is atypical because it is narrated from a woman's perspective, but it confirms Díaz's typical preoccupation with family separation, abandonment, and loss. A twenty-eight-year-old immigrant from the Dominican Republic, Yasmin has been with Tavito for three years. She works in a hospital laundry, he works in a bakery, and they have been trying to buy a house together. Tavito has a wife, Amporo, back home, who sends him letters that Yasmin secretly reads. Her best friend, Ana Iris, also has a family back on the island, but she has been away so long, she tells Yasmin, she has trouble recognizing her children's voices when she calls home. Yasmin is pregnant when the last letter from Amporo arrives, and she puts it before Tavito and closes her eyes as he reads it. All the characters are torn between two worlds, working on the immigrant dream of integration into the society of the United States, while at the same time pieces of them remain in the Dominican Republic.

"THE PURA PRINCIPLE"

"The Pura Principle" returns Yunior to an earlier age, when he is in high school, smoking a lot of marijuana and living in New Jersey with his mother and his brother, Rafa, who is home from a second radiation treatment at the hospital. (In the earlier "Nilda," Yunior meets one of Rafa's old girlfriends after Rafa has died of cancer.) Yunior and Rafa let their mother wait on them, never lifting a finger to help, and the family tensions worsen when Rafa's new girlfriend, Pura, starts showing up at the apartment. When Mami bans Pura from the house, she and Rafa run off and marry, and Rafa later returns to steal his stuff, the television, and his mother's bed. The mother continues to slip money to Rafa when he is living with Pura, and when he gets home after a third hospital stay, the mother gives money to Pura, who then disappears. The story ends when Rafa gets his revenge on Yunior for not helping him with Pura earlier. "The Pura Principle" epitomizes male gender identity, in the sons' treatment of their mother, in Rafa's treatment of all women, in male abandonment (the father and Rafa both flee the home), and in Rafa's brutal attack on Yunior at the end. Díaz paints his characters mired in their gender roles, but Yunior's narration is also riddled with dry humor and colorful street language.

OTHER MAJOR WORKS

LONG FICTION: *The Brief Wondrous Life of Oscar Wao*, 2007.

NONFICTION: "He'll Take El Alto," 2007.

EDITED TEXT: *The Beacon Best of 2001: Great Writing by Women and Men of All Colors and Cultures*, 2001.

BIBLIOGRAPHY

Dalleo, Raphael, and Elena Machado Sáez. *The Latino/a Canon and the Emergence of Post-Sixties Literature*. New York: Palgrave Macmillan, 2007. See chapter 3, "Movin' on Up and Out: Lowercase Latino/a Realism in the Work of Junot Díaz and Angie Cruz," which includes detailed analyses of "Edison, New Jersey" and the title story of *Drown*.

Díaz, Junot. "Becoming a Writer." *O, The Oprah Magazine* (October 13, 2009). Díaz writes about the long gestation of his prize-winning novel and how he overcame his five-year siege of writer's block.

Suarez, Lucia M. *The Tears of Hispaniola: Haitian and Dominican Diaspora Memory*. Gainesville: University Press of Florida, 2006. Chapter 3, "Exposing Invisibility: *Drown*," presents an analysis that leans heavily on a historical understanding of Díaz's

Dominican background to unlock the elements of class, gender, and violence in the collected stories.

David Peck

PHILIP K. DICK

Born: Chicago, Illinois; December 16, 1928
Died: Santa Ana, California; March 2, 1982

PRINCIPAL SHORT FICTION

A Handful of Darkness, 1955
The Variable Man, and Other Stories, 1957
The Preserving Machine, and Other Stories, 1969
The Book of Philip K. Dick, 1973 (pb. in England as *The Turning Wheel, and Other Stories*, 1977)
The Best of Philip K. Dick, 1977
The Golden Man, 1980
I Hope I Shall Arrive Soon, 1985
Robots, Androids, and Mechanical Oddities: The Science Fiction of Philip K. Dick, 1985
The Collected Stories of Philip K. Dick, 1987 (5 volumes)
Selected Stories of Philip K. Dick, 2002 (Jonathan Lethem, editor)
The Early Work of Philip K. Dick, Volume One: The Variable Man, and Other Stories, 2009
The Early Work of Philip K. Dick, Volume Two: Breakfast at Twilight, and Other Stories, 2009

OTHER LITERARY FORMS

Philip K. Dick's large body of science-fiction stories (he published more than one hundred stories in science-fiction magazines) is matched by his large number of science-fiction novels (he published more than thirty). Most of his short stories were first published in the 1950's, whereas he concentrated on the novel form in the 1960's and 1970's.

ACHIEVEMENTS

Philip K. Dick's work received little critical attention during the early part of his career, but he later was regarded as one of the most important writers of science fiction. Dick concentrates less on the technical aspects of science fiction than he does on character and theme, though his stories and novels do involve such things as time travel, space flight to distant galaxies, robots, and androids. In 1963, his novel *The Man in the High Castle* (1962) won science-fiction's Hugo Award as the best novel of the year, and in 1975, he was given the John W. Campbell Memorial Award for *Flow My Tears, the Policeman Said* (1974). The Campbell award may seem somewhat ironic, since Dick has written that Campbell, who edited *Astounding* magazine, considered his work "not only worthless but also, as he put it, 'Nuts.'"

BIOGRAPHY

Philip Kindred Dick was born in Chicago in 1928; his twin sister died at a few months of age. While Dick was still very young, his parents moved to Berkeley, California, and Dick grew up there. Dick's parents were divorced when he was four years old, and he did not see his father for many years after that. Dick attended Berkeley High School and was graduated in 1945. He then went to the University of California at Berkeley but dropped out after a year in order to escape compulsory service in the campus Reserve Officers' Training Corps (ROTC). In 1947, he took a job as a radio announcer for a classical music station in Berkeley, and from 1948 to 1952, he worked as a record store manager.

In 1951, Dick sold his first story, "Roog," to Anthony Boucher at *Fantasy and Science Fiction*, but the story did not appear until 1953. Dick had attended an informal writing class that Boucher taught in Berkeley and considered Boucher a good friend and editorial adviser. Dick's first story to be published was "Beyond Lies the Wub" (1952) in the science-fiction magazine *Planet Stories*.

Most of Dick's short stories were written in the 1950's and 1960's. He published seventy-three short stories between 1952 and 1955, while the last years of his life saw only a few stories. As his output of short stories diminished, however, his production of novels grew, some of them based on material from the stories. For example, his novel *The Penultimate Truth* (1964) draws on the story "The Mold of Yancy." His first published novel was *Solar Lottery* (1955). Many of Dick's novels were published first only in paperback, and it was not until later in his career that his work began to receive critical acclaim.

In 1970, Dick's fourth wife left him, and he plunged into despair. He apparently had experimented with drugs, including lysergic acid diethylamide (LSD), during the 1960's, but he began using them heavily and finally attempted suicide in 1972. He later gave lectures for antidrug organizations. In 1973, Dick married again and had a son in addition to his two daughters from previous marriages. Sometime during this period, he moved from the San Francisco area to southern California. Dick also had a series of religious experiences in the 1970's, and these influenced his later work, particularly the trilogy consisting of *The Divine Invasion* (1981), *Valis* (1981), and *The Transmigration of Timothy Archer* (1982). Dick's novel *Do Androids Dream of Electric Sheep?* (1968) was made into the film *Blade Runner* in 1982, and his story "We Can Remember It for You Wholesale" was adapted for the screen as *Total Recall* (1990).

Dick died in 1982. After his death, the Philip K. Dick Award was established to recognize the best science-fiction novel published in paperback each year.

Analysis

Philip K. Dick often commented that "the two basic topics which fascinate me are 'What is reality?' and 'What constitutes the authentic human being?'" Science-fiction writers are naturally questioners of reality, since they are constantly asking "What if?" Despite his robots and androids, time travel and spaceships, Dick is not a writer of technical science fiction. He is concerned with human values, and his speculative "what ifs" aim to answer his two main questions, if they can be answered. Reality in Dick's stories is fluid; just

when readers think that they understand what is real and what is not, Dick moves the goalposts. Fakes, deceptions, misunderstandings, and differing points of view all cloud the issue of what is real. In each story, the answer might be somewhat different. Ultimately, reality seems to be something defined on personal terms, something slightly different for each individual. Dick's exploration of "what constitutes the authentic human being," however, does yield a fairly clear-cut answer: it is "*caritas* (or agape)," unselfish brotherly love or empathy, the "esteem of good people for one another." Many of Dick's stories portray the exact opposite in the form of political or corporate evil, a desire for power, a selfish lack of concern for others. The underlying theme of love, however, is still there in the little human being who fights for his or her individualism, for his or her own decisions and not someone else's. In some stories *caritas* is overt; in others it either is simply hinted at or is conspicuous in its absence. Despite the importance of Dick's main themes, the stories are not just metaphysical tracts: They are enjoyable, often amusing, sometimes horrifying excursions.

"Roog"

"Roog," Dick's first story to be accepted for publication, already displays his concern for point of view, his idea that for different people, or in this story, dogs, reality is different. "Roog" concerns a dog that is firmly convinced that the garbagemen who pick up his master's trash each week are taking an offering or sacrifice, which prevents them from taking his master, as they would like to do. In commenting on this story, Dick wrote, "I began to develop the idea that each creature lives in a world somewhat different from all the other creatures and their worlds." Obviously, the dog's reality is different from the master's. To the dog's master, the garbagemen are there to take the trash away, and the dog's howls of warning, despair, and fear are simply annoying and likely to bring on the complaints of neighbors. The dog, however, locked in his view of reality, exemplifies *caritas:* He loves his master, and he unselfishly confronts these fearsome beings each week in order to protect him. The story smoothly switches back and forth from the points of view of the dog, his master, and even the Roogs, as the dog calls the evil garbagemen.

"RAUTAVAARA'S CASE"

One of Dick's last stories, "Rautavaara's Case," published in 1980, also contrasts several opposing points of view, none of which can firmly be said to have the true picture. The narrator of "Rautavaara's Case" is a being from the Proxima Centaurus system who has no body but is "plasma." This entity and his colleagues are monitoring the thoughts of Agneta Rautavaara, whose brain, but not her body, has been kept alive after an accident that killed her coworkers. Rautavaara's thoughts seem to reveal the presence of Christ with those killed and the promise of an afterlife, but is it a "genuine window on the next world" or "a presentation of Rautavaara's own cultural racial propensities?" The plasma beings introduce to Rautavaara's thoughts their version of the Savior, and the result horrifies Rautavaara and the Earth people who are also monitoring her case. Rautavaara's brain is taken off its support and the "window" is closed.

"Rautavaara's Case" twists reality in all sorts of ways. Christians have long believed in an afterlife; this story suggests that what kind of an afterlife a person has depends on that person's beliefs. There is also the possibility that all Rautavaara's thoughts have been hallucinations, that her mind was driven mad by complete sensory deprivation. Is what Rautavaara is experiencing real in any way, or has her mind created some sort of reality for her, since she has no other inputs? Reality differs for the Earth people and the beings from Proxima Centaurus as well: Because they cannot understand each other, cannot even agree on right and wrong, because their points of view are so different, there is no consensual reality--nothing that they agree on as being true. The only thing that is sure is what actions were taken, and there are even disagreements about whether those actions were right.

"PROJECT: EARTH"

Many of Dick's stories meditate directly or obliquely on the existence of God. "Project: Earth" concerns a boy, Tommy, who discovers that the boarder at his friend's house is keeping an enormous file on Earth and has a cage with nine tiny people in it. He steals the people, lets them explore his room, and gets a friend to make clothes for them. When the boarder gets them back, they attack him and escape.

There are a number of biblical references in "Project: Earth" which make the story a comment on the nature of human beings. The boarder tells Tommy about the failure of Project A, which he describes as consisting of beings like humans but with wings. Pride brought Project A down. The boarder considers Project B, consisting of men, to have failed because it was influenced by Project A. Project C, the little people, has in turn been influenced by Project B: When the boarder gets the little people back, "They had clothes on. Little suits of clothing. Like the others, a long time before," like Adam and Eve. In this story, there is no confidence in the excellence of God's plan. With each project, it is the creature's individuality and desire for self-determination that make the plan a failure, yet the story seems quietly to approve of this. The boarder seems rather like a scientist who experiments on animals; he does not seem particularly interested in the little people or in men except as they fit into his experiment.

"THE TROUBLE WITH BUBBLES"

In "The Trouble with Bubbles" and "Small Town," human beings themselves are the experimenters. Bubbles are a kind of advanced terrarium: "Sub-atomic worlds, in controlled containers. We start life going on a sub-atomic world, feed it problems to make it evolve, try to raise it higher and higher." Creating these worlds is a popular pastime, but now people are taking their worlds and wantonly destroying them. The story treats the moral issues of humans playing God. The world builders do not allow the cultures they create to determine their own futures, and the cultures can even be destroyed on a whim. Again, Dick supports humans' desire for free will and questions the excellence of God's will. The story ends with an earthquake that kills thousands of people--an "act of God" analogous to the smashing of bubbles. Is it, however, an act of God, or are the characters in the story a bubble civilization themselves?

"Small Town" also portrays human beings creating their own world. Verne Haskel is a henpecked, cuckolded husband who retreats to his basement to work on his electric train layout. The layout re-creates Haskel's hometown, and, one day, when his life becomes unbearable, he starts to change the town, removing the places that he does not like and adding places that he thinks would make the town better. It is a way of regaining power and control, of creating his own reality. Finally, though, Verne's reality becomes everyone's reality: When his wife and her lover go to the police station to report him missing, assuming that he has somehow disappeared into his substitute reality of the train layout, they find that the whole town has changed in accord with Verne's vision, and they realize that they will soon feel Verne's revenge. In Dick's stories, it is often the downtrodden but persevering little guy who is the hero, who is fighting for individualism and self-determination; however in "Small Town," Haskel wants to determine not only his own life but also everyone else's. He is a wrathful god, punishing those who go against him, desiring total control.

"THE MOLD OF YANCY"

"The Mold of Yancy" also describes an attempt to control a population. Yancy is a father figure created by a group of advertising executives to mold the thoughts and opinions of the population of the moon Callisto. Yancy pronounces on everything from garlic in cooking to war; the purpose of the campaign is to get the citizens of Callisto to accept anything he says-- "Yancy does all their thinking for them." One of the advertising executives rebels, however, and tells a representative from Earth the reason behind the campaign: The trading syndicates that operate on Callisto want to expand their territory to Ganymede, which would mean a war. They want the public to accept a war that Yancy will condone. Once the Earth representative, who has been sent to investigate Callisto's drift toward totalitarianism, understands its cause, he calls in the police to arrest the heads of the trading syndicates and develops a plan to have the Yancy campaign start promoting individualistic thought.

"The Mold of Yancy" concerns a manipulation of reality intended to take away a population's individualism. Again, Dick promotes thinking for oneself, making one's own moral judgments. As in many of Dick's stories, here he sees evil in large corporations; in Dick's view, business enterprises are usually looking out for their own good and no one else's. "The Mold of Yancy" is also one of the stories in which the reader can hear Dick speaking out "loud and clear *against* the prevailing hysterias of the times," in Norman Spinrad's words. The story was written in the 1950's, the era of McCarthyism, when anyone who considered questioning the government's policies was suspected of disloyalty to the country. "The Mold of Yancy" is Dick's protest against this kind of thinking.

"SECOND VARIETY"

"Second Variety" also comments on "the prevailing hysterias of the times" in its portrayal of a suicidal end to the Cold War. It is set toward the end of a massive war between United Nations troops (which in this story means the United States and its allies) and the Soviet Union. The end of the war is near because the Americans have devised a kind of robot--a "claw"--that kills soldiers or anyone else not wearing an identification tab. The claws, which are made by automatic machinery below the Earth's surface, have been designed to repair themselves and, most important, to learn. They are, in that sense, alive. When Major Hendricks agrees to meet the Russians on their lines for a conference, he learns that the claws have developed an android--a robot that looks like a human--that pays no attention to the radioactive identification tabs. These robots come in several varieties designed to play on the sympathies of the soldiers: a little boy clutching a teddy bear, a wounded one-legged soldier. The Russians believe that there may be more than only these two types. At the end of the story, Hendricks realizes that the woman he has trusted to go to the moon base and send help back to him is yet another variety of these murderous robots.

Dick commented that in this story "my grand theme--who is human and who only appears (masquerades) as human?--emerges most fully." What defines a human being? Is it the ability to learn, to adapt oneself to the situation? The androids are certainly intelligent. One could say that they are no more murderous than the humans who started the war. Dick suggests, however, that compassion makes the difference; the androids know that they can achieve their aims by appealing to the soldiers' pity. The story also elucidates Dick's antiwar stance: War is an act of suicide.

"THE LITTLE BLACK BOX"

In the afterword to *The Golden Man*, Dick wrote that "The Little Black Box" is "closer to being my credo than any of the other stories here." The story makes Dick's belief in *caritas* explicit in a reworking of the Christ story. The United States and other countries are worried about a new religion sweeping the planet. They treat it as a political movement, believing that it threatens their power. Followers of Wilbur Mercer, the story's Christ figure, are a threat to the political system because they follow different rules. When one of the government's employees becomes a Mercerite, he loses his job after telling authorities that their persecution of the new religion is morally wrong. Mercerites enter into empathy with their leader by grasping the handles of an "empathy box." They then feel what Mercer feels, suffer what he suffers. It is a voluntary act of caring, and the end of the story makes it clear that the government cannot defeat it.

Dick's two main themes--what is real and what is human--run through virtually every story that he has written. He is never didactic, though; the stories are not boring tracts on his own particular worldview. Dick's vision is not always a cheerful one: Governments are perfidious, human beings can be evil, corporate greed is rampant. As he has written, however, "I trust . . . that you will not misread me and see dislike and anger only; please reach out to me at the core below that, the core of love." The core of love defines what is real and what is human.

OTHER MAJOR WORKS

LONG FICTION: *Voices from the Street*, wr. 1953, pb. 2007; *Solar Lottery*, 1955 (pb. in England as *World of Chance*, 1956); *The Man Who Japed*, 1956; *The World Jones Made*, 1956; *Eye in the Sky*, 1957; *Time Out of Joint*, 1959; *Dr. Futurity*, 1960; *Vulcan's Hammer*, 1960; *The Man in the High Castle*, 1962; *The Game-Players of Titan*, 1963; *Clans of the Alphane Moon*, 1964; *Martian Time-Slip*, 1964; *The Penultimate Truth*, 1964; *The Simulacra*, 1964; *The Three Stigmata of Palmer Eldritch*, 1964; *Dr. Bloodmoney: Or, How We Got Along After the Bomb*, 1965; *Now Wait for Last Year*, 1966; *The Crack in Space (Cantata 140)*, 1966; *The Unteleported Man*, 1966 (pb. in England as *Lies, Inc.*, 1984); *Counter-Clock World*, 1967; *The Ganymede Takeover*, 1967 (with Ray Nelson); *The Zap Gun*, 1967; *Do Androids Dream of Electric Sheep?*, 1968 (reissued as *Blade Runner*, 1982); *Galactic Pot-Healer*, 1969; *Ubik*, 1969; *A Maze of Death*, 1970; *Our Friends from Frolix 8*, 1970; *The Philip K. Dick Omnibus*, 1970; *We Can Build You*, 1972; *Flow My Tears, the Policeman Said*, 1974; *Confessions of a Crap Artist*, 1975; *Deus Irae*, 1976 (with Roger Zelazny); *A Scanner Darkly*, 1977; *The Divine Invasion*, 1981; *Valis*, 1981; *The Transmigration of Timothy Archer*, 1982; *The Man Whose Teeth Were All Exactly Alike*, 1984; *In Milton Lumky Territory*, 1985; *Puttering About in a Small Land*, 1985; *Radio Free Albemuth*, 1985; *Humpty Dumpty in Oakland*, 1986; *Mary and the Giant*, 1987; *The Broken Bubble*, 1988; *Four Novels of the 1960s*, 2007; *Five Novels of the 1960s and 70s*, 2008; *VALIS and Later Novels*, 2009.

NONFICTION: *In Pursuit of Valis: Selections from the Exegesis*, 1991 (Lawrence Sutin, editor); *The Selected Letters of Philip K. Dick*, 1991-1993 (Don Herron, editor); *The Shifting Realities of Philip K. Dick: Selected Literary and Philosophical Writings*, 1995 (Lawrence Sutin, editor); *What If Our World Is Their Heaven: The Final Conversations of Philip K. Dick*, 2000 (Gwen Lee and Elaine Sauter, editors).

MISCELLANEOUS: *The Dark Haired Girl*, 1988.

BIBLIOGRAPHY

Aldiss, Brian W., and David Wingrove. *Trillion Year Spree: The History of Science Fiction*. London: Victor Gollancz, 1986. Aldiss's work is useful as an overall survey of themes and writers of science fiction, and he allots several pages to Dick's work. His focus is on Dick's novels, but his comments are useful for looking at the short stories as well.

Dick, Anne R. *Search for Philip K. Dick, 1928-1982: A Memoir and Biography of the Science Fiction Writer*. Lewiston, N.Y.: Edwin Mellen Press, 1995. An important documentation of Dick's life, told in candid detail by his wife.

Gillespie, Bruce, ed. *Philip K. Dick: Electric Shepherd*. Melbourne: Norstrilia Press, 1975. This collection of essays on Dick's work includes an article by Dick himself called "The Android and the Human."

Golumbia, David. "Resisting 'The World': Philip K. Dick, Cultural Studies, and Metaphysical Realism." *Science-Fiction Studies* 23 (March, 1996): 83-102. A discussion of reality and appearance, metaphysics, and politics in Dick's work and thought. Comments on the relationship of his thought to culture studies.

Kucukalic, Lejla. *Philip K. Dick: Canonical Writer of the Digital Age*. New York: Routledge, 2009. Although Kucukalic focuses on an examination of five of Dick's novels, her observations can also apply to the short stories. She argues that Dick is a serious philosophical and cultural thinker whose works examine two key questions: what is reality and what is human.

Lee Zoreda, Margaret. "Bakhtin, Blobels, and Philip Dick." *Journal of Popular Culture* 28 (Winter, 1994): 55-61. A discussion of the story "Oh, to Be a Blobel" from a Bakhtinian perspective. Argues that the story demonstrates the complexities in the presence/absence of dialogism. Discusses how the story demonstrates the misery, suffering, and irreversible injury created by the military-capitalist complex.

Link, Eric Carl. *Understanding Philip K. Dick*. Columbia: University of South Carolina Press, 2010. Link argues that Dick was above all else a novelist of ideas, and his study examines Dick's craft and career and the themes of his works. Includes analysis of six of the novels.

Mckee, Gabriel. *Pink Beams of Light from the God in the Gutter: The Science-Fictional Religion of Philip K. Dick*. Lanham, Md.: University Press of America, 2004. An overview of Dick's religious experiences and his attempts at communicating them in his fiction, as well as his in his journals and personal correspondence.

Science-Fiction Studies 2, no. 1 (March, 1975). This issue of the journal is devoted to the work of Dick and contains essays by writers eminent in the field of science-fiction criticism.

Sutin, Lawrence. *Divine Invasions: A Life of Philip K. Dick*. 1989. Reprint. New York: Carroll & Graf, 2005. Sutin has written a well-researched biography that includes some discussion of Dick's work.

Suvin, Darko. "Philip K. Dick's Opus: Artifice as Refuge and World View." In *Positions and Presuppositions in Science Fiction*. London: Macmillan, 1988. Suvin's essay focuses mainly on Dick's novel *The Man in the High Castle*, but many of his observations are useful in examining the short stories.

Umland, Samuel J., ed. *Philip K. Dick: Contemporary Critical Interpretations*. Westport, Conn.: Greenwood Press, 1995. An indispensable collection of essays on Dick's varied body of work. Umland has compiled extremely valuable primary and second bibliographies. Like Umland's introduction, the essays take careful note of the body of critical literature already published on Dick.

Vest, Jason P. *The Postmodern Humanism of Philip K. Dick*. Lanham, Md.: Scarecrow Press, 2009. Describes how Dick adapted the conventions of science fiction and postmodernism to express humanist concerns about the problems of maintaining identity and autonomy in the last half of the twentieth century. Compares Dick's work to that of writers Jorge Luis Borges, Franz Kafka, and Italo Calvino.

Karen M. Cleveland Marwick

Thomas M. Disch

Born: Des Moines, Iowa; February 2, 1940
Died: New York, New York; July 5, 2008
Also known as: Cassandra Knye, Leonie Hargrave, Thom Demijohn (joint pseudonym with John Sladek)

Principal short fiction

One Hundred and Two H-Bombs, and Other Science Fiction Stories, 1966

Fun with Your New Head, 1968 (also as *Under Compulsion*)

Getting into Death, 1973

The Early Science Fiction Stories of Thomas M. Disch, 1977

Fundamental Disch, 1980

The Man Who Had No Idea, 1982

Ringtime, 1983

Torturing Mr. Amberwell, 1985

The Brave Little Toaster, 1986

The Wall of America, 2008

Other literary forms

Thomas M. Disch (dish) was as versatile as he was prolific, having published, in addition to his short fiction, novels, poetry, and children's books. Among his nonfiction works is *The Dreams Our Stuff Is Made Of: How Science Fiction Conquered the World* (1998). He wrote theater criticism, lectured at various universities, and created a computer-interactive novel entitled *Amnesia* (1985). His other novels include *On Wings of Song* (1979) and *The M.D.* (1991), a fable about a boy's use of supernatural powers to accomplish good deeds and punish evil.

Achievements

Though known primarily as a science-fiction writer, Thomas M. Disch is hard to categorize. He was part of the New Wave science-fiction writers of the 1960's,

many of whose works appeared in the English magazine *New Worlds,* under the editorship of Michael Moorcock, and might be said to belong to an "absurdist" tradition within science fiction. With three titles included among editor David Pringle's list of the one hundred best science-fiction novels--*Camp Concentration* (1968), *334* (1972), and *On Wings of Song*--Disch was one of the serious writers who brought science fiction a little of the intellectual respectability long denied works of popular culture. Two stories won Disch the O. Henry Prize, in 1975 and 1979. The novella *The Brave Little Toaster* won nominations for both the Hugo and Nebula Awards in 1980 and won a British Science-Fiction Award in 1981. In 1999, Disch won the Michael J. Braude Award for light verse.

Biography

Thomas Michael Disch was born in Des Moines, Iowa, the son of Felix Henry Disch and Helen Gilbertson. Thomas M. Disch went to Cooper Union and New York University but never graduated. After working in an advertising agency and a bank, he started writing full time in the mid-1960's. His travels in England, Turkey, Italy, and Mexico provided settings for some of his stories. Disch worked with Charles Naylor, his longtime companion, on various anthologies and the novel *Neighboring Lives* (1981). He also collaborated with John Sladek on *Black Alice* (1968), a thriller about a kidnapping in the South, and a gothic romance published under the pseudonym Cassandra Knye. Disch was a theater critic for *The Nation* from 1987 to 1991 and a theater critic for the *New York Daily News* beginning in 1993. He became artist-in-residence at the College of William and Mary in 1996. Disch died from a self-inflicted gunshot wound on July 5, 2008, in his apartment in New York City.

ANALYSIS

Two themes recur frequently in Thomas M. Disch's short fiction and dominate his best work: the desperate battle to establish and sustain a meaningful identity in a hostile and mercurial world and the uneasy metaphorical relationship between sex and death. The former theme has various manifestations in his work, motivating both sober and nightmarish stories, such as "Descending" and "The Asian Shore," and delicately satirical, sometimes even playful, stories, such as "Displaying the Flag" and "The Man Who Had No Idea." The second theme, however, is restricted to the display of a narrow spectrum of ironic unease, characteristic of such stories as "Death and the Single Girl" and "Let Us Quickly Hasten to the Gate of Ivory."

"GETTING INTO DEATH"

Disch's two main themes are merged and presented explicitly in "Getting into Death," in which a female writer tries to reconcile herself to her impending death from an incurable illness. She reflects on the various roles she has played as wife, mother, and writer, while she studies more closely and critically than ever before the daughter and sister who visit her in the hospital. She is also attended in her death-watch by a series of religious representatives, since she checked all the available categories under the heading "religion" on her admission form. She finds the solace they offer almost useless, and they refuse to satisfy her curiosity about the strategies their other charges use in facing their final hours. Now that she is about to die, she finds herself curiously uncertain as to who she is and has been; even as a writer she has been both B. C. Millar, author of rigorous and rather esoteric detective stories, and Cassandra Knye, author of highly popular and emotionally lurid gothic romances.

Cassandra comes to see new significance in both these literary endeavors. Her detective novels come to be images of a reified world in which death is the central feature of a puzzle to be solved. (She begins work on a new Millar novel, a murder mystery told from the viewpoint of the corpse.) Her gothics, meanwhile, become parables in which the threat of sexual violation is symbolic of the threat of mortality. Her eventual reconciliation with the idea of death emerges from a strange inversion of this symbology, when she comes to see death in the same terms as sex, as a "medium in which relationships may exist."

"LET US QUICKLY HASTEN TO THE GATE OF IVORY"

The relationship between sex and death is further explored in the story that follows "Getting into Death" in the collection of that name: "Let Us Quickly Hasten to the Gate of Ivory." In this story a brother and sister unconsciously subject to incestuous desires go in search of their parents' graves and find themselves lost in an infinite cemetery, alone with each other in an ocean of *memento mori*.

"DEATH AND THE SINGLE GIRL"

Death is the ultimate loss of identity, but it is far from being the only threat to the integrity and the security of consciousness. In "Death and the Single Girl" the demoralized heroine calls Death on the telephone and asks that he visit her with his fatal orgasm. Unfortunately, Death can no longer cope with the demands placed upon him by modern America, and he proves to be impotent. After several unsuccessful attempts to arouse him, she settles for "the next best thing" and becomes his receptionist and switchboard operator.

"THE ASIAN SHORE"

In "The Asian Shore," perhaps Disch's most powerful story, it is not death but alienation of a fearfully literal kind that threatens the protagonist. He is an American tourist wintering in Turkey, who finds himself haunted by a miserable woman and a young starveling, who call out a name when he passes them. Despite the length of his stay his suitcases remain unpacked, and he cannot tear down the emblems of personality abandoned by the previous occupant of his room. Gradually he allows himself to be spiritually absorbed into his environment, unable to assert himself sufficiently to maintain his own identity against a subtle but relentless pressure. He simply does not have the psychic strength to sustain himself against a new personality that possesses him--a personality whose need to exist is, it seems, far stronger than his own. In the end he is claimed by the alien shore that waits on the far side of the Bosporus and by the woman and her child.

"THE JOYCELIN SHRAGER STORY"

The attempt to discover in life a meaning that it does not possess and the futility of trying to impose spurious meanings are the themes of "The Joycelin Shrager

Story," in which an aging member of the avant-garde film community becomes infatuated with a girl who is making her awkward and unremarkable existence the subject of an endless, continuing film called *The Dance of Life*. To woo her he praises her endeavor and exerts pressure on his friends and acquaintances to back up his pandering with fake appreciation and applause. At first this is merely a ploy intended to maintain the sexual relationship between them, but he gradually becomes fascinated by the film as he assumes a leading part in it. In the end he has to face a crisis induced by the prospect of a wedding night surrounded by lights and cameras, when his pretenses are tested to destruction. If a genuinely realistic account of everyday existence does not constitute art, and if in the end everyday life cannot bear the strain of such exposure, what justification is there for either the way one lives or the ways in which one tries to transmute experience into art?

"THE MAN WHO HAD NO IDEA"

Disch's later work recovers something of the iconoclastic enthusiasm of his earlier works. "The Man Who Had No Idea," first published in 1978, is set in a magnificently absurd future America in which free speech--even casual conversation--is a privilege that has to be earned. Licenses to communicate must be won, initially, by passing examinations geared to test adolescents for articulateness. Having been provisionally awarded, they must win two endorsements from established talkers in order to be made permanent. The hero of the story is a marginal case whose struggle to win his full license is a difficult one. His conversational skills seem adequate enough, but he is cursed by the fact that he has nothing to say--he simply is not very interesting to talk to. The world would hardly be impoverished if he were condemned to eternal silence, but his own social prestige and self-esteem are entirely bound up with being licensed.

THE BRAVE LITTLE TOASTER

Disch's short fiction of the 1980's continued in the same relaxed satirical vein as "The Man Who Had No Idea." *The Brave Little Toaster* is a subtle parody that gently extrapolates the anthropomorphic method of moralistic children's animated films to an absurd extreme. The substitution of household appliances for animals was supposed to highlight the fact that cinema

audiences were ridiculously eager to have their responsive buttons pushed, but it proved that the threshold of skepticism was even lower than many people had assumed. This was not the first of Disch's parodies to be so straight-faced and so accurately targeted as to be mistaken for the genuine article, but it eventually proved to be the most successful, finally published in book form in 1986, when it was made into an animated film by Disney Studios, as if it were no more and no less than an earnestly cute heroic fantasy. Disch delightedly sallied forth into even more remote hinterlands of parodic excess in a sequel, *The Brave Little Toaster Goes to Mars*, although a projected third story, *The Brave Little Toaster Splits the Atom*, never materialized.

THE 1990'S

Much of Disch's short fiction of the 1990's reverted to a more caustic vein of satire, in which he scathingly lampooned and lambasted various individuals and collectives who excited his ire. "Abduction of Bunny Steiner: Or, A Shameless Lie" (1992) pulls no punches in parodying the best-selling accounts of the alleged abduction by aliens of horror writer Whitley Strieber and his son. Other fashionable targets on which Disch zeroed in during this critical phase included television-based personality cults, which are subjected to mockery in "Celebrity Love" (1990); millenarian cultists joyously looking forward to the end of the world, whose wishes are ironically granted in "A Family of the Post-Apocalypse" (1993); and emotive fund-raising campaigns, whose exploitative tactics are spoofed in "The Children's Fund to Save the Dinosaurs: A Charity Appeal" (1997). Such sharply pointed tales serve to underline the fact that Disch gradually moved in the course of his career from being a writer of offbeat fantasies and surreal science fiction to becoming one of the leading Swiftian satirists of the twentieth century's close.

THE WALL OF AMERICA

The collection of stories *The Wall of America* was published shortly after Disch's death and consists of stories originally published from 1981 to 2005. The title story, originally published in 1981, is set in a future in which the United States has built a wall on the border with Canada. In a joint venture, the National

Endowment for the Arts (NEA) and the Department of Homeland Security lease space on the American side of the wall to artists to hang their work at no charge. Lester, the main character, has leased a spot in North Dakota and spends two months a year there painting and displaying his work, until he meets a Canadian tourist named Gulliver, a salute to Jonathan Swift. Lester disappears after meeting Gulliver, but this makes his work even more valuable to collectors. A painter is also the main character in "Painting Eggplants" (2002), although he makes a living as a professor of creative writing at a university. During one summer vacation, the painter goes into a creative frenzy, painting portraits of eggplants, but he loses his inspiration after he sells one of them and is never so productive again.

Disch satirizes the process of governments and charities subsidizing artists in "The Man Who Read a Book" (1994) and "The First Annual Performance Arts Festival at the Slaughter Rock Battlefield" (1997). In the first story, the title character is a young man who falls for a scam in which he is supposed to be paid to read a book, but eventually he comes out ahead when he plagiarizes a pastiche of several classic nineteenth century novels, not knowing that it is a pastiche, never having heard of them. After falling for yet another scam in which he pays for publishing an excerpt from the book, the NEA awards him an annual stipend because he is a published author, another organization pays him to teach creative writing to the homeless, and finally another pays him for the right for someone to be videotaped translating the book into sign language for the deaf. No one at those organizations actually bothers to read what he had supposedly written. The title of the completely unoriginal book is *I Iced Madame Bovary*, which shows that Disch also anticipated the fad of combining classics such as *Pride and Prejudice* with genres such as zombie literature. "The Annual Performance Arts Festival at the Slaughter Rock Battlefield" is set during a festival that is subsidized by the state of New York, and the organizer had previously received grants for both her choreography and her poetry. The main character, K. C., is a guitar player who formerly was a member of a rock band but is now trying to make it as a solo musician. "The White Man" (2004)

concerns a refugee from Somalia named Tawana whose family has settled in Minnesota. Tawana discovers that there are vampires in her neighborhood, and they look just like European Americans who do not spent any time in the sun.

OTHER MAJOR WORKS

LONG FICTION: *The Genocides*, 1965; *Mankind Under the Leash*, 1966 (also as *The Puppies of Terra*, 1978); *The House That Fear Built*, 1966 (with John Sladek, both under pseudonym Cassandra Knye); *Echo 'Round His Bones*, 1967; *Black Alice*, 1968 (with John Sladek, both under pseudonym Thom Demijohn); *Camp Concentration*, 1968; *The Prisoner*, 1969; *334*, 1972; *Clara Reeve*, 1975 (as Leonie Hargrave); *On Wings of Song*, 1979; *Neighboring Lives*, 1981 (with Charles Naylor); *The Businessman: A Tale of Terror*, 1984; *Amnesia*, 1985 (computer-interactive novel); *The M.D.: A Horror Story*, 1991; *The Priest: A Gothic Romance*, 1995; *The Sub: A Study in Witchcraft*, 1999; *The Voyage of the Proteus: An Eyewitness Account of the End of the World*, 2007; *The Word of God: Or, Holy Writ Unwritten*, 2008.

POETRY: *The Right Way to Figure Plumbing*, 1972; *ABCDEFG HIJKLM NOPQRST UVWXYZ*, 1981; *Burn This*, 1982; *Orders of the Retina*, 1982; *Here I Am, There You Are, Where Were We*, 1984; *Dark Verses and Light*, 1991.

NONFICTION: *The Castle of Indolence: On Poetry, Poets, and Poetasters*, 1995; *The Dreams Our Stuff Is Made Of: How Science Fiction Conquered the World*, 1998; *The Castle of Perseverance: Job Opportunities in Contemporary Poetry*, 2002; *On SF*, 2005.

CHILDREN'S LITERATURE: *The Tale of Dan De Lion*, 1986; *The Brave Little Toaster Goes to Mars*, 1988; *The Silver Pillow: A Tale of Witchcraft*, 1988; *A Child's Garden of Grammar*, 1997 (with David Morice).

EDITED TEXTS: *The Ruins of Earth*, 1971; *Bad Moon Rising*, 1975; *The New Improved Sun*, 1975; *New Constellations*, 1976 (with Charles Naylor); *Strangeness*, 1977 (with Charles Naylor).

BIBLIOGRAPHY

Clemons, Walter. "The Joyously Versatile Thomas Disch." *Newsweek* 112 (July 11, 1988): 66-67. A biographical account that claims Disch is one of America's most gifted writers whose work is hard to categorize.

Crowley, John. "Fiction in Review." *The Yale Review* 83 (April, 1995): 134-146. A survey of Disch's work in various genres, including his short stories; suggests that Disch was wearying of the constraints of the horror genre.

Delany, Samuel R. *The American Shore: Meditations on a Tale of Science Fiction by Thomas M. Disch.* Elizabethtown, N.Y.: Dragon Press, 1978. The renowned science-fiction author writes about "The Asian Shore."

_____. Introduction to *Fundamental Disch.* New York: Bantam Books, 1980. A master of science fiction introduces his own selection of eighteen Disch stories, with brief commentaries on "Slaves" and "The Asian Shore." This volume also contains several appendixes.

Finkle, David. *Publishers Weekly* 238 (April 19, 1991): 48-49. A sketch of Disch's literary career and an informal interview in which Disch talks about his horror fiction and his plans for work in the future.

Martin, Douglas. "Thomas Disch, Novelist, Dies at Sixty-Eight." *The New York Times*, July 8, 2008, p. A19. Obituary for Disch that covers highlights of his writing career.

Sallis, James. "The Wall of America." *The Magazine of Fantasy and Science Fiction* 116, nos. 4/5 (April-May, 2009), p. 46. A combination of a review of *The Wall of America* and a eulogy for Disch.

Stableford, Brian. "Thomas Disch." In *Science-Fiction Writers: Critical Studies of the Major Authors from the Early Nineteenth Century to the Present Day*, edited by Richard Bleiler. 2d ed. New York: Charles Scribner's Sons, 1999. An overview of Disch's life and writings, updated from the first edition (1982). Of particular interest are brief selections of Disch's commentaries on science fiction. Bibliography.

Brian Stableford
Updated by Thomas R. Feller

CHITRA BANERJEE DIVAKARUNI

Born: Calcutta (now Kolkata), India; July 29, 1956
Also Known As: Chitralekha Banerjee

PRINCIPAL SHORT FICTION
Arranged Marriage, 1995
The Unknown Errors of Our Lives, 2001

OTHER LITERARY FORMS

Chitra Banerjee Divakaruni (CHIH-tra BAHN-ur-jee dih-VAHK-ah-rewn-ee) has written several novels, many of which have received high critical acclaim. Among her novels are *The Mistress of Spices* (1997), *Sister of My Heart* (1999), *The Conch Bearer* (2003), *The Palace of Illusions* (2008), and *One Amazing Thing* (2010). *The Mistress of Spices* has been made into a film, and *Sister of My Heart* has been made into a Tamil television serial.

Divakaruni is also widely acclaimed for her *Shadowland* series of children's novels. There are unique in being set exclusively in India and based heavily on Indian folklore and mythology. With William E. Justice, Divakaruni edited *California Uncovered: Stories for the Twenty-first Century* (2004), a literary anthology of California's new and established writers published in collaboration with the California Council for the Humanities.

Before her fiction career, Divakaruni was an acclaimed poet. Her poems, like her fiction, address a variety of themes and focus heavily on the experiences of immigrants and South Asian women. Divakaruni's work has been translated into more than twenty languages and has been widely popular among international audiences.

ACHIEVEMENTS

Chitra Banerjee Divakaruni's work has received staunch critical acclaim since early in her career. In 1996, she received the Bay Area Book Reviewers Award for Best Fiction, the PEN Oakland/Josephine Miles Award, and American Book Award for *Arranged Marriage*. Her novel *The Mistress of Spices* was included in the *Los Angeles Times*'s Best Books of 1997 and *The Seattle Times*'s Best Paperbacks of 1998. Her novel *The Vine of Desire* (2002) was included in Best Books of 2002 in both the *San Francisco Chronicle* and the *Los Angeles Times*. *The Conch Bearer* was included in *Publishers Weekly*'s Best Books of 2003 and was nominated for the Bluebonnet Award in 2004. Many of her stories have been acknowledged as well: "Mrs. Dutta Writes a Letter" was included in *Best American Short Stories, 1999*, and "The Lives of Strangers" was included in *O. Henry Prize Stories, 2003*.

Divakaruni's other numerous awards include the Hackney Literary Award, Birmingham-southern College, Alabama (1988), the Santa Clara Arts Council Award (1990, 1994), two PEN Syndicated Fiction Awards (1993, 1994), the Pushcart Prize (1994, 2003), the Allen Ginsberg Poetry Prize (1994), the C. Y. Lee Creative Writing Award (1995), the California Arts Council Award (1998), and the South Asian Literary Association Distinguished Author Award (2007).

BIOGRAPHY

Chitralekha Banerjee was born on July 29, 1956, in Calcutta, India, to parents R. K. and Tatini Banerjee. The only girl in a family with four children, Chitra Banerjee Divakaruni lived in Calcutta until 1976, when she came to the United States to continue her education in the field of English language and literature. Following a bachelor's degree from Calcutta University in 1976, Divakaruni earned a master's degree from Wright State University in Dayton, Ohio, in 1978, and a Ph.D. from the University of California, Berkeley, in 1985.

The material for many of her short stories comes from her experience as an immigrant as a worker in the many odd jobs she held to earn money for her education. Though she briefly lived in Illinois, Ohio, and Texas, the backdrop for many of her stories is Northern California, where she has spent most of her life.

Divakaruni moved to Houston, Texas, with her husband, Murthy, and her sons, Anand and Abhay, whose names she has used in her children's novels. There she began to teach in the creative writing program at the University of Houston. She has served on advisory boards of organizations that help educate underserved children in India and that support abused and battered South Asian or South Asian American women who find themselves in abusive or domestic violence situations.

ANALYSIS

Chitra Banerjee Divakaruni's writing is often compared to that of other Asian American women writers, including Jhumpa Lahiri, Amy Tan, and Tahira Naqvi. While the tone and lyricism of Divakaruni's stories reflect those of Ismat Chughtai and Santha Rama Rau, some of India's foremost writers, Divakaruni's stories are deeply rooted in the immigrant and cross-cultural experience. These stories depict strong female protagonists, who, though they may come from traditional Indian backgrounds, refuse to become victims of circumstance. Though Divakaruni does not eschew her native culture overtly, her subtly crafted and often unexpectedly strong female protagonists defy the prevailing caste system and male dominance of that culture.

In her fiction writing, Divakaruni draws heavily on cultural elements of both her native India and the South Asian American community. *Arranged Marriage* even contains a glossary to familiarize readers with some of these cultural elements, including traditional foods, elements of dress, and common Bengali vocabulary. Divakaruni's use of these words and her careful attention to the intricate details of color, sound, and texture add a certain degree of tangibility to her stories, enriching the narrative with descriptions of landscapes, fashion, culture, and language to bring the Indian and Indian American experience to life for a broad reading audience.

The strength of Divakaruni's narrative style is particularly important in her depictions of the immigrant experience and of women's self-discovery. Some critics have suggested that Divakaruni's stories stereotype the incompatibility of eastern and western cultures; however, the vast majority of her stories present well-developed protagonists with plights and inner struggles far too complex to be reduced to such generalizations. Drawn in part from the author's own experiences, Divakaruni's stories are narrated through a number of unique voices and from a variety of rich perspectives to reveal the immigrant experience and a woman's search for identity as intricate and ongoing evolutions without simple resolution.

ARRANGED MARRIAGE

Divakaruni's first collection of short stories provides an apt glimpse at the themes and techniques that characterize much of her writing. Her carefully constructed prose, with its lyricism reminiscent of the poetry for which she initially gained critical acclaim, creates a rich tapestry interwoven with Bengali words and phrases to add texture to the stories of Indian American immigrants and their children. These stories recount the experience of arranged marriage from a multitude of perspectives, none entirely positive or negative, and all drawn against the backdrop of the sometimes fraught cultural exchange between East and West.

In "Clothes," a young woman travels to the United States to live with the husband she has just met and grapples with the decision to adopt a more westernized appearance and lifestyle, even in the face of his untimely death and her in-laws' expectation that she will come to live with and care for them. "The Word Love" tells of a young immigrant woman who faces the consequences of choosing for herself the loose freedoms of American culture against her mother's admonitions. In "The Maid Servant's Story," a story within a story and one of few in this collection to take place in India, a mysterious maid servant, newly arrived, throws a family into an uproar when, after charming the mistress of the house, her insidious past is suddenly revealed. "The Disappearance," told from a young husband's perspective, expresses wonder at a wife and mother who could simply disappear, leaving behind the domestic life that everyone, especially the husband, expected her to enjoy. In "Meeting Mrinal," an abandoned wife faces a friend from her childhood, both of them competing to prove their happiness, in spite of hidden tragedies and grief.

These different voices lend richness to the collection and allow Divakaruni to present arranged marriage as a complex and challenging component of converging cultures. Arranged marriage, as presented in this collection, seems no less complicated than marriages made for love, and its success or failure is equally likely to stem from the two people who make up that marriage. The strength of Divakaruni's female characters and the choices they make for their lives challenge male dominance and the strictures of the Indian caste system but ultimately do not defy the balanced examination of the tradition of arranged marriage.

Divakaruni presents her characters and their situations in a variety of settings. Some stories take place in less-fortunate neighborhoods; others take place in fine middle-class American homes and neighborhoods. Still others provide a glimpse into the rich landscape of Indian estates. The intricacy of the backdrops for these different stories also serves as a platform for Divakaruni to examine other, more universal elements of human experience. Her characters' considerations of marriage, fear, aging, friendship, loss, grief, and parenthood, among other themes, provide portals for diverse readers to enter the stories and find commonality with characters deeply situated in the South Asian American immigrant experience.

"MRS. DUTTA WRITES A LETTER"

Divakaruni considers "Mrs. Dutta Writes a Letter," which opens her second collection of short stories, *The Unknown Errors of Our Lives*, one of her best and favorite pieces, though it was one of the most difficult for her to write; the author worked through nearly ten iterations before arriving at a satisfactory final draft. The smooth poetic cadences of this narrative give evidence of Divakaruni's labors in its creation, as the reader enters the Dutta household and becomes familiar with Mrs. Dutta, her son, her daughter-in-law, their children and the very foreign experience the elderly Mrs. Dutta finds herself trying to navigate.

In this story, as in many of her others, Divakaruni introduces a female protagonist separated from her homeland and struggling to relearn cultural norms and expectations. Mrs. Dutta has arrived in America from India to live in the home of her son and his family, only to find that they have embraced a westernized lifestyle in which there seems to be no room for the good wifely duties on which she prides herself. Mrs. Dutta struggles to adapt to the rhythm of the household and to accommodate viewpoints that clash strongly with her own, but as she rehearses a letter she wishes to write to the best friend she left behind in India, she discovers that what she wants to believe and what her heart really feels may indeed be at odds.

Unique to this story, identifying it as one of Divakaruni's best, is the definitiveness of her protagonist's final decision. The endings of many of Divakaruni's stories remain open and indefinite, allowing the reader to speculate on the ultimate fate of the characters and the resolution of their decisions. Mrs. Dutta's story, however, expresses a surety not often evident in Divakaruni's writing. Though Mrs. Dutta eventually comes to accept a set of truths dear and personal--overcoming intense feelings of guilt, shame, loneliness, and disappointment--she does not come to favor western society and culture but rather returns to that which is familiar. In the finality of this decision, she is unusual among Divakaruni's many strong female characters.

"The Unknown Errors of Our Lives"

In Divakaruni's "The Unknown Errors of Our Lives," the title story of her second collection, readers meet Ruchira, a young Indian American woman preparing for a semiarranged marriage to a man she has known only briefly but has come to love deeply. Ruchira represents the dilemma faced by so many first-generation American children: She clings to the traditions and culture of her immigrant parents and of their parents in another country, even while struggling to forge her own identity in the social context of her own native land. Ruchira agrees to meet Biren, the young man recommended to her mother by a close family friend; however, Ruchira meets the man for coffee before entering an arranged-marriage agreement. Small details--an earring stud, a choice in lovers, a possible history of drug use--indicate without overtly stating that Biren is quite Americanized. Ruchira is perhaps less so: Divakaruni describes in vivid detail the décor of her small apartment, which reflects the culture in which her parents were raised, and the paintings she creates with themes based almost entirely on Indian myth and legend.

From her nostalgia over a notebook in which she recorded her adolescent errors, the reader learns that Ruchira has guided herself through adolescence and young adulthood by asking herself how her grandmother, a woman who never left Calcutta, would have acted in any given situation. Upon learning some unexpected news about Biren's past, Ruchira must face the startling revelation that the rules that guided her grandmother's life might not apply to her own. Ultimately, Ruchira weighs her respect and admiration for Biren against the significance of this news, and decides from her heart rather than out of a sense of duty.

Stylistically, Divakaruni's attention to small details guides the reader through a setting and a series of circumstances that are highly generalized from a distance but deeply personal up close. On the surface, Ruchira faces an experience familiar to many children of immigrants. On a deeper level, the choices and decisions she must make are unique to the first- and second-generation American children of South Asian families, and specifically to the women who struggle against the mores of their grandparents' male-dominated culture.

Ruchira thus represents the cross-cultural middle ground: She struggles to adjust to the news about Biren in the context of the values with which she has been raised and to recognize herself as a product of two sometimes disparate cultures. In this, Divakaruni replicates a theme from her earlier collection of short stories, creating a strong female protagonist who accepts arranged marriage as a practical and even favorable tradition but who asserts her own mind in a manner that may be the product of her western upbringing.

Other major works

LONG FICTION: *The Mistress of Spices*, 1997; *Sister of My Heart*, 1999; *The Vine of Desire*, 2002; *The Conch Bearer*, 2003; *Queen of Dreams*, 2004; *The Mirror of Fire and Dreaming*, 2005; *The Palace of Illusions*, 2008; *One Amazing Thing*, 2009.

POETRY: *The Reason for Nasturtiums*, 1990; *Black Candle*, 1991; *Leaving Yuba City: New and Selected Poems*, 1997.

CHILDREN'S LITERATURE: *Neela: Victory Song*, 2002; *Shadowland*, 2009.

EDITED TEXT: *California Uncovered: Stories for the Twenty-first Century*, 2004 (with William E. Justice).

BIBLIOGRAPHY

Farmanfarmaian, Roxane. "Writing from a Different Place." *Publishers Weekly* 248, no. 20 (May 14, 2001): 46. Provides insight into Divakaruni's childhood and early career and shares the author's advice to developing writers.

Gelfant, Blanche H., ed. "Chitra Banerjee Divakaruni." *The Columbia Companion to the Twentieth Century American Short Story*. New York: Columbia University Press, 2000. Examines several of Divakaruni's popular short stories; situates Divakaruni's writing in the context of works by other South Asian and South Asian American women writers.

Johnson, Sarah Anne. *Conversations with American Women Writers*. Hanover, N.H.: University Press of New England, 2004. Features an interview with Divakaruni in which she discusses the joys and challenges of writing, the differences between her fiction and her poetry, and what she has learned from being a writer. Divakaruni also provides insight into the immigrant experience and how she has incorporated it into her writings.

Kafka, Phillipa. *On the Outside Looking In(dian): Indian Women Writers at Home and Abroad*. New York: Peter Lang, 2003. Offers a critical examination of "Mrs. Dutta Writes a Letter" and analyses of Divakaruni's general themes, in both her short and long fiction, in the context of other Indian and Indian American women writers.

Softky, Elizabeth. "Cross-Cultural Understanding Spiced with the Indian Diaspora." *Black Issues in Higher Education* 14, no. 15 (September 18, 1997): 26. Features comments from Divakaruni and information about her career; focus is primarily on her longer fiction.

Rachel E. Frier

STEPHEN DIXON

Born: Brooklyn, New York; June 6, 1936
Also known as: Stephen Ditchik

PRINCIPAL SHORT FICTION

No Relief, 1976
Quite Contrary: The Mary and Newt Story, 1979
Fourteen Stories, 1980
Movies, 1983
Time to Go, 1984
The Play, and Other Stories, 1988
Love and Will, 1989
All Gone, 1990
Friends: More Will and Magna Stories, 1990
Moon, 1993
Long Made Short, 1994
The Stories of Stephen Dixon, 1994
Man on Stage: Play Stories, 1996
Sleep: Stories, 1999
What Is All This? Uncollected Stories, 2010

OTHER LITERARY FORMS

In addition to his short fiction, Stephen Dixon has published several novels, including *Work* (1977), *Garbage* (1988), *Frog* (1991), *Interstate* (1995), *Gould: A Novel in Two Novels* (1997), *I* (2002), *Phone Rings* (2005), *The End of I* (2006), and *Meyer* (2007).

ACHIEVEMENTS

In 1974-1975, Stephen Dixon received a grant from the National Endowment for the Arts, and in 1977, he received both an O. Henry Award and a Pushcart Prize. He won an American Academy of Arts and Letters prize in 1983 and was awarded a John Simon Guggenheim Memorial Foundation Fellowship in 1984. In 1986, Dixon won the John Train Humor Prize awarded by *The Paris Review*. His novel *Frog*, which contains several short stories, was a finalist for the National

Book Award in 1991 and for the PEN/Faulkner Award in 1992; his novel *Interstate* was a finalist for the National Book Award in 1995. Dixon's stories have appeared in *Prize Stories: The O. Henry Awards* and *The Best American Short Stories*.

BIOGRAPHY

Stephen Dixon was born Stephen Ditchik in Brooklyn, New York, on June 6, 1936, the son of a dentist and an interior decorator. After going to public school in Manhattan, where his father set up a dental practice, he attended New York City College and received a B.A. degree in 1958. Following a short stint as a newsman in Washington, D.C., he returned to New York in 1961 to work as a news editor for Columbia Broadcasting System (CBS) and as an editor for two detective magazines. During 1964-1965, he attended Stanford University on a Wallace Stegner Fellowship and began publishing stories in *The Paris Review*, *The Atlantic Monthly*, and numerous smaller magazines.

In 1979, Dixon began teaching creative writing at New York University's School of Continuing Education, and the following fall he was hired as an assistant professor at Johns Hopkins University, where he eventually became a professor and the chair of the university's writing seminars program. In 1982, he married Anne Frydman, a teacher of Russian literature, with whom he had two daughters.

ANALYSIS

Stephen Dixon's short fiction is almost always characterized as being "experimental," "fabulous," or "quirky" in the tradition of Franz Kafka and Samuel Beckett. However, although Dixon has experimented with a wide range of narrative devices and fictional techniques, many of his stories, as imaginative and inventive as they may be, largely seem to be just that-bloodless experiments with devices and techniques rather than stories about real human events.

Dixon's favorite technique--what some critics have called "experimental realism"--is to create stories that seem grounded in solid, everyday reality and at the same time completely in the style of Gabriel García Márquez, in which fantastic and fabulous events are described as if they were taking place in a specific real world instead of in the "once-upon-a-time" world of fairy tales or in the purely imaginative world of folktales and parables.

"MAN OF LETTERS"

Many of Dixon's stories are experiments with traditional narrative structures. For example, "Man of Letters" from *The Stories of Stephen Dixon* makes use of the epistolary form, in which a man named Newt, who features in a number of Dixon's stories, writes a series of letters to a woman he has been dating. Although he begins the first letter with the sentence, "I don't want to see you anymore," by the time he has verbally examined the relationship and justified his decision by writing a whole stack of letters, he ends by saying, "No matter what I'll be seeing you Friday night." It is as if the very act of writing has so self-consciously engaged the protagonist that he cannot state his feelings; he is too busy trying to impress instead of saying simply what he wants to express. Many of Dixon's stories convey this sense of becoming bogged down in verbal and narrative cleverness, thus never quite expressing a truly human experience.

"THE SIGNING"

In a number of Dixon's stories, characters try to avoid coming to terms with tragedy. For example, in "The Signing," from *Fourteen Stories*, a man's wife dies, and as he leaves the hospital room, a nurse asks him about arrangements for the body. He tells her to burn it or to give it to science, for he wants only to get away from the hospital as quickly as he can. As the man catches a bus to escape, a security guard follows him to try to get him to sign the necessary papers. He not only refuses to return to the hospital but also throws away the wristwatch his wife gave him, says he is going to let their car rot in the street, and even takes off the clothes she bought for him and throws them out the bus window. By wanting to destroy everything connected with his wife, the protagonist seems both to be expressing a grief that goes beyond ordinary responses

and to be rejecting grief by completely obliterating its source. Often characters in Dixon's stories act as if they do not care about the relationships in which they are involved.

"LAST MAY"

A number of male protagonists in Dixon's stories move in and out of relationships in such passive ways that their relationships seem to be tentative and transitory. In "Last May" from *No Relief*, a character named Bud, another recurring Dixon male protagonist, meets a woman while visiting his dying father in a hospital, where the woman's mother is also a patient. A scene in which the two make love in Bud's father's hospital room is described in the same unfeeling way that Bud's care for his father is described. After the death of the two parents, Bud visits the woman at her home, but he does not feel the same way about her and never calls her again. When she visits and asks for an explanation of his failure to call, he says he has none. In the last sentence of the story, she says, "All right, then that's it, then I'm leaving." With no response from Bud, who somehow cannot continue with the relationship outside the context of hospitals and death, she leaves.

"THE INTRUDER"

Dixon can narrate the most shocking and horrifying events in such a flat, deadpan style that the events become transformed into a kind of surrealistic and highly stylized set of gestures that readers accept, only to become appalled by their acceptance. "The Intruder" from *Fourteen Stories*, perhaps the most extreme example of this technique, begins with a man entering his apartment to find his girlfriend being raped by an intruder who is threatening her with a knife. The story describes in graphic detail the intruder's forcing both the woman and the man to engage in sex acts with him. However, it is the stripped-down and matter-of-fact style with which the acts are described that creates the strange, surreal effect of the story. As horrifying as the events are, they seem to take place in a world without emotional response.

FROG

A number of stories, such as "Frog's Nanny," "Frog Dances," "Frog Made Free," "Frog Takes a Swim," and "Frog's Mom," are included in Dixon's 1991 novel *Frog*. Howard, the recurring character in these stories, is more human and vulnerable than earlier Dixon characters, such as Newt and Bud. In "Frog Dances," for example, Howard sees a man dancing with a baby to a slow, tragic movement from a symphony by Gustav Mahler in an apartment window. The man seems so enraptured that Howard thinks he must get married and have a child because he wants to have the same experience. Although, like other Dixon protagonists, Howard seems caught in the trap of transitory relationships, it is a trap that he wishes to escape. The story ends with Howard, after some abortive relationships, getting married, having a baby, and dancing with his baby to Mahler's symphonies.

Poignancy changes to pathos in "Frog Takes a Swim," in which Howard, while on the beach with his daughter, takes a quick swim. When he returns, she has disappeared, and the rest of the story charts his heartbroken search for her. Although Dixon's earlier stories are told in a flat indifferent style, this one is filled with anguish. The story ends with Howard sitting in the snow on the beach where he last saw his daughter, begging her to materialize, and crying that he is heartbroken and that he will never ask her where she has been if she will, by some miracle, reappear.

"MAN, WOMAN, AND BOY"

"Man, Woman, and Boy," chosen for the annual publication *The Best American Short Stories* in 1993 and collected in *Long Made Short*, is one of Dixon's most human and affecting stories. It is a straightforward examination of a couple who have reached a point in their relationship in which they are both together and separate at once. Although they care for each other, they are indifferent to each other. Although they still want each other, they repel each other. They love each other but often hiss, "I hate you." It is a situation familiar to many couples, and Dixon tells it in a sensitive and unembellished way. The husband continually says to himself that he loves his wife and goes to bed thinking he cannot wait until she comes to bed so he can hold her. At the same time, there is a sense of loss, loneliness, and hopelessness. The story communicates in a carefully controlled way the complex realization that both love and hate can exist simultaneously and that most male/female relationships exist as just such an inextricable mix of opposite emotions.

OTHER MAJOR WORKS

LONG FICTION: *Work*, 1977; *Too Late*, 1978; *Fall and Rise*, 1985; *Garbage*, 1988; *Frog*, 1991; *Interstate*, 1995; *Gould: A Novel in Two Novels*, 1997; *Thirty: Pieces of a Novel*, 1999; *Tisch*, 2000; *I*, 2002; *Phone Rings*, 2005; *The End of I*, 2006; *Meyer*, 2007.

BIBLIOGRAPHY

Boyd, Greg. "The Story's Stories: A Letter to Stephen Dixon." In *Balzac's Dolls, and Other Essays, Studies, and Literary Sketches*. Dalphne, Ala.: Légèreté Press, 1987. An essay analyzing the themes and techniques of Dixon's short fiction, written in the form of a letter to him. Argues that Dixon's fiction is unique for its conversational intimacy and its rhythms of seemingly unmediated thought. Discusses themes and narrative devices in several stories; comments on how his books hold together as unified collections.

Daley, Jason. "Spinning Through Possibilities." *Poets and Writers* 35, no. 5 (September/October, 2007): 46-51. A profile of Dixon, in which he discusses the craft of writing. He states that early success forced him to become a self-sufficient writer, describes how the themes of his work have changed over the years, and proclaims his love for the act of writing.

Ferguson, William. "Which Version Do You Prefer?" *Los Angeles Times*, September 4, 1994, p. 12. A review of *The Stories of Stephen Dixon*. Comments on Dixon's themes of relations between the sexes, the plight of the individual in a hostile society, and the unstable nature of truth. Argues that Dixon's characters reinvent themselves in language that is often more substantial than they are; notes that many of his male characters become compulsive talkers when rejected by women.

Klinkowitz, Jerome. "Experimental Realism." In *Postmodern Fiction*, edited by Larry McCaffery. New York: Greenwood Press, 1986. Comments on Dixon as an example of superrealism, which sees the limitations of its form as positive aids. Briefly discusses Dixon's story "Said," which takes the redundant convention of identifying each line of a speaker and makes it a self-apparently opaque sign.

_____. *The Self-Apparent Word: Fiction as Language/Language as Fiction.* Carbondale: southern Illinois University Press, 1984. Claims that Dixon is able to take the most familiar narrative conventions and reinvest them with a sense of novelty new to contemporary realism. Discusses these tactics in several stories, focusing on such self-reflexive devices as how stories need reshaping and how fictions are generated.

Passaro, Vince. "S.A.S.E." *The New York Times*, May 16, 1999, p. 7. A review of *Thirty: Pieces of a Novel* and the short-story collection *Sleep*. Suggests that Dixon's stories are strongly autobiographical and that his strength lies in the quick revelation of a rushing and exhibitionist prose. Discusses Dixon's treatment of sexuality in his stories.

Salzman, Arthur. "To See a World in a Grain of Sand: Expanding Literary Minimalism." *Contemporary Literature* 31 (1990): 423-433. Discusses Dixon as a writer who redefines minimalism as a set of ways of asking questions about the contemporary world. Argues that, in Dixon's fiction, what charges otherwise anonymous, menial jobs with interest is language--urban lingoes, inside dope, and coded cryptics.

Trucks, Rob. "Stephen Dixon." In *The Pleasure of Influence: Conversations with American Male Fiction Writers.* West Lafayette, Ind.: NotaBell Books, 2002. Dixon discusses the origins of his fiction, explains his writing process, and assesses his literary achievements.

Charles E. May

E. L. DOCTOROW

Born: New York, New York; January 6, 1931

PRINCIPAL SHORT FICTION

Lives of the Poets: Six Stories and a Novella, 1984
Sweet Land Stories, 2004
All the Time in the World: New and Selected Stories, 2011

OTHER LITERARY FORMS

E. L. Doctorow (DAHK-tur-oh) is known primarily for his novels, from *Welcome to Hard Times* (1960) and *Ragtime* (1975) through *Loon Lake* (1980), *World's Fair* (1985), *Billy Bathgate* (1989), and *The Waterworks* (1994), to *City of God* (2000), *The March* (2005), and *Homer and Langley* (2009). He also has written plays (*Drinks Before Dinner*, 1978), and screenplays based on his books *The Book of Daniel* (1971), *Ragtime*, and *Loon Lake*, and he has several collections of essays.

ACHIEVEMENTS

E. L. Doctorow has been a major contributor to American literature for more than fifty years, and he has received a number of honors. He was awarded the National Humanities Medal at the White House in 1998; *World's Fair* won the National Book Award in 1985; and *Ragtime*, *Billy Bathgate*, and *The March* have all won National Book Critics Circle Awards. Doctorow is recognized as a prose stylist who rarely repeats himself, with each of his novels exploring new territory. His first three novels, for example, belong to the genres of the western, science fiction, and political-historical fiction, respectively. His short fiction has appeared in a number of national journals, often in *The New Yorker*. He also edited the annual *Best American Short Stories* in 2000.

BIOGRAPHY

Edgar Lawrence Doctorow was born and raised in New York City, and he graduated from Kenyon College in 1952. He served in the U.S. Army in Germany during 1954-1955, and he married Helen Seltzer while still in the service. They have three grown children. He worked as an editor in his early professional life, first at

New American Library and then at Dial Press, where he became editor-in-chief. Doctorow left publishing in 1969 to write full time; since then he has produced a book every three or four years. In addition to his writing, he has taught at several universities, including the University of California, Irvine; Sarah Lawrence College; and New York University, where in 1982 he became the Loretta and Lewis Glucksman Professor of English and American Letters.

ANALYSIS

Although primarily known for his novels, E. L. Doctorow is also a major practitioner of short fiction, and his stories have appeared frequently in recent years in the leading venue for short fiction in the United States, *The New Yorker*. Doctorow's stories often involve innocent people learning about the world or misfits and outsiders working on the edges of society. Many characters pursue the American Dream, but it is often a dream tempered by the difficulties of social class. Realistic and often straightforward in narrative technique, Doctorow's stories are sometimes mysteries, stories that contain a haunting feeling reminiscent of the work of Joyce Carol Oates, Stephen King, and other contemporary gothic writers.

LIVES OF THE POETS: SIX STORIES AND A NOVELLA

The stories collected in 1984 in *Lives of the Poets* had first appeared in various magazines--*The Atlantic*, *Esquire*, *Vanity Fair*, *The Paris Review*--but the volume has much more coherence than most short-story collections. The six short stories that make up roughly the first half of the volume make sense only when filtered through the title novella, which concludes it. The first story, for example, "The Writer in the Family," is a coming-of-age story about a young boy, who, after his father's death, is forced by his family to write letters to his frail grandmother pretending the father is well and living in Arizona. The "writer" in the story, Jonathan, is the fifty-year-old author, struggling with his writing, who narrates the title novella. In between these two authorial stories are five stories that make other connections and share recurrent ideas and images. "The Water Works" is a fragment that anticipates an incident in Doctorow's 1985 novel of that name."Willi" is another initiation story, in this case an Oedipal tale set in

Galicia in 1910, in which a young boy betrays his mother when he reveals her affair with his tutor to his father. "The Hunter" is a disturbing tale about a young teacher in a poor upstate New York town, struggling with her isolation and sexual frustration. "The Foreign Legation" is a story about a recently separated husband (like Jonathan in the novella), waiting for something to happen, with a nightmare explosion at the end. "The Leather Man," like "The Water Works," is a fragment, this one about outsiders in society. Critics understand that these first six stories are all connected to and extensions of the Doctorow persona, Jonathan, who is struggling to finish a novel in the concluding novella and wrestling with his isolation and the questions of his chosen profession. They are, in other words, products of Jonathan's imagination. Some critics even refer to *The Lives of the Poets* as fragments of a novel. The novelist of the title novella is estranged from his wife and family in Connecticut, living in an apartment in New York City, and trying to understand his life and his work. The story is a monologue by a writer in a midlife crisis, trying to figure out the relationship between his private role and his public responsibility. The story concludes with the artist breaking out of his isolation and taking a refugee family into his apartment. The best stories in *Lives of the Poet* are "The Writer in the Family" and "Willi," and both initiation stories have been reprinted in other collections, "Willi" in *American Short Story Masterpieces* (1989) and "The Writer in the Family" in *Early Sorrow: Ten Stories of Youth* (1986).

SWEET LAND STORIES

Doctorow's second collection of short stories is less cohesive than the six stories and a novella linked together in *Lives of the Poets*, but it focuses more narrowly on misfits working on the American Dream. The collection comprises five stories, four of which first appeared in *The New Yorker*. The lead story, "A House on the Plains," selected for *Best American Short Stories* in 2002, combines gothic and historical elements. An accomplice son narrates the story of how his mother kills her husband for insurance money and then uses it to move them from Chicago to the title location, where she adopts three orphans and lures prospective partners to invest in a scheme, kills them for their money, and ends up burning down the house and framing an alcoholic handyman for the dead people inside. What makes the story unique is the slightly comic tone maintained throughout this horrific tale. "Baby Wilson," another *New Yorker* story selected for *Best American Short Stories*, is narrated by the shiftless Lester, who knows his girlfriend is crazy when she steals a baby from a hospital, but he flees with her, dropping the baby at a church and making an odyssey to Alaska. "Baby Wilson" is, like "A House on the Plains," a flawed American Dream tale. "Jolene: A Life" concerns another working-class character, who narrates the story of her odyssey in search of the dream, only this one ends, after a series of losing relationships, with the narrator no better off than when she started.

"Walter John Harmon" is narrated by a lawyer, who is working in a cult (not unlike the Branch Davidians near Waco, Texas, in 1993) run by the charismatic title character. When Harmon runs off with the narrator's wife and the commune's money, the narrator takes over to build a wall around the compound that seems to foreshadow military action. The concluding story,

E. L. Doctorow (AP Photo/Mike Albans)

"Child, Dead in the Rose Garden," differs in subject and tone from what precedes it in the collection, for it is a political mystery narrated by an agent of the Federal Bureau of Investigation, trying to figure out how a dead child ended up on the White House lawn. He solves the puzzle in spite of political interference and amid vague environmental and class issues. Most of the works in *Sweet Land Stories* are gothic, in their violence and mystery, and most contain characters pursuing the American Dream, with violent and sometimes comic results.

"WAKEFIELD"

Doctorow's later stories focus even more insistently on the seemingly opposed themes of isolation and the American Dream, of outside-inside. In "Wakefield," the title character, Howard Wakefield, becomes a hermit in the unused attic space over his garage, hiding for months from his wife and twin daughters and, like an animal, foraging for food at night in his suburban neighborhood. When he finally spies his wife entertaining an old beau, Wakefield cleans himself up, and the story ends with him reentering his house as if he had just returned from work. "Hello? I shouted. I'm home!" Like the title character in Nathaniel Hawthorne's gothic sketch "Wakefield" (from his *Twice-Told Tales* of 1837), who leaves his home and remains on a nearby street for twenty years and thus becomes "the Outcast of the Universe," before returning home, Doctorow's protagonist has dropped out of "the system" and then reenters the world. It is significant that the title story of Doctorow's third collection of short stories, *All the Time in the World*, focuses on another outcast, an exile running the crowded streets of Manhattan until the apocalyptic, science-fiction ending in an otherwise empty city.

"ASSIMILATION"

If "Wakefield" explores the idea of becoming invisible to society, "Assimilation" is a complex tale of trying to get into that society and the American Dream it embodies. Mestizo Ramon is a busboy in a Brooklyn restaurant, who is promoted to waiter when the East European owners learn he is an American citizen and can help their niece emigrate to the United States by marrying her. Ramon's brother, a crime boss finishing a prison sentence, advises Ramon to be wary, and when the brother is released from prison, he helps Ramon and Jelena flee from the restaurant owners and their criminal gang. "Assimilation" thus plays with complex levels of entrance into the American Dream. Leon is successful in the United States, restaurant owner Borislav is a little further down the social scale, and Ramon and Jelena are two innocents caught between the criminal groups who hold the real power in society. As in "Jolene: A Life" and other early Doctorow stories, "Assimilation" plays with the ideas of making it in an America of powerful class differences.

OTHER MAJOR WORKS

LONG FICTION: *Welcome to Hard Times*, 1960; *Big as Life*, 1966; *The Book of Daniel*, 1971; *Ragtime*, 1975; *Loon Lake*, 1980; *World's Fair*, 1985; *Billy Bathgate*, 1989; *The Waterworks*, 1994; *City of God*, 2000; *The March*, 2005; *Homer and Langley*, 2009.

PLAYS: *Drinks Before Dinner*, 1978.

SCREENPLAYS: *Three Screenplays*, 2003.

NONFICTION: *Jack London, Hemingway, and the Constitution: Selected Essays, 1977-1992*, 1993; *Poets and Presidents*, 1993; *Conversations with E. L. Doctorow*, 1999; *Reporting the Universe*, 2003; *Creationists: Selected Essays, 1993-2006*, 2006.

EDITED TEXT: *The Best American Short Stories 2000*.

MISCELLANEOUS: *American Anthem*, photographs by Jean-Claude Suares, 1982; *Scenes and Sequences: Fifty-Eight Monotypes*, photographs by Eric Fischl, 1989; *The People's Text: A Citizen Reads the Constitution*, 1992; *Lamentation 9/11*, 2002 (photographs by David Finn).

BIBLIOGRAPHY

Bloom, Harold, ed. *E. L. Doctorow*. Philadelphia: Chelsea House, 2002. This volume collects the best previously published criticism, including that of John G. Parks, "Art and Memory: *Lives of the Poets* and *World's Fair*," and of Stephen Matterson, "Why Not Say What Happened? E. L. Doctorow's *Lives of the Poets*."

Fowler, Douglas. *Understanding E. L. Doctorow*. Columbia: University of South Carolina Press, 1992. Chapter 6 is devoted to the seven pieces that make up *Lives of the Poets*.

Harter, Carol C., and James R. Thompson. *E. L. Doctorow*. Boston: Twayne, 1990. Chapter 6 of this study of the writer, "A Mind Looking for Its Own Geography," explores the interrelationships among the six stories and novella that make up *Lives of the Poets*.

Siegel, Ben, ed. *Critical Essays on E. L. Doctorow*. New York: G. K. Hall, 2000. Collection includes two reviews of *Lives of the Poets* and an essay, Susan Brienza's "Writing as Witnessing: The Many Voices of E. L. Doctorow," which discusses *Lives of the Poets*.

Ulin, David. "Pangs of an Aimless Existence." *Los Angeles Times*, March 20, 2011, p. E7. Review of the stories in *All the Time in the World*, which notes that Doctorow's short stories are set pieces to the symphonies of his novels. His themes are emotional exhaustion and the tension between longing and obligation.

David Peck

ANTHONY DOERR

Born: Cleveland, Ohio; October 27, 1973

PRINCIPAL SHORT FICTION

The Shell Collector, 2002
Memory Wall, 2010

OTHER LITERARY FORMS

Anthony Doerr (door) writes primarily short fiction, but he has written a novel, *About Grace* (2004), and a memoir, *Four Seasons in Rome* (2007).

ACHIEVEMENTS

Anthony Doerr's work has been widely recognized, garnering him a range of prizes. In 2007, the British literary magazine *Granta* named him one of the twenty-one best young American novelists; he also was appointed writer-in-residence for Idaho, a three-year position. In 2005, he was awarded the Rome Prize from the American Academy of Arts and Letters, and the ensuing year in Rome led to his writing of *Four Seasons in Rome*. Doerr has been awarded both a Guggenheim and a National Endowment for the Arts Fellowship. *The Shell Collector* won the Barnes and Noble Discover Prize, the New York Public Library's Young Lions Fiction Award, an Ohioana Book Award, a Pushcart Prize for "For a Long Time This Was Griselda's Story," and two O. Henry Prizes for "The Shell Collector" and "The Hunter's Wife." *About Grace* earned Doerr another Ohioana Book Award. *Memory Wall* received a National Magazine Award for Fiction, a Pushcart Prize for "The River Nemunas," and an O. Henry Prize for "Village 113."

BIOGRAPHY

Although Anthony Doerr kept a journal in high school and had been writing stories since he was nine, he never thought he would be a professional author. It was not until he was twenty-two that he started writing seriously, and a few years after that he began sending his stories to be published. He holds an undergraduate degree in history from Bowdoin College in Maine, which boasts among its graduates Nathaniel Hawthorne and Henry Wadsworth Longfellow. Doerr earned his M.F.A. in fiction writing from Bowling Green State University in Ohio, where he met his wife, Shauna Eastland. The two moved to Boise, Idaho, with their twin sons. Doerr has previously lived and worked in Alaska, Colorado, Ohio, New Zealand, Kenya, and Italy.

Doerr served as writer-in-residence for Idaho from 2007 to 2010, a position that entailed being a literary ambassador for Idaho and doing readings around the state. He has written a regular column reviewing science books for the *Boston Globe* and has been an occasional contributor to *The Morning News,* an online magazine that publishes daily features by the Web's best writers. He also has taught in the low-residency M.F.A. program at Warren Wilson College in North Carolina.

ANALYSIS

Anthony Doerr's fiction often centers on location. The many places where he has lived appear frequently in his stories. Because of his familiarity with them, the locations come alive in his stories. His stories also address place in a metaphorical way: Where does a person belong? What is his place in life? The characters in his stories sometimes actively search for answers to these questions and sometimes avoid the questions, but they are always present. In "The Shell Collector," the main character goes as far as to acknowledge that "you spend your life avoiding these things; you end up seeking them out."

Acceptance of place and situation is another theme in Doerr's stories. His characters repeatedly face the death of family members, severed relationships, and the denial of dreams. The stories work through these issues without being moralistic. Instead, Doerr turns his characters to the power of nature for healing.

It is often said that time heals all wounds, but time can also erase the memory of those wounds. Doerr's second collection, *Memory Wall*, is focused particularly on memory, from memories extracted onto tapes to haunting memories from the afterworld. Each of the stories provides a different take on the way memory functions and how it does not. As in all of his stories, Doerr's writing gracefully weaves in these ideas without being heavy-handed. He presents stories of great beauty that call for reflection and rereading.

"THE SHELL COLLECTOR"

This title story is probably Doerr's most widely taught. Its main character is an unnamed man of sixty-five, who went blind as a child and subsequently became fascinated with shells because he could "see" them with his hands. He read everything he could about shells, eventually getting a Ph.D. in malacology and becoming a professor. However, at age fifty-eight, he retired early and moved to a small beach house in

Anthony Doerr (Getty Images)

Kenya, where he can simply appreciate the beauty of the shells and the ocean. Doerr discusses all of this with a scientific specificity that does not alienate his readers, instead offering an air of authority and knowledge. The shells provide an interesting metaphor for the collector's life and the way he tries to hide inside of it. Doerr skillfully weaves the various types and characteristics of shells into the story and into his character's life.

Much of this story is told in reminiscences. In the present, two reporters named Jim have come to see the shell collector to ask about cone shells. Two years prior, a woman named Nancy showed up on his beach, incoherent and feverish, and is only completely healed after she is bitten by a deadly poisonous cone shell. It is not long before a local religious leader comes to the shell collector to heal his sick daughter with a cone shell. Amazingly, the cone shell does not kill her but heals her. No one understands why the cone shells kill the well and heal the sick, but the seemingly miraculous events spur research and visits from others who are sick. Soon, the shell collector is surrounded by the ailing waiting to be healed. People lie outside his door and follow him into the sea to collect shells. He quits shelling for fear one of his followers will stumble upon a dangerous shell and be hurt.

With news of the shell collector's miracles traveling the world, his "goody-goody" son Josh comes for a visit and immediately begins caring for the sick and suffering who linger around the house, giving them money and inviting them in for meals. The shell collector begins taking walks to escape the commotion in his house, but he begins to "see" cone shells everywhere--in a rock, in a pine cone, in empty shells in the path. After Josh begins to read about shells to three orphan boys, the shell collector decides to take them all shelling. On that first day back in the water, Josh picks up a cone shell and is bitten. Within an hour, he is dead.

Within a month, the Jims are there to interview the shell collector, and the story returns to the present. They do not ask the shell collector about his son, but the shell collector knows the story they write about him will be one of pity. He goes out to the water to search for cone shells for the men, but just as he decides he will not risk their lives by showing them the shells, he realizes he is bitten. He is finally found by the young girl he saved with the bite of a cone shell. She nurses him back to health. The story ends a year later, the two of them walking on the beach. The young girl is more relaxed because she does not have to worry about what the man sees. The shell collector displays his initial boyish wonder at a shell walking across the sand, content in its own small home.

"So Many Chances"

"So Many Chances" is the story of fourteen-year-old Dorotea, whose family moves from Ohio to Maine. Her father thinks he will be able to get a job shipbuilding, and he wants to seize this opportunity because "a man only gets so many chances"--a lesson Dorotea takes to heart. The story is written with short, descriptive sentences, like the ebb and flow of the ocean they will live near. In Ohio, Dorotea was invisible in school, walking with her head down and not making a stir. When she goes to explore the seashore in Maine, she is first surprised by its seeming emptiness. However, when she sees a lone fisherman near the shore, she, emboldened by the beauty of the sea, walks toward him, head up. The sixteen-year-old boy is fly-fishing and makes her a present of his pocketful of hand-tied lures. Importantly, he shows her that the sea is not empty, but that in a handful of mud there are a hundred living creatures, allowing her to later appreciate her surroundings on her own: "the silence of Harpswell rises up in her ear like a wave and breaks into a rainbow of tiny sounds." When Dorotea goes home, she asks her father for a fishing rod. That night, she sneaks out of the house and meets the boy at a bonfire.

Over the following weeks, Dorotea teaches herself to fish and looks for the boy. She blossoms on the seaside and becomes a "new" Dorotea. When she does not see the boy for some time, she goes back to the site of the bonfire, but she discovers he has left with his family as he is only one of the "summer people." Distraught, Dorotea wanders the woods for the rest of the night, and in the morning, she makes her way to her father's shipyard. She finds her father on the docks with a broom. She realizes instantly that he did not get a job shipbuilding but instead is merely a janitor at the shipyard. Her confidence is shaken, and she retreats to her room, no longer fishing every day as she once did.

She finally is persuaded to leave her room when the man who sold her the rod shows up at the door and invites her to fish. She discovers in this day by the sea that even after disappointment, she is still the same girl and that "there are still plenty of chances left in this world." After the fisherman leaves, she finally catches her first fish. After reeling it in, she admires it, then ducks underwater with it and lets it go.

"Village 113"

The story begins nearly a year before the scheduled submergence of Village 113 in China. After multiple bouts of severe flooding, city commissioners decide to move everyone out of the affected villages and release the dam. They have prepared for the displaced villagers resettlement districts, where they purportedly will be able to gain half a century's advancements just by moving in. The story focuses on two elderly members of Village 113: the seed keeper, who is never named, and Teacher Ke. The seed keeper's son, Li Qing, is a "security liaison" for the resettlement and visits his mother's village to encourage her and other doubters to move. Teacher Ke is skeptical, almost to the point of paranoia, about the move. It is clear the seed keeper is also skeptical, but she withholds voicing her concerns, instead focusing on what is present in the village.

During his visit, Li Qing takes his mother on a walk by the water to convince her she does not need to "remain loyal to one place" all her life. The seed keeper does not respond. She continues to watch others leave the town and makes an accounting of what they take--the bones of three generations of housecats rolled into an apron--and what they leave, "dustless circles on a mantel where statuettes once stood." As the city empties, the seed keeper finds herself with an excess of seeds and so plants them not methodically, as she usually would, but rather by tossing them by the handful into this garden and that. The seeds represent the memories that are sown in the village and attached to the place--each seed is "a link to every generation that has gone before it."

The seed keeper goes downriver to visit Li Qing in his forty-eighth-floor apartment. After nine days, she asks how the water will arrive when the dam is released. She returns to Village 113 and begins to bring pots of soup and stew to Teacher Ke, but he does not leave the house. One day when she arrives, he opens his door and asks her to stay to talk. He tells her about the three letters he writes a day, one hundred words each, protesting the flooding. She sends his letters with traders at the waterfront. After a few weeks, he arrives at her house with one last mailing. He has a bag full of fireflies, attracted with honey and water. She empties all of her seed jars, and they stuff the jars with letters and fireflies. The two wade into the water and release the jars into the current one by one.

On the final day prior to the submergence, the seed keeper empties all of her seeds into a blanket and makes a bundle. She does not see the schoolteacher again. Li Qing picks her up in a boat and brings her to her new apartment, where he visits her once a week with his fiancé and her nine-year-old son. The seed keeper feels her memories are trapped, almost underwater, and her seeds remain in a drawer. It is only when the nine-year-old wants to grow something for a school project that the seeds are brought to life to be used again.

OTHER MAJOR WORKS

LONG FICTION: *About Grace*, 2004.

NONFICTION: *Four Seasons in Rome: On Twins, Insomnia, and the Biggest Funeral in the History of the World*, 2007.

BIBLIOGRAPHY

Hughes, Carolyn T. "A Profile of Anthony Doerr." *Poets and Writers* 32, no. 6 (November/December, 2004): 44-47. Chronicles Doerr's path to becoming a writer and includes an excerpt from *About Grace*.

Mukherjee, Neel. "Dream Lover." *The New York Times Book Review*, November 7, 2004, p. 29. Review of *About Grace*.

Rafferty, Terrence. "Time and Inner Space: Anthony Doerr's Stories Contemplate the Restorative Power of Memory." *The New York Times Book Review*, August 1, 2010: 12. Review of *Memory Wall*.

Willard, Nancy. "Rivers Run Through It." *The New York Times Book Review*, March 3, 2002: 7. Review of *The Shell Collector*.

Katy L. Leedy

HARRIET DOERR

Born: Pasadena, California; April 8, 1910
Died: Pasadena, California; November 24, 2002
Also known as: Harriet Huntington

PRINCIPAL SHORT FICTION

"Edie: A Life," 1989
Under an Aztec Sun, 1990
The Tiger in the Grass: Stories and Other Inventions, 1995

OTHER LITERARY FORMS

Harriet Doerr (dowr) is best known for her 1984 autobiographical novel *Stones for Ibarra*, about a woman who moves to Mexico with her husband and lives in a small village. It is a book, Doerr said, about how "memories are like corks left out of bottles. They swell. They no longer fit." She also is the author of a another novel about Mexico, *Consider This, Señora*, published in 1993.

ACHIEVEMENTS

The fact that Harriet Doerr was seventy-five when her first novel *Stones for Ibarra* was published was a source of fascination and even wonder for reviewers and interviewers. However, when the novel won the American Book Award the following year, critics were forced to admit that the most significant thing about Doerr was not her age but her talent. The book was a best seller and has since become a twentieth century classic. Her novel *Consider This, Señora* also was a national best seller. Her story "Edie: A Life" was included in *The Best American Short Stories 1989*.

Biography

Harriet Doerr was born in Pasadena, California, in 1910; her grandfather was Henry Edwards Huntington, the railroad tycoon, whose reputation as both a philanthropist and a robber baron would always haunt Doerr. Doerr's father was Howard Huntington, Henry Huntington's only son; she had five brothers and sisters. During her childhood, her grandfather's estate, now the Huntington Library, Art Collections, and Botanical Gardens in San Marino, California, was a playground for her and her brothers and sisters. She also remembers Christmas parties at her Uncle Fred's place in Long Beach, the Bixby Ranch, center of the historic twenty-eight-thousand-acre Rancho Los Alamitos.

Doerr had a tutor when she was a child but entered Polytechnic Elementary School in Pasadena in the fourth grade. She went to Smith College in Northhampton, Massachusetts, in 1927 but returned to Pasadena the following year. She then traveled to Palo Alto, where Albert Doerr, whom she would marry in 1930, was attending Stanford University. Their first child, Mike, was born in 1931, and their daughter Martha was born in 1935. Beginning in the 1930's, Doerr and her husband made several extended trips to Mexico to oversee her husband's family mining business there; much of her fiction derives from the times she lived in Mexico, particularly a year-long sojourn in 1950.

After her husband's death in 1972, on a dare from her children, Doerr went back to school, taking courses at Scripps College and then attending Stanford University on a Wallace Stegner Fellowship, during which time she received encouragement from Wallace Stegner and John L'Heureux to write *Stones for Ibarra*.

Doerr died in Pasadena on November 24, 2002, at the age of ninety-two.

Analysis

Called by one reviewer the "mother of spare prose, a patron saint of life's enduring details," Harriet Doerr published a small body of fiction that has been highly praised for its classically spare style and its ability to evoke the personal past. All of Doerr's fiction was based on her own long life, most of it focusing on the times she and her husband lived in Mexico as the only Americans in a small village.

Doerr's short stories, like all her fiction, are so thoroughly enmeshed with autobiography that the question of whether events she describes actually occurred matters little. Referred to by reviewers as essays, recollections, stories, and sketches, her short fictional pieces in *The Tiger in the Grass*, which she subtitled *Stories and Other Inventions*, derive their power from the unassuming voice of their narrator, who delights in language's ability to stimulate discovery. Doerr's short fiction admirably reflects what she once told an interviewer: that everything and everyone one meets rubs off on him or her and is never lost. "That's what's eternal," Doerr said, "these little specks of experience in a great, enormous river that has no end."

"Edie: A Life"

Although "Edie: A Life," like many of the short fictions in her collection *The Tiger in the Grass*, is highly autobiographical, it is the most popular choice of short-story anthology editors primarily because it has the kind of well-made unity that critics expect of the modern short story. As the title suggests, the story is an account of the life of one person, Edith Fisk, governess to the five half-orphaned children of the Ransom family. However, unlike book-length biographical accounts, this "life" of Edie narrowly focuses on the governess's relationship to the family, a stylistic limitation that, typical of the short story, transforms her into a significant symbolic character rather than a well-rounded realistic individual.

Brought over from England to California after the mother has died during the birth of twins, Edie immediately transforms the grieving family, becoming as much a part of their lives as food and water. In a twelve-year period, while the father brings three different wives into the home, Edie is the "mast" the children cling to in a "squall of stepmothers." While mysterious adult affairs disrupt the house, Edie creates an alternate world of sheltering security.

When Edie is sixty years old and the children have all left, she moves to a beach cottage with a pension for the rest of her life. The story ends in the late 1940's, when Edie is dying of cancer and the children imagine the two little girls she once cared for in England, Alice and Anne, living in a tower, still seven and eight years old, writing to express their sorrow at her illness. "Edie: A Life" is an interesting example of how Doerr uses familiar literary conventions and a crystalline prose style to transform mere reality into a magical realm. There is a curious old-fashioned nineteenth century feel to the story, even though it is told in the modern economic style for which Doerr is famous.

Although the story is ostensibly about the "life" of Edie, she is little more in the story than a stable center, a fantasy fulfillment in the fashion of Mary Poppins, an adult who is able to respond to children as if they were adults even as she is willing effortlessly to enter into their childlike experience. The events of this autobiographical recollection may be based on real life, but the story itself is a highly stylized literary convention.

"THE TIGER IN THE GRASS"

The title piece of Doerr's short-fiction collection is largely a reminiscence motivated by the fact that the narrator's son, who has lung and brain cancer, has given her a stuffed tiger for her eighty-fifth birthday to remind her to write an account of her life. The tiger motif is further emphasized by her glaucoma doctor, who tells her that peripheral vision is how "we see the tiger in the grass," adding, "It's also how the tiger sees us." These two tiger references provide the structural link for the recollections, which reflect both opportunities for experience, as well as the inevitable dangers always lurking in one's life.

The sketch focuses primarily on three different flawless periods of the narrator's life: the summers in the 1930's which she and her husband and two children spent at a beach house, the times she and her husband spent in Mexico (much more detailed in Doerr's two novels), and the time she went back to school in 1975 and took writing classes. The accounts are separated by brief anecdotal paragraphs about her ailing son.

The series of reminiscences ends with Doerr's rumination about the pleasure of writing as a discovery of things she did not know she had lost. Echoing the "tiger in the grass" metaphor that introduced the sketch, Doerr concludes, "Let us celebrate our vision, clear or clouded, central or peripheral." Sidelong she sees the tiger in the grass as half threat and half friend, accepting the fact that, "We are still in step after all this time, my tiger in the grass and I."

MEXICO

The longest section of fictionalized reminiscences in Doerr's short-fiction collection focuses on, as might be expected by those familiar with Doerr's novels, her experiences in Mexico. Although some of these pieces, such as "The Seasons," are brief lyrical descriptions, others are longer narrative accounts. "Sun, Pure Air, and a View," for example, focuses on a widow named Morgan Sloane who comes to live among the dozen exiles in the Mexican town of Santa Felicia. As Morgan tries to deal with her loneliness after the death of her husband, she settles into the rhythmic routine of village life.

When her daughter, who has come for a brief visit, leaves, the Mexican caretaker who has helped her adjust reminds her of the pleasures of a simple life in the words of Doerr's second novel. "Consider this, señora," he says, "On a day like today you can tell from here what kind of ice cream the vendor is selling." With full acceptance of her age and her solitary life, Morgan glances without mercy into her mirror and then crosses to the window to "consider the view."

OTHER MAJOR WORKS

LONG FICTION: *Stones for Ibarra*, 1984; *Consider This, Señora*, 1993.

BIBLIOGRAPHY

Doerr, Harriet. "Enough About Age." Interview by Pamela Warrick. *Los Angeles Times*, August 27, 1993, p. E1. An interview with Doerr on the publication of *Consider This, Señora*. Doerr talks about her decision to get her college degree after her husband's death in 1972 and her experience in the creative writing program at Stanford University. She discusses the importance of memory, saying that no experience one has had is ever lost.

_____. "Harriet Doerr: When All of Life Is Important, the Search for the Right Word Is Endless." Interview by Steve Profitt. *Los Angeles Times*, December 31, 1999, p. 31. In this interview, Doerr talks about the lessons she learned from her life in Mexico, her matter-of-fact style, the importance of memory in her work, and her attitude toward mortality. Doerr says she sees no harm in the fact that the older one gets, the more memory and imagination become the same.

_____. Interview by Lisa See. *Publishers Weekly* 240 (August 9, 1993): 420. Doerr discusses her youth, family history, and marriage to Albert Doerr; she talks about how she turned to writing after her husband's death, her love of Mexico, and the differences between her two novels.

King, Rosemary A. *Stones for Ibarra*: Harriet Doerr. In *Border Confluences: Borderland Narratives from the Mexican War to the Present*. Tucson: University of Arizona Press, 2004. Focuses on the depiction of the borderlands between the United States and Mexico in Doerr's first novel but can pertain to the short fiction, in which Doerr also drew upon her experiences in Mexico.

Lacy, Robert. "Harriet Doerr Discloses She Has Few Regrets." Review of *The Tiger in the Grass*, by Harriet Doerr. *Minneapolis Star Tribune*, January 18, 1996, p. 16F. Comments on the importance of Mexico to Doerr's work. Argues that "Edie: A Life" is the best story in the collection, for it shows the wealthy being instructed by the poor while Doerr's prose shows wit and keenness of observation.

Martin, Douglas. "Harriet Doerr Is Dead at 92: Writer of Searing, Sparse Prose." *The New York Times*, November 27, 2002, p. 9. Obituary provides an overview of Doerr's life and literary career.

Reynolds, Susan Salter. "Haunted by Memory." *Los Angeles Times Magazine*, (February 8, 1998): 12. In this extensive article, based on an interview, Reynolds provides a biographical sketch supplemented by Doerr's memories of her childhood. Doerr talks about her nurse Edie Pink, the subject of her best-known story, "Edie: A Life," and other autobiographical sources of her work. She explains her use of detail by noting that a great deal comes from a small thing if "you see it in a certain light and you leave yourself open."

_____. "Memories of Pleasure and Pain." Review of *The Tiger in the Grass*, by Harriet Doerr. *Los Angeles Times*, December 15, 1995, p. E4. Focuses on the importance of memory in the stories. Reynolds says Doerr has one of those sly memories that is sharpest and clearest when focusing on life's best times; notes that her memories of childhood are fragmented, but her memories of Mexico are the source of metaphors and connecting tissue in the work.

Silko, Leslie Marmon. "Pablo, Domingo, Richard, and Sara." Review of *Stones for Ibarra*, by Harriet Doerr. *The New York Times Book Review*, January 8, 1984, 8. Silko argues that the village of Ibarra takes over as the central interest in the story and the American couple serve only as a point of departure for the reader. Calls the work a poet's novel and a tribute to the native culture and the basic human impulse to tell a story.

Streitfield, David. "The Strength of Age." *The Washington Post*, September 26, 1993, p. 15. In this interview/review, Streitfield provides biographical background and comments on Doerr's focus on expatriates in Mexico. Doerr says she does not try to understand mysterious things and that what she loves about Mexico is that it is a mysterious country.

Charles E. May

MICHAEL DORRIS

Born: Louisville, Kentucky; January 30, 1945
Died: Concord, New Hampshire; April 11, 1997
Also known as: Milou North (shared with wife
  Louise Erdrich)

PRINCIPAL SHORT FICTION
  Working Men, 1993
  "Queen of Diamonds," 1991

OTHER LITERARY FORMS

Michael Dorris (DOH-rihs) is probably best known for writing *The Broken Cord* (1989), a nonfiction account of his adopted son Reynald Abel's struggle with fetal alcohol syndrome (FAS), and *A Yellow Raft in Blue Water* (1987), his first novel.

ACHIEVEMENTS

Michael Dorris graduated cum laude, Phi Beta Kappa, and Alpha Sigma Nu from Georgetown University in 1967. In 1970, he received his master's degree in philosophy from Yale University in anthropology. In 1971, at age twenty-five, Dorris adopted three-year-old Abel, called "Adam" in Dorris's book *The Broken Cord.* In 1972, Dorris established a Native American Studies program as part of the Anthropology Department at Dartmouth College in Hanover, New Hampshire. In this position, he increased Native American enrollment at the college and successfully retired what many considered to be Dartmouth's demeaning "Indian" mascot. Dorris continued to be an outspoken critic of the use of Native American sports team logos and mascots. His first novel, *A Yellow Raft in Blue Water,* won critical praise. *The Broken Cord* won the 1989 National Book Critics Circle Award for nonfiction, the Heartland Prize, and the Christopher Award. The attention that *The Broken Cord* received brought the dangers of drinking alcohol during pregnancy to national attention. Dorris became a not-always-popular spokesperson for abstinence during pregnancy, using his son Abel as a tragic example of the consequences of alcohol consumption by pregnant women. In 1992, with Dorris as a consultant, *The Broken Cord* was made into a television film starring Jimmy Smits as Dorris.

BIOGRAPHY

Michael Anthony Dorris was born on January 30, 1945, in Louisville, Kentucky. His parents, Lieutenant Jim Leonard Dorris and Mary Besy Burkhardt, met in Louisville while Jim was stationed at Fort Knox. Jim was killed in 1946 in a Jeep accident--possibly a suicide--while serving in Germany, so Dorris never got to know his father. Mary never remarried, and Dorris grew up in Louisville in a household of women, which included his mother, his grandmother, and one of his mother's two sisters, Marion. Even though he spent some summers with relatives of his father on a reservation in Montana, Dorris--Modoc (a tribe of the Northwestern United States), French, and English descent on his father's side and Irish and Swiss descent on his mother's side--felt isolated and lonely as a child. He was, however, an exceptional student, and his family made his education a priority, paying for Dorris to attend religious schools. The gift of a typewriter when he was fourteen along with joining a pen-pal club allowed Dorris to finally collect the friends he had longed to have. The experience of making friends through his writing was one that would serve Dorris well throughout his life.

In 1963, Dorris became the first of his family to attend college. He went to Georgetown University in Washington, D.C., graduating in 1967, and then went to Yale University to study theater history. He later switched to cultural anthropology and eventually earned a master's degree in this field.

In 1971, Dorris adopted three-year-old Abel, a Lakota boy. The fall after adopting Abel, Dorris began teaching anthropology at Franconia College in New Hampshire. Then, in 1972, Dorris moved to Dartmouth College to start a Native American Studies program as part of its Anthropology Department. In 1974, Dorris adopted two-year-old Jeffrey Sava, through the same agent who helped him adopt Abel. In 1975, he adopted a two-month-old Lakota girl, Madeline Hannah.

Along with establishing a Native American Studies program, Dartmouth began recruiting Native American students, and Karen Louise Erdrich (she later dropped the Karen) was one of them. One-quarter Anishinabe on her mother's side and German on her father's side, Erdrich entered Dartmouth as an undergraduate the same year Dorris started teaching there, in 1972. Unlike Dorris, Erdrich comfortably felt part of the Native American community. Her grandfather had been a tribal leader, and her parents had taught at the Bureau of Indian Affairs school in Wahpeton, North Dakota, where she had grown up.

The couple got to know each other on the Dartmouth campus. Erdrich took a course from Dorris while an undergraduate. In her junior year, Erdrich received the American Academy of Poets Prize. After Erdrich left Dartmouth, Dorris and she started writing to one another. This exchange continued during 1980, the year Dorris spent in New Zealand on sabbatical. When Dorris returned to his position at Dartmouth following his sabbatical, Erdrich also returned to Dartmouth, as a writer-in-residence.

Dorris married Erdrich in 1981. During their marriage, they claimed that they not only encouraged each other but also read and edited each other's work to the point where they sometimes no longer knew who had written what. They added three biological daughters to the three children Dorris had adopted while still single, and they appeared to be an idyllic couple, able to successfully combine parenting, collaboration, friendship, romance, and more. In hindsight, these appearances were idealized rather than authentic.

While Dorris presented himself in his writing and in interviews as a gentle and caring father, the reality may have been quite different. In 1992, Dorris's son Abel, by then living on his own and working part-time as a

dishwasher at age twenty-three, died after being struck by a car. In 1991, Dorris's son Sava wrote a threatening letter to Dorris and Erdrich, in which he demanded money in exchange for his silence about alleged abuse he had suffered at their hands as a child. The couple responded by bringing extortion charges against Sava. During the trial that followed, Sava made damaging claims about Dorris's and later Erdrich's abusive behavior toward him and their other children and succeeded in being acquitted in 1994.

In December, 1996, Dorris's twenty-two-year-old adopted daughter Madeline and two of his three biological daughters accused Dorris of physical abuse and inappropriate physical contact. Earlier that year, Erdrich had moved out of the family home in Minneapolis and had started divorce proceedings at the time of Dorris's suicide on April 11, 1997, in a motel in Concord, New Hampshire, the town where he lived first with his adopted children and later with Erdrich and their three biological daughters and where his son Abel was buried. Dorris's body was discovered on the day he was to have been honored at Dartmouth for his work

Michael Dorris (AP Photo/File)

founding the Native American Studies Department and to have been charged by the Hennepin County attorney's office in Minnesota with criminal sexual child abuse. Many mysteries surround the life of Dorris. His writing and the writing about him offer clues but no definitive answers.

ANALYSIS

In his short fiction, Michael Dorris imagines alternative lives wide ranging in economic and ethnic circumstances and in gender and sexual orientation. Though they take place in various time periods, all are set in locations familiar to Dorris, places that at one time or another he called home. Twelve of the fourteen stories in the collection *Working Men* are told in the first person, employing the same narrative tone found in his collection of essays, *Paper Trail* (1994). Ten of the fourteen stories were published in literary magazines, beginning in 1987. The stories reflect Dorris's fascination with the connection between a person's family and personal life and his or her professional life and the often-blurred boundaries between the two, which accounts for one meaning of the title *Working Men.* They also touch on the work of becoming a fully realized person maturing into a productive, actualized adult or failing to do so. The role of others as potential helpmates in the process of maturation is explored in many of the stories, often with disappointing consequences.

The stories in the collection are interesting because, on some level, they are about Dorris, his extensively interwoven professional and personal life, his fears and resentments, his deep loneliness and self-doubt, and his talent for presenting himself as he needed to in order to get the acceptance and approval from others that he wanted. Themes common to the stories in this collection are sacrifice (often but not always human), redemption through relationships, deception, and rebirth and renewal.

"JEOPARDY"

Published for the first time in the collection *Working Men*, "Jeopardy" is the story of a traveling pharmaceutical salesman named Don Banta, the narrator. Don is confronted by his lonely, deceptive life when his father dies in their home while Don is on the road. Don wears a wedding ring though he is not married to provide a barrier between himself and the female receptionists at the doctors' offices he flirts with as part of his sales strategy. Instead of asking one of them out, Don returns to his motel and picks up a man in the bar. However, it is to these women that Don turns after discovering his father has died. None of the women has time for him, suggesting that the wedding ring he has been wearing to keep them at bay never has been necessary. The final telephone number that Don tries is that of the first receptionist he had visited the day before, and he gets a response for which he had not bargained. A sample of an inhaler he had given her for her son was the only thing that had stopped the boy's asthma attack the evening before. She is grateful, and her gratitude opens the door of opportunity for Don to make a deeper human contact. However, he remains speechless, and the woman hangs up. This leaves Don at an emotional dead end. He needs rescuing, there is no one to rescue him, and he seems ill equipped to rescue himself.

The title "Jeopardy" is a double entendre, referring to the game show Don's father enjoys watching and to the position Don is in at the end of the story. Anchorless and alone without his father to care for, Don will have to risk being more authentic--that is, start to have more meaningful and less superficial relationships--or remain achingly alone.

"NAME GAMES"

In this story, featuring a first-person point of view, narrator Alex dreams that he has a more feminine name and that someone is calling to him. He and partner Noel, a flight attendant, are experiencing difficulties in their relationship at the outset of the story. Alex does not want to take the spat of the evening before too seriously. Ready to make up, he snuggles up to Noel, who has spent the night on the couch rather than in their shared bed. However, Noel announces that one of his fellow flight attendants has just left her husband--for Noel. "I'm going to try it . . . I have to know,'" Noel tells Alex, without clearly specifying what "it" is. Like Don Banta in "Jeopardy," Alex, the narrator, is suddenly plunged into frightening isolation. Noel has implied that what he and Alex share is not "it" and cannot be "it," that "it" can only be achieved with a woman. Though Alex, the narrator, is the protagonist of the story, it is Noel, whose occupation hints at both his rootlessness and his eventual flight from his relationship with Alex, who is embarking on a deception that will mean living a lonely and false life like the one Don leads in "Jeopardy."

"THE BENCHMARK"

In this story, the narrator speaks through his profession as a pond builder. The very vocabulary that surrounds the narrator's work creates a metaphor through which he speaks. Pond building is a trade that he has learned from his father but that the narrator will not be passing on to his offspring. Only one of his three children expressed interest in the narrator's work, and that son died in a tragic accident in the pond the narrator had built for his wife. The death of this son weighs down their lives and their marriage, but the narrator never has considered changing professions, and his wife never asks him to, not even after she is diagnosed with terminal cancer. The moment the hospital calls to tell him that his wife has died, he is, in fact, out measuring the land to place yet another pond. Unlike the previous stories, the narrator's profession is almost like another character. As a living presence, pond making is for the narrator both the source of solace and the source of his isolation.

"EARNEST MONEY"

In this story, Sky, a man probably in his thirties, is living in a state of arrested adolescence from which he needs rescuing. As the story opens, narrator Sky is returning to Montana after living many years in Canada to avoid the military draft of the Vietnam War. His father has recently died, and Sky has come to claim his thirteen-thousand-dollar inheritance. His mother and a couple of other women pick Sky up at the bus station. Not particularly ambitious and therefore uncomfortable with his mother's expectations of him, Sky takes up with a slightly older, divorced woman named Evelyn. From the beginning, Evelyn is in charge. About this, Sky says, "I recognized her bossiness for what it was: the instruction booklet that up to then my life had been lacking." When Evelyn takes a job cooking at the state park, Sky spots a deserted gas station and decides to use his inheritance to buy it, foolishly giving the real estate agent much more "earnest money" than he needs to in order to close the deal. In the end, Sky and Evelyn

marry. "You're not doing this for yourself . . . . It's all because you don't want to be left alone," Evelyn correctly deduces. After the wedding, Evelyn wears an expression like "someone who had just woken up and couldn't place where she was." Though Evelyn gets the passive Sky to act, she realizes that she has taken him on more permanently than she perhaps intended. The success of the marriage is in question, since it relies on her willingness to be Sky's "instruction book," a role about which she seems to be having second thoughts.

"OUI"

"Oui" is a funnier story than "Earnest Money" but one with a similar theme. Narrator Dwayne, older than Sky at forty but another directionless man camping out with his mother, hooks up with Cecille, who is "heading out west alone." Again, what brings these two together is their mutual loneliness. Cecille, like Evelyn, takes charge and works to get Dwayne both a place to live and a job. "Living with Mom, I had learned when to shut up and let the other person define a situation," Dwayne explains. Dwayne gets a place to live by marrying Cecille and moving in with her. Then Cecille sends Dwayne to the local high school to interview for a job as a French teacher, even though Dwayne knows only five words in French, the most useful of which is the "Oui" of the title. Dwayne tells the principal that he can also coach football and is hired to do both. At first, this ruse seems safe from detection because of the students' ignorance of French and the school's need for a football coach that can help the team win a championship. Unfortunately, one ambitious student arranges a class trip to France. Snooping through Cecille's things as Dwayne prepares to go on the trip, he thinks he has found evidence that she has been cheating on him and plans to leave her while he is in France. He decides to confess his suspicions and cancel the trip. Before he can speak up, though, Cecille appears at the airport with his suitcases and her own. She announces to the students and their parents that Dwayne has lost his voice cheering at the football game (which his team lost) and that she is coming along on the trip to help out. Surprisingly, her speech is peppered with French phrases, which, of course, Dwayne cannot understand. It seems that she has been taking French classes--not having an affair--and is sufficiently fluent to mask

Dwayne's incompetence. "Anything else, we'll wing it or make the students talk. Tell them it's a test or something," she tells Dwayne. Despite her fear of flying, confessed to early in the story, she is making the trip with him because "there are things I'm scared of worse." Presumably, she means being alone.

In this, the one story in the collection with a truly happy ending, Dorris works through the isolation that comes from telling protective lies to others and to oneself, that the narrator of "Jeopardy" so chillingly faces at the end of that story, to show the comradely and even loving nature of the shared, purposeful deception. The lines between the personal the professional are blurred, as Cecille first plants Dwayne in the job he is not qualified to do and then protects that job by learning to do the job with him. They will reinvent themselves through their collaborative effort, something Cecille has already demonstrated that she is able to do successfully, with the room-sharing arrangement she has at her job. Deception then turns into reinvention, as the lie is converted to the truth.

OTHER MAJOR WORKS

LONG FICTION: *A Yellow Raft in Blue Water*, 1987; *The Crown of Columbus*, 1991 (with Louise Erdrich); *Cloud Chamber*, 1997.

NONFICTION: *Native Americans: Five Hundred Years After*, 1975 (photographs by Joseph Farber); *A Guide to Research on North American Indians*, 1983 (with Arlene Hirschfelder and Mary Lou Byler); *The Broken Cord*, 1989; *Rooms in the House of Stone*, 1993; *Route Two*, 1990 (with Louise Erdrich); *Paper Trail: Essays*, 1994.

CHILDREN'S LITERATURE: *Morning Girl*, 1992; *Guests*, 1994; *Sees Behind Trees*, 1996; *The Window*, 1997.

BIBLIOGRAPHY

Covert, Colin. "The Anguished Life of Michael Dorris." *Minneapolis Star Tribune*, August 3, 1997, p. 1A. This account of Dorris's life published a few months after his death in the newspaper in the city in which his wife and biological children were living presents a particularly positive view of Dorris.

Dorris, Michael. *Paper Trail*. New York: HarperCollins. 1994. Essays by Dorris that explore a wide range of topics, such as children's rights and Native American issues. The essays offer Dorris's unique perspective and the vision of himself he wanted others to see.

Erdrich, Louise. *Shadow Tag*. New York: HarperCollins, 2010. In this novel, Erdrich presents what some have seen as an inside look at her marriage to Dorris.

Erdrich, Louise, and Michael Dorris. *Conversations with Louise Erdrich and Michael Dorris*. Jackson: University Press of Mississippi, 1994. This collects material from the many interviews Erdrich and Dorris gave.

Konigsberg, Michael. "Michael Dorris's Troubled Sleep." *New York Magazine* (June 16, 1997): 32-37. Long and well-researched article that looks at the personal life of Dorris and Erdrich in the wake of his suicide.

Trueheart, Charles. "Marriage for Better or Word: The Dorris-and-Erdrich Team, Creating Fiction Without Friction." *The Washington Post*, October 19, 1988, p. B1. This article, written at the height of the couple's literary and outwardly personal success, presents and interesting contrast to the information revealed after Dorris's suicide.

Laurie Lykken

ELLEN DOUGLAS

Born: Natchez, Mississippi; July 12, 1921
Also known as: Josephine Ayres Haxton

PRINCIPAL SHORT FICTION

Black Cloud, White Cloud, 1963 (revised 1989)
Truth: Four Stories I Am Finally Old Enough to Tell,
1998

OTHER LITERARY FORMS

Ellen Douglas published six novels between 1962
and 1988. Her children's book, *The Magic Carpet, and
Other Tales* (1987), retells familiar fairy tales. Douglas's nonfiction works include a critical study, *Walker
Percy's "The Last Gentleman"* (1969), and numerous
essays published in periodicals, journals. and her collections *A Long Night* (1986) and *Witnessing* (2004).

ACHIEVEMENTS

Ellen Douglas received a Houghton Mifflin Literary
Fellowship in 1961. *A Family's Affairs* (1962) was
named best novel of the year by *The New York Times;*
that newspaper also named *Black Cloud, White Cloud*
one of the five best fiction works of 1963. Her short
story "On the Lake" was included in *Prize Stories: The
O. Henry Awards* in 1961, and "Grant" was included in
the 1996 collection. "Grant" also appeared in *New Stories from the South: The Year's Best* in 1996, and "Julia
and Nellie" was selected for the annual publication the
following year. Douglas has received a National Endowment for the Humanities grant, a Mississippi Institute of Arts and Letters Award for Literature, and grants
from the National Education Association. In 1989, she
was honored by the Fellowship of southern Writers.

BIOGRAPHY

Ellen Douglas was born Josephine Ayres in Natchez, Mississippi, on July 12, 1921. She attended
school in Hope, Arkansas, and Alexandria, Louisiana,
but spent summers with her many relatives in Natchez.
After a year at Randolph Macon Women's College, she
transferred to the University of Mississippi, receiving
her B.A. in 1942. In 1945, she married Kenneth Haxton
and went to live in his hometown, Greenville, Mississippi. They had three children, Richard, Ayres, and
Brooks. After their divorce in 1983, Josephine moved
to Jackson, Mississippi.

Although she has always worked on her writing, Josephine Ayres Haxton did not decide on a literary career until she was thirty-four, and it was several years
after that before her fiction appeared in print. Her first
efforts were short stories, like "On the Lake," which
The New Yorker published in 1961; later she transformed several of her stories into a novel, *A Family's
Affairs.* Because some of her characters were modeled
on family members, she chose to use the pseudonym
Ellen Douglas.

During the next three and a half decades, Douglas
produced a book approximately every five years, lectured frequently, and taught at Northeast Louisiana
University, Hollins College, the University of Mississippi, the University of Virginia, and Millsaps College.
In her seventies she gave up teaching, although she
continued to write, publishing a second collection of
short fiction in 1998.

ANALYSIS

Although Ellen Douglas addresses such twentieth
century problems as racism, alienation, and cultural
breakdown, her approach is unlike that of most contemporary writers. Her characters may be confused
about the direction their lives should take, but the author herself is not in doubt; her works reflect her un-
swerving adherence to Judeo-Christian ethics. Like the
great moralists of the eighteenth and nineteenth centuries, such as Jane Austen and Charles Dickens, Douglas
believes that such happiness as this world can provide
is achieved only by putting principles above selfish

considerations, by placing the needs of others ahead of own's own.

This preoccupation with the way people behave toward one another is evident throughout Douglas's short fiction. "The House on the Bluff," from *Black Cloud, White Cloud*, examines the relationships between a number of characters, primarily members of two white families, who have lived in the same community for generations, and the blacks who were so much a part of their lives. With so many possibilities for kindness, compassion, and pure spitefulness, it is not surprising that a child like Anna McGovern often finds this world quite puzzling.

Whether they are told by first-person narrators or in the third person, Douglas's short stories and novellas generally have a single point of view. Almost always the protagonist is both sincere and sympathetic. "I Just Love Carrie Lee" is an exception; in that story, the reader is expected to see beyond what the unreliable narrator says. Most of the time, however, the reader and the protagonist move together toward the recognition of some truth about human nature or about life. While Douglas is too much of a realist to minimize the difficulties inherent in human relationships, she always holds out hope that, despite their differences, her characters can become more tolerant and more empathetic.

"I JUST LOVE CARRIE LEE"

One of the pervasive themes in *Black Cloud, White Cloud* is how difficult it is for even the best-intentioned whites and blacks to surmount the racial barriers erected by time and tradition. In the satirical monologue "I Just Love Carrie Lee," Emma, the white narrator, thinks of herself as a model employer. She points out an obvious truth: that, unlike transplanted Yankees, southerners take responsibility for their black employees--for instance, making sure that they have an income even when they cannot do their usual work. However, despite her protestations, Emma does not really "love" Carrie Lee. Though the two women do know each other intimately, they are not friends, for while Emma admits she depends on Carrie Lee, she does not respect her. She quotes Carrie Lee's homey truths in order to laugh at them, and even when she allows Carrie Lee to enter the white church for family weddings and funerals, she does so primarily so that

Emma can admire her generosity. Ironically, it is not Emma but Carrie Lee who knows the real meaning of life and love. The very comments that Emma finds so amusing prove how much wiser the servant is than the mistress.

HOLD ON

The novella *Hold On*, from *Black Cloud, White Cloud*, is told from the perspective of Anna McGovern Glover, who appeared as a child in *A Family's Affairs* but who appears here as an adult, living in Philippi, West Virginia, with her husband Richard and their children. The central incident of this novella was first related in "On the Lake." Anna invites a black woman, Estella Moseby, to go fishing with her. During the afternoon, Anna becomes aware of the differences between them; for example, Estella fearlessly kills a cottonmouth, a type of water snake, but she is superstitious about being "marked" during pregnancy and has a profound terror of water. When they start back, the lake becomes rough, and Estella panics, causing the boat to capsize, but Anna manages to hold on to Estella until help arrives, and she survives. The short story ends here, whereas the novella is much more complex. In it, though Estella believes that Anna saved her life, Anna believes she failed her. Not only did she fail to give Estella a life preserver or even to make sure she could swim but also she kicked Estella away so that she herself would not drown. Her search for the truth takes Anna to one of the rescuers, Carl Jensen, who, because of an incident in his own past, can see that Anna's feelings are born out of a pervasive sense of guilt about the past treatment of African Americans. The novella ends with Anna determined to "hold on" to Estella, even if their relationship remains less than perfect.

"ABOUT LOVING WOMEN"

The impact of the past on the present is also the subject of "About Loving Women," which was written for *That's What I Like (About the South) and Other New southern Stories for the Nineties* (1993). The narrator is a high school boy who is desperately in love with a girl named Roseanne. Just when their romance seems to be flourishing, Roseanne's former boyfriend, Henry, moves to town, and Roseanne begins avoiding the narrator. During the inevitable fight between the rivals, Henry begins to cry for Roseanne, and suddenly the narrator remembers his own tears when he was just five and had to say goodbye to an uncle's girlfriend, who had made a pet of him. What he learned then and what Henry has just found out is that once a man has been betrayed by the woman he loves, he can never regain his lost innocence.

TRUTH

Reviewers are divided as to whether *Truth* should be classified as fiction or as nonfiction. However, in her 1977 interview with Charline R. McCord, Douglas referred to the works in the collection as short stories. Douglas has made no secret of the fact that she sets her fiction in actual places and bases her characters on people she knows. Thus in *Black Cloud, White Cloud*, Homochitto can be read as Natchez, and Philippi, as Greenville. In Douglas's first novel, two of her aunts were so thinly disguised that at their request she published the book under a pseudonym. In *Truth*, Douglas describes real events and uses real names for people and places. However, the point of the book is that truth is elusive and that what is called history is essentially indistinguishable from fiction.

Ellen Douglas (AP Photo/Vickie D. King, The Clarion-Ledger)

In all four stories in *Truth*, Douglas has two roles: She is an observer or investigator, on one hand, and a storyteller, on the other. In "Grant," she looks back on the final months of her husband's uncle's life, which he spent in her home; in "Julia and Nellie," she reports the speculations of family members and friends about a scandalous relationship; in "Hampton," she reconstructs the life of a black chauffeur she knows; and in "On Second Creek," she looks into the executions of slaves in 1861 and also discovers some long-concealed secrets. In every case, the author's investigations provide her with more questions than answers, for, even when she is sure of facts, she has to guess or invent the reasons why people felt and thought as they did. Because both history and fiction are mixtures of truth and lies, Douglas suggests, one should focus less on supposed facts and more on moral choices. Those are the real truths that give both fiction and history a lasting significance.

OTHER MAJOR WORKS

LONG FICTION: *A Family's Affairs*, 1962; *Where the Dreams Cross*, 1968; *Apostles of Light*, 1973; *The Rock Cried Out*, 1979; *A Lifetime Burning*, 1982; *Can't Quit You, Baby*, 1988.

NONFICTION: *Walker Percy's "The Last Gentleman,"* 1969; *A Long Night*, 1986; *Conversations with Ellen Douglas*, 2000 (Panthea Reid, editor); *Witnessing*, 2004.

CHILDREN'S LITERATURE: *The Magic Carpet, and Other Tales*, 1987.

BIBLIOGRAPHY

Broughton, Panthea Reid, and Susan Millar Williams. "Ellen Douglas." In *southern Women Writers: The New Generation*, edited by Tonette Bond Inge. Tuscaloosa: University of Alabama Press, 1990. Focuses on Douglas's development as an artist from her early works to *Can't Quit You, Baby*. *Black Cloud, White Cloud* is discussed in detail.

Chappell, Fred. "The Good Songs Behind Us: southern Fiction of the 1990's." In *That's What I Like (About the South), and Other New southern Stories for the Nineties*, edited by George Garrett and Paul Ruffin. Columbia: University of South Carolina Press,

1993. Another important southern writer uses Ellen Douglas's story "About Loving Women," which appears in the volume, to exemplify the importance of memory and history in southern fiction.

Douglas, Ellen. Afterword to *Black Cloud, White Cloud*. Rev. ed. Jackson: University Press of Mississippi, 1989. Douglas identifies the themes and symbolic patterns that dominate this book. She also emphasizes the importance of storytelling in a rapidly changing world.

_____. *Conversations with Ellen Douglas*. Edited by Panthea Reid. Jackson: University Press of Mississippi, 2000. Collection of sixteen interviews with Douglas conducted between 1971 and 1999. The interviews trace her development as a writer, place her within the context of the southern literary tradition, and illuminate the style of her works.

_____. "Interview with Ellen Douglas: February 25, 1997." Interview by Charlene R. McCord. *Mississippi Quarterly: The Journal of southern Culture* 51 (Spring, 1998): 291-321. Deals primarily with the writing process and the teaching of writing. Douglas comments on the short stories in her second collection.

Feddersen, Rick. "An Interview with Ellen Douglas." In *Speaking of the Short Story: Interviews with Contemporary Writers*, edited by Farhat Iftekharuddin, Mary Rohrberger, and Maurice Lee. Jackson: University Press of Mississippi, 1997. Douglas speaks about her experiences with short fiction and comments on story sequences and novels written in that form.

Jones, John Griffin. "Ellen Douglas." In *Mississippi Writers Talking*, edited by John Griffin Jones. Vol. 2. Jackson: University Press of Mississippi, 1983. Douglas reflects on how her family, her southern heritage, and her awareness of racial injustice have influenced her work.

Jones, Suzanne W. "Writing southern Race Relations: Stories Ellen Douglas Was Brave Enough to Tell." *southern Quarterly* 47, no. 2 (Winter, 2010): 24-38. An overview of Douglas's writings, focusing on her treatment of race relations, particularly in *Black Cloud, White Cloud*. Argues that the theme of white ignorance of African American life is a "constant thread" in her works.

Manning, Carol S. "Ellen Douglas: Moralist and Realist." In *Women Writers of the Contemporary South*, edited by Peggy Whitman Prenshaw. Jackson: University Press of Mississippi, 1984. Contends that while, as a realist, Douglas understands yearnings for total freedom, as a moralist she believes human beings should take responsibility for their actions.

McHaney, Thomas L., and Noel Polk, eds. "Ellen Douglas." *The southern Quarterly: A Journal of the Arts in the South* 33 (Summer, 1995). This special issue contains essays on the author and her works, two interviews, and extensive bibliographies. Also includes the text of Douglas's speech "I Have Found It."

Stockwell, Joe. *Ellen Douglas*. Jackson: Mississippi Library Commission, 1977. Douglas is seen as a traditional moralist and satirist. Includes an in-depth analysis of *Black Cloud, White Cloud*.

Weaks, Mary Louise. "Ellen Douglas." In *The History of southern Women's Literature*, edited by Carolyn Perry and Weaks. Baton Rouge: Louisiana State University Press, 2002. Provides a brief overview of Douglas's life and works.

Rosemary M. Canfield Reisman

THEODORE DREISER

Born: Terre Haute, Indiana; August 27, 1871
Died: Hollywood, California; December 28, 1945

PRINCIPAL SHORT FICTION

Free, and Other Stories, 1918
Chains: Lesser Novels and Stories, 1927
Fine Furniture, 1930
The Best Stories of Theodore Dreiser, 1947 (Howard Fast, editor)
Best Short Stories, 1956 (James T. Farrell, editor)

OTHER LITERARY FORMS

Theodore Dreiser (DRI-sur) is best known for his novels. Of the eight that he wrote, *An American Tragedy* (1925), which was twice made into a motion picture, has attracted the most continuing interest. His short fiction is subsidiary to his novels, and his stories are sometimes capsule versions of his longer fiction, or novels in miniature. Additionally, Dreiser, more interested in literature's power to educate than its ability to entertain, experimented with a variety of forms in which to express his ideas, writing several autobiographical volumes, various books of essays, sketches, and accounts of his travels, as well as two books of plays and a collection of poems.

ACHIEVEMENTS

Dreiser remains one of the foremost naturalistic writers of the early twentieth century. Best known for his novels, particularly *Sister Carrie* (1900) and *An American Tragedy,* all the other works help illuminate them. Dreiser's dark outlook and brooding style is leavened by his richness of language and compassion. His life and art have been closely examined in numerous book-length studies and critical pieces that range in the hundreds. He has been hailed as the most influential figure in American letters at the beginning of the twentieth century, the Mount Everest of American fiction, and he was considered the chief spokesman for the realistic novel. Dreiser was a finalist for the Nobel Prize in literature in 1930, but he lost in a close and bitterly contested vote to Sinclair Lewis, a rebuff that he never forgot. In 1944, the year before his death at age seventy-four, Dreiser was given the Award of Merit from the American Academy of Arts and Letters for extraordinary achievement in his art.

BIOGRAPHY

Theodore Herman Albert Dreiser was virtually the first widely recognized American writer whose background lacked connection with the white Anglo-Saxon Protestant establishment; his father was a Catholic emigrant from Germany, and Theodore grew up, with nine siblings, in a relatively impoverished, strictly religious family. Dreiser rejected his father's religion; he maintained a sympathy for the poor and various relations with his brothers and sisters (including Paul Dreiser, the writer of very popular songs, such as "My Gal Sal"), a number of whom provided him with prototypes for his fictional characters. Leaving his Indiana home at fifteen to go to Chicago, Dreiser was fascinated with the raw and vital city, where he worked at a variety of jobs, pausing to spend one term at Indiana University before beginning a career as a journalist.

From Chicago this career took him to St. Louis, Pittsburgh, and New York, where he eventually became established as a successful magazine editor. In 1908 he married his first wife; the marriage lasted until her death in 1941, with many problems, some of them reflected in stories such as "Free" and "Chains."

Although his journalistic experiences had given him potential material and writing practice, Dreiser was late in turning to fiction; his first short story was not completed until he was twenty-eight, but having begun, he went on to write other stories and have his first novel, *Sister Carrie,* appear in 1900. While *Sister*

Carrie, in which the heroine loses her virtue and survives, unrepentant, was in effect suppressed by its publisher because of its unconventional morality, Dreiser was launched upon his career as a writer of fiction.

Subsequent financial troubles, a partial mental breakdown, marital problems not unrelated to Dreiser's apparent constitutional aversion to monogamy, and continual attacks by the literary, moral, and economic establishments, rather than permanently halting this career, provided it with raw material. With the appearance of his novel *An American Tragedy*, Dreiser, at fifty-four, finally achieved significant financial success and wide acceptance, although his difficult personality, sexual varietism, drinking, anti-Semitism, and communist sympathies kept him involved in controversy. Near the end of his life he both developed an interest in eastern mysticism and joined the Communist Party. He died in 1945.

ANALYSIS

A number of Theodore Dreiser's short stories reveal skills not found in the longer works. The reader who comes to the short fiction after reading Dreiser's novels is frequently surprised by both the whimsy and humor of some of the tales, and by their concise clarity of style, hardly a prominent feature of the novels. Nevertheless, the subject matter, techniques, and especially the tone of Dreiser's short fiction more often than not mirror the novels.

Some exceptions may be noted first. "When the Old Century Was New," set in New York in 1801, presents a day in the life of William Walton, a gentleman merchant "of Colonial prestige." Although Walton does propose to, and is accepted by, the fair Mistress Beppie Cruger, very little actually happens in the sketch; its interest arises from the historical verisimilitude that Dreiser gives to the commonplace. Even further removed from the modern reality which Dreiser customarily treats are two stories, "Khat" and "The Prince Who Was a Thief," set in an indefinite time in Arabia, the first focusing on the misfortunes of Ibn Abdullah, an aged beggar; the second, subtitled "An Improvisation on the Oldest Oriental Theme," being a kind of pastiche of a tale from *Alf layla wa-layla* (fifteenth century; *The Arabian Nights' Entertainments*, 1706-1708).

A different sort of fantasy is "McEwen of the Shining Slave Makers," Dreiser's first story, in which the title figure dreams that he is a black ant engaged in a titanic struggle against red ant tribes.

Dreiser's imagination takes another turn in "The Cruise of the *Idlewild*." "Idlewild" is the name assigned to a railroad shop by the workers in it, who pretend that, rather than toiling in a stationary, unromantic workplace, they are sailing on a yacht, taking on imaginary roles as captain, bos'n, able seaman, and so forth. This is a curious tale of a kind of collective escapism, told with somewhat ponderous, but genial, humor. Finally, of Dreiser's various atypical stories, two related to his newspaper days should be noted: "A Story of Stories" and "Nigger Jeff." In both these works there is a strong emphasis on plot; the first tale involves the competition of two reporters in covering the story of a train robber; the second uses a lynching to describe the maturation of a young newspaperman. Focused on action, neither of these stories contains much of the awkward wording and sentence structure often thought characteristic of Dreiser's style. Indeed, the only aspect

Theodore Dreiser (Library of Congress)

common to all these miscellaneous stories, by which their author does something to put his own mark on them, is the sense of the difficult, competitive nature of human existence. This sense appears even in the light sketch "When the Old Century Was New," which ends with the words, "The crush and stress and wretchedness fast treading upon this path of loveliness he could not see"; it surfaces in "The Cruise of the *Idlewild*" when one character, little Ike, becomes the butt of the other men, and the humorous fantasy temporarily threatens to turn nasty.

Dreiser's fundamental view of life is more naturally expressed, however, in stories in which humor, fantasy, or action for its own sake does not dominate. His subject matter is, typically, contemporary and serious; his interest is more in character than in plot. This material and interest can be seen in "Sanctuary," a story more representative of Dreiser's work. It traces the life history of its "heroine" (the short fiction, like the novels, sometimes has a woman as protagonist), Madeline, from her upbringing in the slums through her arrest for prostitution, after which she is "turned over to the care of the Sisterhood of the Good Shepherd." After serving her time, she works at a variety of "honest" jobs, is married and abandoned by her husband, and returns, voluntarily, to find, with the Sisters, a permanent "Sanctuary." The resemblances between this tale and a famous work of naturalism, Stephen Crane's *Maggie: A Girl of the Streets* (1893), are obvious, but superficial. While both stories chronologically trace the inescapable influences of environment in warping the development of a girl not lacking sensitivity, Dreiser's tone, one of Olympian pity, differs from the ironic detachment of Crane. It is Dreiser's sense of "there but for the grace of God go I" that keeps his focus, and his reader's, on the character, whereas Crane, with his remarkable descriptive style that contrasts with Dreiser's flatness, emphasizes the background and setting.

While suggesting greater empathy with his characters than does a more typically naturalistic writer, such as Crane in *Maggie* or Frank Norris in *McTeague* (1899), Dreiser does employ techniques that produce "aesthetic distance." These techniques operate so that the reader, while reacting to the often pathetic situation of a story's protagonist, is able to see that situation in a larger "philosophic" perspective. A believer in the educational importance of literature, Dreiser had little use for the idea of "art for art's sake." His stories, while not crudely didactic, are meant to teach.

"THE OLD NEIGHBORHOOD"

"The Old Neighborhood," quite representative of Dreiser's technique, has a point to make, even if that point may ultimately be reduced to a sad sigh offered in recognition of life's inescapable sorrow. This story, which first appeared in 1918 but was later collected in Dreiser's second book of stories, *Chains*, can be seen as a dehydrated novel, in that the protagonist's whole life story is presented in a relatively few pages. Unlike Dreiser's actual novels, however, which proceed in basically straightforward chronological order, this story is "framed." The central character has returned to visit his "old neighborhood"; the story begins with his walking from his car to his old apartment; it ends, shortly thereafter, with his returning to his car. Within this frame, through a series of flashbacks (a time scheme employed in a number of Dreiser's stories) which are described in the third person but limited to the protagonist's memory (also a typical device in Dreiser's short fiction), the reader learns of all the major events in the protagonist's life. The reader learns the character's reaction to these events, what his reactions were when the events occurred, and what his overall view is in retrospectively considering a life that is drawing toward a close. The reader discovers that the unnamed protagonist has struggled out of poverty, marrying a department store clerk, Marie, when they are still both young and he has little education or apparent prospects; but he has talent as an inventor and visions of a better life. In spite of the economic pressure occasioned by fathering two children, the protagonist studies at night and on Sundays, and eventually, through his inventions, achieves fame and money. In the course of his rise, however, his two children die, and he becomes increasingly estranged from his wife, whose simple loyalty no longer satisfies him.

Driven by his ambition, he leaves his wife, and she does not share in his material success. After her death he remarries, but at the time of the story, he has returned to the scene of his earlier married days--the old neighborhood of struggle, poverty, loss, and dreams--in an attempt to lay to rest the ghosts of the past that still haunt him. In the insight that ends the story, however, he realizes "how futile this errand was" and how his actions were "not right, not fair," and that "there is something cruel and evil in it all, in all wealth, all ambition, in love of fame." He returns to his car, a symbol of "power and success," to be "whirled swiftly and gloomily away."

The moral that is drawn by the protagonist is one that the audience has been prepared by the author to accept. By means of the complex time scheme, in which the inventor's memories occur in roughly, but by no means exactly, an order corresponding to the order of the past events of his life, readers are partially "distanced" from the protagonist's attitudes, recognizing their selfishness before he does, yet maintaining some sympathy for him all the while. When, at last, he expresses a view that the audience has already approached, there is a satisfactory sense of conclusion which allows the reader to judge and pity the central figure simultaneously. A kind of catharsis that depends on "philosophical" acceptance of "the pity of it all" occurs. In some ways the story resembles James Joyce's famous work "The Dead," in which irony is also employed to lead toward an "epiphany" or revelation of a significant insight gained by both the central figure and the reader.

While Dreiser in his consistent use of imagery is certainly less impressive than is Joyce, it is worth noting that the former, often attacked for being a clumsy craftsman, does make effective use throughout the story of symbolic references to the bridge and to water. It seems that Dreiser must have decided to play with, and revitalize, the cliché "It's all water under the bridge," just as Charles Waddell Chesnutt, in his story "Baxter's Procrustes," did with the expression "Don't judge a book by its cover."

If "The Old Neighborhood" is, on balance, a relatively successful story, it suffers from the attempt to cover too many events in too few pages, so that, with his novelist's inclination bound within the limitations of short fiction, Dreiser resorts to "telling" rather than "showing," and the tale produces a certain unfortunate impression of stasis. Two other stories by Dreiser, notable for avoiding this impression while still being, unlike the atypical works noted earlier, representative of his general thought and method, should be briefly mentioned. In them, Dreiser successfully integrates his philosophy of life with writing techniques adjusted to the requirements of short fiction.

"THE LOST PHOEBE"

"The Lost Phoebe," which may owe something to Norris's story in *The Octopus* (1901) of Vanamee and his lost love, tells of an old man who, refusing to accept the death of his wife of many years, wanders over the countryside imagining her return until at last he sees her in a vision that he follows over a cliff to his death. In this work, Dreiser's view of the "terror and beauty of life" emerges through an effective balance of action, setting, and character.

"ST. COLUMBA AND THE RIVER"

Finally, "St. Columba and the River," developed from an earlier nonfiction piece Dreiser had written concerning the work of "sand-hogs," those construction workers who build underwater tunnels, may well be the author's most successful work of short fiction. The story tells of the tribulations of one such worker, McGlathery, who, driven by the need for something approaching a living wage, develops real courage in his dangerous occupation, finally surviving a cave-in through a freak of good fortune. In this story, Dreiser's naturalistic details are never tedious because the material, involving an unusual occupation, requires them. Dreiser's frequently ponderous tone, more out of place in short fiction than in novels, is avoided; the story is lightened with humor. Character, appropriately in a short story, is exposed more than developed, and the plot reaches a definite climax, yet the theme is not made subservient to the plot; rather, it is integrated with it. If, as always, Dreiser teaches the reader about the strange kaleidoscope of life, here he does it while simultaneously being entertaining. With Horace, the reader can, in this story, accept the idea that art's function may be to at once delight and instruct.

In spite of such notable successes, Dreiser's short fiction remains secondary in interest to his novels, on which his reputation correctly rests. Nevertheless, not only are his short stories valuable when used to help understand his more significant work, but they are also interesting in demonstrating other sides of his remarkable talent. Most importantly, there are those successes that are, in their own right, valuable works of art.

OTHER MAJOR WORKS

LONG FICTION: *Sister Carrie*, 1900; *Jennie Gerhardt*, 1911; *The Financier*, 1912, 1927; *The Titan*, 1914; *The "Genius,"* 1915; *An American Tragedy*, 1925; *The Bulwark*, 1946; *The Stoic*, 1947.

PLAYS: *Plays of the Natural and Supernatural*, pb. 1916; *The Girl in the Coffin*, pr. 1917; *The Hand of the Potter: A Tragedy in Four Acts*, pb. 1919; *The Collected Plays of Theodore Dreiser*, pb. 2000.

POETRY: *Moods: Cadenced and Declaimed*, 1926, 1928; *Epitaph: A Poem*, 1929; *The Aspirant*, 1929.

NONFICTION: *A Traveler at Forty*, 1913; *A Hoosier Holiday*, 1916; *Twelve Men*, 1919; *Hey, Rub-a-Dub-Dub!*, 1920; *A Book About Myself*, 1922 (revised as *Newspaper Days*, 1931); *The Color of a Great City*, 1923; *Dreiser Looks at Russia*, 1928; *My City*, 1929; *Dawn*, 1931 (autobiography); *Tragic America*, 1931; *America Is Worth Saving*, 1941; *Letters of Theodore Dreiser*, 1959; *Letters to Louise*, 1959; *Notes on Life*, 1974 (Marguerite Tjader and John J. McAleer, editors); *American Diaries, 1902-1926*, 1982; *An Amateur Laborer*, 1983; *Selected Magazine Articles of Theodore Dreiser*, 1985; *Dreiser's Russian Diary*, 1996 (Thomas P. Riggio and James L. W. West, editors); *Theodore Dreiser's "Ev'ry Month,"* 1996 (magazine articles; Nancy Warner Barrineau, editor); *Art, Music, and Literature, 1897-1902*, 2001 (Yoshinobu Hakutani, editor); *Theodore Dreiser's Uncollected Magazine Articles, 1897-1902*, 2003 (Hakutani, editor); *New Letters*, 2008 (2 volumes; Donald Pizer, editor).

BIBLIOGRAPHY

Cassuto, Leonard, and Clare Virginia Eby, eds. *The Cambridge Companion to Theodore Dreiser*. New York: Cambridge University Press, 2004. A collection of twelve essays that interpret Dreiser's life and work from various perspectives, including discussions of Dreiser and the uses of biography, Dreiser and the history of American longing, his writing style, his representation of women, and his sociological vision.

Elias, Robert H. *Theodore Dreiser: Apostle of Nature*. Ithaca, N.Y.: Cornell University Press, 1970. An excellent scholarly biography of Dreiser, who cooperated on the work. Includes a comprehensive chapter listing a bibliography, biographies, manuscripts and letters, and criticism of the writer.

Gerber, Philip. *Theodore Dreiser Revisited*. New York: Twayne, 1992. Includes chapters on all Dreiser's major works, three chapters on the development of Dreiser studies, a chronology, notes and references, and an annotated bibliography.

Gogol, Miriam, ed. *Theodore Dreiser: Beyond Naturalism*. New York: New York University Press, 1995. Divided into sections on gender studies, psychoanalysis, philosophy, film studies, and popular literature. Gogol's introduction advances the argument that Dreiser was much more than a naturalist and deserves to be treated as a major author.

Hricko, Mary. *Genesis of the Chicago Renaissance: Theodore Dreiser, Langston Hughes, Richard Wright, and James T. Farrell*. New York: Routledge, 2009. Chronicles the origins of Chicago's two literary renaissance periods, 1890-1920 and 1930-1950, by examining the works of Dreiser and three other writers.

Kazin, Alfred, and Charles Shapiro. *The Stature of Theodore Dreiser: A Critical Survey of the Man and His Work*. Bloomington: Indiana University Press, 1965. Provides a good anthology of articles, essays, and personal reminiscences by noted authors and critics on Dreiser the man and the writer. Kazin's perceptive introduction sets the tone. Includes a lengthy bibliography.

Kratzke, Peter. "'Sometimes, Bad Is Bad': Teaching Theodore Dreiser's 'Typhoon' and the American Literary Canon." In *Short Stories in the Classroom*, edited by Carole L. Hamilton and Peter Kratzke. Urbana, Ill.: National Council of Teachers of English, 1999. Discusses how teaching Dreiser's story raises a number of issues about how the canon gets established. Shows how an analysis of the story reveals its poor literary quality and suggests that canonical authors are not infallible.

Loving, Jerome. *The Last Titan: A Life of Theodore Dreiser.* Berkeley: University of California Press, 2005. Written by a distinguished biographer, this engrossing survey of Dreiser's life and work is a welcome addition to Dreiser scholarship

Lydon, Michael. "Justice to Theodore Dreiser." *The Atlantic* 272 (August, 1993): 98-101. Argues that Dreiser should be seen without reservation as a giant of American letters who stood at the vanguard of modernism. Argues that the incongruities and eccentricities of Dreiser's life have always affected the critical reception of his writing.

McAleer, John J. *Theodore Dreiser: An Introduction and Interpretation.* New York: Barnes & Noble Books, 1968. A study of Dreiser that aims to help the reader grasp the whole of his fiction. Includes a lengthy chronology and a bibliography.

Packer-Kinlaw, Donna. "Life on the Margins: The Silent Feminist in Theodore Dreiser's 'Marriage--For One.'" *Dreiser Studies* 32, no. 2 (Fall, 2001): 3. An analysis of one of Dreiser's short stories, focusing on his depiction of women.

Pizer, Donald, ed. *Critical Essays on Theodore Dreiser.* Boston: G. K. Hall, 1981. An excellent compilation of articles and essays. The criticism is arranged around Dreiser's works and ideas in general, while a second section is devoted to analysis of individual novels.

Riggio, Thomas P. "Following Dreiser, Seventy Years Later." *The American Scholar* 65 (Autumn, 1996): 569-577. A biographical sketch that focuses on Dreiser as the most famous American to be invited to Moscow for the tenth anniversary of the Russian Revolution in 1927. Describes a visit to Russia to research an edition of a diary kept by Dreiser in the late 1920's during his three months' stay in the Soviet Union.

Shapiro, Charles. *Theodore Dreiser: Our Bitter Patriot.* Carbondale: Illinois University Press, 1962. Shapiro expands his original dissertation study into a critical and illuminating examination of the underlying themes found in Dreiser's works. He believes that *An American Tragedy* is Dreiser's most important work because of its thematic richness.

Swanberg, W. A. *Dreiser.* New York: Charles Scribner's Sons, 1965. The definitive biography of Dreiser; it has stood the test of time and ranks with the best. Swanberg, who is not a literary critic, is less interested in Dreiser the artist and concentrates on Dreiser the man.

William B. Stone
Updated by Terry Theodore

ANDRE DUBUS

Born: Lake Charles, Louisiana; August 11, 1936
Died: Haverhill, Massachusetts; February 24, 1999

PRINCIPAL SHORT FICTION

Separate Flights, 1975
Adultery and Other Choices, 1977
Finding a Girl in America, 1980
The Times Are Never So Bad, 1983
The Last Worthless Evening, 1986
Selected Stories, 1988
Dancing After Hours: Stories, 1996
In the Bedroom: Seven Stories, 2002

OTHER LITERARY FORMS

Although Andre Dubus (ahn-DRAY duh-BYOOS) wrote an early novel, *The Lieutenant* (1967), which is highly regarded by some critics and readers, and a novella, *Voices from the Moon* (1984), which has been printed separately, his most important contributions to literature are his shorter works. Besides his fiction, Dubus wrote two well-received books of autobiographical essays.

ACHIEVEMENTS

Andre Dubus's literary career is notable because it stands outside the shifting fashions of the American literary scene. During the 1960's and 1970's, when the "postmodernism" of Donald Barthelme, John Barth, and Raymond Carver, Bobbie Ann Mason, and Lorrie Moore came into literary prominence, Dubus remained what might be called a "maximalist" writer, who seemed most at home in the form of the long story, or novella. In a period of shifting male and female definitions, Dubus wrote often about the waywardness of people who continue to define themselves by concepts of masculinity and femininity that the world around them no longer values. Not least of all, in an age of secular values, Dubus often looked to the sacraments of the Catholic Church to find deep values.

BIOGRAPHY

Andre Dubus was born in Lake Charles, Louisiana, on August 11, 1936, and attended the Christian Brothers Catholic School in Lafayette from 1944 until 1954, after which he enrolled in McNeese State University in Lake Charles. Upon graduating from college in 1958 with a B.A. in English and journalism, he married Patricia Lowe and entered the Marine Corps with a commission as lieutenant. Over the next five years, four of the couple's children were born (Suzanne in 1958, Andre III in 1959, Jeb in 1960, and Nicole in 1963), and he was to rise to the rank of captain.

In 1963, he published his first story, "The Intruder," in the *Sewanee Review* and resigned his officer's commission to enter the M.F.A. program at the University of Iowa, the much respected Writers' Workshop program. Upon receiving his M.F.A. in 1965, he taught for one year as a lecturer at Nicholls State University in Louisiana before accepting a position at Bradford College in Massachusetts in 1966, where he was to teach for the next fourteen years, until his retirement in 1984.

Dubus was married and divorced three times, and the pain of these broken marriages provided a source for much of his fiction. His first marriage to Lowe in 1958 ended in divorce in 1970; his second marriage to Tommie Gail Cotter in 1975 ended in divorce in 1977. He married his third wife, writer Peggy Rambach, in 1979, and the couple had two daughters, Cadence, born in 1982, and Madeline, born in 1987; this marriage ended when his wife left in November, 1987, amid family strain stemming from a 1986 automobile accident, which also cost Dubus a leg.

Many of Dubus's stories have been selected for the annual *The Best American Short Stories* and *Prize Stories: The O. Henry Awards* series. Among his national honors, he received a National Endowment for the Arts grant in 1985 and a John Simon Guggenheim Memorial Foundation Fellowship in 1986. Both of these honors came after his retirement from teaching in 1984. His plans to use the monetary freedom provided by these grants to spend more time writing were violently interrupted by an accident in which he had stopped to assist two distressed motorists, only to become the victim of another car. The pain of recovering from this accident, in which he saved a life but lost a leg, is chronicled in the title essay of his collection of essays *Broken Vessels* (1991). On February 24, 1999, Dubus died in Haverhill, Massachusetts.

ANALYSIS

Among American story writers of the twentieth century, the one to whom Andre Dubus is most often compared is Flannery O'Connor. While Dubus's works are not generally marked by the wry, ironic wit that permeates O'Connor's work, both writers demonstrate what critic Thomas E. Kennedy, among others, has called an "existential Christian" sensibility.

"IF THEY KNEW YVONNE"

An early Dubus story, "If They Knew Yvonne," first published in *The North American Review* in 1969 and collected both in *Separate Flights* and *Selected Stories*, displays this sensibility clearly. This story traces the development of a teenager, Harry Dugal, growing into manhood and caught between two powerful forces: his emerging sexuality and his need for the absolution and communion provided by the Catholic Church. Taught by the fathers at the Christian Brothers School to regard masturbation as "self-abuse" and a mortal sin, Harry, as he discovers his own inability to resist the urge to masturbate, goes to confession at every opportunity to confess his sins. Disgusted at his own weakness and at the sexual weakness that he discovers in his family around him, including his parents, whose store of condoms he discovers, and his sister Janet, who gets married while two months pregnant, the young Harry even considers emasculating himself at one point.

At the age of nineteen, however, he has his first sexual encounter with a woman his own age, Yvonne Millet, and discovers a type of sexuality that does not disgust him. When Yvonne implores him, "Love me, Harry, love me," he begins to perceive that this type of love is not the squalid lust that he had been warned to guard against but something else, something he is not sure the Catholic fathers at his school knew anything about. The story ends shortly after he has drifted apart from Yvonne and goes to confession again. After Harry has confessed his sexual affair, the priest quotes a line from St. John, in which Christ prays, "I do not pray that You take them out of the world but that You keep them from evil," a quote that delineates the story's Christian existentialist theme. Harry begins to understand that the higher good depends not on remaining pure and safe from the world but on being a responsible, conscientious member of the world.

"THE PRETTY GIRL"

In his full-length study, *Andre Dubus: A Study of the Short Fiction*, Thomas E. Kennedy points out that almost half of Dubus's first fifty stories deal with violent themes or subjects, but he further points out that violence is only secondary to the central theme, a symptom of the greater condition of "human isolation and disconnection in . . . modern America." This is not to say that Dubus in any way excuses violence, but rather that understanding how violence grows out of an acceptance of superficial values is an important source for his fiction.

His novella-length story, "The Pretty Girl," collected in both *The Times Are Never So Bad* and *Selected Stories*, is one of his best extended examinations of this type of violence. One of the two point-of-view characters is Raymond Yarborough, who is presented as a wildly exploding tinderbox of violence. When the reader meets him, he is divorced from the other main character, Polly Comeau, but still obsessed by her. The reader learns early that Raymond has already raped her, though he considers that he was only "taking back my wife for a while." Before long, he beats up and severely injures a man whom he knows she has slept with and lights a fire around the house where Polly is staying, not to destroy anything but to terrorize her.

If Raymond is in many ways the antagonist in the story, he is also the most interesting character, and his former wife Polly is not presented in particularly sympathetic terms. A waitress by trade, Polly is in many ways best described in the terms of the story's title as a twenty-six-year-old "pretty girl" who has used her beauty to avoid fashioning an adult identity and instead has tended to drift from one sexual affair to another, even during the course of her marriage, without much sense of responsibility or consequences.

Polly is a loner almost as much as Raymond is. She shares a house with a male acquaintance but has no close friends, either male or female. Her relationships with women tend to be competitive, and her friendships with men tend to be brief, quickly sacrificed to her love affairs. She is significantly alone when Raymond breaks into her house at the end of the story to confront her about why she left him and what she really wants. Though he is unarmed, Polly, who has been ill and alone for several days, uses a gun she bought for protection to kill him when he begins to take off his clothes. Both main characters are carefully constructed

Andre Dubus (AP Photo/Marion Ettlinger)

to be unlikable, though only Raymond is presented as truly repugnant. The success of the story is that it compels the reader nevertheless to want to understand each of them and to appreciate each character's struggle, while not inviting the reader to forget or overlook their immature self-obsession or moral rootlessness.

"Finding a Girl in America"

A number of Dubus's stories deal with recurring characters. Two stories of the three that deal with Hank Allison, a middle-aged, philandering college professor, show Dubus's art at both its best and its worst. "Finding a Girl in America" shows both the character Hank Allison and the writer Andre Dubus at their worst. In it, Hank is presented as a divorced college professor who has been having affairs with his female students. As the story opens, he has learned that a former lover had an abortion and feels cheated because he believes that had the baby been born, it would have filled the void left in his life by his daughter growing up; the point of view of the woman who would have had a baby she did not want fathered by a man she did not love is not seriously considered. The attention to detail, which in other stories creates a convincing illusion of reality, in this story seems tedious and self-indulgent. Dubus's insistence on finding moral frameworks to understand his characters, a tendency that in many stories uplifts his art, in this story misleads him. Hank's life is so self-indulgent that it is hard for a reader to take him half as seriously as he takes himself.

"Adultery"

The earlier story, "Adultery," is by contrast one of the finest examples of Dubus's art. To be sure, Hank Allison is the same self-centered, self-justifying man that the reader meets in the later story (as well as in "We Don't Live Here Anymore"). "Adultery," however, is carefully constructed to consider not only marital fidelity but also spiritual fidelity.

The main characters are Hank Allison, his wife Edith, and Father Joe Ritchie, a Catholic priest dying of cancer who renounces his vows and has an affair with Edith. The story also investigates the lives of a number of other men and women whom Hank and Edith choose as lovers. It is Hank who initially brings adultery into his and Edith's marriage, but when she discovers it, he immediately consents to her right to

also have extramarital affairs. The affairs they both have take their toll, especially on Edith, and make a sham of their marriage. The irony of the title--and the element that raises this story to the finest level of American fiction--is that Edith's adultery with a dying Catholic priest is not viewed by her or Father Ritchie as true adultery; the true adultery for her is staying in a marriage based on hypocrisy. Similarly, although this affair compromises Joe Ritchie in more ways than one, he and Edith both understand that their relationship is spiritually as well as personally the right thing to do; what worries Joe Ritchie most is that Edith might remain married to Hank, and he is relieved when she comes to him while he is dying (in the reverse of a deathbed to confession) to say that she is divorcing Hank. By deciding to divorce Hank, Edith upholds at least the *idea* of marital fidelity. Moreover, she realizes that her affair with Joe Ritchie has provided her with a new center for her life and that she would be unfaithful to herself and the belief in marriage to remain with Hank any longer.

"A Father's Story"

"A Father's Story," which was chosen by John Updike for the annual *The Best American Short Stories* in 1984, is in some respects Dubus's most important story. Smaller in scale than stories such as "The Fat Girl" or "Separate Flights," which each compress the story of several years into a few pages, "A Father's Story" focuses on a crucial incident in the life of Luke Ripley and his daughter Jennifer. Like many of Dubus's characters, Luke seems in many ways to be a version of the author, but he is a version that has achieved a deceptive veneer of simplicity. The opening line of the story, "My name is Luke Ripley and here is what I call my life," seems to present the voice of a direct, straightforward man. The life that Luke tells the reader about is one filled with a variety of contradictions: He is a devout Catholic but divorced; he attends Mass regularly but does not always listen; he enjoys talking to his priest but casually, preferably over a few beers, and what they discuss is mostly small talk; he is a self-described lazy man who dislikes waking up early but does so each morning to pray, not because he feels obligated to do so but because he knows he has the choice not to do so. Luke Ripley is a man who lives with contradictions and accepts them.

As such, when his daughter comes to him, frantically telling him that she hit a man with a car, he reacts almost instinctively. Rather than call the police or an ambulance, he drives to the scene of the accident to verify that the young man is in fact dead. When he knows that there is nothing that can be done to help the young man, he drives home and puts his daughter to bed, then takes her car out and runs it into a tree in front of the church to cover up the dent she had already created. The story ends with Luke recalling to the reader how he justifies himself to his God each morning, saying, "You never had a daughter and, if You had, You could not have borne her passion. . . . I love her more than I love truth." God replies, "Then you love in weakness," to which Luke responds, "As You love me."

The power of "A Father's Story" is that it captures perfectly the opposites that Dubus's fiction is constantly exploring. Luke Ripley's love for his daughter is both his strength and his weakness. Similarly, his love for his daughter moves him to deceive, even as his religion demands confession; and when he finds himself unable to confess his sin of covering up his daughter's crime, the story itself, it is clear, is his substitute for the confession that he cannot make to a priest. Like many of Dubus's stories, "A Father's Story" shows a person caught between the confusing, ambiguous demands of his human heart and the by-no-means-clear demands of a religion in which he believes but which speaks of an absolute he can only partially understand.

OTHER MAJOR WORKS

LONG FICTION: *The Lieutenant*, 1967; *Voices from the Moon*, 1984; *We Don't Live Here Anymore*, 1984.

NONFICTION: *Broken Vessels*, 1991; *Meditations from a Movable Chair: Essays*, 1998; *Leap of the Heart: Andre Dubus Talking*, 2003 (Ross Gresham, editor).

BIBLIOGRAPHY

Breslin, John B. "Playing Out of the Patterns of Sin and Grace: The Catholic Imagination of Andre Dubus." *Commonweal* 115 (December 2, 1988): 652-656. An analysis of the Catholic themes in Dubus's literature, written for a lay audience. Breslin focuses particularly on Dubus's early novel *The Lieutenant*, the trilogy of stories dealing with Hank Allison ("We Don't Live Here Anymore," "Adultery," and "Finding a Girl in America"), and "A Father's Story."

Cocchiarale, Michael. "The Complicated Catholicism of Andre Dubus." In *Songs of the New South: Writing Contemporary Louisiana*, edited by Suzanne D. Green and Lisa Abney. Westport, Conn.: Greenwood Press, 2001. Discusses Dubus's writing in the context of Catholicism and its role in the complex morality of his characters.

Dubus, Andre. "The Habit of Writing." In *A Short Story Writer's Companion*, by Tom Bailey. New York: Oxford University Press, 2001. Dubus describes his method of writing short stories.

_____. *Leap of the Heart: Andre Dubus Talking*. Edited by Ross Gresham. New Orleans: Xavier Review Press, 2003. Reprints twenty-four interviews with Dubus ranging in time from his early career to an interview conducted the day before he died in 1999. Includes a chronological bibliography of all of Dubus's interviews, with notes on and excerpts from the interviews not included in this collection.

Feeney, Joseph J. "Poised for Fame: Andre Dubus at Fifty." *America* 155 (November 15, 1986): 296-299. Using the occasion of Dubus's fiftieth birthday, Feeney provides a general introduction to the man, his writing, and his major themes. Aimed at an audience that is generally unfamiliar with Dubus's fiction, Feeney's article presents the major themes of Dubus's work without exploring them in depth.

Gelfant, Blanche H., ed. *The Columbia Companion to the Twentieth-Century American Short Story*. New York: Columbia University Press, 2000. Includes a chapter in which Dubus's short stories are analyzed.

Kennedy, Thomas E. *Andre Dubus: A Study of the Short Fiction*. Boston: Twayne, 1988. The first full-length study of Dubus's fiction to be published, this volume is by far the most helpful work for someone interested in Dubus and his writing. Kennedy groups Dubus's stories together by their thematic content and analyzes them in separate chapters, which are each devoted to one theme. Also included are other critical evaluations, two interviews with Dubus, an extensive bibliography of primary and secondary sources, and a helpfully designed index. If there is a flaw, it is that Kennedy sometimes seems too devoted to Dubus's work to accurately evaluate its occasional shortcomings.

Lesser, Ellen. "True Confession: Andre Dubus Talks Straight." Review of *Selected Stories. Village Voice* 37 (January 17, 1989): 56. Lesser claims that "Dubus writes stories like a pilot pushing the envelope--continually testing fiction's effective limits." She praises his fiction for its deliberate unfashionableness and for its unsimplified Catholic sensibility.

Miner, Madonne. "Jumping from One Heart to Another: How Andre Dubus Writes About Women." *Critique* 39 (Fall, 1997): 18-31. Discusses three stories-- "Anna," "Leslie in California," and "Rose"--in terms of Dubus's ability to write empathetically from a woman's perspective and to speak with a woman's voice about women's experience, while still retaining his "maleness."

_____. "What Cannot Be Told: Gender and the Limits of Storytelling in Andre Dubus's 'Graduation.'" *Critique* 44, no. 3 (Spring, 2003): 227. Examines how Dubus's short story "Graduation" articulates the difficulties that its protagonist, a young, white, middle-class woman living in 1950's America, encounters in trying to tell her own story.

Rowe, Anne E. "Andre Dubus." In *Contemporary Fiction Writers of the South*, edited by Joseph M. Flora and Robert Bain. Westport, Conn.: Greenwood Press, 1993. A general introduction to such Dubus themes as the passage from childhood to the adult world, failed friendships and marriages, and the individual's search for a meaningful center. Includes an analytical survey of criticism of Dubus's fiction.

Todd, David Yandell. "An Interview with Andre Dubus." *Yale Review* 86 (July, 1998): 89-110. Dubus candidly discusses his decision to become a writer and the relationship between his life, his stories, and the authors who have most influenced him. He also considers what motivates his characters, creates their conflicts, and provides them with spiritual and moral significance.

Yarbrough, Steve. "Andre Dubus: From Detached Incident to Compressed Novel." *Critique: Studies in Modern Fiction* 28 (Fall, 1986); 19-27. Argues that Dubus's short stories can be categorized in three different ways, of which the largest category is the compressed novel, which follows the course of characters' lives for several years. This article focuses on a number of short stories, including "The Doctor," "The Dark Men," "Townies," "In My Life," "Separate Flights," and "The Fat Girl."

Thomas J. Cassidy
Updated by Charles E. May

RIKKI DUCORNET

Born: Canton, New York; April 19, 1943
Also Known As: Erica Lynn DeGré

PRINCIPAL SHORT FICTION
The Complete Butcher's Tales, 1994
The Word "Desire," 1997
Gazelle, 2003
The One Marvelous Thing, 2008

OTHER LITERARY FORMS

The artistic output of Rikki Ducornet (RIH-kee dew-kohr-NAY) is deep and varied, consisting as much of visual work--surreal painting and illustration, often inspired by natural history--as it does of long and short fiction, poetry, and essays. In addition to her three collections of short fiction, Ducornet is the author of seven novels, seven collections of poetry, and two children's books. She has collaborated with other artists and writers, including her ex-husband, Guy.

ACHIEVEMENTS

In 1988, Rikki Ducornet won a Bunting Institute Fellowship at Radcliffe University. She won the Lannan Foundation Literary Award for Fiction in 1993 and 2004. In addition, she received a Writing Residency Fellowship from the Lannan Foundation in 2004. In 2008, she won an Academy Award for Literature from the American Academy of Arts and Letters. Her novel *The Jade Cabinet* (1993) was a finalist for the National Book Critics Circle Award, and *The Fan-Maker's Inquisition* (1999) was chosen as a *Los Angeles Times* Book of the Year.

Ducornet has taught at the New Orleans Center for Creative Arts and the Santa Fe Institute of American Indian Arts. She has been honored as novelist-in-residence at the University of Denver and the Eminent Writer-in-Residence at the University of Louisiana.

BIOGRAPHY

Rikki Ducornet was born Erica Lynn DeGré and was raised in New York. Captivated early by the works of Lewis Carroll and natural history dioramas, she spent some of her childhood in Egypt and much of it on the campus of Bard College, in Annandale-on-Hudson, New York, where her father was a professor. She earned a B.A. in fine arts from Bard in 1964. She studied painting, minored in medieval studies, and developed an interest in poetry but did not pursue writing until much later. She met Robert Coover and Robert Kelly at Bard, however, and these writers are considered influential in her work. (It is said that at Bard she met future Steely Dan lead singer Donald Fagen, motivating him to write the *Billboard* hit "Rikki Don't Lose That Number.")

Ducornet moved to the Loire Valley with her husband Guy in 1974, eventually finishing her first novel, *The Stain*, in 1984. She went on to travel and write four more "elemental" novels--*Entering Fire* (1986), *The Fountains of Neptune* (1989), *The Jade Cabinet* (1993), and *Phosphor in Dreamland* (1995)--and many short stories.

Throughout her life, Ducornet has painted and illustrated. Her drawings, lithographs, and paintings have been shown at the Museo de Bellas Artes in Mexico City, the Museu National de Castro Coimbra in Portugal, and the Museo de la Solidaridad in Santiago, as well as in museums in Massachusetts, Berlin, Ixelles, Brno, and Lille. She has illustrated her own works, in addition to those of Jorge Luis Borges and Robert Coover.

Ducornet has lived in Algeria, Egypt, Chile, France, and Canada and in various places across the United States. In 1989, she moved to Denver to teach at the University of Denver. In 2007, she replaced the retiring Ernest Gaines as the Eminent Writer-in-Residence at the University of Louisiana.

Analysis

Rikki Ducornet's fictions are often short--her stories sometimes under five pages, her novels under two hundred pages. Nevertheless, the worlds described in her fiction are deep and rich, full of bizarre details from history, nature, the plant and animal sciences, and painting or other sensual arts: perfume-making, fan-making, and so on.

Her worlds are, moreover, the creations of highly individual voices. Ducornet has said that every story is inspired by a different voice, even if from a distant time or place. Considered a postmodernist, she remains true to the inherent logic of each of the voices, no matter how fragmented its identity may seem at first.

Her miniature fables range in genre from science fiction and historical fiction to erotica and the utterly surreal. Each is a mosaic tile in the larger, marvelous world of Ducornet's writing. *Gazelle*, for example, fuses history, sexuality, and youth in one mysterious short tale that, while less surreal than some of her work, is pervaded with a sense of magic--dark, animistic, and sacrificial--tied to common objects and uncommon smells. In all of her stories, the real and rational world seems only thinly layered over a gnostic realm accessible to the sensitive, the young, and those engaged in the extreme pleasures and pains of the body, far from the entrapments of consciousness.

One way to consider Ducornet's mixture of voices, places, and marvelous moments is the Renaissance wonder cabinet, a proto-scientific display of natural and artificial objects from across the disciplines: taxidermy, skulls, jewels, narwhal horns, bottled freaks, plants, illustrations, and foreign art objects. Captured in a random tableau, the curiosities of the wonder cabinet were treated equally, seriously, even though many were gaffes or would not be valid objects of study within a scientific framework. Ducornet has stated her interest in wonder cabinets and something of her approach--mixing genres and media, reaching back to different eras, traveling literally and literarily to new lands, collecting marvels--validate this reading.

The Complete Butcher's Tales

Her first collection is definitely a cabinet of curiosities, featuring nearly sixty shorts, from the obscure and playfully "scientific" (the alternate universe of "Brillig") to the highly sensuous and historically perfumed ("The Tale of the Tattooed Woman," about a murderess who signifies her crimes directly and voluptuously onto her skin). Some stories are only a few lines long, akin to poetry ("Thrift," "Theft," "Bedtime Story"). Others are narratively robust, with distinct voices, often female, often young. The whole is a network of haiku-like moments of the grotesque and (otherwise) sublime. Anticipating *The Word "Desire"* (there is even a story called "Desire"), many of the stories in *The Complete Butcher's Tales* tackle madness, the erotic, and the almost religious madness of Eros. Perhaps two keys to Ducornet's sublimity are mutability and beauty, as answers Ms. Few Seconds, one of a handful of identifiable characters in "The New Bronx Zoo," when asked "what rules you?"

"Brillig," Fantasy, and (Postmodern) Science Fiction

The story "Brillig" consists of an anthropological team visiting the shifting world of Brillig, home to the Jumblies: bad-tempered, brutish goblins who raise owl-faced dragons from "cult Eggs." Their oral traditions and cultural rituals are the subject of the story, but, true to form, Ducornet hardly builds up a stable of fantastic jargon. She instead plays with the nature of words themselves. As with the self-gene-engineering children in "Egyptian Gum" and the posthuman, faux-animal neohippies of "The New Bronx Zoo," the identities of both the "Jumblies" and the scientists who observe them widen, until the reader is not sure if Ducornet is writing about an imagined world or the reader's own, through a glass darkly. The "owl-faced dragons" and other odd phrases accumulate until they overcome the reader's senses. They cannot mean just one thing, or they cannot mean anything.

As the scientists and their objects mutate, the reader follows their steady voices and is comforted by the strength of the (strange, also mutating) world. If this is the reader's world--if the voice telling the story is in some way the reader's or Ducornet's--its torturous and ecstatic changes, mental and quite physical, are the reader's own, too. Her "fantasy" thus comments harshly and relevantly on playful experiments with fashion, genetics, words, and finally meanings for life. "Brillig" and related quasi-fantasies suggest that the reader should examine his or her notions of beauty and meaning. The story seems to ask: If postmodern life is changing more rapidly than ever, and all changes must be accepted, then where can common values be located?

"SAIDA" AND CHILDHOOD SEXUALITY

In several stories--notably "Saida" from *The Complete Butcher's Tales* and "The Chess Set of Ivory" and "Roseveine" from *The Word "Desire"*--Ducornet delves not only into the emergence of the erotic in children (their first moments of desire and of the confusion of desire unfulfilled) but also into the realization that it is this very emergence that separates childhood forever from the adult world (or even from sanity).

Many of Ducornet's child-voiced stories are told in retrospect or in a shifting tense. The reader is not sure if childhood is happening in the moment, or if the childhood and what it must have felt like are being recalled much later. In "Saida"--voiced by the titular girl's companion, the daughter of missionaries, years after the fact--Ducornet further complicates childhood sexuality by making the narrator desire a female companion and by foreshortening the reader's knowledge of the girls' early lives, so that only a few stark facts compel the story forward: Saida breaks the jar preserving a two-headed snake--a zoological specimen, a wonder-cabinet centerpiece--in her father's study. Her father is a professor. The professor knows about the sexual folklore of southern tribes. The narrator values Saida's touch, her lips.

Ducornet focuses on a single voice: the voice of a woman slipping back into the mystery of her childhood, torn between the comfort of her age and the enticement of all her possible future transgressions, all of which are characterized neatly, compactly, in the opening action of the story--Saida's breaking of the snake's jar. At this moment and other quintessentially grotesque ones within Ducornet's stories, sexuality, ordinary childhood chaos, and atypical objects fuse. Any facile reading is made impossible by the story's shortness and air of mystery. It is not clear that even the narrator knows exactly why she speaks, except that she cannot forget Saida and what Saida meant to her, at the crossroads of youth and nostalgia for it.

THE WORD "DESIRE"

The Word "Desire" consists of twelve stories, longer than those found in *The Complete Butcher's Tales* and generally less surreal, obsessed with tracing desire in some of its most hypnotically human forms, both repressed and (almost infinitely) expressed. Where the stories in *The Complete Butcher's Tales* tend to move quickly, leaping over certain facts, the stories in *The Word "Desire"* consist of whole fables, each a defensive telling of one person's small but important story (and all of them rehearsing the confessional and highly sensuous style of the titular character in *The Fan-Maker's Inquisition*). Again Ducornet focuses on one strong voice per story, and again the voices vary, both in themselves--the mad, "royal-we" abusing boy in "Roseveine" is nothing like the repressed priest in "The Foxed Mirror"--and in time and place.

Ducornet effortlessly moves between epochs, linking them all, again, in a network of desires and human impulses. If it is true that she sees a gnostic truth available in moments of orgasm and loss, lust and love, death and madness, then it is also true that this gnosis takes the form of the human id (Saturn, juxtaposed with Christ on the cross in "The Foxed Mirror"), a natural madness, as opposed to the divine ecstasy sought after by the religious. These are stories of failure as much as of ecstasy, especially in "Das Wunderbuch," "Neurosis of Containment," "The Foxed Mirror," and "Roseveine." However, not all failure is without humor.

"FORTUNÉ," EGYPT, FRANCE, AND THE MARVELS OF THE ANCIENT PAST

Narrated by Empress Josephine's black lapdog, Fortuné, this short tragic love tale chronicles the dog's awakening to Napoleon's glory (though he refers to him only as "Boney"). Paralleling Fortuné's rising desire to see the Pyramids and to see them crushed to help the French usher in modern industry in the Muslim world is the dog's increasing failure to please his girlfriend, a dachshund named Mina. Ducornet's grotesque humor, obsessions with history, and empathy with nature blend expertly in the story's final moments, as Fortuné realizes that his mistress does not love Boney and will not be joining him in the Orient, and Mina does not love him. Thus darkly enlightened, Fortuné jumps into the jaws of the huge kitchen hound, Creon, that Mina does love. Fortuné's death is impossible not to laugh at. As a symbol, as a singular moment, it sums up something raw and admonishing about the French Revolution, Napoleon's orientalism and avarice, and the impotence of the Parisian bourgeoisie.

"ROSEVEINE"

Another French fable, concerning in part colonial Madagascar, "Roseveine" is a madman's lucid reminiscence, which humanizes madness. As a boy, the man was driven insane by his tyrannical father; the man is humanized because he is allowed to recall for himself his youth, and the emblematic tale he chooses to tell is of his first moment of perfect erotic clarity--his introduction to his mother's friend Roseveine, the laughing lady who teaches the boy about mollusks and other sea life and who allows him to lick her foot. His tale is fraught with tension but does not end with a bang. His desire, unlike Fortuné's, is allowed no true outlet.

The sadness of his story is its charm: He has not forgotten and does not distort the events of his childhood. His one moment of enlightenment was his downfall. His obsession is a house like a mollusk's, one that will protect him and outlast him, one that will consume him, so that he is only surface. This desire contains echoes of the earlier "New Bronx Zoo," whose wildly finned and tattooed and pierced inhabitants insist that there is only surface, and that this is positive, liberating. Contrast this with the meaninglessness of the children's continual evolutions in "Egyptian Gum." Perhaps "Roseveine" represents a middle way. Subtly postmodern, "Roseveine" insists that the madman choose the form of his madness (mollusks, one woman glimpsed in childhood, surface, houses), even if it he cannot overcome the affliction itself (the tyranny of the father).

GAZELLE

Gazelle investigates the idea of choosing from failures or using failures to synthesize a new life. The story describes a thirteen-year-old girl's awakening into adulthood in the Cairo of the 1950's, expanding upon many of Ducornet's themes and yielding many strong examples of her precision with the senses. Elizabeth, who loves *Alf layla wa-layla* (fifteenth century; *The Arabian Nights' Entertainments*, 1706-1708), falls for a perfumer, Ramses, who has dedicated himself to simulating the most rare and infamous scents of the distant past.

As do both "Saida" and "Fortuné," *Gazelle* highlights the fact that the past is neither gone nor entirely explicable; it lingers on with a certain hazy quality, becoming over time, in one word, marvelous. Even events that are not ancient can fall rapidly outside of rationality. When Elizabeth's mother leaves the family and her father hires a nomadic magician to bring her back, the girl is forced to concede that there are no ultimate answers or even identities, only temporary constructions. Thus she is able to learn from Ramses and her sad father--even though the former rejects her as a lover (she is a little girl) and the latter is unable to provide her with a solid foundation for reality--an ultimate meaning. Again, mutability and beauty rule.

OTHER MAJOR WORKS

LONG FICTION: *The Stain*, 1984; *Entering Fire*, 1986; *The Fountains of Neptune*, 1989; *The Jade Cabinet*, 1993; *Phosphor in Dreamland*, 1995; *The Fan-Maker's Inquisition*, 1999.

POETRY: *From the Star Chamber*, 1974 (as Rikki); *Wild Geraniums*, 1975; *Bouche à Bouche*, 1975 (as Rikki; with Guy Ducornet); *Weird Sisters*, 1976; *Knife Notebook*, 1977 (as Rikki); *The Illustrated Universe*, 1979 (as Rikki); *The Cult of Seizure*, 1989.

NONFICTION: *The Monstrous and the Marvelous*, 1999; *The Deep Zoo*, 2004.

EDITED TEXT: *Shoes and Shit: Stories for Pedestrians*, 1984 (with Geoff Hancock).

CHILDREN'S LITERATURE: *The Blue Bird*, 1970; *Shazira Shazam and the Devil*, 1970 (with Guy Ducornet).

ILLUSTRATIONS: Robert Coover, *Spanking the Maid*, 1981; Jorge Luis Borges, *Tlön, Uqbar, Orbis Tertius*, 1983; Karen Elizabeth Gordon, *Torn Wings and Faux Pas*, 1997.

BIBLIOGRAPHY

Broening, John. "A Conversation with Rikki Ducornet." *Colorado Springs Independent*, January 6, 2000. Spirited interview with Ducornet, in which she discusses her writing, food, and "the belief in man's innate badness."

May, Charles E. "*The One Marvelous Thing*: Rikki Ducornet Has Still Got It." *Journal-Sentinel*, November 15, 2008. Perceptive review of Ducornet's short stories in her collection *The One Marvelous Thing*.

Pearlman, Ellen. "Rikki Ducornet in Conversation." *The Brooklyn Rail* (August/September, 2003). Ducornet discusses how she finds her characters, how much revision she does, and the thematic threads in her work.

Wythe Marschall

PAUL LAURENCE DUNBAR

Born: Dayton, Ohio; June 27, 1872
Died: Dayton, Ohio; February 9, 1906

PRINCIPAL SHORT FICTION

Folks from Dixie, 1898
The Strength of Gideon, and Other Stories, 1900
In Old Plantation Days, 1903
The Heart of Happy Hollow, 1904
The Best Stories of Paul Laurence Dunbar, 1938
The Complete Stories of Paul Laurence Dunbar,
    2006 (Gene Andrew Jarrett and Thomas Lewis
    Morgan, editors)

OTHER LITERARY FORMS

Known primarily for his verse, Paul Laurence Dunbar published *Lyrics of Lowly Life* in 1896, and this collection vaulted him to fame as a premier dialect poet. He was also the author of five other volumes of original verse, three librettos written alone and with others, a drama, essays, and four novels, the most interesting of which is *The Sport of the Gods* (1901, serial; 1902, book).

ACHIEVEMENTS

Paul Laurence Dunbar was America's first professional black writer and a great popular success. Championed for the dialect verse and stories of the plantation folk he was unequaled in rendering but which he himself despised as limited and compliant with existing stereotypes, Dunbar was hailed by the leading literary minds of his day.

BIOGRAPHY

The child of former slaves, Joshua and Matilda Glass Burton Murphy Dunbar, Paul Laurence Dunbar was raised in Dayton, Ohio. His younger sister died when he was three, and his father died when Paul was twelve. In high school, he was the only African American, but perhaps both despite and because of this he became president of his class, managing editor of his school newspaper, president of the school literary club, and class poet. While still in high school, he published poems in local newspapers and served as editor for the *Dayton Tattler*, published by classmate Orville Wright, coinventor of the airplane. Despite Dunbar's scholastic excellence, Dayton's discriminatory policies forced the young graduate to take a menial position as an elevator operator while he continued to write. Encouraged by other writers and a former teacher, Dunbar published privately his first collection of poetry, *Oak and Ivy* (1893). His second collection, *Majors and Minors* (1895), won praise from writer William Dean Howells and sent him on the road to fame, but for Dunbar it was for all the wrong reasons.

In 1898, Dunbar married Alice Ruth Moore, a Creole writer from New Orleans; the childless couple separated in 1902. Dunbar died in 1906, at the age of thirty-three, of tuberculosis, of the effects of the alcohol prescribed to treat it, and of the melancholy brought on by his belief that his life had been a failure.

ANALYSIS

Paul Laurence Dunbar's life and writing were both impeded and tempered by the racial politics of his day. It was his greatest sorrow as an artist that his public wanted to read only his dialect verse and his stories in the plantation tradition, which were comic and sentimental, depicting black people as ignorant children. The fact that so much of his work contributed to negative stereotypes of his people has compromised his legacy and sometimes eclipsed the fact that, if he had not complied with those stereotypes, the work for which he is justly revered would not have been published at all. For African Americans of his day, his literary success was a symbol of the entire race's intellectual and creative abilities, hitherto unrecognized by white Americans.

The roots of Dunbar's short fiction are to be found in the stories his parents told him of their Kentucky home and servitude. His mother told him gentle stories about plantation community life, but his father had been a fugitive and had fought with the Massachusetts Fifty-Fifth Volunteer Infantry regiment, and his stories were not sentimental. Dunbar's best short fiction is informed by the spirit and example of these stories and by the customs, traditions, and mores of the transplanted black southern community from which he came.

Dunbar's short fiction is often compared to that of his contemporary, Charles Waddell Chesnutt, who was also black and who wrote some accomplished plantation-based tales of black life. Chesnutt's stories are often peopled with characters who resist, undermine, and outsmart the white people, who think they know them. The majority of Dunbar's black characters tend instead to manipulate and subvert white opposition and gain white approval by a show of sterling character: honesty, integrity, faithfulness, loyalty, love, redemptive suffering, and forgiveness. Worse, some Dunbar stories cast uneducated black people as the ignorant, minstrel buffoons his white readers preferred. Nestled among this packing, however, were also great stories for which he is well remembered, stories that reveal righteous anger over ignorance and racial injustice and contempt for those who perpetuate them.

FOLKS FROM DIXIE

There is plenty of "packing" in Dunbar's first story collection. Several stories, such as "Mount Pisgah's Christmas 'Possum," depict uneducated black people as ludicrous bumpkins or grateful, indebted servants. "The Colonel's Awakening" is an extremely sentimental tale, dripping with the sort of pathos that writer Thomas Nelson Page whipped into his plantation tales. In "Anner 'Lizer," Dunbar pokes fun at religious hypocrisy, while affirming the fact that people's emotional and spiritual needs are often deeply linked. "Jimsella," "Aunt Mandy's Investment," and "Nelse Hatton's Revenge" were written primarily for his post-Reconstruction black readers, who were still figuring out how to live now that the structure and restrictions of slavery no longer dictated their circumstances. The timely issues that these stories address include family responsibility; honesty; integrity in businesses, which should serve the black community; and remembering and living the results of slavery and emancipation in ways that are not self-destructive.

"The Ordeal at Mt. Hope" and "At Shaft 11" are satisfying, well-constructed stories. The former is interesting for its autobiographical elements, its social commentary, and its "bootstrap economic" and educational philosophies as advocated by Booker T. Washington. The Reverend Howard Dokesbury steps off the train at Mt. Hope to take up his new post as Methodist preacher. The station house is run-down and filthy, like the rest of the town, and the indolent blacks, whites, and dogs view him with suspicion and malice. Dokesbury, understanding that any reconstruction of this community must happen one individual at a time, befriends 'Lias, one of the defeated young men. They collaborate on a small agricultural venture, and 'Lias gains confidence, feelings of self-reliance and self-esteem, and the financial base to go to the new industrial school to expand his skills. One by one, the townspeople are anxious to follow his example. Possibly Dunbar considered this story to be a blueprint for the betterment of the black masses, though he became increasingly critical of Washington's ideas, and by 1903 he warned of "educating the hand to the exclusion of the head." Dunbar gives Dokesbury his own physical characteristics, an occupation that Dunbar himself seriously considered, and, even more important, some of his doubts and feelings of estrangement.

> He had always been such a loyal Negro, so proud
> of his honest brown . . . but . . . was he, after all,
> different from the majority of the people with

whom he was supposed to have all thoughts, feelings, and emotions in common?

Increasingly, Dunbar discovered that education and class standing were great dividers among his people, and color-consciousness made it all much worse.

"At Shaft 11" takes place in a mining community in West Virginia where a strike is being broken with a crew of black miners. Violence erupts, and two heroes emerge: the Scottish foreman, Jason Andrews, and the black foreman, Sam Bowles, who unite for common cause and mutual benefit. Less believable than the previous story, it is a blueprint for how things might have been in a more perfect world but rarely were. Still, it is revealing as a Dunbar story: The black men fight back here, meeting violence with necessary violence, and winning their share of the American pie.

THE STRENGTH OF GIDEON, AND OTHER STORIES

Dunbar's second collection of short stories reveals a wide spectrum of his thought and style. The title work and "Mammy Peggy's Pride" typify the plantation stories that champion the virtues of the race, such as honor, loyalty, dignity, faithfulness, selflessness, and a sense of duty and responsibility. Mammy Peggy, still the faithful, postemancipation house servant, so identifies with her owners' former aristocratic place in southern society that she almost cannot adapt to the alliances and reconciliation necessary for a new day. Gideon's strength is his sense of duty and responsibility in keeping his word to his old master, even though he loses the woman he loves and who loves him. Dunbar's intent is to glorify race relations of an earlier day in the interest of race relations of his own day, which were marked by increasing enmity and violence. It is as if he hopes to calm would-be lynchers and segregationists and to reassure potential friends of the race with the admonition to "remember who these people are."

"The Ingrate" is based on Dunbar's father's experiences as a slave, a fugitive on the underground railroad to Canada, and a Union soldier. The former slaveholder sees his former slave's name on a Union roster and feels grievously abused that he taught "the ingrate" to read and cipher because he used these accomplishments against him. "The Case of 'Ca'line'," subtitled "A Kitchen Monologue," is a sassy piece, which

Paul Laurence Dunbar (Library of Congress)

anticipates Langston Hughes' Simple and Alberta K. Johnson stories.

Though there is enough melodramatic action in "The Tragedy at Three Forks" for a novel, this anti-lynching story is not entirely unsuccessful. Reflecting the usual circumstances of lynchings, the two victims are innocent, and the reader understands that this evil bloodthirst will continue as long as white people are motivated by guilt, ignorance, immorality, cruelty, base instincts, and mob violence. Other stories point out other kinds of white injustice. In "One Man's Fortunes," a worthy black college graduate goes out to get a job and, like Dunbar himself, meets defeat and deception in the white world. Others warn of the folly of migrating to the urban North, where hardship and evil await. The last story in the collection, "Silas Jackson," could have been a prototype for the beginnings of James Weldon Johnson's *Autobiography of an Ex-Coloured Man* (1912), and Ralph Ellison's *Invisible Man* (1952). Here, too, the young, country innocent has a vision of a better life, and, through a series of ever more blinding incidents involving white "benefactors" and black charlatans, he finds himself in New York City, where he thinks he has "made something of himself." Here Silas's fortunes take a characteristic Dunbarian turn, and he returns home "spent, broken, hopeless, all contentment and simplicity gone." Portending death more than reunion with "the old folks at home," it is an ambiguous, unsettling end to the collection.

In Old Plantation Days

This collection is in the plantation tradition, though there are two stories worth reading. "The Finding of Martha" is really the second half of "The Strength of Gideon," which ended unsatisfactorily in the previous collection, and "The Memory of Martha," which, despite certain weaknesses (omission of painful details of slavery, oversentimentality), is still an affecting love story.

The Heart of Happy Hollow

These stories take place during and after the Reconstruction and are concerned with the strengths and weaknesses of the southern black community in the aftermath of slavery and the strained, even violent circumstances African Americans were forced to endure as they claimed the benefits of freedom. "The Scapegoat" is Dunbar's most successful story about how African Americans were, and are, used as America's political pawns. It is also one of the first stories by a black writer to locate an alternate, undermining seat of power in the barbershop/newsstand. "The Lynching of Jube Benson" is Dunbar's other anti-lynching story, this one narrated by one of the lynchers, as in James Baldwin's work. Though its impact is fueled by sentiment, it is unrelenting and unforgiving in its indictment. Other stories, primarily for a black audience, warn of the dangers of boastfulness, vanity, cowardice, self-pity, class and color consciousness, and the reactionary fear of change and difference. Stories such as "The Promoter" and "The Boy and the Bayonet" reveal that Dunbar had discovered how to use humor and pathos without sacrificing his characters' humanity. At the time of his death, his strongest work was no longer in poetry but in short fiction, a genre that allowed him to be more realistic, relevant, and true to himself and his people.

Other Major Works

LONG FICTION: *The Uncalled*, 1898; *The Love of Landry*, 1900; *The Fanatics*, 1901; *The Sport of the Gods*, 1901 (serial), 1902 (book); *The Collected Novels of Paul Laurence Dunbar*, 2009 (Herbert Woodward Martin, Ronald Primeau, and Gene Andrew Jarrett, editors).

POETRY: *Oak and Ivy*, 1893; *Majors and Minors*, 1895; *Lyrics of Lowly Life*, 1896; *Lyrics of the Hearthside*, 1899; *Lyrics of Love and Laughter*, 1903; *Lyrics of Sunshine and Shadow*, 1905; *Complete Poems*, 1913.

MISCELLANEOUS: *In His Own Voice: The Dramatic and Other Uncollected Works of Paul Laurence Dunbar*, 2002 (Herbert Woodward Martin and Ronald Primeau, editors).

Bibliography

Alexander, Eleanor. *Lyrics of Sunshine and Shadow: The Tragic Courtship and Marriage of Paul Laurence Dunbar and Alice Ruth Moore*. Albany: New York University Press, 2001. Traces the tempestuous romance of this noted African American literary couple. Draws on love letters, diaries, journals, and autobiographies to tell the story of Dunbar and Moore's tumultuous affair, their elopement, Dunbar's abuse of Moore, their passionate marriage, and the violence that ended it. Examines Dunbar and Moore in the context of their time, fame, and cultural ideology.

Best, Felton O. *Crossing the Color Line: A Biography of Paul Laurence Dunbar*. Dubuque, Iowa: Kendall/Hunt, 1996. This biography discusses Dunbar's short fiction as evidence of his restrictions and intentions.

Bone, Robert. *Down Home: Origins of the Afro-American Short Story*. New York: Columbia University Press, 1988. Discusses the "strictures" of Dunbar's time and the "travesties" of his fictional response. Judges Dunbar to be a "purveyor of dead forms."

Dunbar, Paul Laurence. *The Collected Poetry of Paul Laurence Dunbar*. Edited by Joanne M. Braxton. Charlottesville: University Press of Virginia, 1993. Though this is a collection of poetry, its biographical introduction is insightful and useful to researchers in any Dunbar genre.

_____. *In His Own Voice: The Dramatic and Other Uncollected Works of Paul Laurence Dunbar*. Edited by Herbert Woodward Martin and Ronald Primeau. Athens: Ohio University Press, 2002. This collection of previously unpublished works includes numerous short stories, as well as some of Dunbar's dramatic works, essays, and poems.

Fishkin, Shelley Fisher. "Race and the Politics of Memory: Mark Twain and Paul Laurence Dunbar." *Journal of American Studies* 40, no. 2 (August, 2006): 283-309. Fishkin, a Dunbar scholar, analyzes works by Dunbar and Mark Twain that influenced American ideas about racial discrimination and slavery in the United States.

Martin, Jay, ed. *A Singer in the Dawn: Reinterpretations of Paul Laurence Dunbar*. New York: Dodd, Mead, 1975. Contains biographical "reminiscences" and essays about Dunbar's poetry and fiction, including one by Bert Bender on "The Lyrical Short Fiction of Dunbar and Chesnutt."

Pierce, Yolanda I. "That Old Time Religion: Christian Faith in Dunbar's 'The Strength of Gideon.'" *African American Review* 41, no. 2 (Summer, 2007): 313-318. Uses Christian biblical rhetoric to analyze the elements of spirituality in the story "The Strength of Gideon." Argues that Dunbar's short fiction is "a vehicle for both the confirmation and contestation of an old time religion."

Turner, Darwin T. "Paul Laurence Dunbar: The Rejected Symbol." *Journal of Negro History* (January, 1967): 1-13. Provides a balanced response to the pros and cons of Dunbar's work. Points out the restrictions under which Dunbar worked and his artistic ideals. Concludes that "readers have demanded too much of Dunbar as a symbol."

Cynthia Packard Hill

STUART DYBEK

Born: Chicago, Illinois; April 10, 1942

PRINCIPAL SHORT FICTION

Childhood and Other Neighborhoods, 1980
The Coast of Chicago, 1990
The Story of Mist, 1993
I Sailed with Magellan, 2003

OTHER LITERARY FORMS

Stuart Dybek (STEW-urt DI-behk) published a volume of poetry, *Brass Knuckles*, in 1979. His short story "Death of a Right Fielder" was televised in 1991, and his play *Orchids* was produced in 1990.

ACHIEVEMENTS

Editors have chosen many of Stuart Dybek's stories for inclusion in anthologies. He won a Special Citation from the Ernest Hemingway Foundation as well as awards from the Cliff Dwellers Arts Foundation, Friends of American Writers, the Whiting Foundation, and the Society of Midland Authors. In addition, he received a Nelson Algren Award, several O. Henry Awards, and the Church and the Artist Literary Competition Award. Dybek was the recipient of a John Simon Guggenheim Memorial Foundation Fellowship and a National Endowment for the Arts grant. In 2007, Dybek won a MacArthur "genius award" and the Rea Award for the Short Story, which included a thirty-thousand-dollar annual stipend.

BIOGRAPHY

Stuart Dybek was born on April 10, 1942, in Chicago, the son of Stanley Dybek and Adeline Sala. Stuart Dybek grew up in a working-class, ethnic neighborhood, a milieu that figures prominently in his writing. After graduating from a Catholic high school, he enrolled at Loyola University, but he interrupted his education to work in the Civil Rights and anti-Vietnam War movements of the early 1960's. He earned a B.A. from Loyola in 1964 and an M.A. in 1968. He married Caren Bassett in 1966.

After working as a case worker with the Cook County Department of Public Aid, teaching in a Chicago-area elementary school, and teaching high school on the island of St. Thomas for Volunteers in Service to America (VISTA), Dybek returned to school. He earned an M.F.A. degree from the prestigious University of Iowa Writers' Workshop in 1973. In 1974, he began teaching English and creative writing at western Michigan University in Kalamazoo, Michigan. He served as a visiting professor at Princeton University in 1990 and began teaching in the Warren Wilson M.F.A. program for writers in 1985.

Dybek's first book-length publication was his collection of poetry and prose poems, *Brass Knuckles*. His first collection of short stories, *Childhood and Other Neighborhoods*, published in 1980, was well received by the critics. Likewise, his second collection, *The Coast of Chicago* (1990), received considerable critical praise. Since the mid-1970's, Dybek has published a steady stream of stories in such important journals as *Ploughshares* and *TriQuarterly* and such popular magazines as *The New Yorker* and *The Atlantic Monthly*.

ANALYSIS

Chicago has a long tradition of producing fine writers who use the city as their literary landscape. Gwendolyn Brooks, Carl Sandburg, Upton Sinclair, and Theodore Dreiser, among others, belong to this tradition. Stuart Dybek, while drawing heavily on the city for his settings, characters, and images, departs from the tradition with his dreamlike portrayal of life in a postmodern world. Some critics have identified his work with Magical Realism and have suggested a connection with Jorge Luis Borges and Italo Calvino. Dybek reports that after he wrote some of the early stories included in *Childhood and Other Neighborhoods* he began to read Franz Kafka and Gabriel García Márquez. In addition to exploring the intersection between dreams and reality, Dybek has pioneered the genre sometimes known as "sudden" or "flash" fiction. These stories are sometimes called "short short" stories; sudden fiction can be just a few paragraphs long and never longer than three pages. Consequently, readers of sudden fiction often find themselves in the middle of a situation well under way, a situation that will end but not conclude. Some of the prose poems in Dybek's poetry collection *Brass Knuckles* could fall into this category. *The Coast of Chicago* also includes several very short stories.

Many of Dybek's stories draw on his experiences growing up in a Polish Latino neighborhood on the South Side of Chicago. His characters often have Polish surnames, attend Catholic churches, and carry with them the culture and mythology of eastern Europe. Even when his stories are not overtly about the immigrant experience, their settings are rich with ethnic sounds, aromas, and sights. Churches frequently appear in the center of the landscape.

Dybek often places his characters in moments of transformation. Frequently this takes the form of a coming-of-age story, especially in *Childhood and Other Neighborhoods*. In a 1997 interview with Mike Nickel and Adrian Smith, Dybek says that he is always "looking for some door in the story that opens on another world." For some characters, this can be the world of adulthood; for others, it can be an entry into the world of magic or death. The entry into a different world can be a transformative moment for his characters and for his readers.

CHILDHOOD AND OTHER NEIGHBORHOODS

The eleven stories in this collection are about coming of age. With his title, Dybek deliberately suggests that there is both a time and a space to childhood; that is, he sees childhood in the same way one would see a neighborhood, as a place where interconnected people live out their lives, bounded by streets, houses, ethnicity, and religion. The main characters in this collection are generally young people, often second- or third-generation Poles making their homes in Chicago. Dybek identifies the subject of the collection as "perception," reminding his readers that children perceive the world in ways that are different from the ways adults do. For many of the characters in this book, their moment of transformation comes when they leave the familiar streets of their own neighborhood and venture out into the world at large. Sometimes these adventures end tragically, sometimes humorously. Often the world outside the neighborhood is a world infused with magic or horror.

The opening story of *Childhood and Other Neighborhoods*, "The Palatski Man," is about a girl, Mary, and her older brother, John. The story opens on Palm Sunday and continues to use religious imagery throughout. At the center of the story stands the nameless Palatski Man, a vendor who dresses in white and sells taffy apples and *palatski*, a confection of wafers and honey. There is a strangeness to this treat; Mary has never seen *palatski* sold anywhere else. For Mary, eating the *palatski* reminds her of Holy Communion, an image that recurs later in the story.

John and his friend Ray Cruz are fascinated by the Ragmen, who traverse their neighborhood collecting rags. John tells Mary about following a Ragman for a long way and discovering the place where all the Ragmen live. Ray and John are discovered by the Ragmen and become separated. Later, when John calls Ray's home, Ray denies that the adventure ever happened, and John is unable to locate the Ragmen's camp again. Later, John and Mary follow the Palatski Man and find themselves once again at the Ragmen's camp. In a mystical, frightening ceremony, the young people partake of a kind of Eucharist consisting of taffy apple syrup and *palatski*, which tastes surprisingly bitter. That night, Mary discovers that John did not eat his portion. The story closes strangely, with a scene that could be a real event, a vision, or a dream. The Palatski Man comes for Mary, and she knows that she must go with him.

Dybek reports that he wrote this story while listening to the music of Hungarian composer Zoltán Kodály. The music suggested the strange, eastern European images. There are also undercurrents of the Persephone myth, and readers should remember that this myth was the subject of a poem in Dybek's *Brass Knuckles*. In Greek mythology, Persephone eats pomegranate seeds offered her by Hades, the ruler of the underworld. As a result, she is bound to stay with him for six months of the year. Likewise, Mary's ingestion of the minute wafer given to her by the Palatski Man makes possible the final scene.

THE COAST OF CHICAGO

The Coast of Chicago contains both longer stories and very short stories, interconnected by theme and image. Some reviewers suggest that the very short

stories are lyrical in nature and may be autobiographical. Again, Chicago provides the setting for the stories, and, again, Dybek has said that he listened to music, jazz this time, as he wrote the stories. Many of the stories in the collection have a dreamlike, legendary quality. Art and music figure in many of the stories. For example, "Nighthawks," a minicollection of tales within the larger collection, uses Edward Hopper's painting by the same name as its starting point. Likewise, "Chopin in Winter" draws on the music of the Polish composer. In all, the stories are elegiac, somber, nearly hallucinatory. Dybek seems interested in showing the reader the way characters and settings change, subtly and quickly, often before the reader's eyes.

"ANT"

Appearing in the Winter, 1997-1998, issue of *Ploughshares*, "Ant" is a sample of Dybek's very short fiction, of the blend of fantasy and realism characteristic of many of his stories, and of an entry into another world and then back into the ordinary one. The story opens with Martin lying on a blanket under a tree with his lover. When an ant begins to drag him by his toe, Martin remembers stories read to him when he was a boy by his Uncle Wayne. The uncle, a veteran of an unnamed war, acted out the stories after reading them to Martin. The most memorable for Martin was "Lonigan and the Ants." His uncle, who had pretended that he was an ant and Martin was Lonigan, had begun to pursue him. All that saved the frightened Martin from the mad pursuit by his uncle was the reminder that Lonigan does not die and the ants do not win; the "authority of the story" is enough to change his uncle's actions. Dybek seems to be playing with the boundaries of storytelling. In the larger story, he exerts authority over his own story and writes a version in which one ant does win. Eventually, an ant works its way up Martin's back, grabs hold of his belt, lifts him off the ground, and carries him away.

I SAILED WITH MAGELLAN

Although Dybek's *I Sailed with Magellan* was promoted by his publisher as a "novel-in-stories," the only thing novelistic about *I Sailed with Magellan* is that some of the same characters appear in all the stories. In an interview, Dybek said that the overall narrative line of such linked story collections as Sherwood Anderson's *Winesburg, Ohio* (1919) and James Joyce's *Dubliners* (1914) does not suggest what they are about, for a successful story sequence refuses to accept that the design of life is a neat pattern of cause and effect. Thus, to call *I Sailed with Magellan* an ethnic "coming-of-age novel" about a young Polish American named Perry Katzek growing up on the South Side of Chicago in the 1950's and 1960's is to minimize the universal power of the eleven individual stories, for each one is a self-contained, lyrically powerful, literary experience.

"LIVE FROM DREAMSVILLE"

In "Live from Dreamsville," an irresistible story about escape and fantasy, Perry tells his younger brother Mick that there is a secret trapdoor in Perry's bed, going down to a clubhouse full of sodas, malts, and candy. They play a radio game, in which Mick sings a song, "I Sailed with Magellan," he made up, " However, the real world hovers near them; the story ends with the sound of a dog softly whimpering in the next apartment because its owner beats it.

"BREASTS"

After three stories about Perry, suddenly there is a long story, "Breasts," in which a mob hit man, who is supposed to kill a guy for skimming off the top, keeps putting off the inevitable. The piece reads like a parody of gangland Chicago in the 1950's, perhaps because parody is the only way such a story can now be told. The title is echoed in the last section when Mick overhears the murdered man's wife begging for her life and sees her slip fall down her shoulders, giving him his first glimpse of a woman's naked breast.

"BLUE BOY"

"Blue Boy," another long story, centers symbolically on Ralphie, born a blue baby, who becomes a sacred icon in the neighborhood and is protected by his brother, Chester. Perry's eighth-grade class has to write a composition on the meaning of Christmas and dedicate it to Ralphie after his death. However, everyone knows that the winning essay will be written by Camille Estrada, a writing prodigy. In lesser hands this could have been a simple sentimentality, but Dybek makes it an engaging meditation on emotional risk-taking.

"WE DIDN'T"

Even the pieces with the slick professionalism that has often given the short story a bad name are redeemed by Dybek's lyrical style and his refusal to rush to a neat final twist. The best-known story in the collection, "We Didn't" (picked for both *Best American Short Stories* and the O. Henry Awards in 1994), is primarily a clever tour de force, but Dybek makes it into an evocative piece of music. These eleven pieces do not derive their power from being linked novelistically but by being compelling individual short stories.

OTHER MAJOR WORKS

PLAY: *Orchids*, pr. 1990.

POETRY: *Brass Knuckles*, 1979; *Kiddie Corner*, 1981; *Streets in Their Own Ink*, 2004.

BIBLIOGRAPHY

Chung, Jeanie. "An Interview with Stuart Dybek." *The Writer's Chronicle* 38 (October/November, 2005): 38-45. Long interview in which Dybek talks about the stories in *I Sailed with Magellan*, his career, and the writers who have influenced him.

Cook, Bruce. "Walks on the Southwest Side." *Washington Post Book World*, January 13, 1980, p. 1. Places Dybek in the tradition of Chicago writers, including Nelson Algren, Gwendolyn Brooks, and Saul Bellow, in a review of *Childhood and Other Neighborhoods*.

Dybek, Stuart. "An Interview with Stuart Dybek." Interview by Mike Nickel and Adrian Smith. *Chicago Review* 43 (Winter, 1997): 87-101. A revealing interview in which Dybek reflects on what it means to be a "Chicago writer," his ethnic background, how it influences his writing, and his ideas about form and writing.

_____. "Thread." *Harper's* 297 (September, 1998): 34-37. A brief memoir by Dybek, recalling his Catholic upbringing and his First Holy Communion.

Gladsky, Thomas S. "From Ethnicity to Multiculturalism: The Fiction of Stuart Dybek." *MELUS* 20 (Summer, 1995): 105-118. Offers a brief history of Polish immigration to the United States, followed by a consideration of Polish American writers, before turning to an examination of Dybek in this context. Connects ethnicity and memory and discusses the role of Catholicism in Dybek's prose.

Kakutani, Michiko. "Lyrical Loss and Desolation of Misfits in Chicago." *The New York Times Book Review*, April 20, 1990, p. C31. Draws a parallel between *The Coast of Chicago* and Sherwood Anderson's *Winesburg, Ohio*, noting similarities in characters, lyricism, and "emotional forcefulness."

Lee, Don. "About Stuart Dybek." *Ploughshares* 24 (Spring, 1998): 192-198. An in-depth profile of Dybek and his subject matter. Provides biographical information and considers Dybek's contribution to the "short short" genre of short stories.

Shapard, Robert, and James Thomas, eds. *Sudden Fiction: American Short-Short Stories*. Salt Lake City, Utah: Gibbs M. Smith, 1986. The classic collection of the "short short" story. Includes Dybek's "Sunday at the Zoo" and an afterword by Dybek on the genre.

Ward, Robert. "A Review of *Childhood and Other Neighborhoods*." *Northwest Review* 18 (Fall, 1980): 149-157.

Weber, Katharine. "Windy City Dreaming." *The New York Times Book Review*, May 20, 1990, p. 30. Reviews *The Coast of Chicago*, connecting memory, dreaming, and the dreamlike nature of Dybek's stories.

Diane Andrews Henningfeld
Updated by Charles E. May

E

Tony Earley

Born: San Antonio, Texas; June 15, 1961

Principal short fiction

Here We Are in Paradise, 1994
"The Bridge," 1997
"Meteorite," 1998
"Quill," 1998
"Just Married," 1999
"The Wide Sea," 1999
"Have You Seen the Stolen Girl?," 2003
"The Cryptozoologist," 2006
"Yard Art," 2006
"Mr. Tall," 2009

Other literary forms

Tony Earley is the author of *Jim the Boy* (2000), his first work of long fiction. He published a collection of essays, *Somehow Form a Family: Stories That Are Mostly True* (2001). The author's second novel, *The Blue Star*, was published in 2008.

Achievements

In 1999, Tony Earley was included on a list of young writers in *The New Yorker* for a piece on "The Future of American Fiction." In 1996, Britain's *Granta* included Earley among the Best of Young American Novelists. Earley won a PEN Syndicated Fiction Award in 1993.

Biography

Tony Earley's career has included working as a newspaper sports editor and columnist in Forest City, North Carolina, and as a writer of collected short stories, essays, and two novels. A 1983 graduate of Warren Wilson College, which is in the Swannanoa Valley about ten miles east of Asheville, North Carolina, Earley earned his master's degree at the University of Alabama in Tuscaloosa in 1992. In 1993, he married Sarah Bell, who lived in Rutherfordton, North Carolina. Earley also has taught at Carnegie-Mellon University and the University of Alabama, and he was a former Tennessee Williams Visiting Writer at the University of the South. In 1997, Earley moved to Nashville, Tennessee, where he became the Samuel Milton Fleming Associate Professor of English at Vanderbilt University.

Although born in Texas, where his father served in the U.S. Air Force, Earley grew up in and is identified with western North Carolina, and a majority of his short stories and novels are set in the region. He has contributed stories to *Harper's*, *Esquire*, *Tri-Quarterly*, *Oxford Magazine*, *The New Yorker*, *The New York Times Book Review*, *Mississippi Review*, *Southern Review*, and *Tin House* literary magazines. Earley's short stories have been anthologized in annual volumes of *New Stories from the South* and *The Best American Short Stories*.

Analysis

Tony Earley's short stories are a slice of life, but life has many different flavors. The flavor in Earley's stories is often southern, rural, and poor. The delicious characters inhabiting western North Carolina, where many of the stories take place, are not fancy but plain. In their plainness, the characters are not aware of their nature. They are simply themselves, taking each day and each challenge as they come. In the presentation of his characters, Earley does not fall to one side or the other, neither pitying nor praising them. He presents them naturally, without special explanations or apologies. This makes the characters accessible to the reader in an honest way that permits an uncommon closeness.

Lake Glen's dam keeper, for example, keeps the water in the local lake at a constant level, while mourning his wife's unfaithfulness and the loss of his marriage. He dreams of days past, observes the town's local characters, and plots to catch a catfish of near-mythic size that reportedly swims among the long-abandoned houses of Uree, the sunken town lying below the lake's surface. The reverence for local history, the cold ashes of small-town scandals, and the inevitability of change are encompassed in the dam keeper's distant gaze in the story "The Prophet from Jupiter," the first short story in *Here We Are in Paradise*.

"HERE WE ARE IN PARADISE"

In the short story "Here We Are in Paradise," Vernon Jackson is a local baseball pitcher of some reputation. Tall and lean, he is bashful and self-conscious. He is thirty-two when he finally meets Peggy, the love of his life. Like him, she is a local product, but she had grown up in California. This gives her, in Vernon's eyes, an exotic quality. He thinks she is the prettiest girl he has ever seen.

Years later, Vernon and Peggy are married and without children, and Peggy has had a breast removed and is recovering from her chemotherapy and the surgery while living in their mobile home beside a pond. It is Vernon's idea to populate the pond with mallard ducks with clipped wings, so Peggy can sit and watch the ducks all day long and take her mind off her troubles. Though snapping turtles kill all but one of the ducks, Peggy loves Vernon's gesture anyway. She thinks about how Vernon never really knew her, only sees in her what he wants to see. Though truth is prized by many, sometimes a beautiful illusion, stubbornly held and jealously prized, is a better reality. Though Vernon never really knows the real Peggy, it does not matter after all, she decides, because this "had been a good enough way to live."

"GETTYSBURG"

Tully is traveling alone, going back home to North Carolina, driving back from New Jersey, where he had attended his cousin Tina's wedding. He stops in Gettysburg, Pennsylvania, for two reasons. First, he wants to visit the historic battle site, maybe do some research on his Confederate ancestors who fought and died there. The second reason is to visit his old college buddy Frank, who works at Gettysburg College. Gettysburg is the latest stop on Frank's career in academe, and Frank's latest girlfriend is Eileen, a displaced marine biologist, who greets Tully upon his arrival.

Eileen is wearing large yellow rubber gloves that Frank had convinced her to put on, as the two of them are attempting to rescue baby chimney swifts. The birds have fallen from their nest, and Frank had placed them in the gutters of the house, but he decides instead to take them to a veterinarian for better advice. After brief introductions, Frank hastily leaves home with the baby birds, and Eileen, who is less than five feet tall, is left to entertain the six-feet, eight-inch Tully. They go to a local bar, where Eileen tells Tully her life story; she's a marine biologist specializing in starfish. She and Frank often argue about Eileen's lack of career opportunities, since there is only one starfish in all of Gettysburg, and it is dead and hanging on a fish net in the local bar.

Tony Earley (AP Photo/John Russell)

As the conversation continues, Eileen and Tully walk around the Gettysburg battlefield, and Tully talks about his life back in North Carolina. Tully, who, like Frank, is in his early forties, is married to Crystal. She did not travel with Tully because the two of them are fighting. On the face of it, Tully and Crystal are fighting about a girl Tully once slept with in college, a friend of Crystal. Beneath the surface, the deep resentment is Tully's insistence years ago that Crystal have a tubal ligation. It was a decision made when the couple was younger, and presently they both regret their decision never to have children.

"Gettysburg" is a story about regret, poor communication, and missed opportunities. If Tully learns anything in this story, it is that life continues on long after youth's bloom. The impact of decisions made in one's youth can come back to haunt a person in later years. Life should not be treated so casually, and relationships grow and change over time. Tully realizes that Crystal finally agreed to have a tubal ligation and gave in to his insistence out of love for him, similar to the way Eileen has sacrificed her career to be with Frank.

"THE WIDE SEA"

The short story "The Wide Sea," which was published in *The New Yorker* in 1999, features Jim Glass, the main character in Earley's two published novels and several short stories. Young Jim is being raised by his mother and his three uncles, who all live in adjoining houses in Aliceville, North Carolina. Jim's father had died just before Jim was born.

In this story Jim is with his Uncle Al, traveling outside North Carolina for the first time in Jim's life. Driving through South Carolina at night, and then sitting watch while Uncle Al takes a nap in the truck, Jim thinks about his family and his life to this point. Though he would like to have known his father, Jim thinks he has been very lucky to have three loving uncles who have played the role of father in his life.

The purpose of the trip is to look at a team of Belgian draft horses advertised for sale in a regional newspaper. The horses were owned by Harvey Hartsell, and Jim and his uncle find the horses shot dead and attracting buzzards. Hartsell had defaulted on his farm, killed his animals, and been arrested. Before getting back in the truck, Uncle Al takes a handgun and shoots the buzzards. Uncle Al tells Jim never to make fun of the misfortune of others.

As if to save the trip, Uncle Al suggests that he and Jim take a detour to see the Atlantic Ocean. The enormity and power of the ocean, which neither Jim nor his uncle has ever seen, instills the pair with a sense of wonder. They debate whether they should take their shoes off and step in the water. Having already come this far, they decide it would be all right.

"MR. TALL"

In "Mr. Tall," published in *Southern Review* in 2009, the title character lives alone at the top of a mountain ridge. His nearest neighbors, Charlie and Plutina Scroggs Shires, have been married a few years and have never seen him. Mr. Tall, known locally by this name because of his unusual height, is a farmer. Years ago, he lost his wife and only child in a terrible accident. Since that time, neighbors have left him alone.

Plutina has escaped her father's home and the obligation of looking after her invalid mother, foisting this obligation on her sister Henrietta. Plutina's father is not sorry to see her go, and he warns Charlie not to bring her back. Charlie, in turn, warns Plutina's father not to come looking for her. Charlie is not much different from Mr. Tall. They are both bachelor farmers living alone.

To get to Charlie's farm, the couple rode the train as far as they could, and then Plutina rode Charlie's mule the rest of the way up the mountain, with Charlie walking alongside.

Charlie takes work building the highway, and he returns every Friday night to the farm. Plutina is left alone to take care of the farm during the week. As time goes by, Plutina begins to miss human companionship. Except for Charlie, she never sees another person. Of course, she knows about Mr. Tall. Everyone does. Charlie had warned her never to set foot on his farm. Loneliness gets the best of Plutina, and she leaves her farm one day, looking for Mr. Tall. She spies on his farm and sees his chicken coop, his barn, and his farmhouse. All the buildings seem well maintained, she thinks. Day after day, she hides herself at the edge of Mr. Tall's cornfield, hoping for a glimpse of the man himself. She must be spying at the wrong time of day, she thinks, because he never shows himself.

Plutina's curiosity overwhelms her, and she begins to entertain thoughts of girlish games she could play. Maybe she could just run and touch Mr. Tall's barn and run right back into hiding. She does this. Then she becomes bolder. Maybe she could run right up to Mr. Tall's house, touch it, and run right back. She tries it.

Mr. Tall has a dog living under his house. The dog barks loudly and chases Plutina into a feed bin. She thinks she could wait out the dog, but the dog never seems to tire of barking and growling. The tallest man she has ever seen, wearing a long white beard, comes out of the house. Plutina finds Mr. Tall, and he is in no mood for foolishness. After the shock of seeing another human being on his farm, and a girl besides, Mr. Tall accuses Plutina of being a thief.

Eventually, Mr. Tall gives Plutina a ride home on his mule, as she is exhausted from her adventure with his dog. To atone for her trespassing, Plutina offers to make apple pies for Mr. Tall if he would be kind enough to supply apples from his orchard.

When the weekend comes, Charlie returns home. Plutina does not tell him about Mr. Tall. However, she does tell him another secret she has been keeping. She is pregnant. Charlie is delighted, and Plutina is looking forward to raising a family.

In the next week, while Charlie is away, Mr. Tall shows up carrying bushels of freshly picked apples. True to her word, Plutina makes apple pies. When Mr. Tall returns again, a few days later, she gives him some of the apple pies. As Mr. Tall turns to go back home, Plutina says, "Mr. Tall, I'm sorry about your wife and little baby." Mr. Tall flies into a rage, cursing Plutina and her unborn child, spewing hatred."Mr. Tall," one of the best developed of all Earley's stories, presents a violent clash of personalities: male versus female, old versus young, jaded versus naïve. There is a good reason why Mr. Tall's neighbors leave him alone.

OTHER MAJOR WORKS

LONG FICTION: *Jim the Boy*, 2000; *The Blue Star*, 2008.

NONFICTION: *Somehow Form a Family: Stories That Are Mostly True*, 2001.

EDITED TEXTS: *New Stories from the South*, 1999.

BIBLIOGRAPHY

Currie, Ellen. "A Good Enough Way to Live." *The New York Times Book Review*, March 27, 1994, p. 8. This article reviews *Here We Are in Paradise Stories*, stating that the author has "a wonderful gift of deep observation, exact and wise and often funny."

Hamilton, William L. "A Writer Rebuilds a Home Called Childhood." *The New York Times*, July 13, 2000, p. 1. At home in Tennessee with the writer and his wife, soon after the publication of the author's first novel, *Jim the Boy*.

Schultz, Marc. "Not a Moment Too Earley." *Publishers Weekly* 255, no. 5 (February 4, 2008): 35. This article discusses the author's main character, Jim Glass, who appears in Earley's first novel and in three of the short stories collected in *Here We Are in Paradise Stories*.

Summer, Bob. "Tony the Writer Boy." *Publishers Weekly* 247, no. 24 (June 12, 2000): 48. This article discusses the author's bouts with depression, the release of his first novel, and inspirations for his characters, especially Jim Glass and members of Jim's family.

Randy L. Abbott

DEBORAH EISENBERG

Born: Winnetka, Illinois; November 20, 1945

PRINCIPAL SHORT FICTION

Transactions in a Foreign Currency, 1986
Under the Eighty-Second Airborne, 1992
All Around Atlantis, 1997
The Stories (So Far), 1997 (contains the previous
    two short-story collections)
Twilight of the Superheroes, 2006
The Collected Short Stories of Deborah Eisenberg,
    2010

OTHER LITERARY FORMS

Deborah Eisenberg has written almost exclusively short stories. Her first published creative work was a play, *Pastorale* (1982), and she published in 1994 a critical work about the paintings of visual artist Jennifer Bartlett.

ACHIEVEMENTS

Deborah Eisenberg has received multiple awards and recognition for her short stories. She received the Rea Award for the Short Story in 2000 and a MacArthur Foundation Fellowship, also known as a "genius grant," in 2009. Her collected short stories have been noted by five O. Henry Awards.

BIOGRAPHY

Deborah Eisenberg was born in Winnetka, Illinois, in 1945 to a pediatrician and a housewife. In interviews, she says that she was eager to get out of her hometown; she spent time wandering the United States until settling in New York City, where she got a B.A. from the New School. She identifies her long-term relationship with Wallace Shawn as the major event in her life. Shawn is a writer and actor, who might be recognized from his roles in films such as *The Princess Bride* (1987) and *My Dinner with André* (1981). Among other things, he was responsible for her travels in Central America, a location that figures regularly in her stories. Shawn's father was a longtime editor of *The New Yorker*. Eisenberg has taught at the Iowa Writers' Workshop and at other universities, and in 1994 she became a professor at the University of Virginia.

ANALYSIS

Deborah Eisenberg's fiction centers on an inspection of a central character's perspective. In first person or a carefully limited third person, the stories study that central character's attempts to understand his or her world. Often, conflict arises from the character's confusion and lack of understanding, and Eisenberg's stories often end without a sense of epiphany, a sudden glimpse of understanding that regularly characterizes the endings of contemporary short stories. If anything, the reader is left with a broader sense of just how puzzled that central character remains. Conflict in her stories is also created by cultural and sociological differences between main characters and their environment. Often the difference is economic, between privileged classes and lower ones, both inside and outside of the United States. Eisenberg's work is also distinguished by her skillful use of similes and metaphors, as she leisurely describes setting and character. Her typical short story is longer than average, though not long enough to be characterized as a novella.

"WHAT IT WAS LIKE, SEEING CHRIS"

In the collection *Transactions in a Foreign Currency*, "What It Was Like, Seeing Chris," the central character, a young teenager named Laurel, has a regular appointment with a doctor, concerning a problem with her sight, which needs monitoring. Laurel does not understand the cause of concern, just that her mother is worried that Laurel might lose her sight completely. After each appointment, Laurel goes directly to where her younger, more graceful sister has dance lessons, and they will wait for their mother. Secretly, Laurel has gotten into the habit of stopping first at a bar nearby, where she drinks a cola and talks to Chris, a twenty-seven-year-old with whom she has become infatuated. Chris leads a carefree life, with different women and friends, coming and going. Laurel describes her fascination to her friend Maureen, but she also talks about her life to Chris, who has a sympathetic ear. Because the reader's perceptions of Chris are filtered through Laurel's immature and puzzled views, it is hard to determine his motives in befriending a high school-age girl, but he does not take advantage of her when she schemes with her friend, lies to her parents about a sleep-over, and then spends the night at Chris's apartment. The two mostly talk, about issues of growing up, about how she should be old enough to recognize the consequences of her actions. The story ends with Laurel following her friend Maureen in experimenting sexually with a pair of boys their own age, a decision that leaves Laurel contemplating people's isolation from one another, as they all grow older.

"TRANSACTIONS IN A FOREIGN CURRENCY"

The title story from the collection *Transactions in a Foreign Currency* was Eisenberg's first story to be noted by the O. Henry Awards. This story opens with a first-person narrator receiving a summons from an ex-boyfriend. Despite having a job, the narrator immediately leaves for Montreal, Canada, where her former boyfriend, Otto, lives. This is not the first time she has returned to him. As soon as she arrives, though, she finds Otto has female visitors. Then, Otto leaves, to visit his son in the southern United States. The story's narrator explores Otto's life while he is gone. She dresses in the woman's clothes she finds in Otto's closet and visits some local stores, where she creates a new identity for herself. She has a long conversation with a male friend of Otto, who has entered the house uninvited. Otto owes money to the visitor for some drugs Otto had purchased. At first the narrator is frightened, but she grows curious about this aspect of Otto's life. The story ends with Otto's return. The narrator seems finally able to separate her life from Otto, as she ponders how people cannot decide how they might live their own lives.

Deborah Eisenberg (AP Photo/Charles Sykes)

"CUSTODIANS"

Eisenberg's second collection, *Under the Eighty-Second Airborne*, contains the story "Custodians." This story opens in a successful food store, run by the central character Lynnie. She looks up to see Isobel, a girl whose friendship Lynnie pursued when they were both children. Lynnie always has been puzzled about why Isobel suddenly left one day, driven off to live with family in another town. When Isobel was bored, she would be friends with the younger Lynnie because they were neighbors, even though the two girls belonged to different social classes. In the frame story that opens and closes the narrative, Lynnie appears to be the more successful of the pair, but in the main story, set in their childhood, Isobel runs with college-track children, while Lynnie takes the remedial classes. Isobel's father is in management for the company at which Lynnie's single mother works as an hourly employee and worries about layoffs. Both girls spend time with another family they have discovered moving into a huge but hidden old house. The new owner is a faculty member at the local college. He is married to a woman who was once his student. Lynnie is fascinated by her glimpses at this alternate world, with its different sets of rules. She is paid to babysit the family's small children, while Isobel sits as a model for a painting. Lynnie finds this new family wonderful, a feeling her mother does not share. By the end of the story, the reader realizes that Isobel had to leave because of her underage relationship with the teacher. Ignored Lynnie has grown up to be successful, though she is still full of doubt.

"The Girl Who Left Her Sock on the Floor"

Eisenberg's next collection, *All Around Atlantis*, opens with a story regularly found in anthologies, "The Girl Who Left Her Sock on the Floor." The story starts with two school roommates arguing about what a slob one is. As far as the central character Francie is concerned, there is no need to worry about a simple sock that has not been picked up yet. The world is full of far bigger issues, according to Francie. Just how much bigger, she discovers when she is summoned to the headmaster's office. As Francie's mind races through possible problems related to school, she is told her mother has died, leaving Francie all alone. Her single mother had fallen, breaking a hip, but complications led to a heart attack and death. Francie returns to their empty apartment and looks at the lone cup left in the sink. She goes to the hospital to make arrangements for her mother's burial. There she discovers that arrangements have already been made. An even bigger surprise is that Francie's father has made them. She has always been told he died in a car accident. Feeling a bit like that abandoned, out-of-place sock, Francie introduces herself to her father. The story ends with her waiting for his return, as she contemplates life and considers how no one can ever guess what life holds in store.

"Across the Lake"

The O. Henry Award-winning story "Across the Lake" exhibits Eisenberg's skill with the third-person limited point of view, as it explores the perceptions of Rob, a college student visiting an unidentified country in Central America. Wishing to get away from the places in the tourist guidebooks, he accepts a ride from a couple he has met, to visit a small village on the other side of the lake. Rob is full of fear: He has obsessive worries about drinking the water and eating the local food, concern whether the owner of the little hotel is dealing drugs, terror that the revolutionaries in the unstable country will visit the village during the night. Since all perceptions are filtered through Rob's insecure viewpoint, determining what is real and what is worry is impossible. On the one hand, Mick, the male member of the couple with a car, is physically sick. On the other hand, the story ends with Rob starting to undress Mick's girlfriend, about whom Rob has expressed nothing but negative views throughout the story.

"Mermaids"

Another O. Henry Award-winning story in the collection, "Mermaids," also creates puzzles about the central character's motivations and feelings. This story follows Kyla, a middle school-age girl, as she accompanies a classmate, Janey; her little sister; and their father on a spring-break trip to New York. Kyla does not enjoy the trip, and she does not seem to like Janey, but both appear to have gone out of obligation. Kyla watches Janey's father rule his daughters' lives, as he tells them, for instance, they "really" want a fruit cup to eat, at a place that serves delicious ice-cream sundaes. Kyla hides her true feelings, as the reader realizes that Janey, at least, has realized that the true reason for the week-long trip is not so her father can bond with his daughters, as he has claimed, or to give their mother some peace and quiet: The father has a girlfriend along on the trip as well.

Twilight of the Superheroes

Eisenberg's collection *Twilight of the Superheroes* follows the models of the previous collections, though with a deepening and thickening of stories, as each long story contains the material for a whole novel. For the first time, stories exit the limited point of view of either first-person monologues or limited third-person omniscient, to shift between contrasting perspectives. In addition, the events of September 11, 2001, leave a shadow over the collection.

An anthologized story, "Some Other, Better Otto," shows how Eisenberg's stories have deepened, as this story explores what makes the central character Otto so unhappy. Different aspects of his life--his immediate family, from which he is fairly estranged; his emotionally challenged sister, a part of his estrangement; his longtime gay relationship with his partner--are all sorted through, leaving Otto to acknowledge that happiness would require him to be a different person.

The collection contains two stories also noted by the O. Henry Awards, and one, "Windows," was singled out as a jurors' favorite. Its central image, that of a window covered over with plastic sheeting and weatherstripping, rendering it almost opaque, describes how hard it can be to understand the motivation of the central character, Alma, who is on the run from an abusive boyfriend and has a small child, belonging to her boyfriend and another woman, in tow. The other story, "Like It or Not," also challenges the reader's sense of values, when it shifts from the view of an anxious American, to that of an Italian male, who will take advantage of an underage teen.

"Twilight of the Superheroes"

The title story, "Twilight of the Superheroes," explores the events surrounding the terrorist attacks on the Twin Towers in New York. The story skillfully shifts among several characters, each with a different reaction to the powerful event. One group is made up of young adults, somewhat trying to launch their adult lives in New York, somewhat trying to avoid entering adulthood. The main character from that circle of friends, Nathaniel, draws a comic strip about a character named Passivityman, who represents an inability to move forward or even to act, regardless of opportunities, challenges, or problems. However, Nathaniel and his friends must move on, partially because they must vacate the wonderful apartment where they live, because the owner is returning from out of the country. This incredible apartment has lost its perfection, too, in that its beautiful view of New York City also enabled them to watch the Twin Towers collapse.

Nathaniel and his friends are puzzling and frustrating to his uncle, Lucien. Lucien is struggling with the death of his wife, who still visits him at quiet moments as a ghost. This loss has left Lucien feeling old. The third thread in this story concerns Nathaniel's parents. Lucien has married into the family, to the younger sister. Nathaniel's parents were raised by refugees at the end of World War II, people who had lost family members in the Holocaust. All these different characters come together in a story that is a meditation on the horrors in the world.

Other major works

PLAY: *Pastorale*, pb. 1982.

NONFICTION: *Air, Twenty-Four Hours: Jennifer Bartlett*, 1994

Bibliography

Eisenberg, Deborah. "Fiction Versus Consensus." *Michigan Quarterly Review* 48, no. 3 (Summer, 2009): p. 386. A lecture in which the author describes her views on the purpose of fiction.

Kakutani, Michiko. "Sideswiped by Things Unexpected." *The New York Times*, February 7, 2006. A review of the book *Twilight of the Superheroes*, in which the reviewer notes Eisenberg's "playwright's ear for dialogue and a journalistic eye for the askew detail."

Lucas, Craig. "Deborah Eisenberg." *Bomb* (Fall, 1989). A perceptive interview that describes Eisenberg's development as a writer.

Swift, Daniel. "A Writer's Life: Deborah Eisenberg." *The Telegraph*, July 30, 2006. A review that discusses Eisenberg's political viewpoint.

Thompson, Jean. "Don't Have a Nice Day." *The New York Times*, April 16, 2010. A review of Eisenberg's collected short stories, by a noted short-story writer.

Brian L. Olson

STANLEY ELKIN

Born: Brooklyn, New York; May 11, 1930
Died: St. Louis, Missouri; May 31, 1995

PRINCIPAL SHORT FICTION

Criers and Kibitzers, Kibitzers and Criers, 1965
The Making of Ashenden, 1972
Searches and Seizures, 1973
The Living End, 1979
Stanley Elkin's Greatest Hits, 1980
Early Elkin, 1985
Van Gogh's Room at Arles: Three Novellas, 1993

OTHER LITERARY FORMS

In addition to his short fiction, Stanley Elkin produced several novels, including *Boswell: A Modern Comedy* (1964), *The Rabbi of Lud* (1987), and *The MacGuffin* (1991). He also wrote a screenplay, *The Six-Year-Old Man* (1968), a memoir, *Why I Live Where I Live* (1983), and a collection of essays, *Pieces of Soap: Essays* (1992). In addition, Elkin edited several collections of short fiction and wrote numerous reviews and works of literary criticism for scholarly journals.

ACHIEVEMENTS

Over the course of his career, Stanley Elkin received numerous grants and awards. He won the Longview Foundation Award in 1962; the *Paris Review* prize in 1965; a John Simon Guggenheim Memorial Foundation Fellowship in 1966; a Rockefeller Foundation Fellowship and an American Academy of Arts and Letters grant in 1968; a Rosenthal Foundation Award in 1980; a *Sewanee Review* award in 1981; and a National Book Critics Circle Award in 1983. Three of his books were nominated for the National Book Award, and *Van Gogh's Room at Arles: Three Novellas* was a finalist for the PEN/Faulkner Award for Fiction.

BIOGRAPHY

Stanley Lawrence Elkin was born in Brooklyn, New York, on May 11, 1930. He grew up in Chicago and was educated at the University of Illinois at Urbana, where he earned his B.A. and M.A., and his Ph.D. in English in 1961. While still at the University of Illinois, Elkin married Joan Marion Jacobson, an artist; together they became the parents of two sons and a daughter. After serving in the armed forces for two years (1955-1957), Elkin spent several years living in London and Rome with his wife, prior to writing his first novel, *Boswell* (1964). His second novel, *A Bad Man* (1967), was written on a John Simon Guggenheim Memorial Foundation Fellowship. His short fiction, much of it later integrated into his novels, has been collected in many anthologies.

In 1960, before earning his Ph.D., Elkin taught English at Washington University in St. Louis. He was assistant professor (1962-1966) and associate professor (1966-1969) before becoming a full professor of English in 1969. In 1983, he became a Kling Professor of Modern Letters. He was a visiting lecturer and visiting professor at several institutions, including Smith College, the University of California at Santa Barbara, the University of Wisconsin at Milwaukee, Yale University, and Boston University.

Death is a key subject in Elkin's fiction, as is the obverse. Perhaps his heightened sense of death and life stems from the fact that he suffered from multiple sclerosis, which was diagnosed in 1961. He died of a heart attack in St. Louis in 1995.

ANALYSIS

From the time Stanley Elkin emerged in the mid-1960's, critics applauded his novels and short fiction as some of the best satirical writing in American literature. His stories--often labeled black humor--are essentially dark, urban comedies in which unusually articulate, marginal figures struggle to define themselves in a confusing and chaotic modern world. Often the means of definition is essentially linguistic, as the characters attempt to construct an understanding of themselves and their place in the modern world through language itself. The interplay between the characters' harsh circumstances and their ability to overcome those circumstances through language is the hallmark of Elkin's satire. Throughout his work, Elkin depicts extremes of personality--people in crisis, engaging in personal (if, from external perception, trivial) cataclysms. His characters are often grotesque; Elkin has written, "I stand in awe of the outré." His stories do not hinge on plot; in fact, often little "happens" in the stories. Rather, they delineate a situation and resolution of greater internal than external consequence. A key to Elkin's art is rhetoric. He uses a rich variety of language composed of "shoptalk," the lingo of the professions of his characters: grocers, bailbondsmen, hipsters, and collection agents. His characters, however, do not speak consistently "realistic" speech. Many of his characters magically possess the full range of rhetorical possibility, from gutter speech to learned philosophical flights, while many are also conversant with areas of knowledge far beyond their nominal experience--a metaphorical representation of their heightened consciousnesses. Elkin does not seek literal verisimilitude in his characters' speech. This fictive rhetoric, like that of Henry James, is deliberate artifice. Elkin has written, "Rhetoric doesn't occur in life. It occurs in fiction. Fiction gives an opportunity for rhetoric to happen. It provides a stage where language can stand." Elkin's characters obsessively seek to make contact with their worlds, and their "fierce language" is both a symbol and a product of that aggression.

"EVERYTHING MUST GO!"

In "Everything Must Go!," a story that later became a part of *A Bad Man*, along with "The Garbage Dump" and "The Merchant of New Desires," a young Jewish boy has traveled to southern Illinois with his half-mad father, who is a peddler of rags and snatches--a demented master salesman who can sell anything--who, in fact, has defined himself existentially as an archetype of the Jewish peddler fulfilling the biblical prophecy of the Diaspora. His son loves and hates his father, feeling acutely his "otherness," and is alternately amused and horrified by his father's mad intensity. The man sells everything, including individual months torn from calendars: "April," he called in February, "just out. Get your April here." He sells from his wagon "old magazines, chapters from books, broken pencils, ruined pens, eraser ends in small piles, string, rope, cork scraped from the insides of bottle caps. . . . "

The man tries to educate his son in the fine art of hawking wares, insisting that the American-born lad (neither is an immigrant) sound like the archetypal peddler: "Not 'rags' not 'old *clothes*.' What are you, an announcer on the radio? You're in a street! Say 'regs,' 'all cloze.' Shout it, sing it. I want to hear steerage, Ellis Island in that throat." The boy's call decays into "Rugs, oil cloths!" and "Rex, wild clits." "Terrific, . . . wild clits is very good. We'll make our way. . . . "

The story reaches a climax when the father invades a county fair's ox-pulling contest, and in a hilarious and manic display, sells every item on a wagon towering with junk. Throughout the tale the father has referred to one "unsalable thing," which he finally reveals to his son is himself. When at last he dies of cancer, the son, metamorphosing into the true salesman, proves the father wrong. He calls the doctor to tell him that the father has died. "They argued . . . but it was no use. The doctor, on behalf of the tiny hospital, could offer him only fifteen dollars for the body."

The son, named Feldman, grows into a department store magnate, as the reader finds out in the novel. Feldman eventually turns to a life of crime, is arrested, and revolutionizes the prison to which he is sent through the use of the same gifts and manias that possessed his father. (Another story excerpted from the novel, "The Merchant of New Desires," hilariously depicts Feldman's running of the prison commissary, which has become an avatar of his father's wagon.) Together, the stories form a potent and typical introduction to Elkin's work. The language is nonstop; the "vaudeville-like patter" is continuous. The manic events mask a desperate attempt to form an identity and connect with the world. Both the situations and the rhetoric display the art of the bizarre, the grotesque manifestations of feverishly heightened consciousness and wild emotional excess.

The rhetorical aspects of Elkin's fiction combine with an exact description of every setting. Hotel rooms, for example, are described down to the texture and grain of the plastic wood veneers of the dressers and the weave of the drapes. The stark realism of locale combined with the wild multifaceted language of the characters (who often narrate their own stories) form a unique texture. Throughout, the language is not an end in itself, but rather a clue to the personality of the characters, a metaphor for their psychological states. Elkin's typical protagonists are salesmen, con men, and "consumed consumers" who may be down and out but are struggling obsessively and subjectively, acutely conscious of their every impulse and atom of their surroundings. They exist in a world of objective, unthinking, "normal" people whose lack of engagement is a source of alienation and a cause for despair. They are frequently "ordinary" characters with brutally heightened consciousnesses in discontinuity with themselves and their milieu. Their monologues and harangues, often wildly funny, at other times tragically touching, are an attempt to discover their essences through the medium of language itself. The world does not become knowable, if ever, until expressed verbally.

"IN THE ALLEY"

Fearful of losing their identities, Elkin's characters push life to its fatal limits until it retaliates. At times, they give in to their malaise with a brutal intensity. Feldman, the hero of "In the Alley," from the collection *Criers and Kibitzers, Kibitzers and Criers*, is suffering from a terminal disease and has been told that he will die in a year. He uses the time to die gracefully, stoically, with dignity; dying becomes his identity and life. His body, however, perversely refuses to die on schedule, and his new identity becomes absurd to him. He enters a hospital terminal ward to await his end and to immerse himself in his impending demise, to connect with others in the same plight. His body still refuses to cooperate, and he is disabused of his self-concept of the stoic, heroic dier. There is no "fraternity among the sick."

Feldman wanders about the city, a Joycean "Nighttown" of working-class bars, enters one, and takes up conversation with a muscular Slavic woman with a tattooed wrist. He tells her of his imminent but frustratingly deferred death, at first seeking affection and solace. Finally, however, seeking release and using the woman as an agent, he brings about his own doom. He tries to seduce her, and the woman, with the help of a tough female bartender, beats him senseless. He is carried out to the alley, a sign pinned to his suit reading "STAY AWAY FROM WHITE WOMEN." Surrounded by garbage, Feldman, finally dying, thinks of his family, who had anticipated his death with admiration and compassion and "unmasked hope that it would never come to this for them, but that if it should, if it ever should, it would come with grace. But nothing came gracefully--not to heroes."

"THE BAILBONDSMAN"

One of the very best pieces of fiction Elkin has produced is "The Bailbondsman," one of the three novellas (the others are "The Making of Ashenden" and "The Condominium") in *Searches and Seizures*. Shifting effortlessly between first-and third-person narration, the story relates a day in the life of a classically obsessive Elkin protagonist, Alexander Main, a "Phoenecian" bailbondsman in Cincinnati--a member of an extinct race, practitioner of a trade that requires him to consort with all layers of life, from the ermine of the bench to prostitutes. He is greedy for total immersion in his milieu and obsessed by the mystery of the meaning of his life and its relation to the world. "I have no taste, only hunger," he says--a literal pun, for he has no sense of taste, and food is only fuel to Main. He succeeds in his profession because he is a master of rhetoric and can persuade judges to set bail and persuade clients to seek his services rather than those of his competitors. His Whitman-like consciousness absorbs everything--history, science, the codes of the underworld, literature--with total abandon. All experience floods his consciousness with equal priority, filtered through his expansive rhetoric. He dotes on language; even Crainpool, his gray assistant, enjoys his constant patter about everything from the allegorical parasitology of the liver fluke to the prehistoric teeth Main examines in a museum, tears coursing down his face as he thinks of the fugacity of life. Everything is emblemized.

Main is obsessed with the memory of Oyp and Glyp, the only clients who have ever jumped bail. He dreams of them as grave robbers in an ornate Egyptian tomb. The dream is a profusion of opulent archeological imagery. In his dream, Main apprehends the fiends, but the Egyptian judge foils him by refusing to set bail for a crime so horrendous and then compounds the affront by setting the thieves free because there can be no appropriate punishment. Oyp and Glyp represent to Main his potential lack of control over his environment, which is threatened by legal changes that may make his trade obsolete, and his inability to dominate totally his world and the mystery it represents.

Main's obsession with domination leads him to his assistant's apartment, where it is revealed that Crainpool had jumped bail years ago and that Main had harbored him from prosecution by employing him. He is "the only man in the world [he is] allowed to kill." Main prepares to execute Crainpool, and the story ends as Main shoots Crainpool in the hand and chases out after him into the night. The "seizure" that ends Main's search is obsessive, cruel, and destructive, but also a crushing embrace of the life force. Like Feldman, Main is determined to register his presence in the implacable universe.

VAN GOGH'S ROOM AT ARLES

Most critics agree that the title novella in Elkin's collection of three stories is the strongest. The story centers on an undistinguished professor named Miller from a community college in Indiana, who, when granted a fellowship to attend a think-tank retreat in Arles in southern France, ends up being housed in the bedroom of Vincent Van Gogh. Indeed, the room contains the nightstand, the basin and pitcher, and the cane-bottomed chair depicted in Van Gogh's famous painting entitled "Vincent's Bedroom in Arles."

Miller is something of an "innocent abroad," at first unimpressed by the famous room and obviously outclassed by his more distinguished colleagues at the retreat. However, he gradually begins to appreciate the obligation the room places on him and makes a valiant, albeit feeble, effort to do some thinking while at the think tank, cobbling together a research "project" about the attitudes university professors have toward the lowly community college.

Miller's sense of inadequacy is heightened throughout the story by the continual discovery of scenes from some of Van Gogh's most famous paintings, all of which create the illusion of Miller's moving in a world of art: "The Night Café in the Place Lamartine in Arles," "Fishing Boats on the Beach at Saintes-Maries," "The Langlois Bridge at Arles," and "The Railway Bridge over Avenue Montmajour, Arles." Even more challenging is the appearance of a number of Arles residents who look like characters in several Van Gogh paintings. A doctor who comes to see Miller after he faints from stress and jet lag and who looks like Van Gogh's "Portrait of Dr. Félix Rey" tells Miller that descendants of Van Gogh's models still live in Arles. Miller is more disoriented by this mix of past and present, art and reality, when he sees a man who looks like Van Gogh's "The Seated Zouave" and a boy in a field with a great bag of seeds on his shoulder who looks like Van Gogh's "The Sower."

These encounters come to a climax when additional members of the "Club of the Portraits of the Descendants of the People Painted by Vincent Van Gogh" come to Miller's room to give him advice for what the doctor calls his "sprained soul." Miller's final encounter with a Van Gogh painting occurs when he is introduced to Madame Ginoux, who, when they meet, bends her arm at the elbow and presses the knuckles to the side of her face in a pensive salute, exactly like the gesture in Van Gogh's "Madame Ginoux with Gloves and Umbrella."

At the end of the story, although the mundane Miller has not been radically altered by his visit to the art world of Van Gogh, he is not the same either, for the world of art has made him more responsive to the mysteries and beauties of life. He understands that although one cannot create like an artist, one may still try to see as an artist sees.

OTHER MAJOR WORKS

LONG FICTION: *Boswell: A Modern Comedy*, 1964; *A Bad Man*, 1967; *The Dick Gibson Show*, 1971; *The Franchiser*, 1976; *George Mills*, 1982; *Stanley Elkin's the Magic Kingdom*, 1985 (also known as *The Magic Kingdom*); *The Rabbi of Lud*, 1987; *The MacGuffin*, 1991; *Mrs. Ted Bliss*, 1995.

SCREENPLAY: *The Six-Year-Old Man*, 1968.

NONFICTION: *Why I Live Where I Live*, 1983; *Pieces of Soap: Essays*, 1992.

BIBLIOGRAPHY

Bailey, Peter J. *Reading Stanley Elkin*. Urbana: University of Illinois Press, 1985. This study of Elkin's fiction examines his major themes in order to counteract misreadings of him as another in a series of black humorists, especially given Elkin's association with black humorists of the 1960's. Each of the seven chapters discusses a separate theme or thematic element in Elkin's work. Includes a comprehensive index.

Bargen, Doris G. *The Fiction of Stanley Elkin*. Frankfurt, Germany: Verlag Peter D. Lang, 1980. The first book-length work of criticism on Elkin. Examines his association with the literary movements of metafiction, black humor, American Jewish writers, and popular-culture novels. Bargen argues that Elkin's work is similar in some ways to all of these movements but dissimilar enough to resist categorization. Includes an extensive biography, an interview with the author, and a comprehensive bibliography and index.

Cohen, Sarah Blacher, ed. *Comic Relief: Humor in Contemporary American Literature*. Urbana: University of Illinois Press, 1978. Several authors engage in a discussion of the role of humor in the writers who emerged in the 1960's and 1970's, with Elkin figuring prominently in the discussion. Cohen aligns Elkin with black humorists, identifying their common traits--for example, their need to laugh at the absurdity of modern culture.

Dougherty, David C. *Shouting Down the Silence: A Biography of Stanley Elkin*. Urbana: University of Illinois Press, 2010. The first full-length biography of Elkin, which describes the writer's thwarted desire to attain popular acclaim as well as critical praise. Includes analysis of some of the short stories.

_____. *Stanley Elkin*. Boston: Twayne, 1990. Dougherty discusses all of the fiction through *The Rabbi of Lud*, including stories and novellas, emphasizing Elkin's almost poetic use of language and sense of vocation. The chronology, brief biography, bibliography of secondary works, and discussion of the uses and limitations of classifying Elkin as a Jewish American writer, a satirist, a black humorist, and a metafictionist make this an especially useful work.

Gelfant, Blanche H., ed. *The Columbia Companion to the Twentieth-Century American Short Story*. New York: Columbia University Press, 2000. Includes a chapter in which Elkin's short stories are analyzed.

New England Review 27, no. 4 (Fall, 2006). This entire issue is devoted to Elkin. It features recollections from writers and other people who knew him, as well as two of his previously unpublished short stories, "Baseball Story" and "Colin Kelly's Kids." In addition, Elkin biographer David C. Dougherty contributes a seven-page review of these two stories.

Olderman, Raymond M. *Beyond the Waste Land: The American Novel in the Nineteen Sixties*. New Haven, Conn.: Yale University Press, 1972. Olderman's study is the first treatment of Elkin's fiction in the context of other emerging authors of the 1960's. He discusses Elkin and others of his generation, repudiating the image of modern society as the "wasteland" depicted in T. S. Eliot's landmark 1922 poem. Olderman identifies a new kind of idealism emerging in contemporary fiction.

Pinsker, Sanford. "Sickness unto Style." *Gettysburg Review* 7 (1994): 437-445. Discusses Elkin's collection of novellas *Van Gogh's Room at Arles* and his collection of essays *Pieces of Soap* primarily in terms of prose style. Discusses how the Van Gogh novella focuses on pictures within pictures and is an example of Impressionism in the Van Gogh manner.

Pughe, Thomas. *Comic Sense: Reading Robert Coover, Stanley Elkin, Philip Roth*. Boston: Birkhäuser Verlag, 1994. Explores the humor in each author's fiction.

The Review of Contemporary Fiction 15 (Summer, 1995). Special issue on Elkin, with essays by Jerome Klinkowitz, Jerome Charyn, William H. Gass, and others. Features an interview with Elkin in which he discusses the mystery in his fiction, the nature of plot, the essence of story, and his prose style.

Robins, William M. *Stanley Elkin: A Comprehensive Bibliography*. Lanham, Md.: Scarecrow Press, 2009. An extensive compilation of all of Elkin's writings, nonprint media adaptations, quotes, and editorial ventures, as well as all of the significant writings about Elkin and his work, such as interviews, criticism, awards, obituaries, manuscripts, and Internet references. An indispensable reference for researchers.

Vinson, James, ed. *Contemporary Novelists*. 2d ed. New York: St. Martin's Press, 1976. A comprehensive and broad study. Vinson includes Elkin in an overview of writers from the 1960's and 1970's. The section that covers Elkin most comprehensively is the section written by David Demarest, Jr., who discusses Elkin's place among his contemporaries.

David Sadkin
Updated by Edward Huffstetler
and Charles E. May

GEORGE P. ELLIOTT

Born: Knightstown, Indiana; June 16, 1918
Died: New York, New York; May 3, 1980

PRINCIPAL SHORT FICTION
Among the Dangs, 1961
An Hour of Last Things, and Other Stories, 1968

OTHER LITERARY FORMS

George P. Elliott's published works include poetry; personal, philosophical, and literary essays (originally published in such journals as *Commentary, Commonweal, The Nation, The Atlantic Monthly, Harpers,* and *The Writer*); and novels. He is best known for his short stories, however--particularly those collected in *Among the Dangs*.

ACHIEVEMENTS

As an American novelist and short-story writer, George P. Elliott proved himself as a craftsman of modern realistic fiction. His work was influenced by earlier masters of that tradition, such as Henry James, Joseph Conrad, and James Joyce, as well as prose stylists of the eighteenth and nineteenth centuries. The thoughts of early modern poets, such as William Butler Yeats and W. H. Auden, also had an impact on his writing. While incorporating experimental elements into his work, Elliott consistently affirmed the vitality of the traditional. His honors and awards include a

Hudson Review Fellowship in fiction from 1956 to 1957; a John Simon Guggenheim Memorial Foundation Fellowship from 1961 to 1962; the Indiana Authors' Day Award in 1962 for *Among the Dangs*; the D. H. Lawrence Fellowship at the University of New Mexico in 1962; a Ford Foundation fellowship for writing in connection with the theater from 1965 to 1966; and the National Institute of Arts and Letters award in 1969.

BIOGRAPHY

George Paul Elliott was the eldest of four children (he had two younger brothers and a sister), and he was born on a farm near Knightstown, Indiana, a small country town. His father, Paul Revere Elliott, descended from several generations of Quaker farmers. His mother, Nita Gregory, came from a Methodist family. Since his father did not succeed in making a living from farming in Indiana, the family moved to Southern California, near Riverside, in 1928. There, his father worked on a carob plantation. When the plantation failed in the 1930's, Elliott's father worked as an irrigator until he retired.

After reading Samuel Taylor Coleridge's *The Rime of the Ancient Mariner* (1798) when he was a child, Elliott decided that he would spend his life writing stories and poems. From the time he graduated high school in 1934 until after World War II, he held a variety of jobs. Working his way through college, he first attended Riverside Junior College, then the University of California at Berkeley, where he received his M.A. in English in 1941, the year he married Mary Emma Jeffress; the couple's only child was born in 1943. Elliott was exempted from military service during World War II for medical reasons.

In 1947, Elliott assumed his first teaching post at St. Mary's College, near Oakland, California, and he taught English there for eight years. He then taught for a year at Cornell University and the University of Iowa Writers' Workshop, spent one semester at that University of California at Berkeley, spent three years at Barnard College, and finally remained at his post at Syracuse University for the remainder of his life.

Elliott, more concerned with content than form, explored his fundamentally Christian convictions in a number of novels and short stories. At the beginning of his career, his writing, according to him, consisted of "deadly naturalism, conventional versification, and bloodless fantasy." His dominant literary aim, however, later turned to the idea of infusing "poetic fantasy with the blood of life." Elliott died on May 3, 1980, in New York City.

ANALYSIS

In the fictions of George P. Elliott, individuals discover the limitations or the wrongness of their beliefs or, at least, the complications in their motives, actions, and relations with the world. Quite often, the reader shares in a character's embarrassment or horror from a close distance; but at best, the characters come to revelations to which the mind, senses, and emotions all contribute, as do chance and the acts (or meddling) of other humans. Individuals struggle with various forms of pride; social, psychological, and sexual confusions; blinding imprisonment by fixed ideas; and the need for integration in a marketplace of specialists. The characters appear in groups (microcosms) which they belong to blindly or intrude upon with their motives mixed; and the strains operating upon these groups, particularly the families, make concrete universal stresses. Traditional values are never far from mind, although they are likely to be acted upon by doubting and nihilistic characters. When the characters are hopeful, their hope springs from their discovery of mute pride and zeal and the unmasking of their insecurities, resulting in sympathy.

Because the characters generally are real and their failures elicit compassion, and the reader is not put off by utter condemnations of humanity or stylistic trivialities, the experience of reading Elliott encourages questing among the mysteries of human nature. What makes his more hopeful visions convincing in their optimism is that they are not exaggerated; Elliott's characters make small adjustments in a style that has been called "cool" and from which irony, satire, and other deflators of pretension are never distant. The difficulties in reading his work are never great because the storytelling carries readers through the complications and close attention to the characters brings readers to feel and see. Elliott called the style that achieves this moral end "formal-seeming, of a certain polish, rather distancing." He explained his didacticism as depending upon the "complex relationships among storyteller, characters and readers" and an "aesthetic distance," without which "there is not likely to be much moral clarity."

"THE NRACP"

In the popular anthology piece "The NRACP," collected in *Among the Dangs*, Elliott accomplishes this end by a satirical use of first-person narration. Andrew Dixon's letters imply related and recurrent themes, the ironic disparity between appearance and reality, humans' inhumanity to humans, and humans' misuse of thought and language to obscure the truth. Set near the present (when Christian morality is considered to be relic of which to rid oneself), the story unfolds a government plot to deal with "the negro problem in America" by exploiting prejudices at work within an apparent democracy. On the surface, the government appears to be relocating African Americans, a program that does not upset more than a few dissidents; but in truth, the blacks are to be reprocessed into meat for export and fed to the unwitting white bureaucracy. Like Jonathan Swift's, Elliott's satire is often painfully lucid.

Andy Dixon is one of these bureaucrats. His job, he thinks, is to rewrite the interned blacks' letters before they are sent out. By the time he discovers what is happening, he lacks the moral will to oppose it, and he struggles to put the horror from his mind. The story is chilling, first, because it is not far from other episodes in actual history, and second, because Andy, although obtuse, is credible and not entirely unscrupulous or inhumane. He represents a middle path between extremes, an educated Everyman. Elliott's characters are not simply allegorical, but, like the characters in morality tales, they face elemental problems. It takes Andy a long time to see the truth, much longer than it takes the reader; this delay allows the irony to take root. To feed the irony, other characters see the truth much sooner but are incapable of acting or are unconcerned. O'Doone's suspicious nature causes him to bring invisible ink for messages, but when the truth crumbles him, he kills himself. Ruth, a secretary whom Andy marries, may know the truth, but whether she does matters little because she is not bothered by moral scruples. Her philosophy excludes the relevance of morality: "There are those who get it and those who dish it out," she says, and she intends "to be on the side of the dishers."

What blinds an apparently educated person to the nature of things? The question, implied by a number of Elliot's stories, could be answered variously, but Andy's case is representative. Although his reading--including Swift, Auden, and Joyce--suggests sophistication, Andy admits that he has never known himself. This may be true, but even if it is, it sounds theatrical; indeed, a large part of his problem is his infatuation with the way he sounds. In the first letter, he enjoys sneering at the place, at those who love reading mysteries, and at the black culture. In the second letter, he enjoys admitting his former ignorance and then congratulates himself on his newfound "largeness of spirit"; he is eating up the rhetoric. By the time Ruth enters, Andy has shown off a large vocabulary, but he has also raised some suspicions about whether he can use language truthfully. When he escalates Ruth's "dishers" and "getters" maxim into a "post-Christian golden rule" and her tired dig at his love of guilt into "Dostoevskian notions," he is, indeed, "a balloon" in a "rarefied atmosphere." Andy, like other characters in Elliott's canon, is a sentimentalist, prejudiced against blacks and peers alike and in love with the sound of his own voice.

Indicative of Elliott's wisdom, he does not overwork the obtuseness of the first-person narrator but develops Andy's character, thus complicating judgment

by soliciting compassion. This development is clearly on its way in the eighth letter, when Andy sees a black woman's yearning for her man and is moved by it. Andy's rhetoric is still exaggerated ("I have been discovering that the wells of pity, which have lain so long locked and frozen in my eyes, are thawed in me now"); and, in invisibility, he still allows himself to sneer. When however, he says plainly, "I cannot tell you how I pitied both these unhappy people," he has stopped taking his own pulse and is now feeling empathy for someone else. The last letter shows him splitting dangerously in two. In discussing Ruth's pregnancy, he launches into a visible, cosmic rhetoric that apes Shakespearean flights; but he invisibly recounts O'Doone's actual and his own contemplated suicide in short, deflated sentences. After the guard's indictment of his cannibalism, Andy stays invisible, disgusted but desiring to forget. Finally, he elicits some degree of sympathy because in a world that does not encourage "felt understanding," he has known someone else's hurt, and his numbing chant masks nervousness and pain.

Elliott has a painter's or an architect's regard for form, and, as a critic of the theater, he knows how the treatment of space can effect a mood or work upon the feelings of his characters. He is a master of juxtaposition (as a cool stylist needs to be), and he can use a pattern of scenes to turn ideas nearly palpable. In "The NRACP," Andy blames his initial depression on "the rasping, blinding landscape." Retreating from the overcrowded reading room, he finds his only other choice indoors to be his "own cell" and "cot." Eventually, relief appears to come from the walks he takes "toward two" vast "realities": himself and the natural world. These walks, however, bring him also to the entrapment of long windowless sheds and fences and, finally, to enlightenment. After a dose too great to stand, he stays entrapped; even on a good day, when a bird sings outside, he thinks only of his cot and sleep, murmuring the narcotic chant, "My wife is going to have a baby, my wife is going to have a baby, my wife is going to have a baby."

AN HOUR OF LAST THINGS, AND OTHER STORIES

Such images of adult humans reduced almost to fetal sleep appear increasingly in Elliott's second volume, *An Hour of Last Things, and Other Stories*. For example, the reduction of hope and promise of paranoia and a pathetic death-in-life controls the nightmarish "Better to Burn." Occasionally, a good Samaritan intrudes--as Anna tries to do (but fails to help) in "Better to Burn" and as Brother Nicholas succeeds in doing in "Into the Cone of Cold," the collection's opening story. This novella-length quest narrative, reminiscent of Joseph Conrad's *Heart of Darkness* (1899, serial; 1902, book), employs the science-fiction premise that a man can be projected into the void and brought back to write about it. What occurs, however, is a blank "in his memory," an unsettling reversal of some bodily parts, and the fear that "the void has spread into" him and fills the place where his soul had been. In this world (as in the reader's), there has been a threatening complication of the orders of power. The Catholic fathers of St. Anselm's, where Stuart, the central character, is teaching, are more convincing as scientists, engineers, and bureaucrats than as Christians. Under the pall of physical and psychological reverses, Stuart sets out to find his Kurtz, former Brother Carl, the brains behind the experiment at St. Anselm's. Carl, a genius, has been so affected by his role in the experiment that he has left the order and gone off to dive into a mystery that, unlike the cone of cold, at least yields actual abalone. Still curious about the experience of the void, Carl agrees to meet with Stuart, but their verbal wrestling helps little, if at all. Then, by chance, Stuart stumbles onto where Carl dives and focuses on the "granite oceanic sculpture" where Carl swims. Stuart feels he has "participated in a ritual of revelation"--an archetype of a man at work in the most mysterious depth in the world from which a man may bring back something tangible, chipped by a kind of art from stubborn stone.

When Stuart returns to his wife, Marguerite, he finds her under such a strain from his experience that she leaves him, crying that his respect for her is not enough "to think up a story" she "could at least swallow enough of to keep one little shred of self-respect." Feeling he is a failure, Stuart finds himself a furnished room and withdraws into bed. On the fifth day, when Stuart is nearly a bearded zombie, help comes from an unexpected source. Brother Michael intrudes, forces

Stuart to clean himself and eat, and springs him from this cell. When they reach the freer space of Echo Lake, where Stuart's wife vacations, Brother Nicholas tells her a tale that she cannot understand, but she nevertheless believes it. As the reunited couple settles down to sleep, and Marguerite snuggles Stuart toward intimate security, he starts to feel the stir of words, a poem on its way. A good marriage is hard to find and even harder to keep together, but it helps those who have the magic.

Through the third-person viewpoint, Elliott conveys sufficient sound and surface of the minor characters to make them credible types, and by entering the thoughts and feelings of the main character, he conveys how an intelligent and sensitive man can cause trouble for himself. Stuart does not control his tone of voice, bad enough for anyone, but a major failing in a poet. To his superior he says, "St. Anselm's doesn't mean too awfully much to me" and "I got my own crisis." The narrator explains,

> Because the voice in which he uttered such words was bland and slick instead of abrasive, he sort of thought no one would notice what the words implied; and he did not believe--though it had been suggested to him one way or another by a friend or two--that the smoothness of his voice made the implications of his words penetrate the deeper.

In the present case, the tension builds and the blandness flees, causing his words to come out "openly sarcastic" but "unvenomous"--*that* amounts to paying dearly for no return at all--and, later on, as "piteous bleat" and barking "No"--welcome to the pasture. Because from this viewpoint the readers feel the struggle and the pathos, the readers are is ready to rejoice when "the sanctioned buzz of words begins."

From its position at the beginning of *An Hour of Last Things, and Other Stories*, "Into the Cone of Code" connects with others in the volume. "Tourist and Pilgrim" contains a search for religious fulfillment. A family experiences great strains but tolerates them in "Is He Dead?" "Words Words Words" involves intrusions with promising results; "Invasion of the Planet of Love" reveals disastrous events. There are quite a few imprisoned souls. One of these souls who is deeply in pain haunts "Better to Burn," and one who is still alive enough to continue his "complaining" speaks out from

"In a Hole." This last piece, a fable of civilization's crisis, issues from what starts out as the stunned first-person narrative of a forty-year-old man caught permanently within a hole after an earthquake. His reflections project an allegory of unpreparedness: The city planners built upon a fault, ancestral myths are all but gone, civilizing customs are lost, the police maintain order, and prayers and patriotic speeches fail. There is, however, still something that can be done. The poet, buried near the bedrock, can use "our language" in his "own way"; he can "speak" for himself, "as though" he "were being listened to." These are articles of Elliott's modernist faith, a humanism that does not scorn the mysteries. The tale is obvious, but it is a fable and short enough that readers may "swallow" it while keeping their "self-respect."

"Miss Cudahy of Stowe's Landing"

The characters mentioned thus far have been faceless and almost bodiless sorts, as one might expect in a fiction focusing on thoughts and feelings, such as Elliott's. In "Miss Cudahy of Stowe's Landing," the main character, Bingham, is of this sort. Bingham's opponent, the lady of the title, is Elliott's most vivid character, a "huge old woman" whose "heavy, pale, sensual face" makes her seem older than she is and whose "white arms" might once have called forth the admiration of men. What is most important, however, is the suggestiveness in this external portraiture. By careful selection of detail, gesture, and glance, Elliott has made a tale almost Jamesian in its ability to tease. Fitted out in the trappings of romance--the cast includes a crippled queen (the old stepmother type), a gothic troll of a gardener, a speechless maiden named Phoebe, and an intrusive courtier--this tale promises adventures but shuts the door with many of its mysteries intact. The self-styled courtier is discomfited. Miss Cudahy manipulates her guest: Bingham is the mouse, her house is the trap, the girl the cheese. Miss Cudahy offers Bingham enough to tease him into coming back and staying longer than he had planned; the newel, the decorated bedroom, hints about the history of the house, statements that the girl needs some companionship, and, most of all, Miss Cudahy's way of touching Phoebe in Bingham's presence are sexually suggestive. At the same time, Miss Cudahy pulls Bingham back by

attacking his unspoken motives, uttering knowing exclamations, and erupting puritanically. He knows he is flirting with a bomb but does so just the same. Finally, demanding more than he can get, he loses Phoebe.

Many of the mysteries remain intact; maybe all readers wanted was a picture. If Bingham had stayed, what kind of family would this have been? Is this a mother and a daughter, or a mistress and a servant girl? Miss Cudahy can almost seem like a madam selling flesh, and the complicated sexual themes of modern gothic may lurk behind the door. To these mysteries contribute the wordlessness of Phoebe, the muttering of the gardener, the speech-restraining cat and mouse of guest and hostess, and the many gestures of the hands and glances of the eyes that take the place of words. These gestures hold back as much as they express, and the reader's imagination runs forth to fill out every vein until the courting couple's touches, conveyed in language of Keatsian eroticism, leaves one tingling. Bingham is no courtly knight, however, he is more like a Peter Brench, a character in one of James's short stories.

George P. Elliott is generally thought of as a modern realist, but he was competent in many forms, including various kinds of fables. Whatever the form, he was capable of investing it with tones that bite, amuse, and mend, thus educating readers' minds and feelings to a life among appearances but one that casts an "affirming flame."

Other major works

LONG FICTION: *Parktilden Village*, 1958; *David Knudsen*, 1962; *In the World*, 1968; *Muriel*, 1972.

POETRY: *Fever and Chills*, 1961; *Fourteen Poems*, 1964; *From the Berkeley Hills*, 1969; *Reaching*, 1979.

NONFICTION: *A Piece of Lettuce*, 1964 (essays); *Conversions*, 1971 (essays).

EDITED TEXT: *Fifteen Modern American Poets*, 1956.

MISCELLANEOUS: *A George P. Elliott Reader: Selected Poetry and Prose*, 1992.

Bibliography

Gelfant, Blanche H., ed. *The Columbia Companion to the Twentieth-Century American Short Story*. New York: Columbia University Press, 2000. Includes a chapter in which Elliott's short stories are analyzed.

Hills, Rust, ed. *Writer's Choice*. New York: David McKay, 1974. In the introduction to this collection of short stories by notable contemporary American writers, Hills discusses the reasons why he chose to include Elliott's story "Children of Ruth" in the collection. He also mentions several reasons why the story can be considered one of Elliott's representative works.

McCormack, Thomas, ed. *Afterwords: Novelists and Their Novels*. New York: Harper & Row, 1969. In one section of this informative collection of essays written by novelists about the task of writing, Elliott offers some interesting insights about the writing of his collection *Among the Dangs*. Aside from shedding light on the general process of fiction writing, the essay illustrates Elliott's particular blend of the personal and the universal in his writing.

Morse, J. Mitchell. "A Warm Heart and a Good Head." *The Hudson Review* 3 (Autumn, 1964): 478-480. In this review of Elliott's nonfiction book, *A Piece of Lettuce*, Morse views the work as a mix between literary criticism and autobiography. Most praiseworthy, according to Morse, is Elliott's attempt to discuss literature and politics as human activities with serious consequences.

Podhoretz, Norman. "The New Nihilism in the Novel." In *Doings and Undoings*. New York: Farrar, Straus & Giroux, 1964. Podhoretz comments on the novel *Parktilden Village*, stating that it is a revealing document about contemporary religious values. He also points out that the protagonist reveals sheer habituation to the nihilism of American life. Argues that Elliott treats a religious solution to the problem with mild irony and controlled outrage.

Sale, Roger. "High Mass and Low Requiem." *The Hudson Review* 1 (Spring, 1966): 124-138. Sale reviews Elliott's novel *In the World*, among other works by prominent twentieth century authors. He asserts that the work's strength derives from the impact of William Makepeace Thackeray rather than Leo Tolstoy, as Elliott had professed. He complains that Elliott does not illustrate or describe what it means to be "in the world," other than in the academic world.

Solotaroff, Theodore. "The Fallout of the Age." In *The Red Hot Vacuum, and Other Pieces on the Writing of the Sixties*. New York: Atheneum Press, 1970. Discusses Elliott's *David Knudsen* as a topical novel deserving more critical attention than it has received. Argues that the novel is concerned, in a concrete and sensitive way, with the contemporary problems of what it means to live in the nuclear age--a topic little discussed in previous fiction.

Tisdale, Lyn Camire. "George P. Elliott and the Common Reader." *The American Scholar* 58 (Summer, 1989): 421-428. A general discussion of the life and work of Elliott. Discusses Elliott's love of literature and his belief in the power of literature to create both anguish and delight in the reader.

William P. Keen
Updated by Genevieve Slomski

HARLAN ELLISON

Born: Cleveland, Ohio; May 27, 1934
Also known as: Cheech Beldone, Cordwainer Bird

PRINCIPAL SHORT FICTION

The Deadly Streets, 1958, 1975

A Touch of Infinity, 1960

Gentleman Junkie, and Other Stories of the Hung-Up Generation, 1961

The Juvies, 1961

Ellison Wonderland, 1962 (also known as *Earthman, Go Home,* 1964)

Paingod and Other Delusions, 1965

From the Land of Fear, 1967

I Have No Mouth, and I Must Scream, 1967

Perhaps Impossible, 1967

Love Ain't Nothing but Sex Misspelled, 1968

The Beast That Shouted Love at the Heart of the World, 1969

Over the Edge: Stories from Somewhere Else, 1970

Alone Against Tomorrow: Stories of Alienation in Speculative Fiction, 1971 (pb. in England as *All the Sounds of Fear,* 1973)

The Time of the Eye, 1971

Approaching Oblivion: Road Signs on the Treadmill Towards Tomorrow, 1974

Deathbird Stories: A Pantheon of Modern Gods, 1975

Partners in Wonder, 1975

Strange Wine: Fifteen New Stories from the Nightside of the World, 1978

The Illustrated Harlan Ellison, 1978

The Fantasies of Harlan Ellison, 1979

Shatterday, 1980

Stalking the Nightmare, 1982

The Essential Ellison: A Thirty-Five-Year Retrospective, 1986 (revised and expanded in 2001 as *The Essential Ellison: A Fifty-Year Retrospective*)

Angry Candy, 1988

Footsteps, 1989

Dreams with Sharp Teeth, 1991

Mefisto in Onyx, 1993

Mind Fields: The Art of Jacek Yerka, the Fiction of Harlan Ellison, 1993

"Repent, Harlequin!" Said the Ticktockman: The Classic Story, 1997

Slippage: Precariously Poised, Previously Uncollected Stories, 1997

Troublemakers, 2001

OTHER LITERARY FORMS

Though his reputation rests primarily with the short story, Harlan Ellison (HAR-lan EHL-ih-suhn) has produced abundantly: novels, essays, anthologies, and scripts for the motion-picture industry and television. Two highly influential anthologies, *Dangerous Visions* (1967) and *Again, Dangerous Visions* (1972), critique his own work and that of others. He contributed scripts to many popular television series in the 1960's and 1970's and adapted his story "A Boy and His Dog" for film in 1975. His essays, which comment on a broad range of social issues, have been collected in a number of volumes, including *The Glass Teat: Essays of Opinion on the Subject of Television* (1969), *An Edge in My Voice* (1986), *Harlan Ellison's Watching* (1989), and *The Harlan Ellison Hornbook* (1990). He also published *I, Robot: The Illustrated Screenplay*, an adaptation of Isaac Asimov's novel, in 1994.

ACHIEVEMENTS

As the author of more than seventeen hundred published pieces and as author or editor of more than seventy-five volumes, Harlan Ellison is perhaps the most influential writer of science fiction and fantasy to have emerged in the 1960's. His stories have won three Nebula Awards, eight and a half Hugo Awards, and four Writers Guild of America awards for television scripts. Acclaimed as a leader of the New Wave writers who sought greater sophistication in science fiction--a movement that he has hotly rejected as nonexistent--Ellison nevertheless brought "crossover" qualities to genre fiction, winning new audiences and exploring new literary possibilities. His talent definitely lies in the short story. As an artist, he is a risk taker, seeking out a preposterous central image vital enough to contain his moral outrage and screaming rhetoric. When he succeeds--and he has succeeded often enough to have created several of the best modern stories--then he casts a memorable metaphor, "Do you remember the story in which . . . ?" When he fails, as risk takers often do, he comes up empty and shrill. His fiction from the 1980's onward crosses genre boundaries of mystery, horror, fantasy, science fiction, magic realism, and postmodern slipstream.

BIOGRAPHY

Harlan Jay Ellison's fiction often seems like an extension of the author's vibrant and dominating personality. His stories are frequently dressed up with long titles, quotations, and other effects, as if they cannot stand by themselves but rather serve as the basis for platform performances. Ellison has been a much-sought-after participant at fan conventions and academic groups, where he characteristically strews insults and abuse upon audiences, who howl for more. His friends and associates, nevertheless, find him charming, witty, and generous.

Despite his enormous energy and productivity, Ellison developed slowly as a writer. Born in Cleveland, Ohio, on May 27, 1934, he attended Ohio State University and was soon asked to leave, one reason being his insults to a creative-writing instructor who told Ellison that he could not write. In Cleveland, he edited a science-fiction "fanzine," showing a hero-worship of writers that is still reflected in his work. In New York, he joined a street gang to get authentic material and poured out stories to establish himself, publishing his first, "Glowworm," in 1956. After two years in the Army, he supported himself for a time as an editor. His first novel, *The Man with Nine Lives*, appeared in 1959. In 1962, he moved to the Los Angeles area.

In the 1960's, Ellison became a successful television writer, contributing scripts to *Route Sixty-Six*, *The Alfred Hitchcock Hour*, *The Untouchables*, *The Outer Limits*, *Star Trek*, and *The Man from U.N.C.L.E.* In the same period, he began writing the stories upon which his reputation is based. Hugo and Nebula Awards were presented to him for "'Repent, Harlequin!' Said the Ticktockman" in 1966, and thereafter critical acclaim flowed to him in a remarkable string of honors. His activities have continued to be energetic and broad, both socially and intellectually, leaving him surrounded by many friends and thirty-seven thousand books, leaving many observers to wonder when Ellison could possibly find time to write. In his California period, he has been a book reviewer for *The Los Angeles Times* (1969 to 1982), an editorial commentator for the Canadian Broadcasting Corporation (1972 to 1978), a newspaper columnist, a commercial spokesperson for General Electric, and a television writer, while continuing to write short fiction.

In 1991, Ellison won a lawsuit against James Cameron and his film *The Terminator* (1984); Ellison claimed the film stole from stories written by Ellison for *Outer Limits*, "Soldier" and "Demon with a Glass Hand." In 2006, Ellison won a settlement against America Online (AOL) for allowing his stories to be pirated and posted on the Internet. He also won the Science Fiction Grandmaster Award for Science Fiction that year. His television work includes acting as creative consultant and screenwriter for the *New Twilight Zone* series in 1985-1986, as *Sci-Fi Buzz* commentator in 1993, and as creative consultant for *Babylon Five* (1994-1999). A teleplay based on his story "The Discarded" was produced for *Masters of Science Fiction* in 2007. Independent filmmaker Eric Nelson made a documentary on Ellison (over several years) called *Dreams with Sharp Teeth* (2007).

ANALYSIS

Harlan Ellison is a stern moralist. Despite his self-appointed role as a Hollywood pacesetter, a professional bad boy, and an outrageous commentator, he is at heart thoroughly conventional, a description he might disavow. However, his work declares the necessity of love, loyalty, discipline, personal responsibility, and a Puritan ethic, outside which life decays into horror, a wasteland depicted in violent and grotesque imagery. Despite his antireligious beliefs, he is resolutely on the side of the angels, and his standards are often as simple as the message on a bumper sticker. His work evokes dramatic patterns in which eternal truths become vivid. The works mentioned here have been highly praised and frequently anthologized, showing his range of themes, images, and methods.

"SHATTERED LIKE A GLASS GOBLIN"

"Shattered Like a Glass Goblin" (from *Deathbird Stories*) shows the expressionist at work, using images to express his disgust for the drug culture's special claims about morality and its hypocritical expropriation of "love." Seeking his girlfriend, who has been missing for eight months, Rudy finally locates her in a decaying Los Angeles house, a hippie commune of eleven persons who drift in and out with little attachment to one another. Kris, the girlfriend, is strung out on drugs and tells him to leave. Rudy stays nevertheless and is steadily absorbed into the character of the house.

> It was a self-contained little universe, bordered on the north by acid and mescaline, on the south by pot and peyote, on the east by speed and redballs, on the west by downers and amphetamines.

From the beginning, Rudy hears strange noises. The inhabitants, who care about nothing except their own sensations, are degenerating into beasts: "[He] had heard squeaking from the attic. It had sounded to him like the shrieking of mice being torn to pieces." Far from being committed to love, the members of the commune cannot extend the simplest commitment to one another. In time, Rudy notices that some of them have disappeared. Changes have started to come upon him, too: "He wore only underpants. His hands and feet hurt. The knuckles of his fingers were larger, from cracking them, and they were always angry crimson."

Eventually, he cannot find any of the inhabitants and goes into the basement and upstairs to explore.

> On the first floor he found the one who was the blonde girl. . . . She lay out thin and white as a tablecloth on the dining room table as three of the others he had not seen in a very long while put their teeth into her, and through their hollow sharp teeth they

drank up the yellow fluid from the bloated pus-pockets that had been her breasts and her buttocks.

Rudy, locating Kris "sucking out the moist brains of a thing that giggled like a harpsichord," pleads with her to escape with him. By this time, however, he discovers that he has turned into a glass goblin. Showing little concern, the werewolf behind him says to the glass goblin, "Have you ever grooved heavy behind *anything* except love?" and then smashes him into a thousand pieces. The vision of hell, which is both felt and believed, is produced by the intense language and the grotesque violence.

This vision of hell frequently uses the city--New York, Los Angeles, New Orleans, or elsewhere--as the threatening habitation of demons and strange gods lusting for the souls of those who falter. Again and again, Ellison invents his own pantheon of the supernatural, rejecting ordinary religious imagery but nevertheless showing a fundamental puritanism that emphasizes humankind's moral weakness and the eternal damnation that follows it. "Croatoan" (collected in *Strange Wine*) illustrates the constantly repeated connection between individual morality and the mythological creatures underlying the story.

Carol, who has an abortion and flushes the fetus down the toilet, quarrels with her boyfriend, Gabe. She demands that he go down into the sewer to retrieve the fetus. To please her, he goes out into the street and lifts the manhole cover.

> It had finally overtaken me; the years of casual liaisons, careless lies, the guilt I suppose I'd *always* known would mount up till it could no longer be denied.

Gabe is so irresponsible that abortionists regard him as a steady customer. He therefore feels compelled to enter the sewer, and he proceeds deeply into the bowels of the earth, fascinated by the smell of rot and his guilty reflections about Carol and his long string of abandoned girlfriends. He passes a group of bums, and one of them follows Gabe, pleading with him to go back and leave the underworld to its inhabitants. The man has no hands, only chewed stumps. Gabe comes upon an alligator, with no feet, chewing up a nest of rats. (He remembers the legend that the sewers are occupied by alligators originally bought as children's curiosities and then disposed of down the toilet, as he had once done, paralleling the treatment of the fetus.) Gabe follows the hideous animal and is finally stopped by a heavy door that has "CROATOAN" carved on it in heavy gothic lettering. He remembers that this was the word carved in a tree left by the vanished community at Roanoke, Virginia, in 1590, and source of the legend of Virginia Dare, the first baby born in the Americas to English parents. Gabe enters the door and realizes that he is surrounded by alligators. Then he sees the children: "And the light came nearer, and the light was many lights. Torches, held aloft by the children who rode the alligators." He stays in the sewer, the only adult among them, and says, "They call me father." In this story, Ellison does not build the plot on clever imagery but on layers of narrative: moral indignation about personal irresponsibility leading to abortion, the sewers underlying the city as a central image of moral disgust, the popular belief that alligators remained alive after being disposed of in toilets, the historical legend of Roanoke and Dare, and, finally, a translation of the action into a personal mythology, with the children riding on the backs of the alligators.

"The Face of Helene Bournouw"

"The Face of Helene Bournouw" continues the pattern of connecting moral responsibility to a central image and ultimately to the supernatural, though its language is subtle and not apocalyptic. A celebrated model, Helene is the withered hag made beautiful, "the most beautiful woman who had ever seen man through eyes of wonder." She creates adoration in whomever she touches: a gossip columnist declares her "the most memorable succubus he had ever encountered." The reader follows her throughout her day. Her first engagement is with her lover, Jimmy, at lunch at Lindy's. She tells him that their affair, which had seemed perfect to him, is finished. Later that day, he commits suicide, and Helene goes on to her second appointment. Quentin Deane is a struggling artist for whom she has been a patron. Now she ridicules his latest work, which had been important to him, and tells him she is going to withdraw her support if he persists with these ideas. He rips up his canvases and returns to Ohio. Her third appointment is with a Catholic priest, who is alarmed to see her because she knows his weakness. She dresses up as a little girl and indulges his sexual fantasies.

Her day, however, is not over. She leaves her fashionable Sutton Place apartment and takes a cab to the Bowery. In a filthy alley, she knocks on a door and is admitted to a room containing eight hideous demons from hell. They turn her off, for Helene is only a machine: "Ba'al, wipe her off; you know we've got to keep the rolling stock in good condition." The technological detail pushes the reader over the fine line separating fantasy from science fiction:

> Later, when they wearied of formulating their new image, when they sighed with the responsibility of market trends and saturation levels and optimum penetration campaigns, they would suck on their long teeth and use her, all of them, at the same time.

"On the Downhill Side"

"On the Downhill Side," a modern ghost story and a fantasy without science-fiction elements, has a delicacy in its imagery not characteristic of Ellison's gothic horror, but the story is insistently moral nevertheless. The action takes the reader through the Vieux Carré of New Orleans, using familiar landmarks. Paul, accompanied by his unicorn, meets the beautiful Lizette on the street (she must be a virgin because she is able to stroke the mane of his unicorn, a symbol of moral perfection, with its ivory horn and platinum hoofs clattering on the pavement), and as they wander from place to place, they tell their stories without directly responding to each other, as if they were talking at cross-purposes. Their lives are at opposite ends of a scale: She has been silly, selfish, and trivial, rejecting love; he, on the other hand, has overcommitted himself to his insane wife and demanding mother-in-law, smothering himself in guilt. They have but one night out of all eternity to redeem themselves and to escape their fate. Now it is already after midnight, "on the downhill side."

After her flirtation with a flamenco dancer in a café and her pleas about her hopeless condition, Paul reluctantly allows her to go her own way. With dawn approaching, however, he and the unicorn fly over the fence of Saint Louis Cemetery, the archetype of all cemeteries, because they know that Lizette must return there. The naked Lizette lies upon an altar, attended by eyeless creatures, the agents of the god of love, who are about to claim her. Paul cries out to her in one last effort, and she comes to him at last in an act of love. As she does, however, the faithful unicorn disappears in the mist, symbolizing Paul's abandonment of "loving too much," in contrast to Lizette, who "loved too little." Thus, the lovers meet on a middle ground in which their faults are worked through in a compromise. Though the resolution is too abstract, its concluding imagery too vague to support the moral action, the story nevertheless has a fine touch and a appealing restraint. The image of the unicorn, with its "silken mane and rainbow colors, platinum hoofs and spiral horn," is powerful and memorable. The pattern is familiar in Ellison's stories: A moral preoccupation is tied to a vivid central image and realistic elements give way to the supernatural.

"JEFFTY IS FIVE"

"Jeffty Is Five," winner of the Nebula Award for the best science-fiction story of 1977, brilliantly uses nostalgia to attack the empty vulgarity of modern technology, especially television, one of the author's favorite targets. Donny and Jeffty are five when they meet. As friends, they engage in fun activities, which Donny lovingly recalls: eating nickel Clark Bars covered with real chocolate, attending Saturday matinees that featured Lash LaRue and Wild Bill Elliott, listening to radio programs such as *The Lone Ranger* and *The Shadow*. They all form a flood of memories, made real by Ellison's descriptions of popular culture. Donny moves away and comes back several times. He continues to grow up, but Jeffty mysteriously remains at age five--not retarded but with the interests and concerns of a lively child of that age. When Donny returns from college to go into business at his own electronics store, he continues to befriend the child, frequently taking him to see a film. Jeffty's parents are terrified by Jeffty's lack of development and have left him in limbo, without love.

Donny then discovers Jeffty's radio, which plays programs long since discontinued. Furthermore, Jeffty receives a *new* Captain Midnight Secret Decoder Badge in the mail, buys *new* versions of old comic books, and is even able to project at a local theater a film based on Alfred Bester's science-fiction novel *The Demolished Man* (1952), which ought to exist but does not. He is reordering others' reality, especially

Donny's. One Saturday, Donny is forced to send Jeffty on to the theater alone because the store is busy selling color television sets. While waiting in line at the theater, Jeffty takes the radio of another to listen to one of his favorite programs. This causes a fight, in which Jeffty is seriously injured. Thereafter, he lies in his room upstairs, listening to rock music on his radio, the old programs no longer available. His escape into the past is clearly tied to the indifference of the parents, and Donny's placing of business before Jeffty is a betrayal. A paragraph of science-fiction boilerplate, mentioning that "the laws of the conservation of energy occasionally break," unnecessarily tries to hold the story within the science-fiction genre.

TROUBLEMAKERS

The short-story collection *Troublemakers* does not come up to the standard of *Slippage*, *Angry Candy*, and *Shatterday*, but it can be described as unusual. First, it is mostly a retrospective, with only one new story, and it recycles ten of its seventeen stories from Ellison's early professional efforts from 1956 and 1957. Unlike *The Essential Ellison: A Fifty-Year Retrospective* (2001), which presents a variety of works and "best of" from Ellison, the bulk of these 1956-1957 stories are only workmanlike science-fiction-genre material at best. Second, *Troublemakers* is the only story collection that, according to Ellison's short introductions, was requested by his publisher for a young adult market; as a consequence its stories center on the themes of revolt, rebellion, and nonconformity. This restriction of market audience and purpose sets up a number of unsatisfying tensions in the collection. Although Ellison starts by insulting young readers and calling them Daffy Duck "maroons," he insists they must heed his stories' lessons. His choice of material and language is compromised because, as he admits in the preface to "On the Downhill Side," libraries will be stocking the book. Rather than using the vulgarities he prefers, he must resort to such euphemisms as "horse-puckey" and "patoot," inhibited by the marketplace blinders forced on him. Third, the famous Ellison introductions (which can be as long as the stories) have shrunk to a page or two and respond to the publisher's directive that he point out the moral lesson in each story. This creates a weird collection of fantastic Aesop fables, except, as Ellison notes in the introduction, they constitute a "book of warnings" with "lessons to be learned" that derive from his adolescent experiences. However, in two other introductions, he admits there may be no real moral involved: The story is either about too small a subject or is merely meant for entertainment.

Many young readers will enjoy reading for the first time classics reprinted from 1960's and 1970's, such as "'Repent, Harlequin!' Said the Ticktockman," a manifesto on an exaggerated Henry David Thoreau-style "civil disobedience" of a future "troublemaker;" and "On the Downhill Side;" and "Jeffty Is Five." They will also enjoy the simple 1950's classics such as "Soldier," about a future warrior waging mental warfare who accidentally time-travels back to present Earth and eventually becomes the poster boy for present Earth's disarmament, and "Deeper Than the Darkness," about a pyrotic telepath who chooses to become an outcast, a lonely wanderer among the planets, rather than be used as a military weapon to destroy the sun of Earth's enemy in war. Other 1950's and early 1960's stories seem saturated with the clichés of the period: improbable alien invasions, rebelling robots, telepaths, and O. Henry surprise twist endings, such as those in "Invasion Footnote" and "Voice in the Garden." Later comic efforts, such as "Djinn, No Chaser," the old yarn about the couple who finds Aladdin's Lamp in an antique shop, and the newer "Never Send to Know for Whom the Lettuce Wilts," about a deity with the slowest alien invasion plans ever, manage to rise above well-worn themes by virtue of Ellison's sharp wit, crackling dialogue, and stylistic bravura.

Ellison's explosive imagination scores often enough to believe that his best work will live after him. If, as the poet Randall Jarrell said, a great poet is one for whom lightning has struck half a dozen times, all the rest being mere competence, then Ellison may already have won his place. Other noteworthy stories are "A Boy and His Dog," which won a Nebula Best Novelette in 1969; two stories that Ellison names as his personal favorites, "Pretty Maggie Money-Eyes" and "At the Mouse Circus"; "O Ye of Little Faith," which Ellison wrote in one hour on the basis of three words given to him in the central hall of a science-fiction convention; "I Have No Mouth, and I Must Scream," a Hugo Award winner in 1968; "The Deathbird," which Ellison has said best represents his work; and "The Man Who Rowed Christopher Columbus Ashore," a postmodern fragmented series of fantasy vignettes about a rogue time traveler, selected for *The Best American Short Stories* 1993 annual.

OTHER MAJOR WORKS

LONG FICTION: *Rumble*, 1958 (also known as *The Web of the City*, 1975); *The Man with Nine Lives*, 1959; *Spider Kiss*, 1961 (also known as *Rockabilly*); *All the Lies That Are My Life*, 1980; *Run for the Stars*, 1991.

SCREENPLAY: *I, Robot: The Illustrated Screenplay*, 1994 (adaptation of Isaac Asimov's novel).

NONFICTION: *Memos from Purgatory*, 1961; *The Glass Teat: Essays of Opinion on the Subject of Television*, 1969; *The Other Glass Teat*, 1975; *Sleepless Nights in the Procrustean Bed*, 1984; *An Edge in My Voice*, 1985; *Harlan Ellison's Watching*, 1989; *The Harlan Ellison Hornbook*, 1990.

EDITED TEXTS: *Dangerous Visions*, 1967, 2002; *Again, Dangerous Visions*, 1972.

BIBLIOGRAPHY

Adams, Stephen. "The Heroic and Mock-Heroic in Harlan Ellison's 'Harlequin.'" *Extrapolation* 26 (1985): 285-289. The often-anthologized "'Repent, Harlequin' Said the Ticktockman" is convincingly viewed as a mock-heroic epic, parodying epic conventions through the central character and the narrator: "They both upset established rules (social or literary) and interject spontaneous, anarchic humor into an otherwise joyless, predictable, over-regulated world."

Atheling, William, Jr. *More Issues at Hand*. Chicago: Advent, 1970. An early view of Ellison's impact upon science fiction, especially concerning the anthology *Dangerous Visions*, its significance being that it consisted entirely of literary experiments then called "New Wave." Ellison is highly (but skeptically) praised: "a born writer, almost entirely without taste and control but with so much fire, originality, and drive, as well as compassion, that he makes the conventional virtues of the artist seem almost irrelevant."

Ellison, Harlan. "An Ill-Begotten Enterprise." *Harper's* 294 (May, 1997): 31-32. Describes the controversy over a 1966 *Star Trek* episode that Ellison wrote, "The City on the Edge of Forever." According to Ellison, Gene Roddenberry, the creator of the series, claimed in public that he had rescued the episode from the original script; Ellison strongly criticizes the various people who have claimed that they saved the teleplay.

Francavilla, Joseph. "The Concept of the Divided Self and Harlan Ellison's 'I Have No Mouth, and I Must Scream' and 'Shatterday.'" *Journal of the Fantastic in the Arts* 6, nos. 2-3 (1994): 107-25. Uses a psychoanalytic approach to explain how the divided self figures prominently in Ellison's stories.

Fredericks, Casey. *The Future of Eternity*. Bloomington: Indiana University Press, 1982. Contains an analysis of Ellison's mythmaking capacity, especially the story "The Place with No Name," which allows no settled interpretation.

Harris-Fain, Darren. "Created in the Image of God: The Narrator and the Computer in Harlan Ellison's 'I Have No Mouth, and I Must Scream.'" *Extrapolation* 32 (Summer, 1991): 143-155. Analyzes changes in the different editions of the story and identifies mythological allusions to the Bible and to H. G. Wells's "Country of the Blind."

McMurran, Kristin. "Harlan Ellison." *People Weekly* 24 (December 2, 1985): 97-100. A biographical sketch that claims Ellison's genius is often overshadowed by his bluster; discusses how Ellison's childhood was marred by anti-Semitic insults, how he went through a bout of depression for several years, and how he is driven to work hard.

Nicholls, Peter, ed. *The Science Fiction Encyclopedia*. Garden City, N.Y.: Doubleday, 1979. An excellent, fact-filled summary of Ellison's career, which carries the reader through the period of the writer's greatest accomplishments. Just the list of his activities demonstrates his extraordinary energy and ambition. The article emphasizes, however, that he will be remembered largely for his short fiction.

Platt, Charles. *Dream Makers*. New York: Berkeley Books, 1980. In this book of interviews and interpretations, Platt talks to Ellison in his Los Angeles home, crowded with books and memorabilia. The discussion covers the wide ground of Ellison's interests and serves as a good introduction to his personality.

Salm, Arthur. "Harlan Ellison Is fearless, and a Fearless Writer: 'I Place Ethics and Courage Way Way Above Everything Else.'" *The San Diego Union-Tribune*, March 20, 2005. In-depth interview with Ellison, with vivid descriptions of his home, complete with Hobbitt-style doors and 250,000 books.

Slusser, George Edgar. *Harlan Ellison: Unrepentant Harlequin*. San Bernardino, Calif.: Borgo Press, 1977. Examines the mythological basis of many stories in *The Deathbird* collection.

Weil, Ellen, and Gary Wolfe. *Harlan Ellison: The Edge of Forever*. Columbus: Ohio State University Press, 2002. Examines Ellison's entire output in fiction, nonfiction, and screenplays, beginning from his first days in 1950's New York City.

Bruce Olsen
Updated by Joseph Francavilla

RALPH ELLISON

Born: Oklahoma City, Oklahoma; March 1, 1914
Died: New York, New York; April 16, 1994

PRINCIPAL SHORT FICTION

Flying Home, and Other Stories, 1996

OTHER LITERARY FORMS

Invisible Man, Ralph Ellison's 1952 novel, is one of the most important American novels of the twentieth century. Ellison also published two well-received collections of essays, *Shadow and Act* (1964) and *Going to the Territory* (1986), which were combined into one volume in *The Collected Essays of Ralph Ellison* (1995). A posthumous edition of his long-awaited second novel was published as *Juneteenth* in 1999 and revised as *Three Days Before the Shooting* in 2010.

ACHIEVEMENTS

Though he won a Rosenwald grant in 1945 on the strength of his short fiction, and though two of his short stories, "Flying Home" and "King of the Bingo Game," are among the most commonly anthologized short stories in twentieth century American literature, Ralph Ellison is best known for his 1952 novel *Invisible Man*, which won the National Book Award and the Russwurm Award. In 1975, he was elected to the American Academy of Arts and Letters, which in 1955 awarded him a Prix de Rome Fellowship. He received the French Chevalier de l'Ordre des Arts et des Lettres in 1970 and the National Medal of Arts in 1985. In 1984, he was awarded the Langston Hughes medallion by City College in New York for his contributions to arts and letters.

BIOGRAPHY

Ralph Waldo Ellison was born March 1, 1914, in Oklahoma City to Ida and Lewis Alfred Ellison, who had moved out of the South in search of a more progressive place to live. An ambitious student, he distinguished himself locally and was rewarded with a scholarship to attend the Tuskegee Institute, in part because the local white population did not want Ellison, an African American, to integrate the white colleges in Oklahoma. Unable to afford the fare to Alabama, he rode a freight train to Tuskegee, in which he enrolled in 1933. A voracious reader in college, he pursued interests in literature, history, and folklore. At the end of his junior year, Ellison, like the narrator of *Invisible Man*, was refused financial aid, and so traveled to New York City, where he hoped to make enough money to finish his studies. While in New York, he met another African American author, Richard Wright, who encouraged Ellison's literary ambitions. Instead of returning to Tuskegee, he began to contribute short stories and essays to various literary journals and anthologies. From 1938 to 1944, he worked with the Federal Writers Project, and in 1945, he was a awarded a Rosenwald grant to write a novel. The result was *Invisible Man* (1952), a landmark work in African American fiction that won for its author numerous honorary degrees, literary awards, and worldwide fame.

Though Ellison would publish two well-received collections of essays, *Shadow and Act* and *Going to the Territory*, he would never follow up his first novel with a second in his lifetime. He began writing his next novel around 1958, and over the years he was to publish numerous excerpts from it as a work-in-progress. A fire at his Plainsfield, Massachusetts, summer home destroyed much of the manuscript in 1967, causing him to have to painstakingly reconstruct it. Though he was to work on this project for the rest of his life, he never found a final form for the novel with which he felt comfortable, and it remained unfinished when he died of a heart attack in 1994. His literary executor, John F. Callahan, published his short fiction in one volume as *Flying Home, and Other Stories* in

1996 and a self-contained portion of his final novel as *Juneteenth* in 1999.

ANALYSIS

Because most of Ralph Ellison's short fiction was written before his career as a novelist began, his short stories are often analyzed biographically, as the training ground for the novelist he was to become. This is not entirely unjustified because a biographical overview of his literary output reveals that he tried out the voices, techniques, and ideas that he was to present so boldly in *Invisible Man* and almost completely abandoned the short-story form after his success as a novelist, devoting himself to his essays and to his never-to-be-completed second novel.

It is true that in his two most accomplished stories, "King of the Bingo Game" and "Flying Home," he develops themes of the chaos of the modern world and the affliction of racial conflict that would later be combined and expanded in his famous novel. On the other hand, his earlier stories show him working out many of the same ideas from different perspectives. While the voice that informs his most accomplished work is a mature voice that is uniquely Ellison's own, the voices in his other stories show more clearly the influences of Ernest Hemingway, Richard Wright, and James Joyce.

In relating his short fiction to his overall work, Edith Schor in *Visible Ellison: A Study of Ralph Ellison's Fiction* (1993) has aptly observed that Ellison's short stories provided experimental laboratories for testing the translation of the forms and experiences of African American life into literature. In evaluating the stories themselves, however, critic Robert Bone best summarized their lasting value when he observed in "Ralph Ellison and the Uses of Imagination" (1966) that Ellison's short stories are about "adventurers" testing "the fixed boundaries of southern life."

FLYING HOME, AND OTHER STORIES

Flying Home, and Other Stories is a posthumous collection of stories edited by Ralph Ellison's literary executor, John F. Callahan, which brings together in one volume all of the principal short fiction Ellison wrote, with the exception of pieces that were published as excerpts of his novels. Callahan arranged the stories according to the age of the main characters, thereby highlighting the stories' thematic unity regarding the growth of young persons' ideologies, which might not otherwise be evident.

The collection opens with "A Party Down by the Square," a story told in an intentionally flat style by a young man from Cincinnati who visits his uncle in Alabama and witnesses a lynching on a stormy night. Confused by the cyclone that moves through the town, an airplane pilot mistakes the fire of the lynching for an airport flare and flies too low through the town, knocking loose a wire and electrocuting a white woman. Undaunted, the crowd continues with the lynching and the anonymous narrator watches a nameless black man being burned, marveling at the victim's resiliency but showing no moral awareness of the horror of the act.

Four of the stories in the collection focus on two young friends, Buster and Riley, as they explore their world and their friendship. The first story, "Mister Toussan," finds them making up imaginary exploits for Haitian liberator Toussaint-Louverture, a name they have heard but with which they have only vague associations and upon which they hang various

Ralph Ellison (National Archives)

fantasies. Similarly, "Afternoon" and "That I Had Wings" find the boys involved in imaginative games to stave off boredom. "A Coupla Scalped Indians" focuses on Riley, who has just been "scalped" (circumcised) at the age of eleven, having a sexually charged encounter with old Aunt Mack, an eccentric healer Riley sees naked in her shack as he is making his way home from a carnival. "All was real," Riley tells the reader after leaving her shack, in wonderment about his discovery of encroaching adult reality.

"Hymie's Bull" and "I Did Not Learn Their Names" are stories about riding freight trains, and together with "The Black Ball" and "A Hard Time Keeping Up," they are about young men finding their way in a world that can be violent and harsh but that can also contain friendship and tenderness in unexpected places. The importance of learning to discern the tenderness amid the harshness of the world becomes the central theme of two of the most important stories in the collection, "In a Strange Land" and "Flying Home." "King of the Bingo Game," by contrast, is a story about a young man trying to make his way in a world that offers little in the way of tenderness and much in the way of danger. Though "Flying Home" and "King of the Bingo Game" are the most significant stories in this collection, the collection offers a startling group of works, each of which is a semiprecious jewel and which, when taken together, mark the growth of the author's artistry.

"KING OF THE BINGO GAME"

One of Ellison's most durable statements about the harsh chaos of the modern world can be found in "King of the Bingo Game." The main character is an unnamed black North Carolina man living in Harlem, who has wandered into a motion-picture theater in the hope of winning the door prize that might pay for a doctor for his wife. By playing his own and several discarded bingo cards simultaneously, he manages to win the bingo portion of the game, which gives him the opportunity to spin the bingo wheel. While on stage, he spins the bingo wheel by pressing a button but is then unable to take the chance of letting the button go. Only double zero will win the jackpot of $36.90, and he realizes that as long as he keeps the wheel spinning, he has not lost, so he refuses to let the wheel stop. The wheel takes on the symbolic importance of a mandala, a wheel of life,

something the main character realizes when he exclaims, "This is God!" Because he has taken much too long to let go of the button, security guards try to take it from him and knock him out in an altercation. The wheel stops at double zero, but as he fades into unconsciousness, he realizes that he will not get the prize he sought. Though this story is among Ellison's harsher fictions, it is also one of his most poetic presentations of the unfeeling chaos of the modern world.

"IN A STRANGE COUNTRY"

Though not as artistically satisfying as the longer "Flying Home," "In a Strange Country" tells a similar tale of self-discovery through the acceptance of a previously despised group identity. Parker is an intelligent black merchant seaman who lands in Wales during World War II only to be promptly attacked by a group of American soldiers simply for being a black man. A group of Welshmen, led by Mr. Catti, rescues him but not before his eye is injured and begins to swell. Over several drafts of ale, Catti learns that Parker is a music enthusiast and takes him to a singing club. There, Parker is swept up in the emotions of the songs about Welsh national pride but reminds himself that he is from Harlem, not Wales. He feels at first alienated and then deeply connected to the men around him, who, he believes, see his humanity much more clearly than do his fellow Americans who are white. As the evening is ending, the band begins to play "The Star-Spangled Banner" in his honor, and he finds himself singing along with deep feeling.

On one hand, the "strange country" of the title is Wales, but on a deeper level, it is the part of himself that is opened up by the bond of common humanity he shares with these Welshmen and that, for the first time in his life, disallows any easy cynicism.

"FLYING HOME"

Ralph Ellison's longest short story, "Flying Home," is also his most richly satisfying accomplishment in the form. At the center of the story is Todd, a young black man whose lifelong dream of becoming a pilot crashes along with his plane when he flies into a buzzard on a training flight. Jefferson, an old black man who comes to Todd's rescue after the crash, tells him the buzzards are called "jim crows" locally, setting up an important level of symbolism about what has really caused Todd's crash. In fact, Todd has been training with the Tuskegee Airmen, a group of black World War II pilots who trained at the famed Tuskegee Institute but were only reluctantly deployed for combat missions. For Todd, this crash landing on a routine flight almost certainly means he will never get another chance to fly and, in his mind, will become the common black man he considers Jefferson to be, the worst fate he can imagine for himself.

Despite the younger man's hostility, Jefferson distracts the injured Todd by telling him a story about dying, going to heaven, and flying around so fast as to cause "a storm and a couple of lynchings down here in Macon County." In his story-within-a-story, Jefferson is stripped of his wings for flying too fast and is sent down to earth with a parachute and a map of Alabama. Todd, seeing only that this story has been twisted to mirror his own situation, snaps, "Why are you making fun of me?"--which, in fact, the old man is not doing. A feverish dream into which Todd drifts reveals not only the depth of his lifelong desire to fly but also the power of his grandmother's admonition:

Young man, young man
Yo arm's too short
To box with God.

To Todd, becoming a pilot means taking a position higher than the majority white culture wants to allow black men of his time to occupy; it is the equivalent of boxing with God in his mind. To have failed as a pilot means not only to have made a mistake but also to have let his entire race down, something he cannot allow to happen.

When Dabney Graves, the racist landowner on whose property Todd has crashed, arrives at the site, Todd snaps at the man and places his own life in danger. Jefferson saves him by intervening and telling Graves that the Army told Todd never to abandon his ship. Graves's temper is assuaged, and Jefferson and a young boy are allowed to take Todd to safety in a stretcher. The final image is of Todd watching a buzzard flying against the sun, glowing like a bird of flaming gold. This image suggests that though Todd will never fly again, his spirit will rise up like a phoenix from the ashes of his defeat, a victory made possible by the current of goodwill he can now allow himself to feel for

Jefferson. Todd will begin to learn to love himself for who he is by loving others for who they are.

OTHER MAJOR WORKS

LONG FICTION: *Invisible Man*, 1952; *Juneteenth*, 1999, revised 2010 (John F. Callahan, editor; revised 2010 as *Three Days Before the Shooting*, Callahan and Adam Bradley, editors).

NONFICTION: *Shadow and Act*, 1964; *The Writer's Experience*, 1964 (with Karl Shapiro); *Going to the Territory*, 1986; *Conversations with Ralph Ellison*, 1995 (Maryemma Graham and Amritjit Singh, editors); *The Collected Essays of Ralph Ellison*, 1995 (John F. Callahan, editor); *Trading Twelves: The Selected Letters of Ralph Ellison and Albert Murray*, 2000; *Living with Music: Ralph Ellison's Jazz Writings*, 2001 (Robert O'Meally, editor).

BIBLIOGRAPHY

Bloom, Harold, ed. *Modern Critical Views: Ralph Ellison*. New York: Chelsea House, 1986. Though this widely available collection of essays focuses mainly on *Invisible Man*, it provides insights from which any reader of Ellison may profit. Berndt Ostendor's essay, "Anthropology, Modernism, and Jazz," offers much to the reader of "Flying Home."

Bone, Robert. "Ralph Ellison and the Uses of Imagination." *TriQuarterly* 6 (1966): 39-54. An important essay on the uses of transcendentalism and jazz in Ellison's fiction and of his writings' importance to the Civil Rights movement and black culture in general.

Butler, Robert J., ed. *The Critical Response to Ralph Ellison*. Westport, Conn.: Greenwood Press, 2000. Includes three essays focusing on Ellison's short fiction: "Ralph Ellison's 'Flying Home'by Joseph F. Trimmer, "In Need of Folk: The Alienated Protagonists of Ralph Ellison's Short Fiction." by Mary Ellen Doyle, and "Ellison's 'Black Eye': Transforming Pain into Vision," by Robert J. Butler.

Callahan, John F. Introduction to *Flying Home, and Other Stories*, by Ralph Ellison. Edited by John F. Callahan. New York: Random House, 1996. Callahan's introduction to this collection of short stories is essential reading for anyone interested in Ellison's fiction, not only for the literary insights it provides but also for the basic editorial information about how these stories were selected and edited.

Jackson, Lawrence. *Ralph Ellison: Emergence of Genius*. New York: Wiley, 2001. The first book-length study of Ellison's life, providing a good background source for Ellison's early life and career. Jackson, however, ends his study in 1953, shortly after the publication of *Invisible Man*.

Muyumba, Walton M. *The Shadow and the Act: Black Intellectual Practice, Jazz Improvisation, and Philosophical Pragmatism*. Chicago: University of Chicago Press, 2009. Examines how jazz influenced the works of Ellison, James Baldwin, and Amiri Baraka, who drew on their understanding of improvisation to analyze race and politics. Includes discussions of some of Ellison's short stories, which are listed in the index.

Rampersad, Arnold. *Ralph Ellison: A Biography*. New York: Alfred A. Knopf, 2007. The definitive biography. Rampersad not only recounts the events of Ellison's life and literary career but also provides a complete portrait of a complex personality.

Schor, Edith. *Visible Ellison: A Study of Ralph Ellison's Fiction*. Westport, Conn.: Greenwood, 1993. Published a year before Ellison's death, this is an excellent full-length study of the fiction that was generally available at the time, including his short fiction, which had not yet been collected in book form.

Skerret, Joseph. "Ralph Ellison and the Example of Richard Wright." *Studies in Short Fiction* 15 (Spring, 1978): 145-153. An examination of the influence of Richard Wright on Ellison's short fiction.

Thomas, P. L. *Reading, Learning, Teaching Ralph Ellison*. New York: Peter Lang, 2008. A guide aimed at introducing teachers to Ellison's work and advising them how to teach students about his writings. Devotes a chapter to Ellison's short fiction.

Tracy, Steven C., ed. *A Historical Guide to Ralph Ellison*. New York: Oxford University Press, 2004. Collection of essays providing various interpretations of Ellison's work, including examinations of gender and sexuality in his writings and his "politics of integration." The index lists the pages on which the short stories are discussed.

Wright, John S. *Shadowing Ralph Ellison*. Jackson: University of Mississippi, 2006. A critical analysis of Ellison writings, from his novels to his nonfiction and personal correspondence.

Thomas Cassidy

NATHAN ENGLANDER

Born: New York, New York; 1970

PRINCIPAL SHORT FICTION

For the Relief of Unbearable Urges, 1999
"*How We Avenged the Blums,*" 2005
"*Everything I Know About My Family on My
    Mother's Side,*" 2008
"*Free Fruit for Young Widows,*" 2010

OTHER LITERARY FORMS

Nathan Englander entered the literary scene with his debut collection of nine short stories, each featuring Jewish characters. Eight years later, Englander released *The Ministry of Special Cases* (2007), his first novel and a long-awaited follow-up to his debut. The novel, which takes place in 1976 in Buenos Aires during Argentina's Dirty War and tells the story of the Jewish son of a prostitute, received great critical acclaim and has lived up to the expectations set by his earlier collection of stories. Englander had begun this novel before publishing his collection of short stories; he used the money earned from the collection to take his time crafting his novel.

ACHIEVEMENTS

For the Relief of Unbearable Urges was a national best seller and debuted to widespread critical acclaim; critics compared Nathan Englander's style to that of such prominent writers as Philip Roth, Saul Bellow, Isaac Bashevis Singer, and James Joyce. The collection earned Englander the 2000 PEN/Faulkner Malamud Award and the American Academy of Arts and Letters Sue Kauffman Prize. The title story of his collection received the Pushcart Prize, and "The Gilgul of Park Avenue" received the O. Henry Prize. Englander later received a Guggenheim Fellowship, the Bard Fiction Prize, and a fellowship at the Dorothy and Lewis B.

Cullman Center for Scholars and Writers at the New York Public Library. "The Gilgul of Park Avenue" appeared in the 2000 edition of *The Best American Short Stories*, and "How We Avenged the Blums" appeared in the 2006 edition. Englander also was a Fall, 2009, Mary Ellen von der Heyden Fellow for Fiction at the American Academy in Berlin.

BIOGRAPHY

Born in New York, in 1970 and raised in the Orthodox Jewish community in West Hempstead, Nathan Englander is a prominent contemporary Jewish American author. Englander attended high school at the Hebrew Academy of Nassau County and earned a bachelor's degree from Binghamton University; he also has studied at the Iowa Writers' Workshop at the University of Iowa. Englander moved to New York to teach fiction in Hunter College's Master of Fine Arts Program in Creative Writing at City University of New York.

Englander is best known for his short-story collection *For the Relief of Unbearable Urges*, the themes of which address many elements of culture and religion from Englander's upbringing. Though he grew up in a Orthodox community of strict Jewish observance, and though his early schooling emphasized adherence to Jewish laws and customs, Englander later opted to attend a secular university and eventually departed from the traditional lifestyle in which he was raised.

After visiting Israel during his college years, Englander grew enamored of the Holy Land but thereafter adopted a more secular lifestyle, pursuing interests in photography and later in writing. Nevertheless, Jewish religion and traditions remain a quintessential part of Englander's life and his writings. His first published short story, "The Twenty-Seventh Man" (1993), contains Jewish characters and reveals the influence on Englander's writing of Nikolai Gogol and Singer; themes of Jewish and Eastern European heritage pervade his work.

ANALYSIS

Nathan Englander's highly acclaimed prose earned him a hefty advance for his short-story collection and generated positive critical attention. Even before his collection was published, critics had compared Englander's writing style to that of some of the most established American Jewish writers. Englander's stories treat themes of Jewish identity, among both members of Englander's generation and those of generations past, often in the context of significant historical events in Jewish history, such as the Holocaust or Israel's wars. A recurring theme is the clash of the secular and the religious, the basis for which may be autobiographical in nature.

Englander's prose style relies heavily on dialogue and free indirect discourse to propel the narrative. Descriptive passages are sparse, and the stories move forward through the characters' rapid development over a series of larger-than-life events. Subtle humor is the lens through which Englander examines myriad elements of culture and human experience. His characters seemingly are universal, but the situations they face are

Nathan Englander (Rex Features via AP Images)

often imbued with elements of dramatic Jewish-centered irony. What imagery is evident often serves to shock or to add a surreal quality to an otherwise straightforward plotline and to hyperbolize specific plot elements to striking effect. However, Englander resists the tendency to stereotype, creating dynamic characters who represent a concept or vision rather than archetypes.

In interviews, Englander has emphasized universality as one of the most important elements of his collection; his hope is that his readers connect with the characters and their experiences. Judaism and Jewish culture thus provide the foundation for Englander's examination of abstract issues of identity, desire, hope, change, and culture. However, while Englander's intent was not to write a book solely for Jewish readership or focusing exclusively on Jewish themes, some of the stories and characters' voices are so deeply steeped in the religion and culture as to be almost inaccessible to those with little knowledge of Judaism and its mores. Englander does not always offer translations of his Yiddish turns of phrase, and he frequently references components of Jewish observance that would be familiar only to devoutly observant readers.

"THE GILGUL OF PARK AVENUE"

Winner of the 2000 O. Henry Prize, this story tells of the Gentile Charles Luger, who, while riding a taxi through the streets of New York City, suddenly realizes he is Jewish. What ensues is a colorful journey in which Charles must face breaking from his secular life, including his marriage of twenty-seven years, to pursue a spiritual and religious journey into devout Judaism. As the character faces the risk of losing his wife to his newfound devotion, Englander explores the individual's relationship with God and partner and examines the choices made to pursue a relationship with God in spite of challenges and criticism.

In this story, as in many of his others, Englander addresses the experiences of the secular Jew, generations removed from the shtetls of his ancestors. As a Gentile suddenly becoming acquainted with Judaism, Charles does not seek a traditional spiritual adviser but instead finds one who lives on the fringes of Jewish society and is himself a convert of sorts. Furthermore, Charles is selective in following particular Jewish customs as he comes to learn about them, not following any particular spiritual path but diving headfirst into the middle of Jewish law.

The process of rebirth or, as Englander describes it, the reincarnation of a Jewish soul--the meaning of *gilgul* in the story's title--characterizes the experience of many secular Jews who find themselves adrift in secular society with little spiritual direction. As such, even as a Gentile, Charles speaks to a generation of Jews cut off from the spiritual guidance of their grandfathers' communities; furthermore, in establishing such a wholly new Jewish identity, Charles becomes the voice of a generation of spiritual seekers of all faiths.

"FOR THE RELIEF OF UNBEARABLE URGES"

The title story of this collection, and one of the shortest stories to appear therein, "For the Relief of Unbearable Urges" tells of Dov Benyamin, a "black hat" or member of the extremely Orthodox Hasidic community. Dov's wife, practicing ritual purity, turns away from him night after night, to the extent that he feels an unbearable pressure and turns to his rabbi for counsel. The rabbi gives Dov special dispensation to visit a prostitute for relief, and Dov, who has never made physical contact with a woman other than his mother and wife, suddenly finds himself uncomfortably close to an American prostitute. Thereafter, Dov is consumed with guilt and with an extreme burning sensation that reminds him of the sin he has committed, and this prevents him from returning to his wife, even after she once again shows interest in their relationship.

The narrative casts no judgment on the lifestyle choices of the ultra-Orthodox but examines the strictures of the culture and the clash with the secular lifestyle prevalent in cities such as Tel Aviv. The prostitute tells Dov that he is not the first "black hat" she has been with, raising briefly the question of how commonly such dispensations are offered, or how often the strictly observant wander outside their faith. The extreme situation of the story may be a hyperbole partly responsive to Englander's own journey away from a strictly observant lifestyle, especially in its setting in Israel and with characters at once so deeply rooted in and so sharply departed from the culture and lifestyle of Englander's upbringing. Again Englander raises questions of iden-

tity and heritage, without judgment but with close attention to personal choice over adherence to dogma.

"FREE FRUIT FOR YOUNG WIDOWS"

This short story narrates the tale of one Professor Tendler through the voice of Shimmy Gezer, a Holocaust survivor and father of the story's protagonist, Etgar. Shimmy and Tendler were in the Israeli army together and, before that, were both survivors of the Holocaust; by the story's end, they have grown old together as neighbors in the Israeli *shuk*, or marketplace. Though Tendler once viciously beat Shimmy, and though Tendler's actions have never seemed acceptable to Etgar, as he has heard them recounted by his father, Etgar listens attentively to his father's stories and lessons and acknowledges the different experiences that have led to their differing responses, ultimately coming to treat Tendler with the same compassion and respect that his father has always shown.

The multiple voices of the narrative--those of Shimmy and of Etgar--and the narration of Tendler's story allow Englander to examine both the personal aftermath of the events of the Holocaust and a series of philosophical perspectives on forgiveness and acceptance. As Etgar ages, Shimmy's stories of wartime provide Etgar with new and different details with each telling and reexamination of the events. Moreover, as Shimmy coaches his son through a series of lessons on humanity, justice, and personal struggle, the reader is left to draw his or her own conclusions about the rightness or wrongness of the characters' actions and responses, ultimately emerging with a series of reflections that are particularly poignant during a period of war.

OTHER MAJOR WORKS

LONG FICTION: *The Ministry of Special Cases*, 2007.

BIBLIOGRAPHY

Behlman, Lee. "The Escapist: Fantasy, Folklore, and the Pleasures of the Comic Book in Recent American Jewish Holocaust Fiction." *Shofar: An Interdisciplinary Journal of Jewish Studies* 22, no. 3 (Spring, 2004): 56-71. Explores contemporary American Jewish authors' use of fantasy in exploring themes related to the Holocaust, with special attention to Englander's short story "The Tumblers," in which the famous Fools of Chelm appear in Nazi Germany. Compares the writings of Englander, Jonathan Safran Foer, and Michael Chabon.

Feuer, Menachem, and Andrew Schmitz. "Hup! Hup! We Must Tumble: Toward an Ethical Reading of the Schlemiel." *Modern Fiction Studies* 54, no. 1 (2008): 91-114. Contextualizes the Fools of Chelm of Englander's story "The Tumblers," comparing the fools as they have appeared in traditional Jewish literature, to Englander's iteration; addresses ethical dilemmas as represented by these fools.

Lambert, Joshua N. *JPS Guide: American Jewish Fiction.* Philadelphia: Jewish Publication Society, 2009. Provides a brief synopsis of the stories contained within *For the Relief of Unbearable Urges* and positions the collection among other samples of American Jewish fiction, both contemporary and less recent. Provides a thorough introduction to the themes and ideas prevalent in the genre more generally.

Lyons, Bonnie. "Nathan Englander and Jewish Fiction from and on the Edge." *Studies in American Jewish Literature* 26 (2007): 65. Situates Englander's writing in the context of the broader genre of contemporary American Jewish fiction.

Stavans, Ilan. *The Inveterate Dreamer: Essays and Conversations on Jewish Culture.* Lincoln: University of Nebraska Press, 2001. Critiques the stories in Englander's debut collection, with specific attention to "The Twenty-Seventh Man"; provides limited insight into and predictions for Englander's career.

Rachel E. Frier

LOUISE ERDRICH

Born: Little Falls, Minnesota; June 7, 1954
Also known as: Milou North (shared with husband Michael Dorris)

PRINCIPAL SHORT FICTION

"The Red Convertible," 1981
"Scales," 1982
"The World's Greatest Fishermen," 1982
"American Horse," 1983
"Destiny," 1985
"Saint Marie," 1985
"Fleur," 1987
"Snares," 1987
"Matchimanito," 1988
The Red Convertible: Selected and New Stories, 1978-2008, 2009

OTHER LITERARY FORMS

Louise Erdrich (LEW-eez URD-rihch) is perhaps best known for her novels, which include *Love Medicine* (1984), *The Beet Queen* (1986), *Tracks* (1988), *The Bingo Palace* (1994), *Tales of Burning Love* (1996), *The Antelope Wife* (1998), and *The Master Butchers Singing Club* (2003), among others. She is also the author of several collections of poetry and a number of children's books.

ACHIEVEMENTS

Several of Louise Erdrich's stories have appeared in the annual *The Best American Short Stories* and *Prize Stories: The O. Henry Awards* series. She received a Nelson Algren Fiction Award for her short story "The World's Greatest Fishermen," as well as a National Endowment for the Arts Fellowship in 1982, the Pushcart Prize and the National Magazine Award for Fiction in 1983, a John Simon Guggenheim Memorial Foundation Fellowship in 1985, a Western Literary Association Award in 1992, and a Lifetime Achievement Award from the Native Writers' Circle of the Americas in 2000. She was named the Associate Poet Laureate of North Dakota in 2005 and won the Scott O'Dell Award for Historical Fiction, for the children's book *The Game of Silence* in 2006. *Love Medicine* received the Virginia McCormack Scully Prize, the National Book Critics Circle Award, the *Los Angeles Times* award for best novel, the Sue Kaufman Prize, the American Book Award, and *Love Medicine* was named one of the best eleven books of 1985 by *The New York Times Book Review*. Erdrich's novel *The Plague of Doves* (2008) was a finalist for the Pulitzer Prize.

BIOGRAPHY

Karen Louise Erdrich was born in Little Falls, Minnesota, on June 7, 1954, the first of seven children of a German father and a Chippewa mother. Erdrich spent much of her childhood in North Dakota, where her parents taught at the Wahpeton Indian Boarding School. A member of the first coeducational class at Dartmouth College in 1972, she received her B.A. in English in 1976. While teaching expository and creative writing on a fellowship at The Johns Hopkins University, she earned an M.A. from The Johns Hopkins Writing Program in 1979. In 1980, she worked as a textbook writer for the Charles Merrill Company, and a year later she became a visiting fellow at Dartmouth, where she was the Writer-in-Residence at Dartmouth's Native American Studies Program. On October 10, 1981, she married the writer Michael Dorris, a professor of anthropology at Dartmouth. The couple had three children and adopted three others. Dorris and Erdrich cowrote two books, *The Crown of Columbus* (1991) and *Route Two* (1991). Erdrich has said that the success of her works is due in great part to the collaboration with her husband. However, they divorced in 1997, and Dorris committed suicide after a lengthy and bitter child-custody battle. Erdrich moved to Minneapolis, Minnesota, where she owns a bookstore, Birchbark Books, and she has continued to write successful works of fiction.In 1981, Erdrich published her first short story, "The Red Convertible," in *Mississippi Valley Review*. Over the next two years, she published such award-winning stories as "The World's Greatest Fishermen" and "Scales." In 1984, she published her first collection of poetry, *Jacklight*, as well as her first novel, *Love Medicine*.

ANALYSIS

Just as fiction in general has opened up to a diverse ethnic spectrum of writers, so, too, has short fiction, and Louise Erdrich's stories stand as excellent examples of contemporary Native American literature. Like Leslie Marmon Silko, Linda Hogan, and Paula Gunn Allen, Erdrich has taken a place as one of the prominent female Native American authors of short fiction. Although many of her characters and settings evoke a Native American context, Erdrich also writes about poverty, rural life, northwestern landscapes, and fallible humanity. Even among American Indian stories, Erdrich's stand out for their multiethnic nature. Erdrich's stories include not only Native American characters but also characters of German, Swedish, and other European descent. Likewise, many of the stories' themes are not specifically Native American themes. Indeed, the themes of Erdrich's stories range from the effects of war on families and personal identity to loss of heritage and family and personal relationships.

Stylistically, Erdrich's stories reveal many similarities to those of writers she said had significant influence on her. The distinct sense of place, of character, and of history that colors the works of Toni Morrison, William Faulkner, and Italo Calvino is similarly prominent in Erdrich's stories. She said of Calvino that "the magic in his work is something that has been an influence," which is clear, especially in such Erdrich stories as "Fleur" and "Snares." As Faulkner does with Yoknapatawpha County, Erdrich creates a world of the Chippewa reservation and the town of Argus, in which and around which nearly all of her stories occur. Many of her characters are employed repeatedly in her stories. Minor characters in one story may be the central characters in another or relatives of characters in one story are featured in later stories. Thus, most of Erdrich's stories connect to create a fictional world, which appears as true as the real world.

Like that of many other Native American authors, Erdrich's writing has been described as Magical Realism by some scholars, who place her work alongside that of Gabriel Garcia Márquez. However, this term is derided by some within the Native American community, who see it as a generic label for writing that does not conform to a strictly rational, western perspective. It may be more accurate to approach Erdrich's style as an emotional landscape representing a multitude of perspectives. Erdrich has said that "the story starts to take over if it is good." Her stories fulfill this criterion, capturing readers' imagination and carrying them along on an intense mental ride. Through her masterful use of metaphor, Erdrich crafts a symbolic landscape of allusion and inference, and she relies heavily on foreshadowing to create a sense of destiny in her tales. Her stories truly "touch some universals" that embrace readers of all ages, cultures, and beliefs.

"THE RED CONVERTIBLE"

"The Red Convertible" was Erdrich's first published story. Like many of her stories, this tale of two brothers later became a chapter in the novel *Love Medicine*. On the surface, "The Red Convertible" appears to be a simple tale of two brothers and the car they share. Lyman Lamartine, a young Indian with a "touch" for money, and his brother Henry save enough money to buy a used red Oldsmobile convertible. Lyman tells the story, describing the early adventures he and his brother shared in the car. However, as the story progresses, it becomes clear that much more than the car is important in this story. Lyman describes how Henry had changed when he returned home from the Vietnam War. While the family tries to help the deeply depressed Henry,

Louise Erdrich (AP Photo/Dawn Villella)

Lyman tricks his brother into fixing up the car that Lyman damaged purposely. While Henry does improve, even the car cannot save him, and he commits suicide in the end. In this story, the red convertible represents the freedom and innocence of youth, yet once those things are lost, because of the war in Henry's case and because of the altered Henry in Lyman's case, they cannot be regained; they must be let go. While the story unfolds mainly on the reservation, part of its success is that the themes (the loss of innocence, the effects of war) are universal, which allows any reader to understand and be intrigued by the tale.

"SAINT MARIE"

Like many of Erdrich's stories, "Saint Marie" also became a chapter in *Love Medicine*. "Saint Marie" is the story of a young Indian girl, who goes to the Catholic convent near the reservation so she might prove she is better than the other heathen Indians. Marie tries hard to keep Satan out of her life, yet one of the nuns, Sister Leopolda, believes Marie to be completely under the devil's control. Leopolda proceeds to torture Marie to the point of stabbing her with a fork in order to expunge the evil. To cover her madness, Leopolda lies to the other nuns, telling them that Marie must be touched by God as she has the signs of the stigmata on her hand; Marie must be a saint. However, Marie uses her knowledge of the truth of what happened to intimidate and humble Leopolda. Once again, this is a story about loss of innocence, about the psychological effects of a traumatic event in a young person's life. Similarly, Marie's struggle with her beliefs and Leopolda's madness are not necessarily specific to Native Americans, so many readers can access the story and enjoy it.

"DESTINY"

A story that later became part of *The Beet Queen*, "Destiny" describes Celestine Duval's visit to see her granddaughter's Christmas play. Wallacette, Celestine's granddaughter, is a large, strong, impulsive girl, who intimidates the other children in her school and town. The destiny of the title is Wallacette's destiny to be strong and independent, just like her grandmother. Celestine adores Wallacette, though she does not get along well with Wallacette's parents. In particular, there is bad blood between Celestine and her daughter-in-law, whose gelatin molds with vegetables in them are a source of great disgust for Celestine. The story turns comic when Wallacette hits a little boy she likes when he does not cooperate in the play, and it ends on a humorous note as Celestine reveals that the secret dish she had taken to the play with her daughter-in-law's name on it was a gelatin mold with nuts and bolts in it. This entertaining story is universal in its depictions of family struggles and of the pains of growing up. The psychological element still exists in this story, but some of the intense emotional pains are absent, which allows a humorous tone to come through.

"FLEUR"

"Fleur" presents the story of one woman's multiple drowning experiences and her influence on the people around her. Told from the point of view of Pauline Puyat, this story later became a chapter in *Tracks* (1988). Pauline describes how Fleur Pillager drowned several times, and every man who rescued her ended up either crazy or dead. Pauline believes that Fleur has special magic powers, and she tells the story of the time Fleur left the reservation and went to the town of Argus. After beating a group of men at cards for a number of weeks, Fleur is attacked by the men in a smokehouse. Pauline stands by and watches the event, doing nothing to help Fleur. However, Fleur has her revenge when, in the midst of a storm that came from nowhere and touched nothing that Fleur valued, the men become locked in a meat freezer. Pauline believes that Fleur called up the storm. While the story is about Fleur, it is also about Pauline. Pauline voices her own feelings and thoughts throughout the story, revealing the guilt she feels for not helping Fleur as well as the envy she feels toward this strong woman. Fleur is an enigma to Pauline, but she is also what Pauline seems to want to be in this story.

"MATCHIMANITO"

Though it was published after "Fleur," "Matchimanito" is the story of how Fleur came to be the last living member of her family and what happened to her when she came back to the reservation from Argus. An old man, Nanapush, tells how he found Fleur amid her dead family and took her away to recover from the "spotted sickness." This story reveals that Fleur, from the beginning, is different from everyone else. She is quiet yet powerful. Upon returning from Argus, she

lives alone in a cabin next to Matchimanito, the lake, which fuels rumors about her relationship with the lake monster, Mishepeshu. However, Fleur soon attracts a young man, Eli Kashpaw, and they live as husband and wife by the lake. Fleur becomes pregnant, and her pregnancy sparks more rumors, as the child's paternity is questioned. The birth of the child is difficult, and though many people believe that Fleur and her baby are dead, both live to prove them wrong. This is a powerful story because it demonstrates the strength of Fleur, the mixing of the old Indian ways with the new ones, the interaction of the community and individuals, and the history of both one person and a people. This story is particularly successful in its ability to show all of these things without force-feeding them to the reader.

THE RED CONVERTIBLE

A collection of previously published and new stories, *The Red Convertible: Selected and New Stories, 1978-2008*, presents many of Erdrich's short texts together for the first time. Erdrich's critically acclaimed stories, such as "The Red Convertible" and "The World's Greatest Fishermen," appear alongside tales previously presented as chapters in her famous novels *Love Medicine*, *The Beet Queen*, and *Tracks*. In some of the pieces, such as "F---- with Kayla and You Die," however, the reader encounters new characters and narrators for the first and only time within the collection, a powerful juxtaposition from the first half of the book. Many stories employ the author's penchant for tales of multigenerational households who face anxiety when confronted with the passage of time. Consequently, *The Red Convertible* reads like a family history orated by a relative who is "in the know." The stories both clarify and hide details about the characters, and different narrative perspectives used in separate stories allow events to unwind from new and surprising vantage points. Although Erdrich's work is noted for its humor, the stories in this collection are rarely of the lighthearted, feel-good variety. Erdrich forces her reader, like her characters must do, to find humor amid the grim desperation of rural poverty and reservation life. However, most of the pieces end with negation, and even though characters often come to a greater awareness of themselves or a realization about their relationship with others, this knowledge often comes with a horrible price. For example, Nector Kashpaw finally ends his affair with Lulu Nanapush, realizing the appreciation he has for his wife, Marie, in "The Plunge of the Brave," but only after he decides to leave his marriage and accidentally burns his lover's house to the ground. Still, these stories are not mere representations of human suffering, for it is the reaction of these characters to the crushing weight of life and fate that redeems them. Although Marie is beaten, humiliated, scalded, and finally stabbed by a zealous nun in "Saint Marie," she wields her wounds with a fierce pride, bearing them as a stigmata of destiny and power.

Viewed as a whole, the stories within *The Red Convertible* assert the necessity of community. The various characters are surrounded by immediate family, distant relatives, small-town acquaintances, and rural gossip. However, *The Red Convertible* also raises provocative questions about the effect of such bonds. For example, in "The Plunge of the Brave," Kashpaw laments that each of his intimate acquaintances wants something from him, provoking the reader to see obligation as a necessary component of human community. In other stories, such as "The Future Home of the Living God," characters both desire closer relationships with their families, and simultaneously strive for an acknowledgment of their individualism. *The Red Convertible* conveys more than one specific theme, showing characters wrestling with a palpable sense of confinement and a longing for physical and emotional intimacy.

OTHER MAJOR WORKS

LONG FICTION: *Love Medicine*, 1984 (revised and expanded, 1993); *The Beet Queen*, 1986; *Tracks*, 1988; *The Crown of Columbus*, 1991 (with Michael Dorris); *The Bingo Palace*, 1994; *Tales of Burning Love*, 1996; *The Antelope Wife*, 1998; *The Last Report on the Miracles at Little No Horse*, 2001; *The Master Butchers Singing Club*, 2003; *Four Souls*, 2004; *The Painted Drum*, 2005; *The Plague of Doves*, 2008; *Shadow Tag*, 2010.

POETRY: *Jacklight*, 1984; *Baptism of Desire*, 1989; *Original Fire: Selected and New Poems*, 2003.

NONFICTION: *The Blue Jay's Dance: A Birth Year*, 1995; *Books and Islands in Ojibwe Country*, 2003.

CHILDREN'S LITERATURE: *Grandmother's Pigeon*,

1996 (illustrated by Jim LaMarche); *The Birchbark House*, 1999; *The Range Eternal*, 2002; *The Game of Silence*, 2005.

EDITED TEXT: *The Best American Short Stories 1993*, 1993.

BIBLIOGRAPHY

Beidler, Peter G., and Gay Barton. *A Reader's Guide to the Novels of Louise Erdrich*. Columbia: University of Missouri Press, 2006. An essential companion to Erdrich's body of work, this concordance contains many helpful research and comprehension tools, including a chronology of historical and fictional events, a genealogy and description of all characters, and a glossary of Native American phrases employed within her fiction.

Bruchac, Joseph. "Whatever Is Really Yours: An Interview with Louise Erdrich." In *Survival This Way: Interviews with American Indian Poets*. Tucson: University of Arizona Press, 1987. Erdrich discusses her poetry in particular but also her inspirations for her stories and her philosophy on what makes a good story. She explains how the characters and their stories are formed as well.

Dyck, Reginald. "When Love Medicine Is Not Enough: Class Conflict and Work Culture on and off the Reservation." *American Indian Culture and Research Journal* 30, no. 3 (2006): 23-43. Approaches Native American literature, and Erdrich's *Love Medicine* stories in particular, through the character's socioeconomic situations. By focusing on work and class, this article departs from the common questions of identity and culture, which inform other critical studies.

Ferguson, Suzanne. "The Short Stories of Louise Erdrich's Novels." *Studies in Short Fiction* 33 (1996): 541-555. An excellent discussion of four short stories-- "Saint Marie," "Scales," "Fleur," and "Snares"--and how they were modified when they became chapters in the novels. Ferguson also argues that alone the short stories should be read differently from when they are presented as chapters in a novel. This is a good article for clarifying the differences between the short stories and their counterpart chapters in the novels.

Pacht, Michelle. "Creating Community: Motherhood and the Search for Identity in Louise Erdrich's *Love Medicine.*" In *Narratives of Community: Women's Short-Story Sequences*, edited by Roxanne Harde. Newcastle, England: Cambridge Scholars, 2007. This chapter holds up Erdrich's stories as examples of "narratives of community," which ignore linear development, preserve the patterns of traditional cultures, and reflect the episodic heritage of the oral tradition. In examining the creation of personal identity, the role of motherhood, and the intersections of community, Pacht explores the common themes in Erdrich's short stories.

Rainwater, Catherine. "Louise Erdrich's Storied Universe." In *The Cambridge Companion to Native American Literature*, edited by Joy Porter. Cambridge, England: Cambridge University Press, 2005. This section offers a comprehensive discussion of Erdrich's major works and themes. Rainwater briefly recounts Erdrich's biography, awards, and major works before discussing the author's inclusive writing style and overall accessibility. The chapter offers a summary of Erdrich's major fictional works, but stops short of close reading and instead presents both praise and criticism of the author's individual works and common themes.

Keri L. Overall
Updated by Ryan D. Stryffeler

BRIAN EVENSON

Born: Ames, Iowa; August 12, 1966

PRINCIPAL SHORT FICTION

Altmann's Tongue: Stories and a Novella, 1994
The Din of Celestial Birds, 1997
Contagion, and Other Stories, 2000
The Wavering Knife, 2004
Fugue State, 2009

OTHER LITERARY FORMS

Known primarily for his short-story collections, Brian Evenson (EH-vehn-suhn) also has written five novels: *Father of Lies* (1998), *Dark Property: An Affliction* (2002), *The Open Curtain* (2006), and *Dead Space: Martyr* (2010). He also has written a novella, *Baby Leg* (2009). He produced a nonfiction book, *Understanding Robert Coover* (2003), and nonfiction essays, including "Magic Realism." Many of his stories have been published as stand-alone works. His work is included in *Young Blood* (1994), an anthology of short fiction.

ACHIEVEMENTS

Brain Evenson has received many awards and worldwide academic and literary recognition for his works. They have been translated into Japanese, Spanish, French, and Italian. Evenson received the American Library Association Prize for Best Horror Novel of 2009 for his novel *Last Days*. Both *Fugue State* and *Last Days* were on *Time Out New York*'s top books list of 2009. *The Open Curtain* received the same distinction in 2006. In 2005, *The Wavering Knife* won the International Horror Guild Award for Best Story Collection. In 1998, his short story "Two Brothers" received an O. Henry Award. Many of his novels and collections of stories have been nominated for awards, often receiving finalist status or honorable mention. These, including the World Fantasy Award (finalist, 2009), O. Henry Award (finalist, 2002; honorable mention, 1998), and the Shirley Jackson Award (finalist, 2009), Evenson's 2006 translation of Claro's *Electric Flesh* (2003) received finalist designation in the French American Foundation's Translation Prize (2007).

BIOGRAPHY

Brian Evenson was born in Ames, Iowa, on August 12, 1966. His parents were liberal, sixth-generation Mormons. He spent most of his childhood in Utah. His parents, the only Democrats in a conservative neighborhood, instilled a love of reading in him. Evenson states that their intense devotion to books sometimes made it hard for him to get their attention while they were reading. He decided that there had to be something intrinsically valuable in books, and he started reading a broad spectrum of literature.

After completing high school, Evenson spent two years in Switzerland, Mexico, and France as a missionary for the Church of Jesus Christ of Latter-Day Saints (LDS). He received his B.A. from Brigham Young University (BYU). His M.A. and Ph.D. (in critical theory and English literature) degrees were received from the University of Washington.

Evenson's first university teaching position was at BYU. While there, his first book, *Altmann's Tongue*, was published in 1994. The violent content of the work met with disapproval from some students, faculty, and administrators at BYU. This eventually led to Evenson resigning from BYU and seeking voluntary excommunication from the LDS church. He resigned his tenured position at BYU and took a position at Oklahoma State University. From Oklahoma, he went on to teach at Syracuse University and the University of Denver. He then became the chair of the Literary Arts Program at Brown University. He also has participated in summer writing programs at various universities. He later partly attributed his divorce from his wife, Connie, to the controversy with BYU and the LDS church. He has two daughters from the marriage, Valerie and Sarah.

ANALYSIS

Brian Evenson writes about fear. His short fictions compel readers to participate psychologically in moments far darker than most would encounter in their own lives. Evenson's textual world is not an explanation of violence; it is violence brought to light without need of justification. Indeed, Evenson wants readers to make their own decisions about the dark side of human capabilities. The stories do not glamorize violent behavior; they confront it. Evenson has stated that evil is part of this world, and he simply exposes it.

There appear to be no limits on the almost hallucinatory nature of the violence and atrocity Evenson brings forth on the pages of his tales. A vagabond aimlessly crosses America, killing numerous women and carving symbols into their flesh; a father unexpectedly discovers the body of his dead daughter and buries it without mentioning the fact to others, who are worried about her disappearance; young people laugh with glee as the kittens they toss from their speeding car hit the surface of the highway with a final short squeal.

Evenson has suffered personally for his dedication to his writing. He was voluntarily excommunicated from the LDS Church. He has stated that the cause of this was the belief by some church authorities that presenting such graphic violence puts him on the side of the devil; how can a writer speak in an evil person's voice and not be a part of that evil? Of course, Evenson has a different stated purpose for his writing style. He creates situations that combine violence and modern America in a text that is meant to repulse readers. In a setting so completely devoid of morality, readers are forced to examine or create their own morality as an

Brian Evenson (Getty Images)

overlay or reaction to the text. The characters in these stories do not react. They simply act. The dialogues are direct results of their actions but do not include any self-evaluation of the events they are living out.

Evenson can be compared to Edgar Allan Poe. Evenson's works have a mysterious side to them; however, they go far beyond the subtly macabre tales of Poe. Evenson's stories do not imply brutality; they graphically expose and even accentuate the brutal horror that his demented protagonists act out. Themes of human fear and powerlessness abound. Psychotic obsessions transform and destroy most characters who appear in these works.

Humor is also present. Evenson's work is sadistic and full of dark parodies, yet the author skillfully and creatively weaves a sinister wit throughout many of his tales. Madness has its comical side, and the author brings it to the surface, thereby presenting readers with another aspect to examine through their own moral lens.

The collections of Evenson's short fiction are also short forays into the dark side of human psychology. The Kafkaesque scenes are full of people struggling against psychological questions. What are the limits of God, religion, and morality? Evenson creates characters caught between the extremes of morality and insanity, but no answers are given; that is up to readers.

Enter these brilliant works at your own risk. Readers who delve into the dark worlds of these stories may find the themes and events presented enter their psyche, subtly affecting personal vision and reasoning well beyond the end of the story. Evenson's works so profoundly enter a realm of violence that it seems to inflict a form of psychological violence on readers.

ALTMANN'S TONGUE

Altmann's Tongue is a collection of short stories, some as short as one page. A novella concludes the book. Evenson's skillful use of language lures the reader into scenes of detached barbarity. The characters and settings range from rural to urban. The unifying factor throughout the book is violence. Protagonists participate in a wide variety of horrific violence but show no emotional response to their own actions. The prose is simple but effectively stuns the reader into filling in the emotional blanks left by apparently

uncaring people in the text. Readers are left to witness brutal acts, and Evenson gives no clues as to the reasons for them.

In "Stung," a teenager is seduced by his mother after murdering his stepfather for no apparent reason. In the title story, the narrator is encouraged to eat the tongue of one of the two men a character has just murdered. In the novella "The Sanza Affair," detective Sanza is killed during his investigation of a series of murders. Another detective, Lund, soon finds the trail of evidence leads closer and closer to himself. As with other Evenson tales, a mystery is presented, but with a skewed and ironic outcome. Several of the tales are short-- just one or two pages. Their titles reveal what will take place. For example, in "Killing Cats," cats are killed. "The Abbreviated and Tragical History of the Auschwitz Barber" follows the title's promise in less than one page. These extremely short works are enigmatic, often sadistic, and without explanation.

The violent stories could have come from the most appalling segments of the evening news. The descriptions border on the prurient side of life. Whether rural or urban, animal or human, death is never far away. Evenson lets readers delve into the mind of the narrators and protagonists. What is found there requires readers either to reject the works outright or to accept the violence as an outside observer. The thoughts of the brutal characters often reveal a perverse sense of humor that Evenson's wit conveys with uncanny skill.

FUGUE STATE

Fugue State is a collection of nineteen short stories. In them, Evenson maintains suspense until the end of the tales. The situations of the characters run a broad range, such as a debilitating and advancing illness, amnesia, and an inability to control the words one speaks. Evenson's masterful use of surprising and sometimes odd textual linguistics allows him to subtly incorporate paranoia, dread, and madness into these tales. Like the tales of Poe, these stories lead readers into mysterious and disquieting realms. True to Evenson's previous works, he includes macabre but hilarious sentences at unexpected points in the stories.

An interesting difference from other Evenson collections is found in the black-and-white illustrations (by Zak Sally) that accompany the stories. However,

Evenson is a master at forcing readers to create their own fantasy world, and the illustrations serve as only one example of endless possibilities that the almost-hallucinatory tales illicit.

Another stylistic element that Evenson uses extensively in this collection is illnesses, debilitating emotional states, and sensory deprivations as background conditions for nightmarelike plots. For example, one character, Mudder Tongue, attempts to communicate an excruciating problem to his daughter, but he cannot control the words that he utters. He never connects and the daughter's decision that he should just interact with others leads to disastrous consequences. In "Dread," insomnia reaches catastrophic proportions, in which waking in the middle of the night leaves a terror-stricken character unable to move. Blindness accentuates the moral dilemmas found in "Helpful." "Fugue State" finds characters acquiring amnesia as a form of illness. They progress from bleeding to forgetting their names; eventually they end up unconscious and die. Similar to Nobel Prize in literature winner José Saramago's novel *Ensaio sobre a cegueira* (1995; *Blindness*, 1997), one character, Arnaud, attempts to survive the strange condition. He travels and experiences quarantines and thieves. He desperately communicates with dying people, but he is unable to remember why he is doing it and what he needs to do next.

This collection of short stories is more cerebral than Evenson's first collection. It does not provide more answers. However, the violence is more mental than physical. The horror of unjustified death is present, but the horridness of sadistic control, frightening pursuit, entrapment, and eventual death also challenge the psyche of readers. The enigmas in this Evenson collection are frightening but not as senselessly violent as some of his other short fiction.

CONTAGION, AND OTHER STORIES

In *Contagion*, Evenson locates several of the stories in the American West, where he spent most of his childhood. The language and themes suggest the author metaphysically has revisited the realm of his past issues with his previous church and western landscape. Examples of this can be found in the titles of several of the stories. Although the tale deals with an odd combination of murder and linguistics, the choice by Evenson to use the word "polygamy" in "The Polygamy of Language" is not coincidental. In "Two Brothers," two sons insist on a futile wait for God to save their father, a minister who has broken his leg. The title story, "Contagion," cryptically overlays an historical accounting of barbed wire onto a tragic tale of a twisted Wild West fantasy.

The author continues his practice of situating his stories in the realm of horror and enigmatic madness. Characters act out and confront the impossibility of their disturbed lives. They attempt to rectify nightmare scenarios without success. One man figures a way to escape a bad relationship, only to find out that it might not even exist. The protagonists are trapped in frightening realities that end up folding back upon themselves. They cannot escape; the problems are surreal psychologies that return time and again. In some ways, these tales are more troubling than Evenson's murderous and sarcastic stories from previous collections. In those, readers cannot feel the security of revulsion of the obscene. The events and emotions of these stories could very well be a part of readers' realities.

THE WAVERING KNIFE

The Wavering Knife could be described as a collection of short fiction that provides readers with a course in shock philosophy. Evenson continues with his presentations of a world of bloody violence. In these tales, however, he cleverly intertwines something more troubling: shapeless characters that force readers to construct philosophical reasons for the characters' existence. Other readers might determine that the opposite of this exists. That is, the allegorical portrayals of horrific violence and fear are like antimatter; they are found only in theory.

Evenson provides excruciatingly brutal and savage details of violent acts in the stories, but the characters and settings are vague to the point of possibly not existing. For example, in "White Square," pastel figures pass for humans. The author requires readers to focus on the frightening deeds and possible reasons for them rather on the atrocious characters that commit them. It could be imagined as a world where the mysteries of Poe mix with the hallucinatory realm of Lewis Carroll. Evenson provides no interpretations; he offers no lessons. It is up to readers either to reject the tales outright or to come up with their own insight into madness.

OTHER MAJOR WORKS

LONG FICTION: *Father of Lies*, 1998; *Dark Property: An Affliction*, 2002; *The Open Curtain*, 2006; *Last Days*, 2009; *Dead Space: Martyr*, 2010.

NONFICTION: "Magic Realism," 1998; *Understanding Robert Coover*, 2003.

TRANSLATIONS: *The Passion of Martin Fissel Brandt* by Christian Gailly, 2002; *Giacometti: Three Essays* by Jacques Dupin, 2003; *Mountain R* by Jacques Jouet, 2004; *Red Haze* by Christian Gailly (cotranslated with David Beus), 2005; *Donogoo-Tonka: Or, The Miracles of Science* by Jules Romain, 2009.

MISCELLANEOUS: *The Brotherhood of Mutilation*, 2003.

BIBLIOGRAPHY

Decker, Mark T, and Michael Austin. *Peculiar Portrayals: Mormons on the Page, Stage, and Screen.* Logan: Utah State University Press, 2010. Essays on authors who stray from the expected value system of the LDS church. Excellent explanation of Evenson's attitudes on the reason for the violence found within his works.

Evenson, Brian, and Marni Asplund-Campbell. "Evenson's Tongue: A Conversation with Brian Evenson." *Sunstone* 18, no. 2 (August, 1995): 71-75. Insightful interview with Evenson. Provides background information on the violence encountered in Evenson's works and, interestingly, the author explains his reasons for leaving his teaching position and church in order to remain true to his writing.

VanderMeer, Ann, and Jeff VanderMeer. *The New Weird.* San Francisco: Tachyon, 2008. Collection of authors who vary markedly from more conventional short fiction writers. Particularly valuable for positioning Evenson in his genre and contains a segment on his career as an emerging author. Includes bibliography.

Paul Siegrist

PERCIVAL EVERETT

Born: Fort Gordon, Georgia; December 22, 1956

PRINCIPAL SHORT FICTION

The Weather and Women Treat Me Fair, 1987
Big Picture, 1996
Damned If I Do, 2004

OTHER LITERARY FORMS

Percival Everett is best known for his novels, chief among them *Erasure* (2001), which garnered attention and debate for its portrayal of race and the world of publishing. His first novel, *Suder* (1983), centered on an African American baseball player, also drew critical attention. Several other novels, such as *The Body of Martin Aguilera* (1997) and *Cutting Lisa* (1986), which had no overt racial theme, were largely ignored. Everett also has published poetry in *Abstraktion und Einfühlung* (2008) and a collaborative work, *A History of the African American People (Proposed)* (2004), with James Kincaid, in which Everett appears as a character. *I Am Not Sidney Poitier* (2009) features a professor named "Percival Everett," who offers advice to the title character, Not Sidney Poitier, after meeting him as a student. Everett has written two novels revising classical Greek material, *For Her Dark Skin* (1990) and *Frenzy* (1997), and a cluster of novels set in the West, *Walk Me to the Distance* (1985), *God's Country* (1994), *Watershed* (1996), *American Desert* (2004), and *Wounded* (2005). *Walk Me to the Distance* was the basis for an American Broadcasting Company television film, *Follow Your Heart* (1990), though Everett did not approve of the adaptation and has said in interviews that the film has little connection to the original text. The novel *The Water Cure* (2007) recounts the harrowing story of the aftermath of the kidnapping and murder of a young girl told through the perspective of her father; it raises questions about the necessity and acceptability of torture that reflect the debate raised by actions of the military and intelligence communities during the Iraq War.

ACHIEVEMENTS

Percival Everett's novel *Zulus* (1990) won the New American Writing Award, and *Erasure*, his biting parody of race in the world of publishing, received the Hurston/Wright Legacy Award. Everett also has been the recipient of a PEN USA Literary Award and of a Literature Award from the American Academy of Arts and Letters. Everett has held fellowships from the Lila Wallace-*Reader's Digest* Foundation and from the University of New Mexico. Longwood University in Farmville, Virginia, awarded Everett the Dos Passos Prize in 2010.

BIOGRAPHY

Percival Everett was born in Fort Gordon, Georgia, and raised in Columbia, South Carolina, where he graduated from A. C. Flora High School. His father was a sergeant in the Army when Everett was born on the military base just outside Augusta but went on to become a dentist. Everett's parents, Percival Leonard Everett and Dorothy Stinson, settled in Columbia. Their son, Percival Everett, received a B.A. in philosophy with a minor in biochemistry in 1977 from the University of Miami in Florida and continued the study of philosophy at the University of Oregon from 1978 to 1980. He left the field of philosophy for creative writing, moving to Brown University, where he studied with novelist Robert Coover and earned an M.A. in fiction in 1982. For a brief time, Everett worked as a jazz musician, as a hand on a sheep ranch, and as a high school teacher. He served as an associate professor on the faculty of the University of Kentucky from January, 1985, to January, 1988; he then joined the faculty of the University of Notre Dame as a full professor. Everett left Notre Dame in 1991 for the University of California, Riverside, and finally moved to the University of Southern California in 1998, where he was named a Distinguished Professor in 2007. He also has taught at Bennington College and the University of Wyoming. In addition to being an accomplished writer, Everett is known for his work as a painter. Everett is married to Danzy Senna, who is also a writer, and they have two children.

ANALYSIS

In a 2010 interview with Isaiah Sheffer, host of the radio program *Selected Shorts*, Percival Everett responded to a question about the meaning of "The Fix" by saying, "I make stories; I don't make meaning." This fairly characterizes the short stories and novella that Everett has published. His stories have appeared in *Callaloo* and elsewhere, but *The Weather and Women Treat Me Fair*, *Big Picture*, and *Damned If I Do* represent his best-known work. Though all three collections feature recurrent threads among the stories, in terms of theme, setting, or characters, the stories vary widely, from an eerie surrealism to a sometimes brutal realism.

As in his long fiction, Everett employs multiple approaches in the short stories, from first-person unreliable narrators to the completely external third-person omniscient. The stories also often mix the comic and the tragic, another feature they have in common with his novels. In that interview with Sheffer, Everett claimed that "humor is a wonderful trap." The reader can be led into deeper waters through laughter. Not only do the stories share strategies with the novels, but several of them also appear in one form or another in the longer works, such as *Glyph* (1999), *Watershed*, and *I Am Not Sidney Poitier.*

The story collections and *Grand Canyon, Inc.* (2001) draw on Everett's background in philosophy, and, more important, they reflect his ongoing dialogue with the American West in relation to American identity. The motif of fly fishing, which plays an important role in his novel *Erasure*, also appears time and again in the stories, where it is strongly linked to father-son relationships and meditative states of mind.

THE WEATHER AND WOMEN TREAT ME FAIR

Everett's 1987 collection holds several tales about cowboys, including the title story. "The Weather and Women Treat Me Fair" retells the familiar story of a cowboy reluctant to commit to marriage with his longtime girlfriend and ends with a comic marriage proposal, when that same cowboy sees his girlfriend with another man. The reverse scenario occurs in "Thirty-Seven Just to Take a Fall," where rodeo rider Luke Ellis has lost his girlfriend to a man he cuttingly refers to as "a Texan." This story takes a dark turn when Luke inadvertently attends a dogfight and frees a pit bull after seeing another dog killed in the arena. Of course, the dog has been trained to fight, and Luke ultimately leaves him tied to the bumper of the Texan's car and heads for Oregon. That signature dark humor yields to a more somber vision in "Gaining the Door," the brief recounting of Old Cody Wilson's decision to end his own life by turning himself out into the snow to die just as an old horse would be turned out. In "Cry About a Nickel," the narrator, Joe Cooper, is the lone black man in that part of Oregon, and he walks into an intense family drama between a father and a son as Joe takes a temporary job looking after their horses. Joe learns that the owner's wife has committed suicide, and he observes the overprotective behavior of the widower toward his son, Charlie. Both the father and the son become friendly with Joe, who comes to believe that Charlie has experienced some trauma that his father wants to deny. When Joe offers his employer advice about the boy, Joe is sent packing.

BIG PICTURE

The title story in this collection ends the book and ties into two other stories, "Cerulean" and "Dicotyles Tacaju." They are not treated as a continuous narrative, but they all deal with the African American artist Michael Lawson and provide a clear sense of development. They connect back to the story "A Home for Hachita" in *The Weather and Women Treat Me Fair*, though the artist in that story is named Evan Keeler. Like Keeler, Lawson suffers from mental illness, a fact that becomes apparent only at the end of "Cerulean." The story begins in a conventional suburban home with a comfortable middle-class couple, Michael and Gail. An enigmatic stranger who never speaks turns up at their door with a lawnmower; he looks so needy that Michael gives him a job, and the stranger returns every day to mow an already perfect lawn. The figure of the mower is ultimately internalized as Michael's conflicted love for his wife. He becomes so absorbed in the cerulean blue abstract painting into which he displaces his emotions that he ingests the paint. He awakes in a psychiatric facility where he resists treatment and recognizes his emotional distance from Gail.

"Diotyles Tajacu" takes its title from the scientific name for the wild boar; Michael is out of the hospital, and Gail has left him for a dermatologist. After burning all his paintings, Michael packs up to drive to New York. When he stops at a diner decorated with hunting trophies, he identifies with the one-eyed boar over his booth. The cook finally sells it to him, and the narrative takes a hallucinatory turn. As Michael drives, he senses the boar as a living presence and begins to identify with it. Michael runs into a sculptor friend near Laramie, Wyoming, and ends up spending the night at his house. There he meets another couple invited for the night, and the wife, a writer, admires Michael's painting and makes sexual overtures, which he rejects. He struggles with one of his recurring headaches and wants to go to the bathroom, but the brilliant white décor of the guest bathroom terrifies him. In an almost farcical scene, he sneaks through the master bedroom, where his hosts are having sex, then meets the woman writer naked on his way out. Michael runs for his truck and leaves. He stops, exhausted, at Medicine Bow, wishing he could set the boar free. These scenes correlate to Michael's earlier break with reality and the breakup of his marriage.

The title story closes the entire collection with another episode from Michael's life. He has a new young wife, Karen, and a gallery show in Washington, D.C., for his new paintings sponsored by a longtime supporter of his work. The show succeeds beyond expectations, and a wealthy art investor offers thirty thousand dollars for Michael's "big picture." Michael feels a headache coming on when he considers this purely commercial transaction over a piece he deeply loves. His refusal to sell is overruled by the gallery owner, and the buyer regards Michael's public resistance to the sale as good publicity. In the end, Michael cannot reconcile himself to the deal and plans to steal the painting back that same night. Karen hesitates before supporting his choice, signaling the thematic return of marital conflict. Everett's signature dark humor closes the story; the couple unwittingly parks in front of the Moroccan Embassy, and Michael finds his wife being searched when he returns with the stolen painting. They must first explain themselves to the embassy guards and then to the D.C. police, but they do leave with the painting. However, in the "big[ger] picture," the relationship between Michael and Karen has been compromised by the incident. Michael twice asks Karen if she thinks he is insane, and though she answers twice in the negative, he no longer trusts her words. These three stories reiterate the patterned dissolution of the marital bond and the troubling intersection between talent and instability.

DAMNED IF I DO

Many of the stories in this collection deal with the American West, but the two best known, "The Fix" and "The Appropriation of Cultures," showcase the breadth of Percival Everett's writing palette. "The Fix," a modern-day parable, introduces the character Sherman Olney through a third-person narration from the point of view of Washington, D.C., sandwich-shop owner Douglas Langley. Langley helps Olney after three men have beaten him severely near the shop. In return for Langley's kindness, Olney offers to fix a noisy old refrigerator. He next moves into the room over the shop and begins fixing everything that comes his way, from the foot massager that belongs to Langley's wife to the toy a child brings with him to the lunch counter. The story escalates when Olney proves able to heal emotional and physical wounds and climaxes with his resurrection of a dead woman. The shockingly successful combination of humor and the mysterious spiritual ability of Olney turns serious at the end of the story. Olney attempts to escape into anonymity, utterly drained by the demands made on him, and Langley last sees him poised in the middle of a bridge ready to jump, besieged from both ends by people screaming for him to fix them.

"The Appropriation of Cultures," set in South Carolina, also has lyrical moments, despite the brilliant comic catalyst that moves the story forward, a reappropriation of the Confederate battle flag. It opens with the main character, wealthy African American Daniel Barkley, being heckled as he plays in his favorite jazz club. The racist in the audience calls for "Dixie," only to be silenced by the beautiful performance Daniel produces. Daniel feels himself drawn into the music on a more personal level, and this sets him on the path toward the story's title action, an appropriation of southern culture. He finds his next object in the Confederate flag displayed in the rear window of a used pickup truck he

buys. The seller offers to remove it, and Daniel makes it clear that he wants the flag as well as the truck. Driving the truck around the community, he is challenged by white racists, but his insistence on treating the flag as a symbol of black power confuses his antagonists and draws in other African Americans. His campaign is so successful that white racists abandon the flag, and it is quietly removed from the state capitol building. Just as he has transformed the perspective of others, Daniel, too, views himself as southern in a new way.

OTHER MAJOR WORKS

LONG FICTION: *Suder*, 1983; *Walk Me to the Distance*, 1985; *Cutting Lisa*. 1986; *Zulus*, 1990; *For Her Dark Skin*, 1990; *God's Country*, 1994; *Watershed*, 1996; *The Body of Martin Aguilera*, 1997; *Frenzy*, 1997; *Glyph*, 1999; *Erasure*, 2001; *Grand Canyon, Inc.*, 2001; *American Desert*, 2004; *A History of African American People Proposed*, 2004 (with James Kincaid); *Wounded*, 2005; *The Water Cure*, 2007; *I Am Not Sidney Poitier*, 2009.

POETRY: *Re:f(gesture)*, 2006; *Abstraktion und Einfühlung*, 2008.

CHILDREN'S LITERATURE: *The One That Got Away*, 1992.

BIBLIOGRAPHY

Monaghan, Peter. "The Satiric Inferno." *The Chronicle of Higher Education* 51, no.23 (Fall, 2005): A18-A20. In this interview and analysis Monaghan gives an overview of Everett's major publications and questions the author about his influences, style, and intended audience.

"Percival Everett: A Special Section. " *Callaloo* 28, no. 2 (Spring, 2005): 291-342. This volume of the noted African American literary journal devotes a substantial section to Everett. It includes an interview, personal tributes, images of Everett's paintings, and substantial critical essays. The essays address *God's Country*, *Glyph*, *Erasure*, and *Watershed*. Fiona Macrae, Everett's editor at Graywolf Press, also writes a brief discussion of *Frenzy*, and the volume contains a dialogue between Everett and James Kincaid, a professor of English at the University of California and Everett's collaborator on *A History of the African American People.*

Ramsey, W. M. "Knowing Their Place: Three Writers and the Postmodern South." *The Southern Literary Journal* 37, no.2 (Spring, 2005): 119-139. Ramsay formulates the concept of the "postmodern South," then places African American authors Yusef Komunyakaa, James McBride, and Everett within that context. Ramsay offers substantive analyses of stories, such as "The Appropriation of Cultures," and of the novels *Glyph* and *Erasure.*

Sanchez-Arce, Ana Maria. "'Authenticism,' or the Authority of Authenticity." *Mosaic* 40, no. 3 (September. 2007): 139. This article frames an analysis of *Erasure* with the concept of "authenticity" as defined by Lionel Trilling, Edward Said, Gayatri Chakravorti Spivak., and Jean-Francois Lyotard.

Shavers, Rone. "Percival Everett." *Bomb* 88 (Summer, 2004): 46-51. In this wide-ranging interview, Shavers discusses with Everett the sources and inspiration for his work.

Stewart, Anthony. "Uncategorizable Is Still a Category: An Interview with Percival Everett." *Canadian Review of American Studies* 37, no. 3 (2007): 293-324. This extensive interview with Stewart preceded the publication of *The Water Cure*, which Everett discusses. Stewart also poses questions on Everett's identity as an American and African American writer, eliciting thoughtful answers. Everett also responds at some length on his relationship to Ralph Ellison and his interests in philosophy and literary theory.

Amee Carmines

F

James T. Farrell

Born: Chicago, Illinois; February 27, 1904
Died: New York, New York; August 22, 1979

PRINCIPAL SHORT FICTION

Calico Shoes, and Other Stories, 1934

Guillotine Party, and Other Stories, 1935

Can All This Grandeur Perish?, and Other Stories, 1937

Fellow Countrymen: Collected Stories, 1937

The Short Stories of James T. Farrell, 1937

$1,000 a Week, and Other Stories, 1942

Fifteen Selected Stories, 1943

To Whom It May Concern, and Other Stories, 1944

Twelve Great Stories, 1945

More Fellow Countrymen, 1946

More Stories, 1946

When Boyhood Dreams Come True, 1946

The Life Adventurous, and Other Stories, 1947

A Hell of a Good Time, 1948

An American Dream Girl, 1950

French Girls Are Vicious, and Other Stories, 1955

An Omnibus of Short Stories, 1956

A Dangerous Woman, and Other Stories, 1957

Saturday Night, and Other Stories, 1958

Side Street, and Other Stories, 1961

Sound of a City, 1962

Childhood Is Not Forever, 1969

Judith, and Other Stories, 1973

Olive and Mary Anne, 1977

OTHER LITERARY FORMS

James T. Farrell's more than sixty volumes of publications include essays, critical writing, plays, novels, and social commentary. His novel, *Studs Lonigan: A Trilogy* (1935), was the basis for a film in 1960, and in 1979 it was adapted for television and presented to critical acclaim.

ACHIEVEMENTS

Although he wrote more than two hundred short stories, many of them closely related to his acclaimed novels, James T. Farrell is seldom discussed as a short-story writer or represented in anthologies of fiction. He is, above all, a novelist, one who has incorporated many of his shorter works into his later novels, thereby subordinating them to the longer works. As a politically committed writer, he was also out of fashion in a country where writers with communist or socialist leanings were unpopular. Since many of his stories do concern the plight of political writers, they seem a bit dated to the contemporary reader unfamiliar with the Leon Trotsky/ Vladimir Ilich Lenin wings of the Communist Party. In some respects, the short stories have suffered from their close ties to the novels, which themselves declined in popularity beginning in the 1950's.

BIOGRAPHY

Born and reared on the South Side of Chicago, James Thomas Farrell was educated at a series of parochial schools, attended the University of Chicago sporadically for three years during the 1920's, and attended New York University in 1941. The son and grandson of Irish teamsters, Farrell was also a teamster for a time and worked, variously, as a cigar store clerk, a filling station attendant, and a part-time newspaper reporter. He married Dorothy Patricia Butler in 1931, but was divorced; married the actress Hortense Alden, whom he also divorced; and remarried Dorothy Butler Farrell in 1955, but they separated three years later. He had one child by his second wife. Farrell received a John Simon Guggenheim Memorial Foundation Fellowship for creative writing in 1936, a Book-of-the-Month Club prize for *Studs Lonigan* in 1937, and a Newberry Library Fellowship in 1949. He was a member of the

National Institute of Arts and Letters and the Overseas Press Club. He died in 1979.

ANALYSIS

James T. Farrell's stories, because of their often graphic language and action and, perhaps, because of their relatively uneven quality, are not often anthologized. His best work comes from the early collections such as *Calico Shoes, and Other Stories*, *Guillotine Party, and Other Stories*, and *$1,000 a Week, and Other Stories*. When his stories remain within the realm of his Chicago youth, he is at his best; and even his later stories set in Chicago reflect the tough vibrance evident in the likes of "Willie Collins," "The Triumph of Willie Collins," and "Saturday Night."

Farrell's characters never seem fabricated. They strut and boast. They cringe at frightening things, and they suffer from the inexorable progress of time--perhaps the dominant theme in Farrell's work. Never conventionally literary, the real nature of Farrell's stories makes them compelling if not always tasteful and appealing. There is no varnish on Farrell's rough exterior.

James T. Farrell (Library of Congress)

The reader is expected to accept the stories in their raw, immediate sense.

The individual is the unsteady center of Farrell's stories; a large number of his stories are almost vignettes of individuals as they function in daily life. It is this attention to the individual that sets Farrell's work apart. Farrell's universe does not admit the presence of predestiny or fortune or, despite his rich Irish Catholic milieu, divine intervention; his individual succeeds or fails by virtue of his own efforts and abilities. The only force beyond the control of the individual is time; along with the freedom of the individual will, time rules Farrell's work. There is a consistent determination on the part of Farrell's characters to recapture the past, elude the present, or rush into the future. In each instance, despite their strivings, they inevitably fail. Farrell does not celebrate the failure, but he portrays it honestly, and failure sets the tone of his stories.

"WHEN BOYHOOD DREAMS COME TRUE"

Both of Farrell's major themes are projected in "When Boyhood Dreams Come True." Tom Finnegan, a man trying to understand and recapture his past, fails in a dream world that is reminiscent of the *Inferno* in *La divina commedia* (c. 1320; *The Divine Comedy*, 1802), *The Pilgrim's Progress* (1678, 1684), and the Catholic catechism. Finnegan, on awakening, forgets the dream except for the one synthetic revelation that "almost explained the meaning of life." Finnegan is made aware that "the past was dead, gone. All his life had led up to this minute. Only this minute was real. The past was unreal. . . . It was gone." Finnegan fails to recapture the past and, at the end of the story, he is uncertain of his future, but the moment of reality, the now, is left for him to manipulate--to use or misuse as he is able. It is this juxtaposition of the impact of the past and of failure on which Farrell thrives.

Joe Eliot, in the story of the same name, struggles with the past in a similar fashion, but, unlike Finnegan, he is trapped--hamstrung by his failure and frustration. What Joe calls failures, however, are merely results of his inability to cope with things over which he has no control. When Joe refuses to ride home on the same car with his supervisor, he reflects "contempt," and the reader sees him as "uninterested," "bored," and passive to the point of giving his unfinished evening paper to his supervisor to get rid of him. Joe's reaction to his supervisor is typical of his relationship with human-kind. His contempt for and passive reaction to other men are direct results of his frustration with past failure and himself.

In the second of five parts, Joe sinks into a reminiscence of his past, which begins with bittersweet memories of the Seine in 1918 while he was in World War I and with remorseful recriminations against his wife, who died of peritonitis while he was in France. The reader learns that Joe has a Harvard University degree, was an All-American halfback, and felt that he "could have been something big." The reader also learns that he has had a break with his rich father (probably over Joe's marriage) and that he refuses a reconciliation despite overtures from his father. Farrell presents Joe as bitter and lonely but does not demand the reader's sympathy or pity. Joe deserves no pity in a situation he will not attempt to alter. The narrator declares of Joe: "He hadn't fitted into the world, and he didn't give a good goddamn."

After eating in a second-rate establishment, Joe walks through the Loop in Chicago. The narrator makes a point of coloring the scene with natural commentary about the soft night and the sunset, but Joe is unaffected by it all until, as he convinces himself he is a "failure," he suddenly notices "as if it were a discovery, a sky streaming with stars that were radiant on the surface of a deep blue." While the vision touches Joe, he belittles the experience and himself for standing on the corner gawking at the stars, "but he walked with the happy feeling that he just sucked a flashing moment from the weltering insignificance of human life." The revelation is only momentary, and the insignificance he attributes to human life brings him back to his "failure." He wanders to Lake Michigan musing over his lost promise, his dead wife and daughter, and the fact that "mistakes could not be rectified." He even berates death for being a "messy conclusion to a mess."

The moment of illumination, Farrell seems to tell the reader, is enough to remind Joe of something other than his self-imposed failure and frustration, but it is not enough to draw him out of himself--it cannot save him from himself. The sojourn beside Lake Michigan nearly allows him to effect a reconciliation with himself. The mesmerizing nature of the waves calms his frustration but reminds him of the fruitless nature of people's efforts when compared to the effortless and inexorable presence of nature. Nature, Joe reminds the reader, will be here when Chicago crumbles, and the waves will go on when the city and humans are no more. The waves also remind Joe of his loss of faith and of his attempt to regain that faith with the Catholics; but he is revulsed by the Catholics' "eating their God" and admits the need for a "Presbyterian God." Joe cannot function socially or spiritually in human society, and nature only reminds him of his isolation and, thus, that he is a stranger. He is alone with himself. He is afraid to die. He "almost ached for the past. . . . He found himself wanting them [events of the past] all back." Despite the turmoil in his mind, Joe reaches "a womb of calm" before leaving the lake, but as he leaves, he watches a young couple making love on the beach. The moment of reconciliation is gone. His examination of himself has culminated in watching man procreating beside the forces of nature that calmed him. As he walks back into the city, his frustration returns.

Joe is frustrated by humankind, by nature, and by himself. He does not want to leave a restaurant because he is anonymous while in that group. He does not want to go home because he will be alone. He is fond of the night in the city because he does not have to cope with all the people who normally fill the empty offices, but he still feels surrounded by the city. The city at night and its "many little worlds and private universes were only reflected things." As a reflection, the city does not intrude on Joe's existence but is a sort of an iron womb in which he can avoid the natural calm of the lake and turn back into the solace of his frustration. As a result, there is no final revelation, no change, no alteration in Joe. His failures are all that are real, and his principal failure is the inability to cope with himself. He cannot regain the past, and he cannot deal with his memories of that past. Farrell's world is full of such isolated, ostracized people. The past is an intrinsic part of their failures, and inordinate attention to or desire for the past enhances its impact. Farrell also makes it clear, however, that lack of concern for the past is just as fatal as preoccupation with it.

"THE FASTEST RUNNER ON SIXTY-FIRST STREET"

In "The Fastest Runner on Sixty-First Street," Morty Aiken is successful, but his preoccupation with the future blinds him to the importance of the present, and his failure to attend carefully to that present is a direct influence on the outcome of the story. The story of the boy who could outrun and outskate everyone in his neighborhood is a classic success story with a twist. The reader knows from the beginning that Morty is the All-American boy. He enjoys running and skating faster than anyone else--he does not revel in the victory, but in the performance itself. He is well liked and respected as a direct result of his abilities, and he is fascinated with his promise for the future. He views the present as little more than a way station to becoming the greatest runner in the world. At every turn the reader is reminded of Morty's self-assuredness and of his dreams: "Although he was outwardly modest, Morty had his dreams." Morty dreams of going to high school and prospering under high school coaching. He dreams of college track meets and, ultimately, the Olympics. He also dreams of girls. He dreams that "girls would all like him, and the most beautiful girl in the world would marry him." He dreams of Edna, his ideal of the moment; when he runs, he dreams he is running for Edna. He dreams of ways to give Edna one of the medals he has won for speed. In all of his dreams, however, running is the all-important thing. Everything else in the world is simply an excuse to run and feel the exhilaration of speed and of his body accomplishing that speed.

Tony Rabuski is another accessory to Morty's speed. Tony, the "toughest" and "poorest" boy in school, is befriended by Morty, and Morty uses his speed to keep other boys from teasing Tony by chasing down Tony's tormentors and holding them until Tony can catch up and "exact his revenge." Morty's friendship changes Tony from a sullen outcast to a member of the "gang," but the change does not materially affect Morty. Morty uses Tony as another excuse to run--just as he uses his dreams of Edna and his hopes for the future. In essence, there is no present for Morty, only the future.

It is only in the final sections of the story, after Morty is graduated from grammar school and begins summer vacation, that any sense of temporality enters his life. As Morty whiles away a summer "as good as any summer he could remember," he becomes embroiled in the racial problems of Chicago. Washington Park and Morty's neighborhood are being infiltrated by blacks, and there is a typical gang reaction to this move. One never sees Morty as a racist, only as the "catcher" for the gang. Morty runs ahead of the mob, tackles the "dark clouds" and holds them until the gang can catch up and beat them; it is precisely the scheme he and Tony had "doped out" earlier. The reader is never led to believe that Morty hates the blacks or has any interest in the situation at all except in the sense that it gives him another reason to run. As he runs after blacks, he dreams the same dreams of Edna, of glory, of running. He does not consider the blacks' fate or why he is catching them; he thinks only of running. It is this lack of concern for the real, present world that is Morty's undoing.

When Morty, in the finale of the story, runs ahead of a mob formed by Tony, he is doing only what he does naturally--running. He chases two blacks who escape behind a funeral train (blatant foreshadowing) and then begins the final race to catch a lone black boy. With the mob howling behind him, Morty runs with the idea of catching the black and for the sheer joy of running. As he chases the black, however, the closer he comes to his quarry, the more he outdistances the mob. The closer he comes to his immediate goal, the further he runs ahead of his world, his present. The black runs into a predominantly black area; Morty, innocently, follows him; the black disappears; Morty is "caught and pinioned . . . his throat slashed," and the mob arrives to find no blacks in sight and to view the remains of the fastest runner on Sixty-First Street lying in a pool of his own blood.

Morty has never had time to live in the present. His dreams, his pleasure with his own body and his own future, and his lack of attention to the present that will become his past are fatal. If he had been attentive, he would have been more aware of the danger of entering the black neighborhood alone. He is trapped not by the past but by his ignorance of it, and the reader is warned against that ignorance by the image of his body.

Farrell was a fatalist, a determinist, a naturalist, and a realist, all in one turn. There is no success for Farrell, only endurance. His stories leave the reader with a very real sense of the characters' failures and with a sense of the ongoing nature of that failure in the everyday world. Farrell's characters are hurt and they scream as a result of the pain, but no one is listening.

OTHER MAJOR WORKS

LONG FICTION: *Young Lonigan: A Boyhood in Chicago Streets*, 1932; *Gas-House McGinty*, 1933; *The Young Manhood of Studs Lonigan*, 1934; *Judgment Day*, 1935; *Studs Lonigan: A Trilogy*, 1935 (collective title for *Young Lonigan, The Young Manhood of Studs Lonigan*, and *Judgment Day*); *A World I Never Made*, 1936; *No Star Is Lost*, 1938; *Tommy Gallagher's Crusade*, 1939; *Father and Son*, 1940; *Ellen Rogers*, 1941; *My Days of Anger*, 1943; *Bernard Clare*, 1946; *The Road Between*, 1949; *This Man and This Woman*, 1951; *Yet Other Waters*, 1952; *The Face of Time*, 1953; *Boarding House Blues*, 1961; *The Silence of History*, 1963; *What Time Collects*, 1964; *Lonely for the Future*, 1966; *When Time Was Born*, 1966; *New Year's Eve/1929*, 1967; *A Brand New Life*, 1968; *Judith*, 1969; *Invisible Swords*, 1971; *The Dunne Family*, 1976; *The Death of Nora Ryan*, 1978; *Dreaming Baseball*, 2007 (Ron Briley, Margaret Davidson, and James Barbour, editors).

PLAY: *The Mowbray Family*, pb. 1946 (with Hortense Alden Farrell).

POETRY: *The Collected Poems of James T. Farrell*, 1965.

NONFICTION: *A Note on Literary Criticism*, 1936; *The League of Frightened Philistines, and Other Papers*, 1945; *The Fate of Writing in America*, 1946; *Literature and Morality*, 1947; *The Name Is Fogarty: Private Papers on Public Matters*, 1950; *Reflections at Fifty, and Other Essays*, 1954; *My Baseball Diary*, 1957; *It Has Come to Pass*, 1958; *On Irish Themes*, 1982.

BIBLIOGRAPHY

Branch, Edgar M. *James T Farrell*. Minneapolis: University of Minnesota Press, 1963. Although his monograph is an overview of Farrell's life and work, Branch devotes considerable attention to Farrell's short stories, which he regards as closely linked to the novels. The stories are often preliminary experiments, deletions, or parts of abandoned projects, and they are consistent in tone and style with the larger works.

Fanning, Charles. "Death and Revery in James T. Farrell's O'Neill-O'Flaherty Novels." *In The Incarnate Imagination: Essays in Theology, the Arts, and Social Sciences, in Honor of Andrew Greeley: A Festschrift*, edited by Ingrid H. Shafer. Bowling Green, Ohio: Bowling Green State University Popular Press, 1988. Although Fanning is primarily concerned with Farrell's novels, he does identify themes that pervade all of Farrell's fiction: the artist as an isolated being, the role of memory and dreaming in achieving the necessary isolation, and the relationship of the isolation to the experience of death.

Farrell, James T. *Selected Essays*. Edited by Lunor Wolf. New York: McGraw-Hill, 1967. This book, which contains an overview of Farrell's literary criticism, reprints many of Farrell's most significant essays, among them "On the Function of the Novel" and "The Writer and His Conscience." Also contains discussions of naturalism, Leo Tolstoy, and the American literary tradition.

Farrell, Kathleen. *Literary Integrity and Political Action: The Public Argument of James T. Farrell*. Boulder, Colo.: Westview Press, 2000. Written by Farrell's former daughter-in-law, this book examines Farrell's role in the debate over the relationship of literature and politics that preoccupied members of the American Left during the 1930's.

Freedman, Samuel G. "Echoes of Lonigan, Fifty Years After." *The New York Times Book Review*, March 17, 1985, 45. Argues that Farrell's *Studs Lonigan* trilogy still conveys the essence of Chicago life and that his portrayal of the Lonigans' bigotry still rings true. Maintains that the trilogy is valuable on aesthetic as well as sociological grounds and that Farrell deserves recognition as a prime influence on writers like Nelson Algren, Saul Bellow, Bette Howland, and David Mamet.

Fried, Lewis F. *Makers of the City*. Amherst: University of Massachusetts Press, 1990. Fried argues that Farrell portrays the city as a liberalizing and democratizing force. Fried does an excellent job of weaving together discussion of Farrell's life, career, and fiction. He also provides a helpful bibliographical essay on other studies of Farrell.

Gelfant, Blanche H., ed. *The Columbia Companion to the Twentieth-Century American Short Story*. New York: Columbia University Press, 2000. Includes a chapter in which Farrell's short stories are analyzed.

Hricko, Mary. *Genesis of the Chicago Renaissance: Theodore Dreiser, Langston Hughes, Richard Wright, and James T. Farrell*. New York: Routledge, 2009. Chronicles the origins of Chicago's two literary renaissance periods, 1890-1920 and 1930-1950, by examining the works of Farrell and three other writers.

Landers, Robert K. *An Honest Writer: The Life and Times of James T. Farrell*. San Francisco, Calif.: Encounter Books, 2004. This well-researched and well-written biography offers a fresh look at Farrell and argues for renewed appreciation for the writer, who has fallen out of popular and critical favor.

Pizer, Donald. "James T. Farrell and the 1930's." In *Literature at the Barricades: The American Writer in the 1930's*, edited by Ralph F. Bogardus and Fred Hobson. University: University of Alabama Press, 1982. Pizer argues convincingly that Farrell's literary roots are in the 1920's, that he owes as much to the Chicago school of philosophical pragmation as to naturalism, and that James Joyce and Sherwood Anderson also influenced Farrell's fiction. To demonstrate his theses, Pizer analyzes the *Studs Lonigan* trilogy.

Smith, Gene. "The Lonigan Curse." *American Heritage* 46 (April, 1995): 150-151. Claims that while the character of Studs Lonigan became Farrell's most popular creation, it was also his biggest personal albatross. Notes that after killing Studs off, Farrell had trouble getting his work published and came to look back at his earlier work with loathing.

Wald, Alan M. *James T. Farrell: The Revolutionary Socialist Years*. New York: New York University Press, 1978. Wald's chapter "The Literary Record" demonstrates the intent of Leon Trotsky's influence on Farrell's fiction, and several short stories ("John Hitchcock," "The Dialectic," "The Renegade") receive extensive political readings. Wald identifies the real persons represented by Farrell's fictional characters and focuses on Farrell's treatment of the plight of the socialist writer. Contains an excellent bibliography with many political entries.

Clarence O. Johnson
Updated by Thomas L. Erskine

WILLIAM FAULKNER

Born: New Albany, Mississippi; September 25, 1897
Died: Byhalia, Mississippi; July 6, 1962

PRINCIPAL SHORT FICTION

These Thirteen, 1931
Doctor Martino, and Other Stories, 1934
Three Famous Short Novels, 1942
The Portable Faulkner, 1946, 1967
Knight's Gambit, 1949
Collected Stories, 1950
Big Woods, 1955
Uncollected Stories of William Faulkner, 1979

OTHER LITERARY FORMS

William Faulkner (FAWK-nur) published more than twenty novels, two collections of poetry, and a novel-drama, as well as essays, newspaper articles, and illustrated stories. His early work has been collected and his University of Virginia lectures transcribed. As a screenwriter in Hollywood, he was listed in the credits of such films as *The Big Sleep* (1946), *To Have and Have Not* (1944), and *Land of the Pharaohs* (1955).

ACHIEVEMENTS

William Faulkner is best known for his novels, particularly *The Sound and the Fury* (1929), *Absalom, Absalom!* (1936), and *As I Lay Dying* (1930), all of which have been translated widely. *A Fable* (1954) and *The Reivers* (1962) won Pulitzer Prizes, and *A Fable* and the *Collected Short Stories of William Faulkner* won National Book Awards. Faulkner received the Nobel Prize in Literature for 1949.

Film versions have been made of several of his works: *Sanctuary* (1961), *Intruder in the Dust* (1949), *The Sound and the Fury* (1959), *The Reivers* (1969), and *Pylon* (1957; or *Tarnished Angels*). Others, such as *Requiem for a Nun*, 1951, and "Barn Burning," have been filmed for television.

Such attention attests the fact that Faulkner has been one of the most influential writers in the twentieth century--both in the United States, where his work suggested to an enormous generation of southern writers the valuable literary materials that could be derived from their own region, and in Europe, particularly in France. He has had a later, but also profound, effect on Latin American fiction, most noticeably in the work of Colombian writer Gabriel García Márquez, who seeks, as Faulkner did, to create a fictive history of a region and a people. Faulkner's work has also been well received in Japan, which he visited as a cultural ambassador in 1955.

BIOGRAPHY

William Cuthbert Faulkner spent most of his life in Mississippi, although as a young man he went briefly to Paris and lived for a time in New Orleans, where he knew Sherwood Anderson. He trained for the Royal Air Force in Canada during World War I, but the war was over before he saw action. He attended the University of Mississippi in Oxford for a year, where he published poems and reviews in a campus periodical; after dropping out, he worked for a time in the university post office. He married Estelle Oldham, and they had a daughter, Jill. Except for periodic and often unhappy stays in Hollywood to work on screenplays--in order to support a large number of dependents--Faulkner lived and wrote in Oxford, where he had available to him in the town and surrounding countryside the prototypes for the characters that inhabit his major works. In the late 1950's, he accepted a position as a writer-in-residence at the University of Virginia and traveled to Japan on behalf of the Department of State. Although his literary reputation waned in the 1940's, when virtually all of his earlier works were out of print, Faulkner's stature as a writer grew after 1946, when *The Portable Faulkner* was published by Malcom Cowley, and especially after 1950, after he accepted the Nobel Prize, when his collected stories were published, and when his novels began to be reprinted. Faulkner drove himself harder physically as he grew older, and he was troubled throughout his life with alcohol binges into which he would often fall after completing a book. These factors contributed to his death in 1962.

ANALYSIS

William Faulkner has been credited with having the imagination to see, before other serious writers saw, the tremendous potential for drama, pathos, and sophisticated humor in the history and people of the South. In using this material and, in the process, suggesting to others how it might be used, he has also been credited with sparking the so-called Southern Renaissance of literary achievement that has produced much of the United States' best literature in the twentieth century.

In chronicling the tragedy of southern history, Faulkner delineated a vision tempered by his historical perspective that has freed the region from the popular conception of its character as possessing a universal gentility and a pervasive aristocracy, and he portrayed realistically a population often idealized and caricatured in songs, films, and pulp fiction. In undercutting the false idealizations, Faulkner often distorted the stereotypes and rendered them somewhat grotesque in the interest of bringing them to three-dimensional life; and he attempted to show in the political and social presumptions of the South the portent of its inevitable destruction--first through war and then through an insidious new social order based on commercial pragmatism and shortsighted lust for progress. In this sense, the New South is shown to have much in common with mainstream America.

Faulkner's themes are often conveyed in an elaborate baroque style noted for its long, difficult sentences that challenge the reader to discern the speaker, the time, and even the subject of the narrative. Faulkner makes considerable use of stream-of-consciousness interior monologues, and his frequent meshings of time reinforce his conviction that the past and present are intricately interwoven in the human psyche.

"A ROSE FOR EMILY"

"A Rose for Emily," frequently anthologized and analyzed, is probably Faulkner's best-known story.

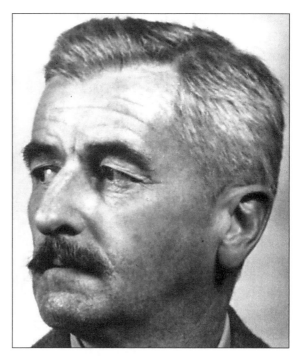

William Faulkner (©The Nobel Foundation)

Because of its elements of mystery, suspense, and the macabre, it has enjoyed a popular appeal. That Emily, an aging southern belle, murders the lover who spurned her and sleeps beside his decaying body for a number of years is only the most sensational aspect of the story. What is more interesting to the serious reader of Faulkner is the interplay between Emily Grierson and the two generations of townspeople who attempt to cope with her--one the old guard and the other a new generation with "modern ideas."

The opening paragraphs of the story inform the reader that when Miss Emily died, the whole town turned out for her funeral. She was a "fallen monument . . . a tradition, a duty and a care; a sort of hereditary obligation upon the town." The townspeople, who are by the time of Emily's death mostly of a generation younger than her own, have never been able to incorporate her into their community. For them, as well as for their fathers, she has stood as an embodiment of an older ideal of southern womanhood--even though in her later years she has grown obese, bloated, and pale as dough. The older generation, under the mayoralty of

Colonel Sartoris ("who fathered the edict that no Negro woman should appear on the streets without an apron"), has relieved Miss Emily of her taxes and has sent its children to take her china-painting classes "in the same spirit that they were sent to church on Sunday with a twenty-five-cent piece for the collection plate." The new generation, however, is not pleased with the accommodations its fathers made with Miss Emily; it tries to impose taxes upon her and it no longer sends its children to take her lessons. Miss Emily has been encouraged in her ways by the old guard, however; she refuses to pay the town's taxes, telling the representatives of the new generation to "see Colonel Sartoris," who has been dead for ten years. The town is unable to handle Emily; it labels her "insane" and likewise comes to see her as the ghost of a feminine ideal out of the past. She becomes a recluse, living alone in her house with her black servant. In her claim to privilege and impunity, she stands as a reminder to the town of the values--and sins--of its fathers, which are visited upon the third generation.

It is tempting to think of Miss Emily as merely a decadent and perverse relic of the South's antebellum past; indeed, this is how the story has often been read. Such a neat interpretation, however, would seem to be defeated by the time element in the story. Emily lives in a house spiraled and cupolaed in the architectural style of the 1870's, on a once-elegant street that has been altered by industry and commercial development. Although the rickety town fathers of the Civil War era come to her funeral dressed in their dusty uniforms and even believe that she was of their own generation and that they had danced with her when she was a young woman, clearly Emily is not of that generation; she is of the postwar South. She has not lingered as a relic from a warped racist culture; she has instead been created by defeated members of that culture who have continued to yearn after a world they have lost, a world that might well have existed largely in their imaginations, but a concept so persistent that the newer generation, for all its modern ideas, is powerless to control it. The reader is told that the town had long thought of Emily and her dead father "as a tableau, Miss Emily a slender figure in white in the background, her father a spraddled silhouette in the foreground, his back to her

and clutching a horsewhip, the two of them framed by the backflung front door." It is clear that the newer generation of the twentieth century has adopted certain popular ideas about the old South. This "tableau" could serve as the dust jacket for any number of romantic novels set in the plantation days.

Thus, the two generations are complicit in ignoring the real Emily and creating and maintaining the myth of Emily as an exemplum of southern womanhood from a lost age, just as the town aldermen-- "three graybeards and one younger man, a member of the rising generation"--have conspired to cover up Emily's horrible crime. When the smell of the corpse of Emily's decaying lover, Homer Barron, had become so strong that it could no longer be ignored by the town, the aldermen had scattered lime around Emily's house secretly at night, although they knew she had recently purchased arsenic from the druggist and that Barron had disappeared; when the smell went away, so did the town's concern about the matter. The old guard cannot bear and does not wish to accept the grim essence of the dream it has spun; the new generation, under the influence of the old, grudgingly accepts its burden of the past, but then wrenches it into a romantic shape that obscures the "fat woman in black" (overindulgent, moribund) that is Emily Grierson.

The story, then, is a comment on the postbellum South, which inherited the monstrous code of values, glossed over by fine words about honor and glory, that characterized the slave era; that postbellum South learns to ignore the unsavory elements of its past by ignoring Emily the recluse and murderess and by valorizing the romantic "tableau." This is, however, a complex matter. The new generation--a generation excluded from the nominal code of honor, valor, and decorum that the old Confederates believed to have sustained them and excluded from the benefits that were to be gained from the slave system of the "glorious" old South--sees the Griersons as "high and mighty," as holding themselves "a little too high for what they really were." The new generation, pragmatic and small-minded, for the most part, has inherited a landscape sullied by cotton gins and garages. Miss Emily Grierson, as a privileged person and as a reminder of what the older generation forfeited in its defeat, is a goad in the minds of the uncharitable newer generation, which, when she does not marry, is "vindicated." When it hears the rumor that she has inherited nothing but the decaying house from her father, it is glad: "At last they could pity Miss Emily." A Miss Emily out of sight, destitute, "insane," and deprived of the lost legacy of the old South can be recreated as a fictional heroine in white, part of the backdrop against which the popularized hero, her father, stands with his horsewhip--a faceless silhouette, cruel and powerful, an "ancestor" who can be claimed by the dispossessed generation as its own.

The incestuous image of the father and daughter suggests the corrupt nature of the new South, which, along with the corrupt nature of the old South, is a favorite Faulknerian concern. Granted, the "tableau" on the face of it appears to be the cover of a romantic novel, and in that sense it seems to be merely a popular rendering of history; but it is the townspeople who arrange father and daughter in the lurid scene. It is the men of the new generation who black out the distinguishing features of Emily's dead father in their creation of the tableau, leaving a dark masculine space (more, one would guess, in the shape of foreman Homer Barron than of Mr. Grierson) into which they can dream themselves, as masters of a glorious age, as potent heroes for whom the wispy heroine pines in the background. The newer generation has the "modern ideas" bred of the necessity of surviving in the defeated, industrialized South; but in its attitudes toward Emily Grierson, it reveals the extent to which the old decadent values of the fathers have been passed along.

The narrator of the story, one of the townspeople himself, has proved unreliable. While it is true that Emily seems to be "a tradition, a duty, a care, . . . an hereditary obligation," a relic of the past miraculously sprung into being in spite of the disparity between her time and the historical time with which she is associated, the narrator only inadvertently reveals the truth of the matter: that both generations of the town are guilty of the desires and misplaced values that not only allow Miss Emily the murderess to come into being but also lead them to cover her crime and enshrine her in a tableau into which they, in their basest longings, can insert themselves. There is an incestuousness to all of this, an

unhealthy interbreeding of values that allows each generation to perform despicable acts in the process of maintaining its ideas of what it would like to be. It is true that Emily is a "fallen monument"; but what the narrator fails to spell out explicitly is that the monument has been erected not only by the historical grandeur of her family but also by the dispossessed generations that interpret her to their own ends. The monument is toppled by death, not by an ethical evolution in the town. The narrator is redeemed to some extent by "his" pity for Emily and by the recognition that the town, by driving her into mad isolation, has treated her badly.

As for Emily herself, she would seem to represent the worst elements of her neighbors, carried to their extreme conclusions. As the antebellum masters of the slaves presumed an all-powerfulness that allowed them to believe that they could own people, so does Miss Emily presume. Alive, Homer Barron--the outsider, the Yankee, a curious vitality in the pallid town--is outside Miss Emily's control. Dead, however, she can own him, can dress his corpse like a groom, can sleep beside him perhaps every night at least until her hair turns gray. As the new generation can blind itself to unpleasant truths about its history and itself, so can Emily become lost in delusion: Her father, dead for three days, is proclaimed not dead and she refuses to bury him; Homer's corpse is a "groom" (and, perhaps in some further depraved vision, connected with the dead father). Emily represents not only the decadence of Colonel Sartoris's racist era but also the decadence of the "modern" generation's use of that era. Thus "A Rose for Emily," often dismissed as Faulkner's ghost story, proves to be a clear expression of a recurring motif in Faulkner's works: the complexity of the connections between the present and the past.

"THE BEAR"

These connections are explored in a less sensational manner in "The Bear." This story, which Faulkner also made the centerpiece of his novel *Go Down, Moses* (1942), is another of the most anthologized, most studied pieces of Faulkner's short fiction. Composed of five sections (although often only four are printed in anthology versions, the long and complex fourth section being omitted), "The Bear" covers the history of Isaac (Ike) McCaslin, heir to the land and to the shame of his slave-owner grandfather, L. P. C. McCaslin, who committed incest with his illegitimate daughter, thereby driving her mother to suicide. After discovering this horrifying ghost in old plantation ledgers, Ike feels bound to repudiate the inheritance that has descended to him from his grandfather--even though the repudiation costs him his wife and any hope of progeny--in an attempt to expiate his inherited guilt and to gain a measure of freedom from the vicious materialism that brought the slavery system into being. Thus he allows his patrimony to pass to his cousin McCaslin Edmonds, who plays devil's advocate in Ike's attempt to understand the South and his own place in it, the tragedy of the blacks and of his own class, and the significance of what he possesses without inheriting: an instinctual knowledge of nature and an infallible sense of what is just.

"The Bear" may be seen as a hunting story, part of the *Big Woods* collection that includes "The Bear Hunt" and "Race at Morning." As a hunting story it is concerned with Ike's maturing, with his pilgrimage year after year to the hunting grounds where he and a group of adult hunters stalk the ancient bear, Old Ben, an enduring symbol of nature. Ike's guide and teacher is Sam Fathers, an aging Native American who still holds a sure instinct for the truths to be found in nature, and under whose tutelage Ike comes to form a system of values that later will lead him to renounce his inheritance. From Sam, Ike acquires a sense of nature's terms and of humankind's need to meet nature on its own terms--of the necessity of according dignity to the force of nature and to all creatures through whom it courses. To meet the embodiment of that force in Old Ben, Ike must leave behind the instruments of civilization: the gun, the compass, the watch. Eventually Ike is able to track down Old Ben with regularity, but even when he encounters the bear and is armed, he refuses to shoot it.

It would seem that the proof of nature's endurance, represented in the bear, is of paramount concern to Ike. When Old Ben is finally killed and Sam Fathers dies, the ritual of the hunt is over for Ike. Two years later, he returns to the woods and sees in its organic and deathless elements, which have incorporated the remains of Old Ben and Sam Fathers, a proof of nature's dualistic power to absorb death and bring forth new life from it.

This force is at the same time awesome and terrifying, and it must be revered and confronted if humanity is to live meaningfully. Even as Ike makes this last pilgrimage, however, a lumber company hacks away at the forest and a train cuts through the wilderness, underscoring the idea of the damage a materialistic civilization can do to even the most powerful aspects of nature. Faulkner shows an era of United States history passing--an era of abundance and of human appreciation of what nature requires from humanity in their mutual interest.

When "The Bear" is examined from the point of view of the intricate fourth section, it goes beyond being merely a hunting story to comment profoundly on the passing age and that which is replacing it. The scene shifts from the vast wilderness of nature to the intense confines of Ike McCaslin's consciousness, which struggles to find a way to atone for the sins of his ancestors and of his class. The entanglement of past and present here is more complex than it is in "A Rose for Emily," for Ike must face the knowledge that bloods mingled in the past--black and white, slave and owner--have flowed in grossly inequitable courses to the present, as reflected in the sufferings of his mixed-blood relatives. Therefore, he renounces his patrimony, he sets out to redress old wrongs with his black relatives, and he seeks to give full recognition to the brotherhood he shares with these relatives by recognizing the strengths they contribute to his family and to southern society--the virtues of "pity and tolerance and forbearance and fidelity and love of children."

In contrast to the self-serving generation of post-bellum townspeople in "A Rose for Emily," Ike--also of that era--is a man of conscience. This is not to suggest, however, that Ike is particularly "modern" in his ideas; rather he has modeled himself on older examples of integrity--not only Sam Fathers but also his father and his uncle, who had turned over their own inherited house to their slaves and built a humbler cabin for themselves. In Ike's own case, the personal sacrifices to integrity and conscience have been enormous--his wife's love; his hope of a son to carry on his mission; living alone and ultimately uncertain that his sacrifice will bear fruit beyond his limited scope to influence events. Nevertheless, Faulkner illustrates through his invention of Ike McCaslin the extent to which idealism can flourish, even when constantly challenged by the grimmest vestiges of past evils.

"BARN BURNING"

"Barn Burning" is an inversion of "The Bear" in that its protagonist, ten-year-old Sarty Snopes, is seeking the world that Ike McCaslin wishes to repudiate. Not of the landed class, but the son of a tenant farmer who is always on the move because arson is his means of creating justice, Sarty associates the landed gentry with a "peace and dignity" and a civilized justice that is the direct opposite of the "fear and terror, grief and despair" that characterizes his life with his father, Ab Snopes. Ab uses fire as a weapon against the ruling class that he sees as the shaper of his economic fate, and he exhorts Sarty to be true to the blood ties, which Ab sees as the only protection for his kind against the forces of an exploitative aristocracy. Sarty, however, rejects the "old blood" that he has not chosen for what seems to him a higher concept of fairness, and he longs to be free of his family and the turmoil it generates in his life.

For Sarty, Major DeSpain is the antithesis of Ab. DeSpain owns the farm on which Ab has most recently contracted to work. To Sarty, DeSpain and his columned house, as big as a courthouse, represent not what Ab sees, the sweat of black and white people to produce someone else's wealth, but rather the peace and dignity for which Sarty yearns and a system of justice that operates on principles of law rather than on personal revenge. Sarty's view is based on a naïve trust in civilization that blinds his inexperienced eyes to the inescapable connections between wealth and the mechanism of civilization.

Ab provokes a confrontation with DeSpain by deliberately tracking horse manure on an expensive rug. A series of moves and countermoves by Ab and DeSpain brings the pair to the point where, although DeSpain cannot begin to recover his loss from Ab, the local court nevertheless rules that Ab must take responsibility, within his means, for his act. This is enough to satisfy Ab yet again that the social system only works in behalf of the rich, and he sets out that night to redress this wrong by burning DeSpain's barn. Sarty cannot bear to allow this injustice, and so he is torn between real loyalty to his family and commitment to an ideal of justice. Specifically, he must decide whether to support his father's crime through silence or to betray the familial bond and warn DeSpain. Sarty chooses the ideal, warns DeSpain even as the barn begins to burn, and then flees the scene, unsure whether the shots he hears wound any of his family. Having made his choice, Sarty must set out alone to forge his own life.

"Barn Burning" offers a helpful picture of how Faulkner sees the economics of the postbellum South, where the poor whites remain the underclass rivals of black sharecroppers. Faulkner shows in other works how a new social order eventually evolved in which the descendants of Ab Snopes slip into the defeated, genteel society like silent bacteria and take over its commerce, coming finally to own the mansions that had previously belonged to the DeSpains and Compsons and Sartorises. Again and again Faulkner reiterates that it was the corrupt systems of slavery and of the plantation that ultimately ensured the fall of the Old South. However, his view of the Snopeses--violent, relentless, insidious men and inert, cowlike women, who by their numbers and crafty pragmatism will wrench the land and the wealth from the depleted gentility--is hardly positive.

In fact, "Barn Burning" is singular in that it is perhaps the only example of Faulkner's fiction in which the Snopeses are depicted sympathetically without first being made to appear ridiculous. As is often the case, Faulkner is extremely sensitive to the young boy caught in a painful rite of passage--as true for Sarty Snopes as it is for Ike McCaslin, Lucius Priest, Chick Mallison, and others not of the threatening Snopes clan. Moreover, "Barn Burning" makes an interesting case for Ab Snopes as the pitiable creation of the landed aristocracy, who seeks dignity and integrity for himself, although his only chance of achieving either would seem to lie in the democratic element of fire as the one defense available to all, regardless of social class. In this story, Ab is placed in the company of Wash Jones, Joe Christmas, and other members of the underclass that Faulkner views with sympathy and whose portrayals are in themselves indictments of the civilization that has forced them to desperate means.

While none of these examples quite suggests the very humorous ends to which Faulkner often turns his southern materials, it should be remembered that he was highly aware of the potential for comedy in all the situations described here and that even such delicate matters as the tensions between the races and the revolution in the social order are, in Faulkner's hands, as frequently the catalysts of tall tales and satire as they are of his most somber and lyrical prose. It is true that "A Rose for Emily" hints at a typically Faulknerian humor in that a whole town is turned on its end by the bizarre behavior of one of its citizens but the grotesque nature of Miss Emily's secret smothers the promise of comedy in the story. Those seeking to experience Faulkner's comic voice are better served by reading such stories as "Shingles for the Lord," "Mule in the Yard," and "Spotted Horses."

In any case, whatever the mode Faulkner adopted in creating his Yoknapatawpha County and thereby recreating the South, he produced a stunning body of work, and in both matter and style, his works have had an equally stunning impact on modern letters.

OTHER MAJOR WORKS

LONG FICTION: *Soldiers' Pay*, 1926; *Mosquitoes*, 1927; *Sartoris*, 1929; *The Sound and the Fury*, 1929; *As I Lay Dying*, 1930; *Sanctuary*, 1931; *Light in August*, 1932; *Pylon*, 1935; *Absalom, Absalom!*, 1936; *The Unvanquished*, 1938; *The Wild Palms*, 1939 (also known by its original title *If I Forget Thee, Jerusalem*, 1990); *The Hamlet*, 1940; *Go Down, Moses*, 1942; *The Bear*, 1942 (novella); *Intruder in the Dust*, 1948; *Requiem for a Nun*, 1951; *A Fable*, 1954; *The Town*, 1957; *The Mansion*, 1959; *The Reivers: A Reminiscence*, 1962; *The Wishing Tree*, 1964 (fairy tale); *Flags in the Dust*, 1973 (original unabridged version of *Sartoris*); *Mayday*, 1976 (fable); *Novels, 1926-1929*, 2006.

SCREENPLAYS: *Today We Live*, 1933; *To Have and Have Not*, 1945; *The Big Sleep*, 1946; *Land of the Pharaohs*(1955);*Faulkner's MGM Screenplays*, 1982.

POETRY: *The Marble Faun*, 1924; *A Green Bough*, 1933.

NONFICTION: *New Orleans Sketches*, 1958; *Faulkner in the University*, 1959; *Faulkner at West Point*, 1964; *Essays, Speeches, and Public Letters*, 1965; *The Faulkner-Cowley File: Letters and Memories, 1944-1962*, 1966 (Malcolm Cowley, editor); *Lion in the Garden*, 1968; *Selected Letters*, 1977.

MISCELLANEOUS: *The Faulkner Reader: Selections from the Works of William Faulkner*, 1954; *William Faulkner: Early Prose and Poetry*, 1962.

BIBLIOGRAPHY

Aiken, Charles S. "Geographical Interpretation of 'The Bear.'" In *William Faulkner and the Southern Landscape*. Athens: University of Georgia Press in association with the Center for American Places at Columbia College, Chicago, 2009. Aiken, a native of Mississippi, focuses on the geography of Faulkner's Yoknapatawpha County and places "The Bear" within the context of that geography.

Blotner, Joseph. *Faulkner: A Biography*. 1964. Reprint. Jackson: University of Mississippi Press, 2005.This extensive but readable two-volume biography is the major source for details about Faulkner's life. It contains many photographs and a useful index.

Brooks, Cleanth. *William Faulkner: The Yoknapatawpha County*. New Haven, Conn.: Yale University Press, 1963. Brooks has written several excellent books on Faulkner, but this venerable classic of Faulkner criticism is one of the best introductions, treating Faulkner's characteristic themes, providing historical and social background, and offering detailed readings of the major stories and novels. His carefully prepared notes, appendixes, and character index can be immensely helpful to beginning readers trying to make sense of mysterious events and complex family relations.

Broughton, Panthea. *William Faulkner: The Abstract and the Actual*. Baton Rouge: Louisiana State University Press, 1974. Of several fine critical studies that attempt to see Faulkner whole and understand his worldview, this is one of the best, especially for readers just beginning to know Faulkner. Broughton sees the tension between the ideal and the actual as central to understanding the internal and external conflicts about which Faulkner most often writes.

Carothers, James. *William Faulkner's Short Stories*. Ann Arbor, Mich.: UMI Research Press, 1985. This study gives special attention to interrelations among the short stories and between the stories and the novels. Carothers offers balanced and careful readings of the stories and a useful bibliography.

Ferguson, James. *Faulkner's Short Fiction*. Knoxville: University of Tennessee Press, 1991. An attempt to redress the critical neglect of Faulkner's short fiction. Discusses Faulkner's poetic and narrative impulses and his themes of loss of innocence, failure to love, loneliness, and isolation. Comments on his manipulation of time and point of view and how his stories relate to his novels.

Ford, Marilyn Claire. "Narrative Legerdemain: Evoking Sarty's Future in 'Barn Burning.'" *The Mississippi Quarterly* 51 (Summer, 1998): 527-540. In this special issue on Faulkner, Ford argues that Faulkner experiments with the doubling of perspective in "Barn Burning," in which the omniscient narrator fuses with the protagonist to create a story with multiple narrative layers.

Gelfant, Blanche H., ed. *The Columbia Companion to the Twentieth-Century American Short Story*. New York: Columbia University Press, 2000. Includes a chapter in which Faulkner's short stories are analyzed.

Godden, Richard. *William Faulkner: An Economy of Complex Words*. Princeton, N.J.: Princeton University Press, 2007. Analyzes Faulkner's late fiction, including *Go Down, Moses*, to trace how it expresses the economic and racial conditions of the South from the 1930's to the 1950's.

Hoffman, Frederick, and Olga W. Vickery, eds. *William Faulkner: Three Decades of Criticism*. New York: Harcourt, Brace, 1960. Though there are more recent collections of critical essays on Faulkner, this volume remains one of the most useful. It contains the important 1956 interview in *The Paris Review*, the Nobel Prize address, and twenty-two essays, many of them seminal, on Faulkner's work and life.

Jones, Diane Brown. *A Reader's Guide to the Short Stories of William Faulkner*. New York: G. K. Hall, 1994. Discusses more than thirty of Faulkner's stories in terms of publishing history, circumstances of composition, sources/influence, and relationship to other Faulkner works. Includes interpretations of the stories and summarizes and critiques previous criticism.

Minter, David. *William Faulkner: His Life and Work*. Baltimore: Johns Hopkins University Press, 1980. Shorter and less detailed than Joseph Blotner's biography (above), this volume gives more attention to exploring connections between Faulkner's life and his works.

The Mississippi Quarterly 50 (Summer, 1997). A special issue on Faulkner, including articles that discuss displaced meaning, dispossessed sons, the wilderness and consciousness, and subjectivity in *Go Down, Moses*.

Rampton, David. *William Faulkner: A Literary Life*. New York: Palgrave Macmillan, 2008. This work divides Faulkner's writings into three eras and discusses how his life impacted his writing, including his use of language and characterization. The book does a good job of showing how his writing evolved throughout his career. Chapter 6 includes several pages of discussion about *Go Down, Moses*.

Ruppersburg, Hugh. "William Faulkner's Short Stories." In *A Companion to the American Short Story*, edited by Alfred Bendixen and James Nagel. Malden, Mass.: Wiley-Blackwell, 2010. Offers an overview and critical examination of Faulkner's short fiction.

Towner, Theresa M., and James B. Carothers. *Reading Faulkner: Collected Stories*. Jackson: University Press of Mississippi, 2006. Aims to make reading Faulkner's short fiction less difficult by providing annotations to more than forty of his short stories. These notes explain the stories' allusions to other writers and thinkers, distinctly southern phrases, and difficult words and help place the stories in their political and literary contexts.

Wagner-Martin, Linda. *New Essays on "Go Down, Moses."* Cambridge, England: Cambridge University Press, 1996. After an introduction that summarizes contemporary reception and critical analysis of *Go Down, Moses*, Wagner-Martin collects essays that approach the work from the perspective of race, environment, gender, and ideology.

Weinstein, Philip. *Becoming Faulkner: The Art and Life of William Faulkner*. New York: Oxford University, 2010. Offers close analysis of Faulkner's texts, including *Go Down, Moses*, while providing a portrait of him that reveals his struggles with family, lovers, racial conflict, and literary success. His life and work are shown to be fused in a way that allows readers to better understand his writing.

Constance Pierce
Updated by Terry Heller

F. Scott Fitzgerald

Born: St. Paul, Minnesota; September 24, 1896
Died: Hollywood, California; December 21, 1940

Principal short fiction

Flappers and Philosophers, 1920
Tales of the Jazz Age, 1922
All the Sad Young Men, 1926
Taps at Reveille, 1935
The Stories of F. Scott Fitzgerald, 1951
Babylon Revisited, and Other Stories, 1960
The Pat Hobby Stories, 1962
The Apprentice Fiction of F. Scott Fitzgerald,
    1907-1917, 1965
The Basil and Josephine Stories, 1973
Bits of Paradise, 1974
The Price Was High: The Last Uncollected Stories of
    F. Scott Fitzgerald, 1979
Before Gatsby: The First Twenty-Six Stories, 2001
    (Matthew J. Bruccoli, editor)

Other literary forms

Four novels, four short-story collections, and a play make up the nine F. Scott Fitzgerald books published in his lifetime. They were issued in uniform editions by Scribner's with a British edition of each. His short stories were widely anthologized in the 1920's and 1930's in collections such as *The Best Short Stories of 1922, Cream of the Jug,* and *The Best Short Stories of 1931.* His play *The Vegetable: Or, From President to Postman* (pb. 1923) was produced at the Apollo Theatre in Atlantic City, and while Fitzgerald was under contract to MGM studios, he collaborated on such screenplays as *Three Comrades, Infidelity, Madame Curie,* and *Gone with the Wind.* There have been numerous posthumous collections of his letters, essays, notebooks, stories, and novels; also since his death, there have been various stage and screen adaptations of his work, including film versions of *The Great Gatsby* (1974, 2012) and *Tender Is the Night* (1934).

Achievements

F. Scott Fitzgerald, considered "the poet laureate of the Jazz Age," is best remembered for his portrayal of the "flapper" of the 1920's, a young woman who demonstrated scorn for conventional dress and behavior. Fitzgerald's fiction focuses on young, wealthy, dissolute men and women of the 1920's. His stories written for popular magazines, such as *The Saturday Evening Post* and later *Esquire,* were very much in demand. Fitzgerald's literary reputation, however, is chiefly based on the artistry of stories such as "Babylon Revisited" and "The Rich Boy," as well as the novel *The Great Gatsby.* In this important novel, Fitzgerald uses rich imagery and symbolism to portray lives of the careless, restless rich during the 1920's and to depict Jay Gatsby as the personification of the American dream, the self-made man whose quest for riches is also a futile quest for the love of the shallow, spoiled Daisy.

Biography

Francis Scott Key Fitzgerald was educated at St. Paul Academy and at the Newman School in Hackensack, New Jersey. While attending Princeton University he wrote for the *Princeton Tiger* and *Nassau Literary Magazine.* He left Princeton without a degree, joined the Army, and was stationed near Montgomery, Alabama, where he met Zelda Sayre. In 1920, they were married in New York City before moving to Westport, Connecticut. Their only child, Frances Scott Fitzgerald, was born in 1921. In the mid-1920's the Fitzgeralds traveled extensively between the United

States and Europe, meeting Ernest Hemingway in Paris in 1925. The decade of the 1930's was a bleak one for the Fitzgeralds; Zelda had several emotional break-downs and Scott sank into alcoholism. They lived variously in Montgomery and on the Turnbull estate outside Baltimore. Fitzgerald went to Hollywood for the second time in 1931. After that they lived for a time in Asheville, North Carolina, where Zelda was hospitalized and where Fitzgerald wrote the Crack-up essays for *Esquire*. In 1937, Fitzgerald met Sheila Graham while he was living in Hollywood and writing under contract to MGM. He began writing *The Last Tycoon* in 1939 and died, before it was completed, on December 21, 1940, at the age of forty-four.

ANALYSIS

F. Scott Fitzgerald was a professional writer who was also a literary artist. In practical terms this meant that he had to support himself by writing short stories for popular magazines in order to get sufficient income, according to him, to write decent books. Indeed, most of the money that Fitzgerald earned by writing before he went to Hollywood in 1937 was earned by selling stories to magazines. In his twenty-year career as a writer, he published 164 magazine stories; other stories were never published. All but eight of the stories that originally appeared in magazines became available in hardcover editions.

As one would expect of a body of 164 stories written in a twenty-year period mainly for popular consumption, the quality of the stories is uneven. At the bottom of this collection are at least a dozen stories, most of them written for *Esquire* during the last years of his life, which have few redeeming qualities; at the top of the list are at least a dozen stories that rank among the best of American short stories. One should not, however, be led to believe that these, as well as the hundred or more "potboilers" in the middle, do not serve a useful role in his development as an artist. Fitzgerald in the 1920's was considered the best writer of quality magazine fiction in America, and his stories brought the highest prices paid by slick magazines; *The Saturday Evening Post*, for example, paid him four thousand dollars per story even during the Depression. Dorothy Parker commented that Fitzgerald could write

F. Scott Fitzgerald (Library of Congress)

a bad story, but that he could not write badly. Thus each story, no matter how weak, has the recognizable Fitzgerald touch--the sparkling prose which Fitzgerald called "the something extra" that most popular short stories lacked. Fitzgerald also learned at the beginning of his career that he could use the popular magazines as a workshop for his novels, experimenting in them with themes and techniques that he would later incorporate into his novels. An understanding of a Fitzgerald story should take into account this workshop function of the story, as well as its artistic merits.

Fitzgerald's career as a writer of magazine fiction breaks logically into three periods: 1919-1924, the years during which he shopped around for markets and published stories in most of the important periodicals of the times; 1925-1933, the central period characterized by a close association with *The Saturday Evening Post*--a relationship that almost precluded his publication of stories in other magazines; and 1934-1940, a period beginning with the publication of his first *Esquire* story and continuing through a subsequent relationship with that magazine that lasted until his death.

During the first of these periods, Fitzgerald published thirty-two stories in ten different commercial magazines, two novels (*This Side of Paradise*, 1920, and *The Beautiful and Damned*, 1922), two short-story collections (*Flappers and Philosophers* and *Tales of the Jazz Age*), and one book-length play (*The Vegetable*). In the second period, during which *The Great Gatsby* and a third short-story collection (*All the Sad Young Men*) appeared, he enjoyed the popular reputation he had built with readers of *The Saturday Evening Post* and published forty-seven of the fifty-eight stories that appeared during this nine-year period in this magazine; the remaining eleven stories were scattered throughout five different magazines. In the final period, Fitzgerald lost the large *Saturday Evening Post* audience and gained the *Esquire* audience, which was smaller and quite different. Of the forty-four Fitzgerald stories to appear between 1934 and his death, twenty-eight appeared in *Esquire*. In addition to *Tender Is the Night*, which was completed and delivered before Fitzgerald's relationship with *Esquire* began, Fitzgerald published his final short-story collection (*Taps at Reveille*); he also drafted *The Last Tycoon* (1941) during the *Esquire* years. Twelve stories, nine of which have appeared in *Esquire*, have been published since his death.

An obvious conclusion may be drawn about Fitzgerald's professional career: He was at his best artistically in the years of his greatest popularity. During the composition of *The Great Gatsby*, Fitzgerald's commercial fiction was in such demand that large magazines, such as *The Saturday Evening Post*, *Hearst's*, and *Metropolitan* competed for it. *Tender Is the Night* was written during the time when Fitzgerald's popularity with slick magazine readers was at its all-time high point; for example, in 1929 and 1930, important years in the composition of *Tender Is the Night*, he published fifteen stories in *The Saturday Evening Post*. In sharp contrast to the 1925-1933 stories, which are characteristically of an even, high quality, and many of which are closely related to two novels of this period, the stories of the *Esquire* years are, in general, undistinguished. In addition, with minor exceptions, the stories written in this final period have little relation to Fitzgerald's last "serious" work, *The Last Tycoon*. The *Esquire* years thus constitute a low point from both a popular and an artistic standpoint. They are years during which he lost the knack of pleasing the large American reading public and at the same time produced a comparatively small amount of good artwork.

In the first two years of Fitzgerald's storywriting, his sensitivity to audience tastes was naïve. "May Day" and "The Diamond as Big as the Ritz"--not only the two best stories from these years but also two of the best stories in the Fitzgerald canon-- were written for sale to mass-circulation magazines. Both, however, were too cynical about American values to be acceptable to a large, middle-American audience. By 1922 and the publication of "Winter Dreams" in *Metropolitan*, Fitzgerald had learned how to tailor his stories for slick magazine readers while at the same time using them to experiment with serious subjects and themes that he would later use in longer works.

"WINTER DREAMS"

Viewed in association with *The Great Gatsby*, "Winter Dreams" provides an excellent illustration of Fitzgerald's method of using his stories as a proving ground for his novels. In a letter to editor Maxwell Perkins, Fitzgerald describes "Winter Dreams" as a "sort of 1st draft of the Gatsby idea," and indeed, it contains sufficient similarities of theme and character to be called a miniature of *The Great Gatsby*. Parallels between Dexter Green and Jay Gatsby are striking: Both men have made a total commitment to a dream, and both of their dreams are hollow. Dexter falls in love with wealthy Judy Jones and devotes his life to making the money that will allow him to enter her social circle; his idealization of her is closely akin to Gatsby's feelings for Daisy Buchanan. Gatsby's idealized conception of Daisy is the motivating force that underlies his compulsion to become successful, just as Dexter's conception of Judy Jones drives him to amass a fortune by the time he is twenty-five. The theme of commitment to an idealized dream that is the core of "Winter Dreams" and *The Great Gatsby* and the similarities between the two men point up the close relationship between the story and the novel. Because "Winter Dreams" appeared three years before *The Great Gatsby*, its importance in the gestation of the novel cannot be overemphasized.

Important differences in Fitzgerald's methods of constructing short stories and novels emerge from these closely related works. Much of the effectiveness of *The Great Gatsby* lies in the mystery of Gatsby's background, while no such mystery surrounds the early life of Dexter Green. In "Winter Dreams," Dexter's disillusionment with Judy occurs suddenly; when he learns that she is no longer pretty, the "dream was gone. Something had taken it from him . . . the moonlit veranda, and gingham on the golf links and the dry sun and the gold color of her neck's soft down. . . . Why these things were no longer in the world!" Because his enchantment could be shattered so quickly, Dexter's commitment to Judy is not of the magnitude of Gatsby's commitment to Daisy. Gatsby's disenchantment could only occur gradually. When he is finally able to see Daisy, "the colossal significance of the green light . . . vanished forever," but his "count of enchanted objects" had only diminished by one. Even toward the end of the novel, there is no way of knowing that Gatsby is completely disenchanted with Daisy. Nick says that "perhaps he no longer cared." The "perhaps" leaves open possibilities of interpretation that are closed at the end of "Winter Dreams." While Dexter can cry at the loss of a dream, Gatsby dies, leaving the reader to guess whether or not he still held on to any fragment of his dreams about Daisy. The expansiveness of the novel obviously allowed Fitzgerald to make Gatsby and his dream believable while he could maintain the mystery of Gatsby's past and the origins of his dream. Fitzgerald could not do this as well with Dexter in "Winter Dreams." The point is that in writing "Winter Dreams" Fitzgerald was giving shape to his ideas about Jay Gatsby, and, after creating the story, he could better see the advantages of maintaining the sense of mystery that made Gatsby a more memorable character than his counterpart in "Winter Dreams."

"THE RICH BOY"

Like "Winter Dreams," "The Rich Boy," published a year after *The Great Gatsby*, clearly illustrates the workshop function that the stories served. The story's rich boy, Anson Hunter, falls in love with the beautiful and rich Paula Legendre, but he always finds some reason for not marrying her, although he maintains that his love for her never stops. Anson, the bachelor, ironically becomes an unofficial counselor to couples with

martial difficulties and, in his role as protector of the family name, puts an end to an affair that his aunt is having. Paula marries another man, divorces him, and, when Anson encounters her late in the story, he finds her happily remarried and pregnant. Paula, whose revered place has been jeopardized by her pregnancy, finally dies in childbirth, symbolically taking with her Anson's youth. He goes on a cruise, disillusioned that his only real love is gone. He is still willing, however, to flirt with any woman on the ship who will affirm the feeling of superiority about himself that he cherishes in his heart.

In "The Rich Boy," then, Fitzgerald uses many of the themes--among them, lost youth and disillusionment in marriage--that he had covered in previous stories; in addition, he uses devices, such as the narrator-observer point of view that had been successful in *The Great Gatsby*, and he pulls from the novel subjects, such as the idealization of a woman who finally loses her suitor's reverence. "The Rich Boy" also blends, along with the themes he had dealt with before, new topics that he would later distill and treat singly in another story, just as he first deals explicitly with the rich-are-different idea in "The Rich Boy" and later focuses his narrative specifically on that idea in "Six of One." Finally, in the use of the theme of bad marriages in "The Rich Boy," there are foreshadowings of *Tender Is the Night* and the stories that cluster around it.

"BABYLON REVISITED"

The best of these *Tender Is the Night* cluster stories is "Babylon Revisited," which earned Fitzgerald his top *Saturday Evening Post* price of four thousand dollars and which is generally acclaimed as his finest story. "Babylon Revisited" represents a high point in Fitzgerald's career as a short-story writer: It is an artistically superior story that earned a high price from a commercial magazine. In the story's main character, Charlie Wales, Fitzgerald creates one whose future, in spite of his heroic struggle, is prescribed by his imprudent past, a past filled with heavy drinking and irresponsibility. He is destined to be haunted by reminders of his early life, embodied by Lorraine and Duncan, drinking friends from the past; to be judged for them by Marion, his dead wife's sister who, like Charlie's conscience personified, is disgusted by his past and demands punishment; and to be denied, for his penance, any right to fill the emptiness of his life with his daughter Honoria, who is in Marion's custody and who is the only really meaningful thing left. Fitzgerald fashions Charlie as a sensitive channel through which the reader can simultaneously view both Paris as it existed for expatriate wanderers before the Depression and the now-dimmed Paris to which Charlie returns.

The contrast is masterfully handled in that the course of Charlie's emotional life closely parallels the changing mood of the city--a movement from a kind of unreal euphoria to a mood of loss and melancholy. The contrast at once heightens the reader's sense of Charlie's loneliness in a ghost town of bad memories and foreshadows his empty-handed return to Prague, his present home. All of Charlie's present misery has resulted, in Fitzgerald's precise summary, from his "selling short" in the boom--an allusion to the loss of his dead wife Helen. Charlie, however, refuses to be driven back to alcohol, even in the face of being denied his daughter Honoria. Although he might easily have done so, Fitzgerald avoids drawing the reader into a sentimental trap of identification with Charlie's plight, the responsibility for and consequences of which must finally be borne only by Charlie. As he later did in Dick Diver's case in *Tender Is the Night*, Fitzgerald has shown in "Babylon Revisited" how one man works his way into an existence with *nada* at the core; how he manages to dissipate, "to make nothing out of something," and thus prescribe for himself a future without direction. It is also in the creation of this mood of Charlie's isolation that the artistic brilliance of the story, as well as its kinship to *Tender Is the Night*, lies.

The popular thrust of "Babylon Revisited" is a dual one in which Fitzgerald plays on what were likely to be ambivalent feelings of popular readers toward Charlie. On the one hand, he is pictured first as an expatriate about whose resolution to remain abroad American audiences may have been skeptical. On the other hand, Charlie appears to have reformed and obviously loves his daughter. Marion, by contrast, is depicted as a shrew, and the reader is left to choose, therefore, between the punishment of a life sentence of loneliness for a penitent wrongdoer and the granting of his complete freedom and forgiveness rendered against the

better judgment of the unsympathetic Marion. Fitzgerald guarantees that the reader will become emotionally involved by centering the story on the highly emotional relationship between a father and his daughter. Because Charlie is, in fact, guilty, to let him go free would be to let wrongdoing go unpunished--the strictest kind of violation of the Puritan ethic. To deprive Charlie of Honoria, however, would be to side with the unlikable Marion. Fitzgerald, then, resolves the conflict in the only satisfactory way--by proposing a compromise. Although Marion keeps Honoria for the moment, Charlie may be paroled, may come back and try again, at any time in the future.

The story, therefore, is successful on three major counts: It served as a workshop in which Fitzgerald shaped the mood of *Tender Is the Night*; it entertained with the struggle against unfair odds of a well-intentioned father for the affection of his daughter; and it succeeded on the mythic level, suggested in the title, as a story in which all ingredients conspire to lead to Charlie's exile--an isolation from the city that has fallen in the absence of a now-reformed sinner, carrying with it not only the bad but also the good that Charlie has come to salvage.

ESQUIRE STORIES

About four years after the publication of "Babylon Revisited," Fitzgerald had lost the knack of writing *Saturday Evening Post* stories, and he began writing shorter pieces, many of which are sketches rather than stories, for *Esquire*. *Esquire*, however, was not a suitable medium to serve a workshop function as *The Saturday Evening Post* had been. On the one hand, it did not pay enough to sustain Fitzgerald through the composition of a novel; even if it had, it is difficult to imagine how Fitzgerald would have experimented in the framework of short *Esquire* pieces with the complex relationships that he was concurrently developing in *The Last Tycoon*. Moreover, there is the question of the suitability of Fitzgerald's *The Last Tycoon* material, regardless of how he treated it, for *Esquire*: The Monroe Stahr-Kathleen relationship in *The Last Tycoon*, for example, and certainly also the Cecelia-Stahr relationship, would have been as out of place in *Esquire* as the *Esquire* story of a ten-year binge, "The Lost Decade," would have been in *The Saturday*

Evening Post. In short, *Esquire* was ill suited to Fitzgerald's need for a profitable workshop for *The Last Tycoon*, and it is difficult to read the *Esquire* pieces, particularly the Pat Hobby stories about a pathetic screenwriter, without realizing that every hour Fitzgerald spent on them could have been better spent completing *The Last Tycoon*. From a practical standpoint, it is fair to say that the small sums of income for which Fitzgerald worked in writing the *Esquire* stories may have interfered with the completion of his last novel, whereas the high prices Fitzgerald earned from *The Saturday Evening Post* between 1925 and 1933 provided the financial climate that made it possible for him to complete *Tender Is the Night*.

Indeed, if the *Esquire* stories in general and the Pat Hobby stories in particular, close as they were in terms of composition to *The Last Tycoon*, marked the distance Fitzgerald had come in resolving the professional writer-literary artist dichotomy that he had been confronted for twenty years, any study of the function of the stories in Fitzgerald's overall career would end on a bleak note. Two stories, "Discard" and "Last Kiss," neither of which was published in Fitzgerald's lifetime, indicate, however, that he was attempting to re-create the climate of free exchange between his stories and novels characteristic especially of the composition period of *Tender Is the Night*. "Last Kiss" provides a good commentary on this attempt. When the story appeared in 1949, the editors remarked in a headnote that the story contained "the seed" that grew into *The Last Tycoon*. The claim is too extravagant for the story in that it implies the sort of relationship between the story and the novel that exists between "Winter Dreams" and *The Great Gatsby*, a relationship that simply does not exist in the case of "Last Kiss" and *The Last Tycoon*. There are, however, interesting parallels.

"LAST KISS"

Fitzgerald created in "Last Kiss" counterparts both to Monroe Stahr and Kathleen in the novel. Jim Leonard, a thirty-five-year-old film producer in "Last Kiss," is similar to Stahr in that he possesses the same kind of power: When the budding starlet, Pamela Knighton, meets Leonard, her agent's voice tells her: "This *is* somebody." In fact, on the Hollywood success ladder he is in Fitzgerald's words "on top," although

like Stahr he does not flaunt this fact. Although Pamela is fundamentally different from Kathleen in her self-centered coldness, they also share a resemblance to "pink and silver frost" and an uncertainty about Americans. Kathleen is no aspiring actress, but her past life, like Pamela's, has an aura of mystery about it. Moreover, the present lives of both are complicated by binding entanglements: Pamela's to Chauncey Ward, and Kathleen's to the nameless man she finally marries. There are other parallels: The first important encounter between Leonard and Pamela, for example, closely resembles the ballroom scene during which Stahr becomes enchanted by Kathleen's beauty. In fact, the nature of Leonard's attraction to Pamela is similar to that of Stahr's to Kathleen; although there is no Minna Davis lurking in Leonard's past as there is in Stahr's, he is drawn to Pamela by the kind of romantic, mysterious force that had finally, apart from her resemblance to Minna, drawn Stahr to Kathleen. Moreover, both attachments end abruptly with the same sort of finality: Pamela dies leaving Jim with only film fragments to remember her by, and Kathleen leaves Stahr when she marries "the American."

That these parallels were the seeds of *The Last Tycoon* is doubtful. The important point, however, is that "Last Kiss" is a popular treatment of the primary material that Fitzgerald would work with in the novel: Jim's sentimental return to the drugstore where he had once seen Pamela and his nostalgic remembrance of their last kiss earmark the story for a popular audience ,which, no doubt, Fitzgerald hoped would help pay his bills during the composition of the novel. Fitzgerald was unable to sell the story, probably because none of the characters generates strong emotion. It is sufficiently clear from "Last Kiss," however, that Fitzgerald was regaining his sense of audience. In the process of demonstrating how well he understood Hollywood, the story also captured much of the glitter that is associated with it in the popular mind. In order to rebuild the kind of popular magazine workshop that he had had for *Tender Is the Night*, it remained for him to subordinate his understanding of Hollywood to the task of re-creating its surface. If he had continued in the direction of "Last Kiss," he would perhaps have done this and thus returned to the kind of climate that had in the past proved to be most favorable for his serious novel work--one in which he wrote handfuls of stories for popular magazines while the novel was taking shape. It is also possible that he might have used such stories to make *The Last Tycoon* something more than a great fragment.

Regarding the role of the stories in Fitzgerald's career, one can finally state that they functioned as providers of financial incentive, as proving grounds for his ideas, as workshops for his craft, and as dictators of his popular reputation. The problem for the serious student of Fitzgerald's works is whether to examine the popular professional writer who produced some 164 stories for mass consumption or to limit the examination of Fitzgerald to his acclaimed works of art, such as "Babylon Revisited," "The Rich Boy," *The Great Gatsby*, and *Tender Is the Night*. To do one to the exclusion of the other is to present not only a fragmented picture of Fitzgerald's literary output but also a distorted one. Just as the stories complement the novels, so do the novels make the stories more meaningful, and the financial and emotional climate from which they all came illuminates the nature of their interdependence.

OTHER MAJOR WORKS

LONG FICTION: *This Side of Paradise*, 1920; *The Beautiful and Damned*, 1922; *The Great Gatsby*, 1925; *Tender Is the Night*, 1934; *The Last Tycoon*, 1941.

PLAY: *The Vegetable: Or, From President to Postman*, pb. 1923.

NONFICTION: *The Crack-Up*, 1945; *The Letters of F. Scott Fitzgerald*, 1963; *Letters to His Daughter*, 1965; *Thoughtbook of Francis Scott Fitzgerald*, 1965; *Dear Scott/Dear Max: The Fitzgerald-Perkins Correspondence*, 1971; *As Ever, Scott Fitzgerald*, 1972; *F. Scott Fitzgerald's Ledger*, 1972; *The Notebooks of F. Scott Fitzgerald*, 1978; *A Life in Letters*, 1994 (Matthew J. Bruccoli, editor); *F. Scott Fitzgerald on Authorship*, 1996; *Dear Scott, Dearest Zelda: The Love Letters of F. Scott and Zelda Fitzgerald*, 2002 (Jackson R. Bryer and Cathy W. Barks, editors); *Conversations with F. Scott Fitzgerald*, 2005 (Matthew J. Bruccoli and Judith S. Baughman, editors).

MISCELLANEOUS: *Afternoon of an Author: A Selection of Uncollected Stories and Essays*, 1958; *The Cambridge Edition of the Works of F. Scott Fitzgerald*, 1991-2010 (12 volumes); *F. Scott Fitzgerald: The Princeton Years, Selected Writings, 1914-1920*, 1996 (Chip Deffaa, editor).

BIBLIOGRAPHY

Bloom, Harold, ed. *F. Scott Fitzgerald*. Updated ed. New York: Chelsea House, 2006. Collection of essays, including an examination of "Babylon Revisited," by Seymour L. Gross. Some of the other essays discuss the moral of Fitzgerald, Fitzgerald and "the authority of failure," and several of his novels.

Bruccoli, Matthew J. *Some Sort of Epic Grandeur*. 1981. Reprint. 2d rev. ed. Columbia: University of South Carolina Press, 2002. Bruccoli, a major Fitzgerald scholar, argues that Fitzgerald's divided spirit, not his lifestyle, distracted him from writing. Bruccoli believes that Fitzgerald both loved and hated the privileged class that was the subject of his fiction.

Conroy, Frank. "Great Scott." *Gentlemen's Quarterly* 66 (December, 1996): 240-245. A reconsideration of Fitzgerald on the centenary of his birth. Argues that one of Fitzgerald's great strengths as a writer was his ability to make the metaphysical beauty of his female characters believable.

Curnutt, Kirk. "The Short Stories of F. Scott Fitzgerald: Structure, Narrative Technique." In *A Companion to the American Short Story*, edited by Alfred Bendixen and James Nagel. Malden, Mass.: Wiley-Blackwell, 2010. Offers an overview and critical examination of Fitzgerald's short fiction.

Eble, Kenneth. *F. Scott Fitzgerald*. Rev. ed. Boston: Twayne, 1977. A clearly written critical biography tracing Fitzgerald's development from youth through a "Final Assessment," which surveys scholarship on Fitzgerald's texts.

Gale, Robert L. *An F. Scott Fitzgerald Encyclopedia*. Westport, Conn.: Greenwood Press, 1998. Provides everything students should know about Fitzgerald's life and works. Indispensable.

Gelfant, Blanche H., ed. *The Columbia Companion to the Twentieth-Century American Short Story*. New York: Columbia University Press, 2000. Includes a chapter in which Fitzgerald's short stories are analyzed.

Kuehl, John. *F. Scott Fitzgerald: A Study of the Short Fiction*. Boston: Twayne, 1991. Part 1 discusses Fitzgerald's major stories and story collections, part 2 studies his critical opinions, and part 3 includes selections from Fitzgerald critics. Includes chronology and bibliography.

Lee, A. Robert, ed. *Scott Fitzgerald: The Promises of Life*. New York: St. Martin's Press, 1989. An excellent collection of essays by Fitzgerald scholars, this book includes an introduction that surveys scholarship on the texts. Topics addressed include Fitzgerald's treatment of women, his notion of the decline of the West, his "ethics and ethnicity," and his use of "distortions" of the imagination.

Mangum, Bryant. *A Fortune Yet: Money in the Art of F. Scott Fitzgerald's Short Stories*. New York: Garland, 1991. Discusses all of Fitzgerald's stories, both those in collections and those uncollected, focusing on their relationship to his novels and their role as a proving ground for his ideas.

_____. "The Short Stories of F. Scott Fitzgerald. In *The Cambridge Companion to F. Scott Fitzgerald*, edited by Ruth Prigozy. New York: Cambridge University Press, 2002. Magnum, the author of a book about Fitzgerald's short fiction, provides a concise overview of Fitzgerald's short stories for this collection of critical essays about the author. Some of the other essays discuss Scott and Zelda Fitzgerald and the culture of celebrity, Fitzgerald and the rise of American youth culture, Fitzgerald's expatriate years and his European stories, women in Fitzgerald's fiction, Fitzgerald and Hollywood, and Fitzgerald's critical reputation.

Meyers, Jeffrey. *Scott Fitzgerald: A Biography*. New York: HarperCollins, 1994. In this biography, which makes use of previously unknown materials about Fitzgerald's life, Meyers discusses how such writers as Edgar Allan Poe, Ernest Hemingway, and Joseph Conrad influenced Fitzgerald's fiction.

Miller, James E., Jr. *F. Scott Fitzgerald: His Art and His Technique*. New York: New York University Press, 1964. An expanded version of *The Fictional Technique of Scott Fitzgerald*, originally published in 1957. Emphasizes Fitzgerald's literary technique, focusing on the impact of the "saturation vs. selection" debate between H. G. Wells and Henry James. Also adds critical commentary and interpretations of the later works.

Noble, Don, ed. *Critical Insights: F. Scott Fitzgerald*. Pasadena, Calif.: Salem Press, 2011. Collection of original and reprinted essays providing biography information and critical readings of Fitzgerald's works. The introductory essay examines the reasons for Fitzgerald's enduring relevance and the persistent significance of the major themes of wealth, success, love, youth, and tragedy in his works. Other essays discuss his interpretation of the American dream, his place within American popular culture, and the critical reception of his short stories and novels.

Petry, Alice Hall. *Fitzgerald's Craft of Short Fiction*. Ann Arbor: UMI Research Press, 1989. A study of Fitzgerald's short stories in relationship to his novels, American society, and his personal life. Summarizes and critiques critical reception to his short-story collections and discusses his relationship with his editor Max Perkins. Analyzes all the major stories and a number of minor ones.

Tate, Mary Jo. *F. Scott Fitzgerald A to Z: The Essential Reference to His Life and Work*. New York: Facts On File, 1998. A comprehensive study of the man and his oeuvre. Provides bibliographical references and an index.

Bryant Mangum
Updated by Mary Ellen Pitts

RICHARD FORD

Born: Jackson, Mississippi; February 16, 1944

PRINCIPAL SHORT FICTION

Rock Springs, 1987
Wildlife, 1990
Women with Men: Three Stories, 1997
A Multitude of Sins, 2001
Vintage Ford, 2003

OTHER LITERARY FORMS

Richard Ford made his reputation as a novelist before turning to short fiction. His first novel, *A Piece of My Heart* (1976), marked him as a southern writer, since it is set primarily in Arkansas and on an uncharted island in the Mississippi River. *The Ultimate Good Luck* (1981) tells the story of a Vietnam veteran, Harry Quinn, in Mexico, on a quest to get his girlfriend's brother out of jail. *The Sportswriter* (1986) is set in New Jersey and involves a failed novelist trying to put his professional and personal life in order. *Independence Day* (1995) is a sequel to *The Sportswriter*. Ford's short-story collection *Rock Springs* and his novella *Wildlife* are set in Montana. In 1991, Ford's screenplay *Bright Angel*, also set in Montana and adapted from stories in the *Rock Springs* collection, was made into a film directed by Michael Fields and released by the Hemdale Film Corporation. *Lay of the Land*, the third in his trilogy, appeared in 2006.

ACHIEVEMENTS

A writer's writer, Richard Ford has been praised for his clean style and craft by other writers such as Raymond Carver, E. L. Doctorow, and Joyce Carol Oates, who described him as "a born storyteller with an inimitable lyric voice." Walker Percy called *The Sportswriter*, which won the PEN/Faulkner Award for Fiction, a "stunning novel." Over the years, Ford earned

several fellowships. From 1971 to 1974, he was a University of Michigan Fellow, and he went on to become a John Simon Guggenheim Memorial Foundation Fellow (1977-1978) and a National Endowment for the Arts Fellow (1979-1980). *A Piece of My Heart* was nominated for the Ernest Hemingway Award for the Best First Novel of the Year in 1976. *Independence Day* won the Pulitzer Prize and the PEN/Faulkner Award in 1996, becoming the first novel ever to win both prizes. Ford won the Rea Award in 1995.

Such recognition, however, was slow in coming. According to Ford's friend and Michigan classmate Bruce Weber, the combined sales of Ford's first two novels amounted to fewer than twelve thousand copies. *The Sportswriter*, which sold sixty thousand copies, was the turning point in Ford's career and encouraged the publisher to put the first two novels back in print. The hardcover edition of *Rock Springs*, published by Atlantic Monthly Press, sold twenty-five thousand copies, and the Vintage paperback edition was then scheduled for an initial run of fifty thousand copies.

BIOGRAPHY

Though he does not consider himself a southern writer, Richard Ford was born in the Deep South in Jackson, Mississippi, in 1944, and he grew up there. Like Sam Newel, one of the two principal characters of *A Piece of My Heart*, Ford's father was a traveling salesman whose territory might have coincided with that of Newel's salesman father in the novel. In 1952, Ford's father suffered a heart attack, after which Ford lived with his grandparents, who ran a hotel in Little Rock, Arkansas. Ford grew into a relatively wild teenager, and, according to Weber, Ford's mother "kept him from serious scrapes with the law." Ford's father died in 1960, and in 1962 Ford went to East Lansing to study literature at Michigan State University, where he met Kristina Hensley, whom he later married. For a year after graduation, Ford taught high school in Flint,

Michigan, and then he enrolled for one semester as a law student at Washington University in St. Louis. Thereafter, he worked briefly in New York City as assistant editor for a trade magazine, *The American Druggist*.

He then seriously began to pursue a career as a writer, studying at the University of California, Irvine, with Oakley Hall and E. L. Doctorow. He also lived in Chicago and Mexico, where his novel *The Ultimate Good Luck* is set. He taught at the University of Michigan, Princeton University, Goddard College, and Williams College. Ford told *People* magazine in 1990 that he had lived in twelve places in twenty-two years.

In an effort to shed his identity as a southern writer, Ford has worked effectively to erase regional traces from his later writing. His first novel, *A Piece of My Heart*, is set mainly in Arkansas, after one of the two central characters crosses the South, coming east from California to get there. Most of the other characters are southern gothic types, and a reader would suppose that it must have been written by a southerner. On the other hand, if the reader turns to a later Ford novel, such as

Richard Ford (AP Photo/Pat Wellenbach, File)

The Sportswriter, set in New Jersey, the reader could easily believe that the novelist had spent all of his life in the New York-New Jersey area. Then, turning to Ford's short-story collection *Rock Springs*, the reader might think that the writer had grown up in Montana. Interviewed in Salisbury, Maryland, in April of 1988, just after the publication of *Rock Springs*, Ford remarked that he did not want to be known as a southern writer, that his stories and characters were universal and did not depend upon the peculiarities of any particular region.

Ford has lived in many places, urban and rural, but he settled in Montana to learn about the locale that would be the setting for his *Rock Springs* story collection and for *Wildlife*. He and his wife have continued to spend part of their time in a rented house in Highwood, Montana, about thirty miles east of Great Falls, and the rest of their time in New York, New Orleans, and other places remote from their Montana hideaway. Ford has lived on fellowships as well as on the income generated from his writing and occasional lectures and readings. Although he has taught and lectured in the past, he clearly takes the vocation of writing seriously. Ford taught at Bowdoin College in Maine in 2005. He became an adjunct professor at the Oscar Wilde Center of the English Department at Trinity College, Dublin, in 2008 to teach in the creative-writing program.

Analysis

Richard Ford's fiction probes the lives of ordinary people, fascinated and troubled by the unpredictability of life. In some cases, the stories involve some catastrophe experienced in adolescence or before, when a family crisis changed comfortable patterns of life.

"Optimists"

In the story "Optimists," in the Rock Springs collection, the narrator recalls a traumatic event that occurred in Great Falls, Montana, when he was fifteen years old, in 1959, "the year my parents were divorced, the year when my father killed a man and went to prison for it." The family situation in this story resembles the one in the later novella *Wildlife*. In both cases, the father reacts badly and emotionally and ruins both his life and the marriage, while the son watches, horrified and dumbfounded.

In fact, the wildlife metaphor of the later novella is explained in the story "Optimists," when the mother tells the boy Frank about a flock of migrating ducks resting on the Milk River that she saw once, when she was a girl and winter was approaching. A friend clapped her hands to startle the ducks into motion, but one stayed, its feet frozen to the ice. The mother's friend explained, "It's wildlife. Some always get left behind." In other words, such things happen in life as a natural consequence. Nature will have its way, and disaster cannot be avoided.

In "Optimists," Frank's father, Roy Brinson, a railway worker, returns home early one night, shaken because he has witnessed a man's death in a railway accident. He finds his wife playing cards and drinking with another couple, Penny and Boyd Mitchell. Boyd has had too much to drink and foolishly baits Roy into an argument about unions. The father loses his temper and hits Boyd "square in the chest," a blow that kills the man. The police come, the father is taken away, and the boy's life is forever changed. "We'll all survive this," Frank's mother reassures him. "Be an optimist." Mere survival, however, is not the issue here. The father serves five months in prison for accidental homicide, but thereafter he loses his job, divorces his wife, turns to drinking, gambling, and embezzlement, and abandons his family. The son survives, but the optimistic title of the story is surely ironic.

"GREAT FALLS"

Fatherhood is a major theme in Ford's fiction, in which men often go haywire, and many of his stories are built on father-and-son relationships, broken families, men trying to be good husbands and fathers, stumbling and failing in their attempts and perplexed by their failures. Jack Russell, the father in "Great Falls," takes his son Jackie duck hunting and attempts to give the boy advice. He remembers something Jackie's mother had once said to him: "Nobody dies of a broken heart," adding "that was the idea she had. I don't know why." The boy has fears: "I worry if you're going to die before I do," he tells his father, "or if Mother is. That worries me."

When Jackie and his father return home, they find a twenty-five-year-old stranger named Woody in the kitchen. The father goes berserk, ordering the mother to pack her bags, after which there is a standoff, with the father holding a loaded pistol just under Woody's chin, out in the yard by Woody's Pontiac, as the mother and son watch. "I did not think she thought my father would shoot Woody," the boy speculates, but he thinks his father did think so, "and was trying to find out how to." When asked in 1988 about his fictive strategy in this story and the dramatic possibilities, Ford explained:

> When I wrote that story, I did something that I almost never do. I didn't know when I was writing the story if someone was going to get shot or not. But I got to the point in writing the story at which . . . I realized that if someone did get shot, that a whole lot of dramatic possibilities that went on beyond that would be foreclosed for me. And in part, at least, for that reason I didn't do it.

Ford also commented on the unpredictability that somehow infects his stories. "Well, when a man is standing in front of another man holding a gun to his chin and he hasn't shot him yet," Ford responded, "he either will shoot him, or he won't. And probably he doesn't know until he does or doesn't do it if he's going to."

"ROCK SPRINGS"

"Rock Springs," the title story of the collection, sets the tone of quiet desperation that dominates the book. Earl Middleton, the central character, is a fugitive and a thief who is trying to escape from Montana to Florida in a stolen Mercedes with his daughter Cheryl and a divorced woman named Edna. When the Mercedes develops mechanical problems, they decide to leave it and steal another car when they get to Rock Springs, Wyoming. Three miles out of town, the car breaks down, and Earl calls a taxi. Their spirits are lifted momentarily when they see a gold mine on the outskirts of town; when they arrive at a Ramada Inn, however, Edna decides to go back to Montana, not because she does not love Earl but because she wants more permanence and security than he can offer. The story ends with Earl casing cars in the dead of night, wondering which one to steal and wondering

> what would you think a man was doing if you saw him in the middle of the night looking in the windows of cars in the parking lot of the Ramada Inn? . . .

Would you think he was trying to get ready for a day when trouble would come down on him? . . . Would you think he was anybody like you?

When asked how he found such a perfect line to end that story, Ford responded,

Sometimes you get lucky. You put yourself at the end of your story, and you know in fact it's the end of your story, and you get down to the last few gestures you've got left. You hope to put yourself in a state of mind where you could write a good sentence. That's . . . what I'm always trying to do--to write a good sentence.

Rock Springs offers the reader a multitude of good sentences.

"Sweethearts"

Earl Middleton, in the story "Rock Springs," is the cousin of Robard Hewes in *A Piece of My Heart*, but with Earl and some of the other characters of the *Rock Springs* collection Ford pushes this prototype toward criminality while still putting the characters' humanity on display. In "Sweethearts," for example, Russ, the narrator, describes the day he and his live-in, Arlene, took her ex-husband Bobby to jail to serve time for passing bad checks and robbing a convenience store. "You have to face that empty moment," Bobby says to Russ. "How often have you done that?"

Bobby looks "like a man who knows half of something and who is supposed to know everything, who sees exactly what trouble he's in and is scared to death by it." Bobby is desperate and pulls a gun just as their car reaches the jail, but finally he decides not to use it to kill Arlene, for whatever crazed motive, though after Bobby surrenders, Russ and Arlene discover the gun was not loaded. As in "Great Falls," the story is not over until Russ and Arlene digest their own feelings and set the course for their own lives, though Russ understands "how you became a criminal in the world and lost it all," like Bobby, and like Earl in "Rock Springs." Again, Ford reveals a sense of closure that is distinctively effective and affecting.

Wildlife

Another character type that recurs frequently in *Rock Springs* and *Wildlife* is that of the disturbed child who senses that his life is being changed by forces beyond his control and that he is powerless to intervene to maintain the status quo. All the child can do is to endure and survive in an unhappily changing world. Ford's adult characters are often faced with the same dilemma, but it is more pathetic when it visits children, such as the boy in "Optimists," Jackie in "Great Falls," or Les in "Communist," who, on a goose hunt with his mother's friend Glen, has "a feeling that something important was about to happen to me, and that this would be a day I would always remember." As Les notes later, "too much awareness too early in life" can be a problem.

Human motivation is always the central puzzle in the fiction of Ford, a mystery that his characters do not pretend to understand. Ford probes the human heart, seeking to understand why it is often disconnected from the human mind. His characters can be painfully sympathetic and wholly decent and admirable as they drift into dilemmas that they cannot control. Fate is a blind mechanism that can cause love to atrophy or die as his characters struggle to control their lives. There is dignity in that struggle and an ineffable melancholy that Ford seeks to convey.

In the novella *Wildlife*, teenager Joe Brinson sees his mother and father drifting apart and their marriage collapsing. He loves his parents and would do anything to save their marriage, but since his parents themselves do not understand what has gone wrong with their marriage after his father loses his job as a golf professional and his self-respect, how could a sixteen-year-old boy do anything to reverse the situation? The unemployed father goes out to fight forest fires for three days. Devastated, and perhaps fearing that her husband will never return, the mother has a fling with an older man, perhaps because she seeks comfort and security, then she leaves the family after the father returns home and discovers that she has been unfaithful. It is not at all clear that she understands her own motives. The son is made to understand that nothing in life is permanent or can be taken for granted. Happiness is a phantom that can dissipate quickly. Grown-ups can be as unpredictable and as irrational as children. The only reality is the coldness of the oncoming winter and, potentially, of life.

Fears, self-doubts, and frustrations flare up and spread as irrationally and as unpredictably as the forest fires that the father fights, which are finally brought under control not by the will of men but by the changing seasons and the passage of time. The fires will run their natural course. "This is a wild life, isn't it, son?" the father asks after the mother announces her intention to leave. The father's reaction to this news is irrational and potentially dangerous to himself and others; at least in this fable, however, all ends well, after a fashion, though relationships cannot be fully restored, despite good intentions, after they are once broken. Life is raw and fragile, and art does not intrude to presume to make it better.

One critic has argued that transience is the major theme in Ford's fiction and in his transient lifestyle. In Montana, Ford seems to have found an appropriate setting for his stories about ordinary Americans, encompassing their hopes and aspirations, their failures, losses, and disappointments. In this respect, Ford seems to be telling the same story over and over, populating it differently, but always demonstrating that life is fraught with frustration and the unexpected and that the measure of a person's character is the ability to endure the worst and hope for the best.

Women with Men

This collection of three novellas develops one of Ford's favorite subjects, the person who finds it difficult to look outside himself and into the life of someone who loves him. Ford has said that he likes the form of the long story and finds it congenial to this subject. In the first of the stories, "The Womanizer," Martin Austin meets a Frenchwoman, Joséphine Belliard, during a business trip to Paris. He is excited and compelled by her apparent self-sufficiency and her resistance to his interest, even by her passivity when he kisses her. Back home, he instigates a quarrel with his wife and returns to Paris and Joséphine. She is surprised but not very interested to hear from him.

When he arranges to meet her, he offers to stay with her six-year-old son Léo while she meets with her lawyer. Austin does not particularly like children, and he is unsure how he will entertain a small child whose language he does not speak. He finally decides to take the child to the nearby park, where Léo disappears. After some hours of searching by Austin and the police, the child is found. He is hysterical after having been attacked sexually. Coldly furious, Joséphine tells

Austin that he is the same as dead. As the story ends, Austin is meditating on the problem of being attached to another human being.

The second story, "Jealous," is set in Montana, where seventeen-year-old Donny is living with his father on a remote farm after his mother has left them to move to Seattle. On this snowy night, Donny's flamboyant aunt, Doris, is driving him to the station in Dutton so that he can visit his mother. While they wait in a bar for the train, they witness a shooting, one more unsettling event in a series for Donny, the last being his aunt's revelations about her bisexuality. The story leaves Donny feeling that his aunt is right in saying that he cannot trust the truth, a claim that leaves him strangely detached and calm.

Like "The Womanizer," "Occidentals" is set in Paris. The central character is a divorced middle-aged novelist, Charley Matthews, who is visiting Paris with Helen Carmichael, a large blond woman for whom he feels a lukewarm affection. Helen is enthusiastic about the trip; she has always wanted to visit Paris. After several uncomfortable experiences, however, Charley develops a distaste for the French and the city, and he erupts in bad temper, despite Helen's cheerfulness. When Helen dies unexpectedly, Charley meets the crisis with the same passive intelligence and vague optimism exhibited by Donny and Martin Austin at similar crises in their stories. Like many of Ford's characters, they ruminate on their futures in the midst of their tattered lives.

A Multitude of Sins

The sins, such as self-centeredness and fear of commitment, explored by Ford in this collection of ten stories are all related to the sin of adultery, a theme so fraught with the dangers of cliché that it takes a wise and conscientious writer to handle it without it becoming predictable and trivialized. Although Ford may be a better novelist than he is a short-story writer, the best stories here are the shortest, least novelistic ones: "Privacy" "Quality Time," "Calling," and "Reunion." The weakest are the three long, novelistic stories: "Crèche," "Charity," and "Abyss." The three mid-range stories-- "Puppy Love," "Dominion," and "Under the Radar"--combine some of the best qualities of the short pieces and some of the worst qualities of the long ones.

The long stories in *A Multitude of Sins* are ineffective because they go on endlessly, padded with pondering, pontificating, philosophizing, all of which Ford may be able to get away with in a novel but not in a short form, where such self-indulgences serve simply to postpone tediously a predictable end. The longest story, "Abyss," about an adulterous couple who leave a sales conference in Phoenix to go see the Grand Canyon, is the most attention grabbing, not only because of its length, which makes it to many critics the most important, but also because it has a shocking ending. A parody of a "family" trip in the midst of an illicit affair convinces the man in the story that although the woman he is with is a "tough, sexy little package" with "strong little bullet breasts," she is intelligent only in bed. The story's central premise--that adultery is an act that erases itself once the performance is over--presumably prepares the reader for the gratuitous ending, when the woman peers over the edge of the Grand Canyon and falls in.

At the other end of the spectrum, the shortest story in the book, "Privacy," about a man who is aroused by watching a woman undress in her bedroom across from his apartment, is tight and effective, working the way fine short stories in the style of Anton Chekhov should work. When the man sees the woman on the street and discovers that she is seventy, he feels in "no way surprisingly betrayed." The story captures economically the mysterious gap between public and secret life, reality and fantasy, action and desire.

Granted, other stories in the collection--such as "Quality Time," which examines the effect of death on an affair; "Reunion," which treats a man who has a compulsion to stop and chat with a husband whose wife the man has slept with; and "Puppy," which surveys a couple's relationship by their treatment of an abandoned dog--intriguingly explore various premises about adultery. However, Ford goes on too long, overplaying his role of the wise old novelist who knows about such things as love, betrayal, gender differences, what holds people together, and what tears them apart.

OTHER MAJOR WORKS

LONG FICTION: *A Piece of My Heart*, 1976; *The Ultimate Good Luck*, 1981; *The Sportswriter*, 1986; *Independence Day*, 1995; *The Lay of the Land*, 2006.

NONFICTION: *Good Raymond*, 1998.

EDITED TEXTS: *The Granta Book of the American Short Story*, 1992; *The Essential Tales of Chekhov*, 1998; *The Granta Book of the American Long Story*, 1998; *The New Granta Book of the American Short Story*, 2007.

BIBLIOGRAPHY

Alcorn, Ellen. "Richard Ford: His Novels Are a Medicine Against Pain." *GQ* 60 (May, 1990): 224-225. A profile of the writer at age forty-six. Attempts to show how Ford found his inspiration for *Wildlife* from his own difficult childhood. For Ford, storytelling is a kind of "medicine against pain."

Ballantyne, Sheila. "A Family Too Close to the Fire." Review of *Wildlife*, by Richard Ford. *The New York Times Book Review*, June 17, 1990, p. 3. This perceptive review finds at the heart of *Wildlife* "a deep nostalgia for that moment when a person recognizes a true perfection in the way things once were, before the onset of ruin and great change." It describes the narrative structure of the story as resembling a memoir, though lacking "a memoir's breadth and scope."

Duffy, Brian. *Morality, Identity, and Narrative in the Fiction of Richard Ford*. New York: Rodolpi, 2008. In addition to discussing the novels in Ford's trilogy about Frank Bascomb, this full-length study analyzes *Women with Men* and *A Multitude of Sins*. Examines relationships between morality and identity by drawing on the narrative theory of Paul Ricoeur. Also contains a long and detailed interview with Ford.

Folks, Jeffrey J. "Richard Ford: Postmodern Cowboys." In *Southern Writers at Century's End*, edited by Jeffrey J. Folks and James A. Perkins. Lexington: University Press of Kentucky, 1997. A discussion of *Rock Springs* as a postmodern Western whose characters are colonials and victims of a restrictive social environment. Argues that Ford's fiction is marginal literature in which all personal relationships are shadowed by political facts.

Ford, Richard. "First Things First." *Harper's Magazine* 276 (August, 1988): 72-77. Ford offers a first-person account of his life and career as a writer, from the early period, when his stories were rejected, and he was forced to deal with disappointment, to his eventual success and recognition. Along the way, Ford comments on the "business" of literary production and book publishing in the United States.

_____. "Interview." In *Speaking of the Short Story: Interviews with Contemporary Writers*, edited by Farhat Iftekharuddin, Mary Rohrberger, and Maurice Lee. Jackson: University Press of Mississippi, 1997. Ford discusses the process of writing such stories as "Rock Springs" and "Empire," talks about the difference between the short story and the novel, and responds to negative criticism of some of the characters in his short stories.

_____. "Interview with Richard Ford." Interview by Matthew Gilbert. *The Writer* 109 (December, 1996): 9-10. Ford discusses his views on the practice of writing, his love of moving to different locales, his rejection of the view that his books appeal more to men than to women, and his approach to writing a novel.

Schroth, R. A. "America's Moral Landscape in the Fiction of Richard Ford." *The Christian Century* 106 (March 1, 1989): 227-230. Schroth believes that Ford's fiction reflects "America's search for integrity," a quest that certainly is central to *The Sportswriter*. The essay also covers *The Ultimate Good Luck* and *Rock Springs*.

Weber, Bruce. "Richard Ford's Uncommon Characters." *The New York Times Magazine*, April 10, 1988, p. 50-51. Weber, a friend and classmate of the writer, offers a biographical portrait and an analysis of Ford's fiction. He discusses Ford's penchant for telling "stories of Americans ennobled by hardship." A full context is given for the writer's interest in changing locales. This profile followed the publication of *Rock Springs*.

James Michael Welsh; Ann Davison Garbett
Updated by Charles E. May

Paula Fox

Born: New York, New York; April 22, 1923

Principal short fiction

"News from the World," 1975
The Little Swineherd, and Other Tales, 1978
Amzat and His Brothers: Three Italian Tales, 1993
    (with Floriano Vecchi)
"Borrowed Finery," 2000
"Grace," 2003
"The Broad Estates of Death," 2004
"Smile," 2004

Other literary forms

Paula Fox has produced more than twenty adult novels, fifty books of fiction for children and young adults, many articles, and two memoirs; she also has retold stories for children and published two children's story collections. Fox is emphatic that her works are not "children's works" or "adult works" but merely "works"; she begins all her writing with the intention of writing well for herself. Fox wants the quality of her writings to be exceptional, regardless of who the reader will be. Librarians, book sellers, and others, however, have found classification of her work to be necessary.

Achievements

Paula Fox's shorts in such publications as *The Yale Review, The New Yorker*, and *The Paris Review* have earned numerous accolades. "The Broad Estates of Death" received the O. Henry Prize as one of the Best Stories of the Year (2006). "Grace" was both an O. Henry Prize Story (2005) and a selection of the Best American Short Story (2004). Fox's article "Borrowed Finery" was a selection for *The Pushcart Book of Essays: The Best Essays from a Quarter Century of the Pushcart Prize* (2002) and for *The Pushcart Prize*

2000. "News from the World" was a selection for the 1982 *Short Shorts: An Anthology of the Shortest Stories.*

Fox's first memoir--*Borrowed Finery* (2001)--was a finalist for the National Book Critics Circle Award for Biography. Her second memoir--*Coldest Winter: A Stringer in Liberated Europe* (2005)--was a *New York Times Book Review* Editors' Choice, a *San Francisco Chronicle* Best Book of the Year, and a *Washington Post* Book World Critics Choice selection.

Fox received a nomination for the National Book Award for Children's Literature for her novel *Blowfish Live in the Sea* (1970). *The Slave Dancer* (1973) received the American Library Association's Newbery award, the yearly prize for the most distinguished American children's book. In 1978, Fox received the Hans Christian Andersen Award, presented by the International Board on Books for Young People every other year to an author living at the time of the nomination and whose complete works make a lasting contribution to children's literature.

One-Eyed Cat (1984) was a Newbery Honor Book. *The Village by the Sea* (1988) and *Western Wind* (1993) received, respectively, the *Boston Globe*-Horn Book Award for Children's and Young Adult Fiction and the *Boston Globe*-Horn Book Honor Award. *A Place Apart* (1980) was the National Book Award Youth Winner.

BIOGRAPHY

Born to itinerant play and film writer Paul Hervey and Elsie Fox, Paula Fox stayed with friends and relatives and in an orphanage until she was six months old. At that point, Reverend Elwood Corning and his invalid mother took Fox. From the minister--a poet, a history buff, a writer, and an avid reader--Fox learned to read and developed her love of writing.

From 1929 until 1931, Fox lived in California. At the age of eight, she moved to a Cuban sugar plantation with her grandmother until the revolution forced Fox to return to New York City in 1934. By this time she had attended nine schools and had seldom seen her parents, who were spending time in Hollywood and Europe. Reading, libraries, and books provided stability for Fox.

After high school, Fox worked as a machinist and an employee at a publishing firm. She wrote for a British news agency and received an assignment in Poland during World War II. Fox married Howard Bird briefly and gave up their child, Linda, born in 1944, for adoption. In 1964, Linda gave birth to Courtney Love, who became an entertainer. Fox's first memoir, *Borrowed Finery*, follows the author from her traumatic childhood through the birth of Linda.

In 1946, Fox left for Europe, where she worked as a model and a reader for both Twentieth Century Fox and a publisher. She worked also as a stringer for Telepress in Great Britain, as a reporter in Paris, and as a writer during reconstruction in Warsaw after World War II. Her biographical *The Coldest Winter: A Stringer in Liberated Europe* tells of her European experiences.

Fox married Richard Sigerson in 1948; the couple had two children, Adam and Gabriel, before their 1954 divorce. Determined to get a college education, Fox enrolled in Columbia University in 1955. She had to drop out in 1958 for financial reasons. With her knowledge of Spanish, she received employment teaching English to Spanish-speaking children; she also secured other teaching positions. In 1962, Fox married English professor Martin Greenberg. While he wrote in Greece on a Guggenheim Fellowship, Fox yearned to write as well

Fox published her first book, *Maurice's Room*, in 1966. She followed this with *A Likely Place*, *Poor George*, and *How Many Miles to Babylon* in 1967. Paramount adapted her adult novel *Desperate Characters* (1970) into a motion picture in 1970. By 1972, Fox had obtained her own Guggenheim Fellowship and had written twelve books; she had earned a grant from the National Endowment for the Arts and had written a total of fourteen books by 1974. She also has taught literature and writing at the University of Pennsylvania and at C. W. Post University through the years.

ANALYSIS

Paula Fox's later works often exemplify a straightforward writing style, little symbolism, succinct dialogue, and a direct approach typical of the news articles she prepared as a correspondent (stringer) for Telepress and as news reporter in Great Britain, Paris, and

Warsaw. The subjects of Fox's work--like news topics--are not always pleasant; her realistic writings include such topics as homeless animals and people, death, disability, addiction, illness, slavery, guilt, acquired immunodeficiency syndrome (AIDS), and abandonment. Fox typically uses concise descriptions and only essential details; she places little emphasis on describing the feelings and the thoughts of the characters and interjecting her opinions.

"News from the World"

In 1975, *Confrontation*--a Brookville, New York, literary magazine--published Fox's six-page short story "News from the World." In it, a forty-year-old housekeeper shares the tragedy of an oil spill and the hopeless love between an older man and herself; this narrator speaks matter-of-factly about the impossibility of their union, the deterioration of his house, and the deadly effects of the spill. Fox concludes by noting that the man's house and the beach remain vacant for the remainder of the winter and the summer. In 1982, Irving and Ilana Wiener Howe selected this story for their anthology of the shortest stories: *Short Shorts*.

Paula Fox (AP Photo/Victoria Will)

More than a quarter of a century later, this story of loss is still relevant.

The Little Swineherd, and Other Tales

Fox's first short-story collection, *The Little Swineherd, and Other Tales*, contains five stories within a main story. The Canada goose narrator tells his tales to a duck (who is a talent agent) and a random number of frogs. Fox's first beast tale features a duck, a goose, a rooster, a swineherd, an alligator, and a raccoon. These moralistic fables are both instructive and humorous.

Amzat and His Brothers

Amzat and His Brothers: Three Italian Tales is Fox's second collection of short stories; most of her short writings appear as articles and not in collections. Fox admits that, like all storytellers, she has injected her own perspective in retelling these pre-World War II tales. The sometimes violent stories are illustrative of prejudice, greed, and revenge; they venerate courage, imagination, and cleverness. Two stories suggest "The Brementown Musicians" and "The Wolf and the Kids."

"Borrowed Finery"

Prior to Fox's full-length memoir titled *Borrowed Finery*, this article with the same name appeared in 2000 in the literary magazine *Threepenny Review*, published in Berkeley, California. Her autobiographical article appears in *The Pushcart Prize 2000* and *The Pushcart Book of Essays: The Best Essays from a Quarter Century of the Pushcart Prize* (2002). Fox begins this factual description of her life with an elderly minister and his invalid mother by describing her inappropriate clothing: donated by the congregation and relatives, purchased for her by the minister, and bought with the ten-dollar bill her father had sent before her fifth birthday. Fox describes sleeping as a ten-year-old in a New York apartment with her grandmother and wearing too-big dresses to school. She notes unemotionally her aunt's clothing and the pieces on the ironing board.

Three or four years after their departure, her parents return--as beautifully attired as film stars--and invite her to meet them in a store to buy some clothes; alone, she reaches the store by subway. They buy her only two pairs of shoes: one black suede and one nonserviceable green suede. Her parents dismiss her twenty minutes after her arrival to return to her grandmother's home by subway. Like the visit, the article concludes abruptly. Fox notes that when she left her grandmother's home permanently, she left behind the shoes.

"GRACE"

Fox's award-winning short story "Grace" features John Hillman and Grace--the animal-shelter dog that Hillman adopts; the fictional story appeared first in *Harper's* magazine. Fox's work was a selection by editor Katrina Kenison for *The Best American Short Stories* in 2004 and was a 2005 O. Henry Prize Story. Like Hillman's relationship with his girlfriend Jean, his relationship with Grace includes both regrettable incidents and happy moments. Like many other animal stories, "Grace" ends with the dog's death. The outcome of John and Jean's relationship remains uncertain; the story leaves the reader with an open denouement.

"THE BROAD ESTATES OF DEATH"

Fox's short story "The Broad Estates of Death" appeared in *Harper's* in 2004. The story tells of Harry's visit with his father Ben Tilson after twenty-three years. The two men show no emotion or affection when they meet or during their visit. Ben spends more time talking with Amelia--Harry's wife--than with Harry. Ben asks Harry to take him to visit some friends. Harry and Amelia leave abruptly that afternoon.

"SMILE"

In 2004, *The Threepenny Review* published]"Smile," an autobiographical article by Fox. The setting of this story is Prague in 1946, when Fox was working abroad as a new "stringer." The characters are Paula and Jan, a man from the news bureau who meets her at the airport. Paula learns of the fate of Jan's family during the Nazi occupation of Czechoslovakia. She decides Jan's frozen semismile is evidence that he will always be between laughter and sadness. "Smile" preceded Fox's memoir titled *The Coldest Winter: A Stringer in Liberated Europe* (2005).

OTHER MAJOR WORKS

LONG FICTION: *Poor George*, 1967; *Desperate Characters*, 1970; *The Western Coast*, 1972; *The Widow's Children*, 1976; *A Servant's Tale*, 1984; *The God of Nightmares*, 1990.

SCREENPLAYS: *Desperate Characters*, 1971; *Side Sho*, 2008.

TELEPLAY: *The Virtues of Madame Douvay*, 1962 (for *The Naked City*).

NONFICTION: *Borrowed Finery: A Memoir*, 2001; *The Coldest Winter: A Stringer in Liberated Europe*. 2005.

CHILDREN'S LITERATURE: *Maurice's Room*, 1966; *How Many Miles to Babylon?*, 1967; *A Likely Place*, 1967; *Dear Prosper*, 1968; *The Stone-Faced Boy*, 1968; *Portrait of Ivan*, 1969; *Hungry Fred*, 1969; *The King's Falcon*, 1969; *Blowfish Live in the Sea*, 1970; *The Slave Dancer*, 1973; *Good Ethan*, 1973; *Literature for Children*, 1974; *A Place Apart*, 1980; *One-Eyed Cat*, 1984; *The Moonlight Man*, 1986; *Monkey Island*, 1987; *Lily and the Lost Boy*, 1987; *The Village by the Sea*, 1988; *In a Place of Danger*, 1989; *Western Wind*, 1993; *The Eagle Kite*, 1995; *Gathering Darkness*, 1995; *Radiance Descending*, 1997; *Traces*, 2007.

BIBLIOGRAPHY

Carroll, Linda. *Her Mother's Daughter: A Memoir of the Mother I Never Knew and of My Daughter, Courtney Love*. New York: Doubleday, 2005. This biography-autobiography of Fox, Linda, and Courtney gives the reader insight into their lives. The abandoned Fox immediately gave up her daughter Linda for adoption in 1944; they did not see each other until 1993, when Linda found Fox. In 1964, Linda had a daughter, Courtney Love, who--like her mother and grandmother--had a troubled childhood.

Daniel, Susanna. *Paula Fox*. New York: Rosen Central, 2004. Daniel discusses the work of Fox, describing her writing process and her inspirations. Includes a biographical timeline and a list of Fox's awards.

Fox, Paula. "Paris: 1946." *The Paris Review* 170 (Summer, 2004): 67-76. In this article, Fox discusses her work for a news service and her stay in Paris at the end of World War II. The terse style of news reporting influenced Fox's style in the years to come.

_____. "Whose Little Girl Are You? Finding a Home from Cuba to Hollywood." *The New Yorker* 77, no. 17 (July 2, 2001): 52-70. This personal narrative by Fox describes her rejection by her playwright father and her young mother. Without emotion, she describes being reared by friends, family, a minister, and strangers. Like most of Fox's other works, this brief article is unsentimental.

Gallo, Donald R., ed. *Speaking for Ourselves: Autobiographical Sketches by Notable Authors of Books for Young Adults.* Urbana, Ill.: National Council of Teachers of English, 1990. Fox discusses her life and writing. She indicates her frequent preoccupation with moral maturation: from moral innocence to moral knowledge. Fox notes suffering and happiness often intertwine in moral knowledge.

Heller, Zoe. "Such Nativity!" *The New Republic* 225, no. 18 (October 29, 2001): 35-37. In a review of *Borrowed Finery*, Heller notes the tension, alienation, and unhappy families that appear in Fox's writings. Fox's works do not resort to sentimentality; rather, the writings are terse--even when Fox discusses her reunion with the child she gave up for adoption.

Anita Price Davis

BENJAMIN FRANKLIN

Born: Boston, Massachusetts; January 17, 1706
Died: Philadelphia, Pennsylvania; April 17, 1790
Also known as: Alice Addertongue, Anthony Afterwit, Miss Busy Body, Harry Meanwell, Silence Dogood, Timothy Turnstone, Richard Saunders, Poor Richard, Celia Single

PRINCIPAL SHORT FICTION

"The Bagatelles," 1722-1784 (miscellaneous tales and sketches)
"Silence Dogood Essays," 1722
"The Busy-Body Essays," 1729
"The Speech of Polly Baker," 1747
Poor Richard Improved, 1757 (also known as *The Way to Wealth*)
"Extract from an Account of the Captivity of William Henry," 1768
The Ephemera, 1778
"Letter from a Gentleman in Portugal," 1786

OTHER LITERARY FORMS

Benjamin Franklin excelled in a dazzling variety of literary forms. He initiated the United States' first successful periodical series, the "Silence Dogood Essays"; he wrote and published *Poor Richard's Almanack*, an annual compilation of weather predictions, jokes, tales, proverbs, and miscellaneous materials; he published numerous scientific papers, such as the description of his famous kite experiment that identified lightning as a form of electricity; he wrote piercing satires, as well as "The Ephemera" and other brilliant bagatelles; and the most important of his many political efforts may have been his editorial contributions to the Declaration of Independence and to the United States Constitution. At the end of his life, he produced one of the most popular, most widely praised, and most influential autobiographies in world literature.

ACHIEVEMENTS

Benjamin Franklin's monumental contributions to science, diplomacy, and politics have been in large measure conveyed through his clear and forceful prose, and the universal recognition accorded to these accomplishments takes into account his literary skills. Franklin was appointed joint-deputy postmaster general of England in 1753; he was awarded the Copley Medal of the Royal Society of London in 1754 and was elected to membership in 1756. He was awarded an honorary degree of doctor of laws from the University of St. Andrews in 1759, and an honorary degree of doctor of civil law from the University of Oxford in 1762. Franklin was also elected president of the American Philosophical Society (1769); chosen as a delegate to the Second Continental Congress (1775); elected minister plenipotentiary to France (1778); elected member of the Royal Academy of History of Madrid (1784); elected president of the Supreme

Executive Council of Pennsylvania (1785); and elected delegate to the Federal Constitutional Convention (1787).

BIOGRAPHY

The fifteenth son of a Boston candlemaker, Benjamin Franklin began America's first genuinely classic success story when he ran away to Philadelphia at age seventeen and achieved both wealth and fame before the age of thirty. He retired from his printing business and lucrative almanac, a wealthy man at age forty-two. Having already excelled as a writer, journalist, and businessman, in the following decades he distinguished himself in science, studying earthquakes, fossils, and the Gulf Stream, and developing experimental gardens in addition to his pioneering work in electricity. He also excelled in technology, inventing bifocals, the Franklin stove, and the lightning rod; in music, creating the glass harmonica for which Wolfgang Amadeus Mozart, Franz Joseph Haydn, and others wrote music; as a public servant, heading the Post Office and founding libraries, insurance organizations, and a charity hospital; as an educator, helping organize the University of Pennsylvania and the American Philosophical Society; and as a statesman, serving as America's first ambassador to France and helping draft the Constitution and the Declaration of Independence. He died the most beloved man in America and the most respected American in the world.

Benjamin Franklin (Library of Congress)

ANALYSIS

No American writer before Washington Irving produced more brilliant short fiction or approached the modern short story quite so closely, or quite so often, as Benjamin Franklin. The modern short story developed in America when Irving and others managed to blend the best of two quite distinct traditions: the essay-sketch tradition and the tale tradition. Scholars agree that Benjamin Franklin was the very first American to imitate the Addisonian periodical essay in America and that he had a genius for manipulating elements of the tale tradition: folklore, hoaxes, tall tales, and others.

Franklin's first published prose, the first of his fourteen "Silence Dogood Essays," appeared on April 2, 1722, in the *New England Courant*. Taking the form of a letter to the paper, the sketch introduces the marvelously characterized persona Franklin adopted for the series, Mistress Silence Dogood; her fondness for gossip, mother wit, humane concern for others, eye for detail, sense of humor, earthiness, and well-deserved vanity make her one of the best-developed and most utterly charming characters of eighteenth century American literature. Apart from her rather more conventional moral system, Mistress Dogood in some respects recalls Daniel Defoe's Moll Flanders, another vital widow powerfully addicted to life.

"THE BUSY-BODY ESSAYS"

Franklin further improved his writing skills in the "Busy-Body Essays," which he penned in 1729, some seven years after the "Silence Dogood Essays," but the lightly sketched persona of this series cannot begin to approach Mistress Dogood's vitality. Some parts of the series, however, such as the eighth essay, do tentatively approach the short story. Somewhat later, as seen on July 10, July 24, and September 12, 1732, Franklin became interested enough in character for its own sake that he abandoned even the quite loose structure of the periodical essay and launched into independent character sketches. Each satirizes a distinct character type. His pseudonym "Anthony Afterwit" is a man who is tricked into marrying a woman without a dowry and nearly ruined by her extravagance, who finally reestablishes a rule of economy and common sense in the household when his wife absents herself for a brief vacation. Another pseudonym, "Celia Single," in a charming scene and with apt dialogue, reports some of the aftermath in the Afterwit household and comments tellingly, with examples, on imprudence in the male of the species. The best of the three--and each is decidedly lively and entertaining--is his character Alice Addertongue, a dedicated scandalmonger and one of Franklin's most brilliantly realized creations.

ALICE ADDERTONGUE

Mistress Addertongue opens her piece, a mock letter to the newspaper (the *Pennsylvania Gazette*, in which all three of these pieces appeared), by commenting about recent newspaper essays on scandal and wittily employing an impeccable logic to demonstrate that only immoral "blockheads" complain of backbiting and gossip:

> They represent it as the worst of Crimes, and then roundly and charitably charge the whole Race of Womankind with it. Are they not then guilty of what they condemn, at the same time that they condemn it?

Let those who accuse Franklin of an incurable didacticism digest that moral and Mistress Addertongue's introduction to the next section: "Let us leave then these Idiot Mock-Moralists, while I entertain you with some Account of my Life and Manners." A "young Girl of about thirty-five," she is unmarried and economically independent but still lives with her mother. Alice first prefers self-praise to scandal of others, but, on the one hand, she is censured and whipped for such display of ill manners and, on the other hand, finds herself much more likely to please an audience by attacking third parties rather than by praising herself. Franklin here as elsewhere economizes, describing the vice, exploring scandalmongers' motives, and vividly characterizing his protagonist at one stroke.

In illustration of the latter principle, Alice recalls an incident wherein she vanquishes her mother's antipathy to the vice. During a tea party in the parlor, her mother brutally bores her company with a drizzling litany of praise of their various neighbors. Alice decamps to the kitchen, where she contrarily entertains the girls with "a ridiculous Story of Mr.----'s Intrigue with his Maid, and his Wife's Behaviour upon the Discovery." Eventually, the mother finds herself destitute of company and in turn adjourns to the kitchen, a convert to Alice's cause.

Mistress Addertongue next describes how she has succeeded in making herself "the Center of all the *Scandal* in the Province." One principle involves sound business practices: Whenever someone tells her one foul story she punctually repays it with two. Another principle dictates that if she has never heard of scandal attached to any given individual's name, she first imputes the lack not to virtue but to "defective Intelligence." Next, if she hears scandal of a woman, she praises her before other women for beauty, wit, virtue, or good management; if her prey is a man, she praises him "before his Competitors in Love, Business, or Esteem on Account of any particular Qualification." The latter technique proves superfluous in the case of politicians. Another principle of Alice's success involves keeping strict accounts (she is trained as a bookkeeper) of those from whom she has received or to whom she has retailed scandalous tales. Alice also generously declares that after profound reflection she determines few people allow more than a fifth of their scandalous behavior to be known; therefore she feels herself justified in improving her stories by inventing sundry details and by modest exaggeration: "I think I keep within Bounds if in relating it I only make it *three times* worse than it is."

In her conclusion, Alice laments that for several days a severe cold and a terrible toothache have prevented her from talking and thus from balancing her accounts; she begs the editor to assist her by printing the material she encloses, an "Account of *4 Knavish Tricks, 2 crakt Maidenheads, 5 Cuckoldoms, 3 drubbed Wives*, and *4 Henpecked Husbands.*" She promises to send more should the toothache continue. In an editorial note the publisher one-ups poor Alice, however, desiring to be excused from printing "the Articles of News she has sent me; such Things being in Reality *No News at all*."

If didactic, Alice Addertongue represents the most enlightened form of didacticism. Franklin does instruct the reader at length in the nature, conduct, and personnel involved in scandal, as if any of this were really necessary. He also underlines the transparent rationalization involved; more charmingly he identifies the true motive for scandal as a perverted impulse of self-praise--prevented from elevating oneself, one denigrates others--as Alice so convincingly demonstrates in her tactics for learning of scandal. Toward the end, in a marvelous twist, she implicitly generalizes her topic by relating scandal in one form to the basis of contemporary political campaigning and of journalism. Who among Franklin's readers could have been innocent of practicing or enjoying scandalmongering in one form or the other? The final mark of genius involves the enormous charm with which Franklin endows Alice. She is vital, magnetic, dynamic, self-assured, and absolutely amoral--rather possessing the attributes of scandal itself. The reader should not like Alice but cannot help it--much the same situation in which one finds oneself regarding scandal. Could Franklin possibly have analyzed scandal more tellingly?

"THE SPEECH OF POLLY BAKER"

Franklin produced a marvelous array of delightful short fictions. "The Speech of Polly Baker" takes the form of a mock oration in which Miss Baker argues on the basis of industry, economy, and nature to defend herself against the calumny associated with her having brought five bastard children into the world; the introduction indicates she represented herself well enough that one of her judges married her the next day and subsequently had fifteen children by her.

THE EPHEMERA

The Ephemera, a bagatelle, gently satirizes human ambition, learning, politics, and art--human life in sum--through the device of recounting the narrator's eavesdropping on a May fly. Franklin's famous letter to Madame Helvétius, another bagatelle, attempts to seduce her by means of a dream in which Franklin learns of "new connections" permitted in the afterlife; in fact, he learns that in this afterlife Mrs. Franklin and Mon-

sieur Helvétius have formed precisely the sort of liaison Franklin devoutly hopes to establish with Madame Helvétius in the here and now.

Franklin's two most impressive works of fiction came from his pen after his sixtieth year. They are genuine tales, not periodical essays, such as the "Silence Dogood Essays" and "The Busy-Body Essays Papers," or short sketches, such as "The Speech of Polly Baker." Their content, moreover, has nothing in common with the satirical character delineations of his newspaper sketches or with the homely wisdom of Poor Richard but is exotic and fanciful. The earliest of these pieces, published during Franklin's middle age, concerns the mythology of Native Americans, and the latter piece, written a few years before his death, concerns everyday life in China.

"EXTRACT FROM AN ACCOUNT OF THE CAPTIVITY OF WILLIAM HENRY"

In 1768, Franklin published in two issues of the *London Chronicle* a pretended "Extract from an Account of the Captivity of William Henry in 1755, and of His Residence Among the Senneka Indians Six Years and Seven Months Till He Made His Escape from Them, Printed at Boston, 1766." Like the "Speech of Polly Baker," the piece is a journalistic hoax. There was no William Henry taken captive by the Indians and no account of such an experience published in Boston. The narrative is based instead on Franklin's personal experience with Native Americans in Pennsylvania and a string of treaties between the colony and the local tribes that he published on his own press. Franklin's main literary source was an anonymous deistical essay that used Native Americans as a vehicle for describing and extolling the religion of nature. Franklin's protagonist details long conversations with the tribal chieftain and younger braves, analyzes Native Americans' principles of rhetoric, and repeats one of the creation myths of the tribe. In this myth, nine warriors while out hunting see a beautiful woman descend from the clouds. Realizing that she is the daughter of the Great Spirit, they go to welcome her and give her food. She thanks them and tells them to return after twelve moons. They do so and discover various new agricultural products where the parts of her body had touched the ground. Franklin introduced this myth in his "Remarks Concerning the Savages of North America" in 1784.

"A LETTER FROM CHINA"

Franklin's narrative concerning China has the same plot structure of an ordinary Englishman forced by circumstances to live in close contact with an alien culture, but it belongs to the literary genre of imaginary voyages. Given the title "A Letter from China," when it appeared in Jared Sparks's edition of Franklin's works in 1839, it should more properly be treated under Franklin's original title in the *Columbia Magazine*, where it was published in 1786 as "Letter from a Gentleman in Portugal to His Friend in Paris, Containing the Account of an English Sailor Who Deserted in China from Capt. Cooke's Ship." This is also the title on Franklin's manuscript copy in the American Philosophical Society Library. The work, which bears a resemblance to both Jonathan Swift's *Gulliver's Travels* (1726, 1727) and the second part of Daniel Defoe's *Robinson Crusoe* (1719), is pure imaginative fiction with no utilitarian purpose. It was partially inspired, however, by Captain James Cook's voyages, which also furnished local color. The sailor whose adventures are recounted was seized by pirates, rescued by the authorities, and sent to work on a farm in the interior of China, where he became a quasi-member of the family with whom he lived. In a style suitable to a literate sailor, who has many characteristics in common with Franklin himself, the narrator introduces in a fictional setting the most popular topics in contemporary Western writing about China.

OTHER MAJOR WORKS

NONFICTION: *Dissertation on Liberty and Necessity, Pleasure and Pain*, 1725; *The Nature and Necessity of a Paper Currency*, 1729; *Poor Richard's Almanack*, 1732-1757; "On Protection of Towns from Fire," 1735; "Self-Denial Not the Essence of Virtue," 1735; *An Account of the New Invented Pennsylvania Fireplaces*, 1744 (science); "The Old Mistresses' Apologue," 1745 (also known as "Advice to a Young Man on the Choice of a Mistress"); *Plain Truth*, 1747; *Proposals Relating to the Education of Youth in Pennsylvania*, 1749; "Physical and Meteorological Observations," 1751

(science); *Idea of the English School*, 1751; *Observations on the Increase of Mankind, People of Countries*, c. 1751 (science); *Papers, Experiments, and Observations on Electricity*, 1751-1754 (3 volumes; science); "The Kite Experiment," 1752 (science); *Post Office Instructions and Directions*, 1753 (state papers); *Some Account of the Pennsylvania Hospital*, 1754; *Albany Plan of Union*, 1754 (state papers); *Treaty of Carlisle*, 1754 (state papers); *The Interest of Great Britain Considered*, 1760; *Cool Thoughts on the Present Situation of Our Public Affairs*, 1764; *Memorandum on the American Postal Service*, 1764 (state papers); *Narrative of the Late Massacres*, 1764; *Examination of Dr. Franklin by the House of Commons Concerning the Stamp Act*, 1766 (state papers); *An Edict of the King of Prussia*, 1773; *Rules by Which a Great Empire May Be Reduced to a Small One*, 1773; *Treaty of Amity and Commerce Between the United States and France*, 1778 (state papers); *Political, Miscellaneous, and Philosophical Pieces*, 1779; *The Whistle*, 1779; *Dialogue Between Franklin and the Gout*, 1780; *The Handsome and the Deformed Leg*, 1780; *Treaty of Peace Between the United States and Great Britain*, 1783 (state papers); *Remarks Concerning the Savages of North America*, 1784; "On Smoky Chimneys," 1785 (science); *The Art of Procuring Pleasant Dreams*, 1786; "Observations Relative to the Academy in Philadelphia," 1789 (science); *On the Slave Trade*, 1790; *Memoirs de la vie privée de Benjamin Franklin*, 1791 (*The Private Life of the Late Benjamin Franklin*, 1793; *Memoirs of the Life*, 1818; best known as *Autobiography of Benjamin Franklin*, 1868); *Writings of Benjamin Franklin*, 1905-1907 (10 volumes; Albert H. Smyth, editor); *Treaties and Other International Acts*, 1931-1948 (state papers; 8 volumes; Hunter P. Miller, editor; also known as *Miller's Treaties*); *The Record of American Diplomacy*, 1947 (state papers; Ruhl J. Bartlett, editor; also known as *Bartlett's Records*); *The Papers of Benjamin Franklin*, 1959-2002 (36 volumes; Leonard W. Labaree et al., editors); *The Portable Benjamin Franklin*, 2005 (Larzer Ziff, editor).

BIBLIOGRAPHY

Aldridge, A. Owen. *Benjamin Franklin and Nature's God*. Durham, N.C.: Duke University Press, 1967.

This study of Franklin's theology treats his religious beliefs in relation to both his practice and his literary works, including "The Speech of Polly Baker," "Extract from an Account of the Captivity of William Henry," and "Letter from a Gentleman in Portugal." Intended for the serious student, it is particularly relevant to Franklin's views on metaphysics and personal conduct.

Anderson, Douglas. *The Radical Enlightenments of Benjamin Franklin*. Baltimore: Johns Hopkins University Press, 1997. A study that focuses on the literary and intellectual career of Franklin in his early years. Provides a close reading of a number of Franklin's texts.

Brands, H. W. *The First American: The Life and Times of Benjamin Franklin*. New York: Doubleday, 2000. A thorough biography that fleshes out the multifaceted Franklin.

Durham, Jennifer L. *Benjamin Franklin: A Biographical Companion*. Santa Barbara, Calif.: ABC-CLIO, 1997. Compendium of information, with topics arranged alphabetically in four categories, one of which is "Franklin's writings." Entries are straightforward and aimed at general readers and high school and undergraduate college students.

Franklin, Benjamin. *Benjamin Franklin's Autobiography*. Edited by J. A. Leo Lemay and P. M. Zall. New York: W. W. Norton, 1986. This critical edition presents the authoritative text of Franklin's *Memoirs of the Life*, superseding those in all multivolume editions of his writings. Particularly useful are thirty pages of biographical notes concerning the contemporary and historical figures mentioned in the autobiography. Other valuable sections contain relevant extracts from Franklin's letters and selected commentaries by outstanding critics from Franklin's times to the mid-1980's.

_____. *Benjamin Franklin's Writings*. Edited by J. A. Leo Lemay. New York: Library of America, 1987. This outstanding anthology--by far the best in print--contains not only the quintessence of Franklin's literary production but also valuable annotations and a thorough index.

Granger, Bruce I. *Benjamin Franklin: An American Man of Letters*. Ithaca, N.Y.: Cornell University Press, 1964. In order to prove that Franklin is an important man of letters, Granger subjects his periodical essays, almanacs, letters, bagatelles, and autobiography to close stylistic analysis, developing the "persona" of his sketches and the tropes of his essays and conversely dissecting "such rhetorical figures as analogy, repetition, proverb and pun." This stylistic analysis is successful as far as it goes, but it fails to consider the intensely human message of Franklin's best writing.

Isaacson, Walter. *Benjamin Franklin: An American Life*. New York: Simon & Schuster, 2003. Well-researched and entertaining biography, in which Isaacson provides a detailed chronicle of Franklin's life and describes the complexities and contradictions of Franklin's personality. Includes information about *Poor Richard's Almanack* and Franklin's other fictional writings, with the references to these works listed in the index.

Locker, Roy N., ed. *Meet Dr. Franklin*. Philadelphia: Franklin Institute, 1981. Sixteen prominent historians contribute to this compilation of essays analyzing various aspects of Franklin's career, including his literary works. Intended for the nonspecialist, the essays cover the essentials of Franklin's life and thought.

Lynch, Jack, ed. *Critical Insights: Benjamin Franklin*. Pasadena, Calif.: Salem Press, 2010. Collection of original and reprinted essays providing critical readings of Franklin's work. A. Owen Aldridge's essay, "Feeling or Fooling in Benjamin's Franklin's 'The Elysian Fields,'" analyzes one of Franklin's bagatelles. Other essays analyze the autobiography and *The Way to Wealth*. Also includes a biography, a chronology of major events in Franklin's life, a complete list of his works, and a bibliography listing resources for further research.

Morgan, Edmund S. *Benjamin Franklin*. New Haven, Conn.: Yale University Press, 2002. Morgan, a senior historian and the chair of the administrative board overseeing the publication of Franklin's thirty-six volumes of published writings, provides a portrait of Franklin's public life, much of it spent in

England and France. Includes information on some of Franklin's short fiction.

Van Doren, Carl. *Benjamin Franklin*. New York: Viking, 1938. This biography, although old, remains readily obtainable, and it is comprehensive and aimed at the general reader. Extensive quotations from Franklin's works provide a "speaking voice" for both the historical figure and the human personality. The text is long but brings the whole of Franklin's life into a single narrative.

Wood, Gordon S. "Not So Poor Richard." *The New York Review of Books* 43 (June 6, 1996): 47-51. Claims that Franklin is the hardest of all the

Founding Fathers to understand. Provides a biographical sketch, noting particularly the apparent contradiction between his image as a rustic, industrious, prototypical American and his image as an urbane and aristocratic European.

Zall, Paul M. *Benjamin Franklin's Humor*. Lexington: University Press of Kentucky, 2005. Examines Franklin's use of various forms of humor in his writings and for diplomatic and political purposes. Analyzes Franklin's writing style.

Walter Evans
Updated by A. Owen Aldridge

MARY E. WILKINS FREEMAN

Born: Randolph, Massachusetts; October 31, 1852
Died: Metuchen, New York; March 13, 1930
Also known as: Mary Eleanor Wilkins, Mary Ella Wilkins

PRINCIPAL SHORT FICTION

A Humble Romance, and Other Stories, 1887
A New England Nun, and Other Stories, 1891
A Pot of Gold, and Other Stories, 1892
Young Lucretia, and Other Stories, 1892
Silence, and Other Stories, 1898
The People of Our Neighborhood, 1898
The Love of Parson Lord, and Other Stories, 1900
Understudies, 1901
Six Trees, 1903
The Wind in the Rose-Bush, and Other Stories of the Supernatural, 1903
The Givers, 1904
The Fair Lavinia, and Others, 1907
The Winning Lady, and Others, 1909
The Copy-Cat, and Other Stories, 1914
Edgewater People, 1918
Best Stories, 1927
The Uncollected Stories of Mary Wilkins Freeman, 1992

A Mary Wilkins Freeman Reader, 1997 (Mary R. Reichardt, editor)

OTHER LITERARY FORMS

While Mary E. Wilkins Freeman's current reputation rests almost exclusively on her numerous collections of short stories for adults, her thirty-nine published works also include poems and stories for children, novels, and a play, *Giles Corey, Yeoman* (1893), a historical tragedy that, in part, dramatizes her ancestors' involvement in the Salem witch trials of 1692. A volume of her previously uncollected stories was published in 1992.

ACHIEVEMENTS

In August, 1890, *Critic* magazine conducted a public opinion poll to establish "Twenty writers whom our readers deem truest representative of what is best in cultivated American womanhood." Mary E. Freeman was included among the twenty, along with Harriet Beecher Stowe, Sarah Orne Jewett, and Rose Terry Cooke. Seven years later the same periodical conducted another poll to determine the twelve best American short stories. The winning list included Freeman's "The Revolt of 'Mother,'" and the second best list included "A Humble Romance." In still another display of public favor, the New York *Herald*'s 1908

"Anglo-American Competition" awarded Freeman five thousand dollars for *The Shoulders of Atlas* (1908). Perhaps the two most significant recognitions of her literary accomplishments were awarded in 1926: Freeman became one of the first four women to be elected to the National Institute of Arts and Letters, and she won the William Dean Howells Gold Medal for Fiction awarded by the American Academy of Letters.

BIOGRAPHY

Reared in an orthodox Congregationalist family, Mary Ella (later altered to Eleanor) Wilkins Freeman spent her early life in Randolph, Massachusetts. She moved with her parents to Brattleboro, Vermont, in 1867; following her graduation from high school, she took courses at Mt. Holyoke Female Seminary and Glenwood Seminary in West Brattleboro, Massachusetts, during 1870-1871. After an unsuccessful attempt at teaching school in 1873, she began writing poetry and short stories; her first significant work appeared in *Harper's Bazaar* and *Harper's New Monthly* in the early 1880's. Her first two collections of stories for adults, *A Humble Romance, and Other Stories* and *A New England Nun, and Other Stories*, generally considered her finest work, established her reputation as a professional writer. Upon her marriage to Dr. Charles Freeman in 1902, she moved to his home in Metuchen, New Jersey, where she resided for the remainder of her life. Personal tragedy marked her later years: She began suffering from deafness in 1909, and she was legally separated from her husband in 1922 as a result of his incurable and destructive alcoholism. Notable among her later works are two novels, *The Shoulders of Atlas*, which won the New York *Herald*'s transatlantic novel-writing contest, and *The Whole Family: A Novel by Twelve Authors* (1908), written collaboratively with William Dean Howells, Henry James, and others.

ANALYSIS

Invariably set in the rural areas of Massachusetts or Vermont, Mary E. Wilkins Freeman's most engaging stories focus on troubled characters who encounter situations that jeopardize their quest for happiness and personal fulfillment. In prose as angular and unornamented as the characters she portrays and with masterful detachment from them, Freeman typically develops a story around the main character's response to a personal crisis. Depending on the degree of resoluteness that they possess and the seriousness of the circumstances that they face, her characters react in several ways: Some openly rebel, exerting their will with great courage and determination; others passively accept their lot, preferring to continue what may be a meaningless existence; still others act self-destructively, revealing a masochistic tendency toward self-punishment. Although she wrote about men, her most fascinating characters are women, especially older ones, and in her best work, *A Humble Romance, and Other Stories* and *A New England Nun, and Other Stories*, from which the following stories are taken, Freeman's heroines are depicted with extraordinary sensitivity and insight. The major theme running through all her fiction is the struggle of every human being to preserve his or her dignity and self-respect when confronted with difficult decisions.

"THE REVOLT OF 'MOTHER'"

As its title indicates, "The Revolt of 'Mother'" has as its protagonist a character who boldly asserts herself. Freeman's most widely anthologized story, it humorously dramatizes the clash of wills between Sarah Penn, a dutiful, God-fearing wife, and her stubborn husband, Adoniram. One spring on the very spot where he had promised to build their new house when they got married forty years earlier, Adoniram begins erecting a new barn for their small New England farm. Having patiently and quietly endured the cramped and outdated quarters of their old house for all these years and wanting her daughter, Nanny, to be married in a new house in the fall, Sarah confronts her husband, accusing him of "lodgin'" his "dumb beasts" better than his "own flesh an' blood." Adoniram refuses to honor his long-standing promise. In fact, he obstinately refuses even to discuss the matter, continually replying with Yankee terseness, "I ain't got nothin' to say." Tearfully reconciling herself to the situation, Sarah chooses not to force the issue, content at present to continue her role as an obedient wife.

When the barn is completed in late July, Adoniram plans to transfer his livestock from the old barn on a Wednesday. On the day before, however, learning of an opportunity to buy "a good horse" in neighboring Vermont, he decides to defer the move until his return on Saturday. Convinced that his absence is an act of "providence," Sarah and Nanny pack the family's belongings and carry them into the spacious new barn. Within a few hours, with a little imagination and ingenuity, Sarah begins to transform the barn into the house of her dreams.

News of her rebellious activities soon spreads, and by Friday she is the main subject of village gossip. The minister, hoping to persuade her to undo the deed before Adoniram returns, tries to reason with her, but his efforts are in vain. When he returns the following day, Adoniram enters the house shed first, only to discover that one of his cows has taken up residence there. In a state of disbelief he then enters the new barn and is flabbergasted when he discovers what has happened during his absence. Assuring him that she "ain't crazy," Sarah releases her pent-up emotions, justifies her

Mary E. Wilkins Freeman (Library of Congress)

actions, and, to his amazement, orders him to complete the conversion. After being served his favorite supper, which he eats silently, Adoniram retreats to the front step and cries. Later comforted by Sarah, he obediently promises to finish converting the barn and humbly confesses to her, "I hadn't no idee you was so set on't as all this comes to."

Like other characters in Freeman's stories who are constitutionally unable to endure the role that they have been forced to play by family or society--for example, Candace Whitcomb in "A Village Singer"--Sarah Penn ultimately resorts to open rebellion as a means of expressing dissatisfaction. Their self-respect threatened, Freeman's psychologically healthy characters refuse to accept the intolerable situation that causes their unhappiness. Most of her protagonists, however, are not as successful in dealing with crises, for their twisted and lonely lives are so devoid of purpose and meaning that they do not even realize that they are partially or wholly responsible for their plight. The tragic vision set forth in these stories is far more typical of her fiction than the comic mood seen in "The Revolt of 'Mother.'" In this regard "A New England Nun" and "A Poetess," two of her most critically acclaimed stories, are more representative in tone, incident, and artistry.

"A NEW ENGLAND NUN"

In the title story of *A New England Nun, and Other Stories*, an illuminating study of self-imposed spinsterhood, Freeman analyzes the crippling emotional paralysis that prevents the heroine, Louisa Ellis, from marrying her fiancé of fifteen years, Joe Dagget. For the first fourteen years of their engagement, Joe had worked in Australia "to make his fortune." Faithful to each other but seldom exchanging letters, Joe and Louisa assume that nothing has happened during their separation that would stop the wedding from taking place as scheduled upon his return. Much, however, has happened to Louisa, and her first reaction to Joe's return is "consternation." His biweekly visits with her are marked by stiff formality, banal conversation, and emotional uneasiness. He is puzzled by her lack of passion; her cool behavior toward him makes him uncomfortable. During one of their awkward meetings for example, Joe unintentionally tracks in some dust, nervously fidgets with her carefully arranged books, and accidentally knocks over her sewing basket, all of which irritates her.

With remarkable insight, Freeman traces the development of Louisa's emotional paralysis and neurotic meticulousness. Following the deaths of her mother and brother while Joe was in Australia, which "left her all alone in the world," Louisa had steadily drifted into the private world of her house and garden. Rather than seeking out the company and friendship of other people, Louisa has retreated into her self-imposed convent and over the years has found comfort and pleasure in growing lettuce "to perfection," keeping her bureau drawers "orderly," cleaning her windowpanes, and "polishing her china carefully." Her sewing apparatus has become "a very part of her personality," and sewing itself one of her great obsessions. Hopelessly inured to her soul-killing routines, Louisa wants nothing to disturb her placid, well-ordered life, including Joe Dagget.

Freeman skillfully employs three important symbols to represent the futility of Louisa's life and the potential unhappiness that Joe would face being married to her. One of Louisa's favorite pastimes is distilling aromatic essences from her roses and mint. The numerous vials of essences that she has collected over the years serve no purpose whatsoever and are clearly a tangible measure of the meaninglessness of her life. Marriage would destroy this self-indulgent hobby, for in being responsible to someone else "there would be no time for her to distil for the mere pleasure of it." What would happen to Joe if he married her is symbolized in part by her caged canary, which always flutters "wildly" when Joe visits as if to warn him of his fate. The most important symbol of bondage, however, is the chain on which for fourteen years she has kept her supposedly vicious dog, Caesar. "A veritable hermit of a dog" and kept "a close prisoner," Caesar has been "shut out from the society of his kind and all innocent canine joys." Joe, knowing that Caesar is not really mean and subconsciously reflecting on what might happen to himself, continually tells Louisa that he will one day set the dog free. For Louisa, too, the chain has symbolic significance: Joe's promise to set the dog free represents a threat to the continuance of her secure, reclusive existence.

Joe does not fully understand the changes that Louisa has undergone and politely continues to tolerate her icy attitude toward him. Louisa, feeling obligated to marry the man who has sacrificed so much of his life for her, is unwilling either to alter her life or to tell him frankly that she prefers monasticism to marriage. Impassive, she does nothing. Having received no passionate responses from Louisa, Joe finds himself becoming attracted to Lily Dyer, a beautiful, warmhearted woman who is helping his sick mother. Lily grows fond of Joe, but neither of the two lets the relationship become serious since both feel that the fifteen-year-old engagement should be sacredly honored.

One evening about a week before the wedding, Louisa, who knows nothing about Joe and Lily, takes a walk and inadvertently overhears them talking. Lily is about to leave town to prevent further complications; with mixed emotions Joe agrees with her decision. Realizing that Joe and Lily love each other and sensing an opportunity to get out of the marriage gracefully, Louisa frees Joe the next night. Without mentioning Lily, Louisa finally admits that "she had lived so long in one way that she shrank from making a change." While Louisa does confess to her inadequacies and while her decision is in part a noble one, it is also self-serving for it allows her to avoid any long-term responsibility to another human being. To achieve this desire, Louisa condemns herself to a life of seclusion.

Freeman's profound understanding of the atrophy of the human will is revealed in a number of stories, most notably "A Symphony in Lavender," "A Lover of Flowers," "A Village Lear," "A Kitchen Colonel," and "Sister Liddy." As in "A New England Nun," Freeman carefully avoids passing judgment on the paralyzed characters in these stories, but she leaves little doubt that total passivity is one of the worst of human failings. The unwillingness to take command of one's life, Freeman demonstrates in these stories, eventually leads to the fatally mistaken assumption that one cannot and should not alter one's pattern of living, even if that life has lost purpose and meaning.

"A POETESS"

If some of Freeman's protagonists aggressively assert themselves or passively accept the status quo, others react in ways that show a tendency toward self-punishment. Such is the case with Betsey Dole in "A Poetess," which traces the invidious effects of gossip on a person who ends up lashing herself rather than the author of her humiliation, the village minister. Fifty years old, unmarried, and consumptive, Betsey has acquired a modest reputation in the town as a writer of poetry, which is every bit as saccharine as the sugar cubes that she feeds her canary. Like Louisa Ellis, Betsey has created a world in which the source of meaning is not other people. Betsey lives only for her poetry. Poor, she has never made any money from her writing. Her only income for the past twenty years has been the interest generated from her deceased father's modest savings account. Impractical as well as poor, she prefers growing flowers rather than the vegetables that she needs for her very nourishment. Her life is characterized by eccentricity.

One summer morning she is visited by Mrs. Caxton, who is dressed in mourning because of the recent death of her young boy, Willie. Wanting her son to be commemorated in verse, she asks Betsey to write a fitting obituary poem. After they weep together for several minutes, Mrs. Caxton informs Betsey that she is going to have copies of the poem printed for friends and relatives. Betsey, promising to do "the best" she can, tells her that the poem will be written in the afternoon.

Raptly working through lunch and even experiencing visions of little Willie as a human and as angel, Betsey looks "like the very genius of gentle, old-fashioned, sentimental poetry." She lies awake all that night mentally revising her sixteen-verse poem; and on the next day she delivers the final copy of the maudlin tribute to a very appreciative and tearful Mrs. Caxton. Having been promised a printed copy, Betsey feels "as if her poem had been approved and accepted by one of the great magazines."

Too poor even to have it framed, she pins the printed copy on her living room wall and subtly calls attention to it when visitors come. Only two weeks later, however, "the downfall of her innocent pride came." The key word is "innocent," for Betsey has naïvely assumed that everyone in the village appreciates her poetry. She is informed by Mrs. Caxton that Reverend Lang, who has some literary taste and who has had some of his poetry published in magazines, has called

her poem "poor." Worse, he is reported to have said that Betsey has never written anything that could rightly be regarded as poetry. Stunned, she says nothing. After Mrs. Caxton leaves, Betsey begins talking as if there were a listener in the room:

> I'd like to know if you think it's fair. Had I ought to have been born with the wantin' to write poetry if I couldn't write it--had I? Had I ought to have been let to write all my life, an' not know before there wa'n't any use in it?

Her listener is God, and her bitter questioning reveals the extent to which she is overly dependent on her poetry for any meaning in her life. Thoroughly humiliated, she proceeds to burn all of her poems: "Other women might have burned their lovers' letters in agony of heart. Betsey had never had any lover, but she was burning all the love-letters that had passed between her and life." Unable to forget the poems, she puts the ashes in her blue china sugar bowl. Burning the poems symbolizes not only her disillusionment with God but also the destruction of her reason for existing. The almost perverse pleasure that she takes in burning the poems and then keeping the ashes as a painful reminder of them suggests the unhealthiness of her will.

Having destroyed the only activity that has ever meant anything to her, she steadily loses her desire to live. By fall she is bedridden and on the verge of death. Shortly before dying, she requests that Reverend Lang visit her. The minister, assuming that Betsey wants to clear her conscience before dying, is unaware that her real purpose is to embarrass him, to make him feel guilty. She asks that he bury the ashes of the poems with her, gets him to admit that he has some literary pretensions, and says that none of her poetry was ever "good." Bewildered by the nature of her death-bed conversation, he remains oblivious to her real intention. Her final request is that he write an obituary poem for her. As Betsey had told Mrs. Caxton, the minister promises to do "the best" he can. Even after this pointed reference, he is completely unaware of the connection between Betsey's behavior and the comments he had made about her poetry several months before. Ironically, Betsey dies falsely believing that Reverend Lang will live with a guilty conscience. Rather than passively living with her limitations as Louisa Ellis chooses to do, or boldly asserting her dignity as Sarah Penn ultimately decides, Betsey Dole follows a self-destructive path.

Thoroughly familiar with the conscience and the will, Freeman created a wide range of literary portraits that are remarkable for their psychological verisimilitude. While most other regional writers represented in their fiction little more than the surface of New England life, Freeman consistently tried to bare the very mind and soul of her compatriots. With the possible exception of Sarah Orne Jewett, none of her contemporaries was as successful in delineating the character of New Englanders. At her best, particularly in *A Humble Romance, and Other Stories* and *A New England Nun, and Other Stories*, her fiction transcends"local color." Although her characters and settings are clearly regional, the underlying subject of her stories--the human condition--is universal. Freeman is not overtly didactic, but the reader may readily infer from her stories that happiness and self-fulfillment are the result of the often difficult struggle to secure and maintain dignity and self-respect. Her fiction is a forceful reminder that while some people succeed, many others fail.

OTHER MAJOR WORKS

LONG FICTION: *Jane Field*, 1892 (serial); 1893 (book); *Pembroke*, 1894; *Madelon*, 1896; *Jerome, a Poor Man*, 1897; *The Jamesons*, 1899; *The Heart's Highway: A Romance of Virginia*, 1900; *The Portion of Labor*, 1901; *The Debtor*, 1905; *"Doc" Gordon*, 1906; *By the Light of the Soul*, 1907; *The Shoulders of Atlas*, 1908; *The Whole Family: A Novel by Twelve Authors*, 1908; *The Butterfly House*, 1912; *The Yates Pride: A Romance*, 1912; *An Alabaster Box*, 1917 (with Florence Morse Kingsley).

PLAY: *Giles Corey, Yeoman*, pb. 1892.

NONFICTION: *The Infant Sphinx: Collected Letters of Mary E. Wilkins Freeman*, 1985 (Brent L. Kendrick, editor).

CHILDREN'S LITERATURE: *Goody Two-Shoes*, 1883 (with Clara Doty Bates); *The Adventures of Ann: Stories of Colonial Times*, 1886; *The Cow with the Golden Horns, and Other Stories*, 1886; *Once Upon a Time, and Other Child Verses*, 1897.

BIBLIOGRAPHY

Daniel, Janice. "Redefining Place: *Femmes Coverts* in the Stories of Mary Wilkins Freeman." *Studies in Short Fiction* 33 (Winter, 1996): 69-76. Discusses the many images in Freeman's stories that suggest covering or containing women. Argues that the women in the stories reject restrictive places imposed from the outside, choose their own places, and enclose themselves in choices that are conducive to their own affirmation of self.

Feinberg, Lorne. "Mary E. Wilkins Freeman's 'Soft Diurnal Commotion': Women's Work and Strategies of Containment." *The New England Quarterly* 62, no. 4 (1989): 483-504. Feinberg questions how women's work is to be valued in the marketplace as she looks at Freeman's short stories dealing with the conception of the "women's sphere" and the economics of women's work. To help answer her question, Feinberg discusses Catherine Beecher and Charlotte Perkins Gilman's ideas on the way value was assigned to women's work. Mentions Freeman's stories "A New England Nun," "An Honest Soul," "A Humble Romance," "A Church Mouse," and "The Revolt of 'Mother.'"

Freeman, Mary E. Wilkins. *The Infant Sphinx: Collected Letters of Mary E. Wilkins Freeman*, edited by Brent L. Kendrick. Metuchen, N.J.: Scarecrow Press, 1985. Kendrick suggests that although the author's letters were written for practical literary reasons and are a bit mundane, they are a valuable source of autobiographical information. Kendrick warns that it may be difficult to recognize and appreciate the autobiographical details tucked away in these letters that reflect Freeman's external and internal life, but he insists that they can be uncovered by the patient reader.

Mann, Susan Garland. "Gardening as 'Women's Culture' in Mary E. Wilkins Freeman's Short Fiction." *The New England Quarterly* 71 (March, 1998): 33-53. Maintains that gardening in Freeman's stories indicates women's culture as imposed by a hierarchical society. Argues that Freeman subverted woman's sphere by focusing on domestic areas in which they received personal gratification.

Marchalonis, Shirley, ed. *Critical Essays on Mary Wilkins Freeman*. Boston: G. K. Hall, 1991. A collection of essays ranging from early reviews to a number of essays influential in starting a revival of interest in Freeman's stories. Includes an essay that surveys one hundred years of criticism of Freeman's work, as well as five essays written especially for this collection.

Reichardt, Mary R. "'Friend of My Heart': Women as Friends and Rivals in the Short Stories of Mary Wilkins Freeman." *American Literary Realism, 1870-1910* 22, no. 2 (1990): 54-68. Reichardt contends that Freeman's work lacks evidence for upholding modern feminist ideas of nineteenth century matriarchal worlds and strong women's friendships. Instead, Reichardt maintains that Freeman's work shows a variegated pattern of domineering or proud women rejected or humbled, while meeker and more dependent women quietly triumph.

_____. "Mary Wilkins Freeman: One Hundred Years of Criticism." *Legacy* 4, no. 2 (1987): 31-44. Reichardt offers an extensive, although not complete, critical and historical context for Freeman and her work. Reveals specific areas of attention given to Freeman over time that serve as a "barometer of our cultural attitudes toward gender in the 100 years that have elapsed since Freeman embarked on her literary career in 1887."

_____. *Mary Wilkins Freeman: A Study of the Short Fiction*. New York: Twayne, 1997. An excellent examination of Freeman's short stories. Includes bibliographical references and an index.

_____. *A Web of Relationship: Women in the Short Fiction of Mary Wilkins Freeman*. Jackson: University Press of Mississippi, 1992. Argues that Freeman's best stories focus on women who struggle against forces that control them, such as marriage, family, and poverty. The book focuses on four types of conflicted relationships in Freeman's stories: women and parents, women and husbands, women and friends, and women alone.

Scofield, Martin. "Rebecca Harding Davis, Sarah Orne Jewett, and Mary Wilkins Freeman." In *The Cambridge Companion to the American Short Story*. New York: Cambridge University Press, 2006. Defines Freeman's place in the history of American short fiction and analyzes several of her short stories.

Toth, Susan Allan. "'The Rarest and Most Peculiar Grape': Versions of the New England Woman in Nineteenth-Century Local Color Literature." In *Regionalism and the Female Imagination: A Collection of Essays*, edited by Emily Toth. New York: Human Sciences Press, 1985. Freeman's use of marriage, or lack thereof, in her short stories is the focus of Toth's article. She maintains that one of Freeman's specialties is the portrait of neurotic single women who eschew marriage and find other sources of emotional fulfillment. Curtailing the theme of marriage, Toth briefly mentions the protectiveness, strength, and sentimentality Freeman develops in her characters who are mothers.

Weinstock, Jeffrey Andrew. "Familial Ghosts: Louise Stockton, Olivia Howard Dunbar, Edith Wharton, Josephine Daskam Bacon, Elia Wilkinson Peattie, Georgia Wood Pangborn, and Mary E. Wilkins Freeman." In *Scare Tactics: Supernatural Fiction by American Women*. New York: Fordham University Press, 2008. Analyzes "The Lost Ghost" by Freeman and other supernatural tales written by women writers. Argues that these stories are feminist attempts to create alternatives to the constrained societies in which they lived.

Westbrook, Perry D. *Mary Wilkins Freeman*. Rev. ed. Boston: Twayne, 1988. With an informative look at Freeman's pre-1900 work written for adults, Westbrook provides background on the socioeconomic and religious situation of backcountry New England. Also offers information on the reception of Freeman's work as it was published.

White, Brian. "'In the Humble Fashion of a Scripture Woman': The Bible as Besieging Tool in Freeman's 'The Revolt of Mother.'" *Christianity and Literature* 58, no. 1 (Autumn, 2008): 81-92. Examines the religious underpinnings of Freeman's story about a dutiful farm wife who successfully defies her husband's plans to build a new barn and in the process strikes a blow to her patriarchal society.

Larry A. Carlson
Updated by Karin A. Silet

NELL FREUDENBERGER

Born: New York, New York; April 21, 1975

PRINCIPAL SHORT FICTION
Lucky Girls, 2003
"The Virgin of Esmeraldas," 2007
"When East Meets West," 2007

OTHER LITERARY FORMS

In 2006, Nell Freudenberger (nehl FROY-dehn-bur-gur) published a novel entitled *The Dissident*, which was nominated for the Orange Prize. She also has written travel memoirs and personal essays for various publications. Two of particular note are "How I Became Afraid of Bugs," which was written for Powell's Books, and "Ambassadors," a piece about travel and culture, which appeared in *Bookmark Now: Writing in Unreaderly Times* (2005).

ACHIEVEMENTS

In 2004, Nell Freudenberger received the PEN/Malamud Award for excellence in short fiction, the Sue Kaufman Prize from the American Academy of Arts and Letters for best first fiction, and an O. Henry Prize and inclusion in *Best American Short Stories* for "The Tutor." In 2005, she was one of the Whiting Writers' Award recipients. She was awarded a Guggenheim Fellowship in 2010.

BIOGRAPHY

Born in New York, Nell Freudenberger is the daughter of Daniel Freudenberger and Carol Hofmann. Her father was the artistic director of the Phoenix Theatre before turning to television film screenwriting and moving to Los Angeles. Nell Freudenberger was educated at the Marlborough School in Los Angeles and then attended Harvard University, graduating magma cum laude in 1997. After college, she traveled in Asia

and spent a year in Thailand teaching English. In 2000, she earned an M.F.A. from New York University. In 2001, she was working as an editorial assistant for *The New Yorker* when the magazine published "Lucky Girls" and featured her as one of four debut writers. She married architect Paul Logan in September, 2006.

ANALYSIS

Nell Freudenberger's stories feature female protagonists of a wide range of ages, who are typically living as expatriates. Four of the five stories in *Lucky Girls* feature American women who are living in or who have lived in Asia, and the fifth protagonist has a strong tie to the region. The two stories that have appeared in *Granta* touch on similar themes of travel and expatriate life, and her novel, *The Dissident*, is about a Chinese immigrant to the United States.

Freudenberger's quick rise to fame brought out some skeptics and detractors. Others have risen to her defense, though, including Curtis Sittenfeld, who admits she approached the book expecting to skewer it, but she found the collection to be "well-written, well-plotted, intelligent, and surprising." Sittenfeld criticizes the characters as sometimes being pretentious and precious, but she praises Freudenberger's realistic dialogue and the unpredictability of the stories--that is, her "willingness to make the stories messier in a way that also makes them more real."

Generally speaking, reviewers seem either to love Freudenberger's work or to hate it. For every review that praises her writing, another finds her prose lacking. Some of the criticisms seem unfair. Rebecca Stuhr describes reading the stories as being "like walking in on the middle of a conversation and having to leave before you catch up on all of the details." The short-story form rarely has the level of detail that a novel can have. Jennifer Schuessler finds that the characters may not have typical human attachments, but that Freudenberger successfully captures place and mood, noting that the characters are loyal "to their own fragile memories, not other people," and that what matters is their connection to home, wherever that may be for them. Jeff Zaleski concurs, noting that Freudenberger is "more inventive and piquant when she probes characters' relationships to their adopted homelands," which she illustrates as being "more passionate and grounded than their ties to the people in their lives."

"LUCKY GIRLS"

The eponymous story of the collection is a first-person narrative told by a woman who never discloses her name. She visited India after graduating from college, as a guest of her wealthy friend Gita Banerjee and her family, a visit so carefully orchestrated that she "saw nothing (she) would not see in New York." The only thing she noticed among the formal parks and the extravagant shopping as being different were the ancient ruins. When she asked a question about them, Gita's mother laughed and responded that she had no idea. During an elaborate party, the narrator met her friend's uncle, Arun, twenty-three years her senior, and soon began an affair with him.

As the story opens, she has lived in India for five years as his mistress, and she is dealing with the aftermath of his sudden illness and death. As if being alone in a foreign country after having lost her romantic partner is not enough, she faces increasingly frequent visits from Arun's mother and the "gift" of a servant named Lata, who spies on that narrator and turns out to be an agent provocateur of sorts for Arun's wife, although even Lata is surprised by the actions of Arun's sons. Since the narrator is in the neighborhood, she visits Arun's wife, who is beautiful and cruel. Laxmi tells the narrator to go, but she insists on thanking the wife for the loan of the servant. Laxmi tells the narrator that Laxmi thought the servant might be useful, reminding the narrator that "I have my sons. And you have no one." At the end of the story, it is not entirely clear whether the narrator will continue living in India, but the story closes with her remembering one of the best times she and Arun spent together.

"THE ORPHAN"

Forty-seven-year old Alice is distressed by many things, including the fact that her husband Jeff has moved out, that they have not told their college-age children, Mandy and Josh, and that Mandy has just called from across the world to report that she has been raped. Mandy is working for a program that takes care of babies with acquired immunodeficiency syndrome (AIDS) in Thailand, and her brother Josh studies at Colby College. The next day, when Alice gets through to Mandy again, Mandy recasts the incident as a misunderstanding with her boyfriend. Since they have already planned a visit at Christmastime, Alice keeps the news to herself and waits to see Mandy. Alice, Jeff, and Josh rendezvous in Thailand, where they suffer through a stereotypically dysfunctional family holiday, made worse by the unease of Alice and Jeff in the unfamiliar setting. A conversation about Josh's activities at Colby reveal his membership in the Cool Rich Kids club, a group devoted to donating their parents' money to worthy causes their parents would not bother to support. Jeff is angered by this characterization, insisting that they are not rich and that they do donate money. When Josh presses him, the reader learns that the extent of their charitable giving is to Yale University. Alice and Jeff spend a few tense days, trying to figure out who their children have become, meeting Mandy's boyfriend, visiting Mandy's workplace, and breaking the news about their divorce.

"OUTSIDE THE EASTERN GATE"

An unnamed narrator recounts her childhood in India, spent with her clinically depressed mother, her father, and her older sister, Penny. When the narrator is seven years old, her mother and her companion Vivian take off on a road trip across the Khyber Pass, taking along Penny but leaving the narrator and her packed suitcase behind with her father. The narrator eventually returns to the United States, where she remains estranged from her family and suffers from depression. The story focuses on her return to India, to visit her father who is in failing health, suffering from the effects of dementia. Vivian also still lives in India and has remained close to the husband of her dead friend and lover. The narrator searches for journals her mother kept, seeking answers to the questions that have haunted the narrator. After more than thirty years, she still wants and needs to know why she was left behind.

"THE TUTOR"

Educated in America and returned to India, Zubin wants to be a poet but works for a living at a firm in Bombay that prepares students for taking the Scholastic Aptitude Test (SAT) and completing applications to American universities. Although his students are typically Indian, Zubin takes on Julia, an American girl whose father works in Bombay, who needs assistance with her application to the University of California, Berkeley. Her SAT scores are high, but her draft essay has been deemed unacceptable by a counselor. Julia's real intention is to pay Zubin extra money to write her essay, not just help her with it. A friendship of sorts develops between the pair, and in the end Zubin does choose to write an essay for her, as a gift. Julia is also intent on losing her virginity, and she uses Zubin for that as well.

"LETTER FROM THE LAST BASTION"

The closing story in the collection is the most polarizing for many critics. Many who like Freudenberger's work are less enthusiastic about this piece, while others who find little positive to say otherwise lavish praise on this story. As one might expect from the title, the story is written as a letter to the department chair of an English department at a prestigious college, and the subject is the school's writer-in-residence, Henry Marks. The narrator introduces herself as a seventeen-year-old from Lancaster, Pennsylvania, who claims to know Henry very well, and notes that although her mother wants her to attend a college like this one, she wants to be an optometrist. The writer, later identified as Miss Fish, recounts the story of Henry's life and how he came to fight in Vietnam, his return to the United States and becoming a successful writer, but with more information and some details that Henry has left out along the way. Readers also learn of his relationships with various women, including a departmental secretary named Maggie, and that Miss Fish is Henry and Maggie's daughter.

Much of the story is focused on Henry's time in Vietnam, but in framing those scenes, Freudenberger successfully captures the tone of a sarcastic teenager, one who is world weary already but still is clearly a girl in many ways. At one point in the letter, she recounts losing her virginity to a classmate, complete with technical anatomical terms and a dispassionate eye on the clock. Afterward, he tells her he loves her, and she responds that she loves Iowa, continuing with "Or that's what I thought. I always think of a better thing to say later, which is why I like letters." She admits that she responded in kind, but she considers this an act of cowardice.

"THE VIRGIN OF ESMERALDAS"

Freudenberger covers familiar ground in this story, although the setting is different and the outcome is clearly defined. Readers are introduced to teenage Marisol Hernandez through a poem she wrote for class about hating her stepmother. Marisol was only two when her mother left, and she was raised mostly by her aunt. Her aunt moved away to Texas to be with her daughter, and Marisol does not feel the same toward her stepmother. She loves her older half-brother, but since he has fallen in love he does not have as much time for her. To make matters more complicated, his girlfriend is their stepsister. The whole family travels to Ecuador, where the parents are building a house. While in Ecuador, Marisol learns that she is going to be an aunt. Because of an injury to her foot, she is left at home alone, while the others go out to dinner one evening. She explores the grounds, runs into the young man who works there as a caretaker, and loses her virginity to him. Unlike Miss Fish, Marisol comes up with good lines on the fly. She asks Pedro how many girls he has had, and he replies that he has been with fifteen. She does not believe him and gets the truth--two--out of him. "You?" he asks her. Marisol "believed him and she didn't want to lie. But she also didn't want to tell him the truth. 'I haven't had any girls,'" she retorts. By the end of the night, she has undergone several transformations and pledges to help her stepsister with the baby and to be a good aunt, like her aunt was to her. Marisol is a smart, witty girl, and although the transformation seems sudden, Freudenberger seems to assure readers that Marisol is going to be just fine.

"WHEN EAST MEETS WEST"

Freudenberger captures the voice of teenagers well, but in this case, her narrator is ninety-four-year-old Tabitha Buell of Rochester, New York. Tabitha was a Latin teacher, misses her husband Frank immensely, is opinionated, and copes with living in a world where people seem to be in too much of a hurry and assume that she cannot do anything on her own. Although her daughter Helen and her family do not live close, Tabitha is friends with her neighbor, George, who after his divorce orders a wife from a Web site. Tabitha is also visited often by that new wife, Amina, whom Tabitha refers to privately as the Bengali girl. Tabitha also has a helper named Serena, who comes in each day. The story finds Tabitha preparing for a visit from her granddaughter, Meryl, and Meryl's new boyfriend, Sam. Phone conversations about sleeping arrangements for the unmarried couple go as one might imagine, and when Helen assures her mother that she thinks Sam is "the one" for Meryl, Tabitha thinks "that if Helen had had Latin, she wouldn't resort to expressions like that." Sam turns out to be Samaj, and Freudenberger deftly explores the issues that emerge between the generations and the cultures represented. In the end, the two announce their engagement, and Tabitha assures her granddaughter that Tabitha is happy for her. She notes to herself that she will not live long enough to see if the marriage works, "as it seems to for 50 percent of American couples. That, to me, is the interesting statistic: that so many stay together, given all the things that can happen to two people these days, in our frighteningly long American lives." Freudenberger wrote this story for her grandmother, and while it is a loving tribute to a woman who was obviously very special to Freudenberger, it is also a story about the power of love.

OTHER MAJOR WORKS
LONG FICTION: *The Dissident*, 2006.

BIBLIOGRAPHY
Ratcliffe, Sophie. "Girl, Willing to Travel." *Times Literary Supplement*, April 30, 2004, p. 22. Ratcliffe finds "Letter from the Last Bastion" to be the strongest of the collection and posits that Freudenberger's main concern is not place but gender.
Schuessler, Jennifer. "Dislocations." *The New York Times Book Review*, September 14, 2003, p. 7. Insightful, extensive review of the collection.
Stuhr, Rebecca. "Lucky Girls." *Library Journal* (August, 2003): 138. Stuhr's negative review of the collection stems from her analysis that the characters and plot elements are not well developed.
Zaleski, Jeff. "Lucky Girls." *Publishers Weekly* (June 30, 2003): 51. Useful review of the stories.

Elizabeth Blakesley

BRUCE JAY FRIEDMAN

Born: Bronx, New York; April 26, 1930

Far from the City of Class, and Other Stories, 1963
Black Angels, 1966
Let's Hear It for a Beautiful Guy, and Other Works of Short Fiction, 1984
The Collected Short Fiction of Bruce Jay Friedman, 1995 (expanded 1997)
Three Balconies, 2008

OTHER LITERARY FORMS

Bruce Jay Friedman has written several novels, the most commercially and critically successful of which have been *Stern* (1962, 1988) and *A Mother's Kisses* (1964). Among his later novels are *The Current Climate* (1989) and *A Father's Kisses* (1996). His other works include essays in popular periodicals; two major plays, both produced in New York; screenplays; a parody of contemporary self-help manuals; book reviews; and journalistic pieces. In 1995, he published a sequel to *The Lonely Guy's Book of Life* (1978), entitled *The Slightly Older Guy.* His play *Have You Spoken to Any Jews Lately?* was produced at the American Jewish Theater in New York in 1995. His book *Violencia!: A Musical Novel* was published in 2002.

ACHIEVEMENTS

Bruce Jay Friedman (FREED-muhn) is an American short-story writer, novelist, playwright, screenwriter, journalist, and editor who has a talent for examining the ironic and often comic aspects of contemporary Jewish life. He named, and has often been linked to, the black humor tradition arising out of the 1960's. In this literary movement, writers emphasize the absurdities of existence through irreverent or grotesque humor. Friedman's central characters are usually middle-class Jews who are alienated from their roots and from mainstream society. They are shallow creatures lost in a fragmented, absurd America, searching for acceptance and strength. Friedman's work has often been compared to that of Saul Bellow, Philip Roth, and Bernard Malamud. He is less intellectual than the aforementioned and more visceral in his approach. Friedman has achieved critical success in different genres, including the short story, the novel, and drama. Although best known as a novelist, he has also devoted time to adapting material for the screen. Friedman won the prestigious Obie Award for his play *Scuba Duba: A Tense Comedy* (1968). *The Collected Short Fiction of Bruce Jay Friedman* was published in 1995 to excellent reviews.

BIOGRAPHY

Bruce Jay Friedman was born in New York City in 1930. He attended the University of Missouri in Columbia, which awarded him a degree in journalism in 1951. After graduation, he joined the Air Force and served as correspondent for the in-house journal *Air Training.* He was discharged in 1953, the same year in which he published his first short story in *The New Yorker.* In 1954, he married actor and model Ginger Howard, and they had three children. In 1977, Friedman and his wife were divorced. From 1954 until 1966, Friedman worked as an executive for the Magazine Management Company in New York. By 1966 he had established himself as an independent writer, having published two novels, two collections of short stories, a play, and the influential anthology *Black Humor* (which he edited). In 1974, he became visiting professor of literature at York College, City University, in New York, a position he held for two years. He continued to produce fiction, and he also began to devote his attention to dramatic and cinematic forms. In the early 1990's, Friedman said he fired his agent because he was too good at getting Friedman work as a screenwriter, which left him too little time for writing stories, novels, and plays. He said he hated screenwriting, although he earned an Academy Award nomination for his screenplay for *Splash* (1984). In 1984, his nonfiction book *The Lonely Guy's Book of Life* was made into the film *The Lonely Guy*, starring Steve Martin.

ANALYSIS

Bruce Jay Friedman condemns his succession of fictional schlemiels, losers, lonely, and fall guys to a violent, morbid, and paranoic world; his terrain is a stark, post-Thurberesque hell haunted by the enfeebled ghosts of Franz Kafka and Søren Kierkegaard (the first "Modern Day Lonely Guy," according to Friedman). The author claims that he has merely attempted to mirror the surreal montage of the first page of *The New York Times*. In such a world, anonymous victims whom no one could imagine to be happy trudge their daily Sisyphean hills. Those sensitive or foolish enough to wonder "Why me?" deserve whatever additional anxieties their hyperconsciousness promises them.

Indeed, the only Friedman characters to escape the avenging furies of their souls are those who cannot or do not think at all, and those who thrive as caricatures of themselves (such as the notorious "Jewish mothers" cluttering the novels and short stories). Such characters possess little genuine self, and, for Friedman, self and suffering form the two halves of a terrible equation. One should not assume something Christ-like in this sacrificial formula, however; Brooklyn and New York City are not exactly Golgotha. Hence, lacking this saving archetypal dimension, Friedman's characters bear their insipid papier-mâché crosses in a cultural and spiritual vacuum. No bands of scraggly disciples witness their travail or await their return, and their passage thus proves all the more torturous. (It takes Stern, in the novel of that title, more than one year to "get even" with a man who has insulted his wife. Meanwhile, Stern develops ulcers and has a nervous breakdown.)

The element of "sick" humor in Friedman's fiction is probably what prompted critics of the 1960's to describe it and similar work by writers such as Vladimir Nabokov, Joseph Heller, James Purdy,

Thomas Pynchon, and Terry Southern as "black humor." Friedman popularized the term when he edited the anthology of short fiction *Black Humor* in 1965. Critic Max Schulz seems to have identified black humor correctly as a phenomenon of its time. Perhaps this is because, as Friedman recognized in an influential introduction to his anthology, the phrase fails to convey the essence as well as the comic seriousness of fiction, which, for whatever reasons, finds itself so classified. Then there is the wider generic question of comedy in general to consider.

Friedman claims in his introduction that black humor has always been and always will be written-- "as long as there are disguises to be peeled back. . . ." Black humor, he suggests, asks "final questions"; it announces to the world, "be preposterous, but also make damned sure you explain yourself." One does wonder, given these qualifications, how black humor differs from the traditional satiric humor of, say, a Jonathan Swift or a Petronius. Critics and theorists, nevertheless, have taken pains to distinguish the two forms. Charles Harris, for one, emphatically denies any satiric function in black humor; so does Robert Scholes, and so, somewhat contradictorily, does Friedman. Black humor apparently shrugs off any hope of personal redemption or social reform; its sole purpose is the exposure of absurdity. In this sense, black humor can be regarded as a kind of vaudevillian naturalism devoid of the scientific and deterministic restraints peculiar to classical naturalism. The only solace it promises is relief through laughter for its own sake. The world, Friedman proclaims, is a tense, brutal affair, and you might as well laugh at what little of it you can; if nothing else, the laughter will discharge muscular tension.

There is, however, more to Friedman's fiction than pure gag and memorable one-liners and perverse comic vision. This extra dimension develops definitively in the novels, but the reader can catch glimpses of it in the short stories that make up the author's first two collections. Beyond the survival motive of Friedman's neurotic antiheroes, certain old-fashioned virtues and values do emerge as possible alternatives to meaninglessness. Courage, for example, would eliminate many otherwise humiliating compromises; love, forever elusive in Friedman's work, might cushion every blow; and compassion would neutralize hatred and egotistical self-centeredness. However, courage, love, and compassion--defenses against what Friedman describes as the "new Jack Rubyesque chord of absurdity [that] has been struck in our land"--lie buried deeply beneath the hill of Sisyphus. Friedman's characters remember them fondly, as they would childhood baubles. With courage, love, and compassion eternally lost, their absence makes them conspicuous themes in Friedman's fiction. Without goodness and order, evil and accident result. Without knowing it, perhaps, the Jewish Friedman delineates an Augustinian world. (Judaism does have its Augustinian equivalents in certain gnostic scriptures.)

Against the fortress of courage, love, and compassion, Friedman assembles an arsenal of germs, disease, physical deformity, violence, humiliation, embarrassment, despair, free-floating anxiety, nervous breakdowns, failure, divorce, infidelity, loneliness, isolation, everyday banalities, and--encompassing them all--the fear of death. In practically every story the central character recognizes but fails to overcome some obstacle.

CASTRATING MOTHER STORIES

In a group of stories involving "castrating" mothers (almost certainly leftover material from the novel *A Mother's Kisses*), the protagonists cannot escape their mothers' omnivorous presence. In "The Trip," for example, a young man's mother accompanies her son to the Midwest to make sure he gets off to a good start in college. The mother, like all Friedman mothers, is loud, crude, brash, and offensive and thrives on the fantasy that strangers will mistake her for her son's lover. The student desperately wants her to act like an ordinary mother, for her power not so much inhibits his style as renders him styleless. "I was marked as a fellow with a mother," he groans. In a related story, "The Good Time," a young soldier's mother visits her son on furlough in Philadelphia to, as she puts it, show him "a good time." She succeeds only in embarrassing and oppressing the anguished son. In still another story, "The Enemy," the men of a typical Jewish family appear weak and impotent when pitted against the voracious, sawtoothed females of the clan.

UNMANAGEABLE WOMEN STORIES

In general, Friedman's literary world is full of unmanageable women. The wives of his characters, who inhabit a different domain, prove no better than the mothers. While the mothers do in a sense remain faithful to their weak sons, the wives constantly drift away from their husbands, emotionally, physically, and legally. Friedman wives, insubstantial intellectually and often vapid emotionally, refuse to remain homebodies, mothers, and kitchen drudges. Their rebellion, if it can be called that, involves nothing so abstract and ideological as the lure of independence or feminist ideals; rather, it takes the form of vague dissatisfaction, diffuse ennui, and an ultimate rejection of the shortcomings of men in general. The husbands, equally fed up and bored with their wives, react in two ways: Either they attempt to make amends and sincerely desire to patch up a shattered marriage, or they abandon their wives for the prospect of nervous one-night stands and ubiquitous nubile flesh in a sexually revolutionized world for which they are little prepared.

Castrating mothers, unsatisfactory wives, problematic girlfriends, and sexual objects--these are the women who populate Friedman's fiction. Their purpose is to expose men where they are most vulnerable, as heroes and/or lovers. Perhaps Friedman grants women no mercy precisely because they undermine the splendid myths men have created about themselves. In "The Punch," a recently married public relations man named Harris describes his marriage as a "series of tense situations." The mere presence of his sexy young wife erodes Harris's confidence and masculinity, and he responds by resorting to violence as "the need to hit someone . . . gathered up like an abscess." Harris feels the only way he can impress his wife is to slug another human being. The fear, however, unsettles him: He knew that "no matter how smoothly things were running, always, at a party . . . there would arise some confrontation in which he would be brought to the edge of violence and then, in some way or other, fail to throw a punch." Finally, to his wife's immense delight, Harris manages to punch a stranger on the street. Once he proves his manhood, Harris realizes that what he really wanted to do was punch the infuriating creature who has so disrupted his life. Thus, violence precipitates more violence.

NEUROTIC MEN STORIES

Missing the comfort of domestic, conjugal, and romantic fulfillment, Friedman's male characters develop numerous real and psychosomatic ailments. Stefano, in "Black Angels," describes his life as a "sea of despair"; the patient in "The Investor" observes his fever rise and fall with the fluctuations of Plimpton Rocket Fuel stock; Gorsline, in "The Death Table," draws a roulette card that promises him an early demise by heart attack; Mr. Kessler, in "When You're Excused You're Excused," claims that bad health excuses him from family and social obligations; Merz, in "A Foot in the Door," arranges a Faustian pact by accepting an ulcer and asthma in order to get the woman he wants; and the lead character in "Mr. Prinzo's Breakthrough" spends his last cent on psychoanalysis. (The paragon of hypochondriacs in Friedman's fiction is Stern in *Stern*.) Freudian critics, particularly those who follow the perceptive analyses of critic Leslie Fiedler, might interpret this widespread hypochondria, as well as the general disrespect for women in Friedman's work, as a sign of latent homosexuality. Homosexuality does not, latent or otherwise, seem to preoccupy Friedman; occasionally, he adds it to the ever-growing list of deleterious options threatening contemporary man. It is altogether safe to assume that the neuroses of Friedman's characters are metaphysical rather than psychological in nature.

Not surprisingly, Jewishness may remain the sole, frayed connection Friedman's comic wretches can make with their culture, their tradition, their heritage, and their brethren. Thematically, Jewishness offers these characters what novelist William Faulkner might have called an "eternal verity." For Friedman, however, one is Jewish by default. In *The Dick* (1970), the protagonist changes his name from Sussman to LePeters in order to enter mainstream America, and in one of Friedman's best stories, "When You're Excused You're Excused," Mr. Kessler seems more interested in avoiding obligatory Jewish holiday rituals than he does in restoring his health at Vic Tanny's gym, where he decides to work out on the eve of Yom Kippur. Throughout the story, Mr. Kessler tries to convince himself that he has been excused from Jewishness for a while. He meets with a group of unsavory characters and indulges himself shamelessly. In the end, however, Mr. Kessler punches a man in the nose for never having heard of the Jewish baseball hero "Phumblin' Phil" Weintraub. That was too much for any Jew on Yom Kippur. "I may have been excused," Mr. Kessler mutters, "but I wasn't that excused."

HARRY TOWNS STORIES

Harry Towns is a black-humor Everyman--a bit of a loser, a bit of a creep, somewhat pathetic, somewhat despicable. In "The Partners," Harry is in Las Vegas with his young son in an effort to spend more time with him in preparation for a divorce. This idealistic notion is spoiled by the fact that Harry has venereal crabs and has trouble getting away from the boy long enough to satisfy his gambling habit and his sexual desires. Although the boy is hurt by a falling barbell in a gym to which Harry takes him, that does not deter Harry from leaving his son in the hotel room while Harry goes to gamble and visit a hooker. When the boy has him paged, Harry is at first angry, but then he feels guilty when the boy, who wants to be with his father regardless of the setting, says he loves Las Vegas more than any place in the world. The only way Harry can show his fatherly love is to give the underage boy a handful of coins with which to play the slot machines and then to stand by him to ward off the casino guard, saying he will kill anyone who dares to come within ten feet of the two of them.

The "lady" in the Harry Towns story "Lady" is cocaine, and Harry is a drug user who also uses cocaine to get women. The death of Harry's mother becomes the opportunity for his meeting a new dealer, who gets Harry some of the best cocaine he has ever had; he has no scruples about exploiting the mother's funeral for the sake of his habit. However, similar to the ending of the story about the father-son bonding around the slot machines in Las Vegas, Friedman creates an ironic version of Harry's saving grace at the end of this story. In the only moral gesture toward his mother's memory that Harry is capable of, he vows to finish the cocaine before dawn of the day of the funeral so he can start off the day clear. He vows that no matter what someone might offer him on the day of the funeral, even cocaine used for brain surgery, he will turn it down. In an ironic and unknowing reference to himself, Harry swears that anyone who sticks so much as a grain of cocaine up his nose on the day of the funeral had to "be some new and as yet undiscovered breed of sonofab----. The lowest."

"Pitched Out" is a black-humor coda to Harry's ignoble adventures. At age fifty-seven, he is a writer sunk so low that he is trying unsuccessfully to pitch a show about a dog to network executives. While in Los Angeles, he meets a friend for dinner and laments that he is getting old and is coming up empty in Hollywood. Both men bemoan their lost youth, which they strive to maintain by hustling women in the bar. As they watch beautiful young girls come out of a night spot, Harry knows that any one of them could have slipped past the fence he had built around himself when he met the woman with whom he lives. Typically, Harry knew "there were still some adventures up ahead."

Friedman's work, in general, exaggerates and exposes the neurotic condition of Jews in America; but as the alienated Jew comes to represent contemporary Everyman, so Friedman's stories transcend their Jewishness and read like absurd vignettes of postindustrial civilization. It would not take much to convert such vignettes into minor tragedies--a laugh less here, a bit more pathos there--making Friedman's humor right for this Age of Anxiety. Saving graces and verities are there, but no one seems to know what to do with them.

THREE BALCONIES

When Friedman edited a paperback collection of plays, stories, and excerpts from novels in 1965 under the title *Black Humor*, he became America's best-known spokesman for a brand of fiction characterized by a quirky kind of comic satire with a sardonic slant. Although in his introduction to that milestone collection, Friedman said that he would have about as much luck defining black humor as he would defining an elbow or a corned-beef sandwich, he described the genre as a "one-foot-in-the-asylum style of fiction," whose typical theme was focused on the absurdity of society and whose typical technique was marked by a "fading line between fantasy and reality." Many of the pieces in his collection *Three Balconies* are typical of his own version of black humor in the short-story form, which Friedman says best represent his work. The collection is a combination of smoothly written, well-constructed conventional stories and rambling realistic accounts of men, mostly writers, who have never quite achieved their goals and are past their prime.

If there is one unifying theme in Friedman's new stories, it is that of the doppelgänger, in which one man tells a story about his relationship with another man, who embodies some aspect of himself. For example, in "The Secret Man," the narrator tells about a bully he knew as a boy, only to discover at the man's death that it is himself who was the bully. In "The Convert," a man, who once taunted a schoolmate that the Jews killed Christ, converts to Judaism and invites the schoolmate to his son's Bar Mitzvah, which ends in a comic confrontation. The concluding novella, "The Great Beau LeVyne," is the capstone "buddy" story, a rambling anecdotal tale of one man's friendship with another, who the man both admires and fears.

Three Balconies features three stories about Friedman's famous character Harry Towns. In "The Thespian," Harry is asked to play a bit part in a film, which he expands into a larger role, which in turn ends up on the cutting-room floor. In "Kneesocks," Harry meets with a woman with whom he was once obsessed, and he discovers that he is well past such nostalgic fantasies. The title story features Harry being tempted to commit suicide by leaping off a balcony but deciding instead to take life "one balcony at a time."

These stories are less biting and ironic than Friedman's early black humor stories. Like his alter ego Harry, Friedman is older and milder. None of Friedman's short fictions spring from the complexity and ambiguity of individual human experience. This is not to say they are poor pieces of fiction, only that they are examples of a rather narrow subgenre--entertaining, amusing and clever, but not profound explorations of the human soul. As Friedman said in his introduction to *Black Humor*, there will always be black humor under one name or another, as long as there are "disguises to be peeled back" and as long as there are thoughts about which no one else cares to think.

OTHER MAJOR WORKS

LONG FICTION: *Stern*, 1962; *A Mother's Kisses*, 1964; *The Dick*, 1970; *About Harry Towns*, 1974; *Tokyo Woes*, 1985; *The Current Climate*, 1989; *A Father's Kisses*, 1996; *Violencia!*, 2001.

PLAYS: *Scuba Duba*, pr. 1967, pb. 1968; *Steambath*, pr. 1970, pb. 1971; *Have You Spoken to Any Jews Lately?*, pr. 1995.

SCREENPLAYS: *The Owl and the Pussycat*, 1971 (based on William Manhof's play); *Stir Crazy*, 1980; *Doctor Detroit*, 1983 (with Carl Gottlieb and Robert Boris; based on a story by Friedman); *Splash*, 1984 (with Lowell Ganz and Babaloo Mandel).

NONFICTION: *The Lonely Guy's Book of Life*, 1978; *The Slightly Older Guy*, 1995; *Even the Rhinos Were Nymphos: Best Nonfiction*, 2000.

EDITED TEXT: *Black Humor*, 1965.

BIBLIOGRAPHY

Fowler, Nick: "Bruce Jay Friedman: Making Sense of Entropy." *Antioch Review* 63 (Winter, 2005): 151-162. Discusses Friedman's influence, his place in pop culture, his humor, and his critical reception.

Gefen, Pearl Sheffy. "Bear of a Man." *The Jerusalem Post*, December 5, 1996, p. 4. A biographical sketch combined with an interview of Friedman. Friedman talks about the ups and downs of his career, his encounters with Hollywood screenwriters, his relationship to his family, and his reaction to reviewers.

Nolan, Tom. "Master of His Universe." Review of *The Collected Short Fiction of Bruce Jay Friedman*, by Bruce Jay Friedman. *The Los Angeles Times Book Review*, March 3, 1996, p. 4. Nolan discusses Friedman's flair for bizarre comedy, his talent for fantasy, and his focus on the recurring character Harry Towns in several of his stories.

Schulz, Max. *Black Humor Fiction of the 1960's: A Pluralistic Definition of Man and His World*. Athens: Ohio University Press, 1973. Schulz has made a career of examining black humor writers in general, Friedman in particular. Schulz describes the emergence of black humor in the 1960's, defines it, and examines its leading exponents. In a separate chapter on Friedman, his novel *Stern* is compared and contrasted to Charles Wright's *The Wig* (1966).

_____. *Bruce Jay Friedman*. New York: Twayne, 1974. Schulz is a critical admirer of Friedman and a leading essayist on his work. Schulz places Friedman directly into the mainstream of black humor (a term coined by Friedman), considering him its leading exponent. The author carefully examines Friedman's wide range of tastes, with separate chapters on the various genres. The author predicts a bright future for him. A good introduction to Friedman's work. Supplemented by a chronology and a select bibliography.

_____. *Radical Sophistication: Studies in Contemporary Jewish American Novelists*. Athens: Ohio University Press, 1969. Limiting his study to a handful of Jewish writers, such as Isaac Bashevis Singer, Bernard Malamud, Saul Bellow, Normal Mailer, and Leslie Fiedler, Schulz includes a separate chapter on Friedman and compares his handling of the theme of love in *Stern* to Edward Lewis Wallant's *The Pawnbroker* (1961). The chapter is a reprint of a 1968 article in *Critique: Studies in Modern Fiction*.

Seed, David. "Bruce Jay Friedman's Fiction: Black Humor and After." *Thalia: Studies in Literary Humor* 10 (Spring/Summer, 1988): 14-22. A good, brief look at Friedman's major work and his importance as a writer. Seed points out that Friedman has been overlooked by critics, except for Schulz, and that Friedman's work deserves greater attention. Seed finds Friedman at his best when he turns everyday notions completely upside down through his characters and their bizarre adventures.

Taylor, John. "The Funny Guy's Book of Life." *New York* 22 (October 9, 1989): 46-50. A biographical sketch that comments on Friedman's success in the 1960's, his slide from fame, his scriptwriting, and his efforts to make a comeback with fiction in the 1980's.

Trachtenberg, Stanley. "The Humiliated Hero: Bruce Jay Friedman's *Stern*." *Critique: Studies in Modern Fiction* 7 (Spring/Summer, 1965): 91-93. Trachtenberg briefly examines Friedman's *Stern*, the novel about a Jew looking for someone to torment him, who finds his nemesis in an anti-Semitic neighbor. Trachtenberg praises the book and considers it significant, noting that Friedman can vividly bring out the laughter behind the grotesque horror.

Louis Gallo; Terry Theodore
Updated by Charles E. May

G

ERNEST J. GAINES

Born: Oscar, Louisiana; January 15, 1933

PRINCIPAL SHORT FICTION
Bloodline, 1968
A Long Day in November, 1971
Mozart and Leadbelly: Stories and Essays, 2005

OTHER LITERARY FORMS

Aside from his short fiction, Ernest J. Gaines (gayns) published several novels: *Catherine Carmier* (1964), *Of Love and Dust* (1967), *The Autobiography of Miss Jane Pittman* (1971), *In My Father's House* (1978), *A Gathering of Old Men* (1983), and *A Lesson Before Dying* (1993).

ACHIEVEMENTS

Ernest J. Gaines won the Joseph Henry Jackson Award of the San Francisco Foundation in 1959 for the short story "Comeback." He received a Rockefeller Foundation grant (1970), a John Simon Guggenheim Memorial Foundation Fellowship (1971), and a John D. and Catherine T. MacArthur Foundation Fellowship (1993). The Commonwealth Club of California honored him with the fiction gold medal in 1972, for *The Autobiography of Miss Jane Pittman*, and in 1984 for *A Gathering of Old Men*. Gaines also won the American Academy of Arts and Letters literary award in 1987 and the National Book Critics Circle Award in 1993, for *A Lesson Before Dying*, which was nominated for a Pulitzer Prize. A few of Gaines's novels, including *The Autobiography of Miss Jane Pittman*, *A Gathering of Old Men*, and *A Lesson Before Dying*, were turned into made-for-television films, and "The Sky Is Gray," a short story, was dramatized for the Public Broadcasting Service short-story series.

BIOGRAPHY

As a boy, Ernest James Gaines lived in rural Louisiana, where he often worked in the fields. At the age of fifteen he moved to Vallejo, California, to live with his mother and stepfather. In 1955, after his release from the Army, he entered San Francisco State College, from which he graduated in 1957. In 1958, two of his stories helped him win a Wallace Stegner Creative Writing Fellowship for graduate study at Stanford University. After 1966, when he received a grant from the National Endowment for the Arts, Gaines garnered many awards and honors, especially in the wake of the 1974 television version of *The Autobiography of Miss Jane Pittman*. He also enjoyed a successful career as lecturer and teacher, working at Stanford, California's Whittier College, and the University of Louisiana at Lafayette. Although semiretired, he holds a lifetime appointment at the latter. He married for the first time at age sixty.

ANALYSIS

Strongly influenced by the folkways of rural Louisiana, Ernest J. Gaines's narratives reflect a cultural heritage enriched by a strong oral tradition. Although his fiction's main focus is on the African American community, the author's work also reflects the cultural diversity of his native parish, Pointe Coupee, by Creoles, Cajuns, and Anglo-American entrepreneurs, overseers, and law officials. Among Gaines's acknowledged literary mentors are the nineteenth century Russian masters, for their treatment of peasantry; Ernest Hemingway, for his understatement and "grace under pressure" theme; and William Faulkner, for his mastery of locale and the oral narrative.

BLOODLINE

Gaines, although popular, is a serious and methodical writer. He works hard to fashion a distinct voice richly imbued with unique traditions. He also spins compelling stories, which are collected in *Bloodline*, first published in 1968. *Bloodline* contains five long stories, all of which deal with a place and a people Gaines expresses so fully and so vividly that they are recognized as his exclusive fictional property: the southern African American communities living on a stretch of low-lying cotton and sugarcane country between the Atchafalaya and Mississippi Rivers, west and northwest of Baton Rouge. Setting is a central force in Gaines's work, and his fiction often focuses on this distinctive Louisiana region.

All the stories in *Bloodline* take place in and around the fictional town of Bayonne, a small country town not too far from the city of Baton Rouge. The lives of Gaines's men and women are shaped by fields, dirt roads, plantation quarters, and the natural elements of dust, heat, and rain. Whatever the differences among his characters--he has a rich diversity of race and culture to work with--the Cajun sharecroppers, the African American tenants, and the white plantation owners all consider the soil and the crops part of their daily weather. Bayonne and the surrounding countryside provide local and cultural unity for the stories in *Bloodline*.

Equally important to the unity of *Bloodline* is the way the stories are presented. All of them are written in the form of oral narratives told by the characters in their own words. The first four stories are told by individual African Americans who participate in or are deeply affected by the stories they tell. The tellers range in age from the six-year-old boy of "A Long Day in November" to a seventy-year-old man in the title story. The final story, "Just Like a Tree," is told by a group of relatives and friends, each in turn, as they attend the leave-taking ceremonies surrounding Aunt Fe, an old black woman who has been invited North to escape white reprisals against the Civil Rights movement. In all these stories the sound of individual voices rings out clearly and convincingly. Gaines has a keen, sure ear for native speech patterns and recognizes the power of language in a predominantly oral culture to assert, affirm, and keep hold of personal and collective values. His stories deliberately call attention to the special virtues of the spoken word as a rich storehouse capable of keeping alive an otherwise impoverished community.

There is, however, a deeper unifying force to the stories than a common setting, race, and dependence on the spoken word. It consists of the movement of the stories through individual lives toward a communal consciousness. There is a hint of this movement in the successive voices of the five stories. The first two are accounts of two young boys, the third of a young man in jail, the fourth of an old man of seventy, and the fifth of a household of friends, relatives, and one stranger. *Bloodline* begins with the private experience of a little boy and ends with a public event that affects the entire community.

The impression of development is strengthened by the recurrence in each story of one of Gaines's major themes, the impact of personal and communal codes of honor colliding with various forms of hostility, especially, in the last four stories, the discrimination, injustice, and violence the African American faced in the segregated South. This is not to imply that polemics or ideologies ever prevail over character in Gaines's stories. What interests him first and foremost is African American experience, and some of his best writing centers on the lives and relationships of southern African Americans within their own community, with sometimes little direct reference at all to the world of the whites around them. Inasmuch as discrimination and the crimes of segregation were an inescapable fact of southern African American experience, the world Gaines describes is always--overtly or not--conditioned by the tensions of racial claims. In *Bloodline*, the questions raised by such claims become progressively more insistent, and the stories themselves roughly follow the chronology of the changing mood among African Americans in modern times. Specific dates are not mentioned, but the stories obviously stretch back to the 1940's rural South of "A Long Day in November" up to the 1960's Civil Rights movement in Louisiana alluded to in the last story, "Just Like a Tree."

"A LONG DAY IN NOVEMBER"

In the first story, "A Long Day in November," there are no direct references to racial struggles. It is a long tale told in the voice of a six-year-old boy, Sonny, whose world is suddenly shattered by the separation of his parents. His mother, Amy, leaves her husband,

Eddie, because she feels he has become overenthusiastic about his car to the point of neglecting his family. She takes Sonny to her mother's house, and the remainder of the story charts Eddie's unsuccessful attempts to bring his wife home. Finally, on the advice of the local Voodoo woman, Madame Toussaint, Eddie burns his car publicly, and Sonny and Amy return home. For the entire story, Sonny does not act; he observes and suffers. He sees the world in terms of basic feelings--warmth, cold, hope, fear--and desires simply that his disrupted world be restored. The story ends where it began, with Sonny in bed, snug and safe under the blankets, only this time the night is not disturbed by his mother's calls or crying. Instead, Sonny is rocked to sleep by the sound of the springs in his parents' bed.

Gaines is a master at re-creating the words and sensations of children, and one of his main concerns in "A Long Day in November" is to contrast Sonny's simple, innocent needs of love and security with the complex world of adult conflicts. Neither his parents nor his grandmother seems to offer him what he needs most. His mother has become hard and bitter, and his father, more gentle, shows a weak streak and tends to use Sonny to win back his wife. The grandmother's irritability may be comic for the reader, but for Sonny she is the most hateful person in his life, rough spoken, harsh, and complaining. She is the one person Sonny would most like to be free of: "Lord knows I get tired of Gran'mon fussing all the time." The main character in the story, however, is Sonny's mother. She may be harsh and bitter, but she has forged for herself a code of personal behavior that finally brings her family into a new relationship. She forces the change at a great cost, especially in regard to her son.

One important feature of "A Long Day in November" is the presence of a well-defined community--the schoolteacher, the preacher, the schoolchildren, the Voodoo woman, Eddie's friends, and Amy's relatives--where conflict and separation may occur but whose shared assumptions are not questioned. Increasingly, as the stories progress, not only individual codes but also communal values are brought under pressure.

"THE SKY IS GRAY"

The second story in *Bloodline*, "The Sky Is Gray," is also narrated by a small boy. One of the most successful stories in the volume, it consists of thirteen episodes spanning the day James, eight years old, goes with his mother to a dentist in Bayonne. Like Sonny in "A Long Day in November," James suffers more than he acts, but already, even at eight years old, he is beginning to adopt the code of stoic pride his mother is constantly encouraging. His world is even bleaker than Sonny's. His father has been called into the Army, and his mother is left with three children and great poverty. Throughout the story, her hard words and harsh judgments must be measured against the fact that she has been placed in a situation in which mere survival is not always certain. She feels compelled to teach her oldest son how to take care of his family and to survive with dignity as a man.

While waiting in the dentist's office, James watches a young, educated African American argue with an older man who looks to James like a preacher. The young African American has no faith in religion but reacts in such an extreme, self-confident way that he challenges religious beliefs. Still, when he is hit by the "preacher," a man who maintains that no questions at all should be asked about God or traditional beliefs, it is the young man who wins the admiration of James: "When I grow up I want be just like him. I want clothes like that and I want keep a book with me, too."

The point seems to be that, given the extent of African American suffering, most reactions tend to assume extreme, absolute forms that destroy man's full nature. The preacher is at once too submissive and too aggressive; the young man asserts his right to disbelieve but is unable to make sense out of his contradictory certitudes; James's mother so overemphasizes stoic resistance that, in a later episode, she is incapable of compromising her rigid pride even when it means a meal for her son. Fortunately, the white lady who offers the meal knows exactly how to circumvent such pride so that natural help is not construed as demeaning charity. Such generosity has been too rare in the past, however, even among her fellow African Americans, and the mother's attitude remains unchanged. At first, the story as a whole seems to reveal a world where gentleness and love and flexibility have no place: "The sleet's coming down heavy, heavy now, and I turn up my coat collar to keep my neck warm. My mama tells me to turn it right back down. 'You not a bum,' she says. 'You a man.'" James nevertheless knows that his mother loves her children and that they love her.

"THREE MEN"

The third story, "Three Men," may have been placed at the center of the collection as a sort of hub toward which the first two stories approach and around which the whole book swings to return to the traditional rural society of the final stories, still rural and traditional, but now in the new context of the Civil Rights movement. Certainly it is the only story in which the central character undergoes anything resembling a change of heart or self-discovery.

Again, like the other stories, "Three Men" centers on a personal code of honor, this time specifically related to racial domination. A nineteen-year-old youth, Proctor Lewis, turns himself in to the law in Bayonne after stabbing another man in a fight over a girl. The story takes place in jail, where his cellmates--an old convict, Munford, and a homosexual, Hattie--argue with each other and talk to Proctor. Munford, full of hate for a society based on racial stereotypes, hates himself for allowing his life to gratify the expectations of those same stereotypes. Recalling the way his own past has swung back and forth between fights and jail, he poses the dilemma of the story: whether Proctor should choose to get out of jail by accepting the bond he initially hopes the white plantation owner will pay, or whether he should stay in jail, suffer the certain beating of the guards, and eventually go to the state penitentiary. Munford claims that the latter choice is the only way for Proctor to keep his manhood, something both Munford and Hattie have surrendered.

As the story ends, Proctor has almost made up his mind to refuse the bond and to abide by the code Munford has described. Although Proctor is not sure if he can stand by his decision, a shift of attitude has been made, and the right questions have been articulated clearly. "Three Men" looks back to the seemingly fatalistic rounds of poverty, frustration, and rigid codes of the first two stories and anticipates the last two stories, in which individual acts of self-affirmation seem to offer something more than mere stoic resistance.

"BLOODLINE"

The last two stories are best treated together, since they both return to the rural world of the plantation

suddenly introduced to the rising violence of African American activism. "Bloodline," the title story of the collection, raises the old southern problem of mixed blood, but in a new context, the "postsegregation" South. The story is told by a seventy-year-old African American, Felix, who works for the plantation's present owner, Walter Laurent. Copper, the half-white illegitimate son of Laurent's dead brother, has returned to the plantation seeking what he considers his birthright, the land on which his "father" raped his mother. He calls himself the General and refuses to go through the back door of the plantation house to meet his uncle. Finally, after Copper has thwarted all attempts by Laurent to force him through the back door, Laurent relents and goes to meet him. Their meeting symbolizes the old order making way for the new. Laurent does not change his mind about the old rules; he simply stops applying them for a time. Copper represents the transformation that will eventually change the caste system of white over black and rewrite the rules Laurent is talking about constantly: "I didn't write the rules, and I won't try to change them."

The old men, Laurent and Copper, are clearly part of the old order, but Gaines is careful to show how they both, especially Copper, manage to retain their individual dignity even though bound to the established tradition. There is a give and take between "master" and "servant" common to men who speak the same language, know the same people, and who have lived near each other all their lives. From this perspective, Copper comes back to his birthplace as an outsider, isolated from the rest of the African Americans, whom he considers childlike lackeys. He embodies the same sort of absoluteness and aloofness represented earlier by the young man in the dentist's office in "The Sky Is Gray," but he also embodies the necessary wave of change that will eventually sweep through the plantation, a change whose consequences are already being felt in the final story, "Just Like a Tree."

"JUST LIKE A TREE"

"Just Like a Tree" revolves around Aunt Fe, an old African American woman who is being taken North to escape the violence that has begun on the plantation. A young man, Emmanuel, has begun working for change, and in retaliation a tenant house has been bombed and a woman and her two children killed. More than any other story in the collection, "Just Like a Tree" affirms the force of the community. The only outsider, an African American from the North, is clearly alien to the shared assumptions and beliefs of the others. He speaks a different "language"; he sets himself apart by his loud manners, his condescension, and his lack of feeling. The other people gathered in the house, even the white lady who has walked to the house to say good-bye, form a whole, united by shared speech and shared feelings. The ceremony of farewell and the narrative mode of the story--told in turn by several of the visitors--affirm the strong communal bonds of rural African American society. Unlike the young man in "The Sky Is Gray" or the General in "Bloodline," Emmanuel belongs to the community even as he acts to change the old ways. He is a type of activist represented best in Gaines's work by Jimmy in *The Autobiography of Miss Jane Pittman.*

Aunt Fe's longtime presence in the community, her having touched, in some loving way, every member of the community, and her impending removal to the North provide clues to the tree symbolism of the story's title: Like a great, old shade tree, she has protected and sheltered other living creatures, and her departure will leave a spiritual hole in the life of the community, like the hole that the removal, roots and all, of a large tree will leave in a meadow. Aunt Clo predicts that Aunt Fe will die when she is "transplanted" to the North. The personal diaspora being forced upon Aunt Fe also represents the mass diasporas suffered by African Americans through the centuries.

The story and the book end with Aunt Fe's death. She has refused to be moved, and once again the strong vital roots of individual pride show their strength. The difference is that Aunt Fe's pride affirms its strength within the community, not in aloof isolation from it. In terms of *Bloodline* as a whole, "Just Like a Tree" offers the conclusion that change must involve sacrifice, but that change must take place. The farewell ceremony and Aunt Fe's death also offer the reminder that the traditional community had values that the new order can deny only at its own peril and loss.

The stories of *Bloodline* illustrate two other major themes in Gaines's writing. First, there is the presence and influence of strong female figures such as Octavia, Aunt Fe, and Amy, who are, in various ways, early prototypes of such heroines as Miss Jane Pittman in Gaines's later fiction. Manhood becomes a significant achievement for several male characters in *Bloodline*--James, Eddie, and Proctor--who anticipate even larger treatment of the male-maturation theme in Gaines's novels from *The Autobiography of Miss Jane Pittman* through *A Lesson Before Dying*, one of his most powerful works.

"MOZART AND LEADBELLY"

Mozart and Leadbelly: Stories and Essays consists of five short stories preceded by six essays and succeeded by a seventh. The contents were compiled and edited by Marcia Gaudet and Reggie Young, colleagues of Gaines at the University of Louisiana at Lafayette. The first section of essays were originally written as talks, ranging from 1971 to 2001. The final essay is a wide-ranging conversation with Gaudet and Darrell Bourque, recorded on December 17, 2002.

In "Miss Jane and I," Gaines says that even some sophisticated readers (for example, a representative of *Newsweek* and a San Francisco newspaperman) took Miss Jane to be a real person, while she is a character solely of his own invention. The theme of the title essay argues that while the artist should embrace Western culture (Wolfgang Amadeus Mozart), the African American artist should not abandon the rich culture represented by Leadbelly performing the blues. "A Very Big Order: Reconstructing Identity" is the first of three essays examining the effect that moving from Louisiana to California at age fifteen had upon Gaines. Interestingly, he writes it in the third person. "Bloodline in Ink" and "Aunty and the Black Experience in Louisiana" address and expand upon the outcome of this dislocation. "Writing *A Lesson Before Dying*" charts for the reader the composition of the novel from its conception through the final draft.

A pattern soon develops in the five short stories. Four are narrated by three young protagonists ("The Turtles" and "Boy in the Double-Breasted Suit" are both narrated by a fourteen-year-old boy, Max). The first story, "Christ Walked Down Market Street," is set in San Francisco. It features a mysterious panhandler whom, apparently, no one but the narrator sees. His outstretched hand bears the marks of stigmata, and references to the Chosen, the Trinity, and the Twelve provide further Christian imagery. The ambiguous conclusion may suggest that the narrator himself is the mysterious bum. "The Turtles" was Gaines's first published story, appearing in 1956 in *Transfer*, a literary magazine at San Francisco State College. It deals with the efforts of two fathers to introduce their adolescent sons, Max and Benny, to sex, as taught by Amy, a local girl of dubious reputation. The experience proves quite traumatic for Benny. The title, though probably meant figuratively, refers to the little turtles the boys catch as they fish. In the other story narrated by Max, his father has been enjoying a satisfactory affair with a widow, Mrs. Adele, until she attempts to draw him to church by inviting both him and a heavy-handed preacher, Reverend Johnson, to dinner. The meal does not go well. Max's father breaks up with Mrs. Adele. Max now fears he will be forced to return the double-breasted blue suit Mrs. Adele gave him. "Mary Louise" is a story of loss, wherein the twenty-year-old narrator's childhood sweetheart, Jackson, tells her gently, but nonetheless painfully, that he has outgrown their relationship. The final story, "My Grandpa and the Haint," is an amusing account of how the dalliance of the boy Bobby's grandfather, Pap, with Miss Molly Bee is thwarted by the grandmother, Mom. She enlists the powers of the feared Madame Toussaint, who conjures a phantom serpent to harry Pap on the way home from his latest tryst. Pap is scared straight, and marital harmony is restored.

OTHER MAJOR WORKS

LONG FICTION: *Catherine Carmier*, 1964; *Of Love and Dust*, 1967; *The Autobiography of Miss Jane Pittman*, 1971; *In My Father's House*, 1978; *A Gathering of Old Men*, 1983; *A Lesson Before Dying*, 1993.

MISCELLANEOUS: *Porch Talk with Ernest Gaines*, 1990.

BIBLIOGRAPHY

Babb, Valerie Melissa. *Ernest Gaines*. Boston: Twayne, 1991. A solid introduction to the author and his works. Includes a bibliography and an index.

Burke, William. "*Bloodline*: A Man's Black South." *College Language Association Journal* 19 (1976): 545-558. This study centers on the design of the five stories in *Bloodline* and argues that they are a coherent record of changing race relations prompted by the African American male's recovery of his masculinity.

Chase, Henry. "A Novel and Poetic View of Louisiana." *American Visions* 11 (August/September, 1996): 44-48. The term "novel" is used ambiguously, referring both to Gaines's work and to his attitude toward his home state. Illustrated.

Gaines, Ernest J. "Where Have You Gone New Orleans?" *National Geographic* 210, no. 2 (August, 2006): 54-65. The author laments the catastrophe of Hurricane Katrina that befell New Orleans. Illustrated.

Gaines, Ernest J., Marcia G. Gaudet, and Carl Wooton. *Porch Talk with Ernest Gaines: Conversations on the Writer's Craft*. Baton Rouge: Louisiana State University Press, 1990. A transcription of an intimate interview conducted by colleagues of Gaines, this work offers an insightful look at how the author has transmuted his Louisiana heritage, familial experiences, literary influences, and strong folk tradition into fiction with a distinct voice.

Jones, Suzanne W. "New Narratives of Southern Manhood: Race, Masculinity, and Closure in Ernest Gaines's Fiction." *Critical Survey* 9 (1997): 15-42. Discusses Gaines's deconstruction of stereotypes and presentation of new models of African American and white southern manhood. Asserts that Gaines suggests that in order to reconstruct the South, black and white men must reject the traditional Western model of manhood that links masculinity and violence.

Lowe, John, ed. *Conversations with Ernest Gaines*. Jackson: University Press of Mississippi, 1995. A selection of interviews in which Gaines speaks about his life, his themes, and his works. Includes an index and chronology of his life.

Magnier, Bernard. "Ernest J. Gaines." *The UNESCO Courier* 48 (April, 1995): 5-7. In this interview, Gaines discusses his childhood and family background, the books that most influenced him, his feelings about Africa, and other topics.

Papa, Lee. "'His Feet on Your Neck': The New Religion in the Works of Ernest J. Gaines." *African American Review* 27 (Summer, 1993): 187-193. Claims that Gaines is concerned with characters who must make a personal test of religion, not accept it as imposed by institutional Christianity.

Peterson, V. R. "Ernest Gaines: Writing About the Past." *Essence* 24 (August, 1993): 52. A brief biographical sketch that discusses Gaines's background, his typical themes, and the development of his writing career.

Shelton, Frank W. "Ambiguous Manhood in Ernest J. Gaines's *Bloodline*." *College Language Association Journal* 19 (1975): 200-209. Shelton notes that although the African American males in Gaines's

stories strive for manhood and dignity, they are only partially successful in their quests.

Simon, John. "Review of *A Lesson Before Dying*." *New York Magazine* 33, no. 38 (October 2, 2000): 86-88. A review of the dramatic adaptation. Illustrated.

Simpson, Anne K. *A Gathering of Gaines: The Man and the Writer*. Lafayette: Center for Louisiana Studies at the University of Louisiana at Lafayette, 1991. Simpson's study, well documented with excerpts from Gaines's personal papers, offers a biographical sketch, an examination of his stylistic influences and characteristics, and a critical overview of his fiction. It includes an unannotated but thorough bibliography.

Ben Forkner; John W. Fiero and Philip A. Tapley
Updated by Patrick Adcock

MARY GAITSKILL

Born: Lexington, Kentucky; November 11, 1954

PRINCIPAL SHORT FICTION
Bad Behavior, 1988
Because They Wanted To, 1997
Don't Cry: Stories, 2009

OTHER LITERARY FORMS

Mary Gaitskill (GAYTS-kihl) published her first novel, *Two Girls, Fat and Thin*, in 1991. She has published articles, especially on feminist issues, in major magazines, most notably her essay, "On Not Being a Victim: Sex, Rape, and the Trouble with Following Rules," in *Harper's Magazine* (1994). Her novel *Veronica* appeared in 2005.

ACHIEVEMENTS

In 1981, Mary Gaitskill received the Jule and Avery Hopwood Award from the University of Michigan for "The Woman Who Knew Judo, and Other Stories." Her story "The Nice Restaurant" was anthologized in *Nothing But You: Love Stories from "The New Yorker"*

(1997).Gaitskill was nominated for the 1998 PEN/ Faulkner Award for Fiction, and she received a Guggenheim Fellowship in 2002. *Veronica* was nominated for the National Book Award in 2005 and was also a finalist for the National Book Critics Circle Award.

BIOGRAPHY

Mary Gaitskill was born in Lexington, Kentucky, on November 11, 1954. Her mother, Dorothy Jane Mayer, was a social worker and homemaker; her father, Lawrence Russell Gaitskill, was a teacher. Mary Gaitskill grew up in Livonia and Northville, suburbs of Detroit, Michigan, in an environment that she once described in an interview as "a whole huge mess." At age sixteen Gaitskill ran away from home and became, among other things, a stripper. She lived in Toronto for a few years and later returned to Michigan to attend the University of Michigan as a journalism student. After she received her B.A. in 1981 and won her first adult award for her fiction, she moved to New York and worked on her first collection of short stories, *Bad Behavior*, until it was published in 1988. In 1991, she published *Two Girls, Fat and Thin*, her first novel. Gaitskill has spent time in mental institutions and for a while bounced back and forth between her New York home and her quieter home in Marin County, California, before settling in San Francisco. In 1997, she published her second collection of short stories, *Because They Wanted To*. Another collection, *Don't Cry*, was published in 2009.

ANALYSIS

In his 1997 review of *Because They Wanted To*, Craig Seligman compared Mary Gaitskill's writings favorably with those of Flannery O'Connor. The driving forces behind most of Gaitskill's characters are the need for self-understanding and the need to connect with other people, both of which are irrevocably linked to each character's fight for identity. Most of the characters in Gaitskill's first collection of stories, *Bad Behavior*, share one huge problem: Each of them tries desperately to cling to the wrong person. Sometimes this mistake leads a character closer to self-discovery, but, as often as not, it leads to that simplest of literary ironies, where the reader can clearly see what the character cannot. The motivation of the characters in Gaitskill's second collection, *Because They Wanted To*, is essentially escape from a past they feel defines them in a way they cannot fully accept. Both collections are filled with what might be called "weird" sex (prostitution, sadomasochism, rapes, gang bangs, date rapes, fetishes, role playing), often presented in graphic detail, but the stories are less about sex than they are about the opportunity for connection, escape from isolation, and feelings of alienation. Even when the opportunities are missed--as they usually are--the characters and the story are enriched by revelations. The major difference in the two collections of stories is maturity. As should be expected, the newer stories show a more stylistically even hand. The message consistently delivered in Gaitskill's fiction is that separation and isolation are often necessary, even desirable.

"DAISY'S VALENTINE"

"Daisy's Valentine" showcases three characters, none of whom has any hope of ever experiencing a normal, enduring relationship. Joey, a delusional epileptic speed freak, lives with Diane, a paranoid epileptic speed freak existing on government checks.

When Diane learns that Joey has slept with Daisy, Diane attacks him, rips out his earring, and throws him out of their apartment. Joey thinks he is falling in love with Daisy, a poster child for the insanely insecure, who works with him at a bookstore. Daisy lives with an abusive man, the only kind of man she thinks she can love. Joey spends much of his time daydreaming about rescuing Daisy from muggers, terrorists, and natural disasters. The heart of this story is in the disparities between how each character interprets his or her own motivations, how each of the other characters views them, and the impressions their actions and reactions leave on the reader. One major accomplishment of this story is that Gaitskill makes the reader care about people who are otherwise hard to care about.

"SOMETHING NICE"

"Something Nice" is one of the few Gaitskill stories in which the leading male character is not a clear-cut villain. This is a story filled with ironies, the greatest of which is that readers see some of the man's better qualities through an affair he has with a prostitute while his wife is out of town. After his first visit with the

Mary Gaitskill (AP Photo/Henny Ray Abrams)

prostitute, he becomes so enamored of her that he comes back every night, except for one he takes off so she will not get bored with him. She is different from any prostitute he has ever seen. He offers her five hundred dollars to take a night off from the escort service and spend it with him alone--a night on the town with dinner and a film that he has arranged for the night before his wife returns. The prostitute stands him up, and when he calls the escort service to set up an appointment, he is told that she no longer works for them. Almost a year later, he sees her in a restaurant with a young man and learns by eavesdropping that her job in a museum may be in jeopardy and that she may have to "survive on free-lance work."

"TINY, SMILING DADDY"

Stew, the father in "Tiny, Smiling Daddy," and his daughter Kitty suffer from a malady common to many of Gaitskill's characters: the failure to understand each other in the face of facts and circumstances that make communication with each other all but impossible. Both are products of their generations and victims of the chasm that separates them, but the large part of the blame for their inability to reach each other rests on Stew. He cannot understand that her changes in behavior, her rebelliousness, and her frequent need for time alone are part of her growing up. The most visible problem is that he cannot accept that his daughter is a lesbian. At the beginning of the story, he is awakened from a dreamy afternoon nap and sent into a panic by a phone call from a friend informing him that the latest issue of the magazine *Self* contains an article "that Kitty wrote about fathers and daughters talking to each other." While waiting for his wife to come home with their only car, so he can go buy a copy of the magazine, he broods over confrontations that he and Kitty had as she was growing up. He recalls with great pain the miserable ways his father treated him as a child, but he never seems to make the connection.

"BECAUSE THEY WANTED TO"

"Because They Wanted To" is the story of a girl who fails to mature because there has been no nurturing person in her life. Elise is a sixteen-year-old runaway, trying to escape a home made unbearable by an incestuous relationship with her brother. She lies about her age so she can hitch a ride across the Canadian border

with a couple of horsemen, who curse her and chase her off when they find out how young she is. In Vancouver, she panhandles for food money and shares housing with Mark, another runaway. She answers an ad for a baby-sitting job, and the woman who placed the ad, Robin, asks if Elise will watch the kids while Robin looks for a job, promising to pay her out of her first paycheck. Desperate for money, Elise agrees to take the job and to wait for her pay. Robin promises to be back home by six. Elise is a wreck long before six, and as it gets later and later, she loses patience and finally tells a man who lives downstairs that she has to leave. As she walks by the house the next morning, she sees that the window she left open is still open, a metaphor for her past and possible future.

"THE GIRL ON THE PLANE"

As in many of her stories, one of the main themes in Gaitskill's "The Girl on the Plane" is the seeming impossibility of defining "consensual sex" objectively. On a flight to Cincinnati, a man sits next to a woman, who reminds him, after a bit of scrutiny, of a girl who had a crush on him in college. The girl on the plane reveals to him, in the spirit of Alcoholics Anonymous, that she has had problems with alcoholism, and he confesses to her that once the college girl with the crush became drunk at a party and willingly had sex with most of the men at the party, including him. This game of "true confessions" continues until he says to her, "If you want to talk about mistakes . . . I raped somebody. Somebody I liked." Instantly, her entire demeanor changes. She wrestles her hand away from his and says, "Don't touch me again." In spite of all his attempts to explain that it was not really rape-- "it was complicated"--she throws up an impenetrable wall. When the plane lands, he tries to follow her and explain, but she pushes her way past him and never looks back.

"COLLEGE TOWN, 1980"

"College Town, 1980," the opening story of Gaitskill's third collection, *Don't Cry*, focuses on four young people living together in Ann Arbor, Michigan, just after the election of Ronald Reagan. The central character, Dolores, has been hospitalized for mental illness and has to wear a scarf because she has taken to pulling out large clumps of her hair. Relatively plotless, the story's underlying tension stems from Dolores's depression and the fact that she blames her unhappiness on her former boyfriend's having dumped her. She also blames her father, an adulterous alcoholic, and her mother, who is "murderously unhappy." The story ends with Dolores thinking she will work on her research papers and graduate, feeling that she is strong, but strong like a bombed-out building, stripped, and imperious. This is less a story than it is a set piece about young people who feel victimized, helpless, and trapped in a stagnant situation at a certain transitional point in American society.

"AN OLD VIRGIN"

"An Old Virgin" in *Don't Cry* focuses on Laura, a woman filled with self-loathing, who has a habit of walking around her apartment, muttering how ugly and valueless she is. Even while she seems to cope with everyday activities and her job at a medical clinic, she feels like a bug tunneling through the earth with fragile insect legs. Her father, a man who was abused as a child and who in turn abused his own children, is ill, emaciated, and fragile. The central titular metaphor of the story is a forty-three-year-old woman who is given a preliminary examination at the clinic by Laura. Because the woman is a virgin, Laura wonders what it would be like to be a virgin at her own age of forty. She imagines virginity as the source of her strength, making everything in her extra alive. However, although she feels her body is vibrant with strong feelings, the feelings seem broken or incomplete.

"THE AGONIZED FACE"

In "The Agonized Face," the unhappy women, who seem to be Gaitskill's obsessive focus, are close to her persona as a writer and a commentator on contemporary society. The divorced mother of a ten-year-old girl, the narrator has been assigned to write a piece on a feminist author who is giving a talk at an annual literary festival. Much of "The Agonized Face" reads like a personal essay on whether feminists have made girls into sluts, who think they have to have sex all the time, or whether feminists have overprotected girls into thinking they have been raped when they were just having sex. The narrator wonders if the feminist author is suggesting that rape and prostitution are the same thing, concluding, in her essayistic tone, that for the

purposes of her "discussion," they are close enough. The article the narrator finally writes takes the feminist writer to task for pretending that female humiliation is an especially smart kind of game, while leaving out the "agonized face" of women's humiliation in modern society. She insists the "agonized face" is one of the few mysteries left to women and must be protected.

OTHER MAJOR WORKS

LONG FICTION: *Two Girls, Fat and Thin*, 1991; *Veronica*, 2005.

NONFICTION: "On Not Being a Victim: Sex, Rape, and the Trouble with Following Rules," 1994; "My Inspiration: Vladimir Nabokov, Sorcerer of Cruelty," 1995; "Men at Extremes," 1999.

EDITED TEXT: *Best New American Voices, 2009*, 2008.

BIBLIOGRAPHY

Contemporary Literary Criticism. Vol. 69. Detroit: Gale, 1992. Contains a comprehensive collection of reviews of the stories in *Bad Behavior* from Michiko Kakutani, Barry Walters, George Garrett, Carol Anshaw, and many more. Especially interesting is Regina Weinreich's explanation of how Gaitskill, inspired in her youth by *Playboy* cartoons, aspired to become a prostitute and how that experience later leaked into her fiction.

Deresiewicz, William. "When the Whip Comes Down." *Nation* 288 (May 11, 2009): 25-30. A long, largely unfavorable review of *Don't Cry*, summarizing Gaitskill's career and arguing that the book is awkwardly self-conscious, marking an artistic midlife crisis for Gaitskill, casting doubt on whether she can make a transition from her early stories of youthful suffering to complex stories of maturity.

Gaitskill, Mary. "On Not Being a Victim: Sex, Rape, and the Trouble with Following Rules." *Harper's Magazine* (March, 1994): 35-44. Gaitskill gives straightforward accounts of times when she was raped and explanations of other experiences in her life that have led her to explore definitions of "rape," "date rape," and "consensual sex." Such terms play major parts in several of her stories, including "The Blanket," "The Girl on the Plane," and "The Nice Restaurant." She provides in-depth description of how she evolved from a "politically correct" feminist into an individual thinker and writer concerned with personal responsibility and trying to understand what really motivates her characters and the characters of other writers.

Graff, E. J. "Mixed Emotions." *Women's Review of Books* 14 (May, 1997): 8-9. Review of several stories from *Because They Wanted To*, critical

comments on *Bad Behavior*, and comparisons of the works of Gaitskill to those of Amy Bloom. Both authors use sex as a dramatic tool in their writing. Both write fiction that has been categorized as "postqueer."

Edmund August
Updated by Charles E. May

JOHN GARDNER

Born: Batavia, New York; July 21, 1933
Died: Susquehanna, Pennsylvania; September 14, 1982

PRINCIPAL SHORT FICTION

The King's Indian: Stories and Tales, 1974
The Art of Living, and Other Stories, 1981

OTHER LITERARY FORMS

Extraordinary variety and productivity marked John Gardner's literary career: He published two collections of short fiction, numerous novels, three books of tales and one of verse for young readers, an "epic," a book of poems, opera librettos, a radio play, and reviews. An academic as well as an imaginative writer, Gardner also published scholarly books and articles--most, however, directed chiefly at nonspecialists, with the aim of making the literature more accessible, such as his translations of medieval poetry or his biography of Geoffrey Chaucer. His interest in contemporary fiction and in teaching fiction writing resulted in his most controversial book, *On Moral Fiction* (1978), and in two related books of advice and encouragement for young writers, *On Becoming a Novelist* (1983) and *The Art of Fiction: Notes on Craft for Young Writers* (1984).

ACHIEVEMENTS

The publication of his third novel, *Grendel* (1971), a postmodern retelling of *Beowulf* (c. 1000) from the monster's point of view, brought John Gardner critical

acclaim and a measure of commercial success. His next three novels--*The Sunlight Dialogues* (1972), *Nickel Mountain: A Pastoral Novel* (1973), and *October Light* (1976)--all became best sellers, and the last one won the 1977 National Book Critics Circle Award for fiction. Gardner's other awards and honors include Woodrow Wilson, Danforth, and John Simon Guggenheim Memorial Foundation fellowships (1955, 1970-1973, and 1973-1974, respectively), election to the American Academy of Arts and Letters, the Armstrong Prize for his radio play *The Temptation Game* (pr. 1977), and a Lamport Foundation award for his essay "Moral Fiction." The book from which that essay was drawn, *On Moral Fiction*, became the focus of a national literary debate over the nature and purpose of contemporary fiction.

BIOGRAPHY

John Champlin Gardner, Jr., was born on July 21, 1933, in the farming community of Batavia in western New York, the setting of a number of his stories and novels. His literary interest can be traced back to his mother, an English teacher, and to his father, a farmer, lay preacher, and opera lover. "Bud" (Welsh for poet) began writing stories when he was eight, but it was the death of his brother Gilbert on April 4, 1945, in a farm accident for which Gardner held himself responsible, that appears to have influenced him most deeply. Gilbert's death and the part that Gardner believed he played in it are the subject of one of his finest stories, "Redemption," and serve as the subtext of nearly all of his fiction.

During his high school years, Gardner studied the French horn at the Eastman School of Music in nearby Rochester. He later attended DePauw University for two years, majoring in chemistry, before marrying Joan Patterson, a cousin, on June 6, 1953, and transferring to Washington University in St. Louis, where he began writing *Nickel Mountain*. He did his graduate work at the University of Iowa, dividing his time between the Writers' Workshop and medieval studies, submitting a collection of stories for his M.A. thesis and a novel, "The Old Men," for his Ph.D. dissertation. From Iowa, Gardner went on to hold faculty appointments at a succession of colleges and universities, including Oberlin College, San Francisco State University, Southern Illinois University (his longest, 1965 to 1976), Bennington College, Williams College, George Mason University, and finally the State University of New York at Binghamton, where he directed the writing program.

The early years of Gardner's literary career were marked by obscurity; the next ones, from 1971 to 1976, by critical and commercial success; the last by notoriety; and all by unflagging, almost demonic, and at times certainly self-defeating energy. The heated debate at the National Book Critics Circle over the relative merits of *October Light* and Renata Adler's *Speedboat* (1976), the book that it narrowly defeated for that year's fiction prize, set the stage for the difficult times that soon followed: the breakup of his first marriage, a charge of plagiarism, a bout with cancer, trouble with the Internal Revenue Service, and the publication of *On Moral Fiction* and the sudden downturn in Gardner's critical reputation--all grist for the mill of his most autobiographical novel, *Mickelsson's Ghosts* (1982). Gardner died in a motorcycle accident on September 14, 1982, a few months after his amicable divorce from the poet L. M. (Liz) Rosenberg and a few days before he was to marry Susan Thornton.

ANALYSIS

Although he published only two short-fiction collections during his brief but nevertheless prolific career, John Gardner took a serious and historically informed interest in short fiction's various forms. In addition to the nineteen stories, tales, and novellas collected in *The King's Indian: Stories and Tales* and *The*

Art of Living, and Other Stories, Gardner published five uncollected stories (the earliest in 1952 while still an undergraduate, the latest posthumously in 1984); a textbook, edited with Lennis Dunlap, significantly titled *The Forms of Fiction* (1962); three books of stories for children (1975-1977); a novella aimed at adolescent readers; one novel, *Grendel*, which initially appeared in abbreviated version (edited as a short story by *Esquire*'s Gordon Lish, not Gardner); and another novel, *Nickel Mountain*, originally conceived as a set of interrelated stories. *The King's Indian* and *The Art of Living* do not, therefore, adequately represent the extent of Gardner's interest in the short story and its allied forms. They do, however, evidence the consistency of Gardner's aesthetic vision and, more important, his remarkable technical virtuosity, ranging from the fantastic and parodic at one extreme to the realistic and didactic at the other. Neither *The King's Indian* nor *The Art of Living* merely collects previously published works; rather, they are carefully and cleverly constructed. *The King's Indian* explores and celebrates the art of narrative, whereas *The Art of Living* pursues the moral fiction idea, which, by the late 1970's, had become the author's chief obsession.

THE KING'S INDIAN

The King's Indian offers an oblique and exuberant commentary on contemporary writing, which Gardner believed was unnecessarily pessimistic and overly concerned with its own verbal texture. *The King's Indian* is divided into four parts, the first entitled "The Midnight Reader." Against the progressive darkness of the first four stories of the first part, Gardner posits both the hopeful vision of the fifth story and--less overtly but also perhaps more effectively--the wildly playful voices of all five narrators, metafictional and moral-fictional versions of Samuel Taylor Coleridge's Ancient Mariner.

"PASTORAL CARE"

In "Pastoral Care," the voice belongs to a John Updike-type minister beset by doubts about his congregation, his world, and himself. Unable to raise the social consciousness of his congregation in Carbondale, Illinois, the Reverend Eugene Pick, standing on a footstool that he keeps hidden behind the pulpit, does reach a tall, bearded stranger who acts on Pick's advice, though in a way that the minister never intended: The stranger bombs the local police station and, as Pick later learns, a church (perhaps his own). Implicated, the minister flees, only, like Jonah, to learn that there is no escape from either the stranger or responsibility (pastoral care). When a girl high on drugs falls from the train, Pick, full of misgivings, attempts to comfort her boyfriend, another bearded stranger. Although he believes that "all systems fail," Pick also believes (adapting William Shakespeare) that "flexibility is all." "I force myself to continue," he says at the story's end. "I have no choice."

"THE RAVAGES OF SPRING"

Another person who apparently does not have a choice is the anonymous country doctor, identified only by the alias William Thorp, in the story "The Ravages of Spring," also set in Carbondale, sometime in the nineteenth century. The tornado, which sets the story in motion, is formidable but no match for the vortex of intertextual forces from which Gardner spins the story's befuddled, unprepossessing narrator and his playfully self-conscious narrative--bits and pieces from Edgar Allan Poe, Herman Melville, and Franz Kafka being the most prominent. Against the awed doctor's appreciation of "the beauty and grandeur of Nature in her rage," Gardner posits the geneticist Dr. Hunter (a cloned copy of the original doctor, dead some thirty years), and against cloning (the reproduction of exact copies), Gardner employs his own parodic method, part put-down, part homage. The tornado topples the Poesque House of Hunter; the doctor disappears, replaced by three infant copies whom the narrator, a bachelor, leaves in the care of an old woman who, believing them mad (and perhaps thinking she has the doctor's consent), subjects them to the "mandrake cure" from which the doctor is only able to save two. The good doctor is puzzled by events but accepting of them, including the fictively real children, the presumed offspring of a Dr. Hunter who may be little more than a character in a dream, the result of a storm-induced bump on the narrator's head.

"THE TEMPTATION OF ST. IVO"

Affirmation in the face of uncertainty is a major theme in all Gardner's fiction and more particularly in the three remaining stories of "The Midnight Reader."

In "The Temptation of St. Ivo," the narrator, Brother Ivo, is a copyist who possesses a firm belief in order and a genius for decorating sacred manuscripts. Ivo manages to successfully balance the imperatives of his fantastic art and the rules of his religious order, as well as his faith in those rules, until Brother Nicholas arrives on the scene. "Your rules are absurd," Nicholas whispers, "The order of the world is an accident." Claiming to have found where the phoenix--the symbol of the resurrection and, not incidentally, the most artful of Ivo's many artful creations--lives, Nicholas in effect forces Ivo to choose between obeying the rules governing monastic life and acting on his faith in order to save not the phoenix, a myth, mere art, but whatever the phoenix may represent--perhaps a child whom Nicholas intends to kill, or even Nicholas's soul. Ivo chooses action over obedience, complex faith over simple order. He leaves the monastery at night and enters the dark Dantean wood where he soon loses his way: "The rules, techniques of a lifetime devoted to allegory, have ruined me." According to the usual Christian plot, Ivo must lose himself before he can be saved, but in Gardner's story, Ivo's salvation proves at best ambiguous--as ambiguous as the advice given by the knight errant whom he meets: "Nothing means anything."

"THE WARDEN"

The next story, "The Warden," does to the existentialist preoccupation with Nothing what much of postmodern fiction does: puts it to comic use, as in the joke line from Thomas Pynchon's *V.* (1963), "Nothing was coming; nothing was already here." The story draws heavily on Poe and Kafka, adds a dash of Samuel Beckett, and ends with the opening lines of Jean-Paul Sartre's *L'Être et le néant* (1943; *Being and Nothingness*, 1956). "The Warden" also leaves its narrator, Vortrab (perhaps a variant of the German *Vortrag*, meaning "performance"), in a far worse, and also more humorous, predicament than the soon-to-be-sainted Ivo, cut off from the guards and prisoners whom he nominally (but without any real authority) commands, from the warden who may be dead, and from his own family (especially his father, a painter). Josef Mallin, the villain of the piece, is a composite of the anarchist figures of the previous three stories, "a nihilist, destroyer of churches, murderer of medical doctors," who, until his execution, opposed all ideas on the grounds that they led people to believe in the possibility of a better world (according to Mallin, an illusion). Not much has changed by the story's end. Vortrab is still waiting for the warden to open his door ("The Parable of the Law" from Kafka's *Der Prozess* (1925; *The Trial*, 1937) and even says to the guard Heller what the warden previously said to Vortrab: "You and I are the only hope."

"John Napper Sailing Through the Universe"

Vortrab's situation is not so much existentially tragicomic as it is comically parodic. The fifth of "The Midnight Reader's" five stories strikes a slightly different note and depends less on virtuoso technique than on willed affirmation. Gardner drops the literary masks (Poe, Melville, Kafka, and others) to speak, which is to say to narrate, in his own voice, the voice of "John Gardner," a fictive character and therefore, autobiographical appearances aside, another mask. Adrift in the same southern Illinois as the Reverend Pick and the country doctor, John and Joan Gardner take off for Europe in search of the jovial John Napper, a character based on the actual artist who illustrated Gardner's 1972 novel *The Sunlight Dialogues*. Arriving in Paris, they find that the Nappers are in London, but disappointment gives way to dismay when the house sitter shows them some paintings from an early period, the work of an artist the Gardners cannot recognize: "dark, furious, intellectual, full of scorn and something suicidal. Mostly black, with struggles of light, losing." Simply put, Napper was what Gardner the narrator/character now is. Gardner soon learns that what saved Napper was his discovery that the cheerful "nonsense" of his later paintings "lighted his sad wife's eyes." In the eyes of his own young daughter, in the painting that Lucy has "commissioned" for seven dark English pennies, Gardner sees the beginning of the very conflict that Napper's art--indeed any art--must depict and, even if only temporarily, offset: "In the pretty flowers, the pretty face, my daughter's eyes were calculating." It is an image that leaves Lucy poised between innocence and experience, between the taking of selfish advantage and paying the price, as Napper has, of selfless, although self-conscious, affirmation.

"Tales of Queen Louisa"

The three "Tales of Queen Louisa," which make up the second part of *The King's Indian*, take the form of fairy tales and so can afford to be less ambiguously affirmative. In drawing on the fairy-tale form here and in his books for young readers, Gardner was contributing to what was fast becoming a postmodern practice: the retelling and defamiliarizing of simple narrative structures--myths and epics as well as fairy tales--by John Barth (*Chimera*, 1972), Donald Barthelme (*Snow White*, 1967; "The Glass Mountain"), Robert Coover (*Pricksongs and Descants*, 1969), Angela Carter (*The Bloody Chamber, and Other Stories*, 1979), and others, including Gardner himself (*Grendel*). Dotted with allusions to contemporary affairs (for example, the war in Vietnam and the kidnapping of Patty Hearst), the three stories recycle traditional plots and character types for decidedly metafictional, but also moral-fictional, purposes. In the only kingdom where imagination rules (the mad Queen's imagination), art wins, righting all wrongs, transforming pregnant chambermaids into long-lost princesses.

"The King's Indian"

In "The King's Indian," the Queen's metamorphosing imagination and the transcendent truth that it makes real by royal decree are outdone by the narrative gamesmanship of John Gardner and Jonathan Upchurch. "The King's Indian" is a strange and exuberant work in the American tall-tale tradition, with characters, plots, and themes borrowed from Edgar Allan Poe, Nathaniel Hawthorne, Herman Melville, Jack London, Samuel Taylor Coleridge, William Shakespeare, Percy Bysshe Shelley, Homer, and Frank L. Baum, among others, and told in a parodically and self-consciously metafictional manner through a relay of narrators. There is the tale's ostensible narrator, the walleyed Upchurch, who tells his tale in the manner of Coleridge's Ancient Mariner to a "guest" whose responses to Upchurch's alternately mesmerizing and infuriatingly "overblown" tale are duly noted. Then there is the barely perceptible narrator who apparently contrives Jonathan's "crafty fabulation" in a prison cell to pass the time before his execution and thus to keep his mind from the existential abyss into which Jonathan nearly tumbles. Finally, near the tale's end, John Gardner makes a "guest" appearance to announce that "The King's Indian" is not "a cynical trick, one more joke on exhausted art" but instead a monument, a collage, a celebration of all literature and life. It is, however, a claim about which even "John Gardner" has his doubts, doubts that the reader--recalling the conundrum of the Cretan barber who claims that all Cretans are liars-- must necessarily share.

The relay of narrators mirrors the story's infinite regress of tales within tales, all stacked like a nest of Chinese boxes. Following the plot of Poe's *The Narrative of Arthur Gordon Pym* (1838), Upchurch finds himself aboard the whaler *New Jerusalem*, where Captain Dirge turns out to be a ventriloquist's dummy crafted by the pseudonymous Swami Havananda (disguised as the mate Wilkins) and manipulated by master mesmerist and archtrickster Dr. Luther Flint (disguised as the blind seer Jeremiah). Like Harry Houdini, born Ehrich Weiss, Flint and his assistant play and prey upon the credulity of others yet nevertheless long for some one, stable, absolute truth in the world of illusion, which their theatrical artistry mimics and extends. Tricksters by "maniacal compulsion," they, like so many characters in Gardner's fiction (Grendel and the Sunlight Man in particular), long for a state that is unattainable and may not even exist (outside art and religion). Failing in their quest, they end up feeling betrayed. Upchurch learns that a wise man settles for less, "for Ithaca," which in his case translates to the cry "On to Illinois the Changeable," accompanied not by Dirge's beautiful daughter Augusta but by Flint's battered Miranda (Augusta unmasked). The reader faces a similar choice in judging a story that, on the one hand, offers the literary equivalent of "the magnificence of God and of all his Creation" and, on the other hand, suggests "mere pyrotechnic pointlessness."

THE ART OF LIVING, AND OTHER STORIES

That is not a choice that a reader of *The Art of Living, and Other Stories* must face. None of the ten stories is stylistically pyrotechnic; all are, if anything, too pointed. Except for "Trumpeter" (another "Queen Louisa" story, told from a dog's point of view), "The Library Horror" (a sophomoric response to William H. Gass's position on the autonomy and self-reflexiveness of all art), and "Vlemk the Box-Painter" (an overlong

fairy tale that proves less imaginative and more didactic than *In the Suicide Mountains*, a novella that Gardner wrote around the same time), the stories take a more of less realistic approach, rather than the self-consciously parodic style of *The King's Indian*. Realism, however, had always been an essential part of Gardner's immensely varied repertoire of narrative tricks, as demonstrated in his novels *The Resurrection* (1966), *The Sunlight Dialogues, Nickel Mountain, October Light*, and *Mickelsson's Ghosts*, but not in the novels *The Wreckage of Agathon* (1970), *Grendel*, or *Freddy's Book* (1980). "The Joy of the Just" was originally part of *Nickel Mountain* before Gardner decided to turn his collection of interrelated stories into a "pastoral novel," and "Stillness" was drawn from a novel (posthumously published) that Gardner wrote as a form of marriage therapy (the marriage failed but the novel, even though never revised for publication, is remarkable).

"REDEMPTION"

"Redemption" was also written as "bibliotherapy" and became the means by which Gardner began to come to terms with the guilt that he felt over the accidental death of his younger brother Gilbert in 1945. The story is deeply autobiographical and, from its opening sentences, quietly devastating:

> One day in April--a clear, blue day, when there were crocuses in bloom--Jack Hawthorne ran over and killed his brother David. Even at the last moment he could have prevented his brother's death by slamming on the tractor's brakes, easily in reach for all the shortness of his legs; but he was unable to think, or, rather, thought unclearly, and so watched it happen, as he would again and again watch it happen in his mind, with nearly undiminished intensity and clarity, all his life.

After a long period of self-hatred, rage, and withdrawal into music in order to escape from others, especially his family, Jack will be redeemed--not, however, by his own playing but by that of his teacher, a master musician whose own sufferings during the Russian Revolution match Jack's. Realizing that he will never play as well as Yegudkin, Jack returns home, finding in the human herd that he, like Friedrich Nietzsche, had formerly scorned, a sense of belonging to something larger, more important, and more forgiving than himself. "Redemption" succeeds so well because it creates, but does not attempt to resolve, the tension between the greatness of what Gardner liked to call "true art"--its visionary power--and the failure of artists and indeed individuals to make their lives art's equal.

"COME ON BACK"

In "Come on Back," the immense gap between the visionary and the quotidian leads one character to take his life but leads the survivors to join in song and thus overcome their individual grief. In the title story, a small-town cook, Arnold Deller, overcomes the loss of a son in Vietnam by preparing a dish that his son had praised in a letter and that, despite their misgivings, members of a local motorcycle gang share with him in a bizarre but nevertheless religious communion. As the cook explains, "'Love by policy, not just instinct.' That's the Art of Living." Rewarding and quietly effective as "Redemption," "Stillness," "Come on Back," and the title story are, *The Art of Living, and Other Stories* as a whole lacks the disruptive energies that characterize *The King's Indian* and that make its affirmations aesthetically as well as morally interesting.

OTHER MAJOR WORKS

LONG FICTION: *The Resurrection*, 1966; *The Wreckage of Agathon*, 1970; *Grendel*, 1971; *The Sunlight Dialogues*, 1972; *Nickel Mountain: A Pastoral Novel*, 1973; *October Light*, 1976; *In the Suicide Mountains*, 1977; *Freddy's Book*, 1980; *Mickelsson's Ghosts*, 1982; "Stillness" and "Shadows," 1986 (Nicholas Delbanco, editor).

PLAYS: *The Temptation Game*, pr. 1977 (radio play); *Death and the Maiden*, pb. 1979; *Frankenstein*, pb. 1979 (libretto); *Rumpelstiltskin*, pb. 1979 (libretto); *William Wilson*, pb. 1979 (libretto).

POETRY: *Jason and Medeia*, 1973; *Poems*, 1978.

NONFICTION: *The Construction of the Wakefield Cycle*, 1974; *The Construction of Christian Poetry in Old English*, 1975; *The Life and Times of Chaucer*, 1977; *The Poetry of Chaucer*, 1977; *On Moral Fiction*, 1978; *On Becoming a Novelist*, 1983; *The Art of Fiction: Notes on Craft for Young Writers*, 1984; *On Writers and Writing*, 1994 (Stewart O'Nan, editor); *Lies! Lies! Lies! A College Journal of John Gardner*, 1999.

TRANSLATIONS: *Tengu Child*, 1983 (of Kikuo Itaya's *Tengu dōji*; with Nobuko Tsukui); *Gilgamesh*, 1984 (with John Maier).

CHILDREN'S LITERATURE: *Dragon, Dragon, and Other Tales*, 1975; *Gudgekin the Thistle Girl, and Other Tales*, 1976; *A Child's Bestiary*, 1977; *The King of the Hummingbirds, and Other Tales*, 1977.

EDITED TEXTS: *The Forms of Fiction*, 1962 (with Lennis Dunlap); *The Complete Works of the Gawain-Poet*, 1965; *Papers on the Art and Age of Geoffrey Chaucer*, 1967 (with Nicholas Joost); *The Alliterative "Morte d'Arthure," "The Owl and the Nightingale," and Five Other Middle English Poems*, 1971.

BIBLIOGRAPHY

Chavkin, Allan, ed. *Conversations with John Gardner*. Jackson: University Press of Mississippi, 1990. Although the nineteen interviews collected here represent only a fraction of the number that the loquacious Gardner conducted, they are among the most important and are nicely complemented by Chavkin's analysis of the larger Gardner in his introduction.

Cowart, David. *Arches and Light: The Fiction of John Gardner*. Carbondale: Southern Illinois University Press, 1983. Like so many Gardner critics, Cowart is too willing to take Gardner at his (moral fiction) word. Cowart is, however, an intelligent and astute reader. He devotes separate chapters to *The King's Indian*, the children's stories, and *The Art of Living, and Other Stories*.

Fenlon, Katherine Feeney. "John Gardner's 'The Ravages of Spring' as Re-creation of 'The Fall of the House of Usher.'" *Studies in Short Fiction* 31 (Summer, 1994): 481-487. Shows how Gardner re-creates Edgar Allan Poe's story and Americanizes its details, providing a comprehensive interpretation of "The Fall of the House of Usher." Argues that Gardner's story, which compares dreaming to artistic creation, interprets what happens in Poe's story as the construction of the artwork.

Haswell, Janis. "John Gardner's Moral Worldview: Queen Louisa Incarnate." *Antigonish Review* 153 (Spring, 2008): 119-138. Analyzes Gardner's unpublished manuscripts, plays, interviews, nonfiction works, and other writings to examine his moral theory. Haswell argues that this analysis demonstrates Gardner's faith in the "moral dimensions of human experience," and she provides a detailed reading of Gardner's series of four short stories about Queen Louisa in order to further prove her thesis.

Henderson, Jeff. *John Gardner: A Study of the Short Fiction*. Boston: Twayne, 1990. Henderson provides a detailed and comprehensive analysis of *The King's Indian, The Art of Living, and Other Stories*, the tales for children, and Gardner's last published story, "Julius Caesar and the Werewolf." Includes previously unpublished Gardner materials and excerpts from previously published studies.

_____, ed. *Thor's Hammer: Essays on John Gardner*. Conway: University of Central Arkansas Press, 1985. Of the fifteen original essays collected here, two will be of special interest to students of the short fiction: John Howell's excellent and groundbreaking essay on "Redemption" and Robert A. Morace's overview of Gardner's critical reception.

McWilliams, Dean. *John Gardner*. Boston: Twayne, 1990. McWilliams includes little biographical material and does not try to be at all comprehensive, yet he has an interesting and certainly original thesis: that Gardner's fiction may be more fruitfully approached via Mikhail Bakhtin's theory of dialogism than via *On Moral Fiction*. Unfortunately, the chapters on the novels and his poetry collection *Jason and Medeia* tend to be rather introductory in approach and only rarely dialogical in focus.

Morace, Robert A. *John Gardner: An Annotated Secondary Bibliography*. New York: Garland, 1984. Morace lists and annotates in detail all known speeches and interviews with Gardner and reviews and criticism of his work.

Morace, Robert A., and Kathryn Van Spanckeren, eds. *John Gardner: Critical Perspectives*. Carbondale: Southern Illinois University Press, 1982. This first book devoted to criticism of Gardner's work includes a discussion of "Vlemk the Box-Painter" (in Morace's introduction), separate essays on *The King's Indian* and the children's stories, and Gardner's afterword.

Morris, Gregory L. *A World of Order and Light: The Fiction of John Gardner*. Athens: University of Georgia Press, 1984. In his chapters on *The King's Indian* and *The Art of Living, and Other Stories*, Morris, like David Cowart, stays within the framework that Gardner himself established. Unlike Cowart, however, Morris contends that moral art is a process by which order is discovered, not, as Cowart believes, made.

Silesky, Barry. *John Gardner: Literary Outlaw*. Chapel Hill, N.C.: Algonquin Books of Chapel Hill, 2004. Recounts Gardner's life from his childhood near Batavia, New York, to his death in a motorcycle accident at the age of forty-nine. Maintains that Gardner strove frantically to attain literary greatness as the result of a childhood accident, in which his brother was killed by a farm machine that Gardner was driving, leaving the writer with a lifelong sense of guilt and of his own mortality.

Yardley, Jonathan. "The Moral of the Story." *The Washington Post*, April 17, 1994, p. X3. A review of Gardner's *On Writers and Writing*, a collection of his reviews and literary essays. Discusses Gardner's controversial insistence on fiction that was moral and affirmative and his distaste for fiction that celebrated technique for its own sake or for the sake of the author's personal amusement.

Robert A. Morace

HAMLIN GARLAND

Born: West Salem, Wisconsin; September 14, 1860
Died: Hollywood, California; March 4, 1940

PRINCIPAL SHORT FICTION

Main-Travelled Roads: Six Mississippi Valley
    Stories, 1891
Prairie Folks, 1893
Wayside Courtships, 1897
Other Main-Travelled Roads, 1910
They of the High Trails, 1916
The Book of the American Indian, 1923

OTHER LITERARY FORMS

Hamlin Garland's published works include nearly every literary type--novels, biography, autobiography, essays, dramas, and poems. His best and most memorable novels are *Rose of Dutcher's Coolly* (1895), similar in plot to the later Theodore Dreiser novel, *Sister Carrie* (1900), and *Boy Life on the Prairie* (1899), chronicling the social history of Garland's boyhood. One book of essays, *Crumbling Idols: Twelve Essays on Art* (1894), presents his theory of realism ("veritism"). His autobiographical quartet, *A Son of the Middle Border* (1917), *A Daughter of the Middle Border* (1921), *Trail-Makers of the Middle Border* (1926), and *Back-Trailers from the Middle Border* (1928), recounts the story of his family. *A Daughter of the Middle Border* won the Pulitzer Prize for 1922. These books contain episodes that are treated in greater detail in some of his short stories.

ACHIEVEMENTS

Hamlin Garland's work stands at an important transition point from Romanticism to realism, playing a role in ushering in the new literary trend. His best works are important for their depiction of a segment of society seldom delineated by other writers and for the relationship they show between literature and its socio-economic environment. He used American themes, rather than Americanized European themes, and commonplace characters and incidents that turned American writers away from their colonial complex, even away from the New England tradition of letters. His realism emancipated the American Midwest and West, and the American farmer particularly, from the romanticized conception that kept their stories from being told before. Like Walt Whitman, Garland wanted writers to tell about life as they knew it and witnessed it. His realism foreshadowed the work of young writers such as Stephen Crane, E. W. Howe, and Harold Frederic. His naturalistic inclination, apparent in his belief that environment is crucial in shaping people's lives, preceded the naturalistic writing of Crane, Frank Norris, and Dreiser. Aside from their value as literature, Garland's best stories are a comprehensive record of an otherwise relatively unreported era of American social history. Much read in his prime, he enjoyed considerable popularity, even while antagonizing with his merciless word pictures the very people about whom he wrote. Garland was awarded honorary degrees from the University of Wisconsin, the University of Southern California, Northwestern University, and Beloit College. In 1918, he was elected to the board of directors of the American Academy of Arts and Letters. He won the Pulitzer Prize for Biography and Autobiography in 1922.

BIOGRAPHY

Of Scotch-Irish descent, Hannibal Hamlin Garland moved with his family from Wisconsin, where he was born in West Salem on September 14, 1860, to an Iowa farm while still a child. Years spent on the farm made him seek escape through a career in oratory. To this end, he attended Cedar Valley Seminary, from which he was graduated in 1881. He held a land claim in North Dakota for a year, but mortgaged it for the chance to go East and enroll in Boston University. He succeeded in getting to Boston but was unable to attend the university; however, he embarked on a self-directed program of reading in the holdings of the Boston Public Library. While in Boston, he began writing, his first attempts being lectures, then stories and books. It was also around this time that he joined the Anti-Poverty Society and became an active reformer. He read Henry George and embraced the Single Tax theory as a solution to some of the many contemporary social problems.

Donald Pizer, along with many scholars, divides Garland's career into three general phases: a period of political and social reform activity that coincides with his most memorable fiction set in the Middle West (1884-1895); a period of popular romance writing in which his settings shifted from the Midwest to the Rocky Mountains (1896-1916); and a period of increasing political and social conservatism, during which he wrote his major autobiographical works (1917-1940). In 1899, Garland married Zulime Taft, and they became parents of daughters born in 1904 and 1907. His list of acquaintances and friends grew to include such literary figures as William Dean Howells, Eugene Field, Joseph Kirkland, Edward Eggleston, Frank Norris, Stephen Crane, George Bernard Shaw, and Rudyard Kipling.

Garland lived the last years of his life in Hollywood, where he could be near his married daughter. In these later years, he turned more seriously to a lifelong fascination with the occult, producing two books on the subject. He died of cerebral hemorrhage in Hollywood on March 4, 1940.

ANALYSIS

Hamlin Garland's most enduring short stories are those dealing with the Middle Border--the prairie lands of Iowa, Wisconsin, Minnesota, Nebraska, and the Dakotas. Collected for the most part in four books, they touch on nearly every subject of everyday life, from birth through youth, adulthood, courtship, and marriage, to death. They deal with the unromantic life of harassed generations on the farms and in the small towns of the prairie. Garland's belief that an author must write of "what is" with an eye toward "what is to

be" causes him alternately to describe, prophesy, suggest, and demand. Although often subtle in his approach, he is sometimes, when championing the cause of the farmer, more the reformer than the artist. Social protest is the single most recurrent theme in his work. "A Stopover at Tyre" and "Before the Low Green Door" show with some skill the unrelenting drudgery of the farmer's life.

"UNDER THE LION'S PAW"

"Under the Lion's Paw," Garland's most anthologized story, is his most powerful statement of protest. In it, one man, Tim Haskins, like thousands of struggling farmers, is exploited by another man, representative of scores of other land speculators. Haskins, through months of arduous labor, pushing his own and his wife's energies to their limits, has managed to make the dilapidated farm he is renting a productive place of which he can be proud. He has begun to feel confident that he can buy the farm and make a success of it. The owner, however, has taken note of the many physical improvements Haskins has made and recognizes its increased value. Thus, when Haskins talks to

Hamlin Garland (Library of Congress

the owner about buying the place, he is astonished to learn that the purchase price has doubled and the rent has been increased. Haskins is "under the lion's paw," caught in untenable circumstances that will hurt him no matter what he does. If he gives up the farm, as his angry indignation dictates, he will lose all the money and time he has invested in the farm's improvements. If he buys, he will be under a heavy mortgage that could be foreclosed at any time. If he continues to rent at the higher fee, all his work will almost literally be for the owner's benefit, not for himself and his family. The personally satisfying alternative of simply striking the man dead is wildly considered by Haskins momentarily until the thought of the repercussions to his family brings him to his senses, and he agrees to buy on the owner's terms. The situation in itself is cruel. Garland clearly shows that it is even worse when one realizes that the exploitation of Haskins is only one of thousands of similar cases.

"Lucretia Burns"

"Lucretia Burns," another social protest story, is longer and has more action and a more complex major character than the similar "Before the Low Green Door." Although some of its impact is diminished by its tiresome discussions of reform and by its weak denouement, Garland has created in Lucretia an unforgettable character who makes the story praiseworthy. Lucretia is a strong personality who had "never been handsome, even in her days of early childhood, and now she was middle-aged, distorted with work and childbearing, and looking faded and worn." Her face is "a pitifully worn, almost tragic face--long, thin, sallow, hollow-eyed. The mouth had long since lost the power to shape itself into a kiss. . . ." She has reached a point of desperation that calls for some kind of action: confrontation (with her husband), capitulation, or a mental breakdown. She chooses to renounce her soul-killing existence and operate on a level of bare subsistence, with no more struggling to "get ahead" or do what is expected. When the spirit of rebellion overcomes her, she simply gives in to her chronic weariness and refuses to do more than feed her children and the husband for whom she no longer cares.

For a successful conclusion to this powerful indictment against the farm wife's hopeless life, Garland had several choices. Unfortunately, he chose the ineffectual ending in which a dainty, young, idealistic schoolteacher persuades Lucretia to give life another try. The reader, having seen Lucretia's determination to stop the drudgery in her life forever, is dissatisfied, knowing it would have taken a great deal more than a sympathetic stranger to convince Lucretia that her life was worth enduring.

"A Sociable at Dudleys"

This kind of lapse is not Garland's only flaw. Occasionally, he leads on his readers, telling them what they should think about a character. In "A Sociable at Dudleys," for example, he describes the county bully: "No lizard revelled in the mud more hideously than he. . . . His tongue dropped poison." Garland apparently abhorred the "vileness of the bully's whole life and thought." Moreover, in most of the stories, one can tell the heroes from the villains by the Aryan features and Scottish names of the former and the dark, alien looks of the latter. His heroes are further categorized into two prevailing physical types: Either they are tall, imposing, strong, even powerful and handsome (Tim Haskins is an older, more worn version of this type) or they are stocky, sturdy, ambitious, cheerful, and optimistic counterparts of the young Hamlin Garland as he described himself in *A Son of the Middle Border*. Will Hannan of "A Branch Road" falls into the latter category.

"A Branch Road"

"A Branch Road" develops another favorite theme of Garland--a romantic one in which boy meets girl; misunderstanding separates them; and then adversity reunites them. Although this plot is well worn today, in the late 1800's and early 1900's, the reading public still liked it, and Garland occasionally catered to the larger reading public. "A Branch Road" is long enough for the author to develop character, setting, and plot in a more leisurely, less personal manner than in some of his other stories on the same theme, such as "A Day of Grace," "A Sociable at Dudleys," and "William Bacon's Man." In "A Branch Road," young Will Hannan and Agnes Dingman have fallen in love. Will is ecstatic when he goes to the Dingman farm to help with the threshing, secure in his belief that she cares as much for him as he for her.

Once at the farm, however, listening to the other men, both young and older, making casual, joking comments about Agnes's prettiness and her attraction to most of the young swains in the county, Will becomes apprehensive that they will notice her obvious preference for him and make light of his deep private feelings. To prevent this, he repays her smiling attentions to him with curt words and an aloof manner. Agnes is hurt and confused by his behavior, not understanding his masculine pride and sensitivity to ridicule. She responds by keeping up a lighthearted demeanor by smiling and talking to the other men, who are delighted, a response that makes Will rage inwardly. The day is a disaster for Will, but because he is to take Agnes to the fair in a few days, he is confident that he will be able then to set things right.

On the morning of the day of the fair, however, the hopeful lover sets out early, but promptly loses a wheel from his buggy, requiring several hours of delay for repair. By the time he gets to Agnes's house, she has gone to the fair with Will's rival, Ed Kinney. Will is so enraged by this turn of events that he cannot think. Dominated by his pride and jealous passion, blaming her and considering no alternatives, he leaves the county, heading West, without a word of farewell or explanation to Agnes.

Seven years later he returns to find Agnes married to Ed Kinney, mother of a baby, daughter-in-law to two pestering old people, and distressingly old before her time. Will manages to speak privately to her and learns how he and she had misunderstood each other's actions on that day long ago. He finds she had indeed loved him. He accepts that it is his fault her life is now so unhappy, that she is so abused and worn. In defiance of custom and morality, he persuades her to leave her husband and go away with him. They flee, taking her baby with them.

In outline, this is the familiar melodrama of the villain triumphing over the fair maiden while the hero is away; then, just in time, the hero returns to rescue the heroine from the villain's clutches. Actually, however, Garland avoids melodrama and even refrains from haranguing against farm drudgery. He avoids the weak denouement and chooses instead a rather radical solution to the problem: The abduction of a wife and baby by another man was a daring ending to an American 1890's plot. Garland, however, makes the justice of this action acceptable.

Will Hannan, a very sensitive young man living among people who seem coarse and crude, is propelled through the story by strong, understandable emotions: love, pride, anger, fear of humiliation, remorse, pity, and guilt. Love causes the anger that creates the confusion in his relationship with Agnes. Pride and fear of humiliation drive him away from her. Remorse pursues him all the time he is away and is largely responsible for his return. Pity and guilt make him steal Agnes away from the life to which he feels he has condemned her. Many of Garland's other stories do not have the emotional motivation of characters that "A Branch Road" has (in all fairness, most are not as long); nor are Garland's characters generally as complex. He seems less concerned with probing a personality's reaction to a situation than with describing the consequences of an act.

The theme of the return of the native to his Middle Border home is used in several stories, among them "Up the Coolly," "Mrs. Ripley's Trip," and "Among the Corn Rows."

"THE RETURN OF A PRIVATE"

Less pessimistic and tragic and more sentimental than these stories is "The Return of a Private," an elaboration of Garland's father's return from the Civil War as told in the first chapter of *A Son of the Middle Border*. The story describes the sadness which old war comrades feel as they go their separate ways home. It describes the stirring emotions that the returning soldier feels as he nears his home and sees familiar landmarks; when he first catches sight of the homestead; and when he sees his nearly disbelieving wife and the children who hardly remember him. They are tender scenes, but Garland the artist cannot contain Garland the reformer, who reminds the reader of the futility facing the soldier, handicapped physically from war-connected fever and ague and handicapped financially by the heavy mortgage on his farm. The soldier's homecoming is shown as one tiny, bright moment in what has been and will continue to be an endless cycle of dullness and hardship. Garland obviously empathizes with the character and shows the homecoming as a sweet, loving time, but, like so many of his stories, "The Return of a Private" is overcast with gloom.

Garland's stories depict the ugly and the beautiful, the tragic with the humorous, the just with the unjust. He tries always to show the truth, reporting the speech and dress of the people accurately, describing their homes and their work honestly. Truth, however, is not all that he seeks; he wants significance as well. To this end, his stories show the effects of farm drudgery on the men and women, of the ignorant practices of evangelists, and of the thwarted ambitions of the youth because of circumstances beyond their control. Garland does not always suppress his reformer's instincts, and so in some stories he offers solutions. In his best stories, however, he simply shows the injustice and moves the reader, by his skillful handling of details, to wish to take action. Although his stories are often bitter and depressing, there is a hopefulness and optimism in Garland that compels him to bring them to a comparatively happy ending. In his best stories, he does for the Middle Border what Mary E. Wilkins Freeman does for New England, brings the common people into rich relation with the reader and shows movingly the plights of the less fortunate among them, especially women.

OTHER MAJOR WORKS

LONG FICTION: *A Little Norsk*, 1892; *A Member of the Third House*, 1892; *A Spoil of Office*, 1892; *Jason Edwards: An Average Man*, 1892; *Rose of Dutcher's Coolly*, 1895; *The Spirit of Sweetwater*, 1898 (reissued as *Witch's Gold*, 1906); *Boy Life on the Prairie*, 1899; *The Eagle's Heart*, 1900; *Her Mountain Lover*, 1901; *The Captain of the Gray-Horse Troop*, 1902; *Hesper*, 1903; *The Light of the Star*, 1904; *The Tyranny of the Dark*, 1905; *Money Magic*, 1907 (reissued as *Mart Haney's Mate*, 1922); *The Long Trail*, 1907; *The Moccasin Ranch*, 1909; *Cavanagh, Forest Ranger*, 1910; *Victor Ollnee's Discipline*, 1911; *The Forester's Daughter*, 1914.

PLAY: *Under the Wheel: A Modern Play in Six Scenes*, pb. 1890.

POETRY: *Prairie Songs*, 1893.

NONFICTION: *Crumbling Idols: Twelve Essays on Art*, 1894; *Ulysses S. Grant: His Life and Character*, 1898; *Out-of-Door Americans*, 1901; *A Son of the Middle Border*, 1917; *A Daughter of the Middle Border*, 1921; *Trail-Makers of the Middle Border*, 1926; *The Westward March of American Settlement*, 1927; *Back-Trailers from the Middle Border*, 1928; *Roadside Meetings*, 1930; *Companions on the Trail: A Literary Chronicle*, 1931; *My Friendly Contemporaries: A Literary Log*, 1932; *Afternoon Neighbors*, 1934; *Joys of the Trail*, 1935; *Forty Years of Psychic Research: A Plain Narrative of Fact*, 1936; *Selected Letters of Hamlin Garland*, 1998 (Keith Newlin and Joseph B. McCullough, editors).

MISCELLANEOUS: *Hamlin Garland, Prairie Radical: Writings from the 1890s*, 2010 (Donald Pizer, editor).

BIBLIOGRAPHY

Garland, Hamlin. *Selected Letters of Hamlin Garland*. Edited by Keith Newlin and Joseph B. McCullough. Lincoln: University of Nebraska Press, 1998. The introduction serves as a good entry into Hamlin's biography.

Joseph, Philip. "The Artist Meets the Rural Community: Hamlin Garland, Sarah Orne Jewett, and the Writings of 1890's Regionalism." In *American Literary Regionalism in a Global Age*. Baton Rouge: Louisiana State University Press, 2007. A study of regionalist authors who, in Joseph's opinion, share a vision of local communities engaged in "open discourse" with a wider world. Examines Garland's short and long fiction to demonstrate how his work fits this definition.

_____. "Landed and Literary: Hamlin Garland, Sarah Orne Jewett, and the Production of Regional Literatures." *Studies in American Fiction* 26 (Autumn, 1998): 147-170. Compares some of Garland's early stories with the stories in Jewett's *Country of the Pointed Firs* to examine ideological conflict within literary regionalism. Argues that while Garland's support for social reform leads him to challenge some of the conventions of late nineteenth century realism, Jewett does not see class differences as a hindrance to American destiny.

Kaye, Frances. "Hamlin Garland's Feminism." In *Women and Western Literature*, edited by Helen Winter Stauffer and Susan Rosowski. Troy, N.Y.: Whitston, 1982. Kaye discusses Garland's deliberate feminism, identifying him as the only male author of note at the end of the nineteenth century who spoke in favor of women's rights, suffrage, and equality in marriage.

Martin, Quentin E. "Hamlin Garland's 'The Return of a Private' and 'Under the Lion's Paw' and the Monopoly of Money in Post-Civil War America." *American Literary Realism* 29 (Fall, 1996): 62-77. Discusses how Garland made money and power the central features in these two stories. Discusses the connection between the stories and the financial system of Gilded Age America in the 1890's.

McCullough, Joseph. *Hamlin Garland*. Boston: Twayne, 1978. Follows Garland through his literary career, dividing it into phases, with major attention to the first phase of his reform activities and the midwestern stories. A primary bibliography and a select, annotated secondary bibliography are included.

Nagel, James, ed. *Critical Essays on Hamlin Garland*. Boston: G. K. Hall, 1982. Nagel's introduction surveys the critical responses to Garland's work. This volume is especially rich in reviews of Garland's books, and it also includes twenty-six biographical and critical essays.

Newlin, Keith, ed. *Hamlin Garland: A Bibliography, with a Checklist of Unpublished Letters*. Troy, N.Y.: Whitston, 1998. Basically a primary bibliography, with one section listing articles that address Garland extensively. The introduction surveys the availability of primary and secondary sources. Newlin includes a chronology and title index.

_____. *Hamlin Garland: A Life*. Lincoln: University of Nebraska, 2008. A comprehensive look at Garland's life and career, including his political activity, his interest in the American West, and his memoirs. By far the most thorough biography of Garland to date.

_____. "Melodramatist of the Middle Border: Hamlin Garland's Early Work Reconsidered." *Studies in American Fiction* 21 (Autumn, 1993): 153-169. Discusses Garland's development of a dramatic method to express the privation of the Middle Border. Argues that he was torn between his admiration for the universal truths of melodrama and his realization that melodrama was limited in its realistic presentation of life.

Pizer, Donald. *Hamlin Garland's Early Work and Career*. Berkeley: University of California Press, 1960. Pizer treats in careful detail Garland's intellectual and artistic development during the first phase of his literary and reformist career, from 1884 to 1895. He discusses Garland's development of his creed, his literary output, and his reform activities in society, theater, politics, and the arts. Includes a detailed bibliography of Garland's publications during these years.

Scofield, Martin. "Realism, the Grotesque, and Impressionism in Hamlin Garland, Ambrose Bierce, and Stephen Crane." In *The Cambridge Introduction to the American Short Story*. New York: Cambridge University Press, 2006. Defines Garland's place in the history of American short fiction and analyzes several of his short stories.

Silet, Charles, Robert Welch, and Richard Boudreau, eds. *The Critical Reception of Hamlin Garland, 1891-1978*. Troy, N.Y.: Whitston, 1985. Contains thirty-three essays that illustrate the development of Garland's literary reputation from 1891 to 1978. The introduction emphasizes the difficulty critics have had trying to determine the quality of Garland's art.

Teorey, Matthew. "Escaping the Lion's Paw: Jungle Cat Imagery and Late-Nineteenth-Century Political Reform." *ANQ* 18, no. 1 (Winter, 2006): 42-47. Examines how Garland and political cartoonist Thomas Nast symbolically used the lion or tiger to criticize American corruption, greed, and oppression. Analyzes Garland's story "Under the Lion's Paw" to demonstrate how his writing depicted the hardships of American farmers.

Jane L. Ball
Updated by Terry Heller

GEORGE GARRETT

Born: Orlando, Florida; June 11, 1929
Died: Charlottesville, Virginia; May 25, 2008

PRINCIPAL SHORT FICTION

King of the Mountain, 1958
In the Briar Patch, 1961
Cold Ground Was My Bed Last Night, 1964
A Wreath for Garibaldi, and Other Stories, 1969
The Magic Striptease, 1973
To Recollect a Cloud of Ghosts: Christmas in England, 1602-1603, 1979
An Evening Performance: New and Selected Stories, 1985
The Old Army Game: A Novel and Stories, 1994
Bad Man Blues: A Portable George Garrett, 1998
A Story Goes with It, 2004
Empty Bed Blues, 2006

OTHER LITERARY FORMS

Although early in his career George Garrett was best known as a poet, he later gained recognition as an important contemporary novelist. He wrote several plays and screenplays, and his screenplay *The Young Lovers* (1964) has become a cult favorite. Garrett received particular acclaim for his historical novels, *Death of the Fox* (1971) and *The Succession: A Novel of Elizabeth and James* (1983), both set in Elizabethan England. Garrett also wrote a biography and critical studies, and he wrote, edited, and contributed to many books and journals on film, writing, and literary criticism. In 1998, *Days of Our Lives Lie in Fragments: New and Old Poems, 1957-1997,* a collection of his poems, was published. In the twenty-first century, he published a novel, *Double Vision* (2004), and two nonfiction books, *Going to See the Elephant: Pieces of a Writing Life* (2002) and *Southern Excursions: Views on Southern Letters in*

My Time (2003), in addition to two short-story collections, *A Story Goes with It* and *Empty Bed Blues.*

ACHIEVEMENTS

Through his teaching, editing, and writing, Garrett influenced contemporary American letters directly and significantly, and he was the recipient of many awards and honors. He was awarded fellowships from the National Endowment for the Arts and the John Simon Guggenheim Memorial Foundation, the Rome Prize of the American Academy of Arts and Letters, and a Ford Foundation grant. He also received the T. S. Eliot Award for creative writing from the Ingersoll Foundation (1989), the PEN/Malamud Award for short fiction (1991), the Hollins College Medal (1992), an honorary doctorate from the University of the South (1994), the Aiken-Taylor Award (1999), a Lifetime Achievement Award from the Library of Virginia (2004), the Cleanth Brooks Medal for Lifetime Achievement from the Fellowship of Southern Writers (2005), and the Carole Weinstein Poetry Prize (2006).

BIOGRAPHY

George Palmer Garrett, Jr., was born on June 11, 1929, in Orlando, Florida, one of three children and the only son of George Palmer and Rosalie Toomer Garrett. He was graduated from Sewanee Military Academy in 1946 and prepped at the Hill School in 1946-1947 before entering Princeton University. He was graduated from there in 1952 magna cum laude and a member of Phi Beta Kappa. He earned his M.A. in English from Princeton University in 1956 with a thesis on the poetry of William Faulkner, a work of scholarship that is still read by scholars who want to know the early Faulkner's work. Garrett enlisted in the U.S. Army Reserves in 1950, and he was soon called to perform two years of active duty in Yugoslavia and Austria before finishing his M.A. Garrett completed all work for a doctorate except for the dissertation;

Princeton accepted his novels *Death of the Fox* and *The Succession* as fulfilling the dissertation requirement and awarded him a Ph.D. in 1985. Active in mentoring young writers, Garrett held teaching positions at a number of universities, including the University of South Carolina, Columbia University, Princeton University, and the University of Virginia. In 1984, he became the Hoyns Professor of English at the University of Virginia at Charlottesville. In 1952, he married Susan Parrish Jackson, and the couple had three children. Garrett died at his home in Virginia on May 25, 2008.

ANALYSIS

George Garrett's work spans many genres. Considered both a poet and fiction writer of considerable importance, Garrett produced a body of work that is varied, substantial, and highly regarded. In his two historical novels, *Death of the Fox* and *The Succession*, Garrett is considered to have elevated the level of a popular literary form to that of serious art. In his poetry and his fiction, Garrett's topics alternately range from classical to popular cultures, thus revealing and providing a unique perspective, which at once embraces the ancient and the modern.

"COLD GROUND WAS MY BED LAST NIGHT"

One of Garrett's persistent themes has been that of man's experience as prisoner. In "Cold Ground Was My Bed Last Night," all the characters are prisoners, no matter what side of the bars they live on, or whether, like the Goat Man, they live in the shifting netherworld between imprisonment de facto and imprisonment de jure. The story opens as deputy Larry Berlin, coming back to the county seat after patrolling all night, is almost hit by a car coming around a curve too quickly. Enraged, he turns around and chases the car, overtakes it, and slides to a halt across its front, forcing the driver to stop. The driver gets out and, pulls out a gun, and the deputy kills him with one shot. Then he discovers that there is someone else inside.

Meanwhile, the sheriff, Jack Riddle, is waiting for Berlin and his prisoner at the sheriff's office and half-seriously threatening the Goat Man, a habitué of the jail, with ninety days if he is caught drunk and disorderly again. He saves a little face, mostly for the sake

of the Goat Man, by saying he does not want the goats to starve. The Goat Man, or the Balloon Man, is a leitmotif in Garrett's work, surfacing in places as disparate as the last scene of *The Young Lovers* and the long story about Quirk. Here, he represents Nature, mindless, oblivious to law or regulation, and incorrigible, something that can imprison one if one believes that Nature will yield to rationalities. The sheriff is unusual; he carries no gun and is not without some compassion. Like most of Garrett's best characters, he is a man of the religious mode. In the office, there is a magazine open to the picture of a naked woman. She is the banal and two-dimensional embodiment of that goddess whom Riddle serves--respectability. The pinup is joined in the close, hot, dirty office by a fly, another objective correlative, this time of life itself, oblivious, buzzing, annoying life. Moreover, the fly seems to be the presiding genius of the place, its totem animal.

Ike Toombs, the other man in the car, is brought in. The sheriff envies him because he represents the open road; he is a shabby modern version of the wayfaring life, but he is a wayfarer nevertheless, and he even sings a verse of the traditional song that gives its name to this story. The sheriff sees in him almost a kindred spirit: Both men are chivalric figures, knight and troubadour.

This illusion, however, soon begins to break down. The prisoner tries to wheedle his release from the sheriff, who has established some kind of tacit understanding with the prisoner. Next, officers from the state police call and report that a service station has been held up and a teenage boy was shot the night before by a man driving the car in which Toombs was riding. His friend of the moment has decided Toombs's fate for him, and Toombs has had no hand in it; for now the disappointed sheriff is thrown back on his resources, which are meager once his confidence in himself and his faith in freedom are shaken. The sheriff angrily rejects the wayfarer even though he knows the jury will no doubt convict him on the basis of the circumstantial evidence. He refuses him his old cheap guitar, an act that brings tears to the eyes of the prisoner, and he throws the magazine away. One man has been killed, another sentenced, and another has died a spiritual death.

"A WREATH FOR GARIBALDI"

In another story, "A Wreath for Garibaldi," an American in Rome who "works" at the American Academy, a man who never names himself or is named, is at a party at which an Englishwoman he admires wants to recruit a volunteer to lay a wreath under the huge bronze statue of Giuseppe Garibaldi. There is an awkward silence. Political tension is very strong in Rome that year, old fascists and new radicals are looking very portentous, and a huge scandal has occurred because of an "orgy" at a big party. The government is obsessed with the idea that because Garibaldi Day is April 30 and the next day is May Day, the international holiday that in Europe is New Year, Easter, and Christmas all rolled into one for the Second, Third, and Fourth Internationals, any wreath honoring Garibaldi is probably a communist provocation.

The American volunteers to lay the wreath at Garibaldi's statue on the condition that he do it alone, without any press, just a simple gesture, but he has to go through the ambassador to get permission. He is also asked to leave "a little bunch of flowers" at the bust of the antifascist poet Lauro di Bosis. In the course of his official dealings with the government, he finds that the bureaucrats do not know who di Bosis is. It is all too evident that everyone knows who Garibaldi is. The American is supposed to lay the wreath the next day, but he decides not to go through with it; it was not going to measure up to what the English lady had wanted done. He goes to where the statue of Garibaldi is. Garibaldi looks imperial. The equestrian statue of his wife, Anna, baby in arms, firing behind her, horse at full gallop, looks silly. He goes across to the bust of di Bosis-- "Pale, passionate, yes glorious, and altogether of another time. . . ." He thinks of those who died rushing the village in France in a stupid, pointless frontal attack, of those killed in police stations all over the civilized world, and his feelings change toward di Bosis: "It was a forlorn, foolish adolescent gesture. But it was a kind of beginning." He looks at the bust with "the feelings usually attributed to young girls standing at the grave of Keats."

"THE MAGIC STRIPTEASE"

The theme of mutability and the problem of the artist's acceptance are the two themes of Garrett's long short story, "The Magic Striptease," in the collection of the same name; the odd paradigms of grace and election have been set aside for the critics in this fable, which also has considerable stature as a moral fable. The story is about one Jacob Quirk, "Proteus of Impersonators," as he is briefly known, and the story is told through entries in Quirk's secret journal, through an omniscient narrator, and through trial transcripts. Through his racy, slangy, topical, simple-minded, vulgar, skeptical, weary, and thoroughly American diction, Garrett achieves some of his finest effects and creates a much-needed tension between the burdens of this long fiction and the expectations of his audience. The story follows Quirk through rapid, unremitting change, which happens, as does most change, as a result of inner and spiritual developments that inevitably bring about outer and tangible transformations.

In the State Orphan's Home, no one will adopt Quirk because, as the director says, no one wants a smart-aleck kid. Once grown, he becomes a nightclub performer specializing in impressions. At first, he impersonates famous persons, but this bores him, so he turns to people he has seen on the street, but he finds this approach unsuccessful. Quirk, therefore, tells his agent that he does not want to be funny any more, that he wants to be an artist. His agent explains that performing is a business, while art is for kids, and Quirk decides to leave him. He intends at first (as he says in his journal) to go where no poet or novelist has ever trod, despite the fact that he will be living characters that are fictional--in other words, that have no life once he leaves them. Moreover, he intends to use his talent coolly and logically.

Quirk's first impersonation is that of the neighborhood postman, whose duties he takes on. It is a sad and sobering experience for him. He discovers that a young man in the neighborhood is a drunkard. A woman upstairs offers herself for an eight-cent postage-due stamp; although her closets are overflowing with good clothes, she sleeps on an old ripped-up mattress, the only furniture in her apartment. Quirk's short tour of duty as a postman gives him "an intoxicated, dizzying sense of his own freedom" because he finds out that most people are totally incurious.

After more impersonations, all of them wildly successful, Quirk changes himself into a beautiful young man and through mere looks prompts a beautiful woman, obviously the mistress of an old, rich, and powerful man, to slip him a note suggesting an assignation at the intermission of the opera where they have just met for the first time. They leave, passing a legless beggar. "Beautiful people are a law unto themselves," she says, and Quirk decides to teach her a badly needed object lesson in humility--or at least this is how he explains it to himself; the reader will be wiser. So, after they have made love and the girl is asleep, Quirk changes into the legless beggar, wakes her up, and crab-scuttles out of the room. He has miscalculated, however--her mind is ruined by the experience. For the first time in his life, he has intentionally hurt another human being. Quirk decides to atone. He too becomes maimed, ugly, despised; now he mimes those who are prisoners of fate or their ugly bodies, just as he is a prisoner of his special talent, unique in all the world. Quirk learns that the types and varieties of suffering "exceeded all the possibilities and subtleties of pleasure."

Quirk decides to go forth and tell humanity what he has learned. Unfortunately, when he decides to do so through his impersonation of Jesus Christ, he is arrested and sent to an insane asylum. Now, with Quirk as artist and man, citizen and student of the human condition, at the end of his rope, Garrett expands the allegorical content of his story and has Quirk decide that insanity and suicide are the only options left to a man of sense, feeling, and breeding in this world. However, the drill of the insane asylum, once settled into, unfortunately leaves plenty of time to think, and once more Quirk ponders his art. After all his experiences, Quirk now realizes in a momentous revelation that all along he has been ignoring whole new realms that could be conquered by his art: the animal kingdom, even in the form of a stray dog. Even more extreme, he can become, because of his great artistry, inanimate--even a fire hydrant, which is below the dog, which is below the crazy, which is below the religious teacher, below the untouchable, and so on back up the spiral. His journal ends: "Just look for me where you find me."

BAD MAN BLUES

In the foreword to this collection of stories, essays, sketches, and anecdotes, Richard Bausch insists that there is no writer in America with a more versatile and "restless" talent than George Garrett. Indeed, this miscellany is eloquent testimony to Bausch's accolade. The most significant part of the book is the section of eight stories, the two most important of which are "A Letter That Will Never Be Written" and "Genius Baby." The former is set in 1626 and features characters from Garrett's well-known Elizabeth trilogy: *Death of the Fox, The Succession*, and *Entered from the Sun* (1990). In a short space, Garrett tackles religious obsession, political turmoil, and the creative vitality of Tudor England in an economical précis of the world of his trilogy treatment of the same material.

"Genius Baby," the most engaging story in the collection, is a comic rendering of a writer by a writer who refuses to take himself too seriously. Assuming the form of notes written on a yellow legal pad in a hospital lounge, the narrator tells about his decision to become a writer when, discovering that his wife was turned on by reading pornography and unable to find any of a literary quality, he began writing the stuff himself. However, the central focus of his account is his troubles with his gifted son Genius Baby, whom he cannot tolerate. The conflict between the two comes to a comic head when the child will not let his father in his room to watch Captain Kangaroo on Saturday morning, whereupon the narrator chops down the door with an ax and then destroys the television set and the rest of the furniture. The story ends when Genius Baby gets his revenge by putting alum in a glass of punch the father drinks, drying him up to absolute silence.

The title story of the collection, "Bad Man Blues," is a racial romp told with risky good humor by an African American man about the "last lynching" in Quincy County, Florida. The story is a classic tall tale, albeit about one of the most horrendous and stereotypical forms of racial persecution to take place in the South before the age of civil rights--the lynching of a black man accused of the rape-murder of a white woman. When the accused man, Buster Ford, the "baddest man to come out of Quincy County," is thrown to the lynch mob by the sheriff, he tricks them into chasing another black man and gets away; the ironic result is that the white folks in the town are so embarrassed at being outwitted by Buster that there has not been a lynching in Quincy County since.

In his essay, "Going to See the Elephant: Why We Write Stories," Garrett says the only advice he can give to aspiring young writers is that they are summoned to an "ancient and honorable enterprise" as old as the caves, where the people painted animals on the wall to illustrate stories. For Garrett, people become story-tellers because there is no choice; writers are like small boys "whistling in the dark, in a graveyard" to assure the dead that they are fearless.

OTHER MAJOR WORKS

LONG FICTION: *The Finished Man*, 1959; *Which Ones Are the Enemy?*, 1961; *Do, Lord, Remember Me*, 1965; *Death of the Fox*, 1971; *The Succession: A Novel of Elizabeth and James*, 1983; *Poison Pen*, 1986; *Entered from the Sun*, 1990; *The King of Babylon Shall Not Come Against You*, 1996; *Double Vision*, 2004.

PLAYS: *Garden Spot, U.S.A.*, pr. 1962; *Sir Slob and the Princess: A Play for Children*, pb. 1962; *Enchanted Ground*, pb. 1981.

SCREENPLAYS: *The Young Lovers*, 1964; *The Playground*, 1965; *Frankenstein Meets the Space Monster*, 1966 (with R. H. W. Dillard and John Rodenbeck).

POETRY: *The Reverend Ghost*, 1957; *The Sleeping Gypsy, and Other Poems*, 1958; *Abraham's Knife, and Other Poems*, 1961; *For a Bitter Season: New and Selected Poems*, 1967; *Welcome to the Medicine Show: Postcards, Flashcards, Snapshots*, 1978; *Luck's Shining Child: A Miscellany of Poems and Verses*, 1981; *The Collected Poems of George Garrett*, 1984; *Days of Our Lives Lie in Fragments: New and Old Poems, 1957-1997*, 1998.

NONFICTION: *James Jones*, 1984; *Understanding Mary Lee Settle*, 1988; *My Silk Purse and Yours: The Publishing Scene and American Literary Art*, 1992; *The Sorrows of Fat City: A Selection of Literary Essays and Reviews*, 1992; *Going to See the Elephant: Pieces of a Writing Life*, 2002 (Jeb Livingood, editor); *Southern Excursions: Views on Southern Letters in My Time*, 2003 (James Conrad McKinley, editor).

EDITED TEXTS: *New Writing from Virginia*, 1963; *The*

Girl in the Black Raincoat, 1966; *Man and the Movies*, 1967 (with W. R. Robinson); *New Writing in South Carolina*, 1971 (with William Peden); *The Sounder Few: Essays from "The Hollins Critic*,*"* 1971 (with R. H. W. Dillard and John Moore); *Film Scripts One, Two, Three, and Four*, 1971-1972 (with O. B. Hardison, Jr., and Jane Gelfman); *Craft So Hard to Learn*, 1972 (with John Graham); *The Writer's Voice*, 1973 (with Graham); *Intro 5*, 1974 (with Walton Beacham); *Intro 6: Life As We Know It*, 1974; *The Botteghe Oscure Reader*, 1974 (with Katherine Garrison Biddle); *Intro 7: All of Us and None of You*, 1975; *Intro 8: The Liar's Craft*, 1977; *Intro 9: Close to Home*, 1979 (with Michael Mewshaw); *Elvis in Oz: New Stories and Poems from the Hollins Creative Writing Program*, 1992 (with Mary Flinn); *The Wedding Cake in the Middle of the Road: Twenty-Three Variations on a Theme*, 1992 (with Susan Stamberg); *That's What I Like (About the South), and Other New Southern Stories for the Nineties*, 1993 (with Paul Ruffin); *The Yellow Shoe: Selected Poems, 1964-1999*, 1999.

MISCELLANEOUS: *Whistling in the Dark: True Stories and Other Fables*, 1992.

BIBLIOGRAPHY
Clabough, Casey. *The Art of the Magic Striptease: The Literary Layers of George Garrett*. Gainesville: University Press of Florida, 2008. Examines how Garrett "sheds skins or layers in his writing, becoming and articulating others while maintaining his own identity." Analyzes Garrett's experiments with form, genre, and storytelling.

_____. "George Garrett's South: A Literary Image." *Virginia Quarterly Review* 82, no. 2 (Spring, 2006): 284-296. Focuses on Garrett's conception of southern literature and its relationship to the rest of the United States and to the world. Examines how this concept is reflected in Garrett's fiction.

_____. "The Primary Story: George Garrett's Initiation Fiction." *Texas Review* 28, no. 1/2 (Spring/Summer, 2007): 57-80. Analyzes Garrett's fiction as a form of initiation story in which the protagonist attains a limited solution to an existential dilemma. Examines Garrett's stated belief that the "initial drama of early published fiction is the drama of finding one's voice."

Dillard, R. H. W. *Understanding George Garrett*. Columbia: University of South Carolina Press, 1988. The first major critical work on Garrett. Contains individual chapters on the novels *The Finished Man, Which Ones Are the Enemy?, Do, Lord, Remember Me, Poison Pen*, and the two historical novels, as well as a chapter on the poems and short stories. Supplemented by a helpful bibliography.

Garrett, George. "Going to See the Elephant: Why We Write Stories." In *Bad Man Blues: A Portable George Garrett*. Dallas, Tex.: Southern Methodist University Press, 1998. Garrett talks about growing up in a large family of storytellers. He discusses the deeper motivation of storytelling, suggesting that storytelling is similar to pygmies hunting an elephant and then relating the story of the hunt.

Horvath, Brooke, and Irving Malin, eds. *George Garrett: The Elizabethan Trilogy*. Huntsville, Tex.: Texas Review Press, 1998. A critical study of a number of historical figures as they relate to Garrett's work, including Sir Walter Raleigh and Christopher Marlowe. Includes a bibliography and index.

Mandelbaum, Paul, ed. *Twelve Short Stories and Their Making*. New York: Persea Books, 2005. Contains Garrett's story "A Record as Long as Your Arm," which Mandelbaum includes in order to exemplify the element of plot in short stories. The story is accompanied by Garrett's comments on this work.

Meriwether, James B. "George Palmer Garrett, Jr." *Princeton University Library Chronicle* 25, no. 1 (1963): 26-39. An introductory article on Garrett's work, acknowledging his excellence in poetry at the time when he was turning his attention more to fiction. Southern and family themes are noted. Complemented by a checklist of Garrett's writings.

Mill Mountain Review 1, no. 4 (Summer, 1971). This special issue on Garrett includes critical essays and personal comments by Fred Chappell, Gordon Lish, and others.

Robinson, W. R. "Imagining the Individual: George Garrett's *Death of the Fox*." *Hollins Critic* 8 (1971): 1-12. An exploration of the mixture of fact and creation that is inherent in fiction and the historical novel in particular, with extensive quotations from Garrett on the subject. Robinson argues that Garrett's work is a serious creation and surpasses conventional historical fiction.

Sheets, Anna J., ed. *Short Story Criticism: Excerpts from Criticism of the Works of Short Fiction Writers*. Vol. 30. Detroit: Gale Research, 1999. Includes excerpts from Garrett, Shmuel Yosef Agnon, Gina Berriault, Theodore Dreiser, Conrad Ferdinand Meyer, Emilia Pardo Bazán, and Leo Tolstoy.

Slavitt, David R. "History--Fate and Freedom: A Look at George Garrett's New Novel." *The Southern Review* 7 (1971): 276-294. In this lengthy first review of *Death of the Fox*, Slavitt examines the novel in relation to Garrett's earlier works and considers the creative process.

Spears, Monroe K. "George Garrett and the Historical Novel." *The Virginia Quarterly Review* 61, no. 2 (Spring, 1985): 262-276. Spears considers how closely *The Succession* and *Death of the Fox* correspond to the traditional definition of the historical novel.

Wier, Allen. "Skin and Bones: George Garrett's Living Spirits." In *Bad Man Blues: A Portable George Garrett*. Dallas, Tex.: Southern Methodist University Press, 1998. Discusses Garrett's interest in the relationship between fact and fiction and the relationship between the present and the past. Comments on Garrett's experimentation with ways of telling stories.

John Carr
Updated by Lou Thompson and Charles E. May

WILLIAM H. GASS

Born: Fargo, North Dakota; July 30, 1924

PRINCIPAL SHORT FICTION

In the Heart of the Heart of the Country, and Other Stories, 1968
The First Winter of My Married Life, 1979
The Cartesian Sonata, and Other Novellas, 1998

OTHER LITERARY FORMS

Besides his collections of short fiction, William H. Gass has published novels, including the well-known *Omensetter's Luck* (1966). He has also written several collections of essays featuring some of the most provocative literary theory of post-World War II literature, and the literary studies *Finding a Form* (1996) and *Reading Rilke: Reflections on the Problems of Translation* (1999).

ACHIEVEMENTS

William H. Gass is one of a handful of contemporary American writers who can justifiably be described as pioneers--that is, writers who eschew the well-trod ways of the mass of their fellow writers and chart new directions for literature. The fact that he has been as frequently assailed--most famously by the novelist John Gardner--as praised for his innovations is perhaps the best proof that Gass has indeed made his mark on the literary world. Along with John Barth, Donald Barthelme and a few other innovators, Gass has shown the reader the artifice behind the art of fiction. At the same time, he has created memorable characters involved in gripping conflicts. Rather than an experimenter or old-fashioned storyteller, however, Gass may best be seen as an impeccable stylist. It is this interest in the relation among the sounds of words that most clearly unifies his short fiction, novellas, novels, and essays.

Among his awards and honors are a Rockefeller Foundation Fellowship (in 1965), the Hovde Prize for Good Teaching (1967), a John Simon Guggenheim Memorial Foundation Fellowship (1969), and the National Institute for Arts and Letters prize for literature (1975). He has also received the National Medal of Merit for fiction (in 1979); three National Book Critics Circle Awards for criticism for *Habitations of the Word: Essays* (1985), *Finding a Form* (1996), and *Tests of Time: Essays* (2002); the Lifetime Achievement Award from the Lannan Foundation (1997); and the Truman Capote Award for Literary Criticism for *A Temple of Texts: Essays* (2007). In addition, Gass has been the recipient of honorary doctorates from Kenyon College, George Washington University, and Purdue University.

BIOGRAPHY

William Howard Gass attended Kenyon College in Gambier, Ohio, for one year and Ohio Wesleyan University in Delaware, Ohio, for a brief period of study. During World War II, he served in the U.S. Navy and was stationed in China and Japan. After the war he returned to Kenyon College and was graduated in 1947 with a B.A. degree in philosophy. He earned his Ph.D. from Cornell University in 1954. Gass has taught philosophy at a number of colleges, including the College of Wooster in Ohio (1950-1955), Purdue University in Lafayette, Indiana (1955-1969), and Washington University in St. Louis, where he began teaching in 1969 and where he held the title of David May Distinguished University Professor in the Humanities. In 1990, Gass became the first director of the International Writers' Center at Washington University. Gass married Mary Patricia O'Kelly in 1952; they had two children. In 1969, he married Mary Alice Henderson; they became the parents of twin daughters.

ANALYSIS

William H. Gass joins a number of contemporary writers--including John Barth and Alain Robbe-Grillet, among others--who have made a significant contribution to the development of short fiction while publishing a relatively small number of stories. Aside from a few uncollected stories published in journals (and most of these are sections of longer works in progress), Gass's initial contribution to short fiction rests on one slender collection, *In the Heart of the Heart of the Country, and Other Stories*, containing only five selections. However, these five are enough to show that Gass is a master of the form, at once innovative and adept at manipulating characterization, plot, and tone--the conventions of the short story.

Calling Gass a master of the conventions of fiction is perhaps ironic, since the bulk of his own criticism seems to lead to the conclusion that one's perceptions of those conventions are generally skewed at best and are often completely wrongheaded. Gass's theories represent less a prescription for writing than a description of what good writing has always involved. Gass emphasizes merely what he feels to be the obvious: that writing is an activity of word choice and placement. Plot, then, is not a sequence of actions but a sequence of words; a character is not a fictive "mirror" of a human being but a set of images, no more. Not surprisingly, Gass's primary concern is style; indeed, he prefers to call himself a "stylist" rather than a novelist or short-story writer. In the novella *The Cartesian Sonata*, he refers to his method of writing as "pencil carving," a habit of repeated light tracings that eventually burn into paper or wood grain. It is this layering of words that constitutes Gass's style.

How does this affect the reader's understanding of Gass's short stories? At the very least, one should be aware that Gass's fictions depend upon a developing pattern of imagery, and that this pattern of imagery does not become more important than characterization or plot, but that characterization and plot are no more than patterns of imagery themselves. Thus, one should see each of Gass's works as a developing metaphor, bound by its own rules, not the rules of the world.

This emphasis on imagery as metaphor indicates that the aesthetic foundation of Gass's work is poetic as well as fictive. As much as any prose writer in American literature, perhaps as much as any *writer* since Wallace Stevens, Gass is concerned with the sound of words and their rhythms. His prose is strikingly rhythmical and alliterative; in fact, in "In the Heart of the Heart of the Country" and *The Cartesian Sonata*, Gass quite deliberately employs prose rhyme. It is impossible, however, to read Gass's stories and be satisfied merely by an examination of his syntax, since the reader is constantly drawn into the characters' lives, their actions and motivations. His readers cannot help comparing the characters' worlds with their own, and Gass nowhere enjoins them from doing so; he simply reminds readers not to weigh down characters and plot with any more "reality" than inheres in the words that compose them.

An overview of Gass's stories reveals that the figures in his carpet of words are structural and thematic, as well as syntactical. Each story, for example, is told from a limited first-person point of view. Characters in effect create the world in which they live through the images in which, consciously or unconsciously, they perceive their world. Thus, the way the worlds appear is less a comment on the worlds than on the narrators. In essence, the fictive worlds are twice removed from "actual" reality: once by virtue of being Gass's creations, twice by virtue of being the narrators' creations.

"ORDER OF INSECTS"

This may perhaps be no more than an overly elaborate way of describing what happens with any limited perspective, yet Gass's fiction causes the reader more problems--intriguing problems--because his narrators are so unreliable. The narrator of "Order of Insects," for example, is a wife and mother who has moved into a new home, only to find it invaded by insects. She quickly becomes obsessed with the bugs; at first horrified, she comes to see their dead bodies as "wonderfully shaped." Her obsession is not shared by other members of the family, however; indeed, the reader is not certain that anyone else is aware of the bugs or that the insects even exist. Rather, her obsession is the chief manifestation of her unhappiness, her horror at her

roles of woman, wife, and mother. She is never so interested in the insects alive as dead; she comes to see
the lifeless husks as the true souls of the insects. To the
wife and mother, what is eternal, what lasts, is not
warmth and love but the dry, physical residue of life.

This reading of "Order of Insects" is not simply
conjecture. The woman herself admits to being "ill":
She is as aware as the reader that her obsession reflects
an abnormal psychological stance toward life in general. Similarly, the narrator of "Icicles" is painfully
aware that he is "not right" and that his obsession with
icicles--he sees them as both beautiful and horrifying-
-is but an extreme symptom of his withdrawal from
life. The motif of the withdrawal from life is found in
all five stories. In "Mrs. Mean" and in "In the Heart of
the Heart of the Country," the narrators have already
retreated, psychologically and physically, to the position of passive observers of life; in "Icicles" and "Order
of Insects," the narrators are in the process of withdrawal; the end of "The Pederson Kid" finds the narrator rejoicing in a "glorious" act of bravery as he sits
curled in a cocoon of psychosis.

"THE PEDERSON KID"

"The Pederson Kid" is overtly Gass's most traditional story. It possesses an identifiable setting, rich,
rounded characters, and action that marches toward a
violent climax. Indeed, in the mind of one critic, the
story recalls nothing so much as the Upper Michigan
stories of Ernest Hemingway. The comparison is understandable, given the story's bleak landscape,
mother/father/son conflict, and violent conclusion; yet
a better comparison would be with William Faulkner's
As I Lay Dying (1930), with its tenuous world built on
the shifting perspectives of unreliable narrators.

A closer reading of "The Pederson Kid" reveals
that, rather than being "traditional," the story is a perfect example of what Gass's theories amount to in practice. Describing the action, for example, *should* be easy
enough. Apparently, one bleak winter morning Big
Hans, a hired hand on a North Dakota farm, discovers
the Pederson Kid, a boy from a neighboring farm, collapsed in the snow. In a delirium, the boy tells of a
stranger in yellow gloves who forced his parents into a
cellar while the boy escaped and ran miles through a
blizzard for help. Jorge (the narrator, a boy a little older

than the Pederson Kid), Jorge's father, and Big Hans
start off on a wagon for the Pederson place. After some
difficulties they get there and hide in the barn, but all
three fear moving across the open space to the house.
Finally, Jorge strikes off across the yard. When his father follows, a shot rings out, and his father falls dead.
Jorge hides in the house, awaiting death, but the
stranger never appears. At the end, Jorge sits in the
Pederson house--convinced that the stranger has killed
Big Hans and his mother, too, by now--but is "burning
up . . . with joy" at the thought of his act of bravery.

Some critics contend that this straightforward plot
summary is indeed an accurate rendering of what "actually" happened in the story. Others maintain that in
all probability the stranger never existed and that "actually" Jorge shot his own father. In Gass's terms, however, nothing "actually" happens; the story is a series of
words creating images that in turn make up a developing metaphor, a virtual world obeying its own rules
and having no meaning beyond the words that compose it.

All the reader can know with any certainty is that
Jorge loathes and fears his father, although at one time
their relationship was at least a little more amicable; he
loathes Big Hans, although once they, too, were much
closer; he initially loathes the Pederson Kid, although
at the end he comes to identify with him. At the end, in
his own mind his act of "bravery" has apparently freed
him from his father's yoke; but this act was largely
without volition, and he has been freed less from his
father than from any connection with the living world.
The reader leaves him thankful for the snow and the
"burning up . . . with joy": fire and ice, the twin images
of Hell. No one interpretation of "The Pederson Kid" is
any more demonstrably valid than another, and this
contributes to, rather than detracts from, the work's
power and endless fascination.

"MRS. MEAN"

A work of less intensity but open to even broader
interpretation, perhaps, is "Mrs. Mean." Mrs. Mean is
the name given by the narrator to a neighbor: the
vulgar, shrill mother of a brood of children. The story is
filled with mythic and religious allusions (as are most
of Gass's stories), which have led certain critics to
rather strained interpretations; once again, however,

the allusions are the unreliable narrator's, and what really happens in his fictive world may be far different from his interpretation of it.

The story is composed almost entirely of the narrator's observations as he and his wife spy on Mrs. Mean from their house across the street. He sees a woman loud, vulgar, violent, and sadistic to her children; indeed, in the narrator's mind she assumes a malevolence of almost mythic proportions. Any parent reading the story, however, might see Mrs. Mean as simply a mother harried to distraction by a pack of children who seem to have very little fear of the "monster" that the narrator perceives. The narrator deems it "unnaturally sacrificial" when the children run *into* their house, not *away* from their house when chased by their mother. What is unnatural, however, is the narrator's inability to understand a simple domestic situation and his obsession with observing life instead of participating in it. At the end, he has withdrawn into his room, locked away even from his wife, but desperate to join the world of Mrs. Mean--which is, after all, simply the world of the living.

Another observer of, rather than participant in, life is the narrator of the title story.

"IN THE HEART OF THE HEART OF THE COUNTRY"

One of the most frequently anthologized stories of contemporary literature, "In the Heart of the Heart of the Country" is strikingly innovative; it achieves what all great writers strive for: the perfect wedding of form and content. The story concerns a poet, the narrator, who has "retired" to a small Indiana town after a failed love affair. He is in the heart of the country geographically, and in the heart of that heart since he is still in the heart's domain: the country of love.

The story is divided into sections ranging from a few sentences to a few pages in length, and each section is entitled with a descriptive phrase, such as "Politics," "Vital Data," "Education," and so forth. In a sense, the story is an anatomy of a rural community, but, as in the other stories, what the narrator describes reveals more about him than about the objects of his descriptions. For example, although the sections may initially appear to be randomly arranged (there is a subtle movement from winter through spring, summer, fall, and back to winter at the story's end),

certain recurring elements bind them together to form a psychological and spiritual portrait of the narrator. As much as he may try to make his descriptions flat and objective, for example, as much as he may try to refine himself out of his own story, the narrator can never escape his memories of love. He as much as admits that his interest in politics, for example, simply fills a vacuum left by lost love.

Even when his memories of love do not intrude directly into certain sections, his despair colors whatever he touches. For example, the persons to whom he returns again and again in his descriptions are the old, the feeble, the lonely: projections of himself. On the rarer occasions when he describes persons who are younger and more vital, he cannot empathize: They are faceless, dangerous. It is a measure of his fall when he thinks of his lost love in terms of "youth and child" but now is obsessed with the lonely and the dying.

The story is fragmented, then, because the narrator's psyche is fragmented; he is out of harmony with his own life. The "organic" qualities of the story, however, go beyond that. The narrator is a poet, and as a result "In the Heart of the Heart of the Country" is a "poetic" fiction. The sentences are rhythmical and alliterative; he even deliberately employs prose rhyme. The descriptions are imagistic, frequently recalling T. E. Hulme, Ezra Pound, Richard Aldington, and Robert Lowell more than any prose masters. Indeed, the first "Politics" section as a poem would rival some of the finest efforts of the contemporary period.

THE CARTESIAN SONATA

Gass's *The Cartesian Sonata* is a further examination of narrative fragmentation. The three-part narrative begins with the Sterne-like promise that "this is the story of Ella Bend Hess," a clairvoyant woman who is subjected to various abuses which she knows about in advance. What follows the opening line, though, are mutterings of the narrator and tergiversations of truth in connected digressive fragments, these all yielding a composite picture of Ella rather than a traditional story about her. The reader moves linearly through the asynchronous images of Ella getting her shoes from a traveling salesman, the salesman's uncle's story of a man shot in the foot, a description of the museum that displays the boot, Peg Crandall's nude portrait session and the artist's lust, the narrator's writing habit and interest in graffiti, an explanation of Ella's talent as the result of her ultrasensitivity ("She was almost totally attention and antennae"), and visits to other seers, including Professor Logrus and Madame Betz. The concluding section is a circular stream-of-consciousness rendering of Ella's husband's thoughts. He reviews his abuse of Ella and the possibility of her death, and the section is peppered with vertical ellipsis and self-deprecation. The effect of these disjunctive elements is that of montage, of the reader's whole understanding of the subject as greater than the sum of the parts.

Hyperbole is hard to avoid when evaluating the work of Gass. He is an enormously talented writer and critic--so talented as to be initially daunting, perhaps, to some readers. That is unfortunate, for enjoyment of his stories never relies on knowledge of his theories or subtle grasp of his technical expertise, although these can add to the pleasure. "The Pederson Kid" and "In the Heart of the Heart of the Country," in particular, are destined to become hallmarks of contemporary short fiction.

OTHER MAJOR WORKS

LONG FICTION: *Omensetter's Luck*, 1966; *Willie Masters' Lonesome Wife*, 1968; *The Tunnel*, 1995.

NONFICTION: *Fiction and the Figures of Life*, 1970; *On Being Blue: A Philosophical Inquiry*, 1976; *The World Within the Word: Essays*, 1978; *The Habitations of the Word: Essays*, 1985; *Finding a Form*, 1996; *Reading Rilke: Reflections on the Problems of Translation*, 1999; *Three Essays: Reflections on the American Century*, 2000 (with Naomi Lebowitz and Gerald Early); *Tests of Time: Essays*, 2002; *Conversations with William H. Gass*, 2003 (Theodore G. Ammon, editor); *A Temple of Texts: Essays*, 2006; *Vanishing America: The End of Main Street*, 2008 (with Michael Eastman).

EDITED TEXTS: *The Writer in Politics*, 1996 (with Lorin Cuoco); *Literary St. Louis: A Guide*, 2000 (with Cuoco); *The Writer and Religion*, 2000 (with Cuoco).

BIBLIOGRAPHY

Busch, Frederick. "But This Is What It Is Like to Live in Hell: Gass's *In the Heart of the Heart of the Country.*" *Modern Fiction Studies* 20 (Autumn, 1974): 328-336. This essay provides one of the earliest, and still one of the best, analyses of theme and style in one of Gass's most important short stories.

Gardner, James. "Transgressive Fiction." *National Review* 48 (June 17, 1996): 54-56. Agues that whereas fiction used to delight as well as edify, now it has split into different forms of fiction, with writers like Stephen King and Jackie Collins being read for entertainment value, while Thomas Pynchon and Gass intentionally suppress the element of pleasure.

Gass, William H. *Conversations with William H. Gass.* Edited by Theodore G. Ammon. Jackson: University Press of Mississippi, 2003. Collection of essays in which Gass recollects incidents from his life, discusses his works, and explains his literary theories. He often repeats his belief that understanding the relationship of language to the world turns upon one's comprehension of metaphor.

_____. "An Interview with William Gass." Interview by Lorna H. Dormke. *Mississippi Review* 10, no. 3 (1987): 53-67. One of the most extensive interviews with Gass.

Gelfant, Blanche H., ed. *The Columbia Companion to the Twentieth-Century American Short Story.* New York: Columbia University Press, 2000. Includes a chapter in which Gass's short stories are analyzed.

Hadella, Charlotte Byrd. "The Winter Wasteland of William Gass's *In the Heart of the Heart of the Country.*" *Critique: Studies in Modern Fiction* 30 (Fall, 1988): 49-58. Hadella explores the wasteland theme and imagery in Gass's collection and compares them with T. S. Eliot's use of the same themes in his great poem.

Hix, H. L. *Understanding William H. Gass.* Columbia: University of South Carolina Press, 2002. Hix provides close analyses of many of Gass's works, devoting a chapter each to *In the Heart of the Heart of the Country* and *Cartesian Sonata.*

Holloway, Watson L. *William Gass.* Boston, Mass.: Twayne Publishers, 1990. A good critical study of Gass's fiction. Includes a bibliography and an index.

Kaufmann, Michael. *Textual Bodies: Modernism, Postmodernism, and Print.* Lewisburg, Pa.: Bucknell University Press, 1994. A thorough study of works by Gass, William Faulkner, Gertrude Stein, and James Joyce. Includes a bibliography and an index.

_____. "The Textual Body: William Gass's *Willie Masters' Lonesome Wife*." *Critique* 35 (Fall, 1993): 27-42. Argues that the voice of the work is not the voice of the protagonist, Willie Masters' wife, but the voice of the text itself. Discusses Gass's experiments with typography and the physical form of the text.

Kellman, Steven G., and Irving Malin, eds. *Into "The Tunnel": Readings of Gass's Novel*. Newark: University of Delaware Press, 1998. Considers the psychological element in Gass's novel; includes a discussion of historians and college teachers in literature, a bibliography, and an index.

Saltzman, Arthur. *The Fiction of William Gass: The Consolation of Language*. Carbondale: Southern Illinois University Press, 1986. Includes seven chapters on various aspects of Gass's fiction. Saltzman claims that Gass's short-fiction collection can best be read as a "series of variations on the theme of the pleasures and pitfalls of aesthetic isolation." The last chapter contains an interesting interview with Gass.

Schwerdtfeger, Barbara. *Ethics in Postmodern Fiction: Donald Barthelme and William Gass*. Heidelberg, Germany: Winter, 2005. Analyzes works by the two authors to demonstrate how they make readers aware of the complexity of ethical issues.

Stone, Robert. "The Reason for Stories: Toward a Moral Fiction." *Harper's* 276 (June, 1988): 71-76. Discusses Gass's argument about the estrangement of art and moral goodness in his essay "Goodness Knows Nothing of Beauty." Claims that Gass does not practice the ideas expressed in his essay, which are at odds with the imperatives of writing. Contends that in order to be independent of morality, fiction would have to be composed of something other than language, for the laws of language and art impose choices that are unavoidably moral.

Dennis Vannatta
Updated by Scott Vander Ploeg

DAVID GATES

Born: Middletown, Connecticut; January 8, 1947

PRINCIPAL SHORT FICTION
The Wonders of the Invisible World: Stories, 1999

OTHER LITERARY FORMS

David Gates is the author of the novels *Jernigan* (1991) and *Preston Falls* (1998) and the editor of *Labor Days: An Anthology of Fiction About Work* (2004).

ACHIEVEMENTS

David Gates was a finalist for the Pulitzer Prize for *Jernigan* and for the National Book Critics Circle Award for *Preston Falls*. He received a Guggenheim Foundation Fellowship in 1999. His stories have been anthologized in *The Best American Short Stories* and *Prize Stories: The O. Henry Awards*. In addition, Gates has published short stories in *Esquire, Ploughshares, GQ, Grand Street,* and *TriQuarterly*.

BIOGRAPHY

David Gates was born in a small Connecticut town and received a B.A. from the University of Connecticut. While in graduate school at that university Gates met and married Ann Beattie, and together they took teaching positions at the University of Virginia and Harvard University, eventually returning to Connecticut when Beattie began to establish herself as a fiction writer. Gates's lack of career success, in tandem with Beattie's fast-growing literary reputation, led to marital tensions and, in 1972, to divorce.

In addition to his teaching jobs, Gates has worked as a wholesale food distributor, a cab driver, a phone operator for Western Union, a stock clerk, and a square dance musician. In 1979, Gates took a job in the correspondence department of *Newsweek* magazine, from which he rose to become a senior writer in the arts section, a position he held until 2008. During this period Gates also began to write fiction. His first novel, *Jernigan*, received high critical praise. In 2010, he taught at the New School in New York City and the graduate writing program at Bennington College in Bennington, Vermont.

ANALYSIS

David Gates's first collection of stories, *The Wonders of the Invisible World*, is regarded as continuing the high caliber of work found in his earlier novels. Here, too, Gates has created an original narrative voice, whose rhythms, intonations, and cultural references seem to capture the tenor of contemporary American life perfectly. In addition to skillfully suggesting the American vernacular, Gates is able to shape the rhythms of the American voice into a highly strung, jazzy stream-of-consciousness that is both humorous and serious.

Although in his first two novels Gates has taken as his protagonists culturally sophisticated but emotionally tormented middle-aged men with a history of difficult or broken marriages, this type of man is the center of consciousness in only a handful of his short stories. Other stories feature the perspectives of contemporary gay men or elderly men from a previous generation. Half of the stories feature female protagonists who are treated with a similar mix of irony and compassion, whether they be bitter, man-hating alcoholics; middle-aged, conflicted feminists; or isolated, desperate housewives. No matter what the age, gender, or sexual preference of Gates's characters, they are all struggling with either their own dark side or the dark sides of those close to them. This may involve alcohol or drug abuse, or relationship problems, such as infidelity, exploitation, abandonment, or divorce.

A clue to the general theme of the stories in *The Wonders of the Invisible World* can be gleaned from the title, which refers to the early American theologian Cotton Mather's description of demonic spirits. For Gates, these demonic forces live within the individual, so that it is largely unconscious or rationalized evil motives and impulses that lead his men and women into loveless, lonely lives and to the subversion of their own best selves.

THE WONDERS OF THE INVISIBLE WORLD

The ten stories in this collection are told from the perspective of a variety of characters, young and old, male and female, straight and gay. However, the plots turn on the universal themes of disintegrating families, broken relationships, and unraveling lives. In the title story, "The Wonders of the Invisible World," the protagonist is divorced and losing touch with his grown daughter. He is having an affair with a woman whose possible pregnancy puts a serious strain on their relationship. The protagonist's hip, jazzy narrative voice, which threatens to disintegrate into incoherence, reflects the ragged quality of his life and his approach to it, which has gradually lapsed into a kind of moral inattention. When he loses his clarinet and alienates his girlfriend in the same evening, the reader sees that he is careless with regard to both his creative life and his love life. Acutely aware of his own fecklessness, he may not be aware, however, of the degree to which his losses may be the product of his own neurotic intentions.

A similar type of character appears in the story "A Wronged Husband." Here the narrator and his wife weave a tissue of lies around their marriage, especially with regard to their infidelities. The lying and adultery, along with drugs and alcohol, are essentially escapist strategies meant to preserve the status quo. The lies and evasions, however, have in reality undermined and destroyed the marriage, an outcome the wife suggests may have been her husband's true intention.

Two other stories have a narrator who is male and homosexual. In each case the man must cope with the presence of a chaotic, self-destructive person in his life. "Star Baby" is told from the perspective of Billy, a gay man and the brother of a drug-addicted, self-destructive woman, Cassie, who has abandoned her seven-year-old son Deke to his care. During the course of looking after Deke, Billy's flippancy and defensive patterns give way to deeper feelings of genuine love. He is stunned by the realization that he will always be the only consistent, caregiving adult in the child's life. Another story, "The Intruder," also features a gay protagonist, a decent older man, whose devotion to a younger, selfish, unfaithful lover has placed his emotional life and his health in danger.

Gates uses a female narrative perspective in four of the stories in this collection. In "The Bad Thing," a pregnant woman feels trapped in her marriage in an isolated house in upstate New York and attempts to rationalize her secret drinking as an emancipatory gesture. In "Beating" the perspective is that of Dinah, a childless day-care worker married to an aging radical. Although a self-described feminist, Dinah is nevertheless responsible for all domestic chores and secretly and compulsively watches the film version of the romantic fairy tale "Beauty and the Beast." Her husband Tobias, who is obsessed with police beatings, is no longer the political idealist she married but has instead become a bitter and paranoid crank. Another unhappy wife can be found in "The Crazy Thought." Here the lonely and childless Faye feels stranded in Vermont and increasingly estranged from her insensitive husband Paul. Daydreaming of an old boyfriend and disturbed by her husband's purchase of a shotgun, she begins to wish for Paul's accidental death. An unhappily married woman in the story "Saturn" tries various ways to relieve her sense of suffocation, including a clandestine love affair and self-improvement schemes, but like the planet Saturn, which is also the brand name of her automobile, which stops cold in a minor traffic accident, she evinces a paralyzing reluctance to change things.

Older men take over the narrative perspective of two other stories. Len, the elderly narrator of "Vigil," is left to hold things together after his daughter Bonnie is hospitalized when her car is struck by a drunken driver. Len, whose alcoholic wife Sylvia ran off to Phoenix with her marginally more successful boss years ago, has long been left in charge of Bonnie, a task he assumed with characteristic stoic competence. When Sylvia returns to see her hospitalized daughter, she frightens her grandson with violent, man-hating fantasies that significantly lessen the value of the domestic skills she also provides for the family. A turning point is reached when Bonnie's husband finally brings out into the open the fact that Bonnie's automobile accident occurred after a tryst with a secret lover. When, for good measure, he also accuses his mother-in-law of

sexual promiscuity, Len can no longer deny the realities that are shattering his family.

An elderly man is also the narrator of the final story, "The Mail Lady," a tour de force reminiscent of the work of Gates's literary hero, the Irish author Samuel Beckett. The story is told from the perspective of an elderly stroke victim named Lewis Coley, whose damaged, sometimes nonsensical thought processes and speech become in Gates's hand a skillful stream-of-consciousness narrative that is both comic and tragic. Lew, once a scientist, heavy drinker, and authoritarian father, who prided himself on the strict discipline meted out to his daughter Wylie, has in his later years undergone a religious conversion that has made him something of a fanatic on the subject. Because of his stroke, he has also become completely dependent on his wife Alice. The female postal worker of the title comes to Lew's rescue after he shuts himself up in his car, which is slowly filling with carbon monoxide. Lew, who had been hoping to die a peaceful, spiritual death in his automobile, sees the Mail Lady as less his salvation than an agent of destiny returning him to a bleak, greatly diminished, and hellish life.

OTHER MAJOR WORKS

LONG FICTION: *Jernigan*, 1991; *Preston Falls*, 1998.
EDITED TEXT: *Labor Days: An Anthology of Fiction About Work*, 2004.

BIBLIOGRAPHY

Gates, David. "David Gates: Voices for Vices." Interview by Michael Coffey. *Publishers Weekly*, May 10, 1999, 42-43. Gates discusses his background, his vocation as a writer, and his two novels, as well as his short-story collection. Much useful material, especially with regard to the influence of Gates's literary hero Samuel Beckett.

Grossinger, Harvey. "David Gates: Life's Hazards, People's Alienation," *Houston Chronicle*, July 18, 1999, p. 23. Interprets stories in *The Wonders of the Invisible World* from an existential perspective, praising them as well-crafted, gritty stories of contemporary malaise, alienation, and spiritual exhaustion. Also analyzes Gates's characters, concluding they are isolated and loveless, have lives marked by regret, and are unable to sustain serious relationships. Lengthy, insightful analyses of "Vigil" and "The Mail Lady."

Hynes, James. "More Hideous Men." Review of *The Wonders of the Invisible World*, by David Gates. *Washington Post*, July 8, 1999, p. X05. Concentrates on Gates's male characters, particularly in terms of their negative attributes. Describes Gates as continuing to mine the territory he staked out in his novels, with heroes who behave badly but are also self-aware and bitterly witty.

Kakutani, Michiko. "Thinking Too Much About Sour Relationships." Review of *The Wonders of the Invisible World*, by David Gates. *The New York Times*, July 6, 1999, p. E-6. Kakutani is critical of the collection's narcissistic, self-absorbed protagonists, finding them too similar to the heroes of Gates's novels. Also faults Gates for overreliance on what she describes as "terminal irony."

Marzorati, Gerald. "Hip, Free, and Middle Aged." Review of *The Wonders of the Invisible World*, by David Gates. *The New York Times Book Review*, July 18, 1999, 11. Praises the collection for its mordant humor and its bleak but sharp-witted vision of contemporary people and situations.

Ulin, David L. "Adrift in the Sea of Adulthood." Review of *The Wonders of the Invisible World*, by David Gates. *San Francisco Chronicle*, August 8, 1999, p. 3. This perceptive review notes that the collection's "low grade existential anguish" is similar to the emotional territory of the novels. Concludes that Gates's protagonists are "adrift in the amorphous sea of adulthood" and are unable to live up to their best possibilities. Especially praises Gates's ability to write endings that pull his stories together in surprising ways and concludes that Gates has developed into a writer to be reckoned with.

Wolfe, Linda. "A Talent for Misery." Review of *The Wonders of the Invisible World*, by David Gates. *Boston Globe*, June 27, 1999, p. D1. Insightful review praises Gates for his ironic approach, his ability to depict depression and bleakness, and his talent for suggesting the cadences and idioms of contemporary American speech. Especially useful comments on the way in which Gates's characters are driven by a hidden dark side. Explores the ways these inner forces of darkness drive Gates's characters to drink, drugs, and isolated, loveless narcissism.

Margaret Boe Birns

TIM GAUTREAUX

Born: Morgan City, Louisiana; October 19, 1947

PRINCIPAL SHORT FICTION

Same Place, Same Things, 1996
Welding with Children, 1999
Waiting for the Evening News: Stories of the Deep South, 2010

OTHER LITERARY FORMS

In addition to his short stories, Tim Gautreaux (gah-TROH) is the author of three novels: *The Next Step in the Dance* (1998), *The Clearing* (2003), and *The Missing* (2009).

ACHIEVEMENTS

Tim Gautreaux's story "Same Place, Same Things" was chosen for *The Best American Short Stories 1992*, "Little Frogs in a Ditch" appeared in *The Best American Short Stories 1997*, "Welding with Children" appeared in that annual collection in 1998, and "The Piano Tuner" in 1999. Gautreaux has been the recipient of a National Endowment for the Arts Fellowship and the National Magazine Award for Fiction. In 1999, *The Next Step in the Dance* received awards from both the Southern Independent Booksellers Alliance Award and the Southeastern Booksellers Association; *The Clearing* won the 2003 Mid-South Independent Booksellers Association Award. Gautreaux also received the 2005 John Dos Passos Prize and the Louisiana Writer Award (2009).

BIOGRAPHY

Timothy Martin Gautreaux was born in 1947 and grew up in Morgan City, Louisiana. His father was a tugboat captain and his grandfather was an engineer on a steamboat. He received his undergraduate degree from Nicholls State University. Although he originally intended to be a business major, he says that when someone stole his accounting books, he changed to English. He received his Ph.D. from the University of South Carolina. He taught creative writing at Southeastern Louisiana University in Hammond, Louisiana, from 1972 until his retirement in 2002, when he became a writer-in-residence at the university. In 1996, he was appointed the John and Renee Grisham Visiting Southern Writer-in-Residence at the University of Mississippi.

ANALYSIS

Tim Gautreaux is but the latest in a long line of fine short-story writers from Louisiana, who include Ellen Gilchrist, Robert Olen Butler, Shirley Ann Grau, and Moira Crone. His milieu is the rural farm country of southern Louisiana, populated with characters who live in small towns, such as Tiger Island, Gumwood, and Pine Oil. Although his people are often down on their luck financially, their moral values are mostly sound, even when they are sorely tried. Gautreaux has said he considers himself a Catholic writer in the tradition of Walker Percy, adding that "if a story does not deal with a moral question, I don't think it's much of a story."

Gautreaux writes of Cajun country, about working-class men and women who come smack up against a challenge to their humaneness, and usually manage to meet it with courage and grace. Comparing him to Flannery O'Connor, critics have praised his stories as being morally complex in their depiction of human frailty and deceptively simple in their pellucid lyrical style.

"SAME PLACE, SAME THINGS"

The title story of Gautreaux's first collection, an anthology favorite, is about Harry Lintel, a forty-four-year-old traveling pump repairman from Missouri who has "followed the droughts" to Louisiana to find work. After finding a dead man who has been electrocuted while trying to fix his pump, Harry is then pursued by the dead man's wife, who says she has spent her life seeing the "same place, same things." Since Harry is the only person she ever met who can go where he wants to go, and since because of poverty she has never been more than a hundred miles from her home, she urges him to take her with him.

However, although Harry is tempted because of the woman's good looks and seductive promise to be good to him, he is bothered by the woman's easy dismissal of her husband and the fact that two previous husbands have died. His revelation comes when he opens the electric fuse box at the woman's house and finds a switch wire cut into the circuit and running into the house. Then he knows that the woman switched on the current while her husband worked on the pump and murdered him. Although Harry is shaken "like a man who had just missed being in a terrible accident," he does not report the crime, happy to leave the town and the woman behind.

The climax of the story comes when he stops at a café and finds the woman hidden under the tarp in his truck bed. Although she begs him to take her with him, he says significantly, "Where you want to go, I can't take you." The woman hits Harry over the head with a heavy wrench, snarling, "I've never met a man I could put up with for long. I'm glad I got shut of all of mine." She then drives away in his truck. When he regains consciousness, Harry knows that whereas she was a woman who would never get where she wanted to go, he was always clear where he was going.

The story is an understated treatment of a man who almost makes a terrible mistake, but who finds meaning in his work. His basic contentment with the "same things" regardless of where he finds himself is contrasted with the discontent of the woman who will never find meaning regardless of the place she occupies.

"LITTLE FROGS IN A DITCH"

In his contributor's notes to this story in *The Best American Short Stories 1997*, Gautreaux says he got the central idea from a radio call-in show that asked listeners to tell about the "meanest trick" they had ever played on someone. One man called in and bragged how he had caught a bunch of common roof pigeons and sold them as untrained homing pigeons, complete with instructions. Gautreaux says he wondered what kind of person would do such a thing and what it would be like to have such a person in his family.

The central character who plays the "mean trick" in Gautreaux's story is Lenny Fontenot, who is out of work and lives with his grandfather, his parents having left him to travel around the country in a Winnebago motor home. The story centers on one man, Mr. Lejeune, who buys a pigeon from Lenny for his crippled little nephew, who is staying with him. The moral conscience of the story is the grandfather, who puts Lenny out until he goes to a priest and makes a confession of what he has done. The title of the story comes from the grandfather's warning Lenny that if he closes his eyes before he goes to confession his sins will make a noise: "They'll cry out like little frogs in a ditch at sundown."

The final revelation of the story occurs when the pigeon sold to Mr. Lejeune returns to the grandfather's house, and he takes it to the new owner to make it appear it has truly "returned home." He discovers that Lejeune knew the pigeon was a fake and that he bought it for his nephew purposely to provide him with a lesson about disappointment. Although the boy has never had a father and his mother is addicted to crack cocaine, he lives in a fairy-tale world in which he thinks his mother will return. Lejeune says he has to toughen up, that maybe if he learns to deal with the little things, it will teach him to deal with the big thing. The story parallels these two men, both of whom are responsible for wards who are crippled in different ways. It ends with the grandfather not being sure about whether what he and Lejeune are doing is the "right thing."

"WELDING WITH CHILDREN"

This is one of Gautreaux's most admired stories, for it combines comic characterization and dialogue with a poignant and deeply felt human realization. The central character is a grandfather whose four unmarried daughters leave their children--who have names such as "Nu-Nu," "Moonbean," and "Tammynette"--with him. He lives in the small central Louisiana town of Gumwood and has an old greasy car engine hanging from a K-Mart chain in his yard. When he takes the kids to the Pak-a-Sak store in his old Chevy Caprice to get Icees, he feels shame when he overhears some men saying, "Here comes Bruton and his bastardmobile."

The highlight of the story is a comic dialogue between Bruton and the grandchildren about their profane language and lack of religious training. The comedy increases when he reads them the Genesis story of creation, which they compare to the film *Conan the Barbarian* because it has swords and snakes in it. When Bruton insists the Bible is not a film, Tammynette says, "I think I seen it down at Blockbuster."

After entertaining fantasies of moving up north with the children and starting over again, Bruton decides to stay and do better by them than he did by his daughters. He turns off the electricity to the television set, begins reading to them, takes them to church, and cleans up his property so it does not look like white trash live there. The story ends with him planning to put a tire swing up on the tree where the old motor once hung.

The story works because of the humanity of the grandfather, who feels badly that he has let things slide with his daughters. Forced into uncomfortably seeing himself as white trash, he makes a last ditch effort to salvage something of his family; if it is too late for his children, he thinks, then maybe it is not too late for his grandchildren.

"THE PIANO TUNER"

This story is similar to "Same Place, Same Things" in that it involves a common Gautreaux technique of focusing on service people. Gautreaux has said that he likes to write about such people who "visit our homes and get just a little entangled in our lives." In this story, Claude, a piano tuner, who, his wife says, "invented reality by saying it," gets entangled in the life of a down-and-out and depressed woman whom he helps get a job playing the piano in the bar at the Lafayette Motel.

As he frequently does in his stories, Gautreaux adroitly mixes comedy with poignant humanism here. In the most hilarious scene, the woman, who has bought a new piano, tries to get her old one out of the house with a tractor the size of a locomotive. In the process, the tractor gets away from her, not only pulling out the piano but also pulling the whole house down, igniting a gas fire that destroys what is left of the house.

However, Gautreaux's characters have staying power above all else. The story ends a year later when Claude goes to hear the woman play and she tells a story about how composer Scott Joplin died crazy from syphilis on April Fool's Day, 1917. She then delivers the defining line of the story, which also describes the characteristic tone of many of Gautreaux's stories: "That's kind of funny and sad at the same time, isn't it?"

OTHER MAJOR WORKS

LONG FICTION: *The Next Step in the Dance*, 1998; *The Clearing*, 2003; *The Missing*, 2009.

BIBLIOGRAPHY

Bauer, Margaret Donovan. *Understanding Tim Gautreaux*. Columbia: University of South Carolina Press, 2010. Bauer's examination of Gautreaux's fiction devotes a chapter apiece to his first two short-story collections, analyzing his character types, major themes, and story structure. She argues that his contribution to southern literature is his authentic insider's view of Cajun culture, and compares his characters to those of William Faulkner.

Blouin, Keith. "People Who Live There Know That Hope Springs Eternal Deep in Louisiana Territory." *The Tampa Tribune*, October 17, 1999, p. 4. Compares Gautreaux to Flannery O'Connor in his ability to portray faithfully "good country people." Discusses his familiarity with the people of Louisiana and his celebration of human strengths and weaknesses and "our everlasting capacity for hope."

Gautreaux, Tim. *Novel Approach: Tim Gautreaux Takes "The Next Step."* Interview by Christina Masciere. *New Orleans Magazine* 32 (March, 1998): 31. Gautreaux repudiates the notion that he is a "southern" writer, allying himself more closely with the frontier humorists. He also acknowledges the role that his Catholic Louisiana milieu has had on his life and work.

Grossinger, Harvey. "A Trip Through Cajun Country." Review of *Welding with Children*, by Tim Gautreaux. *Houston Chronicle*, December 19, 1999, p. 14. Argues that Gautreaux is at the top of the list of gifted American short-story writers. Grossinger discusses what he calls the "brilliant" title story and describes "The Piano Tuner" as a "masterpiece of delicate shading and method."

Jacobs, Hal. "Poignant Messages Emerge in *Welding with Children*." *The Atlanta Journal and Constitution*, November 28, 1999, p. 13K. Says Gautreaux's stories have all the same ingredients as Garrison Keillor's popular stories: humor, warmth, irony, suspense, and uplifting endings.

Larson, Susan. "Swamp Boogie" and "The Writer Next Door." *The Times-Picayune*, May 15, 1998, p. D6, E1. In these two articles, Larson talks about the Louisiana elements in Gautreaux's writing. She says he is a sensualist who can render with equal detail the clank of machinery and the smell of boiled crabs. Provides some biographical background and describes Gautreaux's Acadian home in the woods outside Hammond, Louisiana.

Nisly, L. Lamar. "Wingless Chickens or Catholics from the Bayou: Conceptions of Audience in O'Connor and Gautreaux." *Christianity and Literature* 56, no. 1 (Autumn, 2006): 63-85. Analyzes some of Gautreaux's short stories to compare them with works by Flannery O'Connor. Argues that the two writers have different conceptions of their audiences: O'Connor believes her secular audience is hostile to her Catholic vision, while Gautreaux perceives his readers as "warm and friendly companions."

Paddock, Polly. "*Same Place* Mines Louisiana for Extraordinary Folk Tales." Review of *Same Place, Same Things*, by Tim Gautreaux. *The Arizona Republic*, September 29, 1996, p. E10. Says that although he writes about the Cajun country he knows so well, the stories in this collection transcend locale and plumb the "deepest reaches of the human heart."

Piacentino, Ed. "Second Chances: Patterns of Failure and Redemption in Tim Gautreaux's *Same Place, Same Things*." *Southern Literary Journal* 38, no. 1 (Fall, 2005): 115-133. Focuses on the Cajun characters in this short-story collection, whose class and ethnic group are well known to Gautreaux and whom he treats sympathetically.

Stroup, Sheila. "He's Got the Write Stuff." *The Times-Picayune*, January 26, 1993, p. B1. In this interview story, Gautreaux says he learned to like to tell stories from reading *The Catholic Messenger* out loud when he was in elementary school. He discusses the origins of some of his stories, including how his fascination with obsolete machinery gave rise to the title story of his first collection *Same Place, Same Things*.

Wanner, Irene. "An Imaginative Teller of Tales." Review of *Welding with Children*, by Tim Gautreaux. *The Seattle Times*, October 10, 1999, p. M8. Notes that Gautreaux's "adventurous imagination and perfect pitch for the right phrase" make his stories special. Singles out for particular praise the title story for its "heartbreaking voice" and "The Piano Tuner" for its "generosity of details."

Charles E. May

WILLIAM GAY

Born: Hohenwald, Tennessee; 1943

PRINCIPAL SHORT FICTION

*I Hate to See That Evening Sun Go Down: Collected
Stories,* 2002
Wittgenstein's Lolita/The Iceman, 2006

OTHER LITERARY FORMS

William Gay has produced several novels, including *The Long Home* (1999), *Provinces of Night*
(2000), *Twilight* (2006), and *The Lost Country*
(2011). He first gained notoriety for his short stories, publishing a string of well-regarded stories beginning in 1998. His stories were collected in *I Hate
to See That Evening Sun Go Down: Collected Stories,* and the story "I Hate to See That Evening Sun
Go Down" was adapted into a film *That Evening Sun*
(2009), written for the screen and directed by Scott
Teems. Gay also has written a good deal of nonfiction, publishing essays in many journals, including
the *Oxford American,* to which Gay often contributes essays for the annual music issue. Gay's nonfiction was collected by J. M. White for Wild Dog
Press under the title *Time Done Been Won't Be No
More* (2010).

ACHIEVEMENTS

William Gay's stories have been widely anthologized, including being featured in *Best of the South:
The Best of the Second Decade* (2005). He is the
winner of the 1999 William Peden Award and the
1999 James A. Michener Memorial Prize; he was a
2002 Guggenheim Fellow. He was named a 2007
USA Ford Foundation Fellow and awarded a fifty-
thousand-dollar grant by United States Artists. *Provinces of Night* (2000), Gay's second novel, was turned
into the well-received film *Bloodworth* (2010).

BIOGRAPHY

William Gay was born in Hohenwald, Tennessee, in
1943, the son of Bessie and Arthur Gay, a sharecropper
and part-time saw mill worker. William Gay fell in love
with literature at an early age, and he has credited his
seventh-grade teacher with turning him on to writing.
After noticing that Gay was devouring novels by Zane
Grey and Erle Stanley Gardner, the teacher gave him
Thomas Wolfe's book *Look Homeward, Angel* (1929)
and William Faulkner's *The Sound and the Fury*
(1929), and Gay's life was forever changed. Gay received no education outside of the public school
system, and he was largely self-taught as a writer. He
struggled for years before publishing his first story in
1998 at the age of fifty-five.

After graduating from high school, Gay left Hohenwald and joined the Navy. He served as a radar operator
on a destroyer off the coast of Japan and Vietnam
during the Vietnam War. When his four-year tour of
duty was over, he ended up in New York City, where he
stayed for several years. Always an avid music fan,
Gay became interested in the Greenwich Village music
scene, and his lifelong admiration for Bob Dylan took
shape.

Gay returned to Hohenwald after a few years. When
he could not find work, he moved to Chicago and
worked for a pinball manufacturer. He came back to
Hohenwald again and settled down, less than five miles
from where he grew up, for more than thirty years. Before he experienced success as a writer, Gay paid the
bills by working in construction and as a house painter.
He would write at night after getting off work, or he
would write in his head during the day as he performed
what he considered to be mindless tasks. His success
was a long time coming and then hit him suddenly. His
first story was accepted by *The Georgia Review* in
1998. *The Missouri Review* accepted one soon after
that, and Gay later published stories in *Harper's, GQ,
The Atlantic Monthly, The Southern Review, Oxford*

American, and many other magazines and journals. His work also was anthologized widely in collections as diverse as *Best Mystery Stories* (2001) and *Stories from the Blue Moon Café: Anthology of Southern Writers* (2002). Based on the success of his stories, Gay published his first novel, *The Long Home*, in 1999, and he subsequently published several others, his collected stories, a chapbook of short fiction, and a collection of nonfiction prose.

Gay's relationship with Cormac McCarthy, one of his literary idols, is also noteworthy. While Gay's first stories were being rejected, he was receiving a literary education of the highest order from McCarthy, one of his heroes. Living in Knoxville, Tennessee, at the time, McCarthy had not yet gained an international reputation, and he had only a small cult of followers. Gay, counting himself among that cult audience, looked up McCarthy's phone number and called him. When Gay asked McCarthy about his work, McCarthy was shy, but he was more than willing to talk about Flannery O'Connor, whom both Gay and McCarthy greatly admired. Gay sent McCarthy stories, and McCarthy commented on them. Gay also saw an early draft of *Suttree* (1979), one of McCarthy's masterpieces.

ANALYSIS

William Gay owes a stylistic and philosophical debt to his literary headmasters, Faulkner and McCarthy, yet Gay's voice and vision are uniquely his own. Above all, Gay's love of language comes through in his stories: His has a remarkable ability to render place and landscape in dizzying, beautiful language and he is fascinated with the rhythms of southern and Appalachian speech. Gay's world is tense and dark, and danger and violence lurk around every corner. Characters fend off both interior and exterior darkness with careful and strict codes of values. Characters often confront difficult decisions, and they risk becoming their own worst enemies and alienating the ones that they love. It is of tremendous importance in Gay's world that characters realize what they have before throwing it all away in efforts to maintain sanity and order.

Gay, like his literary heroes, is a writer deeply rooted in place, and Tennessee contains all of the stories he will ever need. Never merely a regionalist, Gay is far more concerned about how his corner of the world is changing over time. Though there is always the threat of encroaching technology and other modern devices, Gay's characters seem to live, in many ways, in a place that does not change at all. All of the eternal verities--love, pity, pride, and sacrifice--hold true, but there is always the threat of random violence and forces that cannot and will not be stopped.

Gay's prose is eloquent, and he mixes elements of realism and surrealism in interesting ways. Though the reader seems to be in a place where real-world rules apply, the reader is often led into a world where there are no rules, where a supernatural chaos governs all. Nature, to Gay, is ominous, mysterious, and wonderful; there is dark divide between man and earth, no matter how close they seem to be. Gay's writing lacks sentimentality and softness, which is not to say that it is without heart. How humans conduct themselves, particularly how they live and love, signifies that there is purpose in humankind's existence.

Gay's characters often keep to themselves, reflecting the economy of his language and the settling motion of his prose. They struggle to maintain relationships, seek human communion, and yet fall back into remote and isolated ways of living. Gay is deeply concerned with broken and damaged characters seeking redemption and atonement in the form of defiant and resilient acts against those who have done them harm. At the center of Gay's stories, there is often a mystery, which is revealed slowly to the reader. The reader may expect common maladies to befall Gay's characters, but the reader also witnesses random and startling acts that go unexplained. Gay's detachment as a writer speaks to his deep concern with human frailty.

"I HATE TO SEE THAT EVENING SUN GO DOWN"

In the title story of Gay's *I Hate to See That Evening Sun Go Down: Collected Stories* (2002), Abner Meecham, an aging farmer who has been living in a nursing home at his son's insistence, escapes and returns home to find that his house has been rented out. Meecham's son not only has rented out his house, where he had lived with his wife until her death, but also has rented it out to Meecham's enemy, Lonzo Choat. Meecham wages a quiet war against Choat, moving into the tenant house on the property and urging his son to kick out the Choats. The story is representative of Gay's best work: both funny and tragic, tender and violent. Meecham is an unlikely hero--think of a softer version of Clint Eastwood's William Munny from the film *Unforgiven* (1992)--and among Gay's most likable characters. He has done wrong things in his life and paid a steep cost. Though the story is about Meecham's attempt to atone for his sins, it focuses on his brilliant and unusual strategic plays against Choat.

"I Hate to See That Evening Sun Go Down" has a mythical quality that defines much of Gay's work. His characters are often the stuff of legend, though, at the same time, real to the core. Meecham is a defiant old man whose exaggerated stoicism transforms him into a hard-boiled hero. Gay treats the American South in a loving way, even as he presents the old hatreds, blood feuds, and narrow thinking that fuel its history. On a technical level, Gay's story is astonishing in its use of lush language intertwined with spare, sharp dialogue. The story has a biblical edge, both haunting and parable-like.

"THE PAPERHANGER"

"The Paperhanger" deals with the disappearance of a child and the turmoil that ensues in the wake of the tragedy. An omniscient narrator tells the story, handling it with a brutal detachment and matter-of-factness. The main characters are a doctor and his wife, a wealthy Pakistani couple who are having a mansion built, their child, and the paperhanger. As the couple's child plays with the paperhanger's hair, the doctor's wife interrogates him, insisting that he has been doing inferior work and overcharging for it. The paperhanger's response is deviant and sexually suggestive. The doctor's wife insults him and storms out of the house, calling for her daughter. Her daughter does not follow and cannot be found. The paperhanger and the rest of the workers conduct a search of the grounds. The police are called. The child, it seems, has fallen off the face of the earth.

The story builds an incredible tension as time passes. The doctor blames his wife for the disappearance of the child, and they grow further apart, sinking into an alcoholic haze. The doctor's wife leaves him, and he seemingly is unaffected, continuing to drink more. After he botches an operation, he, too, leaves

town. Slowly, the narrator reveals the paperhanger to be a troubled man. He does not have any sympathy for the doctor and his wife and observes the search for the child in a detached and distant way. He lives alone in the deep woods, and the narrator reveals his frightening habits, which include digging up bones in an abandoned graveyard and examining them with a haunting aloofness. When the doctor's wife appears a year later, a shadow of her former self, she moves back into their abandoned mansion and sinks further into the depths of alcoholism and despair, hoping for some sort of closure. The paperhanger visits her one afternoon, and she hires him to take her into the deep woods, where she believes her daughter had gone missing. The paperhanger takes her to the abandoned graveyard and tells her a horrifying story that seems to suggest he long ago murdered his unfaithful wife and buried her in a grave under a coffin. He makes sexual advances on the doctor's wife, and she does not resist, allowing herself, in a sense, to be taken out of some sense of despair. As the story winds toward a conclusion, the mystery is unearthed, and the paperhanger is revealed to be one of the most terrifying characters in American literature.

"The Paperhanger" is a story that deals with the ruined world, particularly the ruined American South. A landscape once rich and lush has been overtaken by empty mansions and abandoned graveyards. Characters have no connection to the land and lack values. Both the wealthy doctor and the disillusioned paperhanger stand as examples of characters who move through the world with no connection to it. Gay presents a world where characters go unnamed, identified only by their profession or their station in life: the doctor, the paperhanger, the doctor's wife, and the electrician. Only the child, Zeineb, and the sheriff, Bellwether, are given names, a fact that signals the innocence of the child and parodies the the so-called leader in a community that is dark and chaotic.

The world that Gay paints in "The Paperhanger" is scary on several levels, but especially in light of his examination of the emptiness of the modern world. Like Anton Chigurh in Cormac McCarthy's *No Country for Old Men* (2005), the paperhanger is a sociopathic antagonist, who helps the reader realize that evil is present in a world of collapsing values and cold distance. He has no soul, and he seems to be a form of pure evil. Like Chigurh, the paperhanger comes to symbolize the appalling reality of a world without order.

"Bonedaddy, Quincy Nell, and the Fifteen Thousand BTU Electric Chair"

In "Bonedaddy, Quincy Nell, and the Fifteen Thousand BTU Electric Chair," sixteen-year-old Quincy Nell Qualls is dead set on making Bonedaddy Bowers, an undomesticated ladies' man and roving Casanova, her husband. She finally gives in to his sexual advances, thinking it is the only way to win his heart, but Bonedaddy uses her and moves on. He gives her a stuffed panda and then takes another girl to a dance. Quincy Nell beheads the panda with a razor and seeks revenge on Bonedaddy.

This story, while violent, showcases Gay's great talent for humorous writing. Though Gay deals primarily in the world of isolation and loneliness, of depression and distance, it is important to note that he often does this with his hat cocked to one side, winking all the way. This story is brutally hilarious, satirical and slapstick, moving and disturbing. It calls to mind the dark and funny stories of one of Gay's literary heroes, O'Connor. If the names and situations are reminiscent of O'Connor's world, so, too, is the sharp edge that gives the story its value. Gay's great accomplishment is the affecting whimsy with which he tells the tale.

Other major works

LONG FICTION: *The Long Home*, 1999; *Provinces of Night*, 2000; *Twilight*, 2006; *The Lost Country*, 2011.

NONFICTION: *Time Done Been Won't Be No More;Collected Prose*, 2010.

Bibliography

Giraldi, William. "A World Almost Rotten: The Fiction of William Gay." *The Southern Review* 45, no. 2 (Spring, 2009): 331-344. Giraldi gives a long-needed evaluation of Gay's work, including *The Long Home*, "The Paperhanger," and *Provinces of Night*. The first serious academic work done on Gay's fiction.

Nashville Arts Magazine. "Positively William Gay." An important interview with Gay, in which he talks about his writing process, his love of language, and his literary heroes. Tennessee's embrace of Gay as a literary icon has been crucial to his success.

White, J. M. *Wittgenstein's Lolita/The Iceman*. Brush Creek, Tenn.: Wild Dog Press, 2006. The afterword to this small chapbook of stories provides accurate biographical data for Gay.

William Boyle

ELLEN GILCHRIST

Born: Vicksburg, Mississippi; February 20, 1935

PRINCIPAL SHORT FICTION

In the Land of Dreamy Dreams, 1981
Victory over Japan: A Book of Stories, 1984
Drunk with Love: A Book of Stories, 1986
Light Can Be Both Wave and Particle, 1989
I Cannot Get You Close Enough: Three Novellas,
    1990 (includes *Winter, De Havilland Hand,* and *A*
    Summer in Maine)
Rhoda: A Life in Stories, 1995
The Age of Miracles: Stories, 1995
The Courts of Love: Stories, 1996
Flights of Angels: Stories, 1998
Collected Stories, 2000
The Cabal, and Other Stories, 2000
I, Rhoda Manning, Go Hunting with My Daddy, and
    Other Stories, 2002
Nora Jane: A Life in Stories, 2005

OTHER LITERARY FORMS

Ellen Gilchrist (GIHL-krihst) has found her most
comfortable literary form to be the short story, although
her first published work was a collection of poems, *The
Land Surveyor's Daughter* (1979). She has published
novels, written magazine articles and a television play,
The Season of Dreams (1968), based on writer Eudora
Welty's short stories. *Falling Through Space: The
Journals of Ellen Gilchrist* (1987) is a collection of essays drawn from her journals and presented on National Public Radio. Gilchrist published *The Writing
Life* in 2005, and her novel *A Dangerous Age* (2008)
was brought out by Algonquin Press.

ACHIEVEMENTS

Ellen Gilchrist's fiction features a rich tangle of
family relationships and realistic settings, often

southern locales. Because of that, Gilchrist has sometimes been considered a regional writer, and sometimes
a women's writer, though most reviewers believe that
she rises above the limitations those labels imply. Although her subjects are often the messy lives of the
wealthy and talented, she creates lively pictures of
other types, too, male as well as female. Her portraits
of children are especially vivid, and although she
writes frequently about the South, she has also used
settings from California to Maine. *The Season of
Dreams* won the National Scriptwriting Award from
the National Educational Television Network in 1968.
Gilchrist won Pushcart Prizes for "Rich" (1979-1980)
and "Summer: An Elegy" (1983). In 1984, she won the
American Book Award for *Victory over Japan,* and in
1985 she won the J. William Fulbright Award for literature. The Mississippi Academy of Arts and Sciences
honored her in 1985, 1990, and 1991.

BIOGRAPHY

Ellen Gilchrist was born into a family of plantation
owners in Mississippi and remained in the South almost all of her life, except for several of her adolescent
years during World War II. At that time, her father, an
engineer for the Army Corps of Engineers, moved the
family to several small towns in the Midwest. When
she was fourteen, Gilchrist began her career in journalism by writing a column for a local newspaper in
Franklin, Kentucky. At nineteen, she dropped out of
school and ran away to North Carolina to marry an engineering student. Together they had three children.
Divorced in 1966, Gilchrist entered Millsaps College,
where she studied creative writing under Eudora Welty.
During the next years, Gilchrist continued to write, and
she was married and divorced three more times, once
to her first husband. It was toward the end of that period
that she took significant steps toward a career as a professional writer. The first of those steps was taking a
position as editor for the New Orleans newspaper *Vieux*

Carré Courier.

Gilchrist reported that by the late 1970's she was tired of the social world of New Orleans, where she had lived during her marriages. At about the time she began working at the *Vieux Carré Courier*, she sent some of her poems to Jim Whitehead, poet and novelist in the writing program at the University of Arkansas, Fayetteville. He urged her to join his writing class, and she did so. Gilchrist said that the instant she saw Fayetteville, she felt that she had arrived where she belonged. She liked its unpretentious social world, where people from the university and community met as equals. In 1981, the University of Arkansas Press published Gilchrist's first short-story collection, *In the Land of Dreamy Dreams*. Its sales were remarkable, about ten thousand copies in the Southwest alone-- good sales by any standard but especially for a book brought out with no budget for elaborate advertising and promotion. The word-of-mouth praise that *In the Land of Dreamy Dreams* received brought it to the attention of Little, Brown, the company that published Gilchrist's next two books and that reissued *In the Land of Dreamy Dreams* in 1985. Gilchrist's novel *The Annunciation* (1983) received a cool critical reception, but critical attention to her later work, particularly her short fiction, was more evenly positive. In the mid-1980's, her growing reputation made her an interesting choice for a weekly series of "journal entry" essays on National Public Radio's *Morning Edition* (some of these were later collected in *Falling Through Space*). Many of these essays originated in Fayetteville and dealt with local characters and places (much as *The Annunciation* did). At the same time, they communicated Gilchrist's delight in human relationships, in the demands of her craft, and in the world around her. Gilchrist continued to write fiction and give public readings and lectures, remaining in her beloved Fayetteville. She became an associate professor of creative writing at the University of Arkansas and bought a home in Ocean Springs, Mississippi. In 2004, she won the Thomas Wolfe Prize from the University of North Carolina at Chapel Hill for the body of her work. For 2004 and 2005, she was named an Andrew Mellon Fellow at Tulane University in New Orleans.

ANALYSIS

Any reader of Ellen Gilchrist's fiction quickly comes to recognize her people, places, and preoccupations. She writes about women, often about wealthy southern women coming to terms with their boredom and self-indulgence. Sometimes she writes about creative women, writers and poets and scholars, whose impulses lead them into tight situations from which only drastic action can rescue them. In fact, desperate circumstances--pregnancy, even murder--mark the central action of many Gilchrist stories. Gilchrist also peoples her fiction with children, particularly adolescent girls whose growing self-awareness and sexuality often draw them into the sort of circumstances their creator most enjoys exploring.

Gilchrist frequently revisits favorite characters at several ages in their lives, so that reading successive stories about them becomes a bit like reading a short novel. In fact, Gilchrist frequently interweaves motifs, linking stories within as well as across collections. In her work, characters appear and reappear from one collection to the next, sometimes with new names, sometimes with slightly different families or backgrounds, but always with recognizable characteristics that take on greater depth as the reader sees them from multiple angles. Gilchrist treats settings the same way, using authentic geographic detail about places such as New Orleans, California, or Charlotte, North Carolina, to create the canvas on which she works, linking the various frames of that canvas through repetition.

"RICH"

In "Rich," an early story from *In the Land of Dreamy Dreams*, Tom and Letty Wilson are wealthy New Orleans socialites. Their lives have brought them everything they have ever wanted, including each other. Tom is a banker who likes to quote Andrew Carnegie. "Money is what you keep score with," he says. Letty has loved him since she saw him performing drunken fraternity stunts while they were both students at Tulane University. On one occasion, he stole a Bunny bread truck and drove through the Irish Channel district, a poor area of the city, throwing bread to the housewives. The one thing missing from Tom and Letty's lives is a child, and even that gap is filled when they adopt a baby girl named Helen. After the adoption,

Letty has no trouble conceiving, and in short order, the Wilsons have four additional children. Of their children, only Helen is imperfect; she is plagued with learning disabilities and attention disorders; she must take drugs in order to concentrate.

The Wilsons are also rich in maids, and the maids find Helen hateful to care for, especially because she can turn from loving to vicious in moments, shouting "nigger, nigger, nigger" at the maid who has crossed her will. In one such confrontation, Helen runs from the angry servant, crashes into the bassinet holding the Wilson baby, and sends it rolling off the porch to crash on the sidewalk, killing the infant. The death ruins Tom. He begins to drink too much and makes bad banking decisions. The thought haunts him that people believe Helen is his illegitimate child. His life is crumbling to nothing. At last, driven beyond what he can tolerate, Tom takes Helen out to his duck camp. He takes along his prize Labrador puppy, a rifle, and a revolver. After amusing Helen as tenderly as he can, he shoots first the puppy, then Helen, and then himself. Many things about this story are typical of Gilchrist's work, especially the violent ending and the detailed use of New Orleans for the setting. The reader, however, should also notice the realistic picture of Helen, whose psychic deformities are displayed without melodrama. What is less typical is the shifting point of view in the story; in later work, Gilchrist tends to use limited viewpoints or to write in first person.

"THE FAMOUS POLL AT JODY'S BAR"

"The Famous Poll at Jody's Bar" offers a good example of Gilchrist's fondness for returning to characters. In the story, nineteen-year-old Nora Jane Whittington, whom Gilchrist describes as "a self-taught anarchist," is trying to decide how to get money to go to see her boyfriend, Sandy, in San Jose. She and Sandy had lived together for fourteen months after she had finished high school, during which time Sandy had taught Nora Jane many things, including an appreciation for jazz and an ability to plan holdups. Now she uses that ability, along with her skill in disguise, to hold up Jody's Bar, where the regulars include a judge and Jody, of course, who, ironically, is armed against the holdups he constantly expects. The poll of the title is being taken to let the bar's customers decide whether

Prescott Hamilton IV should go on with his plans to be married. As she cleans out the till, Nora Jane adds her ballot to the jar; then, disguising herself as a nun, she leaves, headed for Sandy.

VICTORY OVER JAPAN

When the reader sees Nora Jane next, she is in California in "Jade Buddhas, Red Bridges, Fruits of Love," from Gilchrist's 1984 collection *Victory over Japan*. The story concerns Nora Jane's efforts to reconnect with Sandy, and it reveals how instead she takes up with Freddy Harwood. As often happens in Gilchrist's stories, biology plays a dramatic role in Nora Jane's destiny, and she becomes pregnant, perhaps by Freddy. In "The Double Happiness Bun" in the same collection, the reader begins to suspect that Nora Jane's baby is really twins. At the end of "The Double Happiness Bun," Nora Jane is caught on the Bay Bridge during an earthquake; she is entertaining the children of a stranger, who is even more desperate than she. In the volume that follows, *Drunk with Love*, the reader experiences part of the story from the point of view of the twin fetuses. Although, like many Gilchrist women,

Ellen Gilchrist (AP Photo/Robert Jordan)

Nora Jane seems trapped by her own sexuality and re-production, it is a mistake to see her as a victim. Like Gilchrist's vivid characters, Nora Jane is also daring and resourceful. Her holdup demonstrates this, and so does her courageous decision to help the stranger and her children in the earthquake disaster.

"Music," in *Victory over Japan*, is the story that am-plifies the character of Rhoda, a woman who appears in several stories over several collections. When readers piece together her background, they know that Rhoda's father is a self-made man, his fortune comes from ge-ology, and he has moved his wife and daughter around the country--heartlessly, his wife says--where his work has taken him. Rhoda appeared as a child in several stories in *In the Land of Dreamy Dreams*, sometimes with her own name, sometimes with another. In "Music," the reader sees a sulky, willful fourteen-year-old Rhoda who embodies many of the qualities of Gil-christ's older heroines. In addition to being unbearably self-centered, she is intelligent and romantic; those parts of her character prevent her from being a bore.

In this story, she becomes the means by which her parents express their ongoing conflict. Furious at being dragged from Indiana to Kentucky by her father while the boy she is sure she loves, Bob Rosen, undergoes surgery for cancer far away in St. Louis, Rhoda does everything she can to make herself obnoxious to her parents. Along with her frequent assertions of her atheism, her constant smoking becomes an instrument of rebellion. Both her parents detest the habit, but her weak mother cannot stop her. At last, her father takes her to see the strip mines in rural Kentucky. He has some limited success in preventing Rhoda from smoking during the trip, but he cannot stop her from seducing a boy she meets in a pool hall, and at last, in the midst of a union dispute, he must send her home in a chartered plane.

The last paragraphs of the story are set thirty years later, when Rhoda reads a letter from her father. In it, he tells her that he and her mother are ashamed of the book she has dedicated to them and that he wants their names removed from it. Rhoda, not surprisingly, has the last word. When she writes back, she tells him to take his name off the checks he sends to television preachers, and she reasserts her old arguments about

evolution. Readers familiar with Gilchrist's women will recognize in Rhoda the spiritual sister of Amanda McCamey of *The Annunciation* and of Anna Hand in many of the later stories.

Victory over Japan also contains an important group of stories that introduce the complicated family ap-pearing in much of Gilchrist's later work. A character who does most to unify these tales is Traceleen, the black woman who has long worked as maid for Crystal and Manny Weiss and as nurse to the family's daughter, Crystal Anne. Like many Gilchrist characters, Traceleen seems to have roots in William Faulkner's vision of the South; she is loyal, intelligent, devoted to the white family she works for but clear-eyed about its many faults. It is through her eyes that readers see Crystal's disintegrating marriage in "Miss Crystal's Maid Name Traceleen, She's Talking, She's Telling Everything She Knows"; this marital conflict forms the theme of several stories in which Traceleen appears. It is Traceleen who observes that Crystal's tragedy is her loveless marriage. "They're rich people, all the ones I'm talking about. Not that it does them much good that I can see," Traceleen says with her characteristic candor. The stories in the "Crystal" section describe Crystal's brother Phelan Manning, her lover Alan, and her son King by her first husband. Gilchrist continues to explore these relationships increasingly in *Light Can Be Both Wave and Particle*, her novel *The Anna Pa-pers*, and her three novellas in *I Cannot Get You Close Enough*.

DRUNK WITH LOVE

Gilchrist's 1986 collection, *Drunk with Love*, con-tains the Nora Jane story, which is concluded from the point of view of her unborn fetuses. As the fetuses speak, they look forward to their appearance on earth, which they know only by reputation. This collection also includes three Rhoda stories: "Nineteen Forty-One," which portrays Rhoda around the age of nine; "The Expansion of the Universe," which details Rho-da's romance with Bob Rosen, before his illness, and which concludes with Rhoda's family moving to Ken-tucky (a move that temporarily unites Rhoda and her mother against her father); and "Adoration," in which readers see nineteen-year-old Rhoda in her hasty new marriage, as she and her husband use her pregnancies as a means of denying their empty relationship.

Drunk with Love concludes with two important stories. "Traceleen at Dawn" is the story of how Crystal quit drinking. Once again, Traceleen is a friendly but not entirely neutral narrator as she relates Crystal's efforts to quit. When Crystal falls off the wagon, she goes on an epic binge, which ends when she deliberately sets fire to her house. That is how she quits drinking at last. The story called "Anna, Part I" introduces Anna Hand on "the day she decided to give up being a fool and go back to being a writer." The story traces Anna's love affair with a married man; as the affair ends, readers see her opening a box of typing paper, determined to turn her experience into art. Anna's story is continued and in a sense concluded in Gilchrist's 1988 novel, *The Anna Papers*. In the course of the novel, Anna discovers her niece Olivia, who is her brother Daniel's child from his failed first marriage to a Cherokee woman, whom he had met in California in the 1960's. Although Olivia is poor and Anna has always had money, once Olivia is brought into the family, she proves to be Anna's spiritual daughter in terms of talent, intelligence, and nerve. At the end of the novel, Anna commits suicide rather than face treatment for a cancer she knows will be fatal. These details become important in *I Cannot Get You Close Enough*.

LIGHT CAN BE BOTH WAVE AND PARTICLE

Light Can Be Both Wave and Particle in many ways distills characters and themes from the earlier collections. "The Tree Fort" and "The Time Capsule" picture Rhoda as a child in wartime, trying to come to terms with her family's constant moving and her first intimations of what death means. Another Rhoda story, "Some Blue Hills at Sundown," confirms that Bob Rosen did indeed die of cancer. "The Starlight Express" documents the birth of Nora Jane's twins. They are delivered by Harwood at his eccentric house far out in the forest. Nora Jane is saved from bleeding to death only by the fortuitous arrival of the medical services helicopter, for in Gilchrist's work, birth is rarely a simple matter.

The title story of the collection involves the meeting of Lin Tan Sing, a third-year medical student from San Francisco, and Margaret McElvoy, from Fayetteville, Arkansas. They meet on a bridge overlooking Puget

Sound, fall in love, and eventually decide to have him meet Margaret's family, in Fayetteville. In Gilchrist's stories, the abrasions that arise from conflicting classes and cultures are often fatal to love. Part of the difficulties of Crystal's marriage, for example, rise from the fact that her husband is a Jew. Olivia, when she reenters the Hand family, is always conscious of her status as a Native American. In the case of Lin Tan and Margaret, however, things go well. Margaret's family is equal to the occasion; the story closes as her father prepares to play chess with his future son-in-law.

The volume closes with a long story, "Mexico," in which the reader sees Rhoda again, now divorced and spending time in Mexico with some of the same wealthy and self-indulgent people who have had roles in other Gilchrist stories; in fact, Crystal's brother, Manning, is here, and the reader also learns that Rhoda knew Anna before she killed herself. At the end of the story, Rhoda has broken her foot, and the resulting confinement leads her to try to make sense of her family and its relationships. As the story concludes, she has written a conciliatory letter to her brother Dudley, with whom her past relationship has been painful. (It is notable that the name Dudley is given to many of Gilchrist's least likable men.)

I CANNOT GET YOU CLOSE ENOUGH

Much of the Anna series is concluded in *I Cannot Get You Close Enough*. The first part is a posthumous manuscript from Anna, explaining her attempts to deal with her brother Daniel's treacherous former wife. The second details the early life in Oklahoma of Anna's niece, Olivia, and her joining the Hands in Charlotte, North Carolina. The last part takes place after Anna's death, when all the family females (including Traceleen and Crystal Anne and Olivia) spend the summer in Maine.

FLIGHTS OF ANGELS

This collection returns some of Gilchrist's liveliest characters--Rhoda, Traceleen, and Crystal--and continues their story, while also introducing new voices into the Gilchrist cast. "Miss Crystal Confronts the Past" is told through the frank voice of Traceleen, who describes herself as "old enough to know better" in reference to her trip with Crystal to Charlotte, North Carolina, to save Crystal's grandmother (a powerful force in her own right) and her estate from the manipulations of Manning. He may be unscrupulous, but he knows how to entertain the bored old woman; it is only after her death that the true nature of Manning's Medicare scam comes to light.

In "A Sordid Tale: Or, Traceleen Continues Talking," Traceleen reveals what Crystal went through to try to keep her recently widowed friend from falling under Manning's spell. Crystal knows that her brother Manning is mainly interested in her friend's money. The story also introduces Traceleen's feisty niece Andria, a television anchorwoman who has told her aunt, "Don't go writing any more of those crazy stories and casting yourself in the role of maid." Traceleen's charm is that while she may call Crystal "Miss Crystal," she is never blind to the truth--good or bad--about her employer.

As the collection's title from Horatio's farewell to the dying Hamlet suggests, many of these stories deal with death or loss. In "Mississippi," Larkin is on death row for the murder of a white supremacist, who killed Larkin's African American friend Someral during a demonstration for integration. Larkin is a typical Gilchrist woman: self-willed, independent, and led by a strong sense of justice. In "A Tree to Be Desired," Juliet takes strength from her dying grandfather to confront her loveless marriage and to begin a love affair with the young black male nurse who tended him.

"The Triumph of Reason" introduces a new Gilchrist narrator, brilliant and outspoken seventeen-year-old Aurora Harris, who relates the story of her romance with a French boy (and justifies her subsequent abortion). In "Have a Wonderful Nice Walk" she chronicles the French boy's difficult visit to the United States, her discovery of her next love, and her comic relationship with her younger sister. The stories demonstrate Gilchrist's skill in creating credible voices of bright adolescents, making them funny and likable without downplaying their self-centeredness. "Down at the Dollhouse," one of the last stories in the collection, returns to the theme of death as it recounts how a spunky old lady spends the last hours of her life at a beauty salon, attending to the needs of her equally elderly friends. As always, the dominant concern is the weight of the past on present human relationships, one of Gilchrist's most persistent themes.

I, RHODA MANNING, GO HUNTING WITH MY DADDY, AND OTHER STORIES

In *I, Rhoda Manning, Go Hunting with My Daddy, and Other Stories*, Gilchrist returns to Rhoda, here aged five-and-a-half, in this title story set in Moundville, Illinois, where her engineer father is supervising the building of levees. As the postscript, written by the adult Rhoda at his death, suggests, this story is a tribute to her powerful and beloved father, or at least the child's impression of him, even as the girl rebels against his sometimes confining notions of how she should be raised so that she becomes a lady and a person of character.

The four stories that follow-- "Entropy," "A Christmas in Wyoming," "On Wind River in Wyoming," and "The Golden Bough"--show the adult Rhoda, first married and raising three sons in New Orleans, where she has settled with a Jewish lawyer named Eric, who does his best to be a good father to the children of her previous marriage, then visiting her parents out West. In fact, as the whole family gathers in "A Christmas in Wyoming," entropy becomes a powerful symbol of how the family seems to fly apart around the strong, clear figure of Rhoda's father, who hopes this reunion will stop the dissolution of his clan, in particular, its men. A recurring theme in these stories is addiction: Rhoda's to alcohol, and her sons' to marijuana, which her father seeks to cure by alternately taking them away from Rhoda and the complicated, decadent South, or having them visit him, exposing them to the beauty and lessons of the outdoors.

In "On Wind River in Wyoming," only Rhoda and her youngest son, Teddy, visit, and her father is now married to the plump Valerie, Rhoda's mother having returned to New Orleans in protest of the miserable cold she can barely endure in the alien West. In yet another attempt to save one of Rhoda's boys, her father takes the pair camping and sends them out alone in a canoe to navigate the river. Though alternately furious and joyful as she and her son wend their way toward her father down-river, taking in the wilderness and even spotting a moose and her calf, in the end Rhoda identifies this test as one of her father's many gifts to her. However, neither her efforts nor those of her father will save her sons from their struggles with addiction.

The final story of this Rhoda section, "The Golden Bough," is told in first person; Big Dudley, her father, had died three years earlier. Her sons are grown with families of their own, and they are largely cured of the addictions their mother and grandfather so feared would ruin the boys. Rhoda, now sixty-four and sober, is savoring her Christmas alone away from them when she decides, while reading Seamus Heaney's 1991 translation of Vergil's *Aeneid* (c. 29-19 b.c.e.; English translation, 1553), that she will seek the sybil and the golden bough in the woods behind her house to find her father somehow just one more time. In the process of climbing a tree, she falls and nearly dies. Pulled back into the world of here and now, a son and grandchildren gathered around her, she recalls talking with her father and hearing him speak of all the rivers he has known. As this series of stories ends, Rhoda commits to passing down to the next generation what she has learned before it is too late.

The five stories that follow feature various characters, the most familiar of which are Nora Jane, Freddy, and Traceleen, Miss Crystal's faithful servant and companion. "Gotterdämerung, in Which Nora Jane and Freddy Harwood Confront Evil in a World They Never Made" is so evocative of 9/11 that Gilchrist says in an author's note that she wrote the story before that tragedy. Nora Jane is invited to sing at a benefit in New York City, but as the plans for this engagement go forward, intercut with the anticipation of the trip is the story of an assassination being planned in that same city, to be carried out as the Harwood family members go about their lives in Northern California. Nora Jane's husband is the target of these Iranians because he carries Salman Rushdie's books in his Berkeley store. At their house away from town, Freddy and his young son are saved by a convergence of Federal Bureau of Investigation (FBI) agents and an ancient mountain lion Freddy has been feeding for years. Despite this close call, the Harwoods do not cancel their trip to New York, where they will be carefully guarded, the FBI agents promise. As the story ends, an ominous sense of impending doom pervades, even as the children joyfully plan the trip with their parents.

In "Light Shining Through Honey," Traceleen, the African American woman who has served and counseled Miss Crystal for years, fears the nanny who is taking care of her niece's twins is not good for them, and she involves herself further in the lives of her niece and the twins as well as in the life of the nanny, Jane. When Jane's drug-addicted boyfriend turns up and takes her hostage in an attempt to score some cocaine from the police surrounding the house, Traceleen has the children safe in her care. Having finally gotten Crystal Anne to live like a grownup, Traceleen is determined to help the twins, Jane the nanny, and even the niece. "Light Through Honey" is what she sees reflected on a countertop before she plunges into these lives, giving comfort and advice from the strange mixture of yoga, Buddhism, and Christianity she has come to practice. In the end, everyone is brought into the safe harbor of Traceleen's wisdom and care. It is on this note that the volume ends.

NORA JANE: A LIFE IN STORIES

As its title suggests, this volume *Nora Jane: A Life in Stories* follows the generally happy arc of Nora Jane's life with her husband Freddy and their children in Berkeley, California. Early stories of Nora Jane's life are reintroduced here: "The Famous Poll at Jody's Bar," "Jade Buddhas, Red Bridges, Fruits of Love," "The Double Happiness Bun," "Drunk with Love," and "The Starlight Express" as well as "Gotterdämerung: In Which Nora Jane and Freddy Harwood Confront Evil in a World They Never Made." Beginning with "Perhaps a Miracle," Nora Jane has decided to go to college, precipitating the romance of Freddy's best friend Nieman Gluuk and Stella Light, which evolves, surprising them both, through courtship, a wedding, and children. They meet in "You Must Change Your Life," in which Nieman hooks up with a time-traveling Leonardo Da Vinci and takes him to see the science labs at Berkeley. "The Affair" and "A Wedding by the Sea" complete this series, though the growing family continues to appear in the Nora Jane and Freddy's lives.

"The Brown Cape," in which Freddy takes his girls, Tammili and Lydia, camping, looks forward to the novella at the end of the collection, "Fault Lines," an account of Freddy's battle with cancer. Though Nora Jane warns him not to make this trip, he persists, is injured, and finds himself the vulnerable one as his quick-thinking daughters manage to shelter him in severe weather, using the brown cape Leonardo has left behind, keeping him warm and dry until they are all rescued. At the end of "Fault Lines," through traditional treatment and with the help of a nun who prays for him daily, Freddy has a good prognosis, though nothing is certain. Tammili and Lydia are contemplating going away to college. As the novella ends, Freddy and his best friend sit in a shaft of sunlight eating croissants and contemplating educating Nieman's children. "It's all good," Freddy says at last.

Gilchrist has said that she never stops wondering what her characters are up to next. This likely will not be the last time readers will see this cast of characters.

OTHER MAJOR WORKS

LONG FICTION: *The Annunciation*, 1983; *The Anna Papers*, 1988; *Net of Jewels*, 1992; *Anabasis: A Journey to the Interior*, 1994; *Starcarbon: A Meditation on Love*, 1994; *Sarah Conley*, 1997; *A Dangerous Age*, 2008.

TELEPLAY: *The Season of Dreams*, 1968.

POETRY: *The Land Surveyor's Daughter*, 1979; *Riding Out the Tropical Depression: Selected Poems*, 1986.

NONFICTION: *Falling Through Space: The Journals of Ellen Gilchrist*, 1987; *The Writing Life*, 2005.

BIBLIOGRAPHY

Allen, Kimberly G. Review of *I Cannot Get You Close Enough*, by Ellen Gilchrist. *Library Journal* 115 (September 15, 1990): 98-99. Praises the work's complex structure, which Allen describes as confusing but effective. Useful in its examination of the novellas' overlapping chronology.

Bauer, Margaret Donovan. *The Fiction of Ellen Gilchrist*. Gainesville: University Press of Florida, 1999. An excellent book-length study of Gilchrist's works and prevalent themes. Includes bibliographical references and an index.

Gilchrist, Ellen. Interview by Wendy Smith. *Publishers Weekly* 239 (March 2, 1992): 46-47. The interviewer claims that Gilchrist creates in her novels an extended family that could no longer be comfortably handled in the short-story form. Discusses characters such as Rhoda Manning, Anna Hand, and others who reappear in Gilchrist's fiction.

Hoffman, Roy. Review of *Light Can Be Both Wave and Particle*, by Ellen Gilchrist. *The New York Times Book Review*, October 22, 1989, p. 13. Analyzes the work as a conclusion to *The Annunciation*; gives particular attention to "Mexico" and to the title story. The themes of the meeting of East and West in that story seem to suggest new directions that Hoffman believes Gilchrist's fiction is about to take.

McCay, Mary A. *Ellen Gilchrist*. New York: Twayne, 1997. Examines Gilchrist's life and her works, with a chapter on the short stories. Includes bibliographical references and an index.

Seabrook, John. Review of *Victory over Japan*, by Ellen Gilchrist. *The Christian Science Monitor*, December 7, 1984, p. 38. This balanced review offers a brief analysis of the stories' major characteristics, praising Gilchrist's prose style and dialogue but faulting the weakness of her character analysis. Seabrook likes her humor but finds the behavior of her characters baffling.

Shapiro, Harriet. "Southerner Ellen Gilchrist Is the Book World's Belle." *People Weekly* 23 (February 11, 1985): 75. A brief biographical sketch written when Gilchrist won the American Book Award for her collection *Victory over Japan*; notes that her stories focus on independent "southern belles."

Thompson, Jeanie, and Anita Miller Garner. "The Miracle of Realism: The Bid for Self-Knowledge in the Fiction of Ellen Gilchrist." In *Women Writers of the Contemporary South*, edited by Peggy Whitman Prenshaw. Jackson: University Press of Mississippi, 1984. A useful close analysis of Gilchrist's early work. The authors see her treatment of women as essentially traditional, despite her interest in unconventional central characters. The essay gives most attention to *The Annunciation*, and it also discusses "Rich," "The President of the Louisiana Live Oak Society," and "Revenge." The authors look particularly at Gilchrist's fondness for central characters who are simultaneously charming and awful.

Ann Davison Garbett
Updated by Susie Paul

CHARLOTTE PERKINS GILMAN

Born: Hartford, Connecticut; July 3, 1860
Died: Pasadena, California; August 17, 1935
Also known as: Charlotte Anna Perkins

PRINCIPAL SHORT FICTION

"The Yellow Wallpaper," 1892

Charlotte Perkins Gilman Reader, 1981 (Ann J. Lane, editor)

The Yellow Wallpaper, and Other Writings, 1989 (Lynne Sharon Schwartz, editor)

Herland and Selected Stories, 1992 (Barbara H. Solomon, editor; also published as *Herland, The Yellow Wall-Paper, and Selected Writings*, 1999, Denise D. Knight, editor)

"The Yellow Wall-Paper" and Selected Stories of Charlotte Perkins Gilman, 1994 (Denise Knight, editor)

The Yellow Wallpaper, and Other Stories, 1995 (Robert Shulman, editor)

OTHER LITERARY FORMS

Charlotte Perkins Gilman published two volumes of poems during her lifetime, *In This Our World* (1893) and *Suffrage Songs and Verses* (1911). Her nonfiction social criticism, notably *Women and Economics* (1898), was the basis of her contemporary reputation and her lecture career. Gilman also wrote utopian novels, including her famous *Herland* (1915, serial; 1979, book), as well as s an autobiography, *The Living of Charlotte Perkins Gilman* (1935).

ACHIEVEMENTS

Charlotte Perkins Gilman was posthumously inducted into the National Women's Hall of Fame in Seneca Falls, New York, in 1994. During her life, she was a delegate to a number of international conventions, including the International Socialist and Labor Congress in London in 1896 and the International Women's Suffrage Congress in Budapest, Hungary, in 1913.

BIOGRAPHY

Charlotte Anna Perkins Stetson Gilman was born in Hartford, Connecticut, on July 3, 1860. Her father was Frederick Beecher Perkins, and her mother was Mary Fitch Westcott. The Beechers, including her early role model, Harriet Beecher Stowe, influenced her social convictions. Gilman married Charles Walter Stetson, a young artist, in 1884. Within the year, their daughter Katharine was born. Thereafter, Gilman suffered bouts of depression stemming from her desire to work as an artist, writer, and advocate of women's rights and the conflict between this desire and her more traditional role as wife and mother.

In 1886, Gilman had a breakdown and was treated for hysteria by neurologist S. Weir Mitchell, who prescribed total rest and abstinence from work. Despite the treatment, Gilman grew worse and feared for her sanity. She decided to take matters into her own hands, separated from Stetson, and moved to California, where she began to publish and lecture on the economic and domestic dependence of women.

In 1892, Gilman published the short story "The Yellow Wallpaper," based on her breakdown and rest treatment. During that time, she also published her first book of poetry, *In This Our World*, and a major volume of social criticism, *Women and Economics*. In 1900, she married George Houghton Gilman. She continued to publish social criticism and fiction throughout the next decades. From 1909 to 1916, she single-handedly wrote and published the monthly magazine *The Forerunner*. Her husband died in 1934. Gilman, diagnosed with incurable breast cancer, took her own life on August 17, 1935.

ANALYSIS

Charlotte Perkins Gilman used her fiction to dramatize her vision of history, sociology, and ethics. Over the course of her career, she published close to two hundred pieces of fiction, mainly short stories, in periodicals or in her own magazine, *The Forerunner*.

Most of Gilman's stories belong to two categories: realistic stories that deal with the unhappy situations of the everyday world and utopian stories set totally in the world of the imagination.

In her fiction, Gilman suggests changes that might be made in preparation for the future world and asserts the need to break away from the traditions that limit human potential. While she is often identified with the feminist movement, her emphasis is on a utopian society in which men and women would be equal, a society she portrays in the novel *Herland*. Her stories are meant to be uplifting examples of her social philosophy. Because many of these stories have an ideal ending, rather than a probable one, many critics find them didactic or formulaic. They are not well regarded for their literary qualities.

Charlotte Perkins Gilman (Library of Congress)

Gilman did not have literary pretensions; she wrote quickly and without much revision. She did, however, aspire to write with "clearness and vivacity," so that her work would "be apprehended with ease and pleasure." Her style is direct; her message is clear.

"THE YELLOW WALLPAPER"

Of all Gilman's fiction, "The Yellow Wallpaper" stands out as a brilliant psychological study, apart from the rest of her work in its emotional intensity and introspection. It is considered by critics the only genuinely literary piece she wrote, in the literary tradition of the nineteenth century American short story, sustaining a single effect: madness, loneliness, and desperation with a psychological intensity best suited to short fiction.

The story is told in the first person by a young wife and mother. The narrator's physician-husband has ordered a rest cure for her nerves. The reference is clearly autobiographical; Gilman's stated intent is to indict the methods of Dr. S. Weir Mitchell, who ordered a similar cure of complete rest and absence of intellectual stimulation for Gilman to cure her depression and breakdown following her own marriage and motherhood. According to Gilman, this medical advice brought her nearer to the brink of "utter mental ruin." This story is unique in Gilman's canon in not resolving happily. The narrator, according to the traditional view of wife as dependent child, believes that her husband-doctor knows best and sinks into horrifying insanity. In her own life, Gilman was able to break out and save herself by moving away from her husband and resuming her work.

John, the well-meaning husband-doctor of the story, rents a large house isolated in the country to provide his ailing wife with perfect rest. Gradually she becomes confined to the nursery at the top of the house, forbidden to write to relieve her anxiety. As her condition worsens, the woman becomes obsessed with the yellow wallpaper in the nursery. She becomes convinced that the wallpaper menaces her, and then believes that it holds a woman trapped behind bars. The poor young woman attempts to escape her confinement and the wallpaper by gnawing at the bed, which is nailed down, and peeling off the wallpaper with her fingernails. Finally, she escapes into total madness, creeping round and round the room on her hands and knees.

"The Yellow Wallpaper" is a small literary gem, the most widely read and admired of Gilman's short fiction. It is the story of a woman's mental breakdown, narrated in a naïve, first-person voice with superb psychological and dramatic precision. The story is consciously autobiographical, achieving a genuine power, directness, and authenticity. From the time of its publication, the story was read and admired as a tale of horror and madness in the tradition of Edgar Allan Poe. Since the 1970's, it has most often been given a feminist reading as a symbolic tale of a woman trying to break free from her cage. Feminist critics view the story as a rare piece of literature by a nineteenth century woman who directly confronts the sexual politics of the male-female, husband-wife relationship.

"MAKING A CHANGE"

Julia is a young wife and mother on the verge of collapse. She is exhausted and hypersensitive from being kept awake at night by her screaming child. She believes it is her duty to care for her child and the home while her husband, preoccupied with earning money, has no understanding of her state of mind. Desperately, Julia tries to kill herself. Fortunately, her mother-in-law arrives in time to stop her, and the two women work out a plan of escape. Secretly, Julia pursues her career as a musician, while the widowed mother-in-law sets up a day care center. Both women find their problems are solved; both pursue meaningful work.

Julia's husband is angry when he discovers the arrangement, but he finally realizes that all of them are happier and better off economically. "Making a Change" is an example of one of Gilman's stories suggesting social change as an alternative to frustrating, meaningless lives for women. The "baby-garden" of the story is a stable environment for children that allows mothers to seek work for which they are better suited and older women to find creative possibilities for their lives after husbands and children are gone. Julia's desperation, realistic and autobiographical for Gilman, is happily resolved through the intervention of a wise older woman.

"WHEN I WAS A WITCH"

First published in *The Forerunner* in 1910, "When I Was a Witch" is one of Gilman's utopian fantasies. The narrator is a modern woman who goes to work in an office in New York City while her sister keeps house. On Halloween, she acquires the magical power to have her wishes come true. Over the course of several days, she doles out punishments to fit the crimes of those who embody her pet peeves: abusers of animals; sellers of bad milk, eggs, and meat; the cruel; the pompous; and those who take excessive profits at the expense of the poor.

Once she realizes what is happening, the narrator sets about reforming the city according to Gilman's imagination. Newspapers stop printing lies, the world becomes kinder and more truthful. In the end, though, when she dares to wish for satisfaction and meaningful work for women, her magic fails her. Gilman's style in this story is light, humorous, entertaining, and mischievous. It is pure fantasy, until the narrator is stopped short at the end, perhaps indicating that Gilman was aware that reform for women would not be so easily accomplished.

"MR. PEEBLES' HEART"

"Mr. Peebles' Heart" is another realistic situation mingled with utopian elements and a happy ending. In this story, the protagonist is an older man, illustrating Gilman's humanistic concern for older people and productive lives for all, men and women alike. Mr. Peebles is a slave of duty. All his life he has labored at work he dislikes in order to support his mother, his silly clinging wife, and his daughters. His sister-in-law, a "new woman" and a doctor, encourages him to travel around Europe for two years, wisely convinced this will improve the lives of all involved. In Gilman's view, conventional domestic arrangements trap men as well as women.

Mr. Peebles returns, healthier and happier. The change does his wife good, too, as she has learned to depend on herself and use her mind. As in "Making a Change," Gilman's formula is a happy ending coming about through the wise intervention of an intelligent person who can envision a better social order.

Other MAJOR WORKS

LONG FICTION: *What Diantha Did*, 1910; *Moving the Mountain*, 1911; *The Crux*, 1911; *The Man-Made World*, 1911; *Benigna Machiavelli*, 1914 (serial), 1994 (book); *Herland*, 1915 (serial), 1979 (book); *With Her in Ourland*, 1916 (serial), 1997 (book).

POETRY: *In This Our World*, 1893; *Suffrage Songs and Verses*, 1911; *The Later Poetry of Charlotte Perkins Gilman*, 1996.

NONFICTION: *Women and Economics*, 1898; *Concerning Children*, 1900; *The Home: Its Work and Influence*, 1903; *Human Work*, 1904; *Women and Social Service*, 1907; *The Man-Made World*, 1911; *His Religion and Hers*, 1923; *The Living of Charlotte Perkins Gilman*, 1935; *The Diaries of Charlotte Perkins Gilman*, 1994 (2 volumes; Denise D. Knight, editor); *A Journey from Within: The Love Letters of Charlotte Perkins Gilman, 1897-1900*, 1995 (Mary A. Hill, editor); *The Selected Letters of Charlotte Perkins Gilman*, 2009 (Denise D. Knight and Jennifer S. Tuttle, editors).

BIBLIOGRAPHY

Cutter, Martha J. "Charlotte Perkins Gilman and the Feminist Tradition of the American Short Story." In *A Companion to the American Short Story*, edited by Alfred Bendixen and James Nagel. Malden, Mass.: Wiley-Blackwell, 2010. Offers an overview and critical examination of Gilman's short fiction. Includes discussions of "The Yellow Wallpaper," "An Honest Woman," and "Dr. Claire's Place."

Davis, Cynthia J. *Charlotte Perkins Gilman: A Biography*. Stanford, Calif.: Stanford University Press, 2010. Scholarly biography that recounts the events of Gilman's life and places her writings within the context of her life.

Davis, Cynthia J., and Denise D. Knight, eds. *Charlotte Perkins Gilman and Her Contemporaries: Literary and Intellectual Contexts*. Tuscaloosa: University of Alabama Press, 2004. A collection of essays by Gilman scholars that offers a wealth of biographical and critical information and places Gilman's opinions among those of her contemporaries.

Gilman, Charlotte Perkins. *Charlotte Perkins Gilman's "The Yellow Wall-Paper": A Sourcebook and Critical Edition*. Edited by Catherine J. Golden. New York: Routledge, 2004. In addition to the text of the short story, this edition republishes contemporary writings, including short stories by Edgar Allan Poe and Kate Chopin, in order to place "The Yellow Wallpaper" in its historical, literary, cultural, and scientific contexts. Also contains select reviews of "The Yellow Wallpaper" written in the nineteenth and early twentieth century, analytical essays written by modern critics, and suggestions for further reading.

Golden, Catherine. *The Captive Imagination: A Casebook on "The Yellow Wallpaper."* New York: The Feminist Press, 1992. The "Backgrounds" section of the volume includes essays on nineteenth century attitudes toward and treatment of women's psychiatric complaints. Also provides an extensive collection of criticism of Gilman's most-discussed story, including Elaine Hedges's 1973 feminist afterword to "The Yellow Wallpaper."

Hill, Mary A. *Charlotte Perkins Gilman: The Making of a Radical Feminist, 1860-1896*. Philadelphia: Temple University Press, 1980. Primarily a biographical exploration of the roots of Gilman's social theories. Hill's insights are based on a reading of Gilman's private journals and letters. Includes comments on the autobiographical short fiction, particularly "The Yellow Wallpaper."

Horowitz, Helen Lefkowitz. *Wild Unrest: Charlotte Perkins Gilman and the Making of "The Yellow Wallpaper."* New York: Oxford University Press, 2010. Describes how Gilman's experiences of receiving a rest cure from neurologist S. Weir Mitchell and her frustration with her traditional marriage to her first husband, Charles Walter Stetson, led her to write "The Yellow Wallpaper." Horowitz draws on personal writings of Gilman and Stetson, as well as Mitchell's papers, to argue that the story was a denunciation of Stetson and the couple's marriage.

Karpinski, Joanne B., ed. *Critical Essays on Charlotte Perkins Gilman*. Boston: G. K. Hall, 1991. This collection includes the Shelley Fishkin essay "Making a Change: Strategies of Subversion in Gilman's Journalism and Short Fiction."

Knight, Denise D., ed. *Charlotte Perkins Gilman: A Study of the Short Fiction*. New York: Twayne, 1997. A most useful volume of critical analysis of the short fiction. Part 1 discusses Gilman's short fiction, its influences, "The Yellow Wallpaper," and other stories. Part 2 provides Gilman's reflections on writing from primary sources, and Part 3 is a collection of criticism of several of Gilman's short stories. The editor makes a point of going beyond "The Yellow Wallpaper" so that readers may expand their appreciation of Gilman's range as a writer of short fiction.

Lane, Ann J. "The Fictional World of Charlotte Perkins Gilman." In *The Charlotte Perkins Gilman Reader*. New York: Pantheon, 1980. Lucid, concise analysis of Gilman's fiction as a whole.

_____. *To Herland and Beyond: The Life and Work of Charlotte Perkins Gilman*. New York: Pantheon, 1990. Primarily a biography. Recognizing the connection between Gilman's life and work, Lane devotes a solid pair of chapters to an analysis of the work. Discussion of the short fiction is brief, but analytic and informative.

Scharnhorst, Gary. *Charlotte Perkins Gilman*. Boston, Twayne, 1985. Scharnhorst, an authority on Gilman who has also compiled an extensive bibliography, has written a literary biography, a study of her imaginative work as a whole, relating her poetry and fiction to her pioneering nonfiction. The theme of this monograph is that Gilman's entire canon shares a unified didactic purpose.

Scofield, Martin. "Charlotte Perkins Gilman, Kate Chopin, Willa Cather, and Edith Wharton." In *The Cambridge Introduction to the American Short Story*. New York: Cambridge University Press, 2006. Defines Gilman's place in the history of American short fiction and analyzes several of her short stories, including "The Widow's Might" and "The Yellow Wallpaper."

Susan Butterworth

ELLEN GLASGOW

Born: Richmond, Virginia; April 22, 1873
Died: Richmond, Virginia; November 21, 1945

PRINCIPAL SHORT FICTION
　The Shadowy Third, and Other Stories, 1923
　The Collected Stories of Ellen Glasgow, 1963

OTHER LITERARY FORMS

Ellen Glasgow (GLAHS-goh) published novels, short stories, poetry, criticism, and an autobiography. She is best known for her novels, particularly *Barren Ground* (1925), *The Romantic Comedians* (1926), *The Sheltered Life* (1932), and *In This Our Life* (1941), which was awarded a Pulitzer Prize in 1942.

ACHIEVEMENTS

Ellen Glasgow spent her lifetime dedicated to the craft of writing, despite the cultural and literary prejudices of her time and place, which deplored the idea of an independent female author. She was at her finest writing fiction about women; many of her female characters' lives were distinctly unconventional for their time. Her exploration of women's lives, male-female relationships, and particularly the destructive effect of romantic notions of chivalry, innocence, and gender roles on the individual and society made her a best seller during her lifetime but earned her limited critical recognition. She was awarded the Howells Medal by the American Academy of Arts and Letters in 1940, *The Saturday Review* Award for Distinguished Service to American Literature in 1941, and the Pulitzer Prize in 1942, three years before her death.

BIOGRAPHY

Ellen Anderson Gholson Glasgow's father was a strict Scotch Presbyterian; her mother was a member of an established Tidewater family. Glasgow was too nervous to attend school, so she was educated at home. In late adolescence, her attention was directed to the work of writers such as Charles Darwin and Friedrich Nietzsche, and she read extensively in philosophy, political economy, and literature. She began to go deaf at the age of sixteen, and throughout her life she felt handicapped in social situations. In 1918, after a quarrel with her fiancé, Glasgow attempted suicide. She was engaged twice, but she never married. Although she always regarded Richmond, Virginia, as her home, Glasgow traveled widely. She received honorary doctorates from the University of North Carolina (1937), the University of Richmond (1938), Duke University (1938), and the College of William and Mary (1939). She was elected to the National Institute of Arts and Letters in 1932, and to the American Academy of Arts and Letters in 1938. Glasgow died in Richmond, Virginia, on November 21, 1945.

ANALYSIS

Ellen Glasgow's most frequently quoted observation is that "What the South most needs is blood and irony." She revolted against the affectedness, romanticism, and excessive picturesqueness of much nineteenth and early twentieth century southern literature, and she set out to produce a more realistic kind of fiction. She emphasized the wastage of life and of human energy which results from prejudice, illusion, impracticality, and a hostile environment; several of her most effective characters portray the frustration which comes from such wastage. Glasgow glorified strength, fortitude, energy, and a sense of duty. In fact, her characters are usually defined in terms of strength or weakness, rather than along the more conventional lines of good and evil.

Although Glasgow did introduce an element of realism into southern literature, she failed to accomplish her objectives fully. She remained a rather genteel southern lady whose attempt to depict the truth of the human situation was hampered by the limited range of her own experiences--she was shocked and horrified at the subject matter described by later southern realists, notably William Faulkner. Further, Glasgow seldom used a personal narrator, preferring an omniscient viewpoint. She often abused the technique, however, by inserting didactic or moralizing editorial observations into her fiction. As a result, much of her work tends to be talky and lacks the immediacy and impact of some other realistic fiction. Glasgow never entirely lost a sense of romanticism or even sentimentality, and although those qualities do appear, she did not associate them with her own writing.

Although Glasgow did not handle realistic materials as convincingly as some other writers have done, she did contribute to the growth of realism by introducing into southern literature a number of topics that had previously been glossed over. Some of these were suggested by her reading; some stemmed from her rebellion against her father's inflexible religion; and some were the product of her frustration with the weakness and ineffectuality of the southern aristocracy, of which she was a member through her mother's family. These comparatively new themes included determinism, social selection, the influence of heredity and environment, positive and negative energy, sexuality, feminism, industrialism, and criticism of the southern class system.

Most of Glasgow's twelve short stories, eleven of which were written before 1925, are adequate but not exceptional. She tended toward a rather diffuse style of writing and found it difficult to confine herself to the limitations of the short-story form. Although Glasgow never deliberately produced inferior work, she evidently wrote at least five of the short stories

Ellen Glasgow (Library of Congress)

primarily for the sake of the high fees that magazines would pay for short fiction. Glasgow's short stories tend to focus on moral themes, particularly those relating to male-female relationships, and these moral themes are not by any means confined to the issue of sexual morality. Glasgow was extremely concerned about the social and personal injustices which occurred because the "double standard" allowed men to behave differently than women.

"THE DIFFERENCE"

Glasgow's best-known story, "The Difference," is a scathing contrast between male and female attitudes toward love and marriage. The protagonist of the story, Margaret Fleming, is horrified when she discovers that her husband has been seeing another woman. Margaret learns about the affair from the mistress, Rose Morrison, who has written to Margaret asking her to give up her husband so that he might find happiness with Rose. Margaret goes to visit Rose, who is living in a villa belonging to George Fleming. Rose assures Margaret that she and George are very much in love, and that she understands George and can offer him far more excitement and satisfaction than Margaret can. Margaret, whose pale, grave beauty is beginning to fade, feels that George must have been attracted by the self-confident good looks of the red-haired Rose. She also wonders whether Rose's uninhibited sexuality is more alluring than her own well-bred reserve. She concludes that George must truly love Rose if he is willing to sacrifice his wife, and she resolves to give him his freedom, even if it costs her own happiness.

Margaret approaches George with the intention of telling him that, although she herself might have been capable of romance and adventure if he had only called forth those qualities in her, she is willing to step out of his life so that he can fulfill the burning love he feels for Rose. This love, she feels, is the only justification for his behavior and the only reason she will forgive him. When Margaret informs George that she has seen Rose, however, and that Rose has asked her to give up George, he stands with his mouth open in amazement. He tells Margaret that he has no intention of leaving her for Rose, and that he thinks of Rose as he thinks of golf-- " . . . just a sort of--well, sort of--recreation." He then considers the subject closed and becomes restless

for his supper. He cannot, in any case, see that Rose has anything whatever to do with Margaret. Remembering Rose's passion, and knowing the depth of her own responses, Margaret feels disillusioned and empty. She recognizes the truth of a remark that a friend had made earlier in the day: "Women love with their imagination and men with their senses." To a woman, love is "a thing in itself, a kind of abstract power like religion"; but to a man, "it is simply the way he feels."

"The Difference" illustrates both Glasgow's feminism and her lingering romanticism. She does not simply conclude that what men call love is frequently sensual and unthinking; she concludes that that view of love is wrong. She speaks of love in terms of "imagination" almost in the sense that Samuel Taylor Coleridge uses the term. Glasgow does succeed in introducing into her story an unconventional but realistic assessment of the moral questions involved in the double standard. George is wrong, not because he slept with another woman, but because he has treated both that woman and his wife as objects for his own convenience. Unlike her Victorian predecessors, Glasgow is not concerned with the religious aspects of extramarital affairs, or with Margaret's and George's mutual duties as husband and wife, as laid down by civil and ecclesiastical authorities. She dismisses the effect of infidelity and possible divorce on the family structure. It is not George's sexuality that Glasgow condemns, but rather his selfishness. Glasgow underlines her point by setting up an unusual relationship in which the wife feels rage on the mistress's behalf because of "the bond of woman's immemorial disillusionment."

"ROMANCE AND SALLY BYRD"

This idea of female solidarity in the face of male selfishness is repeated in a later story, "Romance and Sally Byrd." Unlike "The Difference," this story is told from the point of view of the "other woman," but the effect is the same. In the story, Sally Byrd Littlepage lives with her elderly grandparents and two aging aunts. Her Aunt Louisa is afflicted with neuralgia, and her Aunt Matilda is afflicted with religion. Sally Byrd, at nineteen, finds her dull existence enlivened by an admirer, Stanley Kenton, who has asked her to elope with him. Sally Byrd assumes that he means marriage, but he explains that he is already married, insisting that if she really loves him she will leave with him anyway. Sally Byrd refuses, not because of any strong moral indignation but because of the conviction that, like responding to thirst by getting drunk, this is something that one simply does not do. Having renounced her would-be lover, Sally Byrd feels a sense of romantic melancholy, which she rather enjoys.

Some time after Stanley's departure, Sally Byrd learns that he has been in an accident. His companion is dead, and he himself is badly hurt and will probably be permanently blind. Sally Byrd decides that it is her obligation to go to New York City and nurse him, since he and his wife are estranged and he has no one to care for him. She travels to New York and locates Stanley's luxurious apartment. There she is greeted by a large, firm woman with graying hair and an air of serenity. Sally Byrd explains why she has come. The woman turns out to be Stanley's wife, who gently lets Sally Byrd know that she is one of many women whom Stanley has admired. His latest mistress was the companion who was killed in Stanley's car accident. Mrs. Kenton explains that whenever Stanley needs support, he always returns to her, as he has done in the present instance. She herself is composed and impersonal because, as she explains, once the heart is broken it does not hurt any more. "You can't imagine the relief it is," she tells Sally Byrd, "to have your heart break at last." Sally stumbles out, sure that she is hurt for life, and resolved never to allow anything like this to happen again. On the train going home, however, she meets a personable young man who lives in the same town as she does; as she walks home from the station, she finds herself feeling happier at the thought of meeting him again.

"Romance and Sally Byrd" adds another dimension to the picture of male-female relationships drawn in "The Difference." In "The Difference," neither of the women has the advantage of knowing George's true nature until his wife discovers it in the final scene of the story. As a result, the issue of a woman's knowingly permitting herself to be used as a convenience by a man does not arise. In "Romance and Sally Byrd," however, Mrs. Kenton returns to Stanley whenever he wants her. In fact, she sits darning his silk socks as she talks with Sally Byrd. Her knowledge brings her only the negative satisfaction of a broken heart that no longer hurts. She makes no attempt to shape a life of her own. At the other end of the spectrum of experience, Sally Byrd quickly springs back from her disillusionment and begins daydreaming about another man. Despite her own adventure and the example of Mrs. Kenton, she still thinks of marriage as she had done earlier in the story: "as a passive and permanent condition of bliss."

"DARE'S GIFT"

Although Glasgow reserved most of her experimentation for her novels, she did incorporate into a few of her short stories a technique that she used nowhere else. Realist though she believed herself to be, Glasgow greatly admired the work of Edgar Allan Poe, and she produced a few ghost stories that are indebted to him. The best of these are two stories centering on the image of an old house imbued with an aura or atmosphere that influences or reflects the actions of those who live there.

The earlier of these, "Dare's Gift," focuses on an old Virginia mansion that had been built by a traitor, Sir Roderick Dare. A Washington lawyer takes a lease on the house as a desirable country residence for his wife, who is recovering from a nervous breakdown. At first her health seems to improve, but then her behavior becomes increasingly nervous and erratic. The lawyer, who is involved in a particularly important and delicate case, tells his wife about some evidence, the disclosure of which would greatly injure his client. The evidence is disclosed, and the lawyer realizes that only his wife could have betrayed him. It turns out that this is the most recent of several similar cases that have occurred in Sir Roderick's house. The present owner, who lives in California, left the house because his trusted secretary had betrayed him there, and when the last Dares were living in the house, at the time of the Civil War, Miss Lucy Dare betrayed her fiancé to the soldiers who were seeking him.

"Dare's Gift" combines the occult image of a controlling atmosphere with the more realistic problem of personal loyalty versus loyalty to an ethic or to a cause. This theme is developed most fully in the case of Miss Lucy Dare, who had to decide between the Virginia code of personal loyalty and the duty she felt to the

Confederate cause. The same theme is repeated when the lawyer's wife prevents his client from escaping the consequences of his dishonesty. The issue, however, does not seem to arise in the story of Sir Roderick, who built the house and presumably started the curse, nor in the case of the present owner's secretary. Here, as in her other ghost stories, Glasgow has some difficulty in balancing purely occult manifestations with the psychological elements that writers like Poe and Henry James express so well in their ghost stories.

"JORDAN'S END"

By far the best of Glasgow's ghost stories is "Jordan's End," which, like "Dare's Gift," is influenced by Poe's tale "The Fall of the House of Usher." Like the title "Dare's Gift," which is both the name of the house and an ironic allusion to the inheritance it carries, the title "Jordan's End" has a double meaning. It is the name of the crumbling southern mansion that serves as the main setting of the story, and it is also a reference to the decaying state of the Jordan family.

The opening of "Jordan's End" is very similar to the opening of Glasgow's important novel *Barren Ground*, which appeared two years after "Jordan's End" was published. A doctor, riding in a buggy, approaches a crossroads leading to an ancient southern farm. On the way he gives a ride to an old man, who tells him part of the history of Jordan's End. The present head of the family, Alan Jordan, lives there with his wife and son. The house is also inhabited by three eccentric elderly women: Alan Jordan's grandmother and two aunts. The men in the Jordan family have long been showing symptoms of insanity, and the marked oddity of the three old ladies suggests that the problem is spreading to the women.

When he arrives at Jordan's End, the doctor discovers that the once gracious house is crumbling and the lawns and gardens are unkempt. He meets Mrs. Alan Jordan, who tells him that her husband has begun to show signs of the madness which has already claimed his father, grandfather, and uncles. Her chief fear is that her husband's great physical strength may condemn him to the kind of prolonged existence in a madhouse that his grandfather is presently suffering. The doctor leaves an opiate, and waits for the verdict of a nerve specialist who has promised to visit Jordan's End the next day.

Catching the nerve specialist as he boards a train to return home, the doctor learns that Alan Jordan is incurable. His insanity is the result of a long history of intermarriages within the Jordan family. The specialist has suggested to Mrs. Jordan that she place her husband in an institution. The next morning, however, the doctor is again summoned to Jordan's End, where he finds Alan Jordan dead, and the bottle of sleeping pills empty. His wife, composed and detached, suggests that she has fulfilled a promise she had made to her husband when he first learned of the possibility that he would go mad. The doctor does not inquire further, feeling that Mrs. Jordan's detachment and solitude remove her from any human touch.

"Jordan's End" anticipates the techniques, themes, and characterizations of Glasgow's major novels. For example, the issues of heredity, environment, and euthanasia that appear briefly in this story form the basis of several of her lengthier works. Similarly, her Hardyesque use of setting to reflect character is much more sophisticated here than in "Dare's Gift"; the decaying house, the twilight, the overcast skies, and the ragged vegetation function in "Jordan's End" as external manifestations of internal decay. The fall of the Jordans suggests the recurrent Glasgow theme of the decadence of the South in both blood and environment, and the strong figure of Mrs. Jordan, animated--despite the horrors she has endured--by a sense of duty and compassion, anticipates such major Glasgow heroines as Dorinda Oakley.

OTHER MAJOR WORKS

LONG FICTION: *The Descendant*, 1897; *Phases of an Inferior Planet*, 1898; *The Voice of the People*, 1900; *The Battle-Ground*, 1902; *The Deliverance*, 1904; *The Wheel of Life*, 1906; *The Ancient Law*, 1908; *The Romance of a Plain Man*, 1909; *The Miller of Old Church*, 1911; *Virginia*, 1913; *Life and Gabriella*, 1916; *The Builders*, 1919; *One Man in His Time*, 1922; *Barren Ground*, 1925; *The Romantic Comedians*, 1926; *They Stooped to Folly*, 1929; *The Sheltered Life*, 1932; *Vein of Iron*, 1935; *In This Our Life*, 1941.

POETRY: *The Freeman, and Other Poems*, 1902.

NONFICTION: *A Certain Measure: An Interpretation of Prose Fiction*, 1943; *The Woman Within*, 1954;

Letters of Ellen Glasgow, 1958; *Perfect Companionship: Ellen Glasgow's Selected Correspondence with Women*, 2005 (Pamela R. Matthews, editor).

BIBLIOGRAPHY

Glasgow, Ellen. *The Woman Within*. New York: Harcourt, Brace, 1954. Glasgow's autobiography is one of the best sources for the philosophy behind her fiction. This volume is more of a literary autobiography than a personal one, indicating shifts of perceptions, understanding, and attitude. It was published posthumously.

Godbold, E. Stanly, Jr. *Ellen Glasgow and the Woman Within*. Baton Rouge: Louisiana State University Press, 1972. A literary biography, interesting mainly as an example of a prefeminist interpretation of Glasgow's work.

Goodman, Susan. *Ellen Glasgow*. Baltimore: Johns Hopkins University Press, 1998. A biography that argues for Glasgow's significance as a southern author at the turn of the century. Discusses the gap between her reception by her contemporaries and her later reception.

Matthews, Pamela R. *Ellen Glasgow and a Woman's Traditions*. Charlottesville: University Press of Virginia, 1994. Discusses Glasgow's feminism and her place as a twentieth century southern female author. Includes bibliographical references and an index.

McDowell, Frederick P. W. *Ellen Glasgow and the Ironic Art of Fiction*. Madison: University of Wisconsin Press, 1960. Interesting in-depth analysis of Glasgow's oeuvre primarily in terms of style, irony, and wit. Includes an extensive bibliography.

The Mississippi Quarterly 49 (Spring, 1996). A special issue on Glasgow, with essays on her short stories that discuss her focus on struggling underprivileged farmers, her modernity, the effect of Henry Watkins Anderson on her work, and her use of clothing imagery.

Patterson, Martha H. "Mary Johnston, Ellen Glasgow, and the Evolutionary Logic of Progressive Reform." In *Beyond the Gibson Girl: Reimagining the American New Woman, 1895-1915*. Urbana: University of Illinois Press, 2005. At the end of the nineteenth and beginning of the twentieth century, feminists advanced the idea of a "new woman" who was typically white, well educated, and politically progressive. Patterson describes how Glasgow and other women authors of the period subverted this idea to create other conceptions of the "new woman."

Raper, Julius Rowan. "Ellen Glasgow." In *A Companion to the Literature and Culture of the American South*, edited by Richard Gray and Owen Robinson. Malden, Mass: Blackwell, 2004. An overview of Glasgow's writing, focusing on the novels and placing her work within the context of southern history and culture.

Rouse, Blair. *Ellen Glasgow*. New York: Twayne, 1962. Presents facts, analyses, and interpretations of Glasgow's life, the nature and purposes of her writing, the scope of her work, and her attainment as an artist in fiction. Rouse is a southerner who was one of the first contemporary critics to appreciate Glasgow. Includes an annotated bibliography.

Scura, Dorothy M., ed. *Ellen Glasgow: New Perspectives*. Knoxville: University of Tennessee Press, 1995. Detailed essays on Glasgow's major novels and themes, two essays on her autobiographies, and two essays on her poetry and short stories. Includes a helpful overview in the introduction and a bibliography.

Taylor, Welford Dunaway, and George C. Longest, eds. *Regarding Ellen Glasgow: Essays for Contemporary Readers*. Richmond: Library of Virginia, 2001. These essays examine a broad range of subjects, including a reprint of Edgar MacDonald's *Mississippi Quarterly* article "From Jordan's End to Frenchman's Bend: Ellen Glasgow's Short Stories." Other essays discuss Glasgow and southern history, some of her novels, her representation of southern women and men, and Glasgow and Calvinism.

Wagner, Linda W. *Ellen Glasgow: Beyond Convention*. Austin: University of Texas Press, 1982. An excellent, in-depth analysis of all Glasgow's work, placing it in the context of her time and place, as well as in relation to later work by American authors.

Joan DelFattore
Updated by Mary LeDonne Cassidy

GAIL GODWIN

Born: Birmingham, Alabama; June 18, 1937

PRINCIPAL SHORT FICTION

Dream Children, 1976
Mr. Bedford and the Muses, 1983
Evenings at Five, 2003

OTHER LITERARY FORMS

Gail Godwin has written twelve novels, including *The Odd Woman* (1974), *A Mother and Two Daughters* (1982), *The Good Husband* (1994), *Evensong* (1999), *Queen of the Underworld* (2006), and *Unfinished Desires* (2009). She edited, with Shannon Ravenel, *The Best American Short Stories* (1985). She has also written several opera librettos, including *Remembering Felix* (pb. 1987), for composer Robert Starer, and ventured into nonfiction with *Heart: A Personal Journey Through Its Myths and Meanings* (2001) and *The Making of a Writer: Journals, 1961-1963* (2006).

ACHIEVEMENTS

Gail Godwin received a National Endowment for the Arts grant in 1974-1975, a John Simon Guggenheim Memorial Fellowship in 1975-1976, and the award in literature from the American Academy of Arts and Letters in 1981. *The Odd Woman* received a National Book Award nomination; *Violet Clay* (1978) and *A Mother and Two Daughters* received American Book Award nominations; and *A Southern Family* (1987) received the Thomas Wolfe Memorial Award. In 1988, Godwin received the Janet Heidinger Kafka Prize, presented by the University of Rochester.

BIOGRAPHY

Gail Kathleen Godwin was born in Birmingham, Alabama, on June 18, 1937. She attended Peace Junior College in Raleigh, North Carolina, before matriculating at the University of North Carolina at Chapel Hill, where she received a B.A. in journalism. For two years she was employed as a reporter for the *Miami Herald,* during which time she married Douglas Kennedy, a photographer. The marriage ended in divorce less than a year later. After leaving the *Miami Herald,* Godwin worked and traveled in Europe for six years, settling in London, where she worked in the U.S. Travel Service at the American Embassy. She married Ian Marshall, a British physician; they divorced the following year. Godwin returned to the United States and entered the graduate writing program at the University of Iowa in 1967. She received her M.A. degree in 1968 and her Ph.D. in English in 1971, after which she taught at the Iowa Writers' Workshop, leaving that tenure-track position in the early 1970's to begin a relationship with the composer Robert Starer, whom she had met at Yaddo, the artists' colony, and to write full time. They were companions and collaborators for more than thirty years, until his death of congestive heart failure in 2001. Godwin also accepted teaching positions at Vassar College in 1977 and at Columbia University in 1978 and 1981.

ANALYSIS

Gail Godwin's three volumes of short stories have received little critical attention, in spite of the fact that they anticipate many of the themes Godwin explores in her novels. One such overarching theme, for example, is the relationship between men and women, especially in marriage. Many stories in *Dream Children*, as in Godwin's early novels *The Perfectionists* (1970) and *Glass People* (1972), explore the nature of women's subordination to men and the various strategies women adopt to subvert it. There are prevailing notes of dissatisfaction, rebellion, escape, and revenge, often frustrated revenge. Unlike the realism of Godwin's early novels, however, *Dream Children* contains experiments with form (especially in "Notes for a Story") and explores elements of fantasy and the supernatural, including the nonrational dream world and how it impinges on everyday reality. In the title story, for example, a woman whose child is stillborn has a series of strange nocturnal "spirit" meetings with a child who, as a newborn, was briefly and mistakenly presented to her as her own baby. Sometimes the fantasy elements take on a dark coloring, but these are balanced by stories (such as "An Intermediate Stop" and "The Woman Who Kept Her Poet") that hint cryptically and obliquely at mystical, spiritual moments of realization.

There is a shift in Godwin's second collection, *Mr. Bedford and the Muses*. Almost all the protagonists are writers, people whose lives center on the workings of the creative mind, and these stories tend to reflect an optimistic perspective. The characters find greater possibilities for personal freedom and wholeness, even given the strange twists and turns that life takes--for example, a husband whose young wife leaves him for his son still finds a moment of perfection in his music; a young novelist falls in love with a woman more than twenty years his senior because he cannot help but see her as young. More fully developed and satisfying than many of the somewhat sketchy stories in *Dream Children*, this collection shows Godwin's mastery of the form.

"NOBODY'S HOME"

"Nobody's Home" expresses a highly critical view of marriage that was typical of feminist writers of the 1970's. The story explores the frustration of a lonely, middle-aged, middle-class woman trapped in a tedious marriage and her plan to escape. Mrs. Wakeley decides to leave her husband without explanation and rent an apartment directly opposite their house. It is as if she is an actor in a play she has come to loathe, and she wishes to remove herself from it and then observe the play run into chaos without her. This is the sublimated desire for revenge of a timid, weak-willed woman; Mrs. Wakeley's courage falters at the practical details. How will she open a bank account or get a Social Security card under her new alias of Clara Jones? How will she find a job knowing nothing about the world of work? She concludes she is not fully a person in her own right.

When her husband returns home in the evening, she finds herself diminished even further by his mere presence, although she cannot explain why. The narrator emphasizes the distance between husband and wife that lies behind the polite surfaces. The marriage continues in name only, and the reader is led to the conclusion that Mrs. Wakeley, although continuing to fantasize about her escape, will never muster the means to effect it: She has sacrificed her independence and individual identity (her first name is never mentioned) to her marriage.

"FALSE LIGHTS"

One of several stories in *Dream Children* about second wives or mistresses, "False Lights" is written in the form of an exchange of letters between Violet, the young wife of novelist Karl Bandema, and Annette, Karl's former wife, who is in her fifties. The two opening letters are brief and formal, but then Violet writes to the older woman at length. She reveals herself to be an idealistic, meditative, imaginative woman, given to philosophical speculation, and much in love with her husband, despite the fact that he seems to be a self-centered egotist.

Violet wants to befriend Annette and confides that the category of "wife" seems an ephemeral thing, almost meaningless in an infinite world of perpetual change. She speculates on what marriage will be like in the year 2075. Maybe it will be different, more pure, less petty, "all of us sailing through change as effortlessly as gulls through air." She also wonders whether marriage will even exist a hundred years from now.

As the title of the story may hint, Violet's flights of fancy do not strike a responsive chord within the older woman, who replies formally, rejecting Violet's notion that they could ever be friends. Perhaps Godwin is suggesting that although alternative attitudes to marriage may in theory be possible, for the present, marriages are likely to remain stuck in the familiar groove--temporary, unstable alliances that quickly become unsatisfactory for at least one partner.

"THE LEGACY OF THE MOTES"

In this mystical story about awakening, an American student in London is finishing his Ph.D. dissertation on conceits in metaphysical poetry. Elliott is always in a hurry, impatient with the relaxed pace of living that the English prefer. He develops a problem with his eyes, seeing a pair of wings flying sideways across his line of vision. A librarian friend, Van Buren, hints that he may have been working too hard, a suggestion that Elliott dismisses. Although an eye specialist explains that the *muscae volitantes* (flying flies) pose no threat to his vision, Elliott becomes obsessively worried about them.

After Elliott has a breakdown in the British Museum, the narrative jumps ahead ten years, and the reader learns that Elliott abandoned his studies after making a deal with the *muscae*: If they let him go on seeing, he would not enter a library. Instead, the man who had scoffed at the English and their fondness for parks now finds pleasure in exploring the world, experiencing it at first hand, not through books. He is eventually persuaded by Van Buren to read George Herbert's poem "Easter-Wings." Typographically, this poem about human loss and divine redemption is shaped like a pair of wings. Elliott, weeping, realizes the significance of the real-life images of the *muscae* that were the cause of his own rebirth. Although Godwin does not make this explicit, the implication is that before, Elliott, for all his learning, knew nothing. Now he knows how to experience life fully; the *muscae*, far from being a curse, were divine promptings, nudging him to see things anew.

"AMANUENSIS"

The protagonist of "Amanuensis" is a writer, and the story explores the conditions under which her creativity waxes and wanes. Constance Le Fevre is an ambitious, successful novelist who has lost her inspiration. One day Jesse, a college student, arrives at her house, offering to be Constance's amanuensis; Jesse wants to do the household chores so that Constance can concentrate on her work. This arrangement works well for a time. Constance gets used to Jesse's presence in the house, allows Jesse to nurse her through an illness, and he becomes fond of her. Constance's creativity, however, does not return. The turning point comes appropriately one spring morning, when Constance, inspired by the sounds of Jesse going about her household tasks, for one brief moment realizes "how nice *just being* is," without the self-imposed pressure of ambition or the need to create.

Jesse departs without a trace that very day, and later Constance discovers that she was tricked--a disgruntled former lover planted Jesse in her house so that he could gather material for a novel of his own. What is really important is that Constance somehow finds herself liberated from her need for achievement and the habit of imposing on the world her concepts of events and their patterns. She sells her house and travels, determined to take no notes, simply to let life come and bring her what it will, without interference on her part. The strategy works; her creativity is restored, and she thinks of Jesse as her "angel of release."

EVENINGS AT FIVE

The autobiographical collection *Evenings at Five: A Novel and Five New Stories* features Christina, Godwin's name for herself as she explores various stages of her life. In her introduction to the volume, she also identifies these stories as "ghost" stories of a sort, continuing the interest not exactly in the supernatural, but in the mystical and rich stores of memory. The struggles between women who crave independence and the men they encounter and often love are part of each story. The first, the "novel" of the title, recounts Christina's dealing with her grief in the aftermath of Rudy's (the composer Starer's) death. "Evenings at Five" refers to their sitting down together after working in their separate studios for a drink and their talking over their day. Even after his death, every day at that hour, Christina still feels Rudy's powerful presence, while she sits across from his empty chair, having her drink alone.

In fact, she tells of the many ways in which he lingers, in her memories and in the memories of others--especially in the way people relive their experiences with him in their letters of condolence; in her persisting in certain shared and individual habits and rituals; in the artist's graveyard where he is buried; in the appointment calendar he has left behind and in his voice on their answering-machine; and in the religious ceremonies, both Jewish and Catholic, following his death. At one point she exclaims that he could probably will himself to come back if he wanted to, he was in life such a powerful presence.

"LARGESSE"

In the stories that follow "Evenings at Five," the ghosts are Christina as she lived and learned in various stages of her life. In the first story, fifteen-year-old Christina is treated to a trip by her wealthy Aunt Demaris to visit her for Christmas on her ranch in Texas. The title refers to the Cinderella-like experience waiting for Christina there, as her aunt treats her to luxury and lavish praise and to stories of the aunt's past as a strong-willed young woman. In the end, however, Christina resists the pull of this new life and its possibilities, returning her loyalties to two other independent women: her mother, a junior college teacher who has raised her alone, and her grandmother.

"POSSIBLE SINS"

In "Possible Sins," Christina, eleven years old, thinks about the process of confession and wonders that God does not get bored with the sins she reveals and those she imagines others describing for Father Weir. Later, meeting when Christina is grown up, the two decide that Father Weir will give her a password to let her know he is communicating from the afterlife, an explanation, in part, for the intense expectation she feels when Rudy dies that he is seeking her out.

"OLD LOVEGOOD GIRLS"

Although it begins with a grown-up Christina's conversation with a woman on an airplane, this story is about her experience at a small women's college in North Carolina, where her father, with whom she has recently reestablished a relationship, pays to send her. It is a place that stresses old-fashioned virtues in its students. Although Christina has recently lost her virginity, she falls in love with the place, haunted by its history and its powerful traditions.

Besides the intellectual stimulation she finds there, she must also deal with her nascent recognition that her favorite teacher and the tennis coach she lives with are lesbians and that her father is also in a sexual relationship with Myrna, a woman of whom Christina disapproves and whom her father eventually marries. The story ends with the image of her father as she imagines him, at peace with his image of her as protected by the experience of this venerable place. She is grateful for the respite of this time and place before she is pulled into a tumultuous future.

"WALTZING WITH THE BLACK CRAYON"

Christina is at Iowa learning to be a writer, having two failed marriages behind her. This story, "Waltzing with the Black Crayon," is a loving tribute to her teacher, Kurt Vonnegut, and it details his unorthodox methods. He lets them figure it all out for themselves, and, unlike the others, he is a teacher without his own "agenda."

"MOTHER AND DAUGHTER GHOSTS: A MEMOIR"

The final story, "Mother and Daughter Ghosts: A Memoir," recounts a trip Christina and K., her mother, take to a spirituality workshop, where, instead of falling into their regular roles of gentle troublemakers, Christina finds herself somewhat at odds with her mother, who participates wholeheartedly in the activities of each day. Christina never sees her mother alive again after this, but as the memoir suggests, she has witnessed her mother's spiritual health and the richness of her imagination. As is appropriate for this collection of ghost stories, K. haunts the Episcopal church she attended.

OTHER MAJOR WORKS

LONG FICTION: *The Perfectionists*, 1970; *Glass People*, 1972; *The Odd Woman*, 1974; *Violet Clay*, 1978; *A Mother and Two Daughters*, 1982; *The Finishing School*, 1985; *A Southern Family*, 1987; *Father Melancholy's Daughter*, 1991; *The Good Husband*, 1994; *Evensong*, 1999; *Queen of the Underworld*, 2006; *Unfinished Desires*, 2009.

PLAYS: *The Last Lover*, pr. 1975 (libretto; music by Robert Starer); *Journals of a Songmaker*, pr. 1976 (libretto; music by Starer); *Apollonia*, pr. 1979 (libretto; music by Starer); *Anna Margarita's Will*, pr. 1980 (libretto; music by Starer); *Remembering Felix*, pb. 1987 (libretto; music by Starer).

NONFICTION: *Heart: A Personal Journey Through Its Myths and Meanings*, 2001; *The Making of a Writer: Journals, 1961-1963*, 2006.

EDITED TEXT: *The Best American Short Stories*, 1985.

BIBLIOGRAPHY

Crain, Jane Larkin. "*Dream Children*." *The New York Times Book Review* (February 22, 1976). In this review, Crain argues that the atmosphere of the stories is largely dark and defines Godwin as a "chronicler of life on the edge," depicting states of alienation, isolation, and madness. As in Godwin's novels, the principal concern in the stories is the nature of womanhood.

Gies, Judith. "Obligation, Fascination, and Intrigue." *The New York Times Book Review*, September 8, 1983, p. 14. A critical review of *Mr. Bedford and the Muses*, which faults the stories for being too neatly resolved at the end and regrets the "chatty and oddly schoolmarmish" tone of the book. Regards "A Cultural Exchange" as the most successful story.

Halisky, Linda H. "Redeeming the Irrational: The Inexplicable Heroines of 'A Sorrowful Woman' and 'To Room Nineteen.'" *Studies in Short Fiction* (Winter, 1990): 45-54. Examines the parallels between Godwin's story in *Dream Children* and Doris Lessing's "To Room Nineteen." Argues that because these stories possess similar plots, Lessing's story is an analogue to Godwin's and can help to explain the behavior of Godwin's heroine.

Hill, Jane. *Gail Godwin*. New York: Twayne, 1992. The best study of Godwin for the general reader. Hill concentrates on the novels, while commenting that the stories deserve a study of their own. Hill approaches Godwin's work through plot and character, and although Hill acknowledges the regional and gender-related aspects of Godwin's work as a southern woman writer, Hill points out that Godwin's novels also connect with the larger tradition of novels in America and Europe.

Westerlund, Kerstin. *Escaping the Castle of Patriarchy: Patterns of Development in the Novels of Gail Godwin*. Stockholm, Sweden: University of Uppsala, 1990. Discusses the short stories only briefly, noting that they frequently echo the main themes of Godwin's novels. Analyzes the novels up to *A Southern Family* in terms of female development, which is linked to Godwin's treatment of male-female relationships. Includes a chapter on Godwin and American feminism.

Xie, Lihong. *The Evolving Self in the Novels of Gail Godwin*. Baton Rouge: Louisiana State University Press, 1995. Argues that instead of accepting the postmodern deconstruction of the self, Godwin has constructed a concept of the self as evolving, finding itself not in essence but in process. The book explores the nature of this "self-in-the-becoming."

Bryan Aubrey
Updated by Susie Paul

HERBERT GOLD

Born: Cleveland, Ohio; March 9, 1924

PRINCIPAL SHORT FICTION

Love and Like, 1960
The Magic Will: Stories and Essays of a Decade, 1971
Stories of Misbegotten Love, 1985
Lovers and Cohorts: Twenty-Seven Stories, 1986

OTHER LITERARY FORMS

Herbert Gold's memoirs, *Blind, Blind Date: Memoir* (1980; published in *The Monthly*, a journal then based in Berkeley, California), *Travels in San Francisco* (1990), *Best Nightmare on Earth: A Life in Haiti* (1991), *Bohemia: Where Art, Angst, Love, and Strong Coffee Meet* (1993), and *Still Alive! A Temporary Condition, a Memoir* (2008), are collections of personal reflections on his life and travels. Gold has also published twenty novels, edited collections of short stories, and written the children's book *The Young Prince and the Magic Cone* (1973).

ACHIEVEMENTS

Herbert Gold was a Fulbright fellow at the Sorbonne, University of Paris, in 1950, a *Hudson Review* fellow in 1956, and a John Simon Guggenheim Memorial Foundation fellow in 1957. In 1954, he received an Inter-American Cultural Relations grant to Haiti. He has also received an Ohioana Book Award, a National Institute of Arts and Letters grant, a

Longview Foundation Award, and a Ford Foundation theater fellowship. He received the California Literature Medal in 1968 for *Fathers: A Novel in the Form of a Memoir* (1967), the Commonwealth Club Award for best novel in 1982 for *Family: A Novel in the Form of a Memoir* (1981), and the Sherwood Anderson Prize for fiction in 1989. His short stories have appeared in numerous publications, including *The New York Times Book Review*, *Harper's Bazaar*, *Atlantic*, *Esquire*, *Playboy*, *Partisan Review*, and *Prize Stories: The O. Henry Awards*.

BIOGRAPHY

Herbert Gold was born in Cleveland, Ohio, in 1924. After working for U.S. Army Intelligence from 1943 to 1946, he received his B.A. and M.A. from Columbia University, in 1946 and 1948, respectively. He was married to Edith Durbin from 1948 to 1956 and to Melissa Dilworth from 1968 to 1975; both marriages ended in divorce. Gold has five children: Ann and Judith from his first marriage, and Nina, Ari, and Ethan from his second marriage.

Gold's first published story appeared in *Harper's Bazaar* while he was still in college, and he was firmly established as a full-time writer by the time he was in his thirties. In 1960, Gold left the Midwest permanently; he moved to San Francisco, settling in a small apartment on Russian Hill above North Beach, which continued to be his permanent residence during his extensive travels. Most of his later fiction is set in San Francisco, while his essays reflect his travels, especially in Haiti. Gold has taught at several universities, including the University of California at Berkeley, Stanford University, and Harvard University.

ANALYSIS

Herbert Gold's short fiction depicts realistic themes and settings--most often dealing with male-female relationships or the broader theme of families. He has a keen eye for contemporary manners and mores, and his fiction and essays often investigate how people deal with life, their environment, and one another. Much of Gold's short fiction features middle-aged men, divorced or unhappily married, who have passionate but brief relationships with younger women. In these stories, the men typically are presented as innocent victims of manipulative women. Other stories illuminate the broader network of family relationships, and his treatment of the elderly can be particularly sensitive.

In most of his stories, the situations and personalities are very close to his own life story. Gold has said he writes "semi-automatically" in order to get in touch with his dreams, fantasies, and recollections, especially in his fiction; when he writes less intuitively, he produces essays, which are outlined in advance. Gold's dialogue is frequently wry and witty; his style is often conversational, and he avoids overt symbolism, as he prefers to let the story create its symbols in the reader's mind. Often the story's end is not definitive but leaves the next step in the character's evolution to the reader's imagination. In some stories, Gold objectifies one or more characters by not naming them--in fact, in his novel *He/She* (1980), the names of the main characters, a divorcing couple, are never mentioned.

"THE HEART OF THE ARTICHOKE"

Perhaps Gold's best-known work of short fiction, "The Heart of the Artichoke" (1951) describes the conflicts between twelve-year-old Daniel and his father, whom he deeply loves and admires. His parents insist Daniel work in the family grocery store, a job about which he feels embarrassed. He feels that he has been branded a lower-class immigrant, not only in his own eyes but also, and more devastatingly, in the eyes of Pattie, the wealthy girl on whom he has a crush. His father, who came to America to start a new life against his own father's wishes, does not see that Daniel now faces a similar conflict with his father.

When a class field trip is scheduled for one of the busiest days of the year at the store, Daniel sneaks out of work to join his friends. When Pattie shares her lunch with him and lets him walk her home, Daniel is thrilled and confesses he likes her. Her dismissive response that he is just a grocery boy devastates him. The story concludes with an intensely emotional and physical conflict between Daniel and his father.

In "The Heart of the Artichoke," food is a family symbol of love, security, and abundance, and the father relishes procuring and selling excellent food as much as eating it. Gold uses food analogies, particularly those of the artichoke, to illustrate both the conflicts inherent in the adolescent's struggle to make his or her own way and the problems between immigrant parents and their children.

LOVERS AND COHORTS

Gold's 1986 collection of twenty-seven essays and short stories includes a number of stories already collected in *Love and Like* and *The Magic Will: Stories and Essays of a Decade*, along with later works, several of which were previously unpublished. A number of the selections are set in Haiti; several other stories involve men, often married and often college teachers, who become involved with younger women, often students, then find that they are the ones being used by the vibrant, young women. The men feel betrayed, ignoring the hypocrisy inherent in the fact that they are betraying their own wives and children. The feelings of their wives are barely discussed in most of the stories.

Many of the short stories seem to move toward a predictable ending, until the last paragraph, when a quick remark truncates the story with a different twist than might be expected. Because Gold's essays often incorporate stylistic elements more often associated with fiction and his fiction often draws heavily on his personal life, the reader may not always be sure which selections are fictional and which are not. For example, one of the most amusing stories in *Blind, Blind Date* is a wry look at dating in San Francisco that is so outlandish, it almost has to be true, but it reads like a humorous piece of fiction.

"LOVE AND LIKE"

First published in *The Hudson Review* in 1958, this story is somewhat unusual in Gold's fiction in its in-depth examination of the feelings of the children of a failed marriage. Newly divorced Dan Shaper has moved to New York from Cleveland because he feels unable to live in close proximity to his former wife. The story unfolds when Shaper makes his first visit back to Cleveland to see his young daughters, Paula and Cynthia, and his girlfriend, Sally. While married, his wife was determined to have a son, and she became focused on determining the ideal timing, diet, and techniques for conceiving a boy. The marriage collapsed when she learned that while she had turned their love-making into a clinical pursuit of a son, Shaper had

sought refuge in an affair with a student. Although all the other characters in the story are named, the wife's name is never mentioned: When speaking to her, Shaper always calls her "kid," an appellation she detests; to others, he refers to her as "my wife," although Sally constantly points out that the woman is his former wife.

Shaper insists he likes Sally and claims to like his wife, but he says he loves only his children. When he tries to convince six-year-old Paula that although he and their mother merely like each other, this does not change his love for his daughters, Paula cuts through her father's hypocrisy and word games. As he leaves, Paula challenges him, shouting, "Oh, how I'm sick of those words love and like!" At the end of his visit, the former wife becomes angry when Shaper says he cannot afford tuition at a private school for their older daughter and screams that whereas he never satisfied her sexually, her new boyfriend does. The story ends with Shaper standing in front of Sally's doorway, toying with the idea of suicide but concerned about its effect on his children.

"COHORTS"

In "Cohorts," Gold switches his focus from the problems that men have with women to a touching tale of two brothers spending the day with their aged father. The narrator, who is never named, has flown from California to Cleveland to visit his parents and brother.

The strength of this brief story is in the economical way in which Gold paints a picture of the defeated father Sam, who is waiting to die, and the son's feeling of helplessness in the face of his father's decline. "My father is tired of growing old. . . . He helped me to grow up. Why can't I help him now?" the narrator cries. Sam is often confused, his hearing and sight are fading, his energy is low, and he is embarrassed to admit he now loses control of his bowels and bladder. In one breath, Sam tells his visiting son to go out and have fun but not to leave him.

When the mother, also nameless, goes to a meeting, the visiting son and his brother decide to ignore their mother's wish that they feed their father at home and instead take him to the deli where they often went as a family years earlier. At the deli, waitresses and customers come up to the three men, calling Sam by name, reminding him of their names. Although he has turned off his hearing aid, he cheerfully greets the other customers. After they leave the deli, the brothers ask who all the people were, but Sam laughs as if it were a joke and admits he has no idea.

OTHER MAJOR WORKS

LONG FICTION: *Birth of a Hero*, 1951; *The Prospect Before Us*, 1954 (reprinted as *Room Clerk*, 1955); *The Man Who Was Not with It*, 1956 (published as *The Wild Life*, 1957, with a new introduction by the author); *The Optimist*, 1959; *Therefore Be Bold*, 1960; *Salt*, 1963; *Fathers: A Novel in the Form of a Memoir*, 1967 (reprinted as *Fathers*, 1991); *The Great American Jackpot*, 1969; *Biafra Goodbye*, 1970; *My Last Two Thousand Years*, 1972; *Swiftie the Magician*, 1974; *Waiting for Cordelia*, 1977; *Slave Trade*, 1979; *He/ She*, 1980; *Family: A Novel in the Form of a Memoir*, 1981 (reprinted as *Family*, 1991); *True Love*, 1982; *Mister White Eyes*, 1984; *A Girl of Forty*, 1986; *She Took My Arm as if She Loved Me*, 1997; *Daughter Mine*, 2000.

NONFICTION: *The Age of Happy Problems*, 1962; *A Walk on the West Side: California on the Brink*, 1981; *Travels in San Francisco*, 1990 (memoir); *Best Nightmare on Earth: A Life in Haiti*, 1991; *Bohemia: Where Art, Angst, Love and Strong Coffee Meet*, 1993; *Still Alive!: A Temporary Condition, a Memoir*, 2008.

CHILDREN'S LITERATURE: *The Young Prince and the Magic Cone*, 1973.

EDITED TEXTS: *Fiction of the Fifties: A Decade of American Writing*, 1959; *Stories of Modern America*, 1961 (with David L. Stevenson); *First Person Singular: Essays for the Sixties*, 1963.

BIBLIOGRAPHY

Conrad, Barnaby, and Monte Schulz, eds. *Snoopy's Guide to the Writing Life*. Cincinnati: Writer's Digest Books, 2002. Gold is one of the thirty authors who offers his advice and observations about writing.

Gelfant, Blanche H., ed. *The Columbia Companion to the Twentieth-Century American Short Story*. New York: Columbia University Press, 2000. Includes a chapter in which Gold's short stories are analyzed.

Hicks, Granville. "Generations of the Fifties: Malamud, Gold and Updike." In *The Creative Present: Notes on Contemporary American Fiction*, edited by Nona Balakian and Charles Simmons. New York: Gordian Press, 1973. A critical essay comparing the work of Gold, Bernard Malamud, and John Updike.

_____. *Literary Horizons: A Quarter Century of American Fiction*. New York: New York University Press, 1970. A collection of essays and book reviews of various authors, including Gold.

Tooker, Dan, and Roger Hofheins. *Fiction! Interviews with Northern California Novelists*. New York: Harcourt Brace Jovanovich, 1976. Provides a conversational, noncritical look at Gold's writing style, habits, and literary influences.

Waldon, Daniel, ed. *Herbert Gold and Company: American Jewish Writers as Universal Writers*. Studies in American Jewish Literature 10. Kent, Ohio: Kent State University Press, 1991. A collection of critical essays by various authors focusing on Gold's fiction in terms of his Jewish American background.

Irene Struthers Rush

CAROLINE GORDON

Born: Todd County, Kentucky; October 6, 1895
Died: San Cristóbal de las Casas, Mexico; April 11, 1981

PRINCIPAL SHORT FICTION
  The Forest of the South, 1945
  Old Red, and Other Stories, 1963
  The Collected Stories of Caroline Gordon, 1981

OTHER LITERARY FORMS

Caroline Gordon was a distinguished novelist, short-story writer, essayist, and literary critic. In the field of literary criticism, she is admired for her contributions to New Criticism and to theories of form and symbolic structure. Her most famous work of literary criticism, written with her husband, Allen Tate, is *The House of Fiction: An Anthology of the Short Story* (1950), a collection of short stories designed to illustrate methods for reading and interpreting fiction.

ACHIEVEMENTS

Caroline Gordon's novels and short fiction reveal her concerns with a sense of order and tradition in a world where those qualities are increasingly at risk--the world of the rural South. Her interest in those themes and settings reveals her intellectual ties to the New Critics; like them, she rejected popular, sentimental pictures of the region, finding meaning instead in rituals such as hunting and fishing, which gave dignity and moral order to a chaotic world. Her conversion to Roman Catholicism in 1947 gave an extra dimension to her later work. Her careful style and concern with point of view have also caused her to be compared with Henry James. During her lifetime, Gordon received a John Simon Guggenheim Memorial Foundation Fellowship in creative writing, won the O. Henry Short-Story Award for "Old Red," and

was given honorary doctorates by Bethany College, Purdue University, and St. Mary's College. In 1966, she received a grant of ten thousand dollars from the National Council of Arts.

BIOGRAPHY

Caroline Ferguson Gordon was graduated from Bethany College, Bethany, West Virginia, in 1916. From 1920 to 1924, she served as a reporter for the *Chattanooga News*; an article she wrote in 1923 on the Fugitive Group of writers of Nashville brought her to the attention of members of that group, especially Allen Tate, whom she married in 1924 and divorced in 1959. In 1929, she was awarded a John Simon Guggenheim Memorial Foundation Fellowship in creative writing and traveled to England and France; during that year, she also worked for brief intervals as a secretary to novelist Ford Madox Ford, who was instrumental in encouraging her to publish several of her short stories and her first novel. Gordon taught at the University of North Carolina, the University of Washington, the University of California, Davis, and Purdue University. In 1947, Gordon became a member of the Catholic Church, a fact that a number of critics have seen as influencing the themes and the highly moral cast of her later writings.

ANALYSIS

A modernist in style and technique, Caroline Gordon is decidedly antimodern in the themes of her writings. Among American authors, she is similar to Willa Cather in decrying the spiritual corruption of the modern industrial age and in lauding as an ideal a return to the humanistic values of an agrarian society. While the frontier serves as the backdrop for Cather's idealizations of pastoralism, the South and its heritage provide the setting for romantic explorations of nature's influence upon human beings' ethical development in Gordon's fiction.

The thematics of Gordon's fiction and her own avowed interest in the southern gestalt identify her strongly with the literary movement known as the Southern Renaissance. Initiated around 1920 and encompassing the Fugitive writers, the movement worked to revive through art and literature a rebirth of interest in southern ideals and values, particularly those of the agrarian, pre-Civil War South. The renaissance in southern letters strove to eliminate from portrayals of the South the false sentimentality and excessive romanticism characteristic of the writings of the Old South and to uphold, instead, the view of the South as the repository of humanistic values and a viable alternative to the dehumanizing effects of modern materialism and industrialization. The views of the Southern Renaissance can be seen most clearly in Gordon's choice of heroes in her fiction. Her heroes generally are emblematic of the southern agrarian ideal, individualistic, self-reliant characters exemplifying a deep love of nature and a respect for the values of community and family heritage. A strong sense of place or devotion to the land as symbolic of higher spiritual qualities in human existence is also readily apparent, together with respect for those characters who shape their destinies in accord with ethical values.

A number of Gordon's heroes in her fiction are sportsmen whose dedicated passion for nature is the focal point of their lives and the source of their awareness of aesthetic and spiritual values. From their relationship with nature, they learn moral lessons that inspire them to the higher values of courage, compassion, and sacrifice. Often, the sportsman hero is contrasted directly with those characters of lessened moral awareness who see nature as only a means to an end of self-gratification or materialistic greed.

"THE LAST DAY IN THE FIELD"

Typical of the sportsman hero is Aleck Maury, the protagonist of "The Last Day in the Field" and a character who appears in several of Gordon's short stories in *The Forest of the South* and in the novel *Aleck Maury, Sportsman* (1934), published in London as *Pastimes of Aleck Maury, The Life of a True Sportsman.* In "The Last Day in the Field," Aleck Maury is presented to the reader as a once-vigorous sportsman now grown old and having to confront both his own

physical limitations and his own mortality. Aleck is like "the fall when the leaves stayed green so long." In watching the progress of the frost on the elderberry bushes, he sees symbolized his own existence: "The lower, spreading branches had turned yellow and were already sinking to the ground but the leaves in the top clusters still stood up stiff and straight." Thinking of how the frost creeps higher out of the ground each night, Aleck remarks to himself, "Ah-ha, it'll get you yet!" aware that old age will take its toll upon him soon--but not before he has his "last day in the field."

Aleck's wife, Molly, urges him not to hunt this year, reminding him of the pain in his leg from a previous hunting injury. At first Aleck agrees to her wisdom, but when the killing frost comes, bringing with it the scents and colors of the perfect hunting day, Aleck is off before dawn to awaken Joe Thomas, the young man next door, and go quail hunting. The two men experience the ritualistic pleasure of preparing for the hunt, with Aleck making some sandwiches and coffee to take on the trip, while Joe hitches up the buggy and gathers up the hunting gear. When all is ready in preparation, the

Caroline Gordon (Library of Congress)

men get the dogs, Bob and Judy, a matched set of liver-and-white pointers and two of the finest hunting dogs in the country.

The ride from Gloversville to Spring Creek takes more than an hour, and when the men arrive the dogs are eager to track down some quail. Joe sets the dogs free, and they find their first bevy of quail in the bottomlands of a corn field. Joe takes the easiest shot and bags a bird; Aleck, characteristically, takes the shot requiring the most skill and patience and gets the best bird of the lot. After several more shots at singles, the men stop to eat lunch. Aleck notices Bob, the hunting dog, and senses an empathetic comradeship with his spirit. Aleck reflects, "I looked at him and thought how different he was from his mate and like some dogs I had known--and men, too--who lived only for hunting and could never get enough no matter how long the day was." The men walk through several more fields, and Aleck feels the pain building steadily in his leg. He wonders if he will be able to make it through the day, at the same time that he laments deeply that the day is going by so quickly and soon the perfect hunting day of this season will be over. Joe misses an easy shot, and Aleck shares with him some of his accumulated wisdom gathered through many such days in the field. An empathy develops between the two men, and Aleck feels even more keenly his own age and a deep longing to be young again and have so much time ahead.

At twilight, the men begin the walk back to the buggy. Aleck's leg is hurting him badly, and he fears that he cannot make the journey back. At that moment, the men climb a fence and come out at one end of a long field, "as birdy a place as ever I saw," Aleck thinks to himself, and Aleck knows that no matter how much pain he is in he has to hunt that field, "leg or no leg." Aleck and Joe shoot two quail, and, as Aleck is retreating from the field, he spots Bob making a perfect sighting and points on the last quail from the last covey of the day. "Your shot," Aleck tells Joe, but Joe replies, "No, you take it." In the fading light, Aleck gets the bird with the third shot. "I saw it there for a second, its wings black against the gold light, before, wings still spread, it came whirling down, like an autumn leaf, like the leaves that were everywhere about us, all over the ground."

"The Last Day in the Field" is a descriptive story, working to capture a mood and a setting as a man who loves hunting faces the fact that he must soon give it up and seeks to draw all the beauty, feeling, and meaning he can from his last experience. The story's action line is a simple one, and there are no major plot twists or conflicts to be resolved. What gives the story its effect and power is its sustained tonal qualities of mood, imagery, and setting that subtly suggest much about Aleck Maury and the world he faces. Contrasting images--the green of fall and the frost of winter, the sunrise of the perfect hunting day and its peaceful close at sunset, Aleck's age and Joe's youth, Molly's practical wisdom and Aleck's passionate response to the beauty and energy of nature--combine to create in the reader the mood of "the last day in the field" and to convey the insights acquired in these final moments by a man whose spirit is attuned to the meanings and fulfillment nature has to impart.

"ONE AGAINST THEBES"

The romanticism that pervades much of Gordon's writing reaches its fullest expression in the story "One Against Thebes," a rewritten version of her first published story, "Summer Dust." The line of thematic development presented is almost Keatsian in asserting the primacy of the imagination over the limitations of the real and clearly defined, and there is, too, in the story a strong romantic emphasis upon the beauty of youth and innocence in contrast to the world of experience in which values and the human spirit become corrupted by expediency and failures of moral courage.

The epigraph of the story, "That you shall forever hold this city safe from the men of Thebes, the dragon's sons," indicates that the story's theme is evil and the necessity to protect the city, or human civilization, from evil's encroachment. The inhabitants of Thebes were said to be descended from dragons and to have borne serpent's tails in earlier times. This motif is presented in the story through a number of images that restate the theme of the serpent and emphasize the omnipresence of evil.

The story's protagonist, a small girl, is walking along a dusty road in midsummer. Ahead of her walks a black girl, a black woman, and Son, a black boy; the boy runs behind the woman and lurches from side to side of the road, stirring up clouds of dust that spiral in a trail at his feet. The child looks at the trail and thinks "how it might have been made by a great snake, a serpent as large as any one of them, hurling itself now to one side of the road, now to the other, and thinks, too, how she and the other girl and the boy and even the old woman seem to move in its coils."

The girl's vision of the serpent trail Son has made in the dust as he plays along the road foreshadows her first encounter with evil--a woman, obsessed with greed, who tries to claim for herself peaches that belong to the girl's grandmother; two young men who run a horse several miles, "in August, too, when you're not supposed to lather horses"; and the poverty and loneliness of an old black woman, Aunt Emily, who lives in one of the cabins "in a row back of the big house." The images of imperfection and suffering in the world leave the girl frightened and filled with revulsion, while her older brother's apparent wisdom about the ways of the world and his discussion of "grownup" matters she does not understand leave her confused and isolated. The girl, however, is the only character in the story capable of an act of kindness and of envisioning a better world than the one she encounters. In a moment of empathy and generosity, she slips the *Green Fairy Book* she has read many times into Son's jacket pocket, knowing all the while she will never see the book again. Son runs off to play in the road again, when he comes to a spot where "the trail his feet had made earlier in the afternoon still showed he would whack the dust--as if he were trying the beat a snake to death." The girl follows slowly behind him, "stepping to one side of the road to avoid the serpentine trail that Son's feet had left in the dust." As she walks along the road and clouds of dust envelop her, she recalls the words from the fairy book about how the Fairy Godmother said to the Little Princess that they would ride a cloud to the crystal palace in the woods and there would be waiting for them a gold crown, silver slippers, and a silver veil embroidered with the sun, the moon, and the stars. The concluding image is of the child lost in dream visions of an ideal world in which an escape from ugliness and evil is possible. In the real world, where no such escape is truly possible, the only avenue of amelioration is compassion and the strength to ward off the serpent.

"THE ICE HOUSE"

One of Gordon's most undervalued stories is "The Ice House," a work that expresses both her interest in southern themes and her allegiance to humanistic values. The story takes place a year after the Civil War and is set in an old ice house in the South, where the bodies of Union soldiers were hurriedly buried during a battle in 1862. The story focuses upon two young southern boys, Doug and Raeburn, and a Yankee contractor. The contractor has hired the boys to go into the ice house and dig up the skeletons of the Union soldiers, which he will then place in coffins and deliver to the United States government at so much "a head." After a day of long, hard labor, the contractor pays the boys and tells them he will not be needing them any longer. The boys are surprised, since they were originally told they would be hired for three or four days' work. Doug hangs back in some bushes to see what the contractor will do after they leave and discovers that the man is rearranging the skeletons in the pine coffins. When Raeburn asks Doug what he thinks the contractor is doing, Doug responds, "He dividing up them skeletons so he can get paid double." Later, walking home, Doug stops and tells Raeburn, "There ain't a whole man in any one of them boxes. If that ain't a Yankee fer ye!"

The story would be a slight one in both meaning and impact were it not for the fact that Gordon uses it to contrast, through the characters of Doug and Raeburn, the values of materialism and the values of humanism. Doug shares the values and the worldview of the Yankee contractor; he is a materialist at heart, interested only in opportunity and economic gain. When the boys meet on the road to begin the job, it is Doug who chides Raeburn for being late and for not being excited about all the money they are going to make. When he senses that Raeburn feels uneasy about digging up dead bodies, Doug tells him he can always get somebody else. Digging up the bodies is just a job to Doug, and he is not personally involved with it as Raeburn is. "Handlin' a dead Yankee ain't no more to *me*," Doug says, "than handlin' a dead hawg." As the two boys arrive, the Yankee contractor calls out to them, "Well boys, I see you're like me. Early risers." The emphasis here is upon the work ethic, and Doug is very much a product of this mind-set, while Raeburn prefers to be a little late and at least get his breakfast. Doug is the first to take a pick and begin the gruesome business of unearthing the bodies after the contractor tells them the faster they get done the sooner they will get their money. Raeburn hesitates and moves more slowly, aware of what lies ahead.

As the work progresses, Doug is largely insensitive to the skeletons he unearths and to the lives they once contained. Raeburn, however, pauses to look out over the field where the battle was fought and envisions the suffering that must have occurred. When the boys and the contractor break for lunch, Raeburn cannot eat because of a "sick feeling" that sweeps over him. Doug suffers from no such problem and spends the period discussing with the contractor government jobs and whether the man is paid by the day or by the job. When the boys tell the contractor they plan to do farm work after this job, he tells them that farm work is "all right if you can't get nothing else to do" but that smart young boys like they are should be "looking out for oppertunity." He adds, "The folks at home all thought I was mighty foolish when I come down to this country, but I knew they was oppertunity in the South . . . bound to be."

The contractor, like Doug, sees the South and the skeletons in the ice house as "oppertunity." The reasons the men died and the values they fought to uphold have no meaning. The materialism of the post-Civil War era is rampant; it has invaded the ice house and turned the skeletons of men who died believing in a cause into so many dollars of profit per coffin. The stark contrast in moral values in the story is between the exploiters, who simply profit from other men's battles, and the believers, like the soldiers, who are capable of commitments beyond the self and of sacrifices at great cost. "The Ice House" confirms Gordon's belief, apparent in the entire canon of her writings, that the battle of the modern era is not between sectional rivalries but between those sensitive to man's potential for higher ideals and spiritual purpose in his life and those who wish only to exploit and corrupt for their own self-serving purposes.

OTHER MAJOR WORKS

LONG FICTION: *Penhally*, 1931; *Aleck Maury, Sportsman*, 1934; *None Shall Look Back*, 1937; *The Garden of Adonis*, 1937; *Green Centuries*, 1941; *The Women on the Porch*, 1944; *The Strange Children*, 1951; *The Malefactors*, 1956; *The Glory of Hera*, 1972.

NONFICTION: *How to Read a Novel*, 1957; *A Good Soldier: A Key to the Novels of Ford Madox Ford*, 1963; *The Southern Mandarins: Lettes of Caroline Gordon to Sally Wood, 1924-1937*, 1984; *A Literary Friendship: Correspondence Between Caroline Gordon and Ford Madox Ford*, 1999 (Brita Lindberg-Seyersted, editor).

EDITED TEXT: *The House of Fiction: An Anthology of the Short Story*, 1950 (with Allen Tate).

BIBLIOGRAPHY

Arbery, Virginia L. "'Considerable Emphasis on Decorum': Caroline Gordon and the Abyss." *Modern Age* 36 (Winter, 1994): 157-164. Discusses Gordon's fiction that makes use of American history and her depiction of the hero and the pattern of sacred marriage. Argues that critics have inadvertently depreciated the centrality of her often stated claim that women are always on the lookout for heroes.

Boyle, Anne M. *Strange and Lurid Bloom: A Study of the Fiction of Caroline Gordon*. Madison, N.J.: Fairleigh Dickinson University Press, 2002. Critical interpretation of Gordon's fiction, describing her struggle to gain respect as a writer; her depiction of mothers, daughters, sons, and men; and the exploration of sexual and racial tension in her work.

Folks, Jeffrey J. "Caroline Gordon: Facing the Ethical Abyss." In *In a Time of Disorder: Form and Meaning in Southern Fiction from Poe to O'Connor*. New York: Peter Lang, 2003. Examines how Gordon and other southern writers used their work to restore order and meaning to the disordered society in which they lived.

Fritz-Piggott, Jill. "The Dominant Chord and the Different Voice: The Sexes in Gordon's Stories." In *The Female Tradition in Southern Literature*, edited by Carol S. Manning. Urbana: University of Illinois Press, 1993. Argues that the most general fact about gender in Gordon's stories is that they are told by different male and female voices. Analyzes some of Gordon's stories in which an individual confronts a force as the Other against which the self is defined.

Jonza, Nancylee Novell. *The Underground Stream: The Life and Art of Caroline Gordon*. Athens: University of Georgia Press, 1995. A good, updated biography of Gordon. Includes bibliographical references and an index.

Landless, Thomas H., ed. *The Short Fiction of Caroline Gordon: A Critical Symposium*. Irving, Tex.: University of Dallas Press, 1972. Contains one essay on the Aleck Maury stories and another essay that provides an extensive discussion of "The Captive." Some of the other essays discuss nature, sex, and the political implications of the South in Gordon's short fiction.

Lindberg-Seyersted, Brita, ed. *A Literary Friendship: Correspondence Between Caroline Gordon and Ford Madox Ford*. Knoxville: University of Tennessee Press, 1999. Collection of letters between the two acclaimed authors. Includes an index.

Makowsky, Veronica A. *Caroline Gordon: A Biography*. New York: Oxford University Press, 1989. Although this work is primarily a biography, it contains extensive analysis of Gordon's fiction, including many of the short stories.

Millichap, Joseph R. "Caroline Gordon: Auto/biography, Aleck Maury, and the Heroic Cycle." In *A Backward Glance: The Southern Renascence, the Autobiographical Epic, and the Classical Legacy*. Knoxville: University of Tennessee Press, 2009. Maintains that critics have unfairly excluded Gordon from accounts of southern fiction. Argues that her creation of the character of Aleck Maury, in which she adapts the classical heroic cycle to a modern southern narrative, is her greatest literary achievement.

Rocks, James E. "The Short Fiction of Caroline Gordon." *Tulane Studies in English* 18 (1970): 115-135. Discusses the basic theme of natural and supernatural grace in Gordon's stories. Analyzes the irony in "Her Quaint Honor," the dichotomy between physical and mental insight in "The Last Day in the Field," and the telescoping of time in "Old Red."

Stuckey, W. J. *Caroline Gordon*. New York: Twayne, 1972. A brief biography and a detailed analysis of Gordon's novels and some of the short stories, especially "Old Red," "The Captive," "The Last Day in the Field," "Her Quaint Honor," and "Brilliant Leaves."

Waldron, Ann. *Close Connections: Caroline Gordon and the Southern Renaissance*. New York: Putnam, 1987. A literary biography that concentrates on Gordon's connections with other writers in the Southern Renaissance and their mutual influence.

Christina Murphy
Updated by Ann Davison Garbett

MARY GORDON

Born: Far Rockaway, New York; December 8, 1949

PRINCIPAL SHORT FICTION

Temporary Shelter, 1987
The Rest of Life: Three Novellas, 1993
The Stories of Mary Gordon, 2006

OTHER LITERARY FORMS

Mary Gordon has been most recognized for her novels. *Final Payments* (1978), *The Company of Women* (1980), and *Men and Angels* (1985) all received praise for her examination of themes concerning women, Roman Catholicism, and art. Gordon has also published essays and a personal memoir of her father.

ACHIEVEMENTS

Mary Gordon received t he Janet Heidinger Kafka Prize from the University of Rochester for *Final Payments* in 1979 and for *The Company of Women* in 1981. In 1997, she won the O. Henry Award for Best Story.

BIOGRAPHY

Mary Catherine Gordon was born in 1949 in Far Rockaway, New York, to a working-class, Irish Catholic family. Her father was an important early influence in her life, teaching her to read and encouraging her to write. She was only seven when he died, leaving her devastated. She then grew up in a female household, inhabited by her mother, an aunt, and her grandmother. The latter two were rigid in their piety and unsympathetic toward Gordon's literary interests. Gordon attended religious school and originally planned to become a nun.

Her rebellious nature began to manifest itself during her high school years, and she chose to attend Barnard College instead of Catholic Fordham University. During her university years in the 1960's, she was exhilarated by the sense of freedom and experimentation on campus. Antiwar demonstrations, the women's movement, and the life of the counterculture caused her to question Catholicism's stance on sex and on the role of women in the Church. After college she began graduate work at Syracuse University and participated in a women's writers' group. She began to publish poems and short stories while working on a dissertation on Virginia Woolf. When her third novel was published, she gave up her graduate work.

When Gordon began researching a biography of her father, she was forced to see that most of what he had claimed about himself was untrue. He had come from an immigrant Jewish family and had converted to Roman Catholicism; he had never attended Harvard University or lived in Paris; his writing was labored and pretentious, bigoted and anti-Semitic. These discoveries were painful for Gordon but confronting them marked a new direction in her writing. Gordon married and settled with her husband and children in New York City, teaching creative writing at Barnard College.

ANALYSIS

Mary Gordon's early novels, *Final Payments* and *The Company of Women,* developed religious themes that labeled her a Catholic novelist, a title she rejected. Her later work has moved away from dealing explicitly with religion. In both those early works, a young woman wrestles with conflicts between her repressive Catholic upbringing and her desire for independence. In *Final Payments* the repressive force is a father; in *The Company of Women* it is a priest. Even in *Spending: A Utopian Divertimento* (1998), a novel that seems intent on avoiding expressly religious material, the conflict exists submerged in the novel's narrator.

Parents and children, especially fathers and daughters, play important roles in Gordon's work. The repressive adult, who is unsympathetic to a child's fears, is a common figure and appears repeatedly in the stories of *Temporary Shelter*. In addition, Gordon has been interested in the position of the immigrant Irish person in America, who often faces the same sort of conflict that divides parents and children. How can the children of a New World meet the demands of parents who grew up in the Old World? How can immigrants find a place in the New World? These questions form much of the theme of *The Other Side* (1989), a novel about three generations of an Irish American family.

Many critics found Gordon's early work weak in its portrayal of men and ascribed that weakness to Gordon's own conflicts between the official morality of the Church and her understanding of human passions. Her later work, especially *The Rest of Life* and *Spending*, attempts to correct that weakness by giving close attention to sexual relations between men and women, and in interviews Gordon has wondered how readers of her early work will respond to so much explicit sex.

"DELIA"

"Delia" is one of three stories with interrelated characters from Gordon's early collection, *Temporary*

Mary Gordon (Nancy Kaszerman/ZUMA/Corbis)

Shelter. They focus on four Irish American sisters and their position in America--beautiful Kathleen (whose daughter Nora was born with one leg shorter than the other), sharp-tongued Bridget, tiny Nettie, and Delia, the youngest and best looking of the group, who marries a Protestant and moves away, to the dismay of her sisters. Only Nora's kindly mother defends Delia's husband, John Taylor, because he was kind to Nora. The others assume that he and Delia will have Protestant children and that Delia will be lost to them forever.

After Delia writes that she is pregnant with her first child, no further news is heard. Meanwhile, Kathleen also becomes pregnant. Delia's due date passes without news. At last Kathleen is in labor, and while young Nora is sitting on the porch, listening to her mother's cries, Taylor appears. He intends to speak to Kathleen, but when he learns that she is in labor, he loses courage and instead gives his message to Nora: Delia died two months earlier while giving birth to a stillborn child. He gives Nora a silver dollar to buy her silence for what he mysteriously says will be their secret. Somehow Delia's exposure to American culture proved toxic, just as her sisters had predicted.

"AGNES"

"Agnes" is the second of the *Temporary Shelter* stories to deal with Nora's family. Like "Delia," it is told partly from Nora's point of view. Agnes is the common-law wife of Nora's uncle, Desmond, a bootlegger. For a decade the family suffered both because of Desmond's periodic skirmishes with the law and because of Agnes's sinful living arrangement with him. Nora once liked Uncle Desmond, but as she has matured she has come to see him as an embarrassment. Agnes also embarrasses her; dowdy and common, she has too little self-respect to leave the affair.

Desmond suddenly leaves Agnes to move to California to marry a girl whom Nora's father labels "a rich girl whose family threw her out for marrying a greenhorn." Nora's contempt for Agnes grows as Agnes continues to write Desmond. When Agnes learns that Desmond's wife is pregnant, she even wonders if she should go to California to help with the new baby. When Desmond's wife learns of their correspondence and forces him to break it off, Agnes hangs herself. For that sin, she must be buried in an unsanctified cemetery by a Presbyterian undertaker. After the death, Nora bitterly concludes that the real lesson is that the world has no place for women like Agnes.

"EILEEN"

"Eileen," the last of the Nora stories, chronicles the fate of Eileen Foley, who left her job in a Limerick orphanage to come to America, where she hoped to make enough money to bring over her youngest brother, Tom. Nora liked Eileen when she lived with Nora's family for a few months, but in the intervening years Nora has learned a cruel lesson. The nuns who had encouraged her to apply to a teachers' college failed to mention her disability in their recommendation. She was thrilled to be accepted to the school, but on her arrival she was quickly dismissed on account of her short leg and crutch. She takes an educational course and becomes an excellent secretary, but her idealism has been blasted and her new cynicism convinces her that the bright but childish Tom will never be successful in America. When Tom is killed in a freak accident, Eileen decides to return to Ireland. Like Nora, she has lost faith in America as a land of opportunity, the theme suggested by all three stories.

THE REST OF LIFE

In each of the three novellas of *The Rest of Life*, a woman narrates the story of her most important lover. In *Immaculate Man*, a social worker describes her long affair with Clement, a priest, and the circumstances that have made an ally of Father Boniface, an older priest who also loves Clement. In *Living at Home*, a psychiatrist, who specializes in work with autistic children, describes her marriage to an Italian journalist, Lauro, a man who seems to be her psychic opposite. In *The Rest of Life*, an old woman (from whose point of view much of the story is told) is taken back to the Italian town of her birth by her eager son and his girlfriend. As she travels, she relives her adolescent romance with Leo, a Marxist and a poet, with whom she made a suicide pact.

Each of the novellas examines the ways in which men and women use each other in love. The narrator of *Immaculate Man* loves Clement but suspects that to him she is a means of leaving the priesthood. The narrator of *Living at Home* feeds on Lauro's vitality but

understands that he values her mostly for her body and for the haven their home provides him in his nomadic life. In *The Rest of Life*, the most complex of the narratives, the narrator reveals that Leo used her to massage his own ego. Nevertheless, her guilt at having backed out of the pact while Leo died has tainted her life and added to her guilt at having disappointed her beloved father. Although the three narratives share a focus on character rather than on events, the central character of *The Rest of Life* relives the day of the suicide pact and its humiliating consequences, making this the most conventional of the three works.

THE STORIES OF MARY GORDON

The Stories of Mary Gordon collects new and unpublished short stories alongside previously published stories from *Temporary Shelter*. The lives of women, families, and the Catholic Church continue to appear as thematic influences. Gordon shows slices of American life through close character studies and portraits of personal transition, social and cultural disparity, and a strong sense of place. Such stories as "Separation" and "Death in Naples" address the experience of attachment and loss in motherhood at two distinct stages of life. Through "The Bishop's House," "The Epiphany Branch," and "City Life," Gordon gives voice to the profoundly dissimilar contexts that people inhabit within the same city, same neighborhood, even underneath the same room, revealing poignant aspects of individualism and social, class, and cultural disparity.

The range of characters in this collection is broad and diverse. "The Translator's Husband," for instance, is told through the lens of a middle-aged man, and Gordon creates his character, as she does the others, with humility, wit, and insight. Perpetually aware of the yin and yang of life, she addresses the darkness that lurks below the surface. "Cleaning Up" speaks directly to that understanding: Gordon portrays a young woman who is conscious of her own inclination toward the shadowy corners of existence and the implications of her dark side as she relates to her mother, to men, and to other women.

Gordon channels her own passion for literature and learning through many of her characters. Florence Melnick in "The Epiphany Branch" is a woman whose pursuit of education is so innocent and pure that she ardently resents those who take it for granted. The reader can feel that Gordon knows her characters through and through; even when the reader sees only a small window into the world, the reader believes that the rest is there.

Although the previously uncollected stories do not bear the same consistency of thread as those included from *Temporary Shelter*, there nevertheless exists both thematic and stylistic continuity. The prose is tight, clear, and evocative, which lends to the accessibility of Gordon's work. There is little to distract from the meat and potatoes of her stories, which are, at their core, people. All of her people, regardless of stage or station in life, face conflict at some point in the stories, and through these conflicts, Gordon sheds light upon an internal world and brings to the surface issues that are common to the human experience. "Conversations in Prosperity," for example, confronts head on fears surrounding aging and loss, without for a moment stepping out of character to make a message.

Though most of the stories remain grounded in the day-to-day, covering short sections of daily life, they often weave past into the present, creating a dynamic and complex representation of the characters' journeys. This multilayered effect serves to illuminate the struggles and transitions that confront the characters. With this collection Gordon transcends the categories that have sometimes been imposed upon her work. She is a writer of the human experience, a voice from within.

OTHER MAJOR WORKS

LONG FICTION: *Final Payments*, 1978; *The Company of Women*, 1980; *Men and Angels*, 1985; *The Other Side*, 1989; *Spending: A Utopian Divertimento*, 1998; *Pearl*, 2005.

NONFICTION: *Good Boys and Dead Girls, and Other Essays*, 1991; *The Shadow Man: A Daughter's Search for Her Father*, 1996; *Joan of Arc*, 2000; *Seeing Through Places: Reflections on Geography and Identity*, 2000; *Conversations with Mary Gordon*, 2002 (Alma Bennett, editor); *Circling My Mother: A Memoir*, 2007; *Reading Jesus: A Writer's Encounter with the Gospels*, 2009.

BIBLIOGRAPHY

Becker, Brenda L. "Virgin Martyrs." *The American Spectator* 14 (August, 1981): 28-32. This is a stringent but not unfriendly discussion of Gordon's first two novels. Becker praises depictions of female friendships and the workings of the Catholic Church but faults Gordon for her heavy-handed symbolism and her portrayals of men.

Corrigan, Maureen. "*Spending: A Utopian Divertimento.*" *The Nation* (March 16, 1998): 29-32. In this review of Gordon's work, Corrigan sees the steamy sexuality of this novel's narrator as a reaction to Gordon's earlier models of Catholic guilt. Corrigan praises Gordon's humor and her sharp portrayal of the artist's vision, but Corrigan faults the central theme, which she compares with a Harlequin romance.

Dwyer, June. "Unappealing Ethnicity Meets Unwelcoming America: Immigrant Self-Fashioning in Mary Gordon's *Temporary Shelter.*" *Melus* 22 (Fall, 1997): 103-112. Despite the forbidding title and a rather ponderous introduction, this essay is a thoughtful examination of conflicts inherent in the immigrant experience: Immigrants must face the realities of their new country, while at the same time they must confront the dominant culture's stereotypes of them. Most of the discussion concerns the Nora stories in this collection.

Gordon, Mary. "An Interview with Mary Gordon." Interview by Sandy Asirvatham. *Poets and Writers* (July/August, 1997): 50-61. This meaty interview focuses on Gordon's work methods and influences. It includes some brief analysis of her novels and gives more detailed attention to the significance of her discoveries about her father.

Lee, Don. "About Mary Gordon." *Ploughshares* 23 (Fall, 1997): 218-226. A detailed biography that concentrates on the relationship between Gordon's life and her fiction.

O'Kelly, Kevin. "Collection Provides a Window into Mary Gordon's World." *The Boston Globe*, January 9, 2007, p. C3. O'Kelly provides a general review of *The Stories of Mary Gordon.*

Powers, Elizabeth. "Doing Daddy Down." *Commentary* 103 (June, 1997): 38-42. Powers discusses what she sees as the repudiation of fathers in the work of three writers, including Gordon in *The Shadow Man*. In Powers's rather harsh judgment, Gordon's dismay at the truths she discovered about her father stem from her political liberalism and her quarrels with the Catholic Church rather than from any deeper reasons.

Schlumpf, Heidi. "Informed by the Experience of Being Catholic." *National Catholic Reporter*, February 5, 2010, p. 8A. This article addresses the identities of "woman writer" and "Catholic writer" that have been attached to Gordon. It looks at the era during which she came of age as a writer and the myriad personal, social, and historical influences that have shaped that journey.

Ann Davison Garbett
Updated by Sonia Erlich

WILLIAM GOYEN

Born: Trinity, Texas; April 24, 1915
Died: Los Angeles, California; August 29, 1983

PRINCIPAL SHORT FICTION
Ghost and Flesh: Stories and Tales, 1952
The Faces of Blood Kindred: A Novella and Ten Stories, 1960
Selected Writings of William Goyen: Eight Favorites by a Master American Story-Teller, 1974
The Collected Stories of William Goyen, 1975
Had I a Hundred Mouths: New and Selected Stories, 1947-1983, 1985

OTHER LITERARY FORMS
Although William Goyen asserted that "short fiction is what I most care about . . . the short narrative form most challenges and most frees me," he wrote several highly acclaimed novels, including *The House of Breath* (1950, 1975), *Come, the Restorer* (1974), and *Arcadio* (1983, 1994). Goyen was also a playwright of some distinction, although his plays have never been published. In addition, he wrote two television plays, *A Possibility of Oil* (pr. 1958) and *The Mind* (pr. 1961). Goyen was the playwright-in-residence at Lincoln Center from 1963 to 1964. He was a brilliant lecturer and critic; his essays appeared in *The New York Times*, *TriQuarterly*, *Southwest Review*, and other journals. In 1973, he published a biography of Jesus Christ, *A Book of Jesus*, and at the time of his death, he was at work on studies of Saint Paul and Saint Francis. He was also working on an autobiography/memoir of six influential women in his life. Throughout his life, Goyen was intensely interested in music and was recognized as a composer of considerable ability.

ACHIEVEMENTS
William Goyen won the McMurray Award in 1950 for *The House of Breath*; he was a John Simon Guggenheim Memorial Foundation fellow in creative writing in 1952 and 1954. He received the Texas Institute of Arts and Letters award for the best comic novel of 1962, and he earned a Ford Foundation grant for novelists writing for the theater (Lincoln Center Repertory Company) in 1963 and 1964. In 1965, 1966, 1968, 1969, and 1970, he won the American Society of Composers, Authors, and Publishers award for musical composition. *The Collected Stories of William Goyen* was nominated for a Pulitzer Prize in 1975, and in 1976, Goyen won the O. Henry Award for short stories. The prestigious French journal *Delta* devoted its entire ninth issue to Goyen in 1979. During his distinguished career, Goyen earned what is rarer than any literary award: the unqualified admiration and affection of his peers. He was recognized as being not only a storyteller of originality and consummate skill but also, and more important, an artist and man of genuine integrity, dignity, and spirituality.

BIOGRAPHY

Born in Texas to a lumber salesman, Charles Provine Goyen, and his wife, Mary Inez (Trow), on April 24, 1915, Charles William Goyen has said that his first seven years in the small town of Trinity supplied the material for the short stories he wrote. He then moved to Houston, where he later earned a B.A. and an M.A. in comparative literature from Rice University. From 1940 to 1945, he served in the Navy, and during this time he began his first novel. He lived in Taos, New Mexico, where he met Frieda Lawrence, who was to have a profound influence on the young man: "Frieda brought me a sense of the richness of the great world, and that, together with what I had come through--college, Texas, the war--got me ready to move into the real world that I had never been in." After New Mexico, he lived in Europe for some time, staying with Stephen Spender in London in 1949. In 1951 and 1952, he became friendly with Truman Capote and Carson Mc-Cullers. After another year in Europe (Italy and Switzerland), he returned to New Mexico. In the 1950's, he began to work in theater, film, and television. On November 10, 1963, he married Doris Roberts, an actress. That same year, he won a Ford Foundation grant. He served as senior editor at McGraw-Hill from 1966 to 1972.

Goyen began a distinguished career as a university professor in 1955 at the New School for Social Research, where he taught until 1960. He was a participant in the Columbia University Writing Program from 1963 until 1965; he also taught at Brown University (1972-1973), Princeton University (1976-1978), Hollins College (1978), Stephens College (1979), the University of Houston (1981), and the University of Southern California (1981-1982). In 1975, an anniversary issue of *The House of Breath* brought considerable critical acclaim and renewed attention to his novels. Goyen was, however, more popular and more highly respected in Europe than in the United States. In 1979, the distinguished French journal *Delta* accorded him an honor theretofore granted to only four other writers (Flannery O'Connor, Eudora Welty, William Faulkner, and Herman Melville) by devoting an entire issue to his work. In spite of his failing health, he experienced a great surge of creative energy in his last years; his late

flowering, like that of William Butler Yeats, yielded works of great power, originality, mystery, and beauty. To the end, Goyen wrote eloquently of the ecstasy and the anguish of human life; he championed the diminished and lost things of this world; he insisted on the holy mystery of each human being; and he proved that, as he said, "Art is an act of hope, and faith. Art is redeeming, and art is an affirmation." Goyen died in 1983 after a protracted struggle with leukemia.

ANALYSIS

"The White Rooster" is the story with which *Ghost and Flesh: Stories and Tales*, William Goyen's first collection, opens. The war between the sexes is being fought out in the hen yard. The story opens and centers on an unattractive woman who dominates her absent husband, Walter. In his brief appearances, he says little and does not do much, except to obey his domineering wife. According to the code of the Southwest, a woman needs to be mastered in order to be feminine. Marcy Samuels is homicidal. What is ostensibly driving her "insane" is the omnipresence of her scrawny, "white-faced" father-in-law, who scuttles through her house in his wheelchair, hawking and wheezing through his thin white neck. The second thing that aggravates her to dementia is the presence in her backyard of an old, sick white rooster. The scrawny cock is identified with the annoying old man by his movements, his noise, his appearance, and the rage he arouses in her. She determines to kill it while Mr. Samuels, coughing in his wheelchair behind her, recognizes that it is his neck that she would like to be wringing.

Marcy has had many arguments with Walter about putting his father out of the house. The old man has overheard these and is aware of her hatred for him. Marcy bullies Walter into constructing a trap that functions like a guillotine. She sits by the window, the cord pulled taut in her hand, waiting for the rooster to approach so that she can release the rope and decapitate it. At the murdering instant when the white rooster approaches and is about to "get it" in the neck, the old man slits his enemy's throat from behind with a knife. After murdering her, he devastates the house, smashing everything he can reach from his wheelchair: ripping off the wallpaper, slashing up the pillows, tearing and destroying in impotent fury. Walter finds him dead in this chaos.

The violence initiated by Marcy in her hatred of her father-in-law and deflected to the white rooster ricochets back to the old man, is vented by him against her who began it, and then becomes a storm of passion that demolishes the entire house. Goyen shows that hatred vented against one order of being, the bird, infects the human order, and then grows into a storm that destroys the object world, the house. In parentheses beside the title, it is indicated that this is Walter's story. In narrative terms, the perspective would have to be his, since he is the only survivor. In emotional terms this is also his story, because he, alone, is culpable. As "master" of this house, now savaged, he should have assumed the masculine role; then there could have been order and peace in his house instead of this explosion of destructive force unleashed by hate.

"A SHAPE OF LIGHT"

The last story in *Ghost and Flesh: Stories and Tales* is called "A Shape of Light." Very different in tone from "The White Rooster," it is similar rhetorically. The sentences are made of short, repetitive, incantatory phrases. Instead of a linear plot, there are circlings, stalkings, dancings, and weavings around an action which the language barely lets the reader glimpse. The author describes the setting of this story in words that might equally apply to his syntax. He says, "you had wandered into a landscape of addict elations, hallucinations and obsessions."

In passages of sharply contrasted dictions, a childhood memory is reclaimed, in the guise of a ghost's being fleshed out. The narrator recalls having triumphantly sent up a homemade kite, constructed by him out of shoe-box tissue paper and kindling wood. He sees it in terms of an artifice sent aloft by the artificer, released into a life of its own. Boney Benson, who flags the trains with a lantern, had asked the boy to let him send up a message, which he scribbles in pencil on the page of a lined tablet. The message flies away and the kite falls. The boy wonders what had been written on it. Now an adult, in a dirty city, he identifies with the impulse to send up a message and allow it to fly high above the sordidness. A piece of paper flies up from the street, and on this transitional symbol the narrator imprints Boney's story.

His wife having died in childbirth because the baby rose up in her and choked out her breath, Boney lay on her grave to listen for the unborn baby he had so fatally implanted in her. As restitution, he castrates himself and buries his bloody member in Allie's grave. Each night a light seems to arise from the tomb and Boney follows the flickering light. Four strangers had disinterred Mrs. Benson and found a hole where the child had been, and they join in the search for the light that had issued from the grave. Then the story circles back to its beginning in which a man in a city is writing down "the message that was sent and lost" in that long-ago town that is now "reclaimed and fixed forever in the light of so much darkness." The tale is told of a man who saddles his horse to follow a ghostly light. Interspersed with these passages are balladlike stanzas in which Allie speaks: "Oh where you agoing Boney Benson, and it nightfall? Why are you leaving the supper table so suddenly you have galloped your food; your supper will get cold and I will get cold."

This interplay between the real old man and his lantern, the gossip of the town that turns the actuality into a legend through its whispering, and the ballad form which this orally transmitted material assumes resonates against the figure of the author, seated at his writing table in the present inscribing this fiction. Each level of storytelling is indicated in the style appropriate to it. The educated author is presented in poetic prose, the rumors of the townspeople in colloquial speech, the yearnings of Allie in anapestic meter that stomps itself out in primitive rhythms, and the scenes in which the narrator describes his childhood encounter with Boney Benson are in flat, simple sentences. In this way, Goyen makes language, alone, do the work of setting the stage, changing the scenery, identifying the characters, and establishing the mood. He achieves both lighting effects and background music without employing either.

The denouement is implanted in the opening; it is retrospectively illuminated at the end of the story. The readers must return to the beginning to comprehend what they have just experienced. This imposes on the act of reading the same philosophical point made by the story's theme and by the mode of its narration. All three are engaged in parallel processes symbolized by the pursuit of the flickering light. The quest for the truth is like trying to put flesh on a ghost that ever haunts and eludes the readers. When readers reread the story, they discover that this was the lost message which had been inscribed there in the beginning, which was read, but not yet fully understood:

> Walking one day I found a child let down from Heaven on a piece of string, standing in a meadow of bluebonnets and paint-brush, leashed out to me. This was my lost child and I told him what he did not know, left my words with him, our covenant, and laid this charge upon him: "speak of this little species that cannot speak for itself; be gesture; and use the light and follow it wherever it may lead you, and lead others to it."

By recording a local legend that would otherwise have vanished into the darkness and giving the reader simultaneously the popular form and the philosophical implications, Goyen, in the act of writing a story, gives his readers a history of the narrative form, from its inception in inspiration to its embodiment in artifact.

OTHER MAJOR WORKS

LONG FICTION: *The House of Breath*, 1950, 1975; *In a Farther Country: A Romance*, 1955, 1962; *The Fair Sister*, 1963; *Come, the Restorer*, 1974; *Wonderful Plant*, 1979; *Arcadio*, 1983, 1994; *Half a Look of Cain: A Fantastical Narrative*, 1994.

PLAYS: *The House of Breath*, pr. 1957 (based on his novel; also pr. as *House of Breath, Black/White*, 1975); *The Diamond Rattler*, pr. 1960; *Christy*, pr. 1964; *Aimee!*, pr. 1973.

TELEPLAYS: *A Possibility of Oil*, pr. 1958; *The Mind*, pr. 1961.

POETRY: *Nine Poems*, 1976.

NONFICTION: *My Antonia: A Critical Commentary*, 1966; *Ralph Ellison's Invisible Man: A Critical Commentary*, 1966; *A Book of Jesus*, 1973; *William Goyen: Selected Letters from a Writer's Life*, 1995; *Goyen: Autobiographical Essays, Notebooks, Evocations, Interviews*, 2007 (Reginald Gibbons, editor).

TRANSLATION: *The Lazy Ones*, 1952 (of Albert Cossery).

BIBLIOGRAPHY

Davis, Clark. "'Environment is All': William Goyen's East Texas." *Southwest Review* 94, no. 3 (2009): 430-449. Traces the origins of the themes in Goyen's writings to his upbringing in a small East Texas town. Discusses how in many of Goyen's stories, the principal character is "not so much . . . an autobiographical stand-in but . . . a mouthpiece for Goyen's artistic project--the 'gathering-up' of homegrown myth and memory."

_____. "The Hungry Art of William Goyen." *Southern Review* 40, no. 4 (Autumn, 2004): 816-828. Discusses Goyen's life and analyzes some of his short stories to examine the theme of isolation, estrangement, and leaving in his work.

_____. "William Goyen and the Strangeness of Reading." *Raritan* 28, no. 4 (Spring, 2009): 138-157. Analyzes the themes of strangers and strangeness in Goyen's writings, examining depictions of home, welcome, and houses in some of his stories, including "Precious Door" and "In the Ice-Bound Hothouse."

Duncan, Erika. "Come a Spiritual Healer: A Profile of William Goyen." *Book Forum* 3 (1979): 296-303. Duncan's sensitive essay is part analysis and part personal reminiscence. She suggests that Goyen's stories and novels involve a search "for the radiance of life and the hidden meaning in the darkness."

Gibbons, Reginald. *William Goyen: A Study of the Short Fiction*. Boston: Twayne, 1991. Part of Twayne's Studies in Short Fiction series, this volume provides an excellent overview of Goyen's short stories. Includes bibliographical references and an index.

Goyen, William. *Goyen: Autobiographical Essays, Notebooks, Evocations, Interviews*. Edited and introduced by Reginald Gibbons. Austin: University of Texas Press, 2007. A compendium of materials by and about Goyen, including his previously uncollected autobiographical essays and other writings; interviews he conducted with *Paris Review*, *TriQuarterly*, and other journals; and previously unpublished materials from his papers.

Gumm, Clyde. "William Goyen: A Bibliographical Chronicle." *Bulletin of Bibliography* 35 (1978): 123-131. This bibliography is an invaluable resource for anyone researching Goyen's work.

Gumm has compiled not only the publication data for all of the author's essays, stories, poems, and novels, but also every essay, review, and interview written about Goyen from 1938 through 1976.

Horvath, Brooke, Irving Malin, and Paul Ruffin, eds. *A Goyen Companion: Appreciations of a Writer's Writer*. Austin: University of Texas Press, 1997. Features essays on Goyen by admiring writers, including readings of his short stories and novels.

Paul, Jay S. "Marvelous Reciprocity: The Fiction of William Goyen." *Critique: Studies in Modern Fiction* 19, no. 2 (1977): 77-92. This study of *The Collected Stories of William Goyen* focuses on Goyen's depiction of love, his use of a storyteller as the central character, and the ways in which the manner of telling shapes a story. Paul's thoughtful analyses of numerous stories from this collection leads him to the conclusion that "the whole of Goyen's work must be thought of as a meditation upon storytelling, which is ideally a means of rescuing one's past, one's self, one's listeners. His concern has been art's power to transform human life."

_____. "'Nests in a Stone Image': Goyen's Surreal Gethsemane." *Studies in Short Fiction* 15 (1978): 415-420. "Nests in a Stone Image," from the collection *Ghost and Flesh: Stories and Tales*, is the story of a writer frustrated by his inability to write and by his more profound inability to love. Paul demonstrates that the writer's vigil "is patterned on Jesus' night of prayer and doubt in Gethsemane." He explains that Goyen's theme is love and argues that Goyen believes that each individual "can be as vital and dynamic as Jesus himself."

Wier, Allen. "William Goyen: Speech for What Is Not Spoken." *Black Warrior Review* 10 (Fall, 1983): 160-164. In his moving meditation on Goyen's life and fiction, written shortly after the writer's death, Wier talks about what knowing Goyen meant to him and what reading Goyen's fiction has meant and will mean to him. He focuses his critical comments on *Arcadio*, and he asserts that this novel, like all Goyen's fiction, "gives the reader a sense of intimacy."

Ruth Rosenberg
Updated by Hal Holladay

SHIRLEY ANN GRAU

Born: New Orleans, Louisiana; July 8, 1929

PRINCIPAL SHORT FICTION
The Black Prince, and Other Stories, 1955
The Wind Shifting West, 1973
Nine Women, 1985
Selected Stories, 2003

OTHER LITERARY FORMS

Other than her collections of short stories, Shirley Ann Grau (grow) has written several novels, including *The Hard Blue Sky* (1958), *The House on Coliseum Street* (1961), *The Keepers of the House* (1964), *The Condor Passes* (1971), *Evidence of Love* (1977), and *Roadwalkers* (1994). Her articles and stories have appeared in *Carnival, The Saturday Evening Post, Story,*

The Atlantic, The New Yorker, Gentlemen's Quarterly, Southern Review, Vogue, Redbook, Mademoiselle, Holiday, and *The Reporter.* In 1966, Grau wrote the introduction to Marjorie Kinnan Rawlings's *Cross Creek* (1942).

ACHIEVEMENTS

Shirley Ann Grau's short story "Joshua" was an inclusion in *Prize Stories 1955: The O. Henry Awards.* Her "Eight O'Clock One Morning" was a selection for *Prize Stories 1962: The O. Henry Awards.* Grau received the 1965 Pulitzer Prize for *The Keepers of the House.* Both the Literary Guild and the Book-of-the-Month Club used *The Keepers of the House* as selections; *Ladies' Home Journal* (January/February, 1964) chose the novel as a condensed selection. *The Condor Passes* became a Book-of-the-Month Club selection.

Grau received the LL.D. from Rider College (now Rider University) in New Jersey in 1973 and the D.Litt. from Spring Hill College in Alabama in 1990. In 2004, she earned the Louisiana Writer Award from the Louisiana Center for the Book.

BIOGRAPHY

Born to Adolph Grau and Katherine Onions, Shirley Ann Grau is of German, Scottish, and Louisiana Creole ancestry. Grau attended Booth School in Montgomery, Alabama, from 1940 to 1945 and graduated in 1946 from Ursuline Academy in New Orleans. She was a Phi Delta Kappa of Newcomb College in 1950 and attended Tulane University for two postgraduate years of study. In 1955, she married Tulane philosopher James K. Feibleman; they had four children. Grau found time to hunt duck, sail, enjoy music, and write. Two O. Henry Awards (1955, 1962) and a Pulitzer Prize (1965) followed. Grau taught creative writing (1966-1967) at the University of New Orleans while continuing her writing. Dividing her time between Martha's Vineyard and New Orleans, Grau taught a creative writing workshop in New Orleans in 2009.

ANALYSIS

Identified at the beginning of her career as a southern writer following in the path of such brilliant storytellers as Katherine Anne Porter, Shirley Ann Grau gained quick name recognition based on her effective use of local color and sensory details. Her early settings often reflect mood and tone and articulate, with symbols, their thematic or atmospheric effect on characters.

Grau, however, is more than a regional author bound to a southern heritage. In 1970, she began to shift her settings to other locations, most notably to the Massachusetts coast; she replaced her previously strong emphasis on people living in poverty to a sharp focus on the very wealthy. Whatever the subject matter of Grau's stories, however, she always crafts the work with care. Grau writes in the mode of the modern short story and makes use of a smooth and usually realistic surface of events with an underlying symbolic structure that carries meaning.

Many of Grau's early stories are about characters indigenous to the South. They live in bayou villages, in the foothills of the Appalachians, or near the beaches of the Gulf of Mexico. Usually her plots involve a narrator who resolutely experiences a difficult or a humorous moment in time with no recourse to emotional abandon. For instance, in "Pillow of Stone," from *The Wind Shifting West*, Ann Marie Landry experiences such a moment; although she is pregnant and afraid of water, Ann Marie insists that her husband Raoul take her in a shaky little sailboat in a storm to the wake of her father. As Ann Marie steps from the boat, her unborn child moves. In "The Other Way," some Creole elders insist that a black child not mention quitting and instead return to the all-white school to which she has won a scholarship. The child finds the isolation unbearable, yet she acquiesces. In "The Thieves," a young woman is able to allow both a real thief and her own lover to escape without feeling.

"MISS YELLOW-EYES"

"Miss Yellow-Eyes" describes bravery, cowardice, and racial tensions among siblings. Lena, one of three

Shirley Ann Grau (Library of Congress)

children born to a black couple, is fair-skinned enough to pass for white; the other two, Celia and Pete, have dark complexions. Pete introduces Lena to his white-skinned African American friend, Chris, who becomes Lena's soldier-husband. The couple dream of immigrating to Canada and passing as white, but Pete wants to stay in New Orleans. Chris enlists in the Army and dies fighting in the Korean War; Pete believes Chris's death is a useless waste.

Shortly after Chris dies, Pete loses an arm in a switch-yard mishap. Celia, aware that Pete feared being drafted, questions whether Pete's misfortune was really accidental, for his Army induction notice arrives while he is hospitalized. She also begins noticing contrasts of colors in yellow and blue eyes; white and black taxicabs or beaches; bright moonlight, electric lights, and darkness. She ponders as well the victim-martyr name symbolism of Lena (Mary Magdalene) and Chris (Christ). These environmental elements symbolically project Grau's early ideas and concerns about human subjects and problems.

"JOSHUA"

"Joshua," in *The Black Prince, and Other Stories*, exemplifies the universal experience of growing up. Its setting is Bon Secour, a poor African American fishing community in the bayou region. Unpainted houses with tin roofs, a gulf swamp, and constant rain serve as backdrop for Joshua's struggle to become a man. From the story's beginning, it is clear that eleven-year-old Joshua is the target for many of the tensions between his parents. The immediate difficulty centers on his mother's desire for her husband to return to fishing, so that they will have money to buy Joshua a new coat; the husband refuses because he saw his friend blown up in the Gulf by a German U-boat.

Joshua leaves his argumentative parents, slips on an oil-dipped canvas to keep warm, and, with his friend Henry Bourgeois, spends the night in their hideaway: an abandoned warehouse. During the night a gigantic explosion awakens them; Joshua lights the lamp and leaves it burning as they return to sleep. The next morning Henry suggests that Joshua had kept the lamp burning because Joshua was afraid. Joshua denies his fear, even though Henry heard Joshua crying during the night.

Returning home, Joshua learns that the noise was the explosion of a U-boat. Joshua's drunken father taunts and physically threatens Joshua if he refuses to take the boat and catch fish for supper. Joshua accepts the dare and, with Henry, sets out in the pirogue. After securing fish from the swamp's edge, Joshua steers the boat into the swamp. Despite superstitious fears of evil in the icy, moccasin-filled swamp water, Joshua is intent upon seeing where the explosion took place; he hopes in this way to prove he is not afraid. When they arrive at the backwater of the river, Joshua spies something blue-colored. Determined to get a closer look, and despite Henry's warnings of danger, Joshua wades courageously through the waist-deep waters and debris to find a lifeless body clothed in bright blue pants and a brown leather jacket. His fingers white with cold, Joshua takes the jacket as his tangible reward for courage. In his primal world, Joshua has reached his goal and mastered his test; he has accomplished what his father has been too frightened to do. Additionally, he has proved to his friend that a "real" man refuses to let fear prevent him from taking action or responsibility.

THE WIND SHIFTING WEST

Eighteen years later, after publishing three novels and receiving a Pulitzer Prize, Grau released *The Wind Shifting West*. During those years, she replaced the Gulf Coast settings and shifted character emphasis from the poor to the wealthy. Psychological and motivational insights, along with contrast, serve as basic tools to reveal her characters' universal conflicts or experiences. Many tales in this collection showcase the subject of love, especially love unreturned or denied. Others blend the subject of love with desegregation, tradition, the 1930's Great Depression, and death.

In most of the stories in *The Wind Shifting West*, Grau carefully describes the colors, clouds, and general plan of the scenery in the first paragraphs. In "The Beach Party," she describes the arrival of a jeep at an isolated area of beach. Three men choose a sheltered spot behind a sand dune and dig a pit. The jeep returns later with girls, including Frieda Matthews, and several sacks. Frieda has been invited to the party to be the date of one of her brother's friends--an arrangement insisted upon by their mother. The story, told from Frieda's point of view, is of a young woman who learns from her isolated position as an outsider about dates and about death.

The tone of isolation is set when Frieda refuses to join the group in the water because of her terror of the ocean; she wanders off down the beach by herself. Unexpectedly, she finds in an adjacent cove several people snorkeling. When she returns to her own group, she again asks if she can do anything. When her brother suggests that she help him with the corn in the water, Frieda chooses to leave with John, her date, and they go off to look at the other beach party. The dialogue between Frieda and John illustrates Frieda's naïveté; she is frightened and yet attracted by John's simple physical affection. Their quiet moment is broken by a commotion on the beach.

Everett reports that one of the snorkelers has not come back. John leaves to help, and Frieda is alone once again. Because she cannot join the group at the water, she attempts to help the boy who reported the missing snorkeler, but he requires nothing of her. The young men find the body, and John attempts to revive it with mouth-to-mouth resuscitation. Frieda attempts to help him when he vomits, but he takes care of himself. In the confusion of the police van arriving and the party breaking up, Frieda is left alone on the beach. Finding that she is alone does not terrify her. She decides not to wait for the party; instead she sets out on the four-mile hike home. Grau thus encapsulates in this story the feelings of a young girl not quite ready to participate in adult interaction yet old enough to be aware of the isolation of the environment unpadded by protecting family members.

"THE WAY BACK"

"The Way Back " concerns adultery. A couple has spent two days together, yet the woman, in her internal monologue, reveals no clear memory of any individual moment. Returning to the city, the couple's meaningless conversation underlines the terminal nature of this brief affair. Their formal farewell handshake further emphasizes the absence of love in the relationship. This sterility echoes the closing of the title story, which concerns Carolyn and Giles, a sister-in-law and a brother-in-law. On their way to rescue Carolyn's husband from his damaged boat, they are intimate on the

boat deck. After dressing, Carolyn notices that the only remains of their intimacy are "some weed on the anchor and some salt dried on our skin." Giles replies bluntly, "There isn't ever much left, when it's done."

"THE MAN OUTSIDE"

"The Man Outside" depicts another scenario of love denied. During the Great Depression of the 1930's, a husband deserts his wife and eleven children. Several years later the abandoned wife marries Albert Benton, a foreman of a local lumber mill, who has the funds to make needed farm repairs and to support her family. One evening, one of the children notices a man standing outside watching the house. The mother glances out and insists that Benton send away the man. The children never question the man's identity, but the mother's agitation suggests that she denies her first love--the husband watching the house--in favor of the secure life that Benton's money provides.

NINE WOMEN

The stories collected in *Nine Women* demonstrate Grau's profound understanding of contemporary women's lives, interests, and conflicts. Grau questions what happens to women when they no longer view themselves and their identity solely in relation to traditional male authority figures, who protect and direct the women's lives as if the women are unthinking, irresponsible children. How do women regain control of their lives? Do most women even want to find a separate identity? Death, divorce, or choice in Grau's portraits separates the women from their husbands. Some women prefer to remain sheltered in changeless roles that comfort and protect them from doing anything independently. Others, however, desire the freedom to control and choose their own actions and thoughts.

"HUNTER"

Nancy Morrison, in "Hunter," is the sole survivor of a plane crash that kills her husband and daughter. Nancy courts death on countless plane flights and hopes that perhaps the next plane will crash and end her misery. Symbolically, if Nancy's family were still alive, her dreams of happiness might be similar to Katy Wagner's in "Summer Shore"; Katy prefers--instead of changes in her life--the protection of her sheltering home and the repetitive tasks done regularly for thirty-six years. Even when her husband knows what she is thinking, she considers it comfortable and finds that it "save[s] talking." A widow, Mrs. Emmons in "House-keeper," provides a contrast. She is a strong-willed, independent woman who builds a separate life for herself, against her children's wishes, not once but twice. First, she is housekeeper for a widowed doctor. Nine years later, she remarries. After her former employer dies and leaves her an inheritance, Mrs. Emmons and her husband plan a trip to Egypt, where she has wanted to go since childhood.

"WIDOW'S WALK"

In "Widow's Walk," death separates Myra Rowland from her husband, Hugh. Even his name disappears from her beach-club parking space. On opening day of the summer season, Myra struggles to recall the names of people she has known for years; Hugh had always remembered names for her. Unable to cope with a directionless life, she is a ship without a rudder, drifting aimlessly from place to place.

"LETTING GO"

Divorce and choice combine in "Letting Go." Mary Margaret, bored by the monotony of her marriage, chooses both to divorce her husband and to reject the demands of her controlling parents: She wants personal control of her life. As she drives away from her family, her sense of happiness is similar to the relief that Barbara Eagleton in "Ending" feels after taking the last step to dissolve nearly twenty-five years of marriage. With her first taste of freedom, Barbara comfortably watches the television without turning on the sound.

Grau portrays a different choice in "Home," the story of Angela Taylor, a successful real estate agent, and her lesbian lover, Vicky. Vicky decides to bear a child and wants her and Angela to raise it together. After angry discussion, Angela agrees to the baby. Ironically, without any men in their lives, Angela assumes the role of protective father figure as she makes arrangements to buy a house that will be safe for a baby.

"FLIGHT"

In "Flight," the ninth tale in *Nine Women*, Willie May, a dying woman, refuses to remain in the hospital or with her son any longer. As she flies home, she recalls her life. As a child, Willie May learned that duty comes first and that she would never be free to have

personal choices. Courtship, marriage to her husband John, a war, her son's birth, and the growth of her business happen without any real action on her part. When Willie May discovers that both John and his belongings are gone, his family tells her that John retired after twenty years in the post office. She never searches for his new home because she accepts his absence as something she cannot control. Willie May exemplifies the hopelessness, passivity, and stoic resignation of the black slaves or women in early times who had no control over the things that happened to them. Willie May's story is a negative touchstone against which women may measure their degree of independence.

"THE BEGINNING"

In "The Beginning," Nanda describes how her mother's imaginary creation of a magical kingdom becomes a life-sustaining myth for her. Her father, the absent Hindu shoe salesman, has godlike status, while her mother's constant endearments make Nanda believe in her own personal self-worth. Nanda's acceptance that she is the treasured princess in this fantastic realm is so absolute and powerful that she internalizes castle and kingdom, which become the foundation for her inner world. Nanda carries this sense of self-esteem, along with her wicker basket of toys, to provide continuity and her royal identity as the family moves from place to place. "The Beginning" serves as a positive example of what a strong, determined woman can achieve by herself when she realizes her self-worth and instills this sense of value in her own daughter. The tale of Nanda's and her mother's life concludes in Grau's novel *Roadwalkers*.

In *Nine Women*, self-confidence, determination, and consideration and genuine love for others provide freedom for both males and females to grow and make choices, to have separate identities, and to still join together as two equals who are able to exercise control over their own lives. Through her penetrating examination of national and universal problems in American society, Grau proves that she is far more than just a southern writer of local color.

SELECTED STORIES

In his foreword to *Selected Stories*, Robert Phillips describes the completed collection as "long overdue" because of the favorable reception of Grau's previous collections. He notes the writer's first collection--*The Black Prince, and Other Stories*--went into a second printing within a month of its publication. Grau helped Phillips select the eighteen stories for the 2003 collection *Selected Stories*. All eighteen included stories that came from one of Grau's three earlier collections: *The Black Prince, and Other Stories*; *The Wind Shifting West*; and *Nine Women*.

"BLACK PRINCE"

"Black Prince" and "One Summer" are the only two works in *Selected Stories* to come from Grau's first story collection: *The Black Prince, and Other Stories*. In both, the genteel, Louisiana-born Grau writes about black and white society.

"Black Prince" details the sudden appearance of African American Stanley Albert Thompson and his infatuation with the African American beauty Alberta, who likewise notices him. Stanley establishes his position immediately by winning four bar fights in one night; he also begins wooing Alberta, despite the fact that Willie has been pursuing her.

Willie shoots Stanley with bullets he molded from Stanley's coins--symbolic of who caused the death. With his shattered chest, Stanley and Alberta leave together and are never seen again--except during bad times, when they often appear for an instant. This open-ended story of power and love hints of the supernatural.

"ONE SUMMER"

Grau again weaves power and love into a story. MacDonald, the high school narrator, demonstrates power by stopping a fight near Eunice's school lunch table, and their love develops. This story holds many contrasts: life (MacDonald and Eunice) and death (the passing of MacDonald's grandfather); weakness (the elderly who attend the wake) and strength (MacDonald); whites (MacDonald's family) and African Americans (the servant girl who stays with MacDonald's grandfather). Grau depicts the southern society she knows.

"HOMECOMING"

"Homecoming" from *The Wind Shifting West* describes the unusual reaction of Susan to learning of a soldier-friend's death. The town turns out to support Susan, who displays no love or sorrow. "Homecoming" provides an alternative view of death.

"THE LAST GAS STATION"

"The Last Gas Station" is an apocalyptic story from *The Wind Shifting West*. A girl--left alone to operate the family-owned gas station--watches everyone leaving in cars and realizes she is truly alone. This story symbolizing the end is fittingly the last in *Selected Stories*.

"THREE"

The ghost story "Three" takes its name from the specter of a dead husband returning to live with his wife and her new husband. "Three" is open-ended and shows the continuing relationships that exist in people's lives. The remaining four entries in *Selected Stories*-- "Patriarch," "Wind Shifting West," "Sea Change," and "Lovely April"--are from Grau's second collection; she ably depicts social relationships in the South.

OTHER MAJOR WORKS

LONG FICTION: *The Hard Blue Sky*, 1958; *The House on Coliseum Street*, 1961; *The Keepers of the House*, 1964; *The Condor Passes*, 1971; *Evidence of Love*, 1977; *Roadwalkers*, 1994.

BIBLIOGRAPHY

Allen-Taylor, J. Douglas. "The World According to Grau." *Metro*. (February 19, 2002). African American J. Douglas Allen-Taylor interviewed Grau, and he notes that her most memorable works depict race, class, power, and love--often in a southern setting.

Kissel, Susan S. *Moving On: The Heroines of Shirley Ann Grau, Anne Tyler, and Gail Godwin*. Bowling Green, Ohio: Bowling Green State University Popular Press, 1996. Kissel examines the fictional characters of three contemporary female writers. The book includes bibliographical references and an index.

Rohrberger, Mary. "Shirley Ann Grau and the Short Story." In *Women Writers of the Contemporary South*, edited by Peggy Whitman Prenshaw. Jackson: University Press of Mississippi, 1984. Rohrberger argues that Grau's short stories are models of the form, making use of a surface content and substructures pointing to analogues that carry meaning.

Wagner-Martin, Linda. "Shirley Ann Grau." In *The History of Southern Women's Literature*, edited by Carolyn Perry and Mary Louise Weaks. Baton Rouge: Louisiana State University, 2002. The southern class and caste system, dissonance among characters, and complex human relationships--especially those of African Americans and whites--are recurring themes in Grau's works. The article cites specific examples from Grau's works and predicts that more effective fiction is yet to come from Grau. The volume cites Grau in four other chapters.

_____. "Shirley Ann Grau's Wise Fiction." In *Southern Women Writers: The New Generation*, edited by Tonette Bond Inge. Tuscaloosa: University of Alabama Press, 1990. Wagner-Martin suggests that Grau's highly stylized manner of narration is in many ways suggestive of the style of the folktale and contends that one of Grau's distinctive traits is her interest in ceremony and ritual. Wagner-Martin provides general comments about Grau's writing; for example, Wagner-Martin notes that Grau's best fiction often includes nonwhite culture's impingement on the patriarchal matrix that dominates southern life.

Sylvia Huete; Mary Rohrberger and Betsy Harfst
Updated by Anita Price Davis

JOANNE GREENBERG

Born: Brooklyn, New York; September 24, 1932
Also known as: Joanne Goldenberg, Hannah Green

PRINCIPAL SHORT FICTION
Summering, 1966
Rites of Passage, 1972
High Crimes and Misdemeanors, 1979
With the Snow Queen, 1991

OTHER LITERARY FORMS

In addition to her collections of short fiction, Joanne Greenberg has written several novels. In 1979, her novel *I Never Promised You a Rose Garden* (1964) was adapted as a Hollywood film. Greenberg has also been a regular contributor of articles, reviews, and short stories to many periodicals, including *The Hudson Review, The Virginia Quarterly Review, Chatelaine,* and *Saturday Review.*

ACHIEVEMENTS

The King's Persons (1963), Joanne Greenberg's novel about the York massacre, won the Jewish Book Council of America Award for Fiction in 1963. Another novel, *In This Sign* (1968), a sensitive exploration of the world of the deaf, is studied by those who deal with the hearing-impaired. *I Never Promised You a Rose Garden* was endorsed by Dr. Karl Menninger as a contribution toward the understanding of schizophrenia; in 1967, Greenberg was given the Frieda Fromm-Reichmann Award by the American Academy of Psychoanalysis, an honor seldom accorded to laypersons.

Greenberg also received the Harry and Ethel Daroff Memorial Fiction Award in 1963 and the William and Janice Epstein Fiction Award in 1964, both of them presented to her by the National Jewish Welfare Board for her book *The King's Persons.* In 1971, she won both the Marcus L. Kenner Award from the New York Association of the Deaf and the Christopher Book Award for *In This Sign.* She received the Frieda Fromm-Reichmann Memorial Award from Western Maryland College in 1977 and from Gallaudet College in 1979. In 1983, she was awarded the Rocky Mountain Women's Institute Award, and in 2008 she received Hadassah's Women in the Arts Award.

BIOGRAPHY

Joanne Greenberg was born Joanne Goldenberg in Brooklyn, New York, on September 24, 1932, the daughter of Julius Lester and Rosalie (Bernstein) Goldenberg. She earned a B.A. degree from American

University in Washington, D.C., and at the same time she gained an interest in medieval art and music, which led her to write her historical novel *The King's Persons*. On her summer vacations she sang alto at the Tanglewood Music Festival and "was briefly the only white waitress in a Navajo reservation restaurant"; this period of her life is recounted in her story "L'Olam and White Shell Woman." Other vacation experiences that contributed to the collection *Summering* were herding horses, tutoring the foreign-born, and being a space-control agent for an airline. Greenberg is also a graduate of the University of London, England. Being a qualified teacher of sign language afforded her insights into the silent world she depicted in *In This Sign*.

On September 4, 1955, she married Albert Greenberg, a vocational rehabilitation counselor; they became the parents of two sons, David and Alan. Her involvement in land reclamation led her to write the novel *Founder's Praise* (1976). Her volunteer work on a firefighting and emergency rescue team contributed to her stories "Like a Banner" and "Merging Traffic." Her wide-ranging interests include teaching anthropology and sign language. Greenberg continued to pursue vigorously her writing career and her many and varied interests. She has been a member of the Authors' Guild; the Authors' League of America; the International Association of Poets, Playwrights, Editors, Essayists, and Novelists (PEN); the American Civil Liberties Union; the National Association of the Deaf; and the Colorado Authors' League.

ANALYSIS

A consummate storyteller, Greenberg employs shrewd psychological insights to create characters that draw her readers into the plot, keeping them immersed in her story until the very last page.

"THE SUPREMACY OF THE HUNZA"

Greenberg's "The Supremacy of the Hunza" is about the responses of two men to the ninety-foot towers linked with cables that are erected on their land. Forty-three-year-old Westerbrook is an uncompromising idealist who is looking for a utopia. First he seizes upon the Chontal Indians on the southern isthmus of Mexico, who are reputed to have a society free of violence and crime. Margolin, an anthropologist, who meets Westerbrook at a protest organized against the towers, points out that the absence of crime only means the absence of the idea of private ownership; the Chontals' peacefulness is a result of chronic malnutrition.

Westerbrook tries to enlist Margolin in his causes, conservation groups, fights against pollution, crusades, petitions, and marches. Cynically, Margolin throws away all the pamphlets. Margolin is relieved to be summoned by a therapist at a state institution to interpret the dreams of three Sioux patients so that he can escape from brooding over the towers that are defacing the landscape.

Margolin returns, exhausted by his failures. "The symbols of The People had become cheapened parodies, like Made in Japan trinkets." The dreams that he had taped had been full of phony images from films, consisting of fake feather headdresses from cowboy films, and carried no cultural weight at all. He is oppressed by the pain of these Indians, "tongue-tied with tranquilizers," and by his inability to help. When Margolin discovers a drawer full of leaflets about the air, the water, and the food, he begins, in a rage, to dial Westerbrook's number to tell him that he does not want to be involved in any more of his crusades, but his wife informs him that Westerbrook is sick. Margolin then determines to be kind. He scarcely recognizes the "lowered, pinched quality of the voice; its youthfulness had been conquered, the naïve enthusiasm was gone." There is so much pain in Westerbrook's voice that "suddenly Margolin wanted to beg his forgiveness; for polluting his air and fouling his water and for permitting the hideous towers to stand." When Westerbrook mentions his newest enthusiasm, the Hunza--Muslim herders on the slopes of the Himalayas who live to a vigorous old age because they exist simply on pure food, and whose language has no words for greed or envy--Margolin restrains his usual cynical comments. For his restraint he earns a pounding headache and the reward of hearing Westerbrook's voice recover its normal enthusiasm.

The men's conflict is between two contrasting attitudes toward civilization. The amateur, Westerbrook, romanticizes the simple life; the professional anthropologist, Margolin, refuses to be enlisted in any campaigns to clean the environment because he recognizes the hopelessness of the struggle, as well as the falsity of all the hyped-up reports from utopia. Margolin's compassionate impulse angers him afterward because his fear of further wounding the idealist has cost him his honesty. His conciliatory remarks about the Hunza restore his friend's dignity, however, and Margolin recognizes in this concession how much envy had been mingled with his previous responses to Westerbrook, and this is a humiliating fact to have to accept.

The imagery in this story is so unobtrusive that one has to search for it. The telephone poles that have upset both of the men remain standing. That is an inflexible fact; neither organized protests nor private broodings have budged them an inch. However, the ugly poles support cables that permit telephone conversations like the one that closes the story. The skeptic who had maintained his detachment ends by giving emotional support to a man whose naïveté he had scorned, whose social activism has made him feel guilty, whose faith in primitivism he felt was ill informed, and whose belief that this world could be made better by means of committees he disagreed with. The poles carry the possibility of communication, flawed though it must be by individuals' psychological distances from one another. They bridge the physical distances; one must make the emotional accommodations to bridge the psychic ones. Every technological advance carries its own psychic assault with it. The film versions of Indian identity have supplanted any authentic feelings about what it means to be a Sioux, just as the tranquilizers have obliterated the dark passions that had placed the Sioux patient in the asylum in the first place. Civilization makes primitive truths difficult to recover.

This story is effective precisely because it permits no easy answers to these hard questions. It raises the possibility that there might be a superior language, like that of the Hunza, which has no words for greed (represented by the individual conglomerates that put up more and more poles) or envy (represented by the academic mentality that feels the need to expose myths). If political activism is futile and dreaming of utopias is childish, what hope is there for this earth? The story provocatively raises profound dilemmas, leaving the reader to search for some solution. This is an example of the polemic genre at its most effective. It derives ultimately from the prophetic books of the Bible, whose rhetorical strategy is always to pose a question that demands to be answered in action: What are *you* going to do about this?

"HUNTING SEASON"

"Hunting Season" tells of a mother's anguished pursuit of her little boy, whom she has allowed to play outside while men are shooting their guns and sometimes killing one another. Fearing that he will have an epileptic attack because he has been on some new medicine for only a week, she sets aside the bread she has been baking to follow him in order to make sure he does not have another seizure as the guns go off, and the animals burst the thickets in panic. "He could fall, thrashing, unable to breathe, his face growing gray for lack of air, and then down the rocky gully, falling." She begins to run, listening for him, "smelling the air for danger," tracking him warily like a middle-aged huntress. At the sight of his small, thin figure, staring at the creek, she realizes that she is intruding on his privacy and, full of self-reproach, retreats, leaving him to face his dangers alone. He is shouting at the rocks, a big-boy threat that ends with: "Do you hear me?" "It was her intonation exactly, all the querulous anger of her impatience and all the long-suffering in her tone, captured with unconscious, searing honesty."

She whispers back that she has heard him and that she knows he has to make that murdering world his own. The courage involved in the mother's withdrawal of maternal protectiveness shows that she has successfully negotiated her part of this rite of passage. She hears, in his unconscious imitation of her voice, that she has damaged him enough already. He has internalized all the negative aspects when she had so much wanted him to see her as someone spontaneous, who played and laughed and loved the wind. She is ashamed at having lost her youthful joyousness and turned into a scolding woman. In the instant of grace when she decides to leave him his freedom, however, there is the possibility, if not of recovering her own freedom, at least of permitting him to retain his. The suggestion remains poised in the air.

Again, the symbolism is structural, not decorative. The title, "Hunting Season," is explicitly referring to the men who are stalking game. Implicitly, however, it embodies the plot. The mother has become a hunter of her child. She stalks him, holding her breath, keeping her footsteps noiseless, trying not to extrude the scent of her fear, which he might inhale. When she lets him go, she releases a victim. She allows him to fantasize himself as an aggressive male, to enter the murdering world, protected only by his talismanic turquoise jacket on his pathetically thin shoulders. That instant of swerving away from her maternal impulse to enfold him requires enormous control. The mother's silent surrender of the role of huntress shows she can discipline her feelings. Greenberg's use of a moment of silence to signal emotional growth shows the control she has over her art. The mother's concern builds up, accelerates into anxiety, and mounts into panic, but instead of expending itself, it is suppressed. The pace of the story augments the jolt of the ending. In that instant the mother accepts the end of her season as huntress so that her son can become the hunter of experience in his own hunting season.

HIGH CRIMES AND MISDEMEANORS

All but three of the stories in *High Crimes and Misdemeanors* are Hasidic tales. These trace the cosmic consequences of human lapses. A lie can extinguish a star; an expression of gratitude can make a tree bloom. The narrator of one story says, "Medieval Jewish mystics held that the acts of men have widespread effects in the heavenly realms." Two old ladies afraid of muggers barricade themselves in their house. Their niece consults a professor of religion, who advises her to fortify them through the mystical word as Rabbi Judah Lowe did his golem, when he fed him the Ineffable Name. She inscribes Psalm 22 in Hebrew, leaving out all the vowels, so that its "mystical power retained its primal strength," and bakes it into a honey cake so they can ingest its power. At the end, the elderly aunts are no longer afraid to walk in the streets in the story "The Jaws of the Dog."

"THINGS IN THEIR SEASON"

In "Things in Their Season," intricate calculations are made "from one of the mystical books of

the cabala" to discern where time is stockpiled. Four middle-aged Jews succeed in stealing some time from the Cosmic Bank for Rabbi Jacob, whose fatal illness had threatened to interrupt their Monday night Talmud discussions. "Certain Distant Suns" takes its title from a Yiddish "commercial" on Aunt Bessie's unplugged television set that reproaches her, through the person of a shabbily dressed Hasid, for having stopped praying. He says,

in every relationship a certain amount of resentment builds up over the years . . . this is especially true in regard to mankind and the Master of the Universe, since the relationship is so--so onesided. I beg all of you, not to stop discussing the Master of the Universe, even if you can no longer praise Him. If it be in anger or despair or even, God forbid, in ridicule, keep His Name aloud in your mouths. It is possible that certain distant suns are powered by the mention of His Name.

WITH THE SNOW QUEEN

In her subsequent collection of short stories, *With the Snow Queen*, Greenberg takes readers on an engaging tour of a fantasyland that only she could have created. People travel backward in time, characters harangue their authors, and an incomplete ritual may have had disastrous effects on some innocent bystanders. She uses the search for an authentic sense of self that people in their middle years often embark upon as the bridge for this series of short stories. Personal crises help some of her characters change direction, while other characters come to accept a slightly flawed but more authentic self.

Who can resist Sima's freedom--in the title story--to go back to a turning point in her early years and dramatically change her life? In "Persistence of Memory," a prisoner who trades his memories to the inhabitants of Gehenna for oblivion finds that he can change his life by changing his memories. Only at the very end of "Torch Song" can one find out how the Vatican Ski Team fared in the Olympic Games. While older readers may immediately identify with many characters in this collection, *With the Snow Queen* will appeal to readers of all ages.

OTHER MAJOR WORKS

LONG FICTION: *The King's Persons*, 1963; *I Never Promised You a Rose Garden*, 1964 (as Hannah Green); *The Monday Voices*, 1965; *In This Sign*, 1968; *Founder's Praise*, 1976; *A Season of Delight*, 1981; *The Far Side of Victory*, 1983; *Simple Gifts*, 1986; *Age of Consent*, 1987; *Of Such Small Differences*, 1988; *No Reck'ning Made*, 1993; *Where the Road Goes*, 1998; *Appearances*, 2006.

BIBLIOGRAPHY

Bail, Paul. "Good Mother, Bad Mother in Joanne Greenberg's *I Never Promised You a Rose Garden*." In *Women in Literature: Reading Through the Lens of Gender*, edited by Jerilyn Fisher and Ellen S. Silber. Westport, Conn.: Greenwood Press, 2003. A feminist analysis of Greenberg's novel.

Diamond, R. "The Archetype of Death and Renewal in *I Never Promised You a Rose Garden*." *Perspectives in Psychiatric Care* 8 (January-March, 1975): 21-24. Diamond compares the journey and recovery from schizophrenia to the initiation ritual of shamans; he also discusses the myths of death and resurrection. The incorporation of Carl Jung's archetypes of the unconscious in connection with a search for self makes this article distinctive. Includes a bibliography.

Fromm-Reichmann, Frieda. "Frieda Fromm-Reichmann Discusses the 'Rose Garden' Case." *Psychiatry* 45, no. 2 (1982): 128-136. A transcript of a lecture given by Fromm-Reichmann to the Ypsilanti Psychiatric Institute discussing the treatment of a young female adolescent. Greenberg, using the pseudonym of Hannah Green, wrote about a treatment plan she received. Fromm-Reichmann talks about the treatment plan she devised, the outcome, and the book that her patient wrote.

Greenberg, Joanne. "Go Where You're Sent: An Interview with Joanne Greenberg." Interview by K. L. Gibble. *Christian Century* 102 (November 20, 1985): 1063-1067. Greenberg discusses her motivation and writing techniques with Gibble. He induces her to reveal bits and pieces of her personal philosophy. Some valuable clues to her personality can be found in this interview.

_____. Interview by Susan Koppelman. *Belles Lettres* 8, no. 4 (Summer, 1993): 32. Greenberg discusses her work and when she became a writer. She says she began writing to express her unhappiness while living in New York City.

_____. "Joanne Greenberg." Interview by Sybil S. Steinberg. *Publishers Weekly* 234 (September 23, 1988): 50-51. Notes that each of Greenberg's novels and short-story collections deals with people challenged by a hostile or strange world. Greenberg asserts that she has stood by her publisher, Holt, throughout her writing career because the company gave her a chance when other publishers would not.

Marovitz, Stanford E. "'A Mensh Fights Back' in Joanne Greenberg's Fiction." In *Connections and Collisions: Identities in Contemporary Jewish-American Women's Writing*, edited by Lois E. Rubin. Newark: University of Delaware Press, 2005. Focuses on the what it means for Greenberg and to be both a woman and a Jew, analyzing how she explores these dual identities in her writing.

Stein, Alex. *Made-Up Interviews with Imaginary Artists*. Brooklyn, N.Y.: Ugly Duckling Presse, 2009. Despite the title, this collection of interviews combined with Stein's ruminations and digressions includes a "real" interview with Greenberg.

Wisse, Ruth. "Rediscovering Judaism." Review of *A Season of Delight*, by Joanne Greenberg. *Commentary* 73 (May, 1982): 84-87. This review of Greenberg's novel is set in the context of Jewish life in the United States. Wisse compares the heroine's struggle with issues of faith to a reawakening of spiritual values that can be found in modern society as a whole and the Jewish community in particular.

Wolfe, K. K., and G. K. Wolfe. "Metaphors of Madness: Popular Psychological Narratives." *Journal of Popular Culture* 10 (Spring, 1976): 895-907. An eloquent discussion of an emerging genre using *I Never Promised You a Rose Garden* as an example. This genre, psychological in nature, has a recognizable structure and imagery. The authors turn a spotlight on the implications that many of the protagonists of this type of novel, or autobiography, are women using the

metaphor of a journey. Includes notes and a bibliography.

Ruth Rosenberg
Updated by Maxine S. Theodoulou

JOHN GRISHAM

Born: Jonesboro, Arkansas; February 8, 1955

PRINCIPAL SHORT FICTION
Ford County, 2009

OTHER LITERARY FORMS

John Grisham (GRIHSH-uhm) is best known for his enormously successful series of legal thrillers, but in 2001 he began to write in other fictional forms, including a collection of short stories, and in nonfiction, *The Innocent Man: Murder and Injustice in a Small Town* (2006), about a man wrongly accused and convicted of murder. However, *A Painted House* (2001), a novel of southern rural farm life, was the first of his nonlegal thrillers, followed by a comic novel, *Skipping Christmas* (2001). *Bleachers* (2003) and *Playing for Pizza* (2007) both focused on football as a motif. In addition, Grisham wrote a children's book, *Theodore Boone: Kid Lawyer* (2010), that appears to be the first of a series.

Since many of Grisham's novels have been made into films, it is not surprising that he would try his hand at screenwriting. He wrote an original script for *Mickey* (2004), a made-for-television film about a father with legal troubles and his Little League son.

ACHIEVEMENTS

John Grisham has become one of America's best-selling authors, with each of his novels appearing on *The New York Times* best-seller lists, often reaching the top. Cumulatively, his books have sold in the tens of millions of copies worldwide and have been translated into more than two dozen languages.

Although the phenomenal success of Scott Turow's *Presumed Innocent* (1987) marks the inauguration of the prominence of the contemporary legal thriller, the legal novels of Grisham have become synonymous with the genre. No other modern author has dominated the genre the way he has, both in fiction and on screen.

In addition, he has garnered numerous awards and achieved special recognition from organizations both national and international. In 2009, for example, Grisham was presented the Governor's Award for Literary Achievement from the state of Mississippi. In the same year he received the twelfth annual Library of Virginia award, a recognition previously given to such literary icons as Edgar Allan Poe, Ellen Glasgow, Booker T. Washington, William Styron, Tom Wolfe, and Rita Dove. For Grisham's screenwriting efforts he was nominated for an Edgar Allan Poe Award in 2004 and the University of Southern California Scripter Award in 1998. In 2007, he was recipient of the British Galaxy Award Lifetime Achievement. This list is only partial.

In the more than two decades of his literary career, Grisham has managed not only to sell a great number of books but also to establish himself as one of the masters of contemporary crime fiction. In the last few years, he has added to his literary achievements an increasing number of noncrime books, such as *Ford County*, which offer him opportunities to expand the scope of his writing and to avoid the entrapment many genre authors, especially of the high-selling sort, experience from agents, publishers, and filmmakers who want to continue to benefit from the steady flow of a consistent product.

BIOGRAPHY

John Grisham was born in Jonesboro, Arkansas, on February 8, 1955. His father was a cotton farmer and construction worker, and his mother was a housewife. He graduated from Southaven High School in Southaven, Mississippi, in DeSoto County, where he was the quarterback on the football team. He also played baseball and at one time wanted to become a professional player. Both sports figure in his later fiction.

Grisham graduated from Mississippi State University with a bachelor of science in accounting in 1977. In 1981, he received his law degree from the University of Mississippi Law School. Although he originally planned to become a tax lawyer, he eventually chose criminal and civil litigation. This legal background clearly played a central part in shaping his subsequent literary career.

After graduating from law school, he set up practice in his hometown of Southaven and dabbled in local politics, getting elected to the Mississippi House of Representatives in 1983 as a Democrat, and he has remained active in Democratic politics ever since, and not just in Mississippi. He served in state government until 1990 but curtailed his political involvement after his literary career took off.

Grisham began writing his legal thrillers as a result of witnessing a trial, in DeSoto County in Mississippi, which involved a sensational rape case. It took him almost three years to turn that experience into his first novel, *A Time to Kill* (1989), which was published by a small press in a limited run. Publishing his second book, however, was a very different experience. Just two years later, *The Firm* (1991) became a best seller and the breakthrough novel that launched his successful literary career. After that came a steady stream of fictional works, both legal thrillers and others, many of them adapted into well-regarded films. Grisham's literary rise was truly meteoric. His first novel was published in an edition of five thousand copies, and he traveled around, trying to sell the book himself. His next was sold to Hollywood first, guaranteeing a hefty advance from a publisher. The published book was released in an edition of more than

John Grisham (FilmMagic/Getty Images)

a million copies, and *The Firm* became the highest-selling book of 1991. Since then his books have sold in the millions of copies worldwide and routinely top *The New York Times* best-seller listings.

The films also have proved a lucrative outlet for Grisham. Ten of his books have been adapted for the screen and others are in various stages of development. Grisham has become involved in the film business as a producer, screenwriter, and even as an actor, appearing in a cameo in *Mickey* and providing the uncredited voice-over for *A Painted House*. He also served as a consultant for the television series based on his novel *The Client* (1993).

With the enormous success of his writing, Grisham largely gave up the practice of law, although he did return to it briefly after his early success and still is interested in legal causes. He is married to Renée Jones, and they have two children, Ty and Shea. The Grishams split their time between homes they own outside Oxford, Mississippi, and Charlottesville, Virginia.

ANALYSIS

The seven stories that make up *Ford County* were written over a twenty-year period and are based mostly on ideas that proved too insubstantial for Grisham to use as plots for novels. Although he will undoubtedly remain primarily a writer of long fiction, especially legal thrillers, the short-story form is one more way to break out of the genre in which he gained his initial success. Agents, publishers, film people, and the reading public can apply enormous pressures on a writer to just keep doing over and over whatever has been popular in the past. Grisham's short fiction is one way for him to expand his range and to avoid such pressures.

Although Grisham admits that most of his fiction could be set almost anywhere, the Ford County stories, which include the novels *A Time to Kill* and *The Chamber*, as well as the short fiction of *Ford County*, are all solidly southern in mood, locale, and character. A bit reminiscent of William Faulkner's legendary Yoknapatawpha County, in which Faulkner set so much of his fiction, Ford County is a mythical southern place. Indeed the tales of *Ford County*, with the recurring figure of the southern lawyer, are directly connected to Faulkner's Gavin Stevens stories, in which he examined small-town Mississippi life through the perspective of a local lawyer. However fictional, Ford County is indisputably northern Mississippi, the environs of Grisham's youth and early professional life.

Like his fellow Mississippians Faulkner and Eudora Welty, Grisham has used this small-town rural environment to attack such topics as racism, bigotry in many forms, corruption in the legal system, and what has been called eye-for-an-eye justice. In *Ford County* Grisham explores the eccentricities of the county's isolated, provincial, and just plain crazy inhabitants, while detailing their loyalties, sense of family, and connections to the land long inhabited by their ancestors. Like a great deal of other southern fiction, Grisham mines the layers of history that determine the lives of his characters and employs the traditions of storytelling that permeate southern culture, replete with their own rhetoric, modes of narrative, and topics of conversation. Food, customs, and manners provide touchstones of Grisham's southern fiction.

These sketches of *Ford County* draw on this long and distinguished tradition of southern letters. Readers will find echoes of Faulkner and Welty and also of Flannery O'Connor, Harper Lee, Truman Capote, Erskine Caldwell, Robert Penn Warren, James Dickey, and others. Although there are several lawyers who figure in these stories, Grisham forgoes his usual thriller tactics of blood and mayhem. These gentler tales, with humor, reveal a different side to their author.

"BLOOD DRIVE"

The opening story in the collection is a comic journey tale in which a Box Hill boy, Bailey, has been injured in a construction accident in Memphis. The extent of his injuries and their cause remain the topic of wild and unsubstantiated speculation, as his friends and family try to devise some plan of action to aid Bailey, who is in the hospital. Two young men, Aggie and Calvin, from the rural community volunteer to drive to the city to give blood, which it is assumed will be necessary in Bailey's recovery. When a third, Roger, joins the travelers, things go awry. Roger is an alcoholic petty crook, who claims to know the fleshpots of Memphis; he turns the heads of Aggie and Calvin and eventually lands them in trouble, as the Bailey's plight recedes into the background.

"Blood Drive" contains snippets of other southern tales of wayward journeys, such as Faulkner's *As I Lay Dying* (1930) and *The Reivers* (1962), and reels out its humor in a long, inexorable series of events that lead exactly where the reader feared they would lead. Good intentions gone wrong through the unavoidable frailty of human desires becomes the central motif, with comic rather than dire consequences.

"FETCHING RAYMOND"

There is a fatalistic dark side to this story of a dysfunctional family of dependent criminal brothers and their pathetically supportive mother, who gives up everything to care for her sons. Like a O'Connor story, which it resembles, "Fetching Raymond" sets up a series of events that make sense only at the end. The actions of one brother and his mother, who borrow a local furniture store owner's truck for the trip; why they have to "fetch" Raymond; or even where Raymond is or who he is all remain suspended until the story's final pages.

The stoicism and forbearance of the mother are exasperating and tragic, her illusions about her sons and about life in general are comic and sad. This is a story about people whose actions condemn them to poverty and marginality but who seem powerless to recognize their plight or to change their behavior. Grisham manages to convey his characters' flaws while eliciting sympathy for their failures. It is the mark of truly good fiction if a writer can manage to operate both simultaneously.

"CASINO"

There is something appealing about a con man, and Bobby Carl Leach is the genuine article. With a history of avoiding the Internal Revenue Service and near indictments on any number of legal sleights of hand, Bobby Carl, who has survived divorces and shady deals, drives a Cadillac DeVille and wears three-piece suits with cowboy boots. When Bobby Carl sets his sights on establishing a casino on the outskirts of Clanton, using a questionable Native American connection, the action proves to be as comic as it is predictable.

As is usual with these sorts of stories, the con man gets his comeuppance, the greedy lose out, and the previously duped get a reward. There is certain forbearance in southern culture for the flamboyant rascal, the rapscallion whose fast-talking patter entertains as it deceives, and the con-men adventures contain little morality tales. Living in an enclosed world, as the inhabitants of Ford County do, necessitates forgiveness because the family connections can be close. In the end, Bobby Carl's transgressions injure mostly himself, and things work out for the best, but not, of course, before the comedy plays itself out.

OTHER MAJOR WORKS

LONG FICTION: *A Time to Kill*, 1989; *The Firm*, 1991; *The Pelican Brief*, 1992; *The Client*, 1993; *The Chamber*, 1994; *The Rainmaker*, 1995; *The Runaway Jury*, 1996; *The Partner*, 1997; *The Street Lawyer*, 1998; *The Testament*, 1999; *The Brethren*, 2000; *A Painted House*, 2001; *Skipping Christmas*, 2001; *The Summons*, 2002; *Bleachers*, 2003; *The King of Torts*, 2003; *The Last Juror*, 2004; *The Broker*, 2005; *Playing for Pizza*, 2007; *The Appeal*, 2008; *The Associate*,

2009; *The Confession*, 2010.

TELEPLAY: *Mickey*, 2004.

NONFICTION: *The Innocent Man: Murder and Injustice in a Small Town*, 2006.

CHILDREN'S LITERATURE: *Theodore Boone: Kid Lawyer*, 2010.

BIBLIOGRAPHY

Best, Nancy. *Readings on John Grisham*. Farmington Hills, Mich.: Greenhaven Press, 2003. This is a collection of essays about Grisham edited for younger readers.

Evain, Christine. "John Grisham's Megabestsellers." In *Crime Fictions: Subverted Codes and New Structures*, edited by François Gallix and Vanessa Guignery. Paris: Presses de l'Université de Paris-Sorbonne, 2004. The authors examine Grisham's legal novels, which suggest a new direction for this subgenre of crime fiction.

Nickelson, Katie. "Lawyers as Tainted Heroes in John Grisham's Novels." In *The Image of the Hero in Literature, Media, and Society*, edited by Will Wright and Steven Kaplan. Pueblo: Colorado State University, 2004. Includes a chapter on Grisham's heroic characters in a collection of essays on the wider subject.

Nolan, Tom. "John Grisham Testifies." *Mystery Scene* 79 (Spring, 2003): 12-18. Provides an interview with the author.

Pringle, Mary Beth. *John Grisham: A Critical Companion*. Westport, Conn.: Greenwood Press, 1997. Contains an analysis of Grisham's novels up to its publication date, with biographical and bibliographic materials.

Runyon, Randolph Paul. "John Grisham: Obsessive Imagery." In *Southern Writers at Century's End*, edited by Jeffrey J. Folks, James A. Perkins, and James H. Justus. Lexington: University Press of Kentucky, 1997. Includes a broader view of Grisham's work as a southern writer, not just a crafter of legal thrillers.

Swirski, Peter, and Faye Wong. "Briefcases for Hire: American Hardboiled to Legal Fiction." *Journal of American Culture* 29, no. 3 (September, 2006): 307-320. Surveys the history of legal crime fiction.

Charles L. P. Silet

ALLAN GURGANUS

Born: Rocky Mount, North Carolina; June 11, 1947

PRINCIPAL SHORT FICTION

White People, 1991

The Practical Heart: Four Novellas, 2001

OTHER LITERARY FORMS

The short stories of Allan Gurganus (gur-GAN-uhs) have appeared in such periodicals as *Granta, The New York Times, The New Yorker, Harper's,* and *The Paris Review* and in such collections as *The Faber Book of Short Gay Fiction* (1991). However, the author is best known for his debut novel, *Oldest Living Confederate Widow Tells All* (1989), which spent eight months on *The New York Times* best-seller list. The novel has received much popular acclaim (becoming the subject of a *New Yorker* cartoon and a clue on *Jeopardy*), has been translated into twelve languages, and has sold more than two million copies worldwide. The Columbia Broadcasting Service 1994 adaptation of the book, starring Donald Sutherland and Diane Lane, won four Emmy Awards; in 2003, the novel also was adapted for a one-woman Broadway play, starring Ellen Burstyn.

Though less well known and out of print, Gurganus's novella *Blessed Assurance: A Moral Tale* (1989) has been incorporated into Harvard Business School's ethics curriculum. His novel *Plays Well with Others* (1997) was well received, both by critics and by Gurganus's many fans.

ACHIEVEMENTS

Since the publication in 1974 of his first short story, Allan Gurganus's writing has met with high critical acclaim. Much of his short fiction has been published in *The New Yorker, The Atlantic,* and *The Paris Review;* his stories also have been honored by appearing in such collections as *O. Henry Prize Stories, Best American Stories, The Norton Anthology of Short Fiction,* and *Best New Stories of the South.*

His debut novel, *Oldest Living Confederate Widow Tells All,* won the Sue Kaufman Prize from the American Academy of Arts and Letters and was a main selection of the Book-of-the-Month Club. *White People,* a collection of eleven short stories, received the *Los Angeles Times* Book Prize and the Southern Book Award for Fiction from the Southern Book Critics Circle; it was a PEN/Faulkner Award finalist. *The Practical Heart,* his collection of four novellas, received the Lambda Literary Award in 2001, and the title novella won the National Magazine Prize in 2001. Gurganus was a 2006 John Simon Guggenheim Fellow.

BIOGRAPHY

Allan Gurganus was born in Rocky Mount, North Carolina, on June 11, 1947, to a teacher and a businessman. Before turning to writing, Gurganus first trained as a painter, studying at the University of Pennsylvania and the Pennsylvania Academy of Fine Arts. Though he maintains a love of visual arts--his paintings and drawings have been shown in private and public collections, and he has illustrated three limited editions of his fiction--Gurganus is primarily known for the writing he has produced since his debut novel, *Oldest Living Confederate Widow Tells All.*

Gurganus began his writing career, and this novel in particular, during a three-year stint onboard an aircraft carrier during the Vietnam War. A conscientious objector, Gurganus in 1966 faced charges of draft evasion, so he enlisted as a message decoder on the U.S.S. *Yorktown.* While at sea, Gurganus developed the idea for his novel after reading an article that described pensions granted to Confederate veterans in the 1880's and the subsequent flurry of marriages between older men and younger women.

After the war, Gurganus graduated in 1972 with a bachelor's degree from Sarah Lawrence College, where he worked with Grace Paley, and in 1974 with a masters degree in fine arts from the University of Iowa Writers' Workshop, where he studied under Stanley Elkin and John Cheever. It was Cheever who first submitted Gurganus's writing, unbeknownst to Gurganus, to *The New Yorker* in 1974. Gurganus's first published story, "Minor Heroism," depicted the first gay character that magazine had ever presented.

Gurganus has taught fiction writing at the University of Iowa, Stanford University, Duke University, Sarah Lawrence College, and the University of Iowa Writers' Workshop. His former students--some of whom have written of their experience under his tutelage--include novelists Ann Patchett, Elizabeth McCracken, and Donald Antrim. Gurganus eventually moved to North Carolina, returning to the South from Manhattan, and he rises at six in the morning daily to write and garden. He has been working on *The Erotic History of a Southern Baptist Church*, which is second

Allan Gurganus (Getty Images)

in *The Falls Trilogy* that commenced with *Widow*. Gurganus also has served as a political commentator for *The New York Times* and has continued to write against homophobia, racism, and America's imperial foreign policy.

ANALYSIS

In a 1997 interview with *Salon* magazine, Allan Gurganus explained, "I don't have a career; I have a mission. I'm from a long line of ministers, so I've applied my status as the black sheep--the fallen, queer one--to transforming myself into the ultimate pulpit-pounder." In both his fiction and his political essays, Gurganus has dedicated his career to giving a voice to the social "other," those ostracized by culture and community. Though *Plays Well with Others* takes place in New York during the height of the acquired immunodeficiency syndrome (AIDS) crisis in the homosexual community, most of his writing is situated against the backdrop of the American South and specifically North Carolina. Although he has not produced an autobiography, much of his writing is, in essence, autobiographical.

Gurganus's literary voice has been compared to that of Mark Twain, Walt Whitman, William Faulkner, and Eudora Welty, and Gurganus has been hailed as one of the foremost writers of the contemporary American South. His stories are known for their dark wit and candid eroticism and for their adherence to the tradition of old-time storytellers, recounting tales on their front porches. In this, Gurganus's writing follows neatly along the literary path forged by Twain and Faulkner. However, Gurganus distinguishes himself and his writing by addressing themes outside the mainstream, particularly for the proper southern culture he represents.

Gurganus's short fiction in particular highlights the role of the social other: the senior citizen misunderstood by a younger generation, the married man with homosexual fantasies, the black man who passes for white. Many of his stories and novellas are set against the backdrop of white southern society, which, with all its charms and pretenses, renders the effects of social ostracism that much more poignant. In each of these stories, the point of view of a single key protagonist provides the lens through which the reader examines a particular component of southern culture.

"Minor Heroism"

In 1974, when Gurganus was still an unknown and struggling artist, Cheever--mentor, teacher, and friend--submitted this story to *The New Yorker* on Gurganus's behalf. The result was the start of a literary career that has spanned several decades and produced many highly acclaimed works. Placement of this short story at the beginning of *White People* is apt not only for its recognition as the first of what is to follow in Gurganus's collection but also for its introduction of themes and characters that are prevalent in the author's short fiction.

Gurganus's first short story, subtitled "Something About My Father," appears in three parts, each reflecting a different narrative voice. Bryan--a gay man, Gurganus's literary alter ego, and the story's ultimate protagonist--is revealed to the reader first through his narration of his father, as Bryan looks back on his childhood, then from the perspective of his father, as the father tries to come to terms with his son's atypical behavior, and finally in an addendum that presents one of Bryan's childhood memories of his father.

The story evokes the tropes of authors such as Ernest Hemingway and Eudora Welty, but its narrative success hinges on Gurganus's use of shifting tenses and points of view and other stylistic elements. The brief second-person narration of the story's first section creates intimacy, with the son reaching out to his father and the author reaching out to his reader. The shifting tenses create a flexible timeline that introduces the reader to Bryan's family history and to the cast of characters therein, many of whom will appear in Gurganus's later short stories and novellas.

Underlying this story of his father, with its themes of wartime heroism, discovered identity, the bond between father and son, and life as a big fish in a little pond, Gurganus represents the lifestyle and expectations of middle-class society in the American South. Spanning several decades, the story offers a panoramic view of generations struggling to understand one another and reexamining traditions and values against the backdrop of southern culture.

"Blessed Assurance: A Moral Tale"

This novella, first published in a stand-alone volume and later incorporated into the author's collection of short stories, is the narrator's catharsis for moral misjudgments made in his youth. Jerry, then a young white college student working to save money for his expenses and those of his parents, takes a job selling funeral insurance to impoverished blacks living in a nearby slum. The insurance policy, when it pays, ensures the policyholders a grand sendoff to their final resting place. However, if they miss only three payments at any point, they forfeit the policy and all the money they have put toward it. Recognizing the arrangement for the scam that it is, but desperate to support his ailing and victimized parents, Jerry takes the job and commences lessons in morality from unlikely sources.

The narrator's detailed anecdotes and sharp turns of phrase carry the reader quickly through this tale, in which Gurganus introduces one of his most compelling characters. Vesta Lotte Battle is a formidable woman, precisely because she makes no imposition but knows her mind well; she is the antithesis of the demure southern white woman featured in many of Gurganus's other stories. Vesta becomes the primary source of the narrator's lessons in life and in morality, representing not only the fortitude of the marginalized in society but also the very essence of honesty, faith, and good will.

In this novella, Gurganus abandons the social satire of many of his other stories in this collection and instead offers a realistic portrait of life in the South and the separate existences of African Americans and whites. In the intersection of their lives comes the opportunity for great pain and for great love, and Gurganus guides the reader through challenging lessons in morality and ethics as the narrator describes experiences of each. Reminiscent of his political writings, the story challenges socially accepted mores and compels readers to reexamine their values and judgments.

The Practical Heart

This title novella in a collection of four, winner of the 2001 National Magazine Prize, lays the foundation for themes explored throughout Gurganus's quartet of novellas: heroism, quest, superstition, sexual longing, and personal character and strength. All of the stories in this collection are thus steeped, in theme if not in content, in reminiscences of Gurganus's childhood and wartime experience, and each character reveals an array of self-defining battle scars. Fantasies yield to realities, and each story shows the inevitable legacy left by one person's life on another's.

The Practical Heart tells of the narrator's great-aunt, Muriel Fraser, an impoverished immigrant, and her quest to be painted by John Singer Sargent. The story develops in two parts: the first, a reflection on the adventurous spirit of a beloved aunt and on the life that may have been hers; the second, an admission that the previous reflections are the product of hope, not fact, and their writing is an act of love. The epigraph at the beginning of the novella, the final words of Henry James, lends a recurring reference to the "distinguished thing," an apt phrase for a family whose fortune and land have disappeared and who must struggle to maintain a sense of distinction in spite of impoverishment. In the second part of the novella, Gurganus refers repeatedly to "the actual," to the facts and reality of a situation that is part of a family's history. These competing ideologies represent a changing mentality over the course of three generations and a simultaneously evolving American culture.

The first part of the novella, entitled "The Expense of Spirit," distinguishes itself from Gurganus's other short writing in its sweeping portraiture of late nineteenth century society, a family's loss of fortune, and the American immigrant experience. The section is compelling in its review of the era and the general frankness with which the fate of the Fraser family is described. Against that backdrop, Muriel appears particularly tender, an embodiment of the can-do attitude espoused by so many turn-of-the-century impoverished immigrants, yet a beloved part of a family's proud heritage.

The second part of the novella, "The Impractical Truth," returns the reader to Gurganus's favored Falls, North Carolina, and to a more modern setting, highly reminiscent of the region of Gurganus's upbringing. The chapter reintroduces Bryan and Bradley, the two protagonists of many of Gurganus's semiautobiographical stories collected in *White People*. Descriptions of Aunt Muriel seem to be taken directly from the author's childhood: The narrator refers to the gift of fine

art supplies that ensured his love for his aunt, and with which she half-created him and his art. Such an aunt and her gifts may have been part of Gurganus's childhood and may have steered him toward art and eventually toward writing.

It is perhaps because of this experience that Gurganus reminds the reader again and again, through his characters' words and a recurring quotation from John Ruskin, to see things. Art and the visual experience form the scaffolding for this story, shaping and structuring the novella as the characters fill in the details through their actions and reflections. Images and appearances strengthen the family's history and make truth from the lies. Through this story and its fabrications, Gurganus may indeed be constructing a metaphor for his own works.

OTHER MAJOR WORKS

LONG FICTION: *Oldest Living Confederate Widow Tells All*, 1989; *Plays Well with Others*, 1997.

BIBLIOGRAPHY

Badaracco, Joseph L., Jr., *Questions of Character: Illuminating the Heart of Leadership Through Literature*. Boston: Harvard Business School Press, 2006. Examines Gurganus's *Blessed Assurance: A Moral Tale* in the context of morality and business ethics.

Canning, Richard. *Gay Fiction Speaks*. New York: Columbia University Press, 2000. Features an interview with Gurganus, in which the author describes his literary influences and the themes he addresses in his writing; focuses primarily on longer fiction.

Fellows, Will. *A Passion to Preserve: Gay Men as Keepers of Culture*. Madison: University of Wisconsin Press, 2004. Features a chapter by Gurganus, describing his interest in culture as inspiration for his writing, and situating the gay experience in the context of the Atlantic South; specifically addresses Gurganus's novella *Preservation News*.

Garrett, George. *Southern Excursions: Views on Southern Letters in My Time*. Baton Rouge: Louisiana State University Press, 2003. Offers a critical review of *White People* and Gurganus's narrative technique.

Mandelbaum, Paul. *First Words*. Rev. ed. Chapel Hill: Algonquin Books of Chapel Hill, 2000. Includes a delightful chapter comprising some of Gurganus's early works--a short story written when the author was eighteen and some sketches and photographs--and brief critical commentary on these.

Patchett, Ann. "Writing and a Life Lived Well: Notes on Allan Gurganus." In *Why I Write: Thoughts on the Craft of Fiction*, edited by Will Blythe. Boston: Little, Brown, 1998. Describes Patchett's experience under Gurganus's tutelage; introduces Gurganus as a writer and a writing professor.

Rachel E. Frier

H

ALYSON HAGY

Born: Springfield, Ohio; August 1, 1960

PRINCIPAL SHORT FICTION:
Madonna on Her Back, 1986
Hardware River Stories, 1991
Graveyard of the Atlantic, 2000
Ghosts of Wyoming, 2010

OTHER LITERARY FORMS

Although known primarily for short fiction, Alyson Hagy (AL-ih-suhn HAY-gee) has published two novels. In *Keeneland* (2000), Kerry Connolly, a scrappy young woman recovering from a ruinous marriage to an abusive reprobate, returns to her native Kentucky, specifically to Keeneland, the legendary thoroughbred stables just outside Lexington, near where she had grown up and had worked training horses. Although the novel works best as a character study-- Kerry makes an unforgettable impression, at once vulnerable and tough, tender and brassy--the plot follows Kerry's heroic, if doomed, efforts to save Sunny, a beautiful young horse she loves, from being destroyed so that her husband can use the insurance money to pay off his gambling debts. In *Snow, Ashes* (2007), two men, bonded by the traumas of their service during the Korean War, are reunited more than thirty years later. The narrative centers on the struggle of the comrades, both in their sixties, to start a sheep ranch in the forbidding outback of Wyoming.

ACHIEVEMENT

In a generation of university-educated short-fiction writers who rigorously reinvestigated the elements of narrative in difficult, often highly experimental texts, Alyson Hagy is primarily a storyteller whose sensibility recalls the brutal naturalism of the early twentieth century in the works of writers from Jack London to Ernest Hemingway. Her stories are formally conservative narratives in which solitary characters are pitted against brutal environments, where they confront the elemental realities of existence: fear, survival, courage, and death. Much like the naturalist fictions of an earlier era, Hagy's stories are dark, claustrophobic narratives, written in a stark, plainsong directness; even her most heroic characters succumb to despair--victims, ultimately, of the crushing intrusion of misfortune.

While in graduate school at the University of Michigan, Hagy won one of the university's prestigious Hopwood Awards in Short Fiction for the manuscript draft of what would become her first collection of stories. Since then, her fiction has won a Pushcart Prize and a fifteen-hundred-dollar runner-up prize in the Nelson Algren Short Fiction Competition, a national fiction contest sponsored by the *Chicago Tribune.* Hagy's stories have been included regularly in best-of-the-year anthologies, including the selection of "Search Bay" for inclusion in *Best American Short Stories, 1997.*

BIOGRAPHY

Although Alyson Carol Hagy was born in Ohio, her father, a family doctor, relocated the family soon after Hagy was born to rural southwestern Virginia, to a farm along the Blackwater River near the remote town of Rocky Mount. Along with her sister, Melchora, Hagy grew up enthralled by the unspoiled reaches of the rugged Blue Ridge Mountains all around her. Her father was an old-school doctor who believed in making house calls, and Hagy accompanied him on his rounds. She loved to listen to the stories her father's patients shared, and she developed an ear for the subtle cadences of conversation (both her parents were accomplished vocalists) and a profound compassion for the struggles of ordinary people facing extraordinary challenges in the face of illness and death. She was a voracious reader, and she dreamed of becoming a veterinarian. Hagy attended Williams College, a prestigious liberal arts school in the rolling foothills of the Berkshires. She did well in the sciences, but she began to consider writing as a career and, indeed, published her first stories in campus literary magazines.

After graduating in 1982, Hagy was accepted into the M.F.A. program at the University of Michigan and completed her degree in 1985. After a stint as an adjunct lecturer and creative-writing instructor at the University of Virginia (1985-1986), Hagy returned to Ann Arbor and taught creative writing for nearly ten years, during which she first published her short fiction in a wide range of small presses and university journals. Married and with a son, Hagy spent many of her summers living along the remote stretches of the Outer Banks in coastal North Carolina.

In 1996, Hagy accepted a position at the University of Wyoming, Laramie, drawn by the opportunity to work in one of the most respected creative-writing departments west of the Mississippi River and by the sweeping open expanses of the Rocky Mountains. It was a happy fit. Over the next decade, Hagy published two novels as well as a highly respected collection of short fiction, *Ghosts of Wyoming*, all but one story set in her adopted West. In addition, Hagy found rich reward in her classroom work with fledgling writers of all levels, from undergraduate beginners to postgraduate M.F.A. candidates. She has been recognized with the university's most respected teaching awards.

ANALYSIS

In an impressive body of short fiction that compels with the rugged integrity and stoicism of its primary characters, Hagy's most compelling character may be nature itself, or specifically the force of nature. Her stories are set far from the comforts of contemporary urban living: The remote grazing lands of the West, the desolate stretches of the barrier islands along the Outer Banks, the remote Virginia wilderness ridges of her childhood are all animated under Hagy's naturalist sense of nature's symbolic heft. Her characters are isolates who must confront the most elemental

expressions of nature's brutal force (illness, natural catastrophes, fierce weather, and ultimately death) and the most primitive expressions of humanity (carnality, greed, violence, and ruthless selfishness).

A primary character in a Hagy story likely is haunted by memories, lost to the consolation of companionship, and shaped by the hard friction of the elements. Unavailable to the logic of love but gifted with a primal sense of the sacramental nature of the land (Hagy's fiction often draws on the metaphors of Native American cultures), the characters find profound satisfaction in the simple grace of maintaining and of surviving. Hagy's stories reflect a conservative--that is early twentieth century--sense of form. She is a realist, whose prose style is at once concise, accessible, and suggestive. Her prose elevates to descriptive power when she contemplates the landscape and her characters struggle to articulate their emotional traumas. These primary characters undergo a difficult test and move, through the vehicle of suspense, the subtleties of layered symbols, and the momentum of an epiphany, to a heroic (if harrowing) understanding of the hard reality of their lives spent against the crushing evidence of their own insignificance. Their challenge is to resist the temptation to surrender to hopelessness.

MADONNA ON HER BACK

That *Madonna on Her Back* brings together eight stories Hagy first drafted while still in graduate school testifies to her maturity as a writer in command of her craft, the elements of character revelation, symbol manipulation, and thematic richness. The primary characters are largely women, each locked within an unsatisfying and sometimes toxic relationship with men who at their best disappoint and at their worst frustrate the hopes of the women who fall for them. Hagy's women are passionate, deeply in touch with their sexual nature, aware of their maternal impulses, and trying to sustain the integrity of that identity amid circumstances that make such basic expressions ironic, even inaccessible.

In "Mister Makes," a strong woman scraping along just above the poverty line nurses with tenderness and fierce protectiveness a newborn son born without arms and given only months to live. Leah is alone: Her first child had died shortly after birth (she could not even afford a headstone to mark the tiny grave), and her boyfriend is indifferent to the evident hopelessness of the new child. After the deformed child succumbs--just 157 days old--Leah understands that her brief time with her child had been a blessing. In "Stadia," Laura tries to reconnect with her troubled husband, drifting emotionally after the death of his distant father, by taking him to a Detroit Tigers baseball game, something the father had never done. The trip turns disastrous when stadium security stops the husband when he tries to sneak in a flask. The title story perhaps best reflects the maturity of Hagy's early fiction. It is a contrapuntal narrative: two twenty-something sisters struggle to provide a stable home for the younger sister's baby. The child's father, abusive and violent, is long gone. The older sister, Joelle, is a frustrated artist who teaches art at a local elementary school. She is drawn to the image of her sister nursing her child, and she convinces her sister to pose for her naked. When the two fix up a back room to take a boarder, a handsome college student, both sisters feel the heat of his presence. It is the younger sister, the mother, however, who seduces him (although it is done without much joy or passion), while Joelle agrees to watch the child in the next room. Again and again, Hagy's characters are caught up in inelegant emotional traps, struggling with and against their base instincts, frustrated by the sense that they are somehow entitled to happiness.

"SEARCH BAY"

It was profoundly satisfying for Hagy that her breakthough story, 1997's "Search Bay," would be tied, even indirectly, to E. Annie Proulx, the Pulitzer Prize-winning Wyoming writer to whom Hagy's fiction often has been compared. Proulx personally selected "Search Bay" for inclusion in the prestigious *Best American Short Stories* volume, citing its powerful character development and its expert use of the natural landscape. In ways that recall the classic naturalism of Stephen Crane (and Proulx's own work), the story tracks the emotional reclamation of an old man. Although it is an anomaly in the collection in which it appears--the other stories are all set along North Carolina's Outer Banks-- "Search Bay" offers a template for Hagy's mature fiction.

John Hansen lives by himself along the forbidding shores of Lake Huron, a career sailor and recovering alcoholic, whose memories and dreams are haunted by a lifetime of working freighters on the difficult waters of the Great Lakes. He is obsessed by a stormy passage during which a belligerent passenger was lost at sea under mysterious circumstances that might have involved the ship's cook (the story parallels Crane's "The Blue Hotel" and the death of the belligerent Swede). His wife long dead, his only companion the wild deer he feeds, Hansen has lost his taste for people.

One November day, his solitude is upended by the sudden appearance of a taciturn Chippewa teenager, the son of a bar waitress in town with whom Hansen had a relationship years before. The boy has been hired to check beaver traps along Hansen's property. Inexplicably, Hansen taps into his dormant need for companionship (the boy reminds him of the ship's cook). Weeks later, the boy appears at Hansen's door with his girlfriend; her hand has been caught by a beaver trap and she needs medical help. Socially awkward, Hansen tries to talk to the boy, but they come to blows when the boy insinuates that no woman would ever disturb Hansen's solitude. Weeks later, Hansen is told that the boy has drowned. He had been hauling hay along the shore of the bay when the ice gave way. Hansen is haunted by the image of the boy left at the bottom of the bay, his body too deep to justify rescue or recovery effort, seemingly a symbol of Hansen's isolated life. In the powerful closing passage, Hansen walks out onto the fragile ice of the bay, pays his subdued respects to the drowned boy, and feels the painful warmth of his revived heart.

GHOSTS OF WYOMING: STORIES

The eight stories collected in *Ghosts of Wyoming* reflect Hagy's embrace of the symbolic suggestion of the American West. The stories draw on the familiar archetypal characters of the West in tales that span more than two hundred years, from the early days of the railroad's arrival (a dozen vignettes of men who worked on the railroad are gathered in "Brief Lives of the Trainmen," and "The Sin Eaters" tells of a late nineteenth century quixotic missionary who accepts the call to head West to convert the Native Americans, only to get caught up in a brutal land war between ranchers) to contemporary stories of the boom-and-bust hard life drilling for rapidly dwindling resources of oil and of cattle ranching in an era of encroaching land developers.

Almost all the ghosts in the stories are metaphoric (only one, "Superstitions of the Indians," has a real ghost--a dead librarian who haunts a university library), with Hagy exploring the gravitational pull of recollection, the entangling inescapability of the past. In "Border," Hagy follows a fourteen-year-old hitchhiker, who impulsively snatches a puppy from a farm for company. A demented truck driver, who gives the boy a lift, is infuriated when the puppy urinates on him and coldly tosses the dog out the window. The boy, horrified, quickly gets out and nurses the puppy, as he spends the night at the home of a lonely woman. It is only the next morning when the sheriff, summoned by the woman, arrests the boy that readers are told the boy is on the run because he has killed his abusive father.

In "The Little Saint of Hoodoo Mountain," perhaps the collection's signature work, a young girl, Livia, estranged from a father who is too busy trying to keep his ranch solvent and a psychologically troubled, heavily medicated mother, happens upon the bones of what appears to be a baby buried in a shallow hole near an abandoned cabin. Lonely and gifted with a rich imagination (her only companion is her dog, Nock), she hides the bones in a nearby cave, only to have them discovered by tourists hiking in the mountains, who in turn alert the media and set off a firestorm of indignation from a phalanx of university anthropologists, environmental crusaders, and Native American activists, who assume the cave is a Native American burial ground and that the ranchers (among them her father) have trespassed on sacred territory. Tormented by her

conscience, Livia drives herself out to the site and admits what she has done, but her reward is to return home in time to discover that her mother's lover has accidentally shot and killed Livia's beloved dog. Such tense psychological struggles in a morally ambiguous universe--where innocents are exposed to the compelling urgency of a difficult irony and left haunted, forever scarred--shape the dark, brooding fictions of Hagy's maturity.

OTHER MAJOR WORKS
LONG FICTION: *Keeneland*, 2000; *Snow, Ashes*, 2007.

BIBLIOGRAPHY
Howard, June. *Form and History in American Literary Naturalism*. Durham: University of North Carolina Press, 2009. Helpful introduction to the literary genre that best defines Hagy; explores the tension between individuals who live in the margins and nature, specifically forces beyond their control.
Kakutani, Michiko. "Dark Side of the Human Condition." *The New York Times*, February 12, 1991. Review of Hagy's *Hardware River* salutes her compelling storytelling ability.
McMurtry, Larry. *Still Wild: Short Fiction of the American West: 1950 to the Present*. New York: Simon and Schuster, 2001. Wide-ranging collection of stories by writers whose influence Hagy readily acknowledges. The introduction, by the Pulitzer Prize-winning McMurtry, defines the traditional genre and its elements as expressed in the contemporary model.

Joseph Dewey

NANCY HALE

Born: Boston, Massachusetts; May 6, 1908
Died: Charlottesville, Virginia; September 24, 1988

PRINCIPAL SHORT FICTION

The Earliest Dreams, 1936
Between the Dark and the Daylight, 1943
The Empress's Ring, 1955
Heaven and Hardpan Farm, 1957
A New England Girlhood, 1958
The Pattern of Perfection, 1960
The Life in the Studio, 1969
Secrets, 1971

OTHER LITERARY FORMS

Nancy Hale's many published books include a biography, an anthology, a series of essays on the writing of fiction, two novels for children, and seven novels for adults, as well as collections of short stories and autobiographical fiction. Her novel *The Prodigal Women* (1942) was a great popular as well as critical success; more than two million copies had been sold when it was reissued in paperback in 1980.

ACHIEVEMENTS

The receiver of both the Henry H. Bellamann Award for literature in 1969 and the Sarah Josepha Hale Award in 1974, Nancy Hale is best known for her ability to reveal the depths of the human mind in the style of an acute and objective observer. A common theme in Hale's work is that of maturity attained when one grows out of the dreams and illusions of the past and accepts the present world willingly. This is often manifested through characters moving from one culture to another and facing a new "outer reality" and through her depictions of women in their roles as mothers, friends, and wives.

BIOGRAPHY

The only child of painters Philip L. Hale and Lilian Westcott Hale, Nancy Hale was born in Boston on May 6, 1908. Among her forebears were the patriot Nathan Hale and a number of celebrated writers including Harriet Beecher Stowe, Lucretia Hale (a great aunt), and Edward Everett Hale (her grandfather). Initially she intended to be a painter, like her parents, and, after graduating from the Winsor School in Boston, she studied at the school of the Boston Museum of Fine Arts and in her father's studio. After she married and moved to New York City in 1928, she took a job as an editor first at *Vogue* and then at *Vanity Fair* before becoming a news reporter for *The New York Times*. She began writing at night the short stories and novels that immediately established her as a writer of exceptional talent.

In 1942 Hale married Fredson Bowers, professor of English and later chairman of the English department and dean of the faculty at the University of Virginia, and the couple settled in Charlottesville, Virginia. She had two sons, Mark Hardin and William Wertenbaker, by former marriages, as well as five grandchildren.

In 1933, Hale was awarded the O. Henry Prize for short-short fiction; in 1958, she received the Benjamin Franklin special citation for the short story. In 1971-1972 she was a Phi Beta Kappa visiting scholar, and for eight years, from 1957 to 1965, she gave the lectures on short fiction at the Bread Loaf Writers' Conference. These lectures form the nucleus of *The Realities of Fiction* (1962), one of the best books ever written about the process of writing imaginative prose. Hale died on September 24, 1988, in Charlottesville, Virginia.

ANALYSIS

Most writers of fiction who produce what can be classified as literature, sooner or later, consciously or unconsciously, develop themes that in their various ramifications become identified with their work. With the early Sherwood Anderson of "I Want to Know Why" and the early Ernest Hemingway of the Nick Adams stories, the theme of initiation was established and reiterated; with Willa Cather in *O Pioneers!* (1913), *My Ántonia* (1918), and subsequent shorter pieces, the struggle of immigrants and pioneers to adjust to a new life in a new land provided a theme over and over again; and in the stories collected in *A Good Man Is Hard to Find* (1955), Flannery O'Connor makes it clear that her prevailing theme developed from a conviction that before there could be any illumination or epiphany her characters must undergo some devastating experience of a violent nature.

THE EMPRESS'S RING

Like these writers, Nancy Hale also developed a theme or thesis in her work, which one recognizes most clearly in its various ramifications through reading her stories not singly as they first appeared in magazines at irregular intervals but rather as they were collected in book form. When twenty-four stories published originally in *The New Yorker* and elsewhere were brought together in a single volume entitled *The Empress's Ring*, the underlying theme that unified the collection as a whole clearly emerged. In "Miss August," a story about the mentally disturbed and emotionally ill and maladjusted, a psychiatrist tells a patient, "You are regressing. You are looking for something in the past and when you have found it you will come up again. You feel strangely because you are not living in outer reality." Later the psychiatrist amplifies this statement so that both patient and reader may comprehend more clearly its full import. The reader is to understand that there are two realities: the outer "outer reality," the practical world to which one can touch and document, and "the past," which in these and other stories is also the world of imagination, made up of memories and illusions, which may be considered the reality of fiction.

In one way or another most of Hale's characters in this collection--such as the patient in "Miss August" and the woman in the title story, "The Empress's Ring"--are exploring their past, sometimes trying to resurrect a security they once knew, sometimes trying to free themselves from the world of dreams and illusions in an effort to develop the maturity that will enable them to live in whatever "outer reality" they must

Nancy Hale (Library of Congress)

without loneliness, hurt, or defeat. This choice of alternatives provides thematic material for much of Hale's work. In such stories as "The Secret Garden" and "Object of Virtue," in which a desperately lonely young woman and an unhappy child seek understanding and companionship, the characters remain bewildered and confused because they cannot adjust to "outer reality." Hale's stories, however, are not always records of frustration and failure. In "The Readville Stars" and in those lighthearted recollections such as "The Copley-Plaza" and "Charlotte Russe," the narrators who are looking back and reminiscing have achieved sufficient maturity through experience in living to view the past with humor, objectivity, and understanding rather than with regret and longing. When Hale's women (the men in these stories are essentially negligible) are not immersed in the past searching for something, they are often acquiring self-knowledge in the present. In a beautifully written story, "On the Beach," a mother during a morning with her young son realizes that an atomic world has not after all destroyed what for her are the deepest values; in such ironic pieces as

"Sheltered" and "A Full Life," a girl and a middle-aged woman dramatically discover unsuspected truths about their own lives.

If the stories in this collection represent variations and extensions of a basic theme, they are developed against widely different backgrounds: the North Shore and Litchfield Hills of New England, towns and villages of the South, hospitals and universities, a ballroom, and a highway motel. Whether Hale constructed her stories objectively or as first-person recollections, she quickly established time, place, and situation and created mood and attitude with great economy of language, demonstrating again and again that she was a most accomplished writer.

THE PATTERN OF PERFECTION

In another collection of stories, *The Pattern of Perfection*, Hale presents a similar group of people, this time extroverts instead of introverts but still troubled and bewildered, trying to cope not so much with inner conflicts as with conflicts arising out of unsatisfactory relationships with others. For Hale these conflicts in human relationships--and in these stories the conflicts are usually familial, mostly between parents and children, but sometimes between husbands and wives--are partially solved by replacing indifference and malice with the spirit of understanding and love. In the title story, "The Pattern of Perfection" (a wonderfully ironic title not only for this story but also for the collection as a whole), a house-proud southerner dedicated to her tradition becomes capable of understanding her daughter-in-law's loneliness in an alien land; and in "A Slow Boat to China," a mother made momentarily ill through suppressing manifestations of love for her son finally recognizes the need for yielding to natural impulses. When these conflicts remain unresolved (as in "A Long Summer's Dream," the story of a spinster whose life has been blighted if not destroyed by a dominating mother and aunt), the resulting bitter resignation becomes tragic.

In addition to theme, what contributes largely to the underlying unity of this collection as a whole and to the richness of individual pieces is Hale's skill in fusing story and symbol, her awareness of the discrepancy between the apparent and the real, and her ability to achieve in her narrative the irony so characteristic of

life. That the frustrated spinster of "A Long Summer's Dream" must refuse an invitation to sail because she "cannot swim" suggests that whatever opportunities her life may have offered have never been realized because she has never learned how to keep herself afloat. In "Entrance into Life," in which a mother and her small son watch the ritual of a college commencement, one senses the approach of death in the very midst of all that is most alive; and in the concluding story "Rich People," in which a woman is meditating on her past, one recognizes that to have lived a life no matter how secure financially without love and understanding is to have experienced the most corrosive form of poverty.

HEAVEN AND HARDPAN FARM

In such books as *Heaven and Hardpan Farm* and *Secrets*, stories that originally appeared in *The New Yorker* or elsewhere are linked together with little or no additional material to form novels constructed around a series of experiences and episodes. Reread in this form, the stories possess a continuity formerly lacking when they first appeared as single pieces. In *Heaven and Hardpan Farm*, Hale writes of a group of women, four extroverts and four introverts of various ages and backgrounds, suffering from a variety of neuroses because they are unable to emerge from their worlds of fantasy and adjust to outer reality, in which they must learn to live if they are to become productive, happy human beings. What makes the stories in *Heaven and Hardpan Farm* such absorbing reading is not only the author's extensive knowledge of Freudian and Jungian psychology and her ability to incorporate it into her narrative, but also her skill in the characterization of each of the highly individualistic patients, as well as the wise, lovable, irascible old psychiatrist who is in charge of the sanatorium, of the practical, dependable housekeeper, and of the nurses who come and go. The reader knows them all, their doubts, fears, desires and dreams, as though the reader, too, was in the sanatorium waiting for his or her hour with the doctor.

Hale's special triumph in these stories of the neurotic, however, is her introduction of a humor and caustic wit that she sustains unfalteringly without a sour note. Much of the humor derives from the character, methods, and personality of the doctor but also from the behavior of the patients in their efforts to find those footholds for what might be "a sort of spiral climbing up" into outer reality. Despite the grim situation, for few patients show improvement, the humor never seems cruel or inappropriate but rather is a contribution toward realism, for, in the life most people experience, the linking of opposites is the rule rather than the exception.

SECRETS

In the second short novel, *Secrets*, constructed from stories published in *The New Yorker* with some additional material from *A New England Girlhood*, the narrator, who is also the central character, is a woman in middle life, a wife and a mother who tells in a four-part narrative how she grew from a lonely, sensitive, insecure child, the daughter of artists, into a mature adult capable of coping with her past and present and of appraising herself and others objectively. During the early years the narrator experiences childhood and adolescence with the children next door, "the nearest to brother and sister I ever had," and it is they who provide drama and excitement in the various stages of her life. There is far more to *Secrets*, however, than this skeletal narrative. In the stories Hale deals directly or obliquely with many matters: the difference between imagination and fact, social and racial discrimination, the individual and the group.

As her title announces, her stories are concerned with secrets, not only with childhood secrets, such as secret drawers and secret passages, but also with the more subtle and tragic secrets of later years, and finally with the great secret of all secrets, the riddle of life, which can only be experienced, never solved. Hale excels in her descriptions, whether in her account of a day in the life of a thoughtless, immature debutante, in the devastating picture of Huntington Avenue in the dreary dusk of a Boston winter afternoon, or in the characterization of a friend "with round cheeks, pursed lips, and a button nose." *Secrets* may be enjoyed on several levels. It is both funny and serious, joyous and somber, but above all it is the work of a writer who has always been aware of the conflict between the world of imagination and the world of facts, and who has the experience to know that many must learn to live with both worlds if they are to survive.

THE LIFE IN THE STUDIO

Hale's closest approach to the kind of autobiography that more often than not is based on fact and event, in contrast to "autobiographical fiction," is her *The Life in the Studio*, a collection of stories for the most part published originally in *The New Yorker* and later skillfully arranged in book form as an informal, vivid narrative of her early life growing up in a family of artists. Her reminiscences, whether in the form of cheerful anecdote or serious comment and discussion, are full of affection for her family. For despite an early rebellion against the unconventional life of her hardworking parents whose daily routine followed the pattern established by her father's reiterated statement, "Art first, life afterwards," Hale became an increasingly devoted, admiring daughter. Through her eyes the reader sees these "singular parents" at work in their studios complementing each other as creator and critic; the reader sees them with other artists, especially at the stone studio on Cape Ann during the summer.

In the final stories, now chapters, entitled "Journeys" and "An Arrangement in Parents," there is the account of the memorable and triumphant trip to Italy, where Hale and her mother, who was in her eighties, viewed the works of the great painters in the churches and galleries of Venice, Florence, and Rome. After her mother's sudden death on their return home one has the impression that the author, now reviewing and analyzing the lives of her parents and her relationship to them, has gained a new perspective and understanding that has produced "a calm of mind, all passion spent." These recollections, *The Life in the Studio*, will remain a touching memorial written by one who grew in the kind of understanding and love that so many of the characters in her fiction try to develop and need to receive.

THE REALITIES OF FICTION

The Realities of Fiction is based on Hale's five years of lecturing on fiction at various academic institutions and on her writing of fiction at the Bread Loaf Writers' Conference at Middlebury College. In this work, Hale not only produced one of the most intelligent, lucid, and fascinating books ever written on the role of the imagination in the creative process but also presented criticism, evaluation, and often detailed analyses of the work of writers ranging from Leo Tolstoy, Charles Dickens, and E. M. Forster to Ernest Hemingway, F. Scott Fitzgerald, and William Faulkner, from Jane Austen to Katherine Mansfield and Elinor Wylie, including comments on the genesis and meaning of some of her own stories. In the first chapter, "The Two Way Imagination," and the final chapter, "Through the Dark Glass to Reality," Hale explains her provocative title by showing through ample reference to life and literature that "the realities of fiction" are as real as "outer reality" and closely linked, for without experiencing and understanding the first many cannot successfully make a passage to the second. What is implied in so much of Hale's fiction is made explicit in these chapters.

In this short essay it is impossible to do more than suggest the high quality and variety of Hale's work. Much of her short fiction is not as yet collected in single volumes, but it can be found in various magazines from *The New Yorker* to *The Virginia Quarterly Review*. Such stories as "The Most Elegant Drawing Room in Europe," with its wonderful description of Venice, superb characterizations of the shy, sensitive observer, her dominating mother, and the worldly, ambivalent *contessa*, reaffirm that Hale was an unusually gifted writer with a sure sense of structure and style, a sharp eye for detail, knowledge of many subjects and places, humor and wit, and a profound understanding of human nature.

Although Hale was a highly individualistic writer whose influence cannot yet be measured, she belongs to a great tradition that includes Anton Chekhov, Gustave Flaubert, the Brontë sisters, Katherine Mansfield, J. D. Salinger, and all those whose sympathies are with the alien, the unwanted, the inferior, and the overly sensitive for whom life in outer reality is so difficult and depressing that they must create another more congenial world through their imaginations. For these people Hale had great compassion, but when they find the strength and courage and understanding needed to "climb the spiral" and take their place in outer reality, which none can reject, she was the first to applaud.

OTHER MAJOR WORKS

LONG FICTION: *The Young Die Good*, 1932; *Never Any More*, 1934; *The Prodigal Women*, 1942; *The Sign of Jonah*, 1950; *Dear Beast*, 1959; *Black Summer*, 1963; *Night of the Hurricane*, 1978.

NONFICTION: *The Realities of Fiction*, 1962; *A New England Discovery*, 1963; *Mary Cassatt*, 1975.

BIBLIOGRAPHY

Barron, James. "Nancy Hale, Fiction Writer." *The New York Times*, September 26, 1988, p. B8. Hale's obituary, with an account of her literary career and comments on her fictional treatment of the follies and foibles of well-bred women.

Callahan, Amy. "Nancy Hale." *The Boston Globe*, September 27, 1988, p. 59. A brief biographical obituary that traces Hale's literary career and comments on the proper Bostonian characters in her humorous novels and short stories.

Gray, James. "Dream of Unfair Women." In *On Second Thought*, edited by Gray. Minneapolis: University of Minnesota Press, 1946. Gray discusses Hale's novel *The Prodigal Women*, her short-story collection *Between the Dark and the Daylight*, and several of her individual short stories, drawing the conclusion that Hale "writes her own stuff and writes exceedingly well."

The New Republic. Review of *Between the Dark and the Daylight*. 109 (July 12, 1943): 51. Finds twenty of the twenty-one stories in this collection praiseworthy and admires Hale's neutral treatment of the intense conflict between characters in her stories.

Van Gelder, Robert. "An Analysis of the Feminine." In *Writers and Writing*. New York: Charles Scribner's Sons, 1946. This interview with Hale focuses on her depiction of women and their relationships with men in her novel *The Prodigal Women*. She reveals that many of her character studies are revelations of herself; much of this work is autobiographical.

Walton, Edith H. Review of *The Earliest Dreams*. *The New York Times*, April 19, 1936, 7. In this review of the collection of stories in *The Earliest Dreams*, Walton writer does not commit herself to complete admiration of Hale's work. Instead, Walton points out some of the more "shallow" stories, while balancing that with praise for many of Hale's fine, perceptive works in the collection. The review is favorable overall.

Welty, Eudora. Review of *Between the Dark and the Daylight. The New York Times*, May 2, 1943, 8. Welty is impressed with the scope of subjects that Hale's twenty-one stories cover, as well as with the

sustained "good writing" in them. This article and other book reviews by Welty were reprinted in *A Writer's Eye: Collected Book Reviews*, edited by Pearl Amelia McHaney and published by the University Press of Mississippi in 1994.

John C. Buchanan
Updated by Laurie Coleman

LAWRENCE SARGENT HALL

Born: Haverhill, Massachusetts; April 23, 1915
Died: Orr's Island, Maine; October 28, 1993

PRINCIPAL SHORT FICTION
"The Ledge," 1959
"Twenty-Three, Please," 1982
"The Sequel," 1989

OTHER LITERARY FORMS

Lawrence Sargent Hall received critical acclaim for his novel *Stowaway: A Novel* (1961). He also wrote *Hawthorne: Critic of Society* (1944), *How Thinking Is Written: An Analytic Approach to Writing* (1963), and *A Grammar of Literary Criticism: Essays in Definition of Vocabulary, Concepts, and Aims* (1965), as well as several published essays.

ACHIEVEMENTS

Lawrence Sargent Hall's *Stowaway* was the unanimous winner of the William Faulkner Award in 1961, an award given for the best first novel by an author. "The Ledge" won the O. Henry Award in 1960 for best short story of the year. "The Ledge" was also included in *The Best Short Stories of the Century* (1999; expanded edition, 2000), edited by John Updike.

BIOGRAPHY

Lawrence Sargent Hall was born in Haverill, Massachusetts, on April 23, 1915, and graduated in 1936 from Bowdoin College, where he won several awards, including the Hawthorne Prize. After graduation he

taught at Deerfield Academy in Massachusetts before entering Yale University in 1938. After receiving his doctorate in 1941 (his dissertation was on Nathaniel Hawthorne, also a Bowdoin graduate), he taught at Ohio University and then at the United States Naval Academy until 1942, when he began a four-year tour in the Navy. He served in the South Pacific before being discharged with the rank of lieutenant commander.

After the war Hall returned to Bowdoin as an assistant professor of English and, aside from a year (1955-1956) as a Carnegie visiting professor at Columbia University, he spent the remainder of his teaching career at Bowdoin, retiring in 1986. His O. Henry Award-winning short story, "The Ledge," which appeared in 1959, was followed by his Faulkner Award-winning *Stowaway* in 1961, but despite his phenomenal debut in fiction, he published only two additional short stories. His eclectic interests included taking trips down the Mississippi in his dory, *Way Out*, serving on the Ford Foundation committee that created the Advanced Placement Program of the College Entrance Examination Board, teaching at summer institutes under the National Defense Education Act, and serving on the Maine State Commission for the Arts and Humanities. In addition to academic pursuits, Hall was active in environmental matters, cruising the Maine coast in 1970 to prevent the establishment of oil refineries there. He was also given credit for single-handedly preventing the state of Maine from turning Route 24 into a four-lane highway. After a career in teaching and operating a boatyard on the Maine coast, he died October 28, 1993, at his home in Orr's Island, Maine.

ANALYSIS

Lawrence Sargent Hall's literary accolades are remarkable, considering how few fictional works he wrote. His fiction is, for the most part, concerned with life at sea, hardly surprising given his naval career, his cruises off the Maine coast and down the Mississippi River, and his operation of a boatyard. Hall deprecates contemporary, urban life and exalts life at sea, which he describes in technical detail and which provides him with metaphors for relationships. Like Ernest Hemingway, Hall is concerned with behavior under pressure, and he is skeptical of talk. His protagonists are always taciturn, uncommunicative men's men, who are skilled at their professions but unskilled at interpersonal relationships, which tend to be stormy. Hall's concern seems to be the nature of manhood, and his protagonists are alone but not lonely; they test themselves, usually at sea, by pushing limits and by leading "high-risk lives." Hall also resembles Stephen Crane, whose "The Open Boat" focuses on men's behavior at sea and whose *Red Badge of Courage: An Episode of the American Civil War* (1895) concerns the passage from boyhood to manhood. Hall's style is, for the most part, in the realist tradition, except for "Twenty-Three, Please," which is experimental in that the story consists of a series of impressions on the mind of a character who does not speak.

"THE LEDGE"

"The Ledge," Hall's award-winning and frequently anthologized short story, concerns the accidental drowning of a Maine fisherman, his son, and his nephew. On a Christmas morning, the three go duck hunting on an offshore ledge, which is submerged at high tide. In the excitement of successful hunting, the skiff they take to reach the ledge somehow gets set adrift and, despite their efforts to attract attention and help, they become marooned and drown when the tide covers the ledge. Hall's plot is as simple as Ernest Hemingway's in *The Old Man and the Sea* (1952); Hall and Hemingway both focus on their protagonists' behavior as they react with "grace under pressure."

Hall's fictional universe tends to be bifurcated, split into opposites. He contrasts the masculine, outside world (the fisherman's wife thinks "anyone going out like that had to be incurably male") with the feminine "close bed" and "woman's fears." Similarly, he pits the sea, represented by the fisherman, against the shore, represented by his farming brother. There are even two kinds of fishermen, those who stay close to the shore and those who venture farther out, pushing against limits. In the story the opposing characters seem unwilling or unable to communicate with one another. The other fishermen consider the protagonist a disdainful braggart; even his wife has, in her loneliness, considered leaving him.

In "The Ledge," Hall also presents an initiation story gone awry. The fisherman mentors his thirteen-year-old son, attempting to make him a man. The son's Christmas gift, an automatic shotgun, represents a change in his status; the son "was fierce to grow up in hunting, to graduate from sheltered waters and the blinds along the shores of the inner bay." When they discover the wayward skiff, the son "cried softly for a moment, like a man," unwilling to show pain. In the final moments of the story the son becomes "old enough to know there were things beyond the power of any man." The fisherman's nephew, also the recipient of an automatic shotgun, receives some tutoring in the art of waiting: "Part of doing a man's hunting was learning how to wait." Later, when the nephew is briefly left by himself on the ledge while the fisherman and his son retrieve the dead ducks, he suffers an anticipatory attack of "ledge fever," which leaves him temporarily paralyzed.

"The Ledge" ultimately concerns the competent, hard, insensitive loner proud of his equipment and abilities and intent on defeating the "element of time" by doing more than his peers. On rare occasions the fisherman even has the "grand illusion" of beating the "game." When he has to confront the reality of their impending deaths, he understands that "their situation was purely mathematical," not subject to his control; and he considers the end "quite scientifically." Even though he knows time and tide will destroy them, he puts his son on his shoulders, wedges one foot between the rocks, and vows to hold him "through a thousand tides." He cannot, but when the fisherman is found the next day, his foot is still wedged in the rocks, and his son's boot is under his right elbow. At this sight his wife absolves him "of his mortality," realizing the enormity of his struggle.

"TWENTY-THREE, PLEASE"

Although "Twenty-Three, Please" focuses on a Native American steeplejack, Hall uses sea imagery to portray the city landscape as a "deadly urban reef." The city, with which the steeplejack's wife is associated, is characterized by its "ashen haze" and smog; with their airplanes, people have "lacerated sacred skies." With his telescope, with which he scans the heavens, and his work high above the city, the steeplejack can render the urban landscape "decent by distance." Although in his work he is "selfless as a saint," his wife has forced him to give up the job and become earthbound. Their marriage becomes a battle zone full of military imagery: The telescope is like a machine gun, and her heels "invade the living room."

In the midst of this domestic warfare, a despondent woman in a nearby building strips herself naked and steps out on the ledge of the twenty-third floor. The steeplejack, who is called to rescue her, joins a priest, a psychiatrist, and a police lieutenant. As the scene unfolds, the woman on the ledge becomes dehumanized as she is successively referred to as "it," "thing," "them," "what," "case," and "confrontation," callous responses not lost on the steeplejack, whose silence contrasts with the verbose jargon of the psychiatrist. When he steps out on the ledge and removes his obligatory safety harness, his actions are erroneously interpreted by the three professionals, who see his behavior from their limited perspectives: The lieutenant thinks the steeplejack is excited by the woman's naked body; the psychiatrist sees him as involving the woman in his own problem; and the priest sees him as offering her "the saving expression of love." The woman on the ledge does not respond to their chatter but instead leans forward in "the supreme airfoil embrace of the ballet partner." She and her steeplejack partner experience "no sense of fall but of ascent, through one clear burst of sheer coital light." Their suicide, sexual and cleansing, is one of triumph, not defeat.

"THE SEQUEL"

In "The Sequel" Hall returned to the sea for his subject matter and for his protagonist, Harry, a crusty old salt with a decided preference for sailboats over "stinkpots," or motorboats. As in Hall's other fiction, there are conflicts: In addition to the sail/motor dichotomy, there are class distinctions (Harry is a sailor, whereas yacht club members are mere "yachtsmen"), geographical differences between the "land he went sailing to get away from" and the open sea, and differences between marriage (a "low-risk life") and bachelorhood and freedom. In fact, the title of the short story refers to the aftermath of a romantic relationship between Harry and a twenty-seven-year-old artist.

When Harry takes Josie, a middle-aged divorcée who is sizing up Harry up as a prospective husband, out sailing, all the oppositions surface and are, for the most part, resolved in Harry's favor. Josie, with her "shore-based thoughts," is not the woman for Harry, because they do not speak the same language. Her use of "straighten up," "low side," "up front," and "tippy," in place of nautical terms, makes him realize that she speaks a language "he has to translate." Harry's attitude toward shore women is clearly patriarchal; he compares them to children. However, he is completely entranced by the young artist, who took from him and then mailed him a check with a promise of more money. Although he knows they had "no horizons" together, Harry is still in love with her (the young woman says he is obsessed); when Josie suggests that the young woman might be waiting on the dock for him, he instinctively looks for her, prompting Josie to ask him to take them ashore.

When Harry and Josie sail to secluded Rumrunner Cove, the idyllic mood is shattered by the intrusion of an outboard runabout circling them at full speed. Harry, who compares sailing to falling in love, feels that his beloved yawl has been "ravished." On the way back to shore, Harry spots the runabout, which has developed engine trouble and is now adrift. He gains his revenge and demonstrates the "superiority of sail over steam" by towing them to the yacht club and setting them adrift again. Things end as they began, except the sequel proves to be a continuation of Harry's obsession with the young artist, an obsession without much risk for him.

OTHER MAJOR WORKS

LONG FICTION: *Stowaway: A Novel*, 1961.

NONFICTION: *Hawthorne: Critic of Society*, 1944; *How Thinking Is Written: An Analytic Approach to*

Writing, 1963; *A Grammar of Literary Criticism: Essays in Definition of Vocabulary, Concepts and Aims*, 1965.

BIBLIOGRAPHY

Hall, Lawrence Sargent. *How Thinking Is Written: An Analytic Approach to Writing*. Boston: Heath, 1963. Discusses Hall's method of achieving good writing. Includes sample readings.

"Lawrence Sargent Hall." In *Contemporary Authors*. Detroit: Gale Research, 1967. A good first stop for students. Includes biographical information.

Thomas L. Erskine

MARTHA LACY HALL

Born: Magnolia, Mississippi; August 19, 1923
Died: Summerville, South Carolina; November 1, 2009
Also Known As: Martha Constance Lacy

PRINCIPAL SHORT FICTION

Call It Living: Three Stories, 1981
Music Lesson, 1984
The Apple-Green Triumph, and Other Stories, 1990

OTHER LITERARY FORMS

Although primarily an author of short fiction, Martha Lacy Hall composed a historical genealogical work, published in 1956, *An Historical Sketch of Magnolia, Miss.: Centennial Celebration, Magnolia, Mississippi, 1856-1956.* This book celebrated the hundredth birthday of Hall's birthplace, and compiles many stories concerning the town's citizens and businesses. Published to coincide with Magnolia's centennial celebration, the book contains a brief history of Magnolia, interesting stories of the town and its residents, and genealogical information.

ACHIEVEMENTS

Martha Lacy Hall, a southern writer, received many favorable reviews for her inviting tales of the Deep South. Her stories have appeared in literary journals such as *New Orleans Review, Sewanee Review, Shenandoah, Southern Review, Virginia Quarterly Review*, and *Washington and Lee Journal.* She published three compilations of her stories: *Call It Living, Music Lesson*, and *The Apple-Green Triumph, and Other Stories.*

Her career included more successes, such as the opportunity to edit a novel by John Kennedy Toole titled *A Confederacy of Dunces*, which was published in 1980 and posthumously awarded a Pulitzer Prize in 1981. The book sold many copies through the Louisiana University Press. In 1983, Hall was featured a keynote speaker at the Sandhills Writers Conference in Augusta, Georgia. Her story "The Apple-Green Triumph" won an O. Henry Award in 1991.

BIOGRAPHY

Martha Lacy Hall was born Martha Constance Lacy in Magnolia, Mississippi, on August 19, 1923, to William Monroe Lacy and Elizabeth Hawkins Goza Lacy. Hall had four sisters (Kathryn, Dorothy, Elizabeth, and Lilyan) and two brothers (Walter Maxwell and William). Hall's father owned the *Pike County Herald* daily newspaper in Magnolia, and her mother was an editor. Hall attended Whitworth College for Women in Brookhaven, Mississippi, where for a time she edited the school paper. She graduated with a degree in journalism. On Christmas Day, 1941, she married engineer Robert Sherrill Hall, Jr., of Memphis, Tennessee. The Halls had three children: Martha "Marti" Lacy Hall, Jane Sherrill Hall, and Robert Sherrill Hall, III.

Martha Lacy Hall's work and writing career became intertwined. She worked briefly as a reporter for the *Memphis Press-Scimitar* during World War II, while her husband was in the service. While in Memphis, she became active in theater, playing the lead in *Claudia* (1941), and eventually she won a local acting award.

Later, the Hall family lived in Jackson, Mississippi, for eight years and then moved to Baton Rouge, Louisiana, in 1954. In 1956, Hall produced a genealogical historical publication to mark the one-hundredth anniversary of her hometown, Magnolia. The book, published by W. M. Lacy, contained local information and family stories of Magnolia's residents.

As a writer, Hall dreamed of producing children's stories, but instead she published many fine stories about adults. She worked for approximately eighteen months in publications for Wade O. Martin, the Louisiana secretary of state; in 1968, she went to work for the Louisiana State University Press as a manuscript editor. Two years later, she officially launched her career as a short-story writer with the sale of a story to the *Southern Review* titled "The Peaceful Eye." She became managing editor of the Louisiana State University Press in 1976 and remained there until her retirement in 1983. In the early 1980's, she produced her short-story collections: *Call It Living* and *Music Lesson*. She produced her third book, *The Apple-Green Triumph*, in 1990. While at the Louisiana State University Press, her vocation brought her into contact with many popular authors, whose works were published by the press, including James Lee Burke, Fred Chappell, William Hoffman, and Steve Yarborough. After Hall's retirement, she functioned as a fiction editor for the press until 1993, and she published her final story, "The Snakeshooter," in 2003 in the *Sewanee Review*.

After a lengthy marriage of fifty years, Hall's husband died in 1991. She remarried later in life. Her second husband, Opie L. Shelton, died in 1999. Hall died at age eighty-six in Summerville, South Carolina, on November 1, 2009.

ANALYSIS

Martha Lacy Hall's stories and books received many favorable reviews. Set in the South, a well-known environment for Hall, her stories offer brief slices of the lives of believable characters, who experience challenges, struggles, and losses in the face of time and place, which are important components of her work. These components often reveal a more traditional South in quiet, sometimes quaint, settings. Hall generally avoids high drama but manages to invoke emotion straightforwardly in her readers. In contrast to some writers who employ bolder tactics, Hall uses uncomplicated delivery and descriptive style to suggest and imply her characters' qualities. Many of her protagonists are southern women, and most often they possess inner strength, right-mindedness, tolerance, and compassion. Hall's characters seem familiar, like people one already knows or has met. They resemble a neighbor, a person from the past, a cousin, or possibly oneself.

Hall's work has often been compared to that of Eudora Welty and of Flannery O'Connor, although Hall maintains her unique style, her individuality of expression, and her distinct influence on the realm of southern writing. Her lightweight themes manage to engage her readers subtly and encourage them to think about the relationships and the personalities in the stories. Her plots, enhanced with the scents, sounds, and sights of southern landscapes, occupy her readers and, later, invite reflection.

"THE PEACEFUL EYE"

Hall writes with grace, refinement, and decency, with her earliest tale containing the most punch. "The Peaceful Eye" (bought by Lewis P. Simpson, editor of *Southern Review*) was her first short story sold for publication; it remains one of her most remarkable tales. The protagonist, a sixth-grader named Mary, who leads an ordinary little-girl life, has a soft heart for the elderly. For many years she has befriended an older neighbor, Miss Emma, who lives across the street with her dog, Silky. Mary has spent many hours seeing the woman through her innocent child eyes and visits Miss Emma frequently. However, their friendship changes abruptly after an event that leads to the deaths of Silky and her newborn puppies. Mary witnesses part of the traumatic occurrence and rightly blames Miss Emma, avoiding future contact with the woman but keeping the matter to herself. Toward the end of the tale, the reader realizes that Mary takes a step in the process of growing up, as she experiences the pain of death, the loss of a friend, and a change in perspective, which puts Miss Emma in a different light. Mary feels an emotional distance and fails to grieve openly when Miss Emma commits suicide. Quiet, warm tears come later in a solitary moment.

Mary's experience, the sobering jolt that real life can bring to a child, especially in an area where many children are vulnerable--the tenderness and affection felt for tiny helpless puppies--is an experience to which many readers can relate. A steppingstone on the path to adulthood, a child's quiet heartbreak, is at the center of this tale, and Hall delivers it without illusion.

MUSIC LESSON

Hall's forthright delivery of her themes and her realistic plots make her tales solid, convincing, and impressive. Her skill affords her the ability to narrate from the perspectives of varied characters: a child, an old man, a middle-aged woman. Such is the substance of her second published collection, *Music Lesson.* Published in 1984, this collection was the first of her books to receive critical acclaim.

The characters in this collection are presented mostly in simple, unvarnished, but appealing stories. Subdued and tasteful, the tales tug at the mind, compelling the reader to consider basic life experiences, such as an admired acquaintance grown older ("Doll"), the discovery of a neighbor's exciting secret ("Privacy"), and chuckling at a friend's unusual attitude toward life ("Lucky Lafe"). At first read, these stories seem to be just that--stories. However, the tales linger with the reader, as in "The Man Who Gave Brother Double Pneumonia," when a child unjustly blames herself for her twin brother's illness, leading one to recollect experiences from one's own childhood. The reader's ability to recognize, understand, and identify with Hall's characters is one of the reasons her work is successful. Hall's fiction seems genuinely real.

The titular story is about a woman caught in unexpected financial straits, as her husband lies in a hospital with heart disease. Thrust suddenly into the role of provider, she ponders her situation and worries what will be the outcome: "I have to have some money. Now. But from where?" By the end of the story, however, she has her priorities in order and a temporary solution at hand. As with many of Hall's characters, the inner qualities prevail.

The APPLE-GREEN TRIUMPH AND OTHER STORIES

Hall's third story collection, and the one that received the most attention and review, compiles tales told from a variety of viewpoints. The first is from that of an old woman in the title story who has kept her late husband's green sports car. She drives the car at night in the rain to the airport to retrieve her brother, whom she has not seen in many years. Hall cleverly stages a humorous bugaboo; the old woman must determine how she will accommodate her brother, grown obese since she last saw him, in the tiny sports car for the lengthy ride ahead.

Humor, irony, and poignancy partner up in many of the tales in this collection, such as a proper and genteel woman ("Miss Robbie's Cup of Tea") attempting to serve a nice cup of tea to her beer-swigging, belching husband. More mystery is afoot in "Elinor and Peggy, " when a young woman tells her neighbor the bizarre story of a nude woman on a front lawn. Irony comes to the forefront in "Quicksand" when an aging and ill woman berates her husband by day and writes him love letters in the evenings.

Hall's wit, humor, and insight are evident in her writing but not blatantly. A subtle infusion of joviality does not leave the reader rolling with laughter but rather with a chuckle, a smile, or perhaps a poignant sigh, as the characters' experiences parallel real life.

"THE BIRTHDAY PARTY"

Characterization in "The Birthday Party" demonstrates Hall's ability to use gentle humor as she constructs colorful and credible individuals engaged in a family gathering. The family patriarch, an aged, cranky man, depresses the mood of the dinner party given in honor of his birthday. However, he is not the only one complaining. Other characters in the story display their own various attitudes and idiosyncrasies as the reader recognizes the farces and comic situations that often occur in family groupings.

In addition, apparent in this story is Hall's talent in providing descriptive details: "Willa's fern baskets twisting slowly to the left, then to the right, wagging their long green fronds to some mysterious rhythm conspired between the lake breeze and the ceiling fans." These details lead the reader to believe he or she is witnessing the story particulars in person: "his iced-tea glass was dark with bourbon, and an inch of sugar drifted in the bottom like sand in an hourglass. He took a swallow and made a face, shaking his head."

"THE SNAKESHOOTER"

Hall's final story to achieve publication was "The Snakeshooter." The story is set in Louisiana, and it was written in Hall's later years. The protagonist is an old woman who has outlived two husbands, leaving one to wonder how much autobiography may be stitched into the fabric of the story.

Ouida, arthritic and slow, spends her days caring for her yard and garden, which includes occasionally shooting at rats and snakes among the vines. Mostly she misses her targets, but ironically on the same day she kills a rat, her hired man, Eli, falls ill and unexpectedly dies. Grieved at the loss of her helper, Ouida recalls an earlier time when she and her husband watched the man care for an injured bird. The story concludes with the imagery of the brown wren, healthy and alive, flying away. The imagery remains with the reader as one imagines Eli's spirit on a happy journey, away from the bounds of earth. This comforting imagery is a bittersweet, but fitting, farewell to one of Hall's characters and a tribute to her work, the value of which will endure.

OTHER MAJOR WORKS

NONFICTION: *An Historical Sketch of Magnolia, Miss.: Centennial Celebration, Magnolia, Mississippi, 1856-1956*, 1956.

BIBLIOGRAPHY

Hobson, Linda Whitney. "Inroads to the Deep South." *The Times-Picayune*, September 16, 1990. Newspaper article that provides commentary on the work of Hall.

Koon, George William, ed. "The Man Who Gave Brother Double Pneumonia." In *A Collection of Classic Southern Humor II, More Fiction and Occasional Fact by Some of the South's Best Storytellers*. Atlanta, Ga.: Peachtree, Ltd, 1986. The book is a collection of humorous stories of the South and contains a short story by Hall.

Goldsmith, Sarah Sue. "A Feeling of Being There." *The Advocate*, September 9, 1990. Newspaper article reviewing *The Apple-Green Triumph*.

_____. "Writer Squeezes in Time for Her Craft." *The Advocate*, September 9, 1990. Newspaper article of an interview with Hall, who describes her writing experiences.

Starr, William W. "Hall Bloomed Late But Well." *The Slate*, September 30, 1990. Newspaper article on Martha Lacy Hall and her writing accomplishments.

Weatherby, H. L., and George Core, eds. "Place in My Fiction." In *Place in American Fiction, Excursions, and Explorations*. Columbia: University of Missouri Press, 2004. This essay collection concerning the topic of place in the works of many notable American writers contains a chapter by Hall.

Glenda I. Griffin

DASHIELL HAMMETT

Born: St. Mary's County, Maryland; May 27, 1894
Died: New York, New York; January 10, 1961

PRINCIPAL SHORT FICTION

Secret Agent X-9, 1934 (with Alex Raymond)
The Adventures of Sam Spade, and Other Stories,
   1945
The Continental Op, 1945
The Return of the Continental Op, 1945
Hammett Homicides, 1946
Dead Yellow Women, 1947
Nightmare Town, 1948
The Creeping Siamese, 1950
Woman in the Dark: More Adventures of the Conti-
   nental Op, 1951
A Man Named Thin, and Other Stories, 1962
The Big Knockover: Selected Stories and Short
   Novels, 1966 (Lillian Hellman, editor)
Nightmare Town: Stories, 1999 (Kirby McCauley,*
   Martin H. Greenberg, and Ed Gorman, editors)
Crime Stories, and Other Writings, 2001
Lost Stories, 2005
"So I Shot Him," 2011

OTHER LITERARY FORMS

Dashiell Hammett's published works include seven novels and approximately twenty-five short stories, which he refused to republish during his lifetime. During the 1930's, he wrote "continuing story cartoons," creating the character Secret Agent X-9 to compete with Dick Tracy. Five novels have been filmed, and director John Huston's version of *The Maltese Falcon* (1941), starring Humphrey Bogart as Sam Spade, has been called "the best private-eye melodrama ever made." *The Thin Man* (1934) with William Powell and Myrna Loy as Nick and Nora Charles was the first in a series of "comedy-thrillers" that became for a time a minor film industry.

ACHIEVEMENTS

Publishing short stories mainly in *Black Mask* magazine during the 1920's, Dashiell Hammett had become the preeminent writer, perhaps even the originator, of "hard-boiled" or realistic, action-oriented detective fiction even before he produced any of his novels. Though Carroll John Daly introduced two private eyes in *Black Mask* some months earlier, Hammett's Continental Op generally is considered the prototypical private detective, a credible and unheroic man with whom readers could identify. Drawing from his experiences as a private investigator, Hammett created a thoroughly professional detective: dedicated to his job and usually--though not always--successful at it; more concerned with obtaining facts than with engaging in violent confrontations; and willing to cooperate with the police when necessary. Set in realistic urban America and written in a terse style and often cynical tone, the Continental Op stories to a large extent set the pattern for all subsequent American private eye fiction. Hammett is the first in a continuum that includes Raymond Chandler, Ross Macdonald, Robert B. Parker, and Bill Pronzini.

BIOGRAPHY

Born in Maryland, Samuel Dashiell Hammett spent his early years in Philadelphia and Baltimore. He left school at fourteen and worked at a variety of odd jobs, including that of a manual laborer. Between 1915 and 1918, he worked for the Pinkerton's Detective Agency as an operative, finding this work to be interesting, challenging, adventurous, and at times dangerous. While serving as a sergeant in the U.S. Army Ambulance Corps during World War I, he contracted tuberculosis; although it was cured, his health was permanently impaired. Married with two daughters, Hammett returned to the Pinkerton Agency. (In all, he spent eight years in its employ as an investigator.) He then separated from his family and began to write bits of verse and sketches from his experiences as a detective. In October, 1923, the first story in which the Continental Op appeared was published; by the middle of the 1920's, Hammett was known as an original talent, an innovator in a popular form of fiction, and the central figure in a new school of writing about crime. His writings made him the "darling" of the Hollywood and New York sets. He began to drink heavily and continued to do so despite his meeting with playwright Lillian Hellman, who remained his closest friend for the rest of his life. With the onset of World War II, he enlisted in the Army at the age of forty-eight and served in the Aleutians, where he edited a daily newspaper for the troops. He was discharged in 1945 with emphysema and in poorer health than before. He continued drinking until 1948, when an attack of delirium tremens convinced him never to drink again.

During the 1930's, while he had been writing for the film industry, Hammett had become involved with various left-wing and anti-Fascist causes. He had become a Marxist, and, while he never lost his critical sense regarding the absurdities of many of his associates, he remained loyal to communism. During the McCarthy era of the early 1950's, he served six months in prison for refusing to testify in court. Released and blacklisted, he lived a quiet life with the care and companionship of Hellman. His lung condition was diagnosed as cancerous and he died in 1961.

ANALYSIS

Dashiell Hammett's best-known and most widely read short stories are those in which the Continental Op, a tough, San Francisco-based Continental Detective Agency investigator, serves as the main character and narrator. Unlike the contemporary American private eye, the Continental Op is not a glamorous figure; he is short, somewhat plump, and middle-aged. His name is never revealed in the stories, although he uses several false identities for the people he meets during the course of his investigations. He has no home and no personal life apart from his work; his total identity is that of a private detective. Hired by a society that appears on the surface to be real and respectable, the Continental Op moves through all the social strata from the seediest to the most aristocratic and finds in fulfillment

of his cynicism that all segments of the society are equally deceitful, dishonest, and violent.

Hammett's world is one in which society and social relations are permeated by misanthropic suspicion. The criminal world is a mirror image of the respectable side of the society. It is a reflection of the reputable world in that its existence depends on that world, preys on it for its own ends, and, in effect, is really an actual part of it. These worlds--the respectable and the criminal--are intricately connected and interact with each other. The Continental Op, and for that matter all Hammett's detectives, is the guardian of the official society hired to protect it from the criminal world that is continually threatening to take over. He stands aloof from these worlds in which he must function primarily because he lives by a very stringent "code." There are no rewards for concluding an investigation other than drawing his salary and expenses from the agency, so he cannot succumb to temptations to enrich himself. He expects of himself, and others like him, to accept the failures and disappointments, as well as physical beatings, without complaint. His job is an end in itself, and since his

Dashiell Hammett (Library of Congress)

existential identity comes only from his work, he is protected from the temptation to align himself with either sector of the society against the other. Even his conscious refusal to use the speech of the reputable society becomes a form of self-insulation and serves to establish him as an individual apart.

Written in the realistic style, Hammett's works contain a strong strain of Zolaesque naturalism. The Continental Op, as a narrator, makes no moral claims for himself and is dispassionate in his judgment of other people's actions. The characters of the stories are representative types rather than people. Thefts and killings come naturally out of the forces of the environment. The Continental Op survives in a jungle world in which only the "fittest" can survive. In "The House in Turk Street," for example, the reader is made aware from the very beginning that this detective is different from the Sherlock Holmes type of detective. In the conventional detective story, the sleuth's superior intellect is totally directed toward solving the "challenging puzzle" and discovering the identity of the villain. The actual capture of the criminal does not interest him; this is left to the official police and is usually merely alluded to in passing in the final paragraphs of the stories. In addition, the detective in the conventional story is almost always completely in control of the situation; he makes things happen.

"The House in Turk Street"

In "The House in Turk Street," the Continental Op, acting on a tip from an informant, is searching for a man by going from house to house ringing doorbells. The flat, deliberate tone of the first few paragraphs conveys the sense that most of the work of this private investigator is pure drudgery, a lot of footwork and trial and error. He definitely is not in charge of the situation, and he has no brilliant scheme for finding his man. He is at Turk Street on the advice of his informant, and the events of the story unfold largely by chance rather than because of anything the detective does or plans. The operative is welcomed into the living room of the Turk Street house and given tea, cookies, and a cigar by a harmless-appearing elderly couple. As the Continental Op relaxes and gets comfortable, he is jarred out of his illusions of security by the pressure of a

gun on the back of his neck. Even though he is at this house through sheer happenstance, the criminals assume that he is aware of their dishonest activities and has been tracking them down in order to capture them.

In many ways, Hammett uses the reader's familiarity with the traditional mystery story as a counterbalance for this tale of adventure. What Hammett succeeds in doing in this story and others in the Continental Op series is to introduce a new kind of detective story, one that would replace what the *Black Mask* writer felt was the contrived and unrealistic classical mystery. In "The House in Turk Street," the old and new forms are presented in interaction with each other. When the characters in Hammett's story experience difficulty, they do so because they try to apply the rules of the old world of detective fiction in this new world of adventure, where the old rules no longer operate.

For example, Hook, one of the thieves, is killed because he still tries to live in a world of sentiment where men are inspired by women to achieve great things in the name of love. Tai, the Chinese mastermind with a British accent, also clings to the illusions of the old mysteries. Defeated at the end of the story, he is convinced that he has been thwarted by superior detective work and refuses to consider the possibility that the Continental Op had merely stumbled upon their criminal lair. As the Continental Op matter-of-factly reports: "He went to the gallows thinking me a liar." For the master criminal, the possibility that it was all an accident is unthinkable; but in this house in Turk Street, the unthinkable is what happens. In the world in which the Continental Op does his job, detectives happen upon criminals by chance, criminals such as the young woman in the story escape, the Continental Op survives because he kills in self-defense, and bodies are strewn all around.

Although the "hard-boiled detective" form that Hammett's writings made famous has undergone some significant changes over the years, every writer of the American detective story is indebted to the creator of the Continental Op.

OTHER MAJOR WORKS

LONG FICTION: *$106,000 Blood Money*, 1927 (also known as *Blood Money* and *The Big Knockover*); *Red Harvest*, 1927-1928 (serial), 1929 (book); *The Dain Curse*, 1928-1929 (serial), 1929 (book); *The Maltese Falcon*, 1929-1930 (serial), 1930 (book); *The Glass Key*, 1930 (serial), 1931 (book); *Woman in the Dark*, 1933 (serial), 1951 (book); *The Thin Man*, 1934; *Complete Novels*, 1999.

SCREENPLAYS: *City Streets*, 1931 (with Oliver H. P. Garrett and Max Marcin); *Mister Dynamite*, 1935 (with Doris Malloy and Harry Clork); *After the Thin Man*, 1936 (with Frances Goodrich and Albert Hackett); *Another Thin Man*, 1939 (with Goodrich and Hackett); *Watch on the Rhine*, 1943 (with Lillian Hellman).

NONFICTION: *The Battle of the Aleutians*, 1944 (with Robert Colodny); *Selected Letters of Dashiell Hammett, 1921-1960*, 2001 (Richard Layman with Julie M. Rivett, editors).

EDITED TEXT: *Creeps By Night*, 1931 (also known as *Modern Tales of Horror*, *The Red Brain*, and *Breakdown*).

BIBLIOGRAPHY

Gale, Robert L. *A Dashiell Hammett Companion*. Westport, Conn.: Greenwood Press, 2000. An encyclopedia devoted to Hammett, with alphabetically arranged entries about his works, characters, family members, and acquaintances. Also includes a chronology, a brief bibliography, and bibliographies for especially detailed entries.

Hammett, Jo. *Dashiell Hammett: A Daughter Remembers*. Edited by Richard Layman, with Julie M. Rivett. New York: Carroll & Graf, 2001. A compelling memoir that is well illustrated with photographs drawn from family archives.

Johnson, Diane. *Dashiell Hammett: A Life*. New York: Random House, 1983. The most comprehensive biography of Hammett, this book adds considerable information to the public record of his life but does not provide much critical analysis of the works. More than half the volume deals with the years after Hammett stopped publishing fiction and during which he devoted most of his time to leftist political activism.

Layman, Richard. *Shadow Man: The Life of Dashiell Hammett*. New York: Harcourt Brace Jovanovich/Bruccoli-Clark, 1981. An academic who earlier produced a descriptive bibliography of Hammett, Layman provides lucid interpretations of the works. While he holds Hammett in high regard as a major figure in twentieth century American fiction, he does not present a totally admiring portrait of the man.

Mellen, Joan. *Hellman and Hammett: The Legendary Passion of Lillian Hellman and Dashiell Hammett*. New York: HarperCollins, 1996. Although primarily a biographical study, this scrupulously researched work provides insight into the backgrounds of Hammett's fiction. Includes very detailed notes and a bibliography.

Metress, Christopher, ed. *The Critical Response to Dashiell Hammett*. Westport, Conn.: Greenwood Press, 1994. A generous compilation of reviews and general studies, with a comprehensive introduction, chronology, and bibliography.

Nolan, William F. *Hammett: A Life at the Edge*. New York: Congdon & Weed, 1983. Author of the first full-length study of Hammett in 1969, Nolan here builds upon his earlier work and that of others to present a convincing portrait of a singularly private man with a code of honor that paralleled those of his detectives. The discussions of the works are straightforward and sound.

Orr, Stanley. "The Continental Operations of Dashiell Hammett." In *Darkly Perfect World: Colonial Adventure, Postmodernism, and American Noir*. Columbus: Ohio State University Press, 2010. Traces the development of American crime fiction and film in the twentieth century. Orr argues that the noir detective stories of Hammett and Raymond Chandler derive from late Victorian colonial adventure stories by such writers as Joseph Conrad.

Panek, LeRoy Lad. *Reading Early Hammett: A Critical Study of the Fiction Prior to the "Maltese Falcon."* Jefferson, N.C.: McFarland & Company, 2004. An absorbing analysis of Hammett's earliest work, including his magazine fiction and the last Continental Op stories. The final chapter provides afterthoughts on Hammett's career, style, and place in the history of detective fiction. Includes a chronology of works cited, a bibliography, and an index.

Skenazy, Paul. "The 'Heart's Field': Dashiell Hammett's Anonymous Territory." In *San Francisco in Fiction: Essays in a Regional Literature*, edited by David Fine and Paul Skenazy. Albuquerque: University of New Mexico Press, 1995. A consideration of the importance of history and place in Hammett's fiction. Argues that it is wrong to associate Hammett's concern with expedience, environment, habit, training, and chance with a specifically Wild West tradition.

Symons, Julian. *Dashiell Hammett*. San Diego: Harcourt Brace Jovanovich, 1985. A brief but substantive book by a leading English writer of crime fiction and criticism. Symons believes that Hammett created "A specifically American brand of crime story . . . that transcends the form and limits of [its] genre and can be compared with the best fiction produced in America between the two world wars." His considerations of the works support this judgment. Contains a useful select bibliography.

Van Dover, J. Kenneth. *Making the Detective Story American: Biggers, Van Dine, and Hammett and the Turning Point of the Genre, 1925-1930*. Jefferson, N.C.: McFarland, 2010. A critical analysis of the work of Hammett, Earl Derr Biggers, and S. S. Van Dine, demonstrating how these writers created a new type of detective story in the mid- and late 1920's. Includes appendixes with brief biographies of the three writers, a list of mystery and detective best sellers from 1925 to 1935, and a list of films based on the three writers' works.

Wheat, Edward M. "The Post-Modern Detective: The Aesthetic Politics of Dashiell Hammett's Continental Op." *The Midwest Quarterly* 36 (Spring, 1995): 237-249. Examines the meaning of the postmodern era through the character and world of the hard-boiled detective. Claims that Hammett's Continental Op is a postmodernist who does not find truth and justice but produces a fictive account.

Wolfe, Peter. *Beams Falling: The Art of Dashiell Hammett*. Bowling Green, Ohio: Bowling Green University Popular Press, 1980. Wolfe is especially good in his analyses of Hammett's short fiction, and he surpasses other writers in showing the relationship of each work to Hammett's total output. Wolfe is the author of books on other crime-fiction writers (Raymond Chandler, John le Carré, and Ross Macdonald), and his knowledge and appreciation of the genre are apparent in this excellent study.

Robert W. Millett
Updated by Gerald H. Strauss

BARRY HANNAH

Born: Meridian, Mississippi; April 23, 1942
Died: Oxford, Mississippi; March 1, 2010

PRINCIPAL SHORT FICTION
Airships, 1978
Captain Maximus, 1985
Bats Out of Hell, 1993
High Lonesome, 1996
Long, Last, Happy: New and Selected Stories, 2010

OTHER LITERARY FORMS

Although perhaps a better short-story writer, Barry Hannah was primarily known for his novels, including *Geronimo Rex* (1972), a finalist for the National Book Award; his short novel *Ray* (1980), which was also nominated; *The Tennis Handsome* in 1983; the somewhat autobiographical *Boomerang* (1989); and the darkly comic *Yonder Stands Your Orphan* (2001).

ACHIEVEMENTS

Barry Hannah received the Arnold Gingrich Award for short fiction from *Esquire* (1978), the Henry H. Bellaman Foundation Award in Fiction (1970), the Bread Loaf Fellowship (1971), the William Faulkner

Foundation Prize (1972), and an award in literature from American Academy of Arts and Letters (1979). He has also received a John Simon Guggenheim Memorial Foundation Fellowship, a Mississippi Governor's Award in the Arts, and a Mississippi Institute of Arts and Letters Award. His novel *Geronimo Rex* was a finalist for the National Book Award.

BIOGRAPHY

Born and raised in Mississippi, Barry Hannah graduated from Mississippi College in 1964 and later returned to earn an M.A. and an M.F.A. from that college. In 1966, he began teaching creative writing at Clemson University in South Carolina, where he remained until 1973. It was during this period that he also published his first two novels, establishing himself as a writer of note. Although he did not serve in the Vietnam War, Hannah's most formative influence was that conflict, which was brought home to him by the tales of returning veterans and also by its strong impact on American society. His stories bear witness to the fact that he was of the Vietnam generation and also point to his general interest in war and in military history. For several years he taught at many colleges, including one year at Middlebury and five at the University of Alabama.

In 1980, Hannah moved to Hollywood to write screenplays for director Robert Altman, an interlude that allowed him to overcome a chronic problem with alcohol. After stints at various universities, Hannah settled down as a writer-in-residence at the University of Mississippi, in Oxford, Mississippi, where he lived with his fourth wife, Susan. Hannah died of a heart attack at age sixty-seven, on March 1, 2010, at his home in Oxford.

ANALYSIS

Barry Hannah was among the most prominent southern writers of the post-World War II period and was widely praised for producing some of the finest fiction about the South since the work of William Faulkner. Characterized by a surrealistic style and surprising narrative twists, his stories often depict violent and sexual situations that oscillate between the bleak and the hilarious.

Hannah was especially interested in depicting a generation of southern men scarred by the Vietnam War, a conflict that repeated the Civil War's pattern of loss and defeat but which also was the harbinger of both a crisis in masculinity and a general social unraveling. His largely male characters consistently suffer from physical or emotional pain and cannot escape the destructive patterns in which they find themselves and for which they are, in part, responsible. These stories of disintegration and fragmentation are seen as representative of the difficulties of life in a post-Vietnam America. However, Hannah's jazzy, meandering style and his absurdist sense of humor add rich dimensions of comedy and tragedy that cannot be communicated by simply delineating his narratives, which often consist of a series of chaotic subplots and digressions.

Hannah's distinctive style, which strikes the reader as both manic and depressive, is perfectly suited to the inner lives of his characters, whose emotional weather ranges from a sense of absurd comedy to feelings of anxiety that leave them on the brink of suicide and despair. His capacity to write associatively, as if his stories are as much dreams as histories, also allowed him to develop a unique stream-of-consciousness approach to narrative that is faithful to the strange and intense inner world of his male characters. Notable also are his arresting story titles, which often sum up the themes of his stories.

AIRSHIPS

This first collection by Hannah established both his major themes and his unique style. The theme of war is prominent: "Testimony of Pilot" not only explores the deranging effects of the Vietnam War on a former combatant but also shows the demoralizing impact of the war on those who watched from the sidelines. "Midnight and I'm Not Famous Yet" tells of a pair of Mississippi acquaintances, a soldier and filmmaker, who reunite during the Vietnam War; the two talk about their worship of a professional athlete, somehow juxtaposing both the beauty of athletic prowess and the absurdity of athletic culture with the debacle inherent in the reality of war. War--in this case, the Civil War--also serves as the focus of "Knowing He Was Not My Kind Yet I Followed," about famed Confederate General Jeb

Stuart, who figures centrally in four of the twenty stories in this collection as both hero and fool. Hannah manages to subvert and challenge the cult of the Lost Cause while at the same time understanding its allure to some southerners.

Set in contemporary times, "Love Too Long" and "Constant Pain in Tuscaloosa" depict deserted husbands who cannot let go of their former wives. "Coming Close to Donna" is about a woman whose obsessive sexuality leads to murderous behavior on the part of the men in her life, and "Our Secret Home" is about a man who is obsessed sexually with his mentally impaired sister. One of Hannah's most famous stories, "Water Liars," shows a group of fishermen who enjoy swapping tall tales but who are affronted by a man who makes the mistake of telling the truth about his sexual fears.

The feeling that life is inherently random and disordered is yet another important theme in Hannah's work, which he explores in the domestic vignette "Deaf and Dumb" and in the surreal stories "Green Gets It," "Quo Vadis, Smut?," and "Mother Rooney Unscrolls the Hurt." The latter three stories are vivid

Barry Hannah (Hulton Archive/Getty Images)

stream-of-consciousness stories that attempt to sum up the meaning of lives that seem to be continually in the process of disintegration.

CAPTAIN MAXIMUS

This second collection consists of seven stories, concluding with a long story set in Seattle concerning women employed by an electric power company, a story Hannah originally developed as a film treatment for Robert Altman. The first seven stories draw on material from Hannah's life, including drunken brawls, plane crashes, and relationships with writer friends. Many of the stories also feature what Hannah called "interesting monsters," larger-than-life characters such as war heroes, sports figures, musicians, and writers. The most notable of these is Ned Maximus, who gives this collection its name. Maximus, a one-eyed man with second sight, which allows him to see the dark truths those around him deny, gains no consolation from his gift. He sees in America a wasteland society in which he, too, is a lost soul. His story is summed up by its title, "Ride, Fly, Penetrate, Loiter," which describes a life with no overarching point to it.

Other stories, such as "I Am Shaking to Death," "It Spoke Exactly the Things," and "Getting Ready," also use a series of disjunctive images to depict love stories gone mysteriously wrong. The difficulties of being a man in an unraveling society are also explored in "Even Greenland" and "Jet," which are devoted to masculine role models whose achievements may in fact be dubious. In "Even Greenland," an admired pilot deliberately kills himself in a plane crash; in "Fans," a masochistic man is tortured by the football star he worships. A more positive story, "Idaho," is a montage of reflections on guns, drinking, suicide, male bonding, and the saving influence of writing.

BATS OUT OF HELL

This collection returns to the theme of war so prominent in *Airships*. In the title story, "Bats Out of Hell Division," the Civil War is the occasion for a meditation on war that moves between reality and the surreal nature of dreams. In "Upstairs, Mona Bayed for Dong," the Persian Gulf War serves as a background for meditations on life and death, while "That Was

Close, Ma" is set against the backdrop of Operation Desert Storm. In "Hey, Have You Got a Cig, the Time, the News, My Face?" a veteran of the Vietnam War is overwhelmed by emotional pain.

"High Water Railers" returns the reader to the world of "Water Liars" and to men who are ashamed of their failure to live up to what they understand are infuriating cultural myths about masculinity and whose only recourse is to lie. Other stories deal with bizarre personality changes: "Two Things, Dimly, Were Going at Each Other" is about a disease called "the grofft," which turns men into dogs, and in "Nicodemus Bluff" a boy's father undergoes a strange personality change during a hunting trip.

High Lonesome

This collection is characterized by improbable plots and wildly inventive language. The first story, "Get Some Young," is also typical of Hannah in its gothic approach to sexuality--a middle-aged couple's refusal to accept growing old ends in their corruption of a beautiful young boy. In the title story, "Uncle High Lonesome," a man reflects on the reasons for his special kinship with his alcoholic uncle, Peter, who suffers lifelong guilt after murdering a man during a poker game. This memory has been passed on to his nephew and to his nephew's nephew, so that each is connected in a dreamlike generational tragedy involving violence and alcohol. His nephew eventually realizes that his uncle was unable to overcome the "high lonesomes"--that is, a sense of overwhelming depression. This theme of the "high lonesomes" surfaces in other stories as well. Sometimes, as in "Repulsed," the experience of the "high lonesomes" ends in redemptive acts of generosity, whereas in other stories the outcome is simply diminishment.

Another feature of this collection is the use of biblical language and a strong religious subtext. Christlike figures or references can be found in "Through Sunset into the Racoon Night," "The Agony of T. Bandini," and "Drummer Down." In "A Creature in the Bay of St. Louis," a young boy is pulled under water, where he has a death-and-resurrection experience.

Long, Last, Happy

Long, Last, Happy was published posthumously and collects one early story and four later stories for the

first time. "Trek," originally published in the Mississippi College student magazine *The Arrowhead*, tells of an epic quest for a destination that is eventually revealed to be a football stadium and shows that Hannah's trademark humor has been well in place since his early days as a writer. The four later stories published in the collection, "Fire Water," "Sick Soldier at Your Door," "Lastward, Deputy James," and "Rangoon Green," are intertwined tightly in terms of both plot and theme, and it may be that at least some of them would have been used in a novel or a collection of connected stories. Each of the later stories deals, either overtly or obliquely, with a church burning. These stories use the act as a repudiation of the heritage of hate and bigotry made emblematic by the church burnings that occurred during the civil rights struggles of the 1950's and 1960's. However, in "Lastward, Deputy James" and "Sick Solider at Your Door," the churches burned have white congregations, and the act of arson is a form of cultural revenge. Hannah makes his partial debt to a fellow Mississippi writer clear in "Sick Soldier at Your Door" when Hannah's narrator announces himself as Anse Burden, recalling Faulkner's "Anse Bundren" from *As I Lay Dying* (1930) and the Burdens from *Light in August* (1932). As in Faulkner's work, Hannah's stories reveal the heavy chains imposed on southerners by the past. In the later stories, each of the central characters is unable to turn the particular page in life needed to let go of the past and embrace the future. Still poetic, still comic, still seemingly composed almost from random events, these stories show that Hannah's skills were not abated, and that his early demise (at the age of sixty-seven) deprived literature of one of its great short-story writers.

Other major works

LONG FICTION: *Geronimo Rex*, 1972; *Nightwatchmen*, 1973; *Ray*, 1980; *The Tennis Handsome*, 1983; *Hey Jack!*, 1987; *Boomerang*, 1989; *Never Die*, 1991; *Yonder Stands Your Orphan*, 2001.

Bibliography

Charney, Mark J. *Barry Hannah*. New York: Twayne, 1992. First full-length study of Hannah and an indispensable guide to all his fiction, including the short stories collected in *Airships* and *Captain Maximus*. Makes a case for Hannah as one of the South's freshest and most iconoclastic writers. Features a thorough discussion of *Airships*, which he sees as reflecting a vision of the South as a microcosm of human existence. Also discusses *Captain Maximus* in the light of its preoccupation with violence. Includes an annotated bibliography.

Guinn, Matthew. *After Southern Modernism: Fiction of the Contemporary South.* Jackson: University Press of Mississippi, 2000. Guinn's chapter on Hannah focuses on Hannah's deconstruction of the myths of the southern past; he particularly shows how Hannah's Civil War stories challenge the old assumptions.

Hannah, Barry. "The Spirits Will Win Through: An Interview with Barry Hannah." Interview by R. Vanarsall. *Southern Review* (Spring, 1983): 314-341. A long, thoughtful interview, which connects Hannah's life with the material in his stories. Discusses his alcoholism, his fascination with violence, his work in California as a screenwriter, the influence of other authors, his love of the English language, and his feelings of kinship with rock guitarist Jimi Hendrix.

McHaney, Pearl Amelia. "An Interview with Barry Hannah." *Five Points* 6, no. 3 (August, 2002): 55-66. An insightful interview that queries Hannah on the relationship between his short fiction and novels and the poetic nature of his style.

Shepherd, Allen. "Outrage and Speculation: Barry Hannah's *Airships*." *Notes on Mississippi Writers* (1982): 63-73. Important analysis of many of the stories and major themes in *Airships*. Notes Hannah's ability to render psychologically impaired narrators convincingly, as well as his gift for dialogue and poetic symbolism.

Weston, Ruth D. *Barry Hannah, Postmodern Romantic*. Baton Rouge: Louisiana State University Press, 1998. Important full-length study discusses Hannah's postmodern style and his ability to express hard truths about the conditions of contemporary life. Provides a serious analysis of all of Hannah's work, including his short-story collections. This critique is also notable for its skillful use of current short-story theories to explicate Hannah's work, especially with regard to the idea of "debunking." It is also especially good at discerning the wild, irreverent, "carnivalesque" aspects of Hannah's work and at examining the theme of "the lie" in much of Hannah's work. It correctly identifies a strong religious subtext and sees Hannah as examining the social, cultural, and religious betrayals of the American Dream, especially in terms of defective myths about male prowess. Includes a bibliography.

Wyatt, David. *Out of the Sixties: Storytelling and the Vietnam Generation*. New York: Cambridge University Press, 1993. Analysis of Hannah as a member of a literary generation defined by the Vietnam War, which was experienced as a shared ordeal. Also notes the ways in which Hannah creates parallels between the Vietnam War and the Civil War as unfinished wars in which honor turned to shame, with various issues and emotional wounds remaining unresolved.

Margaret Boe Birns
Updated by Scott D. Yarbrough

RON HANSEN

Born: Omaha, Nebraska; December 8, 1947

PRINCIPAL SHORT FICTION

Nebraska, 1989

OTHER LITERARY FORMS

Ron Hansen is known primarily for his novels: *Desperadoes* (1979), *The Assassination of Jesse James by the Coward Robert Ford* (1983), *Mariette in Ecstasy* (1991), *Atticus* (1996), *Hitler's Niece* (1999), *Isn't It Romantic: An Entertainment* (2003), and *Exiles* (2008). He also has published a book of essays, *A Stay Against Confusion: Essays on Faith and Fiction* (2001), as well as *The Shadowmaker* (1986), a children's book. He also has written a screenplay and a teleplay. Some of his short stories have appeared in anthologies.

In his early works, Hansen adopted the Western as his preferred form, giving to this subgenre a depth and seriousness both spiritual and philosophical. He was at first mildly praised by critics but slowly gained a reputation as a writer of maturity and distinction.

In his later fiction, Hansen moved to novels that explore the nature of religious faith and its impact on life choices. *Mariette in Ecstasy* centers on a young woman who enters a cloistered convent and receives visions of Jesus and the marks of Jesus's crucifixion on her own body. It is not determined whether the young novice is deluded, hysterical, or has indeed been visited by Jesus in this manner. *Exiles* explores the inner life of the poet Gerard Manley Hopkins, showing the poet as a Jesuit novice, reclusive and lonely, deeply moved by a tragedy that claimed the lives of five German nuns on their way to America. This incident became the stimulus and inspiration for "The Wreck of the Deutschland," one of Hopkins's most famous poems.

ACHIEVEMENTS

Ron Hansen's amazing versatility has earned him wide repute. His early Westerns, *Desperadoes*, *Atticus*, and *The Assassination of Jesse James by the Coward Robert Ford*, were praised for crossing from that narrow genre, sometimes considered close to pulp fiction, into serious literature. Critics noted in particular his character development and the beauty of his language. Hansen's later works, particularly *Mariette in Ecstasy* and *Exiles*, transcend what is sometimes called "Catholic" fiction and move into the wider and richer realm of religious speculation. In both novels, the reader is asked to ponder the cost of faith and the ultimate inaccessibility of the religious experience of another person.

Hansen has received a number of significant honors, among them a Guggenheim Foundation Grant, an Award in Literature from the American Academy and National Institute of Arts and Letters, a Lyndhurst Foundation Fellowship, and grants from the National Endowment for the Arts. *Atticus* was a finalist for both a National Book Award and a PEN/Faulkner Award. *Hitler's Niece* was a Literary Guild Alternate for 2001.

BIOGRAPHY

Ron Hansen was educated by Jesuits at Creighton Preparatory School and Creighton University in Omaha, where he received his bachelor's degree in 1970. He then served two years in the Army during the Vietnam War. After his military service, Hansen earned a master of fine arts degree from the Iowa Writers' Workshop. He began writing, selecting the Western as his genre, and publishing *Desperadoes*, his first novel, in 1979.

Later Hansen earned a master's degree in spirituality from Santa Clara University. These educational experiences have deeply influenced his writing; at Iowa, for instance, he had John Irving and John Cheever as teachers. Hansen's fiction is permeated with his reflections on his faith. He explores the relationship between spirituality and writing in his book, *A Stay Against Confusion: Essays on Faith and Fiction*, published in 2001. A Roman Catholic, Hansen was ordained a permanent deacon in the Catholic Church in 2007 and was inducted into the college of fellows at Dominican School of Philosophy and Theology in 2009.

Hansen has earned fellowships from the Michigan Society of Fellows, the National Endowment for the Arts, the John Simon Guggenheim Foundation, and the Lyndhurst Foundation. *The New York Times* included *The Shadowmaker* in the "Books for Vacation Reading" and named it as an outstanding children's book of 1987.

Hansen became the Gerard Manley Hopkins Professor in the Arts and Humanities at Santa Clara University, where he has taught literature and writing. He is married to the writer Bo Caldwell.

ANALYSIS

Although Ron Hansen has published short stories in a variety of literary magazines, *Nebraska* is his only collection; the stories in that volume were published earlier in various respected literary journals. The short stories richly display Hansen's versatility. It is fair to say that no one story prepares the reader for any of the others; each stands alone. Unlike in some collections of short stories, where there is thematic or character progression, *Nebraska* offers eleven stories distinct in setting, tone, character development, moral tone, and language.

There is, however, a unifying theme; it is place, the place of the West, which informs several of Hansen's novels. Place, *Nebraska*, is named in the title of the collection; it is significant, however, that the title story is the last of the eleven. Hansen's stories also share an approach to language that is crafted with absolute precision. Whether he is catching the rhythms of ordinary speech, slang, banality, lyric description, or fast-paced narrative, Hansen's sentences are worthy of a slow, even meditative, read.

The language of Hansen's stories plays with ambiguity; the prose is both wonderfully detailed and simultaneously cryptic. "Wickedness," the first story, begins almost romantically, with a girl from Delaware on a

Ron Hansen (AP Photo/Jim Rogash)

train, heading to her first job as a country schoolteacher. She is reading, ironically and prophetically, *Quo vadis* (1895-1896; *Quo Vadis: A Narrative of the Time of Nero*, 1896). With her the reader is jolted into the great blizzard of 1888. Weather in Nebraska, she is told, could be wicked. The story then details the horrors of the storm, its havoc, its unrelenting fierceness, the speed with which its claims its victims. The ending of the story leaves the reader wondering whether wickedness is natural or moral, deliberate or coincidental.

Nebraska, the state and the place, becomes a metaphor for human nature itself; these events are taking place in Nebraska, the writer suggests, but they take place all over the world and in every time: Women and men dream, plot, experience defeat and death, find love only to let it go, and are fearful of the world around them and of their own inner worlds. In both nineteenth and twentieth century settings the characters in Hansen's stories pass through emotional states, sometimes aware of what is happening but more often unaware, simply moving through an experience without reflecting on it. It is the reader who must reflect.

Hansen's religious sensibilities weave through the stories in *Nebraska*. They are subtle, never center stage. Characters pray, attend mass, believe in the afterlife and in God's providence; they also betray one another, kill, come close to despair. The moral threads are strong. Through all of the stories is a sense of divine care and of sympathy, even for the least appealing characters.

"PLAYLAND"

Set in post-World War I years, this story describes an amusement park built in honor of and for the use of returning veterans. Hansen's account of the building of the park mirrors the admiration the country felt at the end of the war and the national desire to produce something worthy of the sacrifice made by the soldiers. The result is a lavish amusement park, a totally otherworldly American Versailles, adorned, decorated, transformed from unused stables, cow barns, and cornfields into a Utopia destined to become America's Playland. The descriptive details are minute and exhaustive; the tone is wonderfully tongue in cheek. Scantily dressed young women compete for the title of Miss Playland, and more than two million people visit the site each summer.

Into this unreal world Hansen introduces three people: Gordon, a returned corporal with a limp; Bijou, his girlfriend; and Frankie, described as Bijou's cousin. Amid the wonders and glories of Playland, Hansen sketches out a banal flirtation: Bijou primarily concerned with herself and her appearance and what she can gain from her two admirers, Frankie playing a game to amuse himself, and Gordon threatened by Frankie. Bijou's last words to Gordon, telling him to pretend that Frankie is not there, sum up the story as well; it is a story about pretense, about play that becomes painful and futile. Bijou, like Playland itself, is an artificial jewel.

"THE KILLERS"

Following "Playland," "The Killers" makes an abrupt shift from the unreal but sordid to the real and sordid. Once again the cast of characters is spare: Max, the old hit man; Rex, his successor; Ron, the manager; and the narrator, Rex's girlfriend. The story moves between 1926, when Max became the chief hit man, to 1960, when he knows Rex will eliminate him as he eliminated others and instead turns his gun on himself. The reader knows, of course, that there will be another Rex, another Max. Killers come and go, ordering meat loaf, pie, and fried eggs at the local diner and allowing one another to use the restroom before taking them out so that no one will be embarrassed. It is a job.

It is a tribute to Hansen's artistry that the reader is both engaged and sympathetic: This is, after all, life; someone has to do it. No one stays on top forever. The killers, unlike the veterans, have no Playland. They advise one another to see a doctor about a bad cough, discuss guns, and eventually replace one another. The narrator-girlfriend brushes her hair.

"RED-LETTER DAYS"

This brief, poignant story is a series of five months of journal entries made by an elderly man whose life is ordinary and whose appreciation of life is insightful. The writer, Cecil, cares for his wife Etta, his friends, and his regular game of golf. In between he repairs and refurbishes golf clubs and other golf equipment, attends funerals of friends, talks golf with friends, and attends mass at the Catholic Church. During a golf game, he experiences a private but amazing epiphany, reminiscent of those found in the short stories of James Joyce: Suddenly he experiences himself as everywhere he has ever been, on golf courses around the world, with his wife and his good friends. Ordinary days, Hansen suggests, can be red-letter days, even if they have little significance to anyone else. The story ends on the narrator's hope to play nine holes the following day. Hope, like the faith that brings the friends together at funerals, need not be attention-grabbing; it is enough that it sustains. "Red-Letter Days" is perhaps the most tender of the stories in *Nebraska*, partly because of the ordinariness of both the narrator and the golf he loves so much, partly because of the affection the narrator displays for his wife, and partly because, although the story makes several references to friends who have died, both the narrator and his wife are still relatively healthy at the end of the story. It is one of Hansen's few stories in which a character is devout and reflective.

"NEBRASKA"

The title story is the last one in the collection. It might better be described as a tone poem, a musical composition in which Nebraska is the central theme.

The narrative sweeps through, around, up, and down, stopping in October, in January, along the railroad tracks, in kitchens and diners. The cultural mix-- Swedish, Danish, German, Polish--is echoed in the names of the towns. Any town is the quintessential town, with a main street, pickup trucks parked outside the diner, the grocery store, the tavern, the hardware store, two churches--one Protestant, one Catholic.

The story begs to be read aloud, not because of plot- -there is none, there needs to be none--but because of the images and the sounds. The story celebrates the ordinary, grounded in this place, Nebraska. Not for nothing is this place called the heartland. Hansen writes with heart and with an ear so finely tuned to the tiny bits of speech that the reader hears them as well. What could be mundane is transformed into the speech of a people. To call Hansen an American writer is not simply to say that he was born in this country; it is to say that somehow, in these stories and in his other works, he has absorbed America, its rhythms and longings, its sordid parts and its beauty.

OTHER MAJOR WORKS

LONG FICTION: *Desperadoes*, 1979; *The Assassination of Jesse James by the Coward Robert Ford*, 1983; *Mariette in Ecstasy*, 1991; *Atticus*, 1996; *Hitler's Niece*, 1999; *Isn't It Romantic: An Entertainment*, 2003; *Exiles*, 2008.

SCREENPLAY: *Mariette in Ecstasy*, 1996 (adaptation of his novel).

TELEPLAY: *Blue Movie*, 1987.

NONFICTION: *A Stay Against Confusion: Essays on Faith and Fiction*, 2001.

CHILDREN'S LITERATURE: *The Shadowmaker*, 1986.

BIBLIOGRAPHY

Kakutani, Michiko. "Stories That Call an Evil by Its Name." *The New York Times*, February 7, 1989. Thorough review of *Nebraska*, noting Hansen's "meticulous control of his prose."

Poythress, Katherine. "A Conversation with Author Ron Hansen." *The Collegian* (March 13, 2008). Interview with Hansen in which he gives advice to aspiring writers, how being in the Army affected his writing, and in which genre his work fits.

Zenowich, Christopher. "Watchers in an Unquiet Country." *Los Angeles Times*, February 12, 1989. Review of *Nebraska* salutes Hansen's "keen ear for authenticity."

Katherine Hanley

JOY HARJO

Born: Tulsa, Oklahoma; May 9, 1951
Also known as: Joy Foster

PRINCIPAL SHORT FICTION

"Boston," 1991
"Northern Lights," 1991
"The Flood," 1991
"The Woman Who Fell from the Sky," 1996
"Warrior Road," 1997
A Map to the Next World: Poetry and Tales, 2000

OTHER LITERARY FORMS

Joy Harjo is best known as a poet, but some of her work in this form can best be described as prose poetry, so the difference between the two genres tends to blur in her books. In both the poetry and the prose, Harjo frequently uses Native American spiritual myths and symbols and southwestern settings (Oklahoma and New Mexico). She has also edited (with Gloria Bird) *Reinventing the Enemy's Language: Contemporary Native Women's Writing of North America* (1997). Harjo is also the author of two children's books, *The Good Luck Cat* (2000) and *For a Girl Becoming* (2009).

ACHIEVEMENTS

Joy Harjo's two poetry collections published in the 1990's--*In Mad Love and War* (1990) and *The Woman Who Fell from the Sky* (1994)--won numerous awards. Harjo was a National Endowment for the Arts fellow in 1978 and an Arizona Commission on the Arts Creative Writing fellow in 1989, and she won an American Indian Distinguished Achievement Award in 1990. Through her several volumes of poetry, Harjo has become one of the leading Native American poetic voices; in 1995, she received the Lifetime Achievement Award from the Native Writers' Circle of the

Americas. *For a Girl Becoming* received the 2010 Moonbeam Children's Book Award; in addition, Harjo won the Native American Music Award for Best Female Artist in 2010.

BIOGRAPHY

Joy Harjo was born and raised in Tulsa, Oklahoma, where she lived until she was sixteen, and she has been strongly influenced by her Muskogee Creek heritage. She received her B.A. in 1976 from the University of New Mexico and an M.F.A. in creative writing from the University of Iowa two years later. She has been an instructor of poetry at several schools, including the University of New Mexico, Albuquerque. In addition to her other writing efforts, Harjo is a painter, a musician (she plays the saxophone) who has produced several records with her band, "Joy Harjo and Poetic Justice," and a screenwriter. She has lectured widely on poetry and the arts and has been active in Native American affairs, particularly in cultural organizations. She had two children, Phil and Rainy Dawn.

ANALYSIS

As a writer often working in poetry, Joy Harjo's language tends to be highly charged and full of images (such as "the blue bowl of the sky") and visions. Her writing is also often strongly spiritual, encompassing, as it does, a number of Native American myths and a distinctive Native American viewpoint. Harjo also writes of social issues, particularly the plight of Native Americans in the United States, both historically and in the present, and especially (but not exclusively) the condition of the Native American woman. C. B. Clark has accurately described the scope of Harjo's work, saying that she "recalls the wounds of the past, the agony of the Indian present, and dream visions of a better future for indigenous peoples." Her prose work is generally short (three to five pages), it often mingles realistic and mythic modes, and it is strongly autobiographical.

"THE FLOOD"

"The Flood" is representative of the shape of much of Harjo's prose writing--short and yet deeply visionary. This first-person, three-page narrative alternates between a contemporary, realistic mode (cars, a six-pack, and a convenience store) and deeper elements (a mythical water monster and centuries of legend and history). At the heart of the story is the image of a sixteen-year-old woman walking into a lake to marry a mythic Indian water god. However, the narrative is hardly linear, and the girl is simultaneously a tribal daughter carrying her sister to the lake to draw water in the distant past, a contemporary young woman driving a car into the lake, and a third woman watching the girl walk out of the lake twenty years later. Which is she? All of them, in a mixture of the poles of the narrative method used here, which employs memory and imagination. The fiction is heavily multilayered: Myth infuses history with meaning, and there is no objective retelling of the story that can adequately capture truth without undue reduction or simplification. The story is less a fiction than a vision--including the rain at the end "that would flood the world." Readers of "The Flood" may be reminded of another Native American fictionist, the Chippewa writer Louise Erdrich, whose short story "Fleur," for example, also concerns a young Indian girl meeting a water monster in a lake.

"NORTHERN LIGHTS"

Like "The Flood," "Northern Lights" was first collected in 1991 in *Talking Leaves: Contemporary Native American Stories*, edited by Craig Lesley. While it is also in the first person, "the story doesn't belong to me," the narrator concludes, "but to Whirling Soldier who gifted me with it in the circle of hope." The narrator meets Whirling Soldier at a winter dance. He has returned from duty in Vietnam with many scars, most of them mental. His story is also the history of three generations of an alcoholic family (including his father and his daughter). There is no easy answer here as to how Whirling Soldier is saved, but at the conclusion of the story, there is a kind of redemption for all of the characters:

After the dance, we all ran out onto the ice to see the northern lights. They were shimmering relatives returned from the war, dancing in the skies all around us. It was an unusual moment of grace for fools.

Like the work of Native American writers Leslie Marmon Silko (*Ceremony*, 1977) and James Welch (*Winter in the Blood*, 1974), this story of a soldier returning from war is an opportunity for the writer to raise a number of other important Native American issues. As in her other stories, Harjo here writes like a poet ("He snuffed his confusion between honor and honor with wine, became an acrobat of pain in the Indian bars of Kansas").

"BOSTON"

This short story varies from the usual Harjo pattern in its taking place outside the southwestern setting of most of her other fiction, and yet even here the view of the world is Native American, for Boston is perceived as sitting at the edge of the Atlantic, where the horizon divides "the Upperworld and the Underworld," and is infused with myth. Once again the story is short (fewer than one thousand words), told in the first person, and strongly autobiographical (the narrator's first name is "Joy"). "Boston" centers on the narrator's father, who once "found himself" in that city, probably because of a woman. Why did he find himself so far away, she wonders, "ten thousand myths away from Oklahoma"? That speculation leads her to the creation story of the "the first Muskogee rising from the mists of the east" and to other myths, like that of the water monster; ultimately, her thoughts about what might have taken her father from Oklahoma to Boston lead her back to the history and legends of Oklahoma. "At nearly forty," the Harjo persona confesses, "I am thinking of the traps we construct to absent memory." Her father died in 1983 in an aging trailer. The story of her father is thus, like the Muskogee creation story itself, about water, "as if you must wind back through all memory, all history, the water monster the ongoing companion to the left of you." The story of her father has become her own story, the story of her people, and the story of the continuing power of Muskogee myth. Fiction for Harjo cannot leave out history and myth, for all exist on similar planes simultaneously and constantly infuse each other in her writing.

"The Woman Who Fell from the Sky"

This short work is the title piece from Harjo's 1996 prize-winning poetry collection and may be the best example of the ways in which her poetry bleeds into prose, and vice versa. The central image is taken from an old Iroquois female creation myth, but in the Harjo version "that force operates within the dreadful confines of modern urban life," as Paula Gunn Allen notes in the introduction to the story collected in her *Song of the Turtle: American Indian Literature, 1974-1994* (1996). "Once a woman fell from the sky," the story begins, and the reader immediately enters a world where myth and reality coincide. On one plane exists much of the ugliness of modern urban life, like poverty and alcoholism, especially as experienced by Native Americans. The Safeway store parking lot, where Johnny ("Saint Coincidence") witnesses the woman falling from the sky, is also a place of transcendent love and mystery. For Lila, the woman who falls, has also lived in the sky as a star, and her descent into Johnny's arms with her children is the beginning of hope. As the nameless narrator concludes the coda to the story, "*I understood love to be the very gravity holding each leaf, each cell, this earthy star together.*" Native American myth becomes the start of the search for a solution to contemporary Native American problems.

"Warrior Road"

"Warrior Road" is included in *Reinventing the Enemy's Language: Contemporary Native Woman's Writings of North America*, the volume Harjo edited in 1997 with Gloria Bird. It is longer than her other stories and less obviously mythic than her earlier work, but it is linked to other prose pieces in being strongly autobiographical and poetic. The story concerns the birth of Harjo's two children, but she uses these events to talk about the treatment of Native Americans in the United States--and particularly by a medical "system in which the wisdom that had carried my people from generation to generation was ignored." Her son was born when Harjo was seventeen, her daughter four years later. When, at age sixteen, Harjo's daughter bore a daughter herself, the narrator realizes "something *had* changed," and Krista Rae is born into a larger and more loving family. Conditions for Native Americans had improved, as Harjo's own life story demonstrates. Four

days later, she took her grandchild "to the saguaro forest before dawn and gave her the name I had dreamed for her. . . . A female ancestor approaches on a horse. We are all together."

Toward the end of this account, Harjo writes that her work

> has to do with reclaiming the memory stolen from our peoples when we were dispossessed from our lands east of the Mississippi; it has to do with restoring us.

"Warrior Road," which is less fictional and more autobiographical than many of Harjo's stories, is still doing that work and in a language that has Harjo's distinctive poetic stamp.

Other major works

SCREENPLAY: *Origin of Apache Crown Dance*, 1985.

POETRY: *The Last Song*, 1975; *What Moon Drove Me to This?*, 1980; *She Had Some Horses*, 1983; *Secrets from the Center of the World*, 1989; *In Mad Love and War*, 1990; *The Woman Who Fell from the Sky*, 1996; *How We Became Human: New and Selected Poems, 1975-2001*, 2002.

NONFICTION: *The Spiral of Memories: Interviews*, 1996 (Laura Coltelli, editor).

CHILDREN'S LITERATURE: *The Good Luck Cat*, 2000; *For a Girl Becoming*, 2009 (Mercedes McDonald, illustrator).

EDITED TEXT: *Reinventing the Enemy's Language: Contemporary Native Women's Writing of North America*, 1997 (with Gloria Bird).

Bibliography

Clark, C. B. "Joy Harjo (Creek)." In *The Heath Anthology of American Literature*, edited by Paul Lauter et al. Vol. 2. Boston: Houghton Mifflin, 1998. Clark's brief introduction to selections of Harjo's poetry (including the prose poem "Deer Dancer") in this anthology delineates several of the most important qualities of her writing.

Coltelli, Laura, ed. *The Spiral of Memory: Interviews, Joy Harjo*. Ann Arbor: University of Michigan Press, 1996. These interviews with Harjo offer insights into her method of working, as well as the continuing concerns of her writing.

Donovan, Kathleen. *Feminist Readings of Native American Literature*. Tucson: University of Arizona Press, 1998. Donovan's last chapter, "Dark Continent/Dark Woman," is a consideration of Harjo in company with the French literary critic Helene Cixous. Both writers "struggle to reconcile their sense of multiple identities that arise from the displacements of history and family background," Donovan argues, and "by embracing their multiple identities and places of origin, they transform and create, thereby gaining a measured healing that permits them to 'more than survive.'"

Dunaway, David King, and Sara L. Spurgeon, eds. *Writing the Southwest*. Rev. ed. Albuquerque: University of New Mexico Press, 2003. The chapter on Harjo provides a biography, overview of her literary career, analyses of her works, and an interview with Harjo herself.

Monroe, Jonathan. "Untranslatable Communities, Productive Translation, and Public Transport: Rosmarie Waldrop's *A Key into the Language of America* and Joy Harjo's *The Woman Who Fell from the Sky*." In *We Who Love to Be Astonished: Experimental Women's Writing and Performance Poetics*, edited by Laura Hinton and Cynthia Hogue. Tuscaloosa: University of Alabama Press, 2002. Focuses on how the two collections challenge traditional free verse by creating hybrid forms of poetry.

Nixon, Angelique V. "Poem and Tale as Double Helix in Joy Harjo's *A Map to the Next World*." In *Native American Writers*, edited by Harold Bloom. New ed. New York: Bloom's Literary Criticism, 2010. Examines Harjo's blending of poetry and prose, including the narrative style in which she writes her poetry and how storytelling is an important aspect of her verse.

Scarry, John. "Joy Harjo." In *Smoke Rising: The Native North American Literary Companion*, edited by Janet Witalec. Detroit: Gale Research, 1995. Scarry's brief entry on Harjo recognizes her "need for remembrance and transcendence" and includes several poems demonstrating this duality, including the prose poems "Grace" and "Autobiography," both from *In Mad Love and War*.

Witalec, Janet, ed. *Native North American Literature: Biographical and Critical Information on Native Writers and Orators from the United States and Canada from Historical Times to the Present*. New York: Gale Research, 1994. The essay on Harjo in this encyclopedia is a very useful survey of the writer's career and includes long excerpts from three essay-reviews of her work.

David Peck

JOEL CHANDLER HARRIS

Born: Eatonton, Georgia; December 9, 1848
Died: Atlanta, Georgia; July 3, 1908

PRINCIPAL SHORT FICTION

Uncle Remus: His Songs and His Sayings, 1880
Nights with Uncle Remus, 1883
Mingo, and Other Sketches in Black and White, 1884
Free Joe, and Other Georgian Sketches, 1887
Daddy Jake the Runaway, 1889
*Balaam and His Master, and Other Stories and
  Sketches,* 1891
Uncle Remus and His Friends, 1892
Tales of Home Folks in Peace and War, 1898
*Told by Uncle Remus: New Stories of the Old
  Plantation,* 1905
The Complete Tales of Uncle Remus, 1955 (Richard
  Chase, editor)

OTHER LITERARY FORMS

Joel Chandler Harris's literary talents were considerably broader than the Uncle Remus tales for which he is so well known. He was an accomplished editor, essayist, folklorist, and biographer, and he wrote several romantic novels, as well as books for children.

ACHIEVEMENTS

Joel Chandler Harris was best known in his day for his collections of Uncle Remus tales, particularly *Uncle Remus: His Songs and His Sayings* and *Nights with Uncle Remus,* tales that were not created but recorded by him. When the American Academy of Arts and Letters was founded in 1905, Harris was elected to be one of the inaugural members. The black man/white boy pair whom Harris uses in the Uncle Remus stories was highly influential on Mark Twain's portrayal of the Jim/Huck relationship in *The Adventures of Huckleberry Finn* (1884). With the emergence of the Civil Rights movement, however, and with the portrayal of Uncle Remus as a man among cartoons in Walt Disney's film *Song of the South* (1946), the figure of Uncle Remus (who was in part based on Harriet Beecher Stowe's character Uncle Tom from *Uncle Tom's Cabin,* 1852) fell into some amount of literary and political disfavor. Twentieth century studies of folklore have, however, established Harris's importance as a folklorist who collected authentic black folk tales.

BIOGRAPHY

Born in Putnam County, Georgia, the illegitimate son of an Irish laborer who deserted the family just after his birth, Joel Chandler Harris spent a rather ordinary boyhood in rural Georgia. He was not very interested in school and seems to have preferred playing pranks to studying. In 1862, at age fourteen, Harris was given a job as a printer's devil by Addison Turner, an eccentric planter who published a rural weekly newspaper, the *Countryman,* on his nearby plantation. It is impossible to overestimate Turner's influence on young Harris, for in addition to allowing him to contribute pieces to the paper, Turner also encouraged him to read extensively in his private library and to roam around his thousand-acre plantation. It was here that Harris first heard the black folk narratives that were later to become the heart of the Uncle Remus stories. After working for Turner for four years, Harris held brief jobs at several newspapers around the South. In 1873 he married Esther LaRose and soon settled in Atlanta, where he lived until his death in 1908.

In 1876, Harris was hired to do editorial paragraphing for the Atlanta *Constitution.* Soon after his arrival, he was asked to take over a black-dialect column from a retiring writer, and on October 26, 1876, his first sketch appeared, featuring the witty observations of an older black man. A month later the older black was officially called "Uncle Remus," and a major new voice in American humor was born. Uncle Remus began as a rather thin, almost vaudevillian caricature of a black man, an old urban black who supposedly dropped by the Atlanta *Constitution* office to offer practical comments, and some of Harris's own opinions, on corrupt politicians and lazy blacks. The character grew, however, when Harris transferred the locale of the sketches to a plantation and incorporated tales he had heard in the slave quarters during his early days with Turner. In late 1880, Harris collected twenty-one "urban" and thirty-four "plantation" Uncle Remus sketches along with black songs, maxims, and proverbs in *Uncle Remus: His Songs and His Sayings*. The collection was an immediate success, and, much to Harris's astonishment and embarrassment, he was famous.

ANALYSIS

Most of the Uncle Remus stories follow a similar formula. They begin with a frame narrative, which typically opens in Uncle Remus's cabin behind the "big house" as he discusses daily affairs with the young white son of Mars' John and Miss Sally. Usually something that the boy says reminds Uncle Remus of a story about Brer Rabbit or some other "creeturs." Once the tale is over, Uncle Remus draws a moral lesson for the boy and sends him to bed. The friendship between Uncle Remus and the young boy is worth noting, because in many ways it is Joel Chandler Harris's own idealized version of black/white relations. Both Uncle Remus and the boy have a strong love for each other and represent the best qualities of both races--Uncle Remus considers himself superior to the domestic servants, and he tells the boy not to play with the "riff-raff" Favers children, the poor white trash of the area. Uncle Remus is not afraid to discipline the young boy subtly, and he sometimes pretends to withhold a tale because the boy has misbehaved during the day (chucking rocks at chickens, for example). Sometimes, borrowing a trick from Brer Rabbit, he has the boy bring him food from the kitchen as a means of appeasement. Uncle Remus also functions as the boy's teacher, moving him out of the linear chronology of the present and initiating him into the timeless world of the fables--a lesson the young boy sometimes has trouble understanding.

UNCLE REMUS: HIS SONGS AND HIS SAYINGS

In "How Mr. Rabbit Saved His Meat," for example, the boy objects that Uncle Remus is beginning a tale about Brer Wolf, who has already been killed in an earlier story. In mock exasperation, Uncle Remus remarks that the boy "done grow'd up twel he know mo'n I duz." The world of the fables, like the patterns of human nature they depict, is atemporal.

The subtle tensions evident between Uncle Remus and the boy are also reflected in the stories themselves. Most of the Uncle Remus stories center on the best-known trickster in all of folklore, Brer Rabbit, and they present a further allegory of black/white relations in the postwar South. A weaker animal in a world of predatory wolves, foxes, bears, and buzzards, Brer Rabbit is forced to depend on his wits and his creativity for survival. His mischievousness disrupts the traditional roles of success within the established work ethic of the other animals, who raise their own "goobers" and catch their own fish, and his trickery allows him to gain power over, and respect from, a stronger race. Brer Rabbit almost never brings his quarrels to open confrontation, and this reflects Harris's conservatism on racial matters. In "The Wonderful Tar-Baby Story," for example, it is Brer Rabbit's aggressive resistance to the lethargic, silent black tar-baby that gets him trapped by Brer Fox, but his smooth and deceptively conciliatory rhetoric allows him to escape. Brer Rabbit rarely openly accuses the other animals of misdeeds; his struggle for respect in the forest is achieved through the subtleties of role-playing and indirect retribution.

Although the Brer Rabbit tales may represent a projection of the black man's desire for the realignment of the white man's social structure, they have a dark side to them as well. Sometimes Brer Rabbit's overbearing brashness can backfire, as in "Mr. Rabbit Meets His Match at Last." In this tale, Brer Tarrypin and the rabbit agree to a foot race, but the turtle places his wife and children at strategic points around the track and wins the bet, since to Brer Rabbit all turtles look alike. In "Mr. Rabbit Meets His Match Again," Brer Rabbit tries to cheat Brer Buzzard out of some food, but Brer Buzzard flies him high over the river and threatens to drop him until he admits his trickery. On occasion, Brer Rabbit's roguery leads to acts of senseless violence. In

"Mr. Rabbit Nibbles Up the Butter," Brer Rabbit steals butter that communally belongs to himself, Brer Fox, and Brer Possum. He then implicates Brer Possum as the thief by smearing some of the butter on him as he sleeps. Declaring his innocence, Brer Possum suggests that all three jump over a brush fire so that the heaviest animal, being full of butter, will be unmasked as the thief. Both the fox and the rabbit make the jump, but Brer Possum dies. In "The Sad Fate of Mr. Fox," the final tale of *Uncle Remus: His Songs and His Sayings*, Brer Fox offers to show Brer Rabbit how to cut meat from inside a cow without killing it. As soon as they are both inside, however, Brer Rabbit purposefully gives the cow a fatal blow. When the farmer who owns the cow arrives, Brer Rabbit identifies the fox as the thief and the farmer kills him, chopping off his head. Brer Rabbit then takes the head to Mrs. Fox, telling her that it is a fine cut of beef, and Brer Fox's son soon discovers the head of his father floating in the caldron.

The Brer Rabbit tales carry an allegorical message for both blacks and whites. Harris recognizes that white society must learn to make room for a race that it has historically considered to be weak and inferior, yet he advises blacks to be patient and accept a slow rate of change. Too fast a push for power can lead to violence, and killing the fox only angers his son to revenge. Whatever sympathies Harris might have felt for the underdog position of African Americans during Reconstruction were tempered by his political conservatism, which caused him to share some of the racial biases of his time.

NIGHTS WITH UNCLE REMUS

Uncle Remus: His Songs and His Sayings proved so popular that Harris went on to publish six more Uncle Remus volumes in his lifetime. Of these other volumes, his second collection, *Nights with Uncle Remus*, is the most important and the one that most fully shows the fruits of his labor. In it, Uncle Remus is rounded out much more to become a complete character in his own right, and other characters on the plantation are introduced as storytellers, principally Daddy Jack, a character who speaks in a Sea Island dialect called "Gullah," and who Harris used to tell stories he perceived to be of a different cultural origin than the stories that Uncle Remus tells. As popular as these Uncle Remus collections were, Harris never considered that their merit was

inherently literary. He always insisted that in them he was the "compiler" of a folklore and dialect that were fast disappearing in the South at the end of the nineteenth century. He was careful to include only the Uncle Remus tales that could be verified as authentic black oral narratives, and, with his usual diffidence, he minimized his own role in elevating them to artistic short fiction.

MINGO, AND OTHER SKETCHES IN BLACK AND WHITE

In *Mingo, and Other Sketches in Black and White*, Harris surprised his readers by temporarily moving away from the Uncle Remus formula. The collection was favorably reviewed, and Harris showed that his literary talents could be stretched to include what he considered to be more serious forms. The title story, "Mingo: A Sketch of Life in Middle Georgia," is an admirable local-color portrayal of class conflicts. The central conflict is between two white families, the aristocratic Wornums and the poor-white Bivinses. Before the Civil War, the Wornums' daughter, Cordelia, had married the Bivins's son, Henry Clay, much to the displeasure of the Wornum family, who promptly

Joel Chandler Harris (Library of Congress)

disinherited her. Henry Clay was killed in the war and Cordelia died shortly thereafter, leaving a daughter in the care of Mrs. Feratia Bivins, Henry's mother. Mrs. Wornum is overcome with grief after the death of the children and realizes that she has made a mistake in snubbing the Bivinses, but fiercely proud Feratia cannot forgive her. In a comic yet pathos-filled scene, Mrs. Wornum asks Feratia Bivins to let her see her granddaughter, whom she has never seen. Feratia coolly replies, "if I had as much politeness, ma'am, as I had cheers, I'd ast you to set down," and adamantly refuses to let Mrs. Wornum see the baby. The final wise commentary, however, comes from Mingo, a former Wornum slave who is loyal to his old master and acts as the surrogate father for the surviving child. It is the black man's strength of character and endurance that promises reconciliation and social progress. Harris, a poor white by birth himself, is clearly antiaristocratic and sides with the underdog in times of changing social values, yet by applauding the virtues of loyalty and duty in Mingo, he comes very close to advocating a servile and passive acceptance, as some of his critics have charged.

FREE JOE, AND OTHER GEORGIAN SKETCHES

Harris's *Free Joe, and Other Georgian Sketches*, and the frequently anthologized title story, "Free Joe and the Rest of the World," further illustrates his ambivalence on the "Negro question." In 1840, a slave speculator named Major Frampton lost all his property except one slave, his body-servant Joe, to Judge Alfred Wellington in a famous card game. Frampton adjourned the game, went to the courthouse and gave Joe his freedom, and then blew his brains out. Joe, although freed, remains in town because his wife Lucinda is now the property of the judge. All goes well for Joe until the judge dies and his estate is transferred to the stern Spite Calderwood. Calderwood refuses to let Joe visit Lucinda. Joe's easy life comes to an end: The other slaves will have nothing to do with him, and he is an outcast from the white community, sleeping outside under a poplar tree. When Calderwood learns that in spite of his orders Lucinda has been sneaking out to meet Joe, he takes her to Macon and sells her; he even has his hounds kill Joe's dog. Joe, however, even when told the truth about Lucinda, seems incapable of understanding.

Night after night he waits for his wife and his dog to return together in the moonlight, until one night he dies alone under the poplar tree, a smile on his face and humble to the last.

In "Free Joe and the Rest of the World," Harris achieves a balance between sentimentality and realistic portrayal in dramatizing the plight of the freeman in the antebellum South. Even though Joe is the humble, unassuming victim of white cruelty, his freedom also represents the vague, gothic threat of social dissolution to the white community, who come to view him as "forever lurking on the outskirts of slavery, ready to sound a shrill and ghostly signal" of insurrection. Unlike Brer Rabbit, Joe is no ingenious trickster, and Harris obliquely hints that, all things considered, Joe may have been better off a slave since his freedom leaves him "shiftless" and incapable of fending for himself.

BALAAM AND HIS MASTER, AND OTHER SKETCHES AND STORIES

Of the six stories collected in *Balaam and His Master, and Other Sketches and Stories*, three are portraits of loyal blacks and three treat the fate of a white man in a crumbling society. In this collection Harris again illustrates his favorite themes: the changing social values between blacks and whites, and the need for reconciliation through patience and understanding. "Balaam and His Master" is the story of the fiercely loyal manservant of young Berrien Cozart--the sensual, cruel, impetuous, and implacable son of a respected plantation family. As in many of Harris's aristocratic families, the older Cozart practices a benign paternalism toward his slaves, but his young son Berrien is nothing but a spoiled and dissolute gambler who abuses the privileges of his race. Despite his master's excesses, Balaam remains a constant and loyal valet, even to the point of participating in a scam to sell himself to a new master and then returning to Berrien. Berrien is finally arrested for murder, and Balaam breaks into the jail to be with him; but it is too late--Berrien is already dead. The story ends with Balaam loyally crouching over his dead master, who died with a smile as sweet as a "little child that nestles on his mother's breast." Even though Balaam is morally superior to his white master, the message of the story is that loyalty and service are superior to social revolution.

In "Where's Duncan?"--another story in *Balaam and His Master, and Other Stories and Sketches*--Harris gives a more apocalyptic version of the changing social values between blacks and whites. The story is narrated by old Isaiah Winchell, who meets a dark stranger named Willis Featherstone as he is hauling his cotton to market. As they camp for the evening, old Isaiah learns that Willis Featherstone is the mulatto son of a plantation owner who had educated him, grown to hate him, and then sold him. The next evening the group camps near the old Featherstone plantation, and a vampire-like mulatto woman comes to invite them to dinner at the "big house." Willis Featherstone, who seems to know the woman, enigmatically asks her, "Where's Duncan?" and she hysterically replies that old Featherstone has "sold my onliest boy." Later that evening, the camp is awakened by a commotion at the big house. Old Isaiah rushes up to see the house on fire, and through the window he glimpses the mulatto woman stabbing Old Featherstone and screaming , "Where's Duncan?" Willis Featherstone, say some of the observers, was inside enjoying the spectacle. The story ends with a gothic scene of fiery retribution as the old plantation house burns and collapses, and old Isaiah still dreams of the smell of burning flesh. Violent confrontation is possible, Harris suggests, if white society continues to abuse black people.

As an editorialist, essayist, and humorist, Joel Chandler Harris was instrumental in trying to reconcile the tensions between North and South, black and white, left by the Civil War. Although he shared some of the racial prejudices of his time--one detects a paternalism for African Americans in much of the short fiction--he was a progressive conservative who, as one critic has said, "affirmed the integrity of all individuals, whether black or white; and he could not countenance unjust or inhumane actions by any member of the human race." In the 1870's and 1880's, his editorials in the Atlanta *Constitution* consistently argued against sectionalism, both literary and political, and in favor of a united country. Any literature, wrote Harris in 1879, takes its materials and flavor from "localism," yet "in literature, art, and society, whatever is truely southern is likewise truely American; and the same may be said of what is truely Northern."

OTHER MAJOR WORKS

LONG FICTION: *Sister Jane*, 1896; *The Chronicles of Aunt Minervy Ann*, 1899; *On the Wing of Occasions*, 1900; *Gabriel Tolliver*, 1902; *A Little Union Scout*, 1904; *The Shadow Between His Shoulder-Blades*, 1909.

NONFICTION: *Dearest Chums and Partners: Joel Chandler Harris's Letters to His Children*, 1993 (Hugh T. Keenan, editor).

CHILDREN'S LITERATURE: *Little Mr. Thimblefinger*, 1894; *Mr. Rabbit at Home*, 1895; *The Story of Aaron*, 1896; *Aaron in the Wildwoods*, 1897; *Plantation Pageants*, 1899; *Wally Wanderoon and His Story-Telling Machine*, 1903.

BIBLIOGRAPHY

Baer, Florence E. *Sources and Analogues of the Uncle Remus Tales*. Helsinki: Academia Scientiarium Fennica, 1980. Essential to anyone studying the Brer Rabbit stories. For each tale, Baer gives a summary, the tale type number from *The Types of the Folk-Tale* (1928), motif numbers from Stith Thompson's *Motif-Index of Folk Literature* (1955-1958), and a discussion of possible sources. She also includes an excellent essay discussing Harris's legitimacy as a collector of folktales.

Baker, Margaret P. "The Rabbit as Trickster." *Journal of Popular Culture* 28 (Fall, 1994): 149-158. Discusses the image of the rabbit as trickster in popular culture. Concludes that while some of the traditional folk images of the trickster have changed, twentieth century trickster figures help people deal with paradox and irony; trickster figures also show their audiences that they are neither totally victims nor victors but can capitalize on their own weaknesses to better cope with life.

Bickley, R. Bruce, ed. *Critical Essays on Joel Chandler Harris*. Boston: G. K. Hall, 1981. Traces the critical heritage of Harris's work, including contemporary reviews. Of particular importance is an article by Bernard Wolfe, which was printed in *Commentary* in 1949.

_____. *Joel Chandler Harris*. Boston: Twayne, 1978. A full-length study, including chapters on the major as well as the later Uncle Remus tales and on Harris's other short fiction. Includes a brief, useful annotated bibliography.

_____. *Joel Chandler Harris: An Annotated Bibliography of Criticism, 1977-1996*. Westport, Conn.: Greenwood Press, 1997. A good reference for students of Harris.

Brasch, Walter M. *Brer Rabbit, Uncle Remus, and the "Cornfield Journalist": The Tale of Joel Chandler Harris*. Macon, Ga.: Mercer University Press, 2000. A balanced examination of Harris and his stories--part biography, part analysis--aimed at an audience from whom, as children, the Uncle Remus tales had been withheld in deference to the sensitive racial issues encumbering the stories.

Harris, Joel Chandler. *Dearest Chums and Partners: Joel Chandler Harris's Letters to His Children, a Domestic Biography*. Edited by Hugh T. Keenan. Athens: University of Georgia Press, 1993. Reveals aspects of Harris's life through his correspondence with family members.

Hemenway, Robert. Introduction to *Uncle Remus: His Songs and Sayings*, edited by Hemenway. New York: Penguin Books, 1982. Hemenway's introduction is clear and informative, one of the better discussions of the Brer Rabbit stories. Contains a brief bibliography.

Johnson, Ellen. "Geographic Context and Ethnic Context: Joel Chandler Harris and Alice Walker." *Mississippi Quarterly* 60, no. 2 (Spring, 2007): 235-255. Compares the literary styles of the two authors, demonstrating how their ethnic backgrounds influenced the way they portrayed their hometowns in their works. Examines the authors' use of dialect spellings.

Keenan, Hugh T. "Twisted Tales: Propaganda in the Tar-Baby Stories." *The Southern Quarterly* 22, no. 2 (Winter, 1984): 54-69. Updates some arguments that Bernard Wolfe put forth in his *Commentary* article (included in R. Bruce Bickley's entry, *Critical Essays on Joel Chandler Harris*). Better researched than Wolfe's article and more even in tone.

Lester, Julius. "The Storyteller's Voice: Reflections on the Rewriting of Uncle Remus." In *The Voice of the Narrator in Children's Literature*, edited by Charlotte F. Otten and Gary D. Schmidt. New York: Greenwood Press, 1989. Lester discusses the problems he had with his editor when he was trying to get his retelling of the Uncle Remus stories published. He argues that voice is the heart of these stories and he could not be unfaithful to the original folktales.

Rittenhouse, Jennifer. " Reading, Intimacy, and the Role of Uncle Remus in White Southern Social Memory." *Journal of Southern History* 69, no. 3 (August, 2003): 585. Examines the role of the Uncle Remus tales in the social memory of white southerners. Argues that Harris provides authentic representations of African American characters and southern plantation life.

Wagner, Bryan. "Uncle Remus and the Atlanta Police Department." In *Disturbing the Peace: Black Culture and the Police Power After Slavery*. Cambridge, Mass.: Harvard University Press, 2009. Describes the contributions of Harris's Uncle Remus tales to the American political system and to the conceptions of black culture that emerged after the Civil War.

Wyatt-Brown, Bertram. "Trickster Motif and Disillusion: Uncle Remus and Mark Twain." In *Hearts of Darkness: Wellsprings of a Southern Literary Tradition*. Baton Rouge: Louisiana State University Press, 2003. Wyatt-Brown's analysis of southern literature focuses on the themes of melancholy and alienation in works by Harris and Twain and includes a discussion of how the trickster characters in the Uncle Remus tales reflect this sadness.

Robert J. McNutt
Updated by Thomas J. Cassidy

JIM HARRISON

Born: Grayling, Michigan; December 11, 1937

PRINCIPAL SHORT FICTION

Legends of the Fall, 1979 (collection of three
  novellas: *Revenge, The Man Who Gave Up His
  Name*, and *Legends of the Fall*)
The Woman Lit by Fireflies, 1990 (collection of three
  novellas: *Brown Dog, Sunset Limited*, and *The
  Woman Lit by Fireflies*)
Julip, 1994 (collection of three novellas: *Julip, The
  Seven-Ounce Man*, and *The Beige Dolorosa*)
The Beast God Forgot to Invent, 2000 (collection of
  three novellas: *The Beast God Forgot to Invent,
  Westward Ho*, and *Forgot to Go to Spain*)
The Farmer's Daughter, 2010 (collection of three
  novellas: *The Farmer's Daughter, Brown Dog
  Redux*, and *Games of Night*)

OTHER LITERARY FORMS

Although best known for his prose--novels and no-
vellas--Jim Harrison is an accomplished poet (*After
Ikkyu, and Other Poems*, 1996; *The Shape of the
Journey: New and Collected Poems*, 1998), essayist,
and screenwriter. As a man of letters, Harrison made
his poetic debut with the publication of *Plain Song*
(1965). *The Theory and Practice of Rivers* (1985) represents a continuing pursuit of the poetic muse. Essays
concerning food, travel, sports, and critical literary insights appear in *Just Before Dark* (1991). The screenplays *Revenge* (1989), based on the novella in *Legends
of the Fall*, and *Wolf* (1994), which he wrote with
Wesley Strick and which is based on the novel of the
same name, are his noted works in that genre. Harrison
continues to be prolific and eclectic in the early twenty-
first century. His nonfiction reflects his wide-ranging
interests and includes a witty cookbook, *The Raw and
the Cooked* (2001). He continues to write poetry and

novels and, in 2000, he entered a new genre with the
publication of *The Boy Who Ran to the Woods*, a children's book about a seven-year-old boy in post-World
War II Michigan. He indulged in personal reflection
with *Off to the Side: A Memoir* (2002).

ACHIEVEMENTS

The accumulation of Jim Harrison's writing ensures
him a place among important writers of the late twentieth
century. The multifarious concerns addressed in his books
of fiction, poetry, and numerous nonfiction articles are
gleaned from his intense capacity for observation,
memory, and experience. Harrison received a National
Endowment for the Arts Award in 1968 and a John Simon
Guggenheim Memorial Foundation Fellowship in 1969;
he was also honored twice by the National Literary
Anthology.

BIOGRAPHY

James Thomas Harrison was born in Grayling, a
small rural community in northern Michigan, in 1937.
It was there that he developed his love for the outdoors.
At age thirteen, he moved to Lansing, Michigan, when
his father took a position at Michigan State University.

Growing up in a family of voracious readers (his father enjoyed William Faulkner, Ernest Hemingway,
and Erskine Caldwell) proved beneficial to Harrison's
decision at an early age to become a writer. At age nineteen, he left home for New York, where he intended to
write poetry and live the life of a bohemian.

Later, he returned to Michigan and received a
B.A. from Michigan State University in 1960 and
an M.A. in 1964. Shortly thereafter, he took a position as assistant professor of English at the State
University of New York at Stony Brook and taught
there for one year.

After leaving his position at Stony Brook, Harrison
returned to Michigan to take up writing full time.
Grants, fellowships, and articles for magazines such as

Sports Illustrated kept Harrison going until the 1979 publication of *Legends of the Fall*, his first commercially successful book. The film rights for the book's three novellas eventually led to Harrison's career as a screenwriter and the popular film adaptation of the *Legends of the Fall* by screenwriters Susan Shilliday and Bill Witliff in 1995. Harrison's film work and the literary strength of books such as *The Woman Lit by Fireflies* and *The Road Home* (1998) have made him a widely read and critically acclaimed author.

ANALYSIS

As a storyteller who experiments with form, Jim Harrison works in a variety of modes. He borrows techniques and literary conventions from romance, adventure, mystery, and comedy. He does not utilize these categories in a formulaic manner, however, but instead modifies the conventions of literary genre to dramatize contemporary difficulties.

Harrison is often accused of writing "macho fiction." Some critics agree that, if viewed superficially, the stories appear to be rhetorically macho--rendered from a mythic male viewpoint. These stories, however, show the opposite is true. Although his characters display a penchant for sex, violence, and the sporting life, they do not derive any benefit from their macho behavior. In fact, either they become isolated and lonely, or their dignity and integrity are lost.

REVENGE

In *Revenge*, the first novella in *Legends of the Fall*, the persona weaves a violent tale of vengeance, friendship, and love among three people: Cochran, a former fighter pilot; Tibey, a gangster struggling to legitimize himself; and Miryea, Tibey's beautiful wife. As the tale unfolds, Cochran, the protagonist, develops a friendship with Tibey, a powerful and rich Mexican businessman; the friendship results in a dangerous liaison between Cochran and Miryea. Tibey is obsessed with two things: tennis and his beautiful upper-class wife--not because he loves her but because she provides a degree of status for him in the so-called legitimate world.

The story begins in medias res, with vultures hovering over the battered naked body of Cochran, who lies dying in the Mexican desert as a coyote nearby

Jim Harrison (Library of Congress)

watches curiously. The narrative persona informs the reader that "Carrion was shared not by the sharer's design but by a pattern set before anyone knew there were patterns." The natural world is viewed from an objective perspective in Harrison's fiction, and, like the coyote looking on objectively, nature's presence signifies a detached and impersonal environment. Within this environment, Cochran and Tibey find themselves confused and isolated.

When a Mexican worker and his daughter find Cochran in the desert, they deliver him to a mission, where he is nursed back to life by Diller, a Mennonite missionary doctor. Cochran's restoration is slow and painful, as are his memories when he begins to recover. Eventually, Cochran and Tibey must have a showdown. Before Cochran's brutal encounter with Tibey, readers see him several evenings earlier in a bar, drinking with a friend. Cochran talks too much about his relationship with Miryea. His friend listens patiently, but when he realizes that Miryea is Tibey's wife, he turns pale with fear, and he informs Cochran that Tibey is a Spanish sobriquet for *tiburon*, "the shark."

Tibey learns of the affair at the same time that Cochran wins a tennis tournament. He is delighted with Cochran's win and sends him several thousand dollars and a one-way ticket to Paris. This gift, however, is a veiled warning to leave Miryea alone. Cochran and Miryea, however, have already made arrangements to spend a few days at a mountain cabin in Mexico while Tibey is away on business. Unbeknown to the lovers, Tibey and his henchmen have followed them. Miryea is disfigured by Tibey and forced to watch as Cochran is beaten senseless; she is then drugged and delivered to a brothel, where she is kept against her will. Cochran is pulled from the trunk of a car and left to die in the desert.

As Cochran recovers, he is obsessed with finding Miryea and getting revenge against Tibey. Tibey, unable to assuage his guilt for the brutal treatment that Miryea received, has her placed in a nunnery, where she ultimately dies from sorrow and the abuse she received in the brothel. The tale ends in bitter irony when Cochran finally corners Tibey. Tibey asks for an apology, which Cochran gives him; the two men part in misery, realizing that revenge, as the old Sicilian proverb says, "is a dish better served cold." Engaged in this kind of macho behavior, each man loses his love, integrity, and dignity; each is left in the depths of despair.

The Man Who Gave Up His Name

The following novella, *The Man Who Gave Up His Name*, focuses on Nordstrom, a man who at forty-three is in a midlife crisis. His passions consist of cooking and dancing alone in his apartment to "work up a dense sweat and to feel the reluctant body become fluid and graceful." The dance metaphorically represents Nordstrom's life, for this dance, as readers later learn, is for survival. Nordstrom has all the trappings of success; he has plenty of money, a beautiful wife, and his daughter, a university student, is intelligent and lovely. This ideal existence is set up for the reader through flashback via Nordstrom's perspective--a literary convention that Harrison uses to establish the central character's point of view.

Ultimately, though, Nordstrom's classic American Dream disintegrates when his wife divorces him, and even though his daughter loves him, she considers him

a dolt. He is further distressed by the death of his father, which makes him think of his own mortality. During these events, Nordstrom asks himself the question that human beings have been asking since the Industrial Revolution, "What if what I've been doing all my life has been totally wrong?" and he begins his quest to discover the answer.

The story takes a violent and surprising turn at the end, when Nordstrom decides to give his money away and take a long trip. He views his achievements and successes with disdain and thinks that giving away his money will help him turn his life around. At a graduation dinner for his daughter, Sonia, he embarrassingly attempts to give her fifteen thousand dollars in one-hundred-dollar bills for a new car, an act for which he is rebuked by his former wife, Laura, whom he has not seen in four years. Inevitably, Sonia refuses the money, making him regret even more what he feels he has become--a kind of middle-aged fop. The violent twist occurs when Sarah, a beautiful waitress and dancer--after whom Nordstrom lusts when he sees her during forays into his New York neighborhood--is invited to the dinner party by one of Sonia's friends.

A ruckus ensues when an Italian, who looks like "a cutout from the movies of a gangster psychopath," enters, accompanied by a large black man; together, they bodily remove Sarah, but not before Nordstrom strikes the black man and is threatened with a gun held by the Italian. After the party, Nordstrom realizes that he is being set up when Sarah telephones, asking if they can meet. They have lunch together and return to Nordstrom's room, where they have sex. Afterward, Sarah demands ten thousand dollars from Nordstrom to keep her maniacal boyfriend, Slats, from killing him. Nordstrom refuses to be subjected to extortion by these petty, drug-dealing thugs and relishes the thought that his life has been threatened; he waits in his motel room for retribution, feeling more alive and in tune with himself than ever before.

The Italian breaks into his room, unaware that Nordstrom is waiting for him. Nordstrom bursts from the suite, catches the intruder off guard, and throws the man out a seventh-floor window. Nordtrom feels little remorse, however, excusing his actions by noting that this man may have threatened Nordstrom's family. He confronts the extortionists at lunch the next day, refusing to knuckle under to their threats, and explains that it was unfortunate that the Italian had to die. Sarah and Slats are bewildered; they give up their ruse, thinking that they have encountered a genuine madman.

In the epilogue, Nordstrom retreats to a small coastal town in Florida, where he rents a tourist cabin and takes a job cooking seafood in a local restaurant. He buys a boat, fishes in the Gulf, studies marine life, and dances alone at night to music coming from a transistor radio. Nordstrom is an isolated character who resorts to the primitive side of his nature to survive. He searches for self-understanding in a society that constantly negates the natural world. He sheds the burdens of urbanized life--marriage, children, money, and materialism--and for all of his faults, he is an empathetic character, one who is certainly alone and humble in his environment.

BROWN DOG

Harrison's consummate ability to manipulate comedy is exhibited in *Brown Dog*, the first novella in *The Woman Lit by Fireflies*. This humorous tale is about B. D., a footloose scuba diver who shares an illegal salvaging operation with his partner, Bob. The two characters scavenge for artifacts from sunken ships in northern Michigan lakes and sell them to collectors.

The story begins with B. D. writing his memoirs, a mock form that Harrison previously used in *Wolf: A False Memoir* (1971). Having dabbled in psychology, Shelley, B. D.'s girlfriend, convinces B. D. to record, as a form of therapy, the events that led to his eventual arrest for transporting a dead Indian to Chicago in a stolen refrigerator truck. Shelley is an attractive anthropologist twenty years younger than B. D. As B. D.'s version is revealed, readers realize that his reliability as a narrator is questionable, which adds to the story's humor.

The plot revolves around two principal events: Shelley's desire to locate an Indian burial mound on which B. D. had previously stumbled, and the dead Indian chief whom B. D. found during one of his dives in Lake Superior. B. D. has a habit of unexpectedly finding things. When he locates the ancient Indian burial ground, his Chippewa friend, Clause, convinces

him not to divulge its location. Shelly is interested in the burial mounds and continually tries to get B. D. to show her where they are so she can study them.

Upon his dive into Lake Superior, B. D. finds a perfectly preserved Indian (except that his eyes are missing) in seventy feet of water. From that moment, the Indian is referred to as Chief. B. D. does not share his find with Bob, however, until he works out a plan, which he admits in retrospect was not a very good one. The problem is that all good plans must begin without a flaw, and this one unfortunately is flawed from the beginning. B. D. is not Native American, but he looks Indian and is often mistaken for one. Like many other roles that he assumes, B. D. plays at being Indian because it is expected of him. He respects and admires Native Americans, having grown up with them, and so he refuses to show Shelley the ancient burial ground but instead hatches a plan to make a little money from the Chief.

The absurd tale gains momentum when B. D. steals a refrigerator truck, and, after salvaging the Chief, includes Bob in a scheme to transport the dead Indian to an artifacts collector in Chicago. The plan goes awry when B. D. and Bob drink too much and are arrested. Bob is punished with two years in the local penitentiary, but B. D.'s sentence is light--the judge pities B. D. because, as B. D. explains, he got confused when he heard the Chief ask him to bury him.

B. D. describes events in his "memoirs" with alacrity and comic dismay, but while he admits his ordinariness, he does not think himself stupid. Furthermore, although his attitude is predominantly chauvinistic, his commonsense observations provide the reader with viable explanations for his ridiculous behavior.

THE WOMAN LIT BY FIREFLIES

The Woman Lit by Fireflies is the last novella in the collection by the same title. Using a female voice, the narrative presents a sensitive and believable female protagonist. This is not Harrison's first attempt, however, to use a third-person narrative limited to a female-viewpoint character. He accomplished this challenge in *Dalva* (1988), a novel that focuses on the personal and historical aspects of a woman's life in a male-dominated society.

For Clare, a wealthy middle-aged woman married to a man whose only concern is the present status of the stock market, the circumstances are similar. Like most of Harrison's central characters, she is desperately alone. After losing her best friend, Zilpha, and her dog, Sammy, to cancer, Clare's migraines intensify, causing her to give in to the whims of those around her--namely her husband, Donald, who exerts his influence over her.

Returning from a visit to her daughter in Colorado, Clare is plagued by a severe migraine. Donald listens repeatedly to a tape called "Tracking the Blues," which has no connection to music but proves to be an explanation of the current stock-market situation. Clare can no longer tolerate Donald and his obsession with money, and when they exit Interstate 80 in Iowa for a rest stop, she leaves a note in the restroom, stating that she has abandoned her husband because he is physically abusive. She escapes into a nearby cornfield, leaving Donald behind.

Once in the cornfield, Clare resorts to basic survival skills to make it through a rainy night without food or water. Meanwhile, the migraine takes control of her, and she drifts in and out of delirium. Intrusive memories invade her consciousness, and detailed events, retrospective insights into past friendships, and various aspects of her marital relationship are revealed to her. These memories form the basis of Clare's enlightenment--the migraine symbolically paralleling life's suffering and pain. At the end of her ordeal, she is able to subdue the migraine and, in effect, subjugate her inability to act for herself. This character's physical pain allows her to get in touch with her subconscious. She does this while the natural world looks on with a placid eye.

Julip

As in *The Woman Lit by Fireflies*, *Julip*'s female protagonist faces a debilitating masculine world. Unlike Clare, Julip is young, energetic, and capable of correcting the mistakes of male vanity. In *Julip*, Harrison weaves a seamless and comic tale of the protagonist's life. Julip, named for the drink, has a difficult rural Wisconsin childhood. Her father, a trainer of bird dogs, has a weakness for liquor that blunts his success, and his frequent binges often end in physical and mental collapse.

Meanwhile, Julip's emotionally cold mother leaves Julip and her brother Billy to their own resources.

Still, Julip loves her father, and, when he dies, she takes over his profession. Unconsciously, Julip also searches for a connection to her father through her affairs with three middle-aged men--Charles, Arthur, and Ted--collectively called "the boys."

Billy learns of "the boys," and, in a demented attempt to avenge what he calls her "defilement," he begins following them. In disguise, he stalks her lovers for two weeks, finally shooting them in their boat as they are passing under a bridge. However, he uses a .22, and none of the men is fatally wounded. Billy receives seven to ten years in prison, but Julip learns that he may be transferred to a mental institution if he admits to being insane. The judge, prosecutor, and victims all agree to the change in sentence.

Feeling responsible for Billy's plight, Julip sets out to release him. Turning to Billy's psychologist for help, she learns that her father had not committed suicide, as her mother claimed. Instead, a group of drunk teenagers had run over him. Released from two years of guilt over the supposed suicide, Julip heals the wound of her father's drinking and death and finally frees herself from her emotional attraction to older men.

When she confronts "the boys" to sign the agreement to place Billy in the mental institution, she can rise above their empty life of drinking, drugs, and sex with younger women. While they display their foolishness--begging her to marry them between bouts of champagne and fishing--she displays cool affection mixed with rationality and self-confidence.

By the novella's end, Julip attains the agreement and secures a release order from the judge and the prosecuting attorney. Successfully removing Billy from the horrors of prison, Julip, finished with her empty affairs and her brother's insane version of chivalry, returns to Wisconsin to the peace of a rural life training bird dogs. Thus, with her feminine power, wit, and intelligence, she triumphs over an absurd society still shaped by decaying, male-generated notions of lust, honor, and power.

In his fiction, Harrison transcends what some critics have unjustly referred to as macho writing. He uses modes of mystery, adventure, romance, and tragic comedy to reflect men and women in conflict with modern society. His characters are on personal quests, searching for enlightenment in a fast-paced techno-industrial society.

THE FARMER'S DAUGHTER

In *The Farmer's Daughter*, a three-novella collection consisting of *The Farmer's Daughter*, *Brown Dog Redux*, and *Games of Night*, Harrison continues to explore the emotions of yearning, regret, and hope from the male point of view. Each novella exhibits Harrison's dark sense of cringe-inducing humor. Deflowering young girls is no joke, but Harrison uses the young girls as metaphors for innocence. What world-weary male would not lust for that?

Harrison clings to his symbolic geography of Michigan's forests and Montana's rugged countryside. Both bring his wanderers home to, if not decency and happiness, at least temporary satisfaction and protection.

His characters read great writers such as Marcel Proust, Stendhal, and Fyodor Dostoevski. They enjoy classical music, although the repertoire is salted with the country-western songs of Patsy Cline and George Jones. What a perfect world it would be if all girls lived on a remote ranch, read literature, played Franz Schubert at the piano, and looked terrific in shorts.

The title novella centers on lissome Sarah Holcomb, who does live on a remote Montana ranch. The story spans her high school years until she leaves for college. She gets attention from Old Tim and young Karl. Old Tim looks but never touches; young Karl drug-rapes her. She is handy with a 30.06 rifle and loves venison stew. At the end, she leaves Montana for Arizona to consummate her love for Alfredo, a thirty-five-year-old botany professor.

Brown Dog Redux is another adventure in the life of Brown Dog, the half Chippewa man from Michigan. His half-breed status is symbolic of his half-man, half-animal being. He's still howling, sniffing, tracking, and fornicating through the world. Social workers want to institutionalize his stepdaughter Berry, who suffers from fetal alcohol syndrome, so he illegally crosses the Canadian border. Brown Dog and Berry sneak back

into the United States, using the tour bus of an Indian rock band, the Thunderbirds. Returning to Michigan, he copulates in a trash bag with a lesbian friend who wants a baby.

In *Games of Night*, the unnamed narrator practices adolescent sex in a stock watering tank on the plains of West Texas. Emelia, his teenage partner, will reappear thirty-five years later, and they rescue each other. As a boy on a field trip to Mexico with his ornithologist father, he is bitten by a carnivorous hummingbird and a wolf pup; he becomes a werewolf. Relentlessly goaded by wolflike food and sexual appetites, he searches for relief across the United States and Europe. When he and Emelia finally settle in Montana, she understands his "monthly difficulties" and takes him to a wilderness area, where he roams until they subside.

With keen insight into men's basic desires, Harrison asks where it is possible for men to live in a contemporary world. A nearby wilderness and an understanding partner would be best. Is it enough to have a recreation room in the basement, a hunting trip with the guys, a few glances at Internet porn sites? Harrison looks unflinchingly at the male condition.

OTHER MAJOR WORKS

LONG FICTION: *Wolf: A False Memoir*, 1971; *A Good Day to Die*, 1973; *Farmer*, 1976; *Warlock*, 1981; *Sundog: The Story of an American Foreman*, 1984; *Dalva*, 1988; *The Road Home*, 1998; *True North*, 2004; *The Summer He Didn't Die*, 2005 (collection of three novellas: *The Summer He Didn't Die*, *Republican Wives*, and *Tracking*); *Returning to Earth*, 2007; *The English Major*, 2008.

SCREENPLAYS: *Cold Feet*, 1989 (with Thomas McGuane); *Revenge*, 1989; *Wolf*, 1994 (with Wesley Strick).

POETRY: *Plain Song*, 1965; *Locations*, 1968; *Outlyer and Ghazals*, 1971; *Letters to Yesenin*, 1973; *Returning to Earth*, 1977; *Selected and New Poems, 1961-1981*, 1982; *Natural World*, 1983 (includes sculpture by Diana Guest); *The Theory and Practice of Rivers*, 1985; *The Theory and Practice of Rivers, and New Poems*, 1989; *After Ikkyu, and Other Poems*, 1996; *The Shape of the Journey: New and Collected Poems*, 1998; *Braided Creek: A Conversation in Poetry*, 2003;

Saving Daylight, 2006; *In Search of Small Gods*, 2009.

NONFICTION: *Just Before Dark: Collected Nonfiction*, 1991; *The Raw and the Cooked: Adventures of a Roving Gourmand*, 2001; *Conversations with Jim Harrison*, 2002 (Robert DeMott, editor); *Off to the Side: A Memoir*, 2002.

CHILDREN'S LITERATURE: *The Boy Who Ran to the Woods*, 2000.

BIBLIOGRAPHY

DeMott, Robert J., ed. *Conversations with Jim Harrison*. Jackson: University Press of Mississippi, 2002. This is a collection of all interviews given between 1976 and 1999.

Harrison, Jim. Interview by Wendy Smith. *Publishers Weekly* 237 (August 3, 1990): 59-60. A general discussion of some of the basic characteristics of Harrison's writing, followed by comments by Harrison on his work; Harrison notes that, although he still considers fiction and poetry his major work, he is intrigued by the screenplay format.

_____. "Jim Harrison." In *Conversations with American Novelists*, edited by Kay Bonetti, Greg Michaelson, Speer Morgan, Jo Sapp, and Sam Stowers. Columbia: University of Missouri Press, 1997. Harrison discusses how the skills he developed writing poetry were transferred to his fiction; talks about the sometimes negative influence of university writing programs, his reputation as a macho writer, his interest in the novella form, and his work as a screenwriter.

Orr, Greg, and Beef Torrey. *Jim Harrison: A Comprehensive Bibliography, 1964-2008*. Lincoln: University of Nebraska Press, 2009. This is an annotated collection of all works in this time frame arranged by genre. It also includes citations for other writings about Harrison.

Smith, Patrick. *The True Bones of My Life: Essays on the Fiction of Jim Harrison*. East Lansing: Michigan State University Press, 2002. The first full-length collection of Smith's critical essays of Harrison's varied works. Essays tie Harrison's themes and metaphors to contemporary American life.

Allen Learst; John Nizalowski
Updated by Judith L. Steininger

BRET HARTE

Born: Albany, New York; August 25, 1836
Died: Camberley, Surrey, England; May 5, 1902

PRINCIPAL SHORT FICTION

Condensed Novels, 1867
The Lost Galleon, and Other Tales, 1867
The Luck of Roaring Camp, and Other Sketches,
   1870
Stories of the Sierras, 1872
Mrs. Skaggs's Husbands, 1873
Tales of the Argonauts, 1875
Thankful Blossom, 1877
Drift from Two Shores, 1878
The Story of a Mine, 1878
The Twins of Table Mountain, 1879
Flip and Found at Blazing Star, 1882
In the Carquinez Woods, 1883
Maruja, 1885
A Millionaire of Rough-and-Ready, 1887
The Crusade of the Excelsior, 1887
A Phyllis of the Sierras, 1888
Cressy, 1889
The Heritage of Dedlow Marsh, 1889
A Waif of the Plains, 1890
A First Family of Tasajara, 1891
Sally Dows, 1893
A Protégée of Jack Hamlin's, 1894
The Bell-Ringer of Angel's, 1894
In a Hollow of the Hills, 1895
Barker's Luck, and Other Stories, 1896
Three Partners, 1897
Stories in Light and Shadow, 1898
Tales of Trail and Town, 1898
Mr. Jack Hamlin's Meditation, 1899
Condensed Novels: Second Series, 1902
Trent's Trust, 1903
The Story of Enriquez, 1924

OTHER LITERARY FORMS

Bret Harte (breht hahrt) attempted practically every form of *belles lettres* common in the nineteenth century. He wrote several collections of poems, almost entirely forgotten in the years since his death. Indeed, his poetic reputation to modern readers depends completely on the success of one poem, his comic-verse masterpiece "Plain Language from Truthful James," more commonly known as "The Heathen Chinee," published in 1870. He wrote and edited newspaper material, essays, the novel *Gabriel Conroy* (1876), and some excellent satirical work, notably his *Condensed Novels*; and he collaborated with Mark Twain on a play, *Ah Sin* (1877), based on his poem "The Heathen Chinee."

ACHIEVEMENTS

Bret Harte's influence on "local color" fiction, especially the literature of the American West, was profound but not totally fortunate. He was one of the early writers, and certainly the most influential one, to set stories on the mining frontier that evolved from the California gold rush of 1849. His interest in the Western story and his success in transforming his raw material into popular fiction led many subsequent writers to explore American Western themes that they might otherwise have dismissed as unworthy of serious notice. Harte's stories, however, focusing on colorful characters that he deemed worthy of treatment for their own sake, tend to undervalue plot and setting, and his contrived plots and sentimental treatment of character gave subsequent Western fiction an escapist, juvenile bent, which it took a long time to outgrow.

BIOGRAPHY

Born in Albany, New York, as Francis Brett Harte (he would later drop the "Francis" and change the spelling of his middle name to Bret), Harte went to California in 1854, where for a while he lived many of the lives he was later to re-create imaginatively in the biographies of his fictional characters. Among other occupations, he worked an unsuccessful mining claim on the Stanislaus River; he may have been a guard for the Wells Fargo stagecoach lines; and he was employed in various capacities at the San Francisco mint before drifting into journalism. He was associated in 1864 with the founding of C. H. Webb's journal, *Californian*, in which some of his early work was published. Subsequently he became editor of the *Overland Monthly* (1868-1870), in which many of his famous works first saw print. Notable among these are the short story "The Luck of Roaring Camp" and the comic poem "Plain Language from Truthful James," which led to an offer from *The Atlantic Monthly* of a ten-thousand-dollar yearly contract, annually renewable, for exclusive rights to his material. On the strength of this contract Harte moved to Boston, but the contract was not renewed after the first year. Indeed, Harte's later work never came up to the standard of his earlier efforts, and although he was a tireless writer his production rapidly degenerated into hack work. He moved to Europe, serving for a brief time as American consul in Krefeld, Germany, and in Glasgow, Scotland, before finally settling in London, where he lived the rest of his life. He was happy in London, where people viewed his work more charitably than in the United States and where he was respected as an authentic voice of "the '49."

ANALYSIS

Any discussion of Bret Harte must begin by making a clear distinction between *importance* and *quality*--that is, between the influence of an author's work and its intrinsic value. That Harte was an extremely important writer, no one will deny. Almost entire credit should be given to him for the refinement of the gold fields of California into rich literary ore. More than a mere poet of "the '49," he firmly established many of the stock character types of later Western fiction: the gentleman gambler, the tarnished lady, the simple though often lovably cantankerous prospector, all invariably possessed of hearts of gold. These prototypes, so beloved of later Western writers of fiction and of film, seemed to spring, like rustic Athenas, full-grown

from Harte's fertile brain. However, doubts remain about the intrinsic literary quality of his work. After publication of *The Luck of Roaring Camp, and Other Sketches* and the overwhelming success of his famous comic poem "Plain Language from Truthful James," the brilliant tomorrows confidently predicted for him developed instead into a series of remembered yesterdays. What is the reason for Harte's meteoric rise and his equally precipitous fall?

Perhaps a partial answer may be found in a term often applied to Harte's work: It is, critics are fond of saying, "Dickensian." There is much truth in this critical commonplace, for the influence of Charles Dickens is everywhere to be found in Harte's writing, from brilliantly visualized characters and sentimental descriptions to contrived plots. Perhaps the first of these is significant, for, like Dickens, Harte's work is noted for memorable characters rather than memorable stories. What would Dickens be without Bob Cratchit, Mister Micawber, and Little Nell? Similarly, what would Harte be without gambler John Oakhurst and the lovable but

Bret Harte (Library of Congress)

eccentric lawyer Colonel Starbottle? The answer to these rhetorical questions, however, conceals a major limitation in Harte's literary artistry, which a too-facile comparison to Dickens easily overlooks. Dickens also created a series of powerful negative and evil characters, which are completely lacking in Harte's work. Where are the Gradgrinds, Fagins, and Uriah Heeps to be found in Harte's writing? The answer, to the detriment of Harte's stories, is nowhere. Because of this, Harte's stories lack a tragic vision of the world and of human beings' place in it. Misfortune in Harte's stories is uniformly pathetic rather than tragic, and the unfortunate result is that too often these stories settle for a "good cry" on the part of the reader rather than attempting any analysis of humanity's destiny or its place in an unknown and often hostile universe.

"THE OUTCASTS OF POKER FLAT"

A brief glance at one of Harte's best-known stories, "The Outcasts of Poker Flat," may serve at once to indicate both the strengths and the limitations of his work. This story tells of four "outcasts" from the California gold camp of Poker Flat, who have been escorted to the city limits by a vigilance committee, operating in the flush of civic pride, and told never to return on peril of their lives. The four outcasts are John Oakhurst, a professional gambler; "the Duchess" and "Mother Shipton," two prostitutes; and "Uncle Billy," a "confirmed drunkard," suspected as well of the more serious crime of robbing sluices. The four outcasts hope to find shelter in the neighboring settlement of Sandy Bar, a long day's journey away over a steep mountain range; but at noon the saddle-weary Duchess calls a halt to the expedition, saying she will "go no further." Accordingly, the party goes into camp, despite Oakhurst's pointing out that they are only halfway to Sandy Bar and that they have neither equipment nor provisions. They do, however, have liquor, and the joys of alcohol soon replace the will to proceed toward Sandy Bar, where, in all fairness to the outcasts, their reception may not be overwhelmingly enthusiastic. Oakhurst does not drink, but out of a feeling of loyalty he stays with his companions.

Later, the party is joined by two refugees from Sandy Bar, Tom Simson and his betrothed, Piney Woods. They have eloped from Sandy Bar because of the objections of Piney's father to their forthcoming marriage and are planning to be wed in Poker Flat. It transpires that Simson, referred to throughout the story as "the Innocent," had once lost to Oakhurst his "entire fortune--amounting to some forty dollars"--and that after the game was over Oakhurst had taken the young man aside and given his money back, saying simply, "You're a good little man, but you can't gamble worth a cent. Don't try it over again." This had made a friend-for-life of the Innocent and also serves to show that Poker Flat's view of Oakhurst as a monster of iniquity is not to be taken totally at face value. Since it is now too late to travel on, both the outcasts and the young lovers decide to encamp in a ruined house near the trail.

During the night Uncle Billy abandons the group, taking all the animals with him. It also begins to snow. The party, predictably, is snowed in, although the situation is not too grave, since the extra provisions that the Innocent has brought with him, and which Uncle Billy did not steal, are enough, with careful husbandry, to last the party for ten days. All begin to make the cabin habitable, and they spend the first few days listening to the Innocent play the accordion and to a paraphrase of the *Iliad* (c. 750 b.c.e.; English translation, 1611), which the Innocent has recently read and with which, much to Oakhurst's delight, the Innocent regales the company.

The situation, however, deteriorates. Another snowstorm totally isolates the camp, although the castaways are able to see, far below them, the smoke of Poker Flat. On the tenth day, Mother Shipton, "once the strongest of the party," who had mysteriously been growing weaker, dies. Her serious decline, it turns out, is a result of the fact that she had not eaten any of her carefully husbanded rations, which she had selflessly saved for her companions. Oakhurst then makes a pair of snowshoes out of a pack saddle and gives them to the Innocent, whom he sends off to Poker Flat in a last attempt to bring aid. If the Innocent reaches Poker Flat within two days, Oakhurst says, all will be well. He follows the Innocent partway on his journey toward Poker Flat but does not return.

Meanwhile, back at the camp, the situation goes from bad to worse. Only the Duchess and Piney are left, and--although they are properly grateful for the pile of wood that Oakhurst had secretly gathered and left for them--the rigors of a cruel world prove too strong. They die of starvation in the snow, and a rescue party arriving too late is properly edified by their moral courage--and, the reader trusts, properly chastened by recognition of Poker Flat's despicable conduct. Oakhurst, readers discover at the end of the story, in the best tradition of *noblesse oblige*, has committed suicide. The story concludes with a rehearsal of his epitaph, written by himself on a deuce of clubs and pinned to a pine tree with a bowie knife: "Beneath this tree lies the body of John Oakhurst, who struck a streak of bad luck on the 23d of November 1850, and handed in his checks on the 7th of December, 1850."

It is pointless to pretend that "The Outcasts of Poker Flat" does not have a certain power; indeed, the evidence of its continuing popularity, as shown through inclusion in countless anthologies, clearly indicates that the story is not a totally negligible effort. Nevertheless, a thoughtful reader who has finished the story may be conscious of a certain dissatisfaction. Why?

The obvious answer seems to be that the story has little new to say. In European literature, prostitutes with hearts of gold were scarcely novel figures by the 1860's; furthermore, the fact that holier-than-thou individuals, who are likely not only to cast the first stone but also to be sorry when it hits, can scarcely have been new to a reasonably perceptive reader. What Harte no doubt intended was to evoke a set of emotions from the reader, of sorrow and of pity for the poor victims of the social ingratitude of Poker Flat. The argument, from one perspective, is the oldest in the world: the tiresome *tu quoque* statement that the holier-than-thou are little better than the lowlier-than-them. However, this easy answer will not entirely work. As has been pointed out many times, considered purely from the perspective of "ideas," most literature *is* commonplace.

Perhaps a better question is to ask how Harte approached his parable and whether his fictional method works. To this the answer must be "No," for if the reader considers the story carefully, he or she must agree that it simply is not successful, even in its own

terms. The reader has, as Harte's friend and sometime collaborator Twain would have said, been "sold."

If the reader examines the story closely, he or she finds a group of outcasts sent on a long day's journey to another place. They stop only halfway--that is, half a day's journey--there. The place they left, in fact, is clearly visible behind them. Four in number, they are joined by two others; when Uncle Billy deserts, their number is five. Harte tells the reader that with careful management they have ten days' food, even though they have no animals. (What Uncle Billy could possibly have wanted with the seven animals he stole, particularly since he had no provisions to put on them, is never clarified, nor is the bothersome detail of how he could have managed the theft in the first place, considering he had to remove them single-handedly from under the noses of his companions, one of whom, Oakhurst, is, Harte specifically states, "a light sleeper." The animals do not simply wander off; Harte calls attention to the fact that they had been "tethered." Uncle Billy must therefore have released them on purpose.) The unfortunate castaways survive on meager rations for a week, until Oakhurst suddenly remembers how to make snowshoes. Why he could not remember this skill on the second day or perhaps the third is never clarified, but no matter. The reason is obvious, at least from Harte's point of view of the logic of the story. It is necessary for Harte to place his characters in a situation of romantic peril in order that their sterling qualities be thrown into high relief; to place his characters *in extremis*, however, Harte totally sacrifices whatever logic the story may have had in its own terms.

When Uncle Billy leaves, then, the group discovers that it has sufficient supplies for ten days--that is, fifty man days' worth of food. Mother Shipton eats none of hers, dying of starvation at the end of a week. This means that the party now has some twenty-two man days of food left, with at the most only three people to eat it, since Mother Shipton is already dead and Oakhurst is about to commit suicide. This is, according to the data Harte has previously given, an easy week's rations. Why, then, do the two surviving ladies die of starvation before the rescue party arrives some four days later?

The answer has nothing to do with the story, which is designed, rather, for the moral Harte wishes to convey. For in his single-minded pursuit of the commonplace notion that appearances may be deceiving and that there is a spark of goodness in all of us, Harte has totally sacrificed all fictional probabilities. Any potential tragic effect the story might presumably possess evaporates in the pale warmth of sentimental nostalgia.

This inability to allow his stories to speak for themselves is Harte's fictional weakness. Rather than allowing his tales to develop their own meaning, he obsessively applies a meaning to them, a meaning which, in far too many cases, cheapens the fictional material at his disposal. Perhaps the fault is that Harte, in his relentless search for this new California literary ore, did not really know where to find it. The mother lode consistently escaped him, and whatever flakes his search discovered were too often small and heavily alloyed.

"TENNESSEE'S PARTNER"

Harte singles out humor as the factor that finally diminished the influence of English models on the short story in America. It was the type of humor, Harte claimed, common in the barrooms, at the gatherings in the country store, and finally at public meetings in the mouths of "stump" orators. "Tennessee's Partner," one of his best-known stories, is a prototypical example of this barroom humor. After relating how Tennessee's partner went to San Francisco for a wife and was stopped in Stockton by a young waitress who broke at least two plates of toast over his head, the narrator says that he is well aware that "something more might be made of this episode, but I prefer to tell it as it was current at Sandy Bar--in the gulches and barrooms--where all sentiment was modified by a strong sense of humor."

It is from this point of view--sentiment modified by humor--that Harte tells the central episode. Tennessee running off with his partner's wife is related in the same flippant phrases as are used to describe Tennessee's partner's somewhat hazardous wooing. When Tennessee returns from his escapade, and all the boys who gather in the canyon are "naturally indignant" that there is no shooting, Tennessee's partner looks at them in such a way as to indicate "a lack of humorous appreciation"; for he is a "grave man, with a steady application to practical detail which was unpleasant in a difficulty." Tennessee's partner's steady application to practical detail proves unpleasant indeed to Tennessee, who is in difficulty at the trial. For surely, the partner, in his serious and practical way, knows that his attempt to bribe the judge and jury will clinch the case against Tennessee, the final trump in the card game that began with Tennessee's capture. The "popular feeling" that had grown up against Tennessee in Sandy Bar could end no other way.

At Tennessee's trial, the narrator makes it clear that the trial is only to justify "the previous irregularities of arrest and indictment." The men are "secure in the hypothesis that Tennessee ought to be hanged on general principles." It is this knowledge that they are going to hang Tennessee not so much for a concrete wrong as on general principles that makes them begin to waver, until the partner, who has suffered a concrete wrong by Tennessee, enters the game with his attempted bribe. As a result of his taking a hand, the town helps Tennessee's partner avenge himself on Tennessee, and the partner helps the town get rid of a bothersome blight on the body politic. Rather than sentimental, the story is an example of barroom humor at its most sardonic.

"THE LUCK OF ROARING CAMP"

An important aspect of Harte's mastery of the short-story form is the fact that what holds his stories together is not plot but theme. "The Luck of Roaring Camp" is a clear example. In the first three paragraphs, the reader is introduced to the central themes: the all-male world, the men acting as one, and the unusual birth in a place where death is more common (an obvious thematic presage of the story's conclusion). Introduced in the opening paragraphs is the voice of the story--not the voice of the inhabitants of Roaring Camp, but of an educated observer. Moreover, the perspective of this observer is more like that of a man in a theater watching a melodrama than in the town watching the inhabitants. As a result of these melodramatic conventions, the characters are stereotyped and the landscape is stylized.

The addition of a narrative voice to the stage play creates a tragicomic tension. In spite of the fact that the story is moving toward death, the opening birth scenes are inevitably comic, for as the single woman of the camp labor gives birth, the whole camp sits outside and collectively smokes like expectant fathers. Since any one could be the father, all are the father of the child. Harte foregrounds this comic nature of town unity by pointing out that although the individuals may be fragmentary, lacking fingers, toes, or ears, they constitute an "aggregate force." Lest the reader judge the individual by his appearance, the gambler has a Raphael face and the intellectual abstraction of a Hamlet, while the strongest man has only three fingers on his right hand and the best shot only has only one eye. When the newborn baby cries out, they all rise to their feet "as one man."

The surface theme of the story is, of course, the regeneration of Roaring Camp; however, it is not the child who achieves this, but rather the men playing the roles of women. Although the men plan a broad burlesque for the christening of the child, complete with a mock godfather, Stumpy stops it, claiming his own right for that position. "To the credit of all humorists be it said that the first man to acknowledge its justice was the satirist thus stopped of his fun." Thus the christening proceeds seriously, which, the narrator says, makes it more ludicrous than the satirist had planned. Comic also is the notion of "pastoral happiness" set up by the British sailor singing all ninety stanzas of a sea chantey as a lullaby.

However, the idyll works only if perpetuated in a world of men around the baby, bringing it up much as wolves bring up a lost child. When there is talk by some of civilizing the town by bringing in women and families, the threat to the idyll is obvious. Harte makes it clear that the story cannot end that way but that something must prevent the loss of the idyll. The child, the center of the transformation of the men, must be preserved in the only way mythic creatures can, by being made into a holy icon. Thus the story ends with the mighty storm, like the destruction of the earth by flood, in which the camp that formerly roared with male bawdiness now roars with the flood that washes away all in front of it.

OTHER MAJOR WORKS

LONG FICTION: *Gabriel Conroy*, 1876.

PLAYS: *Two Men of Sandy Bar*, pr. 1876; *Ah Sin*, pr.

1877 (with Mark Twain); *Sue*, pr. 1896 (with T. Edgar Pemberton).

POETRY: "Plain Language from Truthful James," 1870 (also known as "The Heathen Chinee"); *East and West Poems*, 1871; *Poems*, 1871; *Poetical Works*, 1880; *Poetical Works of Bret Harte*, 1896; *Some Later Verses*, 1898.

NONFICTION: *Selected Letters of Bret Harte*, 1997 (Gary Scharnhorst, editor).

MISCELLANEOUS: *The Luck of Roaring Camp, and Other Writings*, 2001.

BIBLIOGRAPHY

Barnett, Linda D. *Bret Harte: A Reference Guide.* Boston: G. K. Hall, 1980. With a brief introduction outlining the historical directions of Harte scholarship and criticism, this work provides a good annotated bibliography and checklist through 1977.

Burton, Linda. "For Better or Worse: Tennessee and His Partner: A New Approach to Bret Harte." *Arizona Quarterly* 36 (1980): 211-216. Says the story is not sentimental nonsense or a botched attempt at brotherly love, but depicts a submerged homosexual relationship between Tennessee and his partner.

Conner, William F. "The Euchering of Tennessee: A Reexamination of Bret Harte's 'Tennessee's Partner.'" *Studies in Short Fiction* 17 (1980): 113-120. Points out the relevance of the game of Euchre in the story and discusses the tricks Harte plays on the reader.

Duckett, Margaret. *Mark Twain and Bret Harte.* Norman: University of Oklahoma Press, 1964. Duckett's book is an intriguing and carefully documented history of the friendship between and literary association of Twain and Harte and their eventual falling out and feud. Includes illustrations and a bibliography through 1963.

Hall, Roger. "Annie Pixley, Kate Mayhew, and Bret Harte's *M'Liss*." *ATQ*, n.s. 11 (December, 1997): 267-283. Discusses the struggle in 1878 over the rights to *M'Liss*, a play based on a story by Harte; claims that the struggle indicates the chaotic state of copyright laws, contracts, and play "pirates" in the late nineteenth century.

Morrow, Patrick. *Bret Harte*. Boise, Ida.: Boise State College, 1972. This brief but excellent study analyzes Harte's major work in both literature and criticism. Although concise, it is a helpful introduction. Supplemented by a select bibliography.

_____. *Bret Harte, Literary Critic*. Bowling Green, Ohio: Bowling Green State University Popular Press, 1979. Morrow surveys and analyzes what he considers a neglected part of Harte's work, his literary criticism. He establishes Harte's significance in the "local color" movement. Contains a useful bibliography of primary sources.

_____. "Bret Harte, Mark Twain, and the San Francisco Circle." In *A Literary History of the American West*. Fort Worth: Texas Christian University, 1987. This important chapter covers the contributors to the Western journals between 1865 and 1875, placing emphasis on Harte.

O'Connor, Richard. *Bret Harte: A Biography*. Boston: Little, Brown, 1966. A lively, anecdotal, and gossipy account limited to Harte's life, this work is not critical in focus. It does list Harte's best-known literary characters.

Scharnhorst, Gary. *Bret Harte*. New York: Twayne, 1992. A critical biography of Harte, providing analyses of stories from four different periods of his life, fully informed by critical reception of Harte's work. An afterword summarizes Harte's critical reputation.

_____. *Bret Harte: A Bibliography*. Lanham, Md.: Scarecrow Press, 1995. An excellent tool for the student of Harte.

_____. "Mark Twain, Bret Harte, and the Literary Construction of San Francisco." In *San Francisco in Fiction: Essays in a Regional Literature*, edited by David Fine and Paul Skenazy. Albuquerque: University of New Mexico Press, 1995. Discusses Harte's acceptance of the Eastern canon's taste in such stories as "The Idyl of Red Gulch" and his romanticized depiction of San Francisco as a rough-and-tumble boomtown in several late stories.

Stevens, J. David. "'She War a Woman': Family Roles, Gender, and Sexuality in Bret Harte's Western Fiction." *American Literature* 69 (September, 1997): 571-593. A discussion of gender in Harte's western fiction; argues that what critics have labeled sentimental excess in Harte's fiction is in fact his method of exploring certain hegemonic cultural paradigms taken for granted in other western narratives; discusses stories that deal with the structure of the family and how they critique gender roles.

Stewart, George R. *Bret Harte, Argonaut and Exile*. Port Washington, N.Y.: Kennikat Press, 1964. This is a scholarly and highly regarded Harte biography. It focuses on Harte's life and defends the writer's achievements against his detractors.

Stoneley, Peter. "Rewriting the Gold Rush: Twain, Harte, and Homosociality." *Journal of American Studies* 30 (August, 1996): 189-209. An examination of authority and gender in gold-rush fiction. From the perspective of poststructuralist theories of difference, explores the partnership of Twain and Harte; situates the Harte-Twain relationship within a broader network of late nineteenth century.

James K. Folsom; John W. Fiero
Updated by Charles E. May

ADAM HASLETT

Born: Port Chester, New York; December 24, 1970

PRINCIPAL SHORT FICTION

You Are Not a Stranger Here, 2002

OTHER LITERARY FORMS

Given his legal background, Adam Haslett (HAZ-leht) frequently writes book reviews and essays on legal matters for magazines such as *The Nation, Esquire,* and *The New Yorker.* He also assisted in the writing of several books on U.S. tax politics and policy with Yale law professor and former U.S. Treasury official Michael Graetz. Haslett wrote an introduction and annotations for a 2004 edition of *Adam Haslett on George Washington's Rules of Civility.* Haslett published his first novel, *Union Atlantic,* in 2010.

ACHIEVEMENTS

Adam Haslett's debut collection, *You Are Not a Stranger Here,* was awarded the PEN/Winship Award for the best book for a New England author and was a finalist for both the 2002 National Book Award and the 2003 Pulitzer Prize. Haslett was named *New York* magazine's Writer of the Year in 2002. *You Are Not a Stranger Here* went on to be a *New York Times* best seller, one of *Time*'s five best books of 2002, and one of the best books of the year by *Village Voice, San Francisco Chronicle,* and *The Boston Globe.* It also was selected by author Jonathan Franzen as the second selection for National Broadcasting Corporation's *Today Show* Book Club. It has since been translated into sixteen languages.

Since then, Haslett has been awarded a 2005 Guggenheim Foundation Fellowship, the 2006 PEN/Malamud Award for accomplishment in short fiction, and a 2008 grant from the Rockefeller Foundation. He also has been given residencies at the MacDowell Colony and Yaddo. His story "Devotion" was included in the 2003 edition of *The Best American Short Stories.*

BIOGRAPHY

Adam Haslett was born December 24, 1970, in Port Chester, New York, to a British venture capitalist and an American high school French teacher and spent his early childhood in Kingston, Massachusetts. In 1980, Haslett's father relocated the family to Oxfordshire, England, for a business opportunity; his father suffered a severe bipolar episode when the investment failed soon after their arrival. Haslett's family returned to the United States three years later, and Haslett attended high school in Wellesley, Massachusetts. His father committed suicide shortly after the family's return.

Haslett attended Swarthmore College, where he studied with Franzen, and graduated in 1992. After college, Haslett went to work for George Trescher Associates in New York and the Lambda Legal Defense and Education Fund while debating whether to pursue a career as a writer or as a lawyer. Haslett was then accepted to Yale Law School, but he deferred his enrollment when he was awarded a seven-month fellowship at the Fine Arts Center in Provincetown, Massachusetts, in 1996. Following his fellowship, Haslett again delayed law school and attended the Iowa Writers' Workshop at the University of Iowa, where he received his M.F.A. in 1999.

Still skeptical about whether he could support himself as a writer, Haslett finally enrolled in Yale Law School, where he worked at a U.S. Attorney's office and a prison legal services clinic. In 2002, Haslett's debut collection, *You Are Not a Stranger Here,* was published to critical and commercial acclaim, cementing his career as a promising young writer. Despite his success, Haslett finished law school and received his J.D. in 2003, though he has said that he has no plans to practice law.

In 2002, Haslett returned to New York. Haslett has been a visiting professor at the Iowa Writers' Workshop and Columbia University. His first novel, *Union Pacific*, which he began writing while at the University of Iowa, was published in 2010.

ANALYSIS

As many reviewers noted upon its debut, mental illness is a central theme running throughout Adam Haslett's collection *You Are Not a Stranger Here*. Undoubtedly influenced by his own childhood experiences with his father's mental illness, Haslett writes knowledgeably about mental illness with a deft and sensitive touch. His language is restrained and emotionally precise, allowing the reader to inhabit and experience the thought processes of people in the throes of deep despair. Characters in Haslett's stories frequently suffer from suicidal depression or manic episodes that bring them to extremes of the human experience. Haslett approaches mental illness from a variety of perspectives; he ably describes the experience of mental illness from the perspectives of those who suffer, of their loved ones, and of their doctors. Haslett explores the spectrums of mental illness, debilitating for some, merely alienating for others. In Haslett's stories, mental illness is always incurable.

Despite the bleak nature of his stories, Haslett stresses in *You Are Not a Stranger Here*, as the title suggests, the importance of empathy and understanding, of trying to get his characters and his readers to internalize the experiences of another and make them a little less strange to one another. In the end, Haslett grapples with classical literary anxieties: the problems of alienation, miscommunication, and the gradual dissolution of dreams. Haslett suggests that, through compassion, everyone can find connection with others. It is an optimistic message, and though one not available to all of his characters, it is nonetheless a significant aspect of Haslett's worldview.

"WAR'S END"

This theme is made most clear in "War's End," a story on which Haslett worked continuously during his fellowship at the Fine Arts Center in Provincetown at the beginning of his career. One of Haslett's many stories set in the English countryside, where he spent a formative portion of his childhood, "War's End" is the story of Paul, a suicidally depressed man, who, hopelessly frustrated with his inability to get better and with the pain he is causing his wife, intends to throw himself off the cliffs of St. Andrews. Before he can enact his plan, Paul encounters a kind woman and her dying grandson. Faced with the reality of someone whose physical pain closely mirrors his emotional pain, Paul finds himself able to soothe the young boy by telling him stories from English history. Through this chance encounter, Paul realizes that while he cannot relieve his own pain, he has the ability to lessen the pain of others. By making a connection with another person in pain, Paul finds a previously unknown purpose.

The tone of this story is undeniably bleak, and Haslett does not provide any easy solutions to problems. He does not tend to romanticize his characters' suffering; he is, if nothing else, a realist when it comes to depicting mental health. Paul's depression will not lift; the young boy's life will not be saved. However, Haslett finds meaning in the idea that the despairing can find solace in speaking with others who are sympathetic to the pain of despair.

"DIVINATION"

In "Divination," Haslett elevates his concerns about mental illness to a more symbolic level. The story begins with Samuel, an English schoolboy, being struck by the unshakable belief that one of his schoolmasters, Mr. Jevins, has died in his apartment. When Samuel discovers that his prediction was in fact correct, he struggles with how to tell his family about his strange foreknowledge. He finally confides in his older brother, Trevor, who tells him that their father has experienced similar bouts of clairvoyance and once dreamed of a cousin's death before the actual event. When confronted, however, Samuel's father denies the entire incident and recommends that Samuel never speak about his gift. Once Samuel has a vision of his Trevor's death on a sailboat during a family vacation, he finally decides to speak up and tell others about his gift.

This hints at Haslett's preoccupation with the inheritance of mental illness. Although what is inherited in this instance is not mental illness, clairvoyance acts as a stand-in for more taboo and literal types of ailments. The way Samuel's father both denies his own gift and resists accepting the possibility of his son's clairvoyance is a clear metaphor for the deep shame many feel at admitting to mental illness in contemporary society. Haslett's message seems to be that by accepting and acknowledging mental illness, people can better prepare their families for what they might have inherited. By denying the existence of illness, people are likely to bring about tragedy, which is precisely what happens at the end of "Divination."

As is the case in many classical stories of the supernatural, Samuel's Cassandra-like clairvoyance is proven correct, though not in the way that Samuel anticipated it. His brother does not die on the boat that day but rather in a car accident, when his car collides with another trailing a sailboat. As the story ends, Samuel realizes that he has inherited a terrible gift that will torment him the rest of his life.

"DEVOTION"

Though mental illness seems to be Haslett's main preoccupation throughout *You Are Not a Stranger Here*, several of his stories also explore the stigma of homosexuality and how it, like mental illness, has the potential to alienate and isolate. In the story, the two main characters, Owen and Hillary, a middle-aged brother and sister who have lived together their whole lives after being orphaned at a young age, await the arrival of Ben, an old friend they had both fallen in love with years earlier.

Owen was the first to fall in love with Ben, though his love remains unconsummated, and not simply because Ben is a heterosexual. Owen has been alienated by his homosexuality. Closing himself off emotionally and sexually during the height of the acquired immunodeficiency syndrome (AIDS) epidemic years earlier, Owen finds himself middle-aged, closeted, and alone. As he does with mental illness in other stories, Haslett approaches the stigma of homosexuality with an eye toward compassion and understanding. Though Owen has lacked the courage to live his life the way he intended to, it is his sister, the only person he believes can truly understand him, who makes his life bearable.

Hillary, for her part, understands the importance of their relationship to her brother. Indeed, she needs him as much as he needs her. For, as in "Divination," Haslett provides a twist at the end: Not only has Owen

purposefully hidden all of Ben's letters to Hillary in order to make sure that she never abandons him but also Hillary has known about Owen's subterfuge for years. Though once angry, she has miraculously forgiven him for refusing to allow her to leave. As Ben calls to regretfully announce that he cannot make dinner, the siblings settle back into their normal lives, realizing that they are all each other has, forever. However, in Haslett's grim and disappointing world, this is enough. Haslett once again reasserts the value of compassion and love amid a bleak, sad world.

"NOTES TO MY BIOGRAPHER"

While the prevailing tone of Haslett's short fiction is unequivocally bleak, "Notes to My Biographer" hints at Haslett's more playful side. The story begins: "I have shot Germans in the fields of Normandy, filed twenty-six patents, married three women, survived them all, and am currently the subject of an investigation by the Internal Revenue Service, which has about as much chance of collecting from me as Shylock did of getting his pound of flesh. Bureaucracies have trouble thinking clearly. I, on the other hand, am perfectly lucid." "Notes to My Biographer" is far and away the most colorful story in *You Are Not a Stranger Here*. Told from the perspective of Franklin Caldwell Singer, an aging inventor attempting to reconnect with his estranged son while in the throes of a manic episode, "Notes to My Biographer" contains the only truly humorous moments in the entire collection. The story is carried by the power of the narrator's wildly optimistic voice and his gleeful lack of self-awareness. Franklin delights in providing his biographer with extensive notes about the new kind of bicycle he has just conceived; he is less forthcoming (or honest) about the dissolution of his marriage and his gradual estrangement of his family. When the reader witnesses an awkward dinner between the inventor and his son Graham, it becomes apparent that Franklin is an incredibly unreliable narrator, a man the reader cannot trust not because he lies but because he is not well enough to see things for what they actually are.

Despite the energy and lighter tone, Haslett's deeper serious concerns are still present. At its heart, "Notes to My Biographer" is a story about miscommunication, about a man who is a stranger to his own family. In

Graham's revelation that he, too, suffers from manic depression, though he takes great pains to take better care of himself than his father does (so as not to repeat the mistakes Franklin made), there is a reiteration of Haslett's interest in the inheritance of mental illness. Graham is an example of how it is possible to overcome inherited mental illness, though Haslett makes clear that while Graham can treat his own illness, he cannot cure it, nor can he escape the fears that one day he, like his father, will slip into madness.

OTHER MAJOR WORKS

LONG FICTION: *Union Atlantic*, 2010.

EDITED TEXT: *Adam Haslett on George Washington's Rules of Civility*, 2004 (introduction and annotations).

BIBLIOGRAPHY

Aultman, Julie M., and Delese Wear. "Medicine and Place: An Inquiry." *Perspectives in Biology and Medicine* 49, no. 1 (2006): 84-98. Using Haslett's "The Good Doctor" (2002) as an example, two doctors explore a doctor and a patient's differing experiences of illness.

Seligman, Craig. "I Can't Go On, I'll Go Nuts." *The New York Times Book Review*, July 21, 2002, p. 6. A review of *You Are Not a Stranger Here* focuses specifically on Haslett's facility with depicting mental illness.

Wiegand, David. "A Stranger No More." *San Francisco Chronicle*, September 21, 2002, p. D1. A profile written just prior to Haslett's graduation from law school, it explores his surprise at his sudden fame and the impact of his father's manic depression on his artistic sensibilities.

Stephen Aubrey

NATHANIEL HAWTHORNE

Born: Salem, Massachusetts; July 4, 1804
Died: Plymouth, New Hampshire; May 19, 1864

PRINCIPAL SHORT FICTION

Twice-Told Tales, 1837 (expanded 1842)
Mosses from an Old Manse, 1846
The Snow-Image, and Other Twice-Told Tales, 1851

OTHER LITERARY FORMS

Nathaniel Hawthorne is a major American novelist whose first novel, *Fanshawe: A Tale* (1828), did not lead immediately to further long fiction. After a period largely given to tales and sketches, he published his classic study of moral prejudice in colonial New England, *The Scarlet Letter* (1850). In the next decade, three more novels--he preferred to call them romances--followed: *The House of the Seven Gables* (1851), *The Blithedale Romance* (1852), and *The Marble Faun:Or, The Romance of Monte Beni* (1860). He wrote books for children, including *A Wonder-Book for Boys and Girls* (1852), and travel sketches of England, *Our Old Home* (1863). His posthumously published notebooks and letters are also important.

ACHIEVEMENTS

This seminal figure in American fiction combined narrative skill and artistic integrity as no previous American writer had done. A dozen of Nathaniel Hawthorne's short stories remain anthology favorites, and few modern American students fail to become familiar with *The Scarlet Letter*.

Hawthorne's influence on subsequent American writers, especially on his younger American friend Herman Melville, and on Henry James, William Faulkner, and Robert Lowell, has been enormous. Although he wrote comparatively little literary theory, his prefaces to his novels, preeminently the one to *The House of the Seven Gables*, and scattered observations within his fiction reflect a pioneering concern with his craft.

BIOGRAPHY

It is fitting that Nathaniel Hawthorne's birth in 1804 came on the Fourth of July, for, if American writers of his youth were attempting a literary declaration of independence to complement the successful political one of 1776, Hawthorne's fiction of the 1830's, along with Edgar Allan Poe's poetry and fiction and Ralph Waldo Emerson's essays and lectures of the same decade, rank as the fruition of that ambition.

Undoubtedly his hometown of Salem, Massachusetts, exerted a powerful shaping influence on his work. Nathaniel was the middle of three children and his father, a sea captain, died when Nathaniel was four years old. Nathaniel did not evince much interest in the sea. No one could grow up in Salem without a strong sense of the past, especially a boy whose ancestor, John Hathorne (as the family name was then spelled), had served as a judge in the infamous witchcraft trials of 1695.

In 1813, confined to home by a foot injury for two years, young Nathaniel formed the habit of reading for hours at a stretch. On graduating from Bowdoin College in 1825, where he was a classmate of Franklin Pierce, the future president, and Henry Wadsworth Longfellow, the future poet, the bookish Hawthorne returned to Salem and began a decade of intensive reading and writing. He published a novel, *Fanshawe: A Tale* (later repudiated), in 1828 and began to compose the short stories that eventually brought him into prominence. The first collection of these, *Twice-Told Tales*, appeared in 1837.

In 1838, Hawthorne became engaged to Sophia Peabody of Salem, and the following year he was appointed to a position in the Boston Custom House, but he left in 1841 to join the infant Brook Farm community in West Roxbury, Massachusetts. As a rather solitary man with no prior practical experience of farming, he did not thrive there and left before the end of the year. Marrying in 1842, the couple settled at the Old Manse in Concord. Although he befriended Henry David Thoreau, Hawthorne found the Concord Transcendentalists generally pretentious and boring. During the administration of James K. Polk, he left Concord for another customhouse appointment, this time back in Salem. From this period comes his second short-story collection, *Mosses from an Old Manse.*

Moving thereafter to Lenox in the Berkshires, Hawthorne met the younger writer Herman Melville and produced, in a few weeks in 1850, *The Scarlet Letter*, which was the first of his successful novels; *The House of the Seven Gables* and another collection of short fiction, *The Snow-Image, and Other Twice-Told Tales*, followed the next year. Back in Concord in 1852 at his home, "The Wayside," he wrote a campaign biography for his friend Pierce, which resulted in Hawthorne's appointment as U.S. consul in Liverpool, England. That same year he also wrote the novel *The Blithedale Romance*, based loosely on his Brook Farm experience.

In England, Hawthorne kept an extensive journal from which he later fashioned *Our Old Home*. Resigning his office in 1857, Hawthorne traveled with his family in Europe; in Florence, he began his last novel, published in 1860 as *The Marble Faun*. By the time he returned to Concord, his health was failing, and although he worked at several more novels, he did not finish any of them. In 1864, he set forth on a trip with Pierce but died in Plymouth, New Hampshire, on May 19.

ANALYSIS

Nathaniel Hawthorne's reading in American colonial history confirmed his basically ambivalent attitude toward the American past, particularly the form that Puritanism took in the New England colonies. Hawthorne was especially interested in the intensity of the Puritan-Cavalier rivalry, the Puritan inclination to credit manifestations of the supernatural, such as witchcraft, and the psychology of the struggle for liberation from English rule. He explored these themes in some of his earliest stories. As they did for his Puritan ancestors, sin and guilt preoccupied Hawthorne, who, in his move from Salem to Concord, encountered what he considered the facile dismissal of the problem of evil by the Concord intellectuals. He developed a deeply ambivalent moral attitude that colored the situations and characters of his fiction.

In the early masterpiece "My Kinsman, Major Molineux," his concern with the United States' coming-of-age blends with the maturation of a lad on the verge of manhood. Introduced to the complexities of evil, characters such as Robin of this story and the title character of "Young Goodman Brown" have great difficulty summoning the spiritual strength to resist dark temptations.

Often, Hawthorne's characters cannot throw off the vague but weighty burden of guilt. Frequently, his young protagonists exhibit a cold, unresponsive attitude toward a loving fiancé or wife and can find no spiritual sustenance to redeem the situation. Brown, Parson Hooper of "The Minister's Black Veil," and Reuben Bourne of "Roger Malvin's Burial" are examples of such guilt-ridden and essentially faithless men.

Another prevalent type of protagonist rejects love to become a detached observer, such as the husband of "Wakefield," who for no apparent reason deserts his wife and spends years living nearby in disguise. In the stories of Hawthorne's middle and later periods, these detached characters are usually scientists or artists. The former include misguided idealists such as Aylmer of "The Birthmark" and the scientist Rappaccini in "Rappaccini's Daughter," who experiments remorselessly on female family members in search of some elusive

Nathaniel Hawthorne (Library of Congress)

abstract perfection. Hawthorne's artists, while less dangerous, tend also to exclude themselves from warm and loving relationships.

At their most deplorable, Hawthorne's isolated, detached characters become, like Ethan Brand in the story of the same name and Roger Chillingworth of *The Scarlet Letter*, violators of the human heart, unreclaimable souls whose estrangement from normal human relationships yields them little in compensation, either material or spiritual.

Characteristically Hawthorne builds his stories on a quest or journey, often into the woods or wilderness but always into an unknown region, the protagonist emerging enlightened or merely chastened but invariably sadder, with any success a bitterly ironical one, such as Aylmer's removal of his wife's birthmark, which kills his patient. The stories are pervasively and often brilliantly symbolic, and Hawthorne's symbolic imagination encompasses varieties ranging from more or less clear-cut allegory to elusive multiple symbolic patterns, the significance of which critics debate endlessly.

More than a century and a half after their composition, Hawthorne's artistry and moral imagination, even in some of his seriously flawed stories, continue to engage readers and critics. Two of Hawthorne's most enduringly popular stories-- "Roger Malvin's Burial" and "My Kinsman, Major Molineux"--appeared initially in the 1832 edition of a literary annual called *The Token* but remained uncollected until long afterward. Both seem to have been intended for a book, *Provincial Tales*, that never materialized, and both begin with paragraphs explicitly linking the narratives to historical events.

"Roger MALVIN'S BURIAL"

"Roger Malvin's Burial" is set in the aftermath of a 1725 confrontation with Native Americans called Lovell's Fight. Roger is a mortally wounded soldier; Reuben Bourne, his less seriously injured companion, must decide whether to stay with his older friend on the desolate frontier or make his way back to his company before he becomes too weak to travel. Urged to the latter course by Roger, his prospective father-in-law, Reuben makes the older man as comfortable as he can at the base of a huge rock near an oak sapling, promises to return as soon as he can, and staggers away. Eventually, he is discovered by a search party and taken home to be ministered to by Dorcas, his fiancé. After several days of semiconsciousness, Reuben recovers sufficiently to answer questions. Although he believes he has done the right thing, he cannot bring himself to contradict Dorcas's assumption that he had buried her father, and he is undeservedly lionized for his heroic fidelity.

Eighteen years later, this unhappy and uncommunicative husband takes Dorcas and their fifteen-year-old son Cyrus to the frontier, presumably to resettle but really to "bury" Roger and expiate his own guilt. On the anniversary of the day Reuben had left Roger, Dorcas and Cyrus are led to the rock and the now blasted oak tree, a fatal gunshot is fired, and in a chillingly ambiguous way Reuben relieves himself of his "curse." This pattern of irrational guilt and ambivalent quest would be repeated in other stories, using New England historical incidents and pervasive symbols, such as the rock and oak of "Roger Malvin's Burial."

"MY KINSMAN, MAJOR MOLINEUX"

"My Kinsman, Major Molineux" is justly considered one of Hawthorne's greatest stories. The historical introduction here serves to establish the setting as a time of bitter resentment toward Massachusetts colonial governors. The location is left deliberately vague, except that Robin, the young protagonist, must arrive by ferry in a town where he hopes to meet his kinsman, a colonial official. Robin has come from the country with an idea of getting a boost toward a career from Major Molineux. The town is tense and lurid when he enters at nightfall, and the people act strangely. In particular, whenever Robin mentions the name of his kinsman, he is rebuffed. While frequently described as "shrewd," Robin seems naïve and baffled by the events of this disquieting evening.

Eventually, he is treated to the nightmarish spectacle of the public humiliation of his kinsman, though it appears that Major Molineux is the more or less innocent victim of colonial vindictiveness toward the authority of the Crown. At the climax, Robin finds himself unaccountably laughing with the townspeople at Molineux's disgrace. By the end of the evening, Robin, convinced that nothing remains for him to do but to return home, is counseled by the only civil person he meets to wait a few days before leaving, "as you are a shrewd youth, you may rise in the world without the help of your kinsman, Major Molineux."

At one level, this is clearly a rite-of-passage story. Robin has reached the point of initiation into an adult world of deviousness and obliquity that he has hardly begun to suspect, but one in which he can hope to prosper only through his own efforts. The conclusion strongly implies that he cannot go home again, or that if he does, life will never be the same. As the stranger suggests, he may well be obliged to stay and adjust to the new world that he has discovered. The historical setting proclaims "My Kinsman, Major Molineux" an imaginative account of the colonial struggle toward the challenges and perils of an independence for which the people are largely unprepared. The ferry ride, reminiscent of the underworld adventures of epic heroes, such as Odysseus and Aeneas--and perhaps more pointedly yet, the Dante of the *Inferno* (c. 1320)--leads to a hellish region from which newcomers cannot normally expect to return. The multiplicity of interpretations that this story has provoked attests its richness and complexity.

Several of Hawthorne's best stories first appeared in 1835. One of these, "Wakefield," has been criticized as slight and undeveloped, but it remains intriguing. It poses in its final paragraph an exacting problem: "Amid the seeming confusion of our mysterious world, individuals are so nicely adjusted to a system, and systems to one another and to a whole, that, by stepping aside for a moment, a man exposes himself to a fearful risk of losing his place forever." Wakefield "steps aside" by leaving his wife for no apparent reason and secretly taking up residence in the next street. The setting of this story, unusual for Hawthorne, is London, and the couple have been married for ten years. Wakefield seems to be an embryonic version of the ruthless experimenter of several later stories, but here his action is more of a joke than an experiment. He is "intellectual, but not actively so"; he lacks imagination; and he has "a cold but not depraved nor wandering heart." When he leaves, he promises to be back in three or four days, but he stays away for twenty years. He adopts a disguise, regularly walks by his old home and peers in, and even passes his wife in the street. Wakefield has a purpose that he cannot define, but the author describes his motive merely as "morbid vanity." He will frighten his wife and will find out how much he really matters. He does not matter that much, however, for his wife settles to the routine of her "widowhood." Finally, passing his old home in a rain shower, he suddenly decides to enter, and at this point the story ends, leaving unanswered the question of whether he has lost his place forever.

"THE MINISTER'S BLACK VEIL"

Of the many Hawthorne stories that point toward his masterpiece in the novel *The Scarlet Letter*, "The Minister's Black Veil" boasts the character most akin to Arthur Dimmesdale of the novel. Like Dimmesdale, Parson Hooper has a secret. He appears one morning at a Milford meeting house (a reference to "Governor Belcher" appears to place the story in Massachusetts in the 1730's or early 1740's) with his face shrouded by a black veil, which he never thereafter removes. Unlike Dimmesdale, he thus flaunts his secret while concealing it. The whole story revolves around the veil and its meaning. His sermon, unusually energetic for this mild minister, is "secret sin." That afternoon, Hooper conducts a funeral service for a young woman, and Hawthorne hints darkly that Hooper's sin may have involved her. In the evening, at a third service, Hooper's veil casts gloom over a wedding ceremony. The congregation speculates endlessly but inclines to avoid the minister.

One person who does not avoid him is a young woman named Elizabeth, who is engaged to Hooper. Elizabeth unavailingly begs him to explain or remove the veil and then breaks their engagement. In the years that follow, the lonely minister exerts a strange power over his flock. Dying sinners always insist on his visiting them and never expire before he reaches them, although his presence makes them shudder. Finally, Hooper himself sickens, and Elizabeth reappears to nurse him. On his death bed, he questions the aversion of his onlookers and insists that he sees a similar veil over each of their faces. He then expires and is buried with the veil still over his face. A question more important than the nature of Hooper's transgression concerns his increase in ministerial efficacy. Is Hooper's veiled state a kind of extended stage trick? (In death a smile lingers on his face.) Is it advantageous to be ministered to by a "mind diseased?" Is Hooper's effectiveness an implicit condemnation of his and his congregation's religion? Such questions Hawthorne's story inevitably raises and just as inevitably does not presume to answer directly.

"THE MAY-POLE OF MERRYMOUNT"

"The May-Pole of Merrymount" is simple in plot but complex in theme. One midsummer's eve, very early in the colonial life of the Massachusetts settlement at Mount Wollaston, or Merry Mount, a reenactment of ancient maypole rites accompanies the wedding of an attractive young couple, Edith and Edgar. Into the scene storms a belligerent group of Puritans under John Endicott, who hacks down the maypole, arrests the principals, including the flower-decked priest and the bridal couple, and threatens punishment to all, though Edith's and Edgar's will be light if they can accommodate themselves to the severe Puritan life hereafter.

Hawthorne uses history but does not follow it strictly. The historical Endicott's main motive in attacking Merry Mount was to stop its denizens from furnishing firepower and firewater--that is, guns and liquor--to Native Americans. The real Merry Mounters were not so frivolous, nor the Puritans necessarily so austere as Hawthorne depicts them. His artistic purpose required the sharp contrast of two ways of life among early Massachusetts settlers, neither of which he is willing to endorse. The young couple are caught between the self-indulgence of their own community and the "dismal wretches" who invade their ceremony. Like many of Hawthorne's characters, Edith and Edgar emerge into adulthood in an environment replete with bewildering moral conflicts. It is possible to see the conflict here as one between "English" and "American" values, the Americans being the sober seekers of a new, more disciplined, presumably more godly order than the one they chose to leave behind; the conflict can also be seen as one between a form of religion receptive to "pagan" excesses and a strict, fiercely intolerant one; yet another way of seeing it is as one between hedonists and sadists--for the pleasure principle completely dominates Hawthorne's Merry Mount, while the Puritans promise branding, chopping of ears, and, instead of a maypole, a whipping post for the miscreants.

The resolution of the story echoes John Milton's description of Adam and Eve leaving Eden at the end of *Paradise Lost* (1667, revised 1674), but Hawthorne has Endicott throw a wreath of roses from the Maypole over the heads of the departing newlyweds, "a deed of prophecy," which signifies the end of the "systematic gayety" of Merry Mount, which also symbolizes the "purest and best of their early joys" that must sustain them in the strict Puritan regimen that lies ahead.

"YOUNG GOODMAN BROWN"

"Young Goodman Brown," first appearing in print in 1835, is set in Salem at the end of the seventeenth century--the era of the witchcraft trials. Again, the names of some minor characters are historical, but Brown and his wife, Faith, whom the young protagonist leaves one night to go into the woods, are among Hawthorne's most allegorical. In its outline the allegory is transparent: When a "good man" abandons his faith, he can expect to go to the devil. Hawthorne complicates his story by weaving into it all sorts of subtleties and ambiguities. Brown's guide in the woods is simultaneously fatherlike and devilish. He encounters a series of presumably upright townspeople, including eventually Faith herself, gathering for a ceremony of devil-worship. At the climactic moment, Brown urges Faith to "look up to heaven, and resist the wicked one." The next thing he knows, he is alone in the forest, all his companions having fled--or all having been part of a dream. Brown returns home in the morning, his life radically altered. He can no longer trust his neighbors, he shrinks from his wife, and he lives out his years a scowling, muttering misanthrope.

As in "The May-Pole of Merrymount," Hawthorne's motive in evoking an episode of New England history is not primarily historical: No one proceeds against witches; there is no allusion to Judge John Hathorne. Rather, the setting creates an atmosphere of guilt, suspicion, and unstable moral imagination. Breathing this atmosphere, Brown falls victim not to injustice or religious intolerance but to himself. In a sense it does not matter whether Brown fell asleep in the woods and dreamed the Black Sabbath. Regardless of whether he

has lost faith, he has manifestly lost hope. His apparent capacity to resist evil in the midst of a particularly unholy temptation dispels his own guilt no more than the guilt he, and seemingly only he, detects in others. "Young Goodman Brown" is a masterful fictive presentation of the despairing soul.

All the preceding stories had been published by the time Hawthorne turned thirty-one. For about three more years, he continued to write stories, although most of those from the late 1830's are not among his best. He broke a subsequent dry spell with a series of stories first published in 1843 and 1844, many of which were later collected in *Mosses from an Old Manse* in 1846. Most notable of these later stories are "The Birthmark," "The Artist of the Beautiful," and "Rappaccini's Daughter."

"THE BIRTHMARK"

In these later efforts, the artist-scientist appears frequently. Aylmer of "The Birthmark" becomes obsessed by the one flaw in his beautiful wife, Georgiana, a birthmark on her left cheek that had not previously bothered her or her prior lovers. To Aylmer, however, it is a "symbol of imperfection," and he undertakes its removal. Hawthorne foreshadows the result in many ways, not the least by Georgiana's observation that her brilliant husband's "most splendid successes were almost invariably failures." She submits to the operation nevertheless, and he succeeds at removing the mark but fails to preserve her life, intertwined somehow with it.

Aylmer equates science with religion; words such as "miracle," "votaries," "mysteries," and "holy" abound. He is also an artist who, far from subjecting Georgiana to a smoky laboratory, fashions an apartment with beautiful curtains and perfumed lamps of his creation for her to inhabit during the experiment. Neither hero nor villain, Aylmer is a gifted man incapable of accepting moral limitations and therefore unable to accept his wife as the best that life could offer him.

The artist appears in various guises in Hawthorne's later stories and novels. He may be a wood-carver as in "Drowne's Wooden Image," a poet like Coverdale of *The Blithedale Romance*, a painter like Kenyon of *The Marble Faun*, or, as in "The Artist of the Beautiful," a watchmaker with the ambition "to put the very spirit of beauty into form." Owen Warland is also a peripheral figure, not yet alienated from society like many twentieth century artists real and fictional but regarded as quaint and ineffectual by his companions. Like Aylmer, he attempts to improve on nature, his creation being a mechanical butterfly of rare and fragile beauty. Owen appears fragile himself, but it is part of Hawthorne's strategy to reveal his inner toughness. He can contemplate the destruction of his butterfly by a child with equanimity, for the artifact itself is only the "symbol" of the reality of art. Owen suffers in living among less sensitive and spiritual beings and in patiently enduring their unenlightened patronization, but he finds security in his capacity for beauty.

"RAPPACCINI'S DAUGHTER"

"Rappaccini's Daughter" has three familiar Hawthorne characters. His young initiate this time is an Italian university student named Giovanni Guasconti, whose lodgings in Padua overlook a spectacular garden, the pride and joy of a scientific experimenter, Dr. Rappaccini, whose human subject is his daughter Beatrice. A scientific rival, professor Baglioni, warns Giovanni that Rappaccini much prefers science to humankind, but the young man falls in love with Beatrice and thus comes within Rappaccini's orbit. This scientist is more sinister than Aylmer and exerts his power over Beatrice more pervasively than does Aylmer over Georgiana. Beatrice's very life is bound up with the powerful poison with which he grows the exotic flowers in his garden. Giovanni, who has himself imbibed the poison, tries to counter its effect on Beatrice by offering her a medicine obtained from Baglioni, but its effect on her, whose whole life has depended on the poison, is fatal.

This story and its four main characters have generated a bewildering variety of interpretations. One reason for the critical quarrels is a subtle shift in point of view late in the story. For most of the way, the reader is with Giovanni and knows what Giovanni knows, but about four-fifths of the way, an omniscient narrator begins to comment on the limitations of his perceptions, the truth being deeper than he can plumb. This double perspective creates difficulties in gauging his character and that of the other three principals.

Hawthorne's allegorical propensities also complicate one's understanding of the story. For example, Beatrice can be seen as an Eve, an already corrupted temptress in the garden; as a Dantean, who guides her lover through what is for him, initially at least, Paradise; and as the Pomona of Ovid's tale of Vertumnus, the vegetarian god who wins her love and takes her away. (There is a statue of Vertumnus in Rappaccini's garden.) Obviously, Beatrice is not consistently any of these figures, but each of them leads to further allegorizing.

Perhaps the ultimate explanation of the interpretative difficulties arising from "Rappaccini's Daughter" is the author's profound ambivalence. In this fictional world, good and evil, beauty and deformity, are inextricably intermingled. Is Baglioni, for example, wise counselor or jealous rival, the protector of Giovanni or the vindictive agent of Beatrice's destruction? He fulfills these roles and others. In this story he conjoins with three other familiar Hawthorne types, the young initiate into life's malignities, the trusting victim of a detached manipulator, and the insensitive violator of his victim's integrity. Nearly every conceivable critical method has been applied to "Rappaccini's Daughter"; ultimately each reader must make up his or her own mind about its primary significance.

After these three stories of the mid-1840's, all viewed incidentally as landmarks of science fiction by historians of that genre, Hawthorne, back in Salem and busy with his customhouse duties, wrote little for several years. Before turning his attention to long fiction in 1850, however, he completed a few more short stories in the late 1840's, the most important of which is "Ethan Brand."

"ETHAN BRAND"

Like several of his best stories, "Ethan Brand" occupies the time from nightfall to the following dawn, but unlike "Young Goodman Brown" and "My Kinsman, Major Molineux" it has a contemporary setting. Bartram is a lime burner attending his fire on Mount Greylock in northwestern Massachusetts with his son Joe, when a man appears, a former lime burner who long ago decided to devote his life to searching for the Unpardonable Sin, which, by cultivating his intellect at the expense of his moral sense, he found in his own heart. All this he explains to the unimaginative and uncomprehending Bartram. The sensitive son fears the glint in the stranger's eye, and even Bartram cringes at Ethan Brand's sinister laugh. Since Brand has passed into local folklore, Bartram dispatches Joe to inform the villagers that he is back, and soon a contingent of neighbors comes on the scene. When Brand demonstrates his abrogation of human brotherhood, they retire, and Brand offers to watch Bartram's fire so that the latter and his son can retire for the night to their nearby hut. When Bartram and Joe awake in the morning, they find Brand gone, but a look into the fire reveals his skeleton burned to lime, his hardened heart also burnt but distinctly outlined.

What was the sin? Hawthorne subtitled this story "A Chapter from an Abortive Romance." No fragments of such a romance have ever turned up, although the story alludes briefly to past relationships between Brand and some of the villagers, including an "Esther" on whom Brand had performed a "psychological experiment, and wasted, absorbed, and perhaps annihilated her soul, in the process." Hawthorne seems to have intended no specifying of this or any other of Brand's activities but succeeded in delineating a character who represents the ultimate development--at least in his short fiction--of the coldly intellectual seeker who has denied his heart, exploited others in relentless quasi-scientific experimentation, and isolated himself from humanity. Hawthorne would depict such characters in more detail in his novels but never one who acknowledged his sin so completely and regarded suicide as the only act remaining to him.

At one time, Hawthorne's short stories were viewed mainly as preliminaries to the novels to which he turned shortly after publishing "Ethan Brand" in January, 1850, but he is now recognized as a master of the short story. Unlike all other major American writers of his time, he devoted his creative energies almost exclusively to fiction. Only Edgar Allan Poe, who began to publish his fiction shortly after Hawthorne's early stories appeared, approaches his position as the United States' first artist of short fiction. If Poe excelled at the psychology of terror, Hawthorne prevailed at the psychology of guilt. Both brilliantly characterized the isolated or alienated individual, but only Hawthorne regularly enriched the

cultural significance of his stories by locating these characters within the context of an American past and thus contributing imaginatively to his readers' sense of that past.

OTHER MAJOR WORKS

LONG FICTION: *Fanshawe: A Tale*, 1828; *The Scarlet Letter*, 1850; *The House of the Seven Gables*, 1851; *The Blithedale Romance*, 1852; *The Marble Faun: Or, The Romance of Monte Beni*, 1860; *Septimius Felton*, 1872 (fragment); *The Dolliver Romance*, 1876 (fragment); *Doctor Grimshawe's Secret*, 1883 (fragment); *The Ancestral Footstep*, 1883 (fragment).

NONFICTION: *Life of Franklin Pierce*, 1852; *Our Old Home*, 1863; *The American Notebooks*, 1932; *The French and Italian Notebooks*, 1980; *Letters of Nathaniel Hawthorne*, 1984-1987 (4 volumes); *Selected Letters of Nathaniel Hawthorne*, 2002 (Joel Myerson, editor).

CHILDREN'S LITERATURE: *Grandfather's Chair*, 1841; *Biographical Stories for Children*, 1842; *True Stories from History and Biography*, 1851; *A Wonder-Book for Boys and Girls*, 1852; *Tanglewood Tales for Boys and Girls*, 1853.

EDITED TEXT: *Peter Parley's Universal History*, 1837.

MISCELLANEOUS: *Complete Works*, 1850-1882 (13 volumes); *The Complete Writings of Nathaniel Hawthorne*, 1900 (22 volumes); *The Centenary Edition of the Works of Nathaniel Hawthorne*, 1962-1997 (23 volumes).

BIBLIOGRAPHY

Bell, Millicent, ed. *Hawthorne and the Real: Bicentennial Essays*. Columbus: Ohio State University Press, 2005. Some of the essays look at the totality of Hawthorne's works, including discussions of Hawthorne and politics; Hawthorne, slavery, and the question of moral responsibility; and Hawthorne's feminism. Leland S. Person's contribution focuses on "Hawthorne's Early Tales: Male Authorship, Domestic Violence, and Female Readers."

Bendixen, Alfred. "Towards History and Beyond: Hawthorne and the American Short Story." In *A Companion to the American Short Story*, edited by Bendixen and James Nagel. Malden, Mass.:

Wiley-Blackwell, 2010. Offers a comprehensive overview and critical examination of Hawthorne's short fiction, making reference to many of the individual stories.

Bunge, Nancy. *Nathaniel Hawthorne: A Study of the Short Fiction*. New York: Twayne, 1993. Discusses Hawthorne's major short stories in three categories: isolation and community; artists and scientists; and perspective, humility, and joy. Includes excerpts from Hawthorne's journals, letters, and prefaces, as well as excerpts on Hawthorne from Herman Melville, Edgar Allan Poe, Henry James, and several contemporary critics.

Doubleday, Neal Frank. *Hawthorne's Early Tales: A Critical Study*. Durham, N.C.: Duke University Press, 1972. Doubleday focuses on what he calls "the development of Hawthorne's literary habit," including Hawthorne's literary theory and the materials from which he fashioned the stories of his twenties and early thirties. The index, while consisting chiefly of proper names and titles, includes some features of Hawthorne's work ("ambiguity," "irony," and the like).

Fogle, Richard Harter. *Hawthorne's Fiction: The Light and the Dark*. Rev. ed. Norman: University of Oklahoma Press, 1964. One of the first critics to write full analytical essays about the short stories, Fogle examines eight stories in detail, as well as the four mature novels. He sees Hawthorne's fiction as both clear ("light") and complex ("dark"). He is particularly adept, although perhaps overly ingenious, in explicating Hawthorne's symbolism.

Keil, James C. "Hawthorne's 'Young Goodman Brown': Early Nineteenth-Century and Puritan Constructions of Gender." *The New England Quarterly* 69 (March, 1996): 33-55. Argues that Hawthorne places his story in the seventeenth century to explore the nexus of past and present in the attitudes of New Englanders toward theology, morality, and sexuality. Points out that clear boundaries between male and female, public and private, and work and home were thresholds across which nineteenth century Americans often passed.

Kelsey, Angela M. "Mrs. Wakefield's Gaze: Femininity and Dominance in Nathaniel Hawthorne's 'Wakefield.'" *ATQ*, n.s. 8 (March, 1994): 17-31. In this feminist reading of Hawthorne's story, Kelsey argues that Mrs. Wakefield finds ways to escape and exceed the economy of the male gaze, first by appropriating the look for herself, then by refusing to die, and finally by denying her husband her gaze.

Lynch, Jack, ed. *Critical Insights: Nathaniel Hawthorne*. Pasadena, Calif.: Salem Press, 2010. Collection of original and reprinted essays providing critical readings of Hawthorne's works, including two essays focusing on his short fiction: "'A Small Heap of Glittering Fragments': Hawthorne's Discontent with the Short Story Form," by Kathryn B. McKee, and "Agnostic Tensions in Hawthorne's Short Stories," by Bill Christophersen. Also includes a biography, a chronology of major events in Hawthorne's life, a complete list of his works, and a bibliography listing resources for further research

Mackenzie, Manfred. "Hawthorne's 'Roger Malvin's Burial': A Postcolonial Reading." *New Literary History* 27 (Summer, 1996): 459-472. Argues that the story is postcolonial fiction in which Hawthorne describes the emerging American nation and recalls European colonial culture. Claims that Hawthorne rehearses the colonialist past in order to concentrate and effectively "expel" its inherent violence.

Mellow, James R. *Nathaniel Hawthorne and His Times*. Boston: Houghton Mifflin, 1980. In this substantial, readable, and illustrated biography, Mellow provides a number of insights into Hawthorne's fiction. Refreshingly, the author presents Sophia Hawthorne not only as the prudish, protective wife of the Hawthorne legend but also as a woman with an artistic sensibility and talent of her own. A good introduction to an interesting man, suitable for the student and the general reader.

Miller, Edward Havilland. *Salem Is My Dwelling Place: A Life of Nathaniel Hawthorne*. Iowa City: University of Iowa Press, 1991. A large biography of more than six hundred pages, illustrated with more than fifty photographs and drawings. Miller has been able to draw on more manuscripts of family members and Hawthorne associates than did his predecessors and to develop his subject's family life in more detail. He offers interpretations of many of the short stories.

Newman, Lea Bertani Vozar. *A Reader's Guide to the Short Stories of Nathaniel Hawthorne.* Boston: G. K. Hall, 1979. For each of fifty-four stories, this valuable guide furnishes a chapter with four sections: publication history; circumstances of composition, sources, and influences; relationship with other Hawthorne works; and interpretations and criticism. The discussions are arranged alphabetically by title and keyed to a bibliography of more than five hundred secondary sources.

Person, Leland S. *The Cambridge Introduction to Nathaniel Hawthorne.* New York: Cambridge University Press, 2007. The chapter on Hawthorne's short fiction provides interpretations of fifteen short stories.

Scofield, Martin. "Nathaniel Hawthorne." In *The Cambridge Introduction to the American Short Story.* New York: Cambridge University Press, 2006. Scofield divides his analysis of the short fiction into three categories: tales of Puritan history, tales of sin and guilt, and art and science.

Swope, Richard. "Approaching the Threshold(s) in Postmodern Detective Fiction: Hawthorne's 'Wakefield' and Other Missing Persons." *Critique* 39 (Spring, 1998): 207-227. Discusses "Wakefield" as a literary ancestor of "metaphysical" detective fiction, a postmodern genre that combines fiction with literary theory. "Wakefield" raises many of the questions about language, subjectivity, and urban spaces that surround postmodernism.

Thompson, G. R. *The Art of Authorial Presence: Hawthorne's Provincial Tales.* Durham, N.C.: Duke University Press, 1993. Argues that for Hawthorne the art of telling a story depends on a carefully created fiction of an authorial presence. Examines Hawthorne's narrative strategies for creating this presence by using contemporary narrative theory. Analyzes a small number of early Hawthorne stories and the criticism that has amassed about Hawthorne's fiction.

Wineapple, Brenda. *Hawthorne: A Life.* New York: Knopf, 2003. An account of Hawthorne's often contradictory life in which Wineapple argues that many of Hawthorne's stories are autobiographical.

Robert P. Ellis

ROBERT A. HEINLEIN

Born: Butler, Missouri; July 7, 1907
Died: Carmel, California; May 8, 1988
Also known as: Caleb Saunders, John Riverside, Lyle Monroe, Anson MacDonald

PRINCIPAL SHORT FICTION

The Man Who Sold the Moon, 1950
Waldo and Magic, Inc., 1950
The Green Hills of Earth, 1951
Universe, 1951 (as *Orphans of the Sky,* 1963)
Assignment in Eternity, 1953

Revolt in 2100, 1953
The Menace from Earth, 1959
The Unpleasant Profession of Jonathan Hoag, 1959
    (as *6 x H,* 1962)
The Worlds of Robert A. Heinlein, 1966
The Past Through Tomorrow, 1967
Destination Moon, 1979
Expanded Universe: The New Worlds of Robert A. Heinlein, 1980
Requiem: New Collected Works by Robert A. Heinlein and Tributes to the Grand Master, 1992
The Fantasies of Robert A. Heinlein, 1999
Off the Main Sequence, 2005

OTHER LITERARY FORMS

Robert A. Heinlein (HIN-lin) was prolific in the science-fiction genre, producing many novels, as well as several volumes of short stories. He also wrote a number of science-fiction novels for young adults and a handful of nonfiction pieces about science fiction or the future. In the 1950's he worked as an adviser and occasional script writer for the television program *Tom Corbett: Space Cadet*, and he also worked on the screenplays for two films, *Destination Moon* (1950) and *Project Moonbase* (1953).

ACHIEVEMENTS

With his first published story, "Lifeline," Robert A. Heinlein became a major influence on other science-fiction writers who have emulated his crisp "insider" style, his matter-of-fact acceptance of projected innovations, and his Social Darwinist expansionist philosophy. His name is synonymous with the "realist" school of science fiction in the public mind, and his work is reprinted repeatedly in science-fiction anthologies. Heinlein's stories are generally fast-moving and full of realistic detail, anticipating scientific and technological advances. He has been praised for his ability to create future societies in convincing detail and is considered one of the masters of the science-fiction genre. Heinlein received four Hugo Awards: in 1956 for *Double Star* (1956), in 1959 for *Starship Troopers* (1959), in 1961 for *Stranger in a Strange Land* (1961), and in 1966 for *The Moon Is a Harsh Mistress* (1966). In 1975 he was awarded the Grand Master Nebula Award for his contributions to science-fiction literature.

BIOGRAPHY

Robert Anson Heinlein was born and reared in Missouri and attended the University of Missouri before going to the United States Naval Academy at Annapolis. He served in the Navy for five years until he contracted pulmonary tuberculosis and was forced to retire in 1934. After graduate school at the University of California at Los Angeles, he worked at a variety of jobs, including stints as an architect, a real estate agent, an owner of a silver mine in Colorado, and a civil engineer in a navy yard in Philadelphia during World War

II. After the war, he devoted himself to writing full time. He sold his first story in 1939 to *Astounding Science Fiction* and contributed other stories to various magazines over the years. In the 1960's, he became well known for the Hugo Award-winning novel *Stranger in a Strange Land*, which became a kind of a religious guide for some hippies.

In 1966, he moved to California, where he lived for the rest of his life. In 1969, he was asked to be a guest commentator alongside television news anchorman Walter Cronkite on the Apollo 11 mission that put the first man on the Moon. Heinlein was active at times in Democratic and Libertarian politics, and many of his books reflect his libertarian philosophy that the government should avoid meddling in people's lives. He was married twice, first to Leslyn McDonald and in 1948 to Virginia Doris Gerstenfeld, but he had no children. He died in 1988 in Carmel, California, at the age of eighty.

ANALYSIS

With few exceptions, Robert A. Heinlein's best-known stories are from his Future History series, conceived in 1939-1941 as taking place in a consistent fictional universe over the next two to seven centuries. Ordered by fictional chronology in one 1967 volume, that series is less consistent in detail than in general outlines, leading up to and taking place in "The First Human Civilization," an ideal social arrangement allowing maximum liberty for the responsible individual. This ideal of human progress, not without setbacks, is also evident in tales and novels not explicitly set against the Future History setting, variations of which have also formed the backgrounds of many subsequent writers' works.

As a storyteller, Heinlein seems less concerned with perfect craftsmanship than with what the story can point to; overt didacticism was a feature in his fiction long before the novels of his later career, in which it became a problem. What is the use, Heinlein seems to ask, of thinking about the future except as an arena for testing various strategies for living? Heinlein's characters learn mostly from themselves, however, or older versions of themselves, in a deterministic cycle that leads to social progress and individual solipsism, or to the belief that nothing outside oneself really exists.

Heinlein was a craftsman, however, whose plots are generally adequate and sometimes brilliant, whose style is authoritative and concise at best, whose concern with process did not blind him to human goals, and whose command of futuristic details was often overpowering.

"--WE ALSO WALK DOGS"

The best-crafted story from Heinlein's early, most influential period, "--We Also Walk Dogs," does not strictly fit the parameters of the Future History. It does, however, illustrate the underlying theme of progress by means of roughly equal parts of scientific and social innovation, fueled by the desire for personal gain, and enabled by the freedom to pursue it. Begun for the purpose of walking dogs for a fee, General Services, Inc., the story's "corporate hero," has grown into a multimillion-dollar "credit" business with tens of thousands of employees near the turn of the twenty-first century. A "typical" job is shown at the start, when a wealthy dowager asks the company to help her greet her party guests by "stereo vision," while they speed her by interurban rocket to the side of her injured son. Doing this relatively simple service for her, they revel in their organizational abilities and overcharge her for her spoiled incompetence.

The sideshow she causes is only a prologue to the story's central action, which requires the company to do what is practically impossible. For an interplanetary conclave on Earth, the government wants all the aliens to be provided with approximations of their homeworld environments. The major problem is nullifying gravitation, which requires a new field theory and the practical harnessing of it within ninety days. Locating the one man, O'Neil, who could possibly do it is simple; convincing him to do so is not. Independent and reclusive, he can be bought only by an exquisite china bowl, the Flower of Forgetfulness, the priceless property of the British Museum.

The ease with which the General Services team manipulates people to buy O'Neil off is mirrored by the ease with which he devises an antigravity effect, both accomplishments resulting from proper organization and application of resources. The story does not stop there, however; with an eye on the profitability of the "O'Neil effect" in "space navigation, colonization,

recreation," General Services maneuvers both the naïve inventor and the slow-acting government into an "independent" corporation with Earth as its sole customer and O'Neil as figurehead. The physicist's reluctance finally is overcome when the General Services team request "visiting rights" to the bowl now in his possession.

The pieces dovetail perfectly; the craftsmanship is fine; and the manner of telling and the social attitudes conveyed are vintage Heinlein. The future setting is indicated not only by the existence of planetary governments, intelligent aliens, and powerful "service" occupations but also by abbreviated references to futuristic technology. Some of it is today outmoded ("voders," or wire-spooled vocal recorders), routine (punch-carded data banks), or environmentally unsound (interurban rocket transport). Still exotic are "sky cars," stereo-vision telephones, "pneumatic" lifts in place of elevators, monetary "credits," and "gravity shields." Introduced unobtrusively in action rather than digressive exposition, these developments, taken for granted, underline the alien feel of this future world, even as the story line turns on its essential similarity to readers' own. Fast action, crisp dialogue, and technical ingenuity save the day and serve humankind, thanks to the profit motive. The potential of General Services and new technology for harm is ignored, since these are all good people, competent in science and business and appreciative of good art.

"THE GREEN HILLS OF EARTH"

"The Green Hills of Earth," an often reprinted story, is one of Heinlein's most romantic. Its appeal lies presumably in the figure of its protagonist, Rhysling, "the Blind Singer of the Spaceways," whom it claims to portray, warts and all. Directly addressing his audience, the unnamed narrator alludes to readers' common knowledge of a history yet to come, sketching out an insider's view of solar system colonization and changes in space brought about by progress.

Punctuating the tale with quotations from and allusions to his hero's published and unpublished repertoire, the narrator takes readers from world to world with Rhysling in his dual career as jet-man and minstrel. Part 1 discusses how, as a scapegrace spaceman, he rescues a ship and loses his sight to runaway radioactivity. Part 2 is more complicated, explaining how his doggerel grows to poetry as ribaldry gives way to remembered beauty, the effect of which is poignant on those who can see the despoliation of that which he celebrates in song. Part 2 also ends with heroics, however, as the long-blind former jet-man calls upon memory to save the ship taking him home to Earth at last. Rhysling does not live out the trip, but he does manage to record for posterity the definitive version of the title song.

The story is a model of artistic economy, sketching the outlines of technological and social development, as well as one man's lifetime as a crewman, bum, and artist, in a framework pretending to give an objective account when in fact it sentimentalizes its hero and romanticizes the course of history. Ever cognizant of the frontier motif in American consciousness, Heinlein extends the casual recklessness of the Old West and traditional life at sea into a sphere where it may not belong, given the physical and economic restraints of space travel.

"THE MENACE FROM EARTH"

The Moon is a favorite setting for Heinlein, never more tellingly than in "The Menace from Earth." Like his contemporary "juvenile" novels, it has a teenage protagonist, a girl more believable than her counterpart in *Podkayne of Mars: Her Life and Times* (1963). Contrary to the lurid connotations of the title, the "menace" is a platinum blond entertainer, Ariel Brentwood, whose Luna City vacation precipitates an emotional crisis in the life of the narrator, Holly Jones.

Practical and scientifically educated at fifteen, Holly has no qualms about opting for a career as a spaceship designer in partnership with eighteen-year-old Jeff Hardesty. When Ariel monopolizes the time of Jeff as her guide, Holly does not recognize the emotional cause of her depression. Her neglected emotional education sneaks up on her, causing her first to endanger, then to save Ariel's life. Although she is wary about Ariel's advice on manipulating men, Holly does find there is more to Jeff and to herself than engineering specifications.

Although the plot is trite, Holly's style, replete with unexpected applications of engineering terms, keeps the clichés at a distance. Her lunar provincialism, even

as she is exposing Ariel's terrestrial naïveté, lends charm and verisimilitude to the story. Since Holly finds it difficult to talk about her own emotions, her descriptions are mainly of the artifacts and processes that are the tale's real focal point.

Taking Ariel from the spaceport to her hotel, Holly also gives the reader a guided tour of the multileveled honeycomb of corridors and apartments, shops and labs, patterns and people that make up Luna City. Extended description does not slow the action, however, even when it shifts midway to the Bat's Cave, where residents take advantage of low gravity and convection currents to experience arm-powered winged flight. Heinlein's feeling for process is exhibited in Holly's account, emotionally freighted with mythic references (from Icarus and Lucifer to Circe), of the practice, preparation, and instruction leading to the crucial rescue that gives Ariel a sprained ankle, Holly two broken arms, and the story a happy ending.

"ALL YOU ZOMBIES--"

Alongside his social commentary and technological extrapolation, Heinlein also incorporated softer speculation, less anchored to the real world. Depending more on the artist's ability to make the impossible come true by means of words, many of these stories flirt with solipsism, the belief, perhaps endemic among writers, that nothing and no one outside oneself is real. This is particularly well illustrated in "All You Zombies--," a story of sex change and time travel. Like God and godlike aliens, introducing time travel into a story makes it impossible to say just *what* is "impossible"; what *will* happen is as real as what *has* happened, and either is subject to change at the traveler's option.

To make sure the right choices are made, Heinlein makes his narrator's existence depend on his manipulating events in the past so that boy meets girl, girl has baby, baby is displaced backward in time, and boy joins the Temporal Bureau. All four main characters are versions of the narrator, whose whole existence is a closed loop, himself or herself both creature and creator. Directing readers' attention away from the impossibility of creation out of nothing and the arbitrariness of revising the past, Heinlein focuses on the inevitability of these events and their effect on the narrator. Mixing dialogue with monologue, he preserves the simplest possible narrative sequence to make the story lucid and convincing. For all its machinelike precision, however, the story ends with a hint of terror, since the narrator, aware of his/her own origins, cannot quite believe that anyone else exists.

An ingenious puzzle whose internal consistency defies logical disproof, "All You Zombies--" calls attention to its elaborate stage management and suggests the perpetual dilemma of Heinlein's protagonists. Supremely competent at what they do, they count others only as aids or obstacles. Subject to such authorial determinism, disguised as historical inevitability in the Future History stories, his heroes are projections of the author's will to master the world, which makes them enormously appealing to many readers.

Heinlein's methods for getting the future under control in a fictional setting were highly influential in science fiction. Almost always entertaining and thought-provoking, he often told a superior story in the process.

Other major works

LONG FICTION: *Rocket Ship Galileo*, 1947; *Beyond This Horizon*, 1948; *Space Cadet*, 1948; *Red Planet*, 1949; *Sixth Column*, 1949 (as *The Day After Tomorrow*, 1951); *Farmer in the Sky*, 1950; *Between Planets*, 1951; *The Puppet Masters*, 1951; *The Rolling Stones*, 1952; *Starman Jones*, 1953; *The Star Beast*, 1954; *Tunnel in the Sky*, 1955; *Double Star*, 1956; *Time for the Stars*, 1956; *Citizen of the Galaxy*, 1957; *The Door into Summer*, 1957; *Have Space Suit---Will Travel*, 1958; *Methuselah's Children*, 1958; *Starship Troopers*, 1959; *Stranger in a Strange Land*, 1961; *Glory Road*, 1963; *Podkayne of Mars: Her Life and Times*, 1963; *Farnham's Freehold*, 1964; *The Moon Is a Harsh Mistress*, 1966; *I Will Fear No Evil*, 1970; *Time Enough for Love*, 1973; *The Notebooks of Lazarus Long*, 1978; *The Number of the Beast*, 1980; *Friday*, 1982; *Job: A Comedy of Justice*, 1984; *The Cat Who Walks Through Walls*, 1985; *To Sail Beyond the Sunset*, 1987; *For Us, the Living*, 2004; *Variable Star*, 2006 (with Spider Robinson).

SCREENPLAYS: *Destination Moon*, 1950 (with James O'Hanlon and Rip Van Ronkel); *Project Moonbase*, 1953 (with Jack Seaman).

NONFICTION: *Of Worlds Beyond: The Science of Science-Fiction Writing*, 1947 (with others); *Tramp Royale*, wr.1953, pb. 1992; *The Science Fiction Novel*, 1959 (with others); *Grumbles from the Grave*, 1989; *Take Back Your Government: A Practical Handbook for the Private Citizen Who Wants Democracy to Work*, 1992.

EDITED TEXT: *Tomorrow, the Stars*, 1952.

MISCELLANEOUS: *The Best of Robert A. Heinlein, 1939-1959*, 1973.

BIBLIOGRAPHY

Aldiss, Brian, and David Wingrove. *Trillion Year Spree: The History of Science Fiction*. London: Victor Gollancz, 1986. Aldiss's general survey of the history of science fiction includes a discussion of several of Heinlein's works. His focus is on Heinlein's novels, but Aldiss's comments also provide useful insights into the short stories and place them in a historical perspective. Includes an index.

Franklin, H. Bruce. *Robert A. Heinlein: America as Science Fiction*. New York: Oxford University Press, 1980. Franklin has written an excellent, scholarly, full-length study of Heinlein's work. He assesses Heinlein's important themes and discusses his libertarian politics.

Gifford, J. Daniel. *Robert A. Heinlein: A Reader's Companion*. Sacramento, Calif.: Nitrosyncretic Press, 2000. Provides details on all of Heinlein's short stories, novels, and other works. Readers can locate specific works and information by using the book's cross-references and dual indexes.

Hantke, Steffen. "Surgical Strikes and Prosthetic Warriors: The Soldier's Body in Contemporary Science Fiction." *Science-Fiction Studies* 25 (November, 1998): 495-509. Discusses how the technologically augmented body in the science fiction of Heinlein and others raises issues of what it means to be male or female, or even human, since the use of prosthetics to heal or strengthen the body is accompanied by the dissolution of the body.

Kilgore, De Witt Douglas. "Building a Space Frontier: Robert A. Heinlein and the American Tradition." In *Astrofuturism: Science, Race, and Visions of Utopia in Space*. Philadelphia: University of Pennsylvania

Press, 2003. Examines the scientific, political, and aesthetic movements that advocated the conquest of space as a means of ameliorating the racial differences and social antagonisms on Earth. The chapter on Heinlein analyzes his fictional works, including his story "The Man Who Sold the Moon," to explain his ideas about space exploration and colonization, and it discusses how his ideas influenced American interest in interplanetary exploration.

McGiveron, Rafeeq O. "Heinlein's Inhabited Solar System, 1940-1952." *Science-Fiction Studies* 23 (July, 1996): 245-252. Discusses Heinlein's population of a solar system in his early work by four different extraterrestrial civilizations, which serve the purpose of humbling the brash young human species.

Mendelsohn, Farah. "Corporatism and the Corporate Ethos in Robert Heinlein's 'The Roads Must Roll.'" In *Speaking Science Fiction: Dialogues and Interpretations*, edited by Andy Sawyer and David Seed. Liverpool, England: Liverpool University Press, 2000. Provides an interpretation of the short story.

Nicholls, Peter. "Robert A. Heinlein." In *Science Fiction Writers: Critical Studies of the Major Authors from the Early Nineteenth Century to the Present Day*, edited by E. F. Bleiler. New York: Charles Scribner's Sons, 1982. Nicholl's essay on Heinlein is quite long and an excellent introductory overview of Heinlein's work. His focus is on the novels, but his comments are also useful in looking at the short stories. He also discusses Heinlein's politics.

Contains a Heinlein bibliography and a critical bibliography.

Olander, Joseph D., and Martin Harry Greenberg, eds. *Robert A. Heinlein*. Edinburgh: Paul Harris, 1978. A collection of essays on Heinlein, including discussions of sexuality, politics, and Social Darwinism in his work, as well as an essay on his Future History series. Complemented by a critical bibliography.

Slusser, George Edgar, and Daniele Chatelain. "Space-time Geometries: Time Travel and the Modern Geometrical Narrative." *Science-Fiction Studies* 22 (July, 1995): 161-186. Compares time-travel narratives with modernist geometrical narratives; claims that in both, plot is reduced to a game of logic, and traditional story space and time are transposed into the realm of temporal paradox. Compares Jorge Luis Borges's "Death and the Compass" with Heinlein's "By His Bootstraps."

Wysocki, Ed. "The Creation of Heinlein's 'Solution Unsatisfactory.'" In *Practicing Science Fiction: Critical Essays on Writing, Reading, and Teaching the Genre*, edited by Karen Hellekson, et al. Jefferson, N.C.: McFarland, 2010. In 1941, before the Manhattan Project created an atomic bomb, Heinlein published "Solution Unsatisfactory," a short story about the use of radioactive dust as an atomic weapon. Wysocki traces the circumstances leading to Heinlein's creation of this story.

David N. Samuelson

MARK HELPRIN

Born: New York, New York; June 28, 1947

PRINCIPAL SHORT FICTION

A Dove of the East, and Other Stories, 1975
Ellis Island, and Other Stories, 1981
"Last Tea with the Armorers," 1995
The Pacific, and Other Stories, 2004

OTHER LITERARY FORMS

Though Mark Helprin (HEHL-prihn) is best known as a writer of short fiction, the genre in which he has excelled, he is also the author of several substantial novels. In 1989, Helprin switched genres to children's literature for the writing of *Swan Lake* (1989), with the story taken from the ballet of the same name. It was the first of a trilogy that later would include *A City in Winter: The Queen's Tale* (1996) and *The Veil of Snows* (1997). Two-time Caldecott Award winner Chris Van Allsburg provided the illustrations.

Helprin's stories and essays on politics and aesthetics have appeared in *The New Yorker, The Atlantic, New Criterion, The New York Times,* and *The Wall Street Journal.* He also served as a speechwriter for 1996 presidential candidate Bob Dole, and Helprin wrote Dole's Senate resignation speech in preparation for his candidacy.

ACHIEVEMENTS

Hailed as a gifted voice when his first book of short stories appeared, Mark Helprin confirmed such judgments with *Ellis Island, and Other Stories,* a volume that won the National Jewish Book Award in 1982. That same year, the American Academy of Arts and Letters awarded Helprin its Prix de Rome. Among his other honors are a John Simon Guggenheim Memorial Foundation Fellowship and nominations for both the PEN/Faulkner Award and the American Book Award

for Fiction. In 2006, Helprin's *Winter's Tale* (1983) was nominated by many prominent literary voices as "the single best work of American fiction published in the last twenty-five years."

Helprin has been a fellow of the American Academy in Rome and is a senior fellow at the Claremont Institute for the Study of Statesmanship and Political Philosophy. In 1996, he served as a foreign policy adviser and speechwriter to presidential candidate Dole. In 2006, Helprin received the Tulsa Library Trust's Peggy V. Helmerich Distinguished Author Award, and in 2010 Helprin received the Salvatori Prize in the American Founding by the Claremont Institute. Helprin is one of the most accomplished writers in his generation of Jewish American authors, and his fiction self-consciously attempts to extend and deepen the significant contribution those writers have made to American literature since World War II.

BIOGRAPHY

Born in New York City, Mark Helprin grew up an only child in Ossining, New York. His mother, Eleanor Lynn, was a Broadway leading lady in the late 1930's; his father, Morris Helprin, was a graduate of Columbia University and worked as a reporter, a film reviewer, and an editor for *The New York Times* before entering the film industry. Eventually, the elder Helprin became president of Alexander Korda's London Films.

After graduating from high school in 1965, Mark Helprin attended Harvard University, receiving a B.A. in English in 1969. He then entered the English doctoral program at Stanford University but left after one term and moved to Israel. He returned to Harvard University in 1970, and after finishing an M.A. in Middle Eastern studies in 1972, Helprin went back to Israel, where he was drafted into the Israeli army (he had become a dual citizen). He served from 1972 to 1973 in the army and in the air force. He has also served in the British Merchant Navy. Helprin's main hobby is mountain-climbing, and he has climbed Mount Rainier, which is close to his home in Seattle, and Mount Etna.

Aside from a short stint at Princeton University and a year of postgraduate work at Magdalen College, University of Oxford, in 1976-1977, Helprin concentrated mainly on writing fiction after his return to the United States. In 1986, Helprin moved from New York to Seattle, Washington. A reclusive man, Helprin seldom grants interviews or appears in public forums. Helprin's main hobby is mountain-climbing, and he has climbed Mount Rainier, which is close to his home in Seattle, and Mount Etna.

Helprin's writing has turned increasingly to political and social essays over other forms and genres. He has written essays and a column for the *Claremont Review of Books*, and his essays, articles, and op-eds have appeared in *The New Yorker*, *The Wall Street Journal* (for which he was a contributing editor until 2006), *The New York Times*, *The Washington Post*, *Los Angeles Times*, *The Atlantic*, *The New Criterion*, *National Review*, and *American Heritage*, among others.

ANALYSIS

Mark Helprin is an author whose imaginative resources seem inexhaustible. His prose has economy, grace, and a rich yet accessible metaphorical texture, qualities that combine to make his stories eminently readable. Helprin writes about an astonishing range of times, places, and characters in stories that move from realistic narrative to fable. His fiction, however, is unified by what William J. Scheick has called Helprin's "fascination with the human spirit's impulse for transcendence." Helprin once remarked, "I write only for one reason--and that's a religious one. Everything I write is keyed and can be understood as . . . devotional literature." At their best, his stories disclose a world of values that not only reflects his personal metaphysics but also links Helprin's work to both the Jewish religious tradition and the Transcendentalist heritage of Ralph Waldo Emerson, Walt Whitman, and Henry David Thoreau.

Not surprisingly, the stories often turn on moments of revelation, on various epiphanies. The beauty of nature and the beauty of human action combine to awaken many of his characters to a world that transcends human making. Helprin has noted that "vision and redemption" are two of the principal elements in his writing. Throughout that fiction, he moves his readers toward an enlarged conception of both their own capacities and the wondrous transformations of the world they inhabit.

While Helprin's voice is essentially an affirmative one, his affirmations are usually earned--the product not only of visionary moments but also of experiences of suffering, anguish, and loss. His characters are frequently presented as survivors, sustained by their memories of an earlier love or by their commitments to art. War is one of the most common events in these characters' lives. Like Stephen Crane and Ernest Hemingway, whose influence is often apparent in Helprin's style and subject matter, Helprin makes the experience of war one of his central metaphors.

The most important lessons his characters learn through their varied experiences are spiritual, moral, and emotional. One of the major attractions of Helprin's writing, in fact, is its moral energy and its author's willingness to make assertions of value. "Without sacrifice the world would be nothing," one story begins. In his visionary novel *Winter's Tale*, which projects a transfigured urban world, Helprin describes the four gates that lead to the just city: acceptance of responsibility, the desire to explore, devotion to beauty, and selfless love. These qualities might be said to define the central themes of Helprin's stories as well.

A DOVE OF THE EAST, AND OTHER STORIES

Helprin's first book, *A Dove of the East, and Other Stories*, contains twenty stories, many of them so brief that they depend almost entirely on the creation of a mood rather than on the development of plot, character, or theme. For the book's epigraph Helprin uses a line from Canto 2 of the *Inferno* from Dante's *La divina commedia* (c. 1320; *The Divine Comedy*, 1802; 3 vols.): *Amor mi mosse, che mi fa parlare* (love that has moved me causes me to speak), words that anticipate the book's concern with the redemptive power of love. Helprin has called Dante his single greatest influence, and many of Helprin's portraits of female characters suggest that they function--much as Beatrice did for Dante--to mediate the spiritual vision his male characters strive to attain.

In "Katrina, Katrin'," for example, two young clerks returning home from work are discussing women and marriage, when one of them suddenly launches into an account of his loss of Katrina, to whom he had been engaged some two or three years earlier. Biferman's tale of Katrina's illness and death links this story with the Romantic tradition and its fascination with doomed love and with the strength of human fidelity despite the power of death. Moreover, through allusions to the biblical Song of Solomon, Helprin recalls an even more ancient tradition that conceived of love in terms of both profound passion and passionate commitment, a conception of love all too rare in an age of casual sexual liaisons and disposable spouses. "Katrina, Katrin'" leaves the reader not only with a sense of Biferman's tragic loss but also with a sense of love's shimmering possibilities.

An even greater emphasis on life's possibilities infuses "Katherine Comes to Yellow Sky," which Helprin plays off against a similarly titled story by Stephen Crane. In contrast to Crane's "The Bride Comes to Yellow Sky," in which the bride remains nameless and

Mark Helprin (AP Photo/Sara D. Davis)

the story is told from the perspective of its male characters, Helprin focuses on Katherine, who arrives in Yellow Sky alone. Helprin employs two of his most recurrent symbols--light and a mountain landscape--to emphasize Katherine's potential for personal growth and transcendence. Katherine is a dreamer, in fact something of a visionary, who has come west after her parents' death to begin a new life. In Yellow Sky, with its "lantern mountains glowing gold in all directions, catching the future sun" and its peaks still gleaming after the sun has set, Katherine finds herself in the presence of "the source." Her journey's end is essentially a beginning. What Helprin says about Katherine's dreams might be said about his own approach to fiction. Katherine, he writes, "believed incessantly in what she imagined. . . . And strangely enough these substanceless dreams . . . gave her a strength, practicality, and understanding which many a substantial man would never have." For Helprin, the imagination projects and confirms life's promise.

Among the best of the briefer stories in *A Dove of the East, and Other Stories* are "Ruin," "The Home Front," and "First Russian Summer." In both "Ruin" and "The Home Front," violence is a central, though understated, element. The latter story, set during the Civil War, is again reminiscent of Crane, as Helprin depicts a group of soldiers assigned to burial detail, awaiting a June battle. During an idyllic interlude, the men fraternize with a unit of nurses and luxuriate in the beauty of nature. The air of unreality the war has assumed is soon shattered, however, when the men are commanded to dig five enormous pits. In these mass graves, they later bury more than a thousand dead. The story concludes with a reference to "the high indifferent stars" that oversee the bloodshed below, an image that parallels the "high cold star on a winter's night" in Crane's "The Open Boat."

"The Home Front" is informed by Helprin's awareness of the potential for violence in human nature and the indifference with which the physical world often greets human need. Both humanity and nature have other dimensions, however, as additional stories in *A Dove of the East, and Other Stories* suggest. In "First Russian Summer," for example, an eighty-year-old man named Levi recalls the words of his grandfather some seventy years earlier. Gazing upon forest and mountain, his grandfather had urged the boy to note "the shape of things and how astonishing they are" and had commended the trees, "not any painting or books or music," as "the finest thing on earth." The aged Levi has retained his grandfather's conviction that nature is a miracle that attests to God's creative power. Nevertheless, he knows that he lives in "a world blind to the fact of its own creation." Levi's desire, like Helprin's, is to awaken humanity to the mystery that attends its being.

The most accomplished stories in this first collection are "A Jew of Persia" and the title story, which open and close the book. "A Jew of Persia" combines the fable with elements of literary realism, for it makes use of the supernatural, as Nathaniel Hawthorne does in his tales and romances and as Isaac Bashevis Singer does in his stories. Helprin presents the reader with a protagonist who struggles with the devil himself, a conflict that begins in the mountains of Persia and ends in a barbershop in Tel Aviv, where Najime slays his adversary.

Helprin endows Najime with qualities that are central to Helprin's artistic vision. The Jew not only possesses courage and ingenuity but also demonstrates vital piety. Before his final confrontation with the devil, Najime prays for the strength both to recognize evil and to resist it, and he finds himself endangered in Tel Aviv precisely because he had earlier thwarted an attempt to rob him of the wealth of his village--gold and silver that he had been conveying to the Persian capital to help other Jews emigrate to Israel. Najime resists the robbers not to preserve his own life or his own property but to fulfill his communal responsibilities. Similarly, in Tel Aviv he acts to free the residents of the Ha Tikva Quarter from the misfortunes that have overtaken them on his account. As Helprin presents him, Najime is a heroic figure: not only a survivor but also a savior. In addition to his courage and piety, his greatest weapons are "the strength of the past" and "the power of memory," qualities that Helprin stresses in story after story. "A Jew of Persia" establishes Helprin's relationship to traditional Jewish characters and concerns, including the dramatic conflict between good and evil. Najime's triumphant encounter with the devil also

sounds the note of optimism that predominates in this collection.

In "A Dove of the East," that optimism is again present, though somewhat muted. Like "A Jew of Persia," this story is set in Israel, where its protagonist, Leon Orlovsky, herds cattle on the Golan Heights. Originally from Paris, Leon has become a skilled horseman and an excellent scout. On the day the story opens, he discovers an injured dove that his horse accidentally trampled during a frenzied ride prompted by Leon's desire to exorcize his memories. In a long flashback, Helprin reveals Leon's history: his training as a chemist, his love for Ann in Paris, their courtship and marriage, and her disappearance during World War II. Though Leon endangers the cattle by remaining with the dove, he refuses to abandon it, seeing in the dove an emblem of suffering humanity. Like the bird he nurses, Leon "is moved by quiet love," and his fidelity to the dove's need reflects his continuing commitment to Ann, with whom he still hopes to be reunited. Like the war-torn Nick Adams of "Big Two-Hearted River," Leon carefully ritualizes his daily activities, for such self-discipline helps to insulate him from the ravages of modern history. Though bereft of Ann and unable to save the injured dove, Leon nevertheless affirms love and compassion while awaiting "a day when his unraveled life would again be whole."

ELLIS ISLAND, AND OTHER STORIES

Ellis Island, and Other Stories, published some six years after Helprin's first collection, shows a marked increase in artistic achievement. The book contains the title novella, in addition to ten other stories. Four of those ten deal with war or the threat of war, while two others present characters who must cope with the accidental deaths of their loved ones. In almost all these stories ("White Gardens" is a notable exception), both plot and characterization are much more fully developed than in many of the briefer mood pieces in *A Dove of the East, and Other Stories*.

This second volume opens with one of Helprin's most visionary tales, "The Schreuderspitze," whose central character, a photographer named Wallich, has recently lost his wife and son in an automobile accident. To escape his grief, Wallich moves to a tiny Alpine village, where he takes up mountain climbing.

"He was pulled so far over on one side by the death of his family," Helprin writes, "he was so bent and crippled by the pain of it, that he was going to Garmisch Partenkirchen to suffer a parallel ordeal through which he would balance what had befallen him."

To prepare for his ascent of the Schreuderspitze, Wallich begins a rigorous period of physical training and ascetic self-discipline that lasts nearly two years. The story culminates, however, not in Wallich's ascent of the mountain but in a climb undertaken in a series of dreams that extends over three nights. In this dream vision, Wallich mounts into the *Eiswelt*, the ice world, with an ever-increasing sense of mastery and control. There he achieves a state of mystical insight in which he recognizes "that there was life after death, that the dead rose into a mischievous world of pure light, that something most mysterious lay beyond the enfolding darkness, something wonderful." These discoveries Wallich associates with the quality of light in the *Eiswelt*, but he also links them to the artistry of Ludwig van Beethoven's symphonies, which he compares to "a ladder of mountains" leading into "a heaven of light and the dead." In its use of this imagery of mountains and light, "The Schreuderspitze" resembles "Katherine Comes to Yellow Sky." Like Katherine, Wallich is nourished by his dreams, for they enable him to rise "above time, above the world" to a Blakean vision of eternity ("starry wheels sat in fiery white coronas"). Restored by this experience, Wallich returns to Munich to reenter an everyday world imbued with the extraordinary.

"The Schreuderspitze," perhaps more than any other story in *Ellis Island, and Other Stories*, bears the imprint of Helprin's religious concerns. Moreover, by grounding Wallich's vision in his encounter with the sublime in nature, Helprin places the story squarely in the Romantic tradition. Like his Transcendentalist predecessors, Helprin seeks to promote the reign of wonder as one means of recovering a sense of the sacred, an awareness of mystery.

"Letters from the *Samantha*," one of the most intriguing stories in *Ellis Island, and Other Stories*, records this eruption of the mysterious in a minor rather than a major key. Influenced by the works of Edgar Allan Poe, this story is told through a series of letters that recount events aboard the *Samantha* after it rescues a large monkey adrift at sea. From the first, the creature undermines the ship's morale, and its presence sets many of the sailors against the vessel's master, one Samson Low, the author of the letters. Deciding that the ape must again be set adrift, Low finds himself strangling the creature when it resists him. Although Low informs his crew that the monkey is not a symbol and that no significance invests its coming and going, the power of Helprin's tale lies in just such suggestiveness. As the master's name indicates, Low is a fallen creature who destroys what he cannot understand. Locked in battle, Low and the monkey mirror each other: "I gripped so hard that my own teeth were bared and I made sounds similar to his. He put his hands around my neck as if to strangle me back." This tale, which immediately follows "The Schreuderspitze," counterpoints the initial story. Low's movement, in contrast to Wallich's, is downward.

Several of the stories in *Ellis Island, and Other Stories*-- "Martin Bayer," "A Vermont Tale," "Tamar"-- create or build upon a sense of nostalgia. They are tales that record the loss of innocence, the vanishing of an ideal, while at the same time they affirm the value of that ideal. "A Vermont Tale," for example, recalls the month-long visit the narrator and his younger sister make to his grandparents' farm while his parents contemplate divorce. Though the month is January, with its "murderous ice," the narrator's prose celebrates nature's grandeur. The highlight of this visit is the grandfather's lengthy tale of a pair of Arctic loons. As the old man describes the birds, he humanizes them, so that the marital difficulties he identifies in their relationship seem to parallel those of the narrator's parents. In the grandfather's dramatic and moving story, the unfaithful male loon ultimately reunites with its mate. Helprin's tale ends, however, not on this optimistic note but rather with the boy's recognition that his parents' marriage will not follow his grandfather's plot. However, fidelity remains an ideal that this story discovers, significantly, in nature itself.

Several of the other stories in Helprin's second collection of short fiction return to the concern for war and its effects that is so evident in his first collection. Two of those stories, moreover, appear to draw upon

Helprin's experiences in the Israeli army. The first of these, "North Light," although nominally a first-person narrative, is dominated by the "we" of the soldiers' shared perspective. In only five pages, the story explores the psychology of warfare as an army unit is held back from the battlefield. Helprin's analysis of the anger that this delay generates--an anger that will be the men's salvation in combat--is thoroughly convincing.

The other war story set in Israel, "A Room of Frail Dancers," focuses on a soldier named Rieser, whose brigade has been demobilized. The title of this story becomes a metaphor for human existence itself, especially when Rieser imagines the dancers as "figures of imperfection in constant striving." The frailty of the dancers suggests the fragility of the order they establish, though Helprin's title also hints at humanity's perennial desire to achieve the grace and harmony associated with dance. Rieser's frailty is evinced when he pronounces the dancers' movements "purposeless" and commits suicide.

Another story whose title functions metaphorically is "Palais de Justice." Whereas Rieser's struggle is largely internal, the conflict in this story involves a sculling contest between an attorney in his early sixties and a scornful young man. Using the wisdom of experience, the aging attorney unexpectedly triumphs over his adversary, whom he identifies with the barbarism and violence of the twentieth century, a century contemptuous of tradition and of the older generation that transmits its values, a theme Helprin also addresses in "First Russian Summer." The Palais de Justice is also "the place of the world," Helprin suggests, and he implies as well that every individual has a responsibility to affirm the humane values embodied in this story's protagonist.

The novella that gives Helprin's second collection its title is a comic mixture of realism and fantasy. Divided into four sections, *Ellis Island* recounts the first-person narrator's arrival in the United States and his initial experiences there. The plot is complicated and its events often implausible, but the novella's central thematic concern is the narrator's discovery of selfless love. As is often the case in Helprin's fiction, this discovery is made possible by the protagonist's encounter

with a woman, in this case with two women: Elise, a striking Danish immigrant with whom he falls in love on Ellis Island, and Hava, who attempts to teach him the tailor's trade once he reaches New York City. When Elise, his "pillar of fire" (the title of the novella's first section), is refused entry into the United States because she has no one to support her, the narrator agrees to find a job as a tailor to secure her freedom.

After undergoing several amazing changes of identity on Ellis Island, the narrator continues his extraordinary adventures in New York City, adventures that display Helprin's imagination at its most whimsical. Once the narrator obtains a position as a tailor (a trade about which he knows nothing), he meets Hava. It is from Hava, whose name is the Hebrew word for Eve, that he learns the lesson of selflessness, for she works twice as hard as usual to complete his tailoring along with her own. The narrator moves in with Hava, ironically is given the certificate of employment he needs not for winning a job but for quitting it, and begins a career as a journalist. His very success, however, causes him to forget Elise. Only after he and Hava are married does he recall his pledge "to redeem Elise." Returning to Ellis Island, he learns that she has died while aiding those aboard a typhus-ridden ship. Her death, he recognizes, demands of him "a life of careful amends."

In this novella, as elsewhere in his fiction, Helprin does not shy away from the didactic. Even in so whimsical a tale, he manifests his pervasive concern for health of heart and soul. "Hardened hearts and dead souls" are the price that people pay for ignoring the demands of justice, compassion, and self-sacrifice. "To give to another without reward," writes Helprin's narrator, "is the only way to compensate for our mortality, and perhaps the binding principle of this world."

"LAST TEA WITH THE ARMORERS"

In portraying his characters as survivors, Helprin views them as individuals capable of either being sustained or being restrained by remembrances of their difficult past. In one of his later works, "Last Tea with the Armorers," he once again juxtaposes the beauty of nature with human action to construct an old-fashioned romance with modern-day overtones in which the reality of love is shown to overcome suffocating social influences and human self-perceptions. It is a simple story of a father, a night watchman in a language school, and his thirty-four-year-old daughter Annalise, a hospital microscopist, both of whom are Holocaust survivors, who settled into a small Israeli border community in 1947 following the war in Europe. For the next twenty-five years they spend their lives in a small set of rooms "now impossible to leave because of its perfect familiarity." Their highly structured lives make a turn when the father takes a liking to an Australian immigrant attending the language school where the father works. Immediately, the father begins to sing the praises of the student to his daughter, in the hope she might take a romantic interest in the fellow. The father's role of matchmaker is both simple and complicated--to create a bond between a man whose reason for not being married is simply that he never believed anyone would want to marry him and a woman who "already dismissed him, because she herself had been dismissed so many times before."

Helprin reinforces the powerful pull of self-perception by placing Annalise within the ranks of an Israeli army reserve unit and next to a clerical coworker, Shoshanna, who was "so beautiful that half of her life was closed to her, as she was always the object, and never the observer." The constant presence of Shoshanna and the attraction she represents to the soldiers serves to underscore Annalise's view of herself as a woman almost "invisible to men." It is a classic Helprin theme, that of individuals locked in self-perceptions that limit their capability to experience life's higher emotional callings. Only through her loving father's nudging is Annalise able to take the first step toward her own personal epiphany by initiating a simple dialogue with the Australian, setting in motion a series of events that best can be described as a reaffirmation of the traditional view that beauty is indeed in the eye of the beholder.

Helprin's gift of imagery and his ability to identify the walls that separate individuals, families, and societies, while at the same time making them appear impenetrable, provides a basic framework for his stories. Within the walls reigns a conflux of chaotic experiences fully capable of debasing the human spirit, yet never quite able to extinguish it. Invariably, one of those virtuous absolutes, most notably love, comes

along at a critical juncture to rescue and preserve it. In Helprin's world the absolutes represent eternal truths that can be applied to any age or situation that threatens the human condition.

It is the pursuit of such binding principles that energizes Helprin's fiction. His stories record his character's encounters with or longing for those perennial absolutes: love, goodness, beauty, justice, God. They also celebrate what "Palais de Justice" calls "this intricate and marvelously fashioned world." Though at times too rarefied in plot and character, these stories at their best become windows on the infinite, while grounded in the particular. They thus confirm the claim Helprin makes on his readers in the epigraph to *Winter's Tale:* "I have been to another world, and come back. Listen to me."

THE PACIFIC, AND OTHER STORIES

His first collection of short stories to be published in more than two decades, *The Pacific, and Other Stories* contains tales that continue to reflect the author's vast cultural experience through the voices of his diverse and universally engaging characters. Unlike many of his contemporaries, Helprin does not confine his collected stories to a specific time, character, or culture, but presents a range of narratives that may seem at odds with convention but never with each other.

The blend of fantasy and realism frequently apparent in Helprin's stories features prominently in "Jacob Bayer and the Telephone," which tells of a cell-phone-like technology craze surrounding old-fashioned telephones and set in a 1913 shtetl. Under this premise, Helprin explores themes of spirituality, metaphysics, and community and opens a discourse into love, law, and relationships with God and with one another. Many elements of the story--from the characters' names to the townspeople's crazed fixation on the telephone to the town's warped economic system--are expressed as hyperbole, but they carry stark reminders of his readers' contemporary society and the secularizing sensations wrought by modern technology. The story is representative of Helprin's mature writing; though stylistically similar to his earlier writings, the political and social message is far more pronounced.

The title story, "The Pacific," which closes out the collection, demonstrates the extreme optimism and profound trust in the compassion of humanity that have come to characterize so many of his protagonists. Against the backdrop of the beautiful Pacific coast, a young woman works in a factory while her husband is sent to battles on Pacific beaches. The beauty of the setting serves as a metaphor not only for the beauty of the young woman's hopefulness but also for the possibility of continuance and regeneration after wartime loss. Though the story ends with a hint of extreme sadness and hardship to come, the reader, swept along by Helprin's striking descriptions and the engaging exchanges of the young woman and her husband, cannot help but retain a sense of hopefulness.

Similarly striking imagery and use of rhetorical devices in many of the stories of this collection indicate the maturity of the writing therein and reveal Helprin's literary achievement with this later collection. The writing remains as crisp and authentic as that in Helprin's early collections, but the literary finesse demonstrated in Helprin's prose augments his themes of redemption, hope, love, and faith. His characters are ordinary people experiencing ordinary hardships and tragedies and are realized through Helprin's art and imagery.

OTHER MAJOR WORKS

LONG FICTION: *Refiner's Fire: The Life and Adventures of Marshall Pearl, a Foundling*, 1977; *Winter's Tale*, 1983; *A Soldier of the Great War*, 1991; *Memoir from Antproof Case*, 1995; *Freddy and Fredericka*, 2005.

NONFICTION: *Digital Barbarians: A Writer's Manifesto*, 2009.

CHILDREN'S LITERATURE: *Swan Lake*, 1989; *A City in Winter: The Queen's Tale*, 1996; *The Veil of Snows*, 1997.

BIBLIOGRAPHY

Alexander, Paul. "Big Books, Tall Tales: His Novels Win Critical Acclaim and Hefty Advances, So Why Does Mark Helprin Make Up Stories About Himself?" *The New York Times Magazine* (April 28, 1991): 32-33. This article probably comes closest to penetrating the mystique with which Helprin has surrounded himself. From stories that his mother was once a slave to others that stretch credulity even further, Helprin has fictionalized his life much as he has his books. Alexander calls Helprin a compulsive storyteller, although Helprin himself claims that he has learned "to deal in facts--not dreams," especially when talking to journalists. Alexander provides biographical details and discussion of much of Helprin's work (including critical reaction to it) in addition to interview excerpts with Helprin.

Butterfield, Isabel. "On Mark Helprin." *Encounter* 72 (January, 1989): 48-52. Butterfield views Helprin's writing as following in the footsteps of such American literary giants as Mark Twain, William Faulkner, Nathanael West, William Gaddis, and Thomas Pynchon. The article focuses specifically on two stories from *Ellis Island, and Other Stories*: "Letters from the *Samantha*" and "The Schreuderspitze." Useful for the interpretative information, although no references are included.

Feldman, Gayle. "Mark Helprin's Next Ten Years (and Next Six Books) with HBJ." *Publishers Weekly* 235 (June 9, 1989): 33-34. This piece, found in the "Trade News" section of *Publishers Weekly*, is illuminating for its insight into what Helprin wants out of his writing career. In negotiating a multimillion-dollar, long-term deal with Harcourt Brace Jovanovich, Helprin's real goal was stability--in fact, he could have actually received more money per book if he had negotiated each work individually, a fact that he readily acknowledges. Helprin likens this contract to the arrangement between the publisher Alfred A. Knopf and the writer Thomas Mann; in essence, Knopf said to Mann, "You write for me and I'll take care of you--that's all you have to do." Includes much firsthand (interview) information from Helprin but no outside references.

Goodman, Matthew. "Who Says Which Are Our Greatest Books? The Politics of the Literary Canon." *Utne Reader* (May/June, 1991): 129-130. Discusses Helprin's introduction to *The Best American Short Stories*, in which he attacks revisionists for desecrating the cause of American literature; notes that, although Helprin's argument implies that only revisionists have a political agenda, traditionalists such as former Education Secretary William Bennett use political arguments to advance the cause of Western literature.

Green, Michelle. "Literary Acrobat." *People Weekly* 35 (June 24, 1991): 105-106. A brief biographical sketch that discusses Helprin's childhood, education, and service in the Israeli military.

Lee, Richard E., and Patrick Meanor, eds. *American Short-Story Writers Since World War II (Fifth Series)*. Detroit, Mich.: Thomson Gale, 2007. The entry on Helprin provides biographical information and contextualizes his work among that of other contemporary short-story writers.

Shatzky, Joel, and Michael Taub. *Contemporary Jewish American Novelists: A Bio-critical Sourcebook*. Westport, Conn.: Greenwood Press, 1997. This edition presents a brief biography of Helprin and examines his works, themes, and critical reception in the context of other contemporary Jewish American writers. The collection focuses specifically on longer fiction but provides information relevant to Helprin's shorter works as well.

Shulevitz, Judith. "Research Kills a Book." *The New York Times Book Review*, May 5, 1991, p. 26. This brief article provides insight into Helprin's writing priorities. For example, Helprin believes that impersonal facts, or "research," kills the spirit of his writing, and therefore he does not like to place too much importance on historical accuracy. Helprin also states his belief in the idea that "politics should be the realm of reason and art should be the realm of passion."

John Lang; Jo-Ellen Lipman Boon
Updated by Rachel E. Frier

ERNEST HEMINGWAY

Born: Oak Park, Illinois; July 21, 1899
Died: Ketchum, Idaho; July 2, 1961

PRINCIPAL SHORT FICTION
Three Stories and Ten Poems, 1923
In Our Time, 1924, 1925
Men Without Women, 1927
Winner Take Nothing, 1933
The Fifth Column and the First Forty-Nine Stories, 1938
The Snows of Kilimanjaro, and Other Stories, 1961
The Nick Adams Stories, 1972
The Complete Stories of Ernest Hemingway, 1987

OTHER LITERARY FORMS
During the four decades in which Ernest Hemingway worked at his craft, he published seven novels, a collection of fictional sketches, and two nonfiction accounts of his experiences in Spain and in Africa; he also edited a collection of war stories and produced a considerable number of magazine and newspaper articles. The latter have been collected in posthumous editions. Manuscripts of three unfinished novels, a series of personal reminiscences, and a longer version of a bullfighting chronicle have been edited and published posthumously as well. In 1981, Hemingway's first biographer, Carlos Baker, brought out an edition of the writer's correspondence.

ACHIEVEMENTS
After spending a decade in relative obscurity, Ernest Hemingway finally became a best-selling author with the appearance of *A Farewell to Arms* in 1929. His long association with the publishing firm Charles Scribner's Sons, where the legendary Max Perkins was his editor for more than two decades, assured him wide publicity and a large audience. His passion for high adventure and his escapades as a womanizer made him as famous for his lifestyle as for his literary accomplishments.

For Whom the Bell Tolls (1940) was selected to receive the Pulitzer Prize in 1940, but the award was vetoed. In 1952, the Pulitzer committee did give its annual prize to *The Old Man and the Sea* (1952). Two years later, Hemingway was awarded the Nobel Prize in Literature.

Even more significant than these personal awards has been the influence that Hemingway has exerted on American letters. His spare style has become a model for authors, especially short-story writers. Further, Hemingway has received significant critical attention, though not all of it laudatory. His tough, macho attitude toward life and his treatment of women have been the subjects of hostile reviews by feminist critics during the 1970's and 1980's.

BIOGRAPHY

Ernest Hemingway was born in Oak Park, Illinois, a Chicago suburb, in 1899, the second child of Clarence (Ed) and Grace Hemingway's six children. Growing up in a doctor's house, under the domination of a forceful mother, would provide Ernest grist for his literary mill in years to come. The family's frequent trips to northern Michigan would also figure in his development as a writer, providing him a locale for numerous stories and an appreciation for wild terrain.

After graduating from high school, Hemingway left Chicago to take a job on the Kansas City *Star*. Shortly after the United States entered World War I, he quit his job and went to Italy as a Red Cross volunteer. There, he was wounded while assisting Italian soldiers. He spent several weeks in a Milan hospital, where he met Agnes von Kurowsky, who would serve as a model for Catherine Barkeley in *A Farewell to Arms*.

Hemingway returned to the United States in 1919 and began writing stories--none of which sold. In 1920, he met Hadley Richardson, whom he married the following year. They returned to Europe late in 1921, and for the next decade, Hemingway spent his time in Paris or in other locales on the Continent, sharpening his skills as a short-story writer. Two collections of his work were published by literary presses. The many expatriates whom he met in Paris served as models for his first full-length novel, *The Sun Also Rises*, which appeared to favorable reviews in 1926. In the same year, he and Hadley separated, and Hemingway pursued his relationship with Pauline Pfeiffer, whom he married in 1927.

In 1928, Hemingway began the novel that would establish his reputation, *A Farewell to Arms*. Published in 1929, it sold quite well and freed the novelist to pursue other interests for several years. Though he had his residence in Key West, Florida, during the 1930's he spent considerable time in Spain studying the art of bullfighting and took Pauline on a big-game safari in Africa. Out of these experiences came the nonfiction works *Death in the Afternoon* (1932) and *The Green Hills of Africa* (1935); neither received the acclaim that his earlier novels had enjoyed.

In 1937, Hemingway managed to secure a position as a reporter to cover the Spanish Civil War. While in Spain, he spent most of his time with Martha Gellhorn, a young writer whom he had met the previous year in Florida. They were married in 1939 after Hemingway divorced Pauline. The Spanish Civil War furnished him materials for a major novel, *For Whom the Bell Tolls*, and a play, *The Fifth Column* (1938), which had a brief run on Broadway.

Ernest Hemingway (©The Nobel Foundation)

After the outbreak of World War II, Hemingway found a way to be with the American troops, joining his third wife as a war correspondent in Europe. His relationship with Martha deteriorated as the war progressed, and by 1945, they had agreed to divorce. Hemingway made Mary Welsh his fourth wife in 1946, after courting her for two years. The two spent Hemingway's remaining years together in Cuba or in various retreats in the United States and in Europe. During the years following World War II, Hemingway started several major projects, but few came to fruition. A notable exception was *The Old Man and the Sea*, which ran in *Life* magazine, sold millions of copies in hardback, and became a motion picture. Growing bouts of depression became harder and harder to fight off, however, and in 1961, Hemingway finally committed suicide while staying at his second home, in Ketchum, Idaho.

ANALYSIS

Any study of Ernest Hemingway's short stories must begin with a discussion of style. Reacting against the overblown, rhetorical, and often bombastic narrative techniques of his predecessors, Hemingway spent considerable time as a young man working to perfect the spare form of narration, dialogue, and description that became the hallmark of his fiction. Nowhere does he achieve greater mastery of his medium than in his short stories. He expressed his belief and described his own method in a passage in *Death in the Afternoon:* "If a writer of prose knows enough about what he is writing about he may omit things that he knows and the reader, if the writer is writing truly enough, will have a feeling of those things as strongly as though the writer has stated them." Following this dictum, Hemingway constructed stories that sometimes make readers feel as if they are unseen auditors at some closet drama, or silent observers at intimate moments in the lives of characters struggling with important, although often private, issues.

"HILLS LIKE WHITE ELEPHANTS"

This technique is readily apparent in "Hills Like White Elephants." Set in Spain during the hot summer, the story contains little overt action. Hemingway sketches the background deftly in a single opening paragraph of half a dozen sentences, each of which provides vital information that establishes a physical setting and a symbolic backdrop for the tale. On one side of the little junction station, there are fertile fields; on the other, a barren landscape. Only three characters appear: a man identified as an American, a girl, and a woman who serves them in the little café at which they have stopped to wait for the train that passes through the unnamed town on the route from Barcelona to Madrid. The entire story consists of a single scene in which the man and the girl sit in the café, drink various alcoholic beverages, and converse.

Much of the dialogue seems little more than small talk, but there is an underlying sense of tension from the very first exchange between the man and the girl after they order their beer. The girl mentions that the hills in the distance "look like white elephants," to which her companion replies, "I've never seen one." She immediately responds, "No, you wouldn't have," and he fires back, "I might have. . . . Just because you say I wouldn't have doesn't prove anything." The harshness of their responses contrasts with the inconsequential nature of the subject of their discussion, suggesting that the relationship between them is somehow strained but that neither wishes to discuss openly the real issue over which they are at odds.

For nearly half the story, the two try to make conversation that will ease the tension, but their remarks serve only to heighten it. The man finally mentions, in an almost offhand way, the subject that is really on his mind: He wants the woman to have an abortion. "It's really an awfully simple operation," he tells her. "It's just to let the air in. . . . it's all perfectly natural." The woman, who sits silent through his pleading, finally replies, "Then what will we do afterward?" The man repeatedly assures her that things will be fine if she agrees only to terminate her pregnancy, since in his view the baby will destroy the lifestyle to which they have become accustomed. The woman is wiser; she knows that their relationship has already been poisoned forever and that her pregnancy is not the sole cause. Theirs has been a peripatetic, rootless life, as barren in some ways as the countryside in which they now find themselves.

This summary of the story, like summaries of so many of Hemingway's stories, is inevitably an artificial construct that does not convey the sense of significance that readers get from discovering the larger issues lurking beneath the surface of the dialogue and description. This story is about choice, a vital choice for the woman, who must face the dilemma of either acquiescing to the man's wishes and undergoing what is for her more than a routine operation or risking the loss of a man for whom she has had some genuine feelings of love. Ultimately, either through his insistence or through her own realization that she must try to salvage their relationship, even though she senses it will be futile to do so, she agrees to his demands. Her closing remark, on which the story ends, carries with it the strong note of cynicism that pervades the entire story: "I feel fine," she tells the man as they wait for the train's imminent arrival.

"IN ANOTHER COUNTRY"

In addition to his distinctive style, Hemingway made his mark in the literary world through the creation of a special kind of hero. The "Hemingway hero," as this figure has come to be known, is usually a man scarred by some traumatic experience--war, violence, a love affair gone bad. Often a physical maiming serves as a symbolic reminder of the psychological dysfunction that characterizes these figures. Despite having received a bad deal from the world, the Hemingway hero perseveres in his search for a good life, creating his own meaning out of the chaos of existence--the hallmark of existential heroes in both American and continental literature. These heroes do what is right without expecting reward, either in this life or in the next.

Two fine examples of Hemingway heroes appear in the story "In Another Country." The tale is set in Italy during World War I. A young American officer is recuperating at an Italian hospital, where he mingles with Italian soldiers who have seen considerably more action than he has seen. The extent of their physical injuries mirrors the psychological scars that the war has inflicted on them. One of them, a major who had been a champion fencer before the war, diligently undergoes therapy on a machine designed to restore his withered hand. He is hard on the young American for entertaining thoughts that full recovery for any of them is possible, yet he insists that they all go through the motions--not only with their therapy but also with other activities. He demands that the young man learn Italian

correctly, for example, arguing that one must follow the rules in life, even when they seem meaningless. Clearly bitter over his fate, he nevertheless keeps up his treatment, until an even more ironic blow strikes him: His young wife contracts pneumonia, and while he is going through the motions to recover the use of a hand damaged beyond restoration, she lies dying. His anger at the cruelty of her impending senseless death drives him to lash out at the institution of marriage; when she dies, however, he breaks down in tears and abandons his therapy. The young American, witness to the Italian's great love, comes to understand how nothing of value can last in this world. The lesson is bitter, but it is one that Hemingway heroes must learn if they are to go on living in a world where the only certainties are chance and chaos.

The young American in "In Another Country" is similar to the main figure in many Hemingway stories, Nick Adams. Often seen as an alter ego for the writer himself, Nick appears in almost twenty stories, and from them readers can piece together his history. A youth who spends time in Michigan and who has many of his ideals shattered by his participation in World War I, Nick develops the characteristics of the Hemingway hero: He becomes convinced of the world's essential callousness, yet he steels himself against its cruelties by observing the rituals that give his own life meaning. Hence, in "Big Two-Hearted River," Nick uses the activities associated with fishing as a kind of therapy to recover from the trauma of war.

"THE KILLERS"

One of the most anthologized of the Nick Adams stories is "The Killers." In this tale, Nick is a young man, still quite naïve and still given to romanticizing events in his life. Two Chicago gunmen arrive at the small diner where Nick is eating. They bully the waiter, bind and gag Nick and the cook, and wait impatiently for a boxer named Ole Andresen, a frequent patron of the diner, so that they can kill him. When Andresen fails to come to dinner, the gangsters finally leave. Knowing that they will seek out Andresen, Nick runs to the boxer's boarding house to warn him. Surprisingly, Andresen refuses to run away; he is content to wait for whatever fate brings him. Nick cannot understand how anyone can accept his lot with such resignation. The lesson for him--and for Hemingway's readers--is that there comes a point when it is impossible to keep moving on, to keep effecting changes by running away. All people must stand and meet the destiny allotted to them, no matter how bitter and unfair that may seem.

"Soldier's Home"

Like Nick Adams and the young American in "In Another Country," the hero of "Soldier's Home" has been scarred by his experience in World War I and has discovered upon his return to his hometown that he cannot find a sympathetic audience for his complaints. The people who did not go to war have already formed their opinions of what happened "over there" and have spent their patriotic energies feting the first groups of returning servicemen. Krebs, the protagonist of the tale, had remained in Germany with the occupation forces for a year beyond the declaration of the armistice. He is greeted with suspicion by his fellow townspeople; they cannot understand why he has waited so long to come home. When he tries to tell people what the war was actually like for him, he is rebuffed. He finds that only when he invents tales of heroism do people pay attention to him. Krebs has slipped into a continual state of ennui; no suggestion for action, either from family or friends, strikes him as worthwhile. In this sense, he fails to fulfill the role of typical Hemingway heroes, most of whom go on doggedly with their lives, all the while knowing that their efforts are doomed to failure. The overriding atmosphere of this story is one of pessimism, almost defeatism without hint of defiance--a rather unusual stance for Hemingway.

"The Snows of Kilimanjaro"

Two of Hemingway's greatest short stories are set in Africa, a land to which the author traveled on safari in 1933-1934. Often anthologized and frequently the subject of critical discussion, both "The Snows of Kilimanjaro" and "The Short Happy Life of Francis Macomber" detail relationships between weak men and strong women, displaying Hemingway's hostility toward females who seem to prey upon men, sapping their creativity and in some cases emasculating them.

"The Snows of Kilimanjaro" tells the story of a writer who is no longer able to practice his craft. Harry, the protagonist, has lost his ability to write well, having chosen to live a life of adventure and luxury. When the story opens, Harry is lying on a cot in the African plains, dying of the gangrene that he contracted by failing to take routine care of a scratch. Much of the story is given over to dialogue between Harry and his wife (presumably his second or third wife), a rich woman on whom he depends now for his livelihood; the tension in their marriage is seen by Harry at times as the cause of his inability to produce the kind of work that had once made him the darling of critics and the public. As Harry sees it, "He had destroyed his talent by not using it, by betrayals of himself and what he believed in." In his imagination, he writes fragments of the wonderful tales that he wishes to tell; these are presented in italic passages interspersed throughout the story.

Though the wife holds out hope that she will be able to get Harry back to a hospital, the writer knows that he is condemned to die of his wound--itself a trivial cut, but in this case fatal because of the circumstances in which Harry finds himself. The physical landscape mirrors Harry's failed aspirations. He is dying on the plains in sight of Africa's highest mountain; he can see the summit, but he knows he will never reach it. Similarly, the gangrenous wound and the resultant decay parallels the decay of the writer who fails to use his talents. Both the striving for some imaginary heights and the senseless destruction of the hero are highlighted in the short epigraph that begins the story. In it, Hemingway notes the presence of a leopard carcass, frozen near the summit of Kilimanjaro. "No one has explained," Hemingway writes, "what the leopard was seeking at that altitude." No one can really explain, either, why men such as Harry strive to be good writers, nor can anyone explain why some succeed while others are blocked from achieving their goals.

Hemingway portrays the wife in this story with only a modicum of sympathy. She seems concerned about her husband, but only because she entertains some romantic notion that believing strongly in something will make it so; she is convinced that she can save her husband despite clear evidence that he is beyond hope. Harry calls her names and blames her for his failure, and though he realizes in the moments before he dies that she is not actually the cause of his failure-- "when he went to her [to marry her] he was already over"--she never achieves a level of dignity that truly merits the reader's sympathy.

"THE SHORT HAPPY LIFE OF FRANCIS MACOMBER"

The story that critics often cite as Hemingway's finest is also set in Africa. "The Short Happy Life of Francis Macomber" details the relationship of Francis and Margot Macomber, wealthy Americans on an extended hunt with their professional guide, Robert Wilson. Told nonchronologically, the story reveals Francis's initial cowardice in the face of danger, his eventual triumph over his fear, and his untimely death at the moment when he is able to display his courage.

It would be hard to characterize Francis Macomber as a Hemingway hero. In fact, he is quite the opposite. He has money, but he possesses none of the qualities that Hemingway considers admirable in a man. Francis is dominated psychologically by his wife, and much of what he does is aimed at proving his manhood to her. Their African safari is but another effort on his part to display his worthiness for her continued affection. Unfortunately, Francis is a coward. The story opens with a scene that displays the strain that he is under, having just displayed his inability to stand up to danger. Through conversation among the three principal characters, the reader is able to infer that Francis had failed to complete a kill on a lion he had wounded. When he had gone into the bush to finish off the animal, the lion had charged, and Francis had run away; Wilson had been forced to kill the animal. Margot had observed his behavior, and she is now openly disdainful of her husband. She even plays up to Wilson right in front of Francis. As a final insult, after the Macombers retire to their tent for the evening, Margot slips out and goes to Wilson's tent to spend the night with him.

The following day, Francis has a chance to redeem himself. He and Wilson go out to hunt again; this time the quarry is buffalo. Margot remains in the vehicle once more, and the incident with the lion is repeated: Francis wounds a bull, which slumps off deep into the brush, and he must go in after the beast to finish the job that he started. This time, when the bull charges, Francis holds his ground and fires at the animal, but the beast keeps on coming at him. Almost immediately, Margot fires from the car, but she hits her husband rather than the buffalo. Francis is killed instantly.

Margot Macomber is a classic Hemingway woman-- the kind for which Hemingway has been criticized severely in the years since feminist critics have gained influence in American literary studies. She is physically attractive, though she is reaching the age at which her beauty is starting to fade. She is portrayed as being almost desperate to find some kind of security and is willing to use her sexual wiles to obtain it. She is cruel toward Francis when he shows himself a coward: She rejects physical contact with him and openly fawns over Wilson, though she taunts him too about his rather callous attitude toward killing. When Wilson mentions that hunting from a car (which he had done with the Macombers earlier) is a violation of the sport hunting laws and doing so could cost him his license, Margot leaps on the opportunity to suggest that she will use this information to blackmail him at some later time.

Unlike the Macombers, Wilson, Hemingway's white hunter, possesses several of the qualities that the author admires. He is good at his job. He understands people like Francis and Margot, and he has little respect for either of them because they are essentially fakes. He makes his living by taking advantage of the desires of people like them to dabble in life's more dangerous experiences. Having confronted danger almost every day, Wilson has become accustomed to living with his fears. He has even developed a certain callousness toward hunting and especially toward people who go on safaris. The behavior of the Macombers does not shock him. On the contrary, he is prepared for Margot's gesture of infidelity; he carries a double cot with him so he can accommodate wives like her who find their husbands despicable and the white hunter irresistible. Though Wilson is not admirable, in his self-awareness he achieves a certain esteem that is clearly missing in either of the Macombers.

The major critical question that dominates discussion of this story is: Did Margot kill her husband intentionally, or is Francis's death an accident? This is not idle speculation, for the answer at which one arrives determines the interpretation of the story's central theme. If Francis's death is indeed accidental, one can argue that Hemingway is making an ironic statement about the nature of self-fulfillment. At the moment that Francis achieves his greatest personal triumph, his life is ended. The fates simply destroy the possibility of his taking control of his life now that he has displayed himself capable of facing danger. Few details in the story, however, suggest that Francis should be considered a real hero. He may appear heroic at the instant of his death, but nothing he does before he faces the buffalo makes him worthy of emulation, and little that follows his death indicates that he has won new respect or lasting remembrance. Wilson does remind Margot that, had he lived, Francis would have had the courage to leave his wife. One must remember, though, that Wilson is the person who accuses Margot of murdering her husband, and he is searching to attach a motive to Margot's actions.

If one assumes that Margot shoots her husband intentionally, the ending of the story prompts a different interpretation. Francis is a type of the man struggling to break free of the bond that strong women have placed on weak men--and, by extension perhaps, on all men. This harsh antifeminist viewpoint is supported by Hemingway's portrayal of Margot as a classic femme fatale, valued for her beauty and grasping for security in a world where men ostensibly are dominant but where in reality women use their sexuality to gain and maintain control. Francis's killing of the buffalo is symbolic of his ability to destroy the barriers that are keeping him from breaking free of his wife; when she realizes what the event means, Margot takes immediate action to prevent her husband from carrying through on his triumph. Unfortunately, Hemingway never lets the reader see into the mind of Margot Macomber (though he does share the inner thoughts of Francis, Wilson, and even the lion), so it is impossible to settle on a definitive reading of the wife's motivation and hence of the story itself. As so often happens in real life, readers are left to draw conclusions for themselves from the events that they witness.

A key scene in "The Short Happy Life of Francis Macomber" may serve as a key to understanding Hemingway's philosophy of life. After Macomber has wounded the lion, he and Wilson have a lengthy discussion about the necessity of going after the animal to kill it. "Why not leave him there?" Macomber asks. "It isn't done," Wilson replies; "But," the professional hunter continues, "you don't have to have anything to

do with it [the final kill]." Wilson seems to be speaking for Hemingway here. Once something is started, it must be completed. Society depends on that dictum. This is more profound than it may seem at first. As anyone who has read Hemingway's *The Green Hills of Africa* knows, the author sees the safari as a metaphor for life itself. The activities on the safari are self-generated: No one is forced to undertake anything on the hunt, but once one agrees to participate, one has an obligation to carry through according to the rules of the game. Wilson, who sees himself in terms of his profession, must finish the kill even if his dilettante employer refuses to do so. One's duty, Hemingway says in *Death in the Afternoon*, is what one decides to do. Men and women are free to choose their destiny, knowing their struggle will always end in death; doing well that which they choose to do is what makes people heroic.

OTHER MAJOR WORKS

LONG FICTION: *The Sun Also Rises*, 1926; *The Torrents of Spring*, 1926; *A Farewell to Arms*, 1929; *To Have and Have Not*, 1937; *For Whom the Bell Tolls*, 1940; *Across the River and into the Trees*, 1950; *The Old Man and the Sea*, 1952; *Islands in the Stream*, 1970; *The Garden of Eden*, 1986; *True at First Light*, 1999.

PLAYS: *Today Is Friday*, pb. 1926; *The Fifth Column*, pb. 1938.

NONFICTION: *Death in the Afternoon*, 1932; *Green Hills of Africa*, 1935; *A Moveable Feast*, 1964 (as *A Moveable Feast: The Restored Edition*, 2009); *By-Line: Ernest Hemingway, Selected Articles and Dispatches of Four Decades*, 1967; *Ernest Hemingway: Selected Letters, 1917-1961*, 1981; *Ernest Hemingway on Writing*, 1984 (Larry W. Phillips, editor); *Dateline, Toronto: The Complete "Toronto Star" Dispatches, 1920-1924*, 1985; *The Dangerous Summer*, 1985; *Hemingway on Fishing*, 2000 (Nick Lyons, editor); *Hemingway on Hunting*, 2001 (Seán Hemingway, editor); *Hemingway on War*, 2003 (Seán Hemingway, editor); *Dear Papa, Dear Hotch: The Correspondence of Ernest Hemingway and A. E. Hotchner*, 2005 (Albert J. DeFazio III, editor); *Hemingway and the Mechanism of Fame: Statements, Public Letters, Introductions, Forewords, Prefaces, Blurbs, Reviews, and*

Endorsements, 2006 (Matthew J. Bruccoli, editor; with Judith S. Baughman); *On Paris*, 2008.

BIBLIOGRAPHY

Benson, Jackson J., ed. *New Critical Approaches to the Short Stories of Ernest Hemingway*. Durham, N.C.: Duke University Press, 1990. Section 1 covers critical approaches to Hemingway's most important short fiction; section 2 concentrates on story techniques and themes; section 3 focuses on critical interpretations of the most important stories; section 4 provides an overview of Hemingway criticism; section 5 contains a comprehensive checklist of Hemingway short fiction criticism from 1975 to 1989.

Berman, Ron. "Vaudeville Philosophers: 'The Killers.'" *Twentieth Century Literature* 45 (Spring, 1999): 79-93. Discusses the influence of the modernist reevaluation of vaudeville on Hemingway's short story. Notes that Hemingway's interest in vaudeville resulted from its pervasive presence in society and its acceptance in the intellectual world. Argues that vaudeville scripts inspired Hemingway's interest in the juxtaposition of urban sophistication and rural idiocy.

Dubus, Andre. "A Hemingway Story." *The Kenyon Review*, n.s. 19 (Spring, 1997): 141-147. Dubus, a respected short-story writer himself, discusses Hemingway's "In Another Country." He states that, whereas he once thought the story was about the futility of cures, since becoming disabled he has come to understand that it is about healing.

Flora, Joseph M. *Ernest Hemingway: A Study of the Short Fiction*. Boston: Twayne, 1989. An introduction to Hemingway's short fiction that focuses on the importance of reading the stories within the literary context Hemingway creates for them in the collections *In Our Time*, *Winner Take Nothing*, and *Men Without Women*. Argues that Hemingway devises an echo effect in which one story reflects another.

Gelfant, Blanche H., ed. *The Columbia Companion to the Twentieth-Century American Short Story*. New York: Columbia University Press, 2000. Includes a chapter in which Hemingway's short stories are analyzed.

Goodheart, Eugene, ed. *Critical Insights: Ernest Hemingway*. Pasadena, Calif.: Salem Press, 2010. Collection of original and reprinted essays providing critical readings of Hemingway's works, including Carlos Baker's examination of the short fiction.Also includes a biography, a chronology of major events in Hemingway's life, a complete list of his works, and a bibliography listing resources for further research

Hays, Peter L. *Ernest Hemingway*. New York: Continuum, 1990. A brief but instructive overview of Hemingway's life and his achievement as a writer. Offers brief critical summaries of the novels and many short stories. Contains a useful chronology.

Lamb, Robert Paul. *Art Matters: Hemingway, Craft, and the Creation of the Modern Short Story*. Newcastle upon Tyne, England: Cambridge Scholars, 2010. Lamb has written what is perhaps the definitive examination of Hemingway's short fiction. He discusses the writers who influenced Hemingway, including Anton Chekhov, Guy de Maupassant, Edgar Allan Poe, and Stephen Crane. He also analyzes Hemingway's minimalist writing style, innovative use of dialogue, story structure, and the legacy of his short fiction.

_____. "The Love Song of Harold Krebs: Form, Argument, and Meaning in Hemingway's 'Soldier's Home.'" *The Hemingway Review* 14 (Spring, 1995): 18-36. Claims that the story concerns both war trauma and a conflict between mother and son. Discusses the structure of the story; argues that by ignoring the story's form, one misses the manner of Hemingway's narrative argument and the considerable art that underlies it.

Leonard, John. "'A Man of the World' and 'A Clean, Well-Lighted Place': Hemingway's Unified View of Old Age." *The Hemingway Review* 13 (Spring, 1994): 62-73. Compares the two Hemingway stories in terms of the theme of age. Notes the themes of aloneness, consolation of light, loss of sexuality and physical prowess, depression, violence, and the need for dignity.

Mellow, James R. *Hemingway: A Life Without Consequences*. Boston: Houghton Mifflin, 1992. A well-informed, sensitive handling of Hemingway's life and work by a seasoned biographer.

Monteiro, George. "The Hemingway Story." In *A Companion to the American Short Story*, edited by Alfred Bendixen and James Nagel. Malden, Mass.: Wiley-Blackwell, 2010. Offers a comprehensive overview and critical examination of Hemingway's short fiction, making reference to many of the individual stories.

Nolan, Charles J., Jr. "Hemingway's Complicated Enquiry in *Men Without Women*." *Studies in Short Fiction* 32 (Spring, 1995): 217-222. Examines the theme of homosexuality in "A Simple Enquiry" from Hemingway's *Men Without Women*. Argues that the characters in the story are enigmatic, revealing their complexity only after the reader has looked carefully at what they do and say.

Scofield, Martin. "Ernest Hemingway." In *The Cambridge Introduction to the American Short Story*. New York: Cambridge University Press, 2006. Concise but thorough analysis of the style and content of Hemingway's short fiction. Scofield describes Hemingway as the "foremost American writer of the short story in the first half of the twentieth century."

Stewart, Matthew. *Modernism and Tradition in Ernest Hemingway's "In Our Time": A Guide for Students and Readers*. Rochester, N.Y.: Camden House, 2001. A comprehensive analysis of Hemingway's short-story collection, including discussions of its historical and biographical context, its relation to Hemingway's later works, the collection as a work of modernist literature, the character of Nick Adams, and readings of the individual stories.

Tetlow, Wendolyn E. *Hemingway's "In Our Time": Lyrical Dimensions*. Lewisburg, Pa.: Bucknell University Press, 1992. Argues that the collection is a "coherent, integral work" unified by such elements as the character Nick Adams, image patterns, symbols, and recurrent themes. Claims the book is analogous to a poetic sequence--a group of works that tend to interact as an organic whole. Discusses the lyrical elements in Hemingway's self-conscious juxtaposition of stories and interchapters.

Wagner-Martin, Linda. *Ernest Hemingway: A Literary Life*. New York: Palgrave Macmillan, 2007. Examines Hemingway's life, especially his troubled relationship with his parents. Wagner-Martin makes insightful connections between the writer's personal life, his emotions, and his writing.

_____, ed. *Hemingway: Eight Decades of Criticism*. East Lansing: Michigan State University Press, 2009. Wagner-Martin has updated her previous collections of essays to include criticism published within the past decade. Some of the essays discuss Hemingway's life, including his wounding in World War I, and his treatment of gender, guilt, disability, loss, and mourning.

Laurence W. Mazzeno

AMY HEMPEL

Born: Chicago, Illinois; December 14, 1951

PRINCIPAL SHORT FICTION

Reasons to Live, 1985
At the Gates of the Animal Kingdom, 1990
Tumble Home: A Novella and Short Stories, 1997
The Dog of the Marriage, 2005
The Collected Stories of Amy Hempel, 2006

OTHER LITERARY FORMS

Amy Hempel was a contributing editor to *Vanity Fair* in 1985-1986 and was the editor of *Unleashed: Poems by Writers' Dogs* in 1995.

ACHIEVEMENTS

Amy Hempel's stories have appeared in leading American journals and have been widely anthologized in publications such as *The Best American Short Stories* and *The Best of the Missouri Review, 1978-1990* ("Today Will Be a Quiet Day" appeared in both), *The Pushcart Prize, The Norton Anthology of Short Fiction* (1978), and *New American Short Stories: The Writers Select Their Own Favorites* (1987). Hempel was a finalist for the PEN/Faulkner Prize for Fiction for *Collected Stories* in 2006. She won the 2008 Rea Award for Short Fiction.

BIOGRAPHY

Amy Hempel was born in Chicago, the eldest of three children (she has two younger brothers). Her family moved to Denver when she was in the third grade, and when she was in high school they moved to San Francisco. Her mother committed suicide when Hempel was eighteen, and, at about the same time, Hempel was involved in two serious auto accidents. She spent a number of years in California and studied at both Whittier College and San Francisco

State University, and she held a variety of jobs in her twenties. She attended the Bread Loaf Writers' Conference in Vermont for a while, and she started writing in earnest when she studied with author Gordon Lish in a fiction workshop at Columbia University in 1982. (Lish arranged for her first collection of stories to be published in 1985.) After settling in New York City with her husband, Hempel worked as an editor and contributor to several periodicals and taught and lectured at a number of writing programs and workshops. Hempel has taught at New York University, Saint Mary's College, the University of Missouri, and in the graduate writing programs of Bennington College in Vermont.

ANALYSIS

Amy Hempel is among the original short-story writers upon whom the term "minimalist" was conferred; however, as several critics have noted, "miniaturist" may be a more accurate term. Some of her stories are very short (including the one-sentence "Housewife," which appears in *Tumble Home*). Even in her longer stories the style is compressed and economical in the extreme, the action limited, and the characters constantly make cryptic, ironic comments to one another. In an interview, Hempel said:

> A lot of times what's not reported in your work is more important than what actually appears on the page. Frequently the emotional focus of the story is some underlying event that may not be described or even referred to in the story.

Her stories demonstrate this minimalist philosophy again and again. Hempel's stories often revolve around sadness, loss, and survival: Characters are in hospitals or in recovery or in trouble. However, even in these stories of crisis, Hempel is distinguished by her humor; characters, even children, always have clever things to say to one another, and their conversations are full of metaphors, parables, and symbolic lessons. Hempel's stories often feature dogs, other animals, and best girl-friends, thus often bordering on sentimentality. What saves the stories from falling into that literary condition is their sardonic wit.

"IN THE CEMETERY WHERE AL JOLSON IS BURIED"

"In the Cemetery Where Al Jolson Is Buried" is probably Hempel's best-known work. Originally published in *TriQuarterly*, it has been reprinted in *The Editors' Choice: New American Stories* (1985) as well as in the popular *Norton Anthology of Short Fiction*, and it is quintessentially Hempel. The situation is dire: The narrator is visiting a friend in the hospital whom she has avoided visiting for two months; the friend is dying, and both women are in denial. Their conversation is filled with popular trivia, jokes, and funny stories--but many of these hint at the situation (like the narrator's fear of flying). After an earthquake, the narrator relates, a teacher got her sixth-grade students to shout,"*Bad* earth!" at the broken playground. She asks her friend, "Did you know when they taught the first chimp to talk, it lied?" In the end, the friend dies, although the narrator cannot express the thought and says euphemistically, "On the morning she was moved to the cemetery, the one where Al Jolson is buried." In the last image of the story, the narrator describes what happened when the signing chimp had a baby and it died: "her wrinkled hands moving with animal grace, forming again and again the words: Baby, come hug, Baby, come hug, fluent now in the language of grief." Only the narrator is inarticulate in that language, but the sublimation of her feelings makes the story a powerful emotional experience for readers. As is often the case in reading Hempel, less is surely more.

"TODAY WILL BE A QUIET DAY"

This short story was also published in Hempel's first collection, *Reasons to Live*, and was later included in *The Best American Short Stories*, *The Pushcart Prize XI*, and *The Best of the Missouri Review: Fiction, 1978-1990*, the journal where it first appeared.

The story describes a father in San Francisco taking his son and daughter out for the day. The father drives north across the Golden Gate Bridge; the three eat lunch in Petaluma, and then the daughter drives them home by a different route. Little happens, in other words, and the story is filled with their conversation,

Amy Hempel (AP Photo/Jim Cooper)

joke-telling, and jousting--like the title, an inscription the son once imagined on his tombstone. The father has taken them out for the day because

> He wanted to know how they were, is all. Just--how were they. . . . You think you're safe, the father thought, but it's thinking you're invisible because you closed your eyes.

A friend of the boy has recently killed himself, readers learn, and the father wants to make sure his own kids are okay. The imagery of the story underlines the question of the difference between appearance and reality: The restaurant where they have lunch still looks like the gas station it originally was; the daughter discovers that the dog she thought was taken to live on a ranch has been put to sleep. At the end of the story, all three are in sleeping bags in the master bedroom of their house. Has the mother died recently? Are the parents divorced? Something hidden has given a tension to the simple events of the story. As they fall asleep, the father asks if they want the good news or bad news first and then says he lied, that there is no bad news. For a little while longer, perhaps, he is going to be able to protect his two teenagers from the dangers of the world, but this protective posture, as Hempel intimates to readers, is precarious.

"THE HARVEST"

"The Harvest" was originally published in *The Quarterly* and collected in *At the Gates of the Animal Kingdom*, Hempel's second collection of stories, and it is the best example of her metafictional style, a style that has occasionally appeared in her fiction. The story is narrated by a young woman who has been in an auto accident: She and her date were headed for dinner in his car when they were hit, and in the accident the narrator almost lost her leg--or did she? In the second half of the story, she starts to unravel her narrative, and to describe the things she left out of the story, made up, or exaggerated--the marital status of the man, the seriousness of her injuries--and by the end, readers question what, if anything, took place. A psychiatrist tells the girl that victims of trauma often have difficulties distinguishing fiction from reality, and the insight underlines what Hempel is doing in "The Harvest": telling a story that becomes a narrative about making up a story--or about storytelling itself.

"THE MOST GIRL PART OF YOU"

This story was first published in *Vanity Fair* and was subsequently reprinted in *New American Short Stories* and in *At the Gates of the Animal Kingdom*, and it displays the basic Hempel style. A teenage narrator tells of her relationship with her friend, "Big Guy," whose mother hung herself eight days earlier. While the surface conversation is, as usual, full of jokes, clearly there is something deeper going on. Big Guy sews the girl's name into the skin of his hand, sucks ice to try to crack his teeth, and cuts the insect bites on her body with a razor. When Big Guy starts to make love to her after a dance, the girl claims she is "ready to start to truly be alive," but readers sense something else--his instability, her insecurity, and her obvious pity for his tragedy. The title of the story comes from a film she was forced to watch at school years earlier, *The Most Girl Part of You*, and her own mother has apparently encouraged her sexual initiation. To readers, that introduction to adult sexuality seems wrong. Like the iceberg Ernest Hemingway used to describe a story's hidden content, a large part of this story's cryptic meaning may lie beneath the tense fictional surface.

TUMBLE HOME: A NOVELLA AND SHORT STORIES

This collection contains seven stories and the title novella, an eighty-page letter the narrator is writing to an artist she may or may not have met, describing her life inside a mental hospital. Little happens, and readers learn more about the narrator's friends in the institution--Karen, Warren, and Chatty--than about the narrator's own life. There is hardly anything remarkable in their conversations except the wit and sardonic humor of Hempel's elliptical, first-person style. The other stories in the collection--several of them just a few pages long--reflect typical Hempel concerns. "Sportsman," probably the strongest story here, for example, describes the breakup of Jack and Alex. Jack drives east from California to stay with his friends Vicki and her husband, "the doctor," who live on Long Island. Vicki arranges for Jack to see Trina, a psychic, but then Alex calls from California to say that her mother has suffered a stroke. The story ends with Jack and Trina headed into New York City on a date, but the resolution of the relationships here is far from certain. As usual, appearances can be deceiving. The city looks pretty good, Jack comments; "Give it a minute," the psychic responds. Like Raymond Carver, Hempel often tells deceptively simple stories about contemporary characters in deeper trouble than they realize.

THE DOG OF THE MARRIAGE

When Hempel published her first book, *Reasons to Live*, a collection of stories that promptly placed her in the aggravating category known as "minimalism," Madison Smartt Bell complained that Hempel, like most modish minimalists, just did not have much to say. In *The Dog of the Marriage*, her fourth book, with a career total of less than six hundred pages, Hempel is as tight-lipped as ever. She once told an interviewer that the trick is to find a "tiny way into a huge subject." The question is not whether Hempel has little to say, but whether the few words she chooses to explore the huge subjects in this book--love, loss, divorce, death, grief, betrayal, rape, heartbreak--are the right words to express their inexplicable essence.

What the stories are about is finding a way to live when life is unlivable and language seems inadequate. For example, in the story "Jesus Is Waiting," the reader rides with a woman who, having lost a solid center, stays constantly in motion by putting fifty thousand miles on her car. Feeling she has no place to go, she just drives, listening to a tape of the Reverend Al Green repeating the theme, "Jesus is waiting." It is the "geographic cure" for her suffering, a search for symptoms; her only comfort is the old reassurance that "wherever you go, there you are." In "The Uninvited," a fifty-year-old woman who thinks she may be pregnant but does not know who to blame--the husband that she no longer lives with or the rapist that she did not report--is fascinated by the spooky 1944 Ray Milland-Ruth Hussey film *The Uninvited*. The woman lives a haunted life in which fiction and reality, dreaming and waking, the real and the more-than-real are so bound together that the story ends in a scene of almost pathological pathos.

One very brief piece, "What Were the White Things?" (which seems emblematic of the entire collection), juxtaposes white objects in a gallery of paintings with white spots on an X-ray. The artist of the exhibit, which is significantly called *Finding the Mystery in Clarity*, says the mind wants to make sense of a thing. However, when a doctor tries to tell the central female character the meaning of the spots on her X-ray, she can only repeat helplessly, "What are the white things?" In the title story, a woman facing the breakup of her marriage pre-trains dogs who will then be further trained to be guides for blind partners. Although she is often asked how she can bear always to part with animals she has lived with, the woman struggles with the hard truth that all relationships are weighted with the threat of loss.

A casual first reading of these stories may make one feel short-changed and cheated, but short stories are seldom meant to be read rapidly and once only. The challenge is to try to become the attentive, sympathetic reader they demand. Like most short-story writers, Hempel has a compulsion similar to that of the poet: to struggle with human complexities for which psychologists, sociologists, historians, novelists, and other dispensers of explanatory discourse can never quite account.

OTHER MAJOR WORKS

EDITED TEXT: *Unleashed: Poems by Writers' Dogs*, 1995.

BIBLIOGRAPHY

Aldridge, John W. *Talents and Technicians: Literary Chic and the New Assembly-Line Fiction*. New York: Charles Scribner's Sons, 1992. In a chapter that considers Carver, Ann Beattie, and Frederick Barthelme, Aldridge accuses Hempel of "chronic minimalist constipation" and claims that behind her stories, several of which he analyzes, "there seems to be nothing but a chilly emotional void generated by either an incapacity to feel or a determination to express no feeling if one is there."

Blythe, Will, ed. *Why I Write: Thoughts on the Craft of Fiction*. Boston: Little, Brown, 1998. As one of twenty-six contributors to this collection, Hempel suggests some of the reasons that she creates her short fiction.

Hallett, Cynthia J. "Minimalism and the Short Story." *Studies in Short Fiction* 33 (1996): 487-495. In an essay that uses Hempel, Carver, and Hemingway as primary examples, Hallett attempts to lay down a theoretical foundation for minimalist fiction.

Hemple, Amy. Interview by Suzan Sherman. *BOMB* (Spring, 1997): 67-70. In this wide-ranging interview, Hempel talks about her background as a writer, the origins of many of her stories, and her theories about reading and writing short fiction.

David Peck
Updated by Charles E. May

CRISTINA HENRÍQUEZ

Born: Delaware; 1978

PRINCIPAL SHORT FICTION

Come Together, Fall Apart: A Novella and Stories,
2006

OTHER LITERARY FORMS

Cristina Henríquez (krihs-TEE-nah hehn-REE-kehz) is well known as a writer of short stories. She also writes in long form and published an acclaimed novel, *The World in Half*, in 2009.

ACHIEVEMENTS

Cristina Henríquez's stories have appeared in *The New Yorker*, *The Atlantic*, *Glimmer Train*, *Ploughshares*, and other journals. She was featured in *Virginia Quarterly Review* as one of Fiction's New Luminaries. She also has received the Alfredo Cisneros Del Moral Foundation Award.

BIOGRAPHY

Cristina Henríquez was born in Delaware in 1978. She has lived in Florida, Virginia, Indiana, Iowa, and Texas. Her first writing endeavors started when she was in high school and wrote to a boy she wanted to impress. Her interest in writing continued through her studies at Northwestern University, where she earned a degree in English. Later, she received a master's degree from the renowned Iowa Writers' Workshop. Her first stories, "Carnival, Las Tablas" and "Ashes," were published in magazines. She followed this with her collection of eight short stories and a novella, *Come Together, Fall Apart*, in 2006. After taking a year off to write it, her novel *The World in Half* came out in 2009. Henrique settled in Chicago, Illinois.

ANALYSIS

Cristina Henrique writes about young people coming to grips with transitions to adult life in their particular chronological, geographical, and political space and time. The author grew up in the United States, but she visited her relatives in Panama, her father's native soil, for several weeks each summer. The extent of the autobiographical elements in her stories is known only to Henrique. However, there is an obvious textual parallel between her life and her expressed desire to use her experiences in Panama to give cultural depth to her stories. Henrique draws on her familiarity of her ancestral landscape, as she portrays people coming of age during the same period as her visitations to Panama. The author admits that she writes partially to discover the other half of herself: her Panamanian other.

Henrique, who lives in Chicago, says that she locates her literature in Panama because that is where she finds everyday life surprising. Chicago is normal reality, but the scenes found commonly in the streets of Panama are fodder for the background of her stories (and her novel). Her astute observations of the daily life of her grandmother and others in Panama often end up in her stories. The popsicle vendor with feet larger than his sandals is not just a textual invention. The pleasure that readers derive from the tales comes from Henríquez's heightened awareness as an outsider looking at her ancestral ethnic landscape. She has stated that her family's oral histories do not always coincide; just as with the characters in her works, she chooses what is truth and what is imaginary. To the reader, the line between the author's life and the one she invents is uncertain. This autobiographical link is also present in her novel *The World in Half*, in which a young Chicagoan goes on a journey to Panama to investigate her ancestral roots.

Come Together, Fall Apart comprises tales of growing up, Latin American family values, and love relationships. The stories are located within the social chaos brought about by the American invasion in 1989 that led to the arrest and ouster of Panamanian president Manuel Noriega. The narrators in each story paint a society whose spirit embodies a love for place and country, even amid sweeping changes. They struggle to keep the culture alive and to move on, to an uncertain future. Unlike Ernest Hemingway's Havana, and other foreign lands overly romanticized as surreal and exotic by similar writers, the Panama of Henríquez's tales is revealed as starkly real. This is not a fantasyland; it is an all-too-real Latin American country struggling to evolve without being absorbed by a worldwide pop culture. The reader is confronted by a society that sluggishly attempts to move on from an unstable past to an unsure future.

The characters in Henríquez's tales are mostly young. Nonetheless, her range of personalities includes women, mothers, men, fathers lost to their offspring, boyfriends, girlfriends, grandparents, and friends. These people mirror the dysfunction of their present Panama, and they suffer from fractured families, illness, abandonment, death, and unwanted change at an early age. Henríquez's Panamanians discover ways to rise above what fate has given them. Like Panama itself, they endure despite a complex and indecisive reality.

COME TOGETHER, FALL APART

Unlike her later novel, this collection of eight short stories and a novella are located only in Panama. It is a Panama in transition from the collapsed Noriega regime to an unpredictable future. Each tale is narrated from a different character's viewpoint, and each examines conventional loves and families in unconventional times. Many of the situations portray lives that are teetering on the edge of a psychological, financial, or physical-illness cliff. The inhabitants of these stories cannot go back to a more stable past, and the future requires decisions that cannot be postponed.

Henrique writes about young people, mostly teenagers, at poignant crossroads of their lives. Henrique does not paint these youths as incapable of avoiding tragedy or as super-adolescents who have the wisdom

of age while still young. Instead, her characters are ordinary people in extraordinary situations, who deal with the consequences in an often moving and very human manner. For example, fathers who abandon their children are not presented as evil reincarnate or pious wonders who gave up their children in order to give them a better life. Instead, the neglectful fathers live otherwise normal lives, although they do experience moments of insight when they realize the damage they have inflicted.

In the first story, "Yanina," the reader encounters a recurring theme: young Panamanians at emotional crossroads, personal and societal. In the post-Noriega epoch, everything appears to be in flux: family, love, and society. A young woman, Yanina, wants her boyfriend, Ren, to marry her and end her angst over her father's and godfather's infidelities. Ren lives in a remote beach community and hesitates to take on the responsibility of a marriage. Yanina unsuccessfully petitions Ren forty-five times to marry her. Their conflicted relationship mirrors the uncertainty of Panama.

"Drive" was first published in *Virginia Quarterly Review*. The young woman who narrates "Drive" has a good relationship with her mother, but the girl's attraction to a less-than-ideal first boyfriend threatens this mother-daughter bond. Her father lives a misspent life in Panama City, never having anything to do with her or her mother. Through the words and thoughts of the teenager, the reader learns that her boyfriend uses drugs and encourages her to participate. The mother reacts to this undesirable suitor with fury, putting strain on her relationship with the daughter. Henrique uses the narrator's thoughts to show a daughter that wishes her father were more involved than he is. In a rare encounter, she watches him from behind and tries to will herself into accepting him as any other elderly man with graying hair and the sharp angles of an old man's face and body. Her inability to believe this leads to a form of nonaggressive acceptance.

In "Drive," Henrique shifts the story line into a Magical Realism mode. In this popular Latin American style, she lets the narrator indulge in a fantasy. In the girl's dream, the car she is driving changes into a giant bird. She and her friends soar above the streets, feeling life stream like wind over their graceful, flying bodies.

Henrique brings the reader into wistful fantasy in order to expose the adolescent penchant for immersion in dreamland, in which the narrator escapes the stark realities of a stunted economy, fractured family, and struggling country. The future will wait awhile.

"Ashes" first appeared in *The New Yorker*. Again, a narrator, Mireya, presents a father as mentally lacking. He was generally absent from her and her mother's lives. His infidelity becomes more unbearable when her mother suddenly collapses and dies of a heart attack. The young narrator is working a dead-end and dangerous job, cutting meat in the rear of the Casa de la Carne, when she receives the bad news. Her already troubled life, with its unfulfilled relationships, starts unraveling. Her lover also is unfaithful. She attempts to find good in her memories of her parents, but she cannot remember any signs of true love between them. Henrique describes these fragile memories as the ephemeral vapor that shimmers above a highway on hot humid days. Mireya's only memory of her parents in a loving stance is from long ago, with light laughter and a simple interchange of soft caresses on a couch. The reader is left with a character who has little on which to hang her hopes, but she moves on regardless.

"Mercury" introduces a teenage narrator, Maria, who has been sent to visit her grandparents in Panama while her parents are getting divorced in New Jersey. Just as Henríquez describes herself as half American and half Panamanian, this narrator is caught between two cultures within one family. She feels a desperate need to use her Spanish to bridge the gap between both cultures and her dysfunctional family. Unfortunately, her grandfather is near death and cannot talk to her. Her inability to communicate across geographical and cultural borders reflects the gap some ethnicities experience in America.

The title novella, *Come Together, Fall Apart*, has a teenage boy as narrator. He is in love, and his country is in shambles because of the American invasion of 1989. On the eve of the invasion, his family had to leave Panama City, and he is troubled by the loss of his girlfriend and the seemingly apocalyptic end of the current government and the societal upheaval that will follow. Unlike the other well-structured tales that Henrique includes in this

collection, this novella seems intended to teach the history of Panama and its connection with the United States. There is a short story within its content, but it is clear the author could not decide between creating a story or a novel and settled for neither.

Henrique admits she does not know everything about Panama. Nonetheless, her graceful, uncomplicated prose introduces the reader to young Panamanians at critical junctures in their lives. They confront war, love, and tragedy and somehow come of age amid it all. The everyday language and straightforward story lines are infused with Henríquez's inspiring ability to note the beauty found in simple but meaningful observations of the human spirit under siege, literally and figuratively. She explores various personal conflicts involving generation gaps, first loves, and fiery passions from an unadorned but evocative perspective.

The strongest narrators in these tales are women. They are hard workers, mothers, daughters, and the central features of post-invasion Panama. They somehow maintain a belief in a future that will include all of Panama's social levels. Women of the future, they intend to be a force in constructing a new Panama with the country's culture intact. In these stories, Henrique presents a wide spectrum of manhood, including lost and lazy men and boyfriends and fathers who value love and want to participate in a new cultural reality. At times, they are likable, but the author could have given more weight to the male characterization in this collection. The frequently appalling deportment of the men is somewhat exaggerated.

Henrique textually paints a Panama of stunning geography and geology. Her graceful renditions of city and countryside reveal her love for the physical landscape of Panama. Simple life scenes on remote beaches and in hot and humid cities are told with an obvious love of the land. These remarkable tales are imbued with the subtle lessons of life that all must eventually learn. In this collection, they are crafted into poignant accounts of individual and collective culture that is uniquely Panamanian.

OTHER MAJOR WORKS

LONG FICTION: *The World in Half,* 2009.

BIBLIOGRAPHY

Augenbraum, Harold, and Ilan Stavans, eds. *Lengua Fresca: Latinos Writing on the Edge.* Boston: Houghton Mifflin, 2006. Collection of newer Latino writers. Contains introduction with viewpoints on directions that Hispanic American writers are taking in cultural-driven literature. Contains biographical information.

Merrick, Elizabeth. *This Is Not Chick Lit: Original Stories by America's Best Women Writers.* New York: Random House, 2006. Presents feminist viewpoint of Henrique, along with an unorthodox critique and explanation of newly emerging women writers. Contains biographical information.

Morrison, Susan, ed. "Hello, My Name Is . . ." In *Thirty Ways of Looking at Hillary: Reflections by Women Writers.* New York: Harper, 2008. This article by Henrique presents an insightful look her viewpoint on the American political scene, as opposed to her writings that always reference Panamanian politics and the effect the American invasion had on that country.

Paul Siegrist

O. HENRY

Born: Greensboro, North Carolina;
September 11, 1862
Died: New York, New York; June 5, 1910
Also Known As: William Sydney Porter

PRINCIPAL SHORT FICTION
Cabbages and Kings, 1904
The Gift of the Magi, 1905
The Four Million, 1906
Heart of the West, 1907 *The Trimmed Lamp,* 1907
The Gentle Grafter, 1908
The Voice of the City, 1908
Options, 1909
Roads of Destiny, 1909
Let Me Feel Your Pulse, 1910
Strictly Business, 1910
The Two Women, 1910
Whirligigs, 1910
Sixes and Sevens, 1911
Rolling Stones, 1912
Waifs and Strays, 1917
Postscripts, 1923
O. Henry Encore, 1936
Tales of O. Henry, 1969
The Voice of the City, and Other Stories: A Selection, 1991
The Best of O. Henry, 1992
Collected Stories: Revised and Expanded, 1993
Heart of the West, 1993
Selected Stories, 1993
The Best Short Stories of O. Henry, 1994
One Hundred Selected Stories, 1995

OTHER LITERARY FORMS

While almost all of O. Henry's literary output is in the short-story form, he contributed verse and anecdotes to *Rolling Stone,* the humorous weekly magazine which he founded and edited in 1894. He also experimented with play writing, collaborating with Franklin P. Adams on a musical comedy, Lo(pr. 1909), based on O. Henry's short story "He Also Serves"; this play was staged once in mid-1909. He also prepared a play based on another story, "The World and the Door."

ACHIEVEMENTS

A widely read and published writer, O. Henry's short stories influenced not only the development of magazine fiction as a popular form but also the evolution of modern narrative. Indeed, even very diverse European and South American writers adopt the devices

O. Henry perfected. This phenomenon is no accident: His short stories have been widely reprinted and translated, especially in Russia and France, and have been adapted for radio, stage, and television performances.

O. Henry, however, was especially popular in the United States. Extremely humorous, clever, and entertaining, he also managed to capture all that was recognizably and uniquely American--the variegated language, attitudes, spirit, geographical locations, social environments, and, most important, the inclination to identify with the downtrodden, the underdog. O. Henry's contribution to American letters was so obvious that a long-lived literary prize--the annual O. Henry Memorial Award for Prize Stories--was established in 1918 by the New York Society of Arts and Sciences.

BIOGRAPHY

Receiving little formal education, O. Henry, the pseudonym of William Sydney Porter, found themes and plots for his short stories in his early jobs as pharmacist, ranch hand, draftsman, and bank teller. After being arrested for embezzlement in 1894, he fled to Honduras, where much of the material for *Cabbages and Kings* was acquired. He returned to Texas in 1897 to be with his dying wife and was convicted and sent to prison one year later. During his imprisonment he began to achieve national prominence for his stories and subsequently continued his writing career in New York. He signed contracts with the *Sunday World* and *Munsey's* for weekly stories drawn from his own experiences in the city. In 1907, he married his childhood sweetheart; three years later he died, finally succumbing to alcohol-induced cirrhosis of the liver and diabetes.

ANALYSIS

O. Henry's widely varied background provided not only plots for his tales but also characters drawn from all walks of life. Ham in "The Hiding of Black Chief," Caesar in "A Municipal Report," and Lizzie in "The Guilty Party" are only isolated examples of O. Henry's proficiency in creating a vivid sense of the texture of language for the reader by reproducing native dialect, be it Western, southern, or even "New Yorkese." This linguistic sensitivity contributes to O.

Henry's versatility as a local colorist, as does his literary self-education. Echoes of Charles Dickens appear in "Elsie in New York," allusions to Greek and Roman mythology in "Hygeia at the Solito" and "The Reformation of Calliope," and parodic references to Sir Arthur Conan Doyle in "The Adventure of Shamrock Jolnes."

O. Henry's popularity stems not only from his depiction of commonplace events and human responses but also from the surprise endings of his "well-made" plots. Talented as an ironist, he both comments upon and sympathizes with the ranch hands, bank clerks, and shopgirls whose sorrows and foibles he re-creates. While much of his humor redounds from his likely use of puns and literary allusions, much might be called the humor of recognition--the rueful grin that occurs when a reader sees his or her own petty flaws mirrored in a character and predicts the inevitable downfall. The downfall, however, is often given the comic turn which made O. Henry famous. Kid Brady in "Vanity and Some Sables," for example, would rather go to jail for the theft of furs than tell his girlfriend that her "Russian sables" cost $21.50 in a bargain basement; Maida, the shopgirl in "The Purple Dress" who "starves eight months to bring a purple dress and a holiday together," gives up her carefully garnered money to save a spendthrift friend from eviction. Molly sacrifices her furs--and her vanity--to prove Kid's honesty, and Maida is outdone by her tailor in generosity so that she gets both her dress and the marriageable head clerk: These are the twist endings that turn minor personal tragedies into comic triumphs.

"THE GIFT OF THE MAGI"

Possibly one of the most anthologized of O. Henry's stories is "The Gift of the Magi," a tale about the redeeming power of love. The protagonists, a couple named James and Della Young, struggle to live on a small salary. By Christmas Eve, Della's thrift has gained her only $1.87 for her husband's gift, which she had hoped would be "something fine and rare and sterling." She decides to sell one of the family "treasures"--her long, beautiful chestnut hair--to buy a platinum chain for her husband's prized possession, his watch. The first reversal is that he has bought her a set of pure tortoise-shell combs with which to adorn her long hair; the second, that he has sold his watch to do so.

In this story about the true spirit of gift-giving, both the family treasures and the protagonists take on Old Testamentary significance. Della's hair, the reader is told, puts the Queen of Sheba's wealth to shame; Jim's watch rivals all of Solomon's gold. Both unselfishly sacrifice their most precious possession for the other, thereby ushering in a new dispensation on Christmas Eve. Even more, these "two foolish children" acquire allegorical value in their act of giving insofar as they replicate the giving of the three wise men: "Of all who give and receive gifts, such as they are the wisest," O. Henry tells us: "They are the magi." In O. Henry's version, then, the "Gift of the Magi" turns out not to be gold, frankincense, or myrrh, not even hair combs or a watch chain, but rather selfless love.

"PAST ONE AT ROONEY'S"

This love is what O. Henry posits as a cure for such social ills as the inevitable gang fights and prostitution he portrays in his New York stories. In "Past One at Rooney's," a tale introduced as a modern retelling of William Shakespeare's *Romeo and Juliet* (pr. c. 1595-1596, pb. 1597), a gangster, hiding from the police, falls in love with a prostitute. They lie about their occupations for the sake of the other: Eddie MacManus pretends to be the son of a Wall Street broker, while Fanny claims to be a factory girl. When a policeman recognizes MacManus, however, she gives up her new identity to prevent the arrest. Pulling her night's money out of her garter, she throws it at the policeman and announces that MacManus is her procurer. Once they are allowed to leave, MacManus confesses that he really is wanted by the police but intends to reform; seeing that Fanny still loves him, MacManus saves her (as she had "saved" him by sacrificing her hoped-for respectability) through marriage. Such stories of the "golden-hearted prostitute" are plentiful in the O. Henry canon and in themselves provide another clue to O. Henry's popularity--his emphasis on the remnant of human compassion in the most cynical of characters.

ROADS OF DESTINY

O. Henry is interested as well in what might be called the moment of choice: the decision to act, speak, or dress in a way which seems to determine the whole course of a life. The title story of the volume *Roads of Destiny*, a story allegorical in nature, suggests that the choice is not so much among different fates as among different versions of the same fate. Environment, in short, determines character, unless some modicum of self-sacrificing love as in "The Gift of the Magi" intervenes. More concretely, O. Henry saw poverty and exploitation as the twin evils of urban life. Often cited for his sympathetic portrayal of the underpaid store clerk who struggles to survive, he also is a biting critic of those who perpetuate an inhumane system to satisfy personal greed or lust. "An Unfinished Story," for example, castigates an aging lady-killer who is "a connoisseur in starvation. He could look at a shop-girl and tell you to an hour how long it had been since she had eaten anything more nourishing than marshmallows and tea." Piggy, with whom O. Henry himself ruefully identified, preyed on shopgirls by offering them invitations to dinner. The working girl might thus keep her conscience and starve, or sell herself and eat: This was her condition as well as her choice.

"THE TRIMMED LAMP"

Where a choice need not be made through hunger alone is the middle moral ground on which many of O.

O. Henry (Library of Congress)

Henry's stories take place. "The Trimmed Lamp," the titular story of another volume, suggests two opposing ways to deal with an exploitative economic system. Nancy, a country girl content to work for small wages in a department store, mimics not only the quietly elegant dress but also the manners of her wealthy customers, while her friend Lou, a highly paid laundry presser, spends most of her money on expensive, conspicuous clothing. Nancy exploits the system by educating herself in the best it has to offer; Lou works for the system and profits monetarily. In the long run Nancy's education teaches her the difference between purchased quality, such as the clothes Lou wears, and intrinsic quality, which cannot be bought. She refuses an offer of marriage from a millionaire because he is a liar: As O. Henry writes, "the dollar-mark grew blurred in her mind's eye, and shaped itself into . . . such words as 'truth' and 'honor' and now and then just 'kindness.'" Lou, in contrast, becomes the mistress of a wealthy man, leaving her quiet, serious fiancé to Nancy. The final vignette, a plainly clothed but vibrantly happy Nancy trying to comfort her sobbing, fashionably dressed friend, illustrates the divergence between their two philosophies. While neither can escape completely from the economic system, Nancy refuses to measure human worth in monetary terms; instead, she adopts the same set of values posited in "The Gift of the Magi."

"The Ransom of Red Chief"

Many of the stories O. Henry writes are quite outside the moral framework that is suggested in "The Trimmed Lamp." Like others written about the "gentle grafters" which populated the nether side of his world, the story of "The Ransom of Red Chief" is of the "biter bit" variety. O. Henry's humorous focus on the problems that two kidnappers have with their charge--a redhaired version of Tom Sawyer with the same unflagging energy for mischief--deflects the moral question about the criminal action. Johnny enjoys his adventure; he styles himself Red Chief and tries to scalp one of his captors at daybreak, then rides him to the stockade to "rescue" settlers, feeds him oats, and worries him with questions about why holes are empty. His father's reply to a demand for ransom shows that he understands *who* is in captivity; he offers to take his son back for a sum of $250.

The Gentle Grafter

Similarly, the exploits recounted in *The Gentle Grafter* are modern tall tales, the heroes at times acquiring a mythological aura, at other times appearing to be no different from the average man on the street. Grafting, in short, is an occupation that carries the same code of responsibilities as any legitimate business, as is made clear in "Shearing the Wolf." When two con men, Jeff Peters and Andy Tucker, discover that the leading hardware merchant in town intends to frustrate someone else's scheme to sell forged money, they agree that they cannot "stand still and see a man who has built up a business by his own efforts and brains and risk be robbed by an unscrupulous trickster." The twist is that the "trickster" is the merchant and the "businessman" is the forger.

In a number of respects, then, O. Henry contributed immeasurably to the development of the American short story. To be sure, many of his works are considered ephemeral today, primarily because they first appeared as magazine fiction; but a careful perusal reveals that behind the humor lies the mirror of the social reformer. In the characters and situations one notices common human problems of the beginning of the twentieth century; in the humor one notices the attempt to deal with apparently insurmountable social problems. With his clever plot reversals, O. Henry does more than create a new story form; he keeps the reader alive to the connotations of language and aware that in a world dominated by an unfair economic system, human kindness may be the answer.

Other major works

PLAY: *Lo*,pr. 1909 (with Franklin P. Adams).

NONFICTION: *Letters to Lithopolis*, 1922; *The Second Edition of Letters to Lithopolis from O. Henry to Mabel Wagnalls*, 1999 (with Mable Wagnalls).

MISCELLANEOUS: *O Henryana*, 1920.

Bibliography

Arnett, Ethel Stephens. *O. Henry from Polecat Creek*. Greensboro, N.C.: Piedmont Press, 1963. This entertaining biography of O. Henry's early years goes far in illuminating the character-shaping environment and experiences of both O.

Henry and his fiction. Supplemented by illustrations, notes, a bibliography, and an index.

Current-Garcia, Eugene. *O. Henry: A Study of the Short Fiction*. New York: Twayne, 1993. An introduction to O. Henry's stories, largely drawn from Current-Garcia's earlier Twayne volume. Focuses on O. Henry's frequent themes, his romanticism, and his narrative techniques, such as his use of the tall-tale conventions. Includes critical excerpts from discussions of O. Henry by other critics.

Eichenbaum, Boris. *O. Henry and the Theory of the Short Story*. Translated by I. R. Titunik. Ann Arbor: University of Michigan, 1968. Originally published in Russia in 1925, this study reflects both the Russian interest in O. Henry as a serious writer and the brand of criticism known as Russian Formalism. Because Formalism was more concerned with technical achievement than thematic profundity, O. Henry, who was a technical master, is a perfect candidate for the exercise of this kind of analysis.

Evans, Walter. "'A Municipal Report': O. Henry and Postmodernism." *Tennessee Studies in Literature* 26 (1981): 101-116. Recognizing modern criticism's either trite interpretation or complete indifference to O. Henry's work, Evans embarks on a radical revisioning of his literary contributions by comparing his work to the fiction of postmodernists like Vladimir Nabokov, John Barth, Robert Coover, and William Gass.

Gallegly, Joseph. *From Alamo Plaza to Jack Harris's Saloon: O. Henry and the Southwest He Knew*. The Hague, Netherlands: Mouton, 1970. By investigating contemporary photographs, literature, popular pursuits, news items, and personalities--both real and fictional--from the contemporary scene of the O. Henry, Gallegly provides significant insight into the writer's southwestern stories.

Gelfant, Blanche H., ed. *The Columbia Companion to the Twentieth-Century American Short Story*. New York: Columbia University Press, 2000. Includes a chapter in which O. Henry's short stories are analyzed.

Jennings, Al. *Through the Shadows with O. Henry*. Lubbock: Texas Tech University Press, 2000. Reprint of a classic O. Henry study, with a new introduction by Mike Cox and afterword by Patrick McConal, who consider the reception of Henry's work in the twentieth century.

Langford, Gerald. *Alias O. Henry: A Biography of William Sidney Porter*. New York: Macmillan, 1957. A well-documented biography that considers in detail Porter's marriages and the evidence used in his embezzlement trial. The foreword provides a brief but penetrating overview of O. Henry's critical reputation (including overseas) and his place within the context of American literature. Supplemented by illustrations, an appendix about *Rolling Stone*, notes, and an index.

Monteiro, George. "Hemingway, O. Henry, and the Surprise Ending." *Prairie Schooner* 47, no. 4 (1973-1974): 296-302. In rehabilitating O. Henry and his most famous technique, Monteiro makes comparisons with Hemingway's own--but very different--use of the same device. This significant difference Monteiro ascribes to Hemingway's essentially uneasy reception of O. Henry's work and to the two authors' divergent outlooks on life.

Pattee, Frederick Lewis. *The Development of the American Short Story*. New York: Harper and Brothers, 1923. Although this is an old study of the short story, the O. Henry chapter represents an influential negative criticism of his fiction.

Scofield, Martin. "O. Henry and Jack London." In *The Cambridge Introduction to the American Short Story*. New York: Cambridge University Press, 2006. Discusses O. Henry's "fluctuating" popularity and critical reception. Argues that O. Henry was a precursor of postmodernism, who has "more in common" with Robert Coover and Donald Barthelme than with his contemporaries Sherwood Anderson and Ernest Hemingway.

Stuart, David. *O. Henry: A Biography of William Sydney Porter*. Chelsea, Mich.: Scarborough House, 1990. A good, updated volume on O. Henry. Includes bibliographical references and an index.

Wyatt-Brown, Bertram. *Hearts of Darkness: Wellsprings of a Southern Literary Tradition.* Baton Rouge: Louisiana State University Press, 2003. Discusses the distinctively southern aspects of O. Henry's stories, as well as his influence on other southern American authors. Bibliographic references and index.

Patricia Marks
Updated by Terri Frongia

PATRICIA HIGHSMITH

Born: Fort Worth, Texas; January 19, 1921
Died: Locarno, Switzerland; February 4, 1995
Also known as: Claire Morgan

PRINCIPAL SHORT FICTION

The Snail-Watcher, and Other Stories, 1970 (also known as *Eleven*)

Kleine Geschichten für Weiberfeinde, 1974 (*Little Tales of Misogyny,* 1977)

The Animal-Lover's Book of Beastly Murder, 1975

Slowly, Slowly in the Wind, 1979

The Black House, 1981

Mermaids on the Golf Course, and Other Stories, 1985

Tales of Natural and Unnatural Catastrophes, 1987

The Selected Stories of Patricia Highsmith, 2001

Nothing That Meets the Eye: The Uncollected Stories of Patricia Highsmith, 2002

OTHER LITERARY FORMS

Patricia Highsmith is best known for her highly original psychological studies of the criminal mind, particularly in the Ripley mystery series. She coauthored a children's book and wrote material for television programs, including *Alfred Hitchcock Presents.* A number of her novels were made into films, including the 1951 Alfred Hitchcock production of *Strangers on a Train* (1950) and another version, produced in 1969, entitled *Once You Kiss a Stranger* (1969); *The Talented Mr. Ripley* (1955), produced by Times Film in 1961 as *Purple Noon* and also filmed by Anthony Minghella in 1999; *The Blunderer* (1954) as *Le Meurtrier* (1963) and *Enough Rope* (1966); *This Sweet Sickness* (1960) as the French film *Tell Her That I Love Her* (1977); and *Ripley's Game* (1974) as *The American Friend* (1978). In the 1990's she published the novels *Ripley Under Water* (1991) and *Small g: A Summer Idyll* (1995).

ACHIEVEMENTS

Patricia Highsmith won high critical and commercial acclaim in England, France, Germany, and eventually her native country. A member of the Detection Club, she received both the Edgar Allan Poe Scroll of the Mystery Writers of America and the Grand Prix de Littérature Policière award in 1957 for *The Talented Mr. Ripley.* In 1964, she received the Crime Writers Association of England Silver Dagger Award for the best foreign crime novel of the year, *The Two Faces of January* (1964). She was made an Officier de l'Ordre des Arts et des Lettres in 1990.

BIOGRAPHY

Born on January 19, 1921, the daughter of Jay Bernard Plangman and Mary (Coates) Plangman Highsmith, Mary Patricia Highsmith was reared by her grandmother for the first six years of her life. Her parents, both commercial artists, had separated over her mother's relationship with Stanley Highsmith. When her mother remarried, Highsmith rejoined her in New York City, a time she recalled as "hell" because of constant conflicts and arguments.

Highsmith began writing at the age of seventeen. She was the editor of the Julia Richman High School newspaper and received a B.A. from Barnard College in 1942. For a brief interval after graduation she made her living writing scenarios for comic books. Her first story, "The Heroine," was published in *Harper's Bazaar* in 1945 and selected for inclusion in the collection

O. Henry Prize Stories of 1946. With the help of writer Truman Capote, she was admitted into the Yaddo artists' colony in 1948, where she completed *Strangers on a Train*. The novel, her third written but first published, did not see print until two years later, but the 1951 film adaptation by Alfred Hitchcock and the subsequent sale of its stage rights helped launch her career.

Highsmith traveled extensively in the United States, Mexico, and Europe in 1940's and 1950's, before moving to England in 1963. She lived a solitary life in France from 1967 to 1982, then in Switzerland, where she died in 1995 from a combination of lung cancer and aplastic anemia. She never married, and she left a bequest valued at $3 million to Yaddo.

ANALYSIS

Patricia Highsmith is certainly better known for her novels, especially the Ripley series, than for her short stories. Nevertheless, her work in the demanding shorter medium was diverse and of very high literary quality. She was praised by no less a master of the well-told tale than Graham Greene, who in his foreword to *The Snail-Watcher, and Other Stories* calls her "a writer who has created a world of her own--a world claustrophobic and irrational which we enter each time with a sense of personal danger." Highsmith is not simply a teller of interesting stories but also a master of the intellectually unsettling, a goad and a gadfly who clearly means to upset readers' smug comfort with the everyday world that they take for granted. Greene's word "danger" is precise: Highsmith in a sense threatens the reader with a world in which everything seems normal until a sudden off-kilter event puts all in doubt. Her stories focus on the abnormal psychology of seemingly conventional people, on bizarre natural and supranatural events, and on the animal world upsetting the "natural" superiority of humans.

Highsmith's contributions to the short-story genre have touched a number of very different areas. Her control of the very short, very mordant, and very elegant tale is complete and puts her in the ranks of the French masters of such forms. Not a word is wasted; not a sentence departs from the general train of thought. Her pieces about animals open readers' anthropocentric minds to other possibilities, just as the first-person

(using "person" loosely) narration by animals allows readers to see their world afresh. Animal matters aside, Highsmith's territory is also human psychology, particularly the aberrant and the marginal. She is very skilled at tying the particular psychological quirk to what might be called the psychosocial, the point at which individuals affect the group around them and begin to suffer repercussions because of the complex of reactions of others.

THE SNAIL-WATCHER, AND OTHER STORIES

The Snail-Watcher, and Other Stories features some of Highsmith's sharpest psychological studies. The oft-reprinted title tale is one of several in which a character's neuroses and repressed emotions are reflected grotesquely in the behavior of animals. Peter Knoppert, a proper middle-aged broker with a secure if sexless marriage, develops a passion for keeping snails. The energy he devotes to breeding them as pets provides him with relaxation that has a beneficial effect on his performance at work. As his work becomes more challenging, Knoppert neglects to keep an eye on the snails' reproduction, and they quickly overrun the study where he keeps them, setting up a spectacularly loathsome finale in which he is literally consumed by his hobby.

A similar fate befalls the protagonist of "The Quest for *Blank Claveringi*." Egotistical biologist Avery Clavering is so zealous in his determination to discover and name for himself an appropriately gigantic species of snail reputed to inhabit a remote Pacific island that he fatally miscalculates their predatory behavior. Whereas both these stories reveal Highsmith's underappreciated talent for black comedy, others are deadly earnest in their use of human-animal relationships to explore aspects of failed human intimacy. In "The Terrapin," a young, friendless boy briefly makes a pet from a live turtle his mother has brought home for a stew. The mother's casual indifference toward the animal's fate--she throws it live into a pot of boiling water, then chops it apart--mirrors her domination and emotional brutalizing of her son. In "The Empty Birdhouse," a childless couple approaching middle age (common character types in Highsmith's work) go to increasingly greater extremes to exterminate an unidentifiable animal that has taken up residence in their house, which proves by its indestructibility to be a symbol for the couple's unhappiness and lack of fulfillment.

The Snail-Watcher, and Other Stories also includes some of Highsmith's finest tales about obsessed, perhaps mentally disturbed individuals, conditions she describes with great precision. "When the Fleet Was in at Mobile" tells the story of Geraldine, a country girl from Alabama who is rescued from a Mobile brothel by a Louisiana farmer. When the farmer becomes abusive because of jealousy about her past, she sees no solution except murder, and the description of Geraldine's actions and attempted escape has a dreamlike quality suggestive of a tenuous grasp on reality. Only at the end of the story, however, do readers appreciate how unreliable a source of information Geraldine has been. Highsmith gives an unsentimental picture of the making of a prostitute out of a simple young woman and of her subsequent mental disarray, but in such a way that readers can feel only empathy, in spite of her murderous intentions.

Another fine portrait of a marginally competent young woman pushed over the edge is in "The Heroine." Lucille goes to work for the wealthy and happy Christiansen family as a nurse to the two children. Her pyromaniacal background--she likes to start fires with pieces of paper in ashtrays--is never revealed to the family, and Lucille's subsequent fanatical devotion to the Christiansen children requires, in her own simplistic terms, a heroic act of unselfish devotion. She therefore torches the house with gasoline, before charging in with the intention of saving the children. The story taps the very human fantasy of acting heroically before admiring loved ones but shows a diseased mind blurring the fantasy into reality in a way that can only make readers nervous about the quiet intense strangers who surround them.

"Another Bridge to Cross" focuses on Merrick, a successful businessman who has lost his wife and son in a car accident. Merrick travels to Italy to try to regain some purpose to his life but witnesses the suicide of a poverty-stricken Italian worker. He befriends a street urchin (a theme in Highsmith short stories) who then robs a woman in Merrick's hotel. Merrick next learns that the suicide's wife has killed their children and herself in grief. Like Herman Melville's "Bartleby the Scrivener" (1856) in a parallel that must be intentional, Merrick remains in a garden at his hotel paraphrasing one of Bartleby's lines ("I prefer not to"): "I prefer the garden." Highsmith's story, however, ends more naturalistically than Melville's, for when the hotel staff calls a doctor to examine Merrick, clearly meaning to have him removed and institutionalized, Merrick continues his journey, but no more relieved of his despair than when he arrived. Highsmith's version of "Bartleby" is "modern" in that it does not resolve in a neat literary fashion; Merrick must simply carry on, as usually happens in real life.

LITTLE TALES OF MISOGYNY

Little Tales of Misogyny is accurately named: The longest story is nine pages, most are three or four pages, and all are about the downfall of women and girls. Highsmith does not see women as victims of men or even of other women but rather as--mostly--subject to willful obsessions and compulsions. Flirtatious sexuality ("The Coquette," "The Dancer," "The Victim"), an inexorable drive to procreate ("The Breeder"), a lazy desire to be taken care of by men ("The Invalid: Or, The Bed-Ridden," "The Mobile Bed-Object," "The Fully-Licensed Whore: Or, The Wife")--all familiar but potentially destructive responses by women to the roles they play in society--overcome the individual characters, dominating, controlling, and ultimately destroying the role-players themselves. These reactions include jealousy over imagined betrayal by lovers ("The Female Novelist"); over being the perfect little girl ("The Perfect Little Lady"), the perfect mother-in-law ("The Silent Mother-in-Law"), the perfect mother ("The Prude"), the perfect religionist ("The Evangelist"); or over simply being perfect. A few women in the stories are victims of their own beauty or of their own circumstances or of the equally driven men around them ("The Hand," "Oona, the Jolly Cave Woman"), but most choose their fate, if choice is even possible for people who are virtually humorous characters. The relationship of these women to men, their "meal-tickets," often arises as a theme, yet Highsmith clearly means only to observe, not to analyze causes. All the tales read like sardonic, modern allegories yet with no moral lesson intended beyond the mordant observation of the stubborn foolishness of (female) human nature. The effect has the oddness of medieval misogynist tracts told by a modernist sensibility: There is no comfort here for anyone.

THE ANIMAL-LOVER'S BOOK OF BEASTLY MURDER

The title of *The Animal-Lover's Book of Beastly Murder* puns on British tabloid headlines: Here the murder is *by* (and occasionally *of*) beasts. Each story covers the experience of a different animal, some told in first-person narration. Highsmith's daring in attempting to show the world from inside the brain of elephant and cockroach, cat and camel is admirable for its high credibility and lack of sentimentality. While not all the stories are equally successful, some are among Highsmith's best.

"Chorus Girl's Absolutely Final Performance" contrasts the title's elephant character as a cheerful youngster working for a kind trainer and, thirty years later, as a grumpy oldster under a cruel elephant wrangler. The first-person narration captures a ponderous heaviness to Chorus Girl's thought and "language" that is highly persuasive. "Djemal's Revenge" follows a working camel in an Arab country as he is abused by his master and then as he gets even with a violence most satisfying and quite in accord with his environment. "There I Was, Stuck with Busby" is about The Baron, a large old dog whose master dies, leaving him with an uncaring and nasty new owner. The Baron finally gets to live with Marion, his old master's adored girlfriend, but not until he takes things into his own hands, so to speak.

"In the Dead of Truffle Season" stars Samson the pig, whose greed for truffles overcomes the tenuous control that his master Emile has over him. Pigs are as unsentimental about farmers, readers learn, as farmers are about pigs, and Samson is quite happy to change his loyalties. "The Bravest Rat in Venice," one of the best stories in the book, manages to create sympathy even for a rat that gnaws off a baby's nose--no mean feat. The rat's-eye view of Venice is as precise and as visual as a motion-picture camera. "Engine Horse" traces the revenge of a horse whose pet kitten is carelessly killed by a loutish young man and whose act saves a decent old woman in the bargain. In the other stories, which feature chickens, monkeys, hamsters, and ferrets as their protagonists, Highsmith draws similarly perceptive and provocative parallels between animal and human experience.

SLOWLY, SLOWLY IN THE WIND

Slowly, Slowly in the Wind is hard to categorize. Some stories, notably the title story, continue Highsmith's examination of disturbed characters. Edward "Skip" Skipperton is a highly successful businessman who can barely keep his anger and aggression under control. When poor health puts him into semiretirement as a gentleman farmer, he turns his energy and his fury on a neighbor, losing his daughter, and ultimately his freedom, in the process. While Skipperton's revenge on his neighbor is spectacularly horrible, his motives and uncontrolled emotions are immediately recognizable as very human and thus distressingly familiar: Unable to tolerate the frustration of his wishes, Skipperton responds childishly with simple and overwhelming force. A less common phenomenon, though by no means rare in modern society, is handled in "Woodrow Wilson's Neck-Tie." Serial murderer Clive Wilkes kills to become known, to lift himself out of his banal and mediocre life. He has no emotion, handling his victims like effigies to be posed for comic effect. The result is chilling, evoking newspaper stories of real-life killers of similar coldness. The murderer in "The Baby Spoon" at least has an understandable, if twisted, motive: revenge on a manipulative former professor who has used him and embarrassed him.

Highsmith often writes about New York City, having grown up there, and two works in this collection are in what might be called her New York story mode. "The Network" traces a group of friends who help one another survive the competition and depredations of violence in the city. A young newcomer at first rejects the group's smothering attentions in order to assert his independence but soon changes his mind after a mugging and a robbery. In "Broken Glass," an octogenarian widower is mugged by a teenage thug but responds with unexpected violence that at least gives him the satisfaction of striking back. In the typical Highsmith New York story, there is an "us against them" theme in which a civilized protagonist attempts to ward off the barbarians who run unchecked in the city. Two anomalous stories in this collection are "One for the Islands," an allegory about death and the hereafter expressed in terms of a cruise ship and island destinations, and "Please Don't Shoot the Trees," a futuristic fantasy in which pollution-beset trees grow breastlike protuberances that shoot burning poison at passersby. Highsmith's territory includes the bizarre, the inexplicable, and the satiric, but the usual setting for the aberration is a highly realistic and normal world, not a milieu already topsy-turvy as in these two stories.

THE BLACK HOUSE

Highsmith's juxtapositions of human and animal behavior, most notable in the collections *The Snail-Watcher, and Other Stories* and *The Animal-Lover's Book of Beastly Murder*, are a subtle means of addressing the bestial side of human nature. Animals are less in evidence in *The Black House*, but the book's eleven stories can be read as interpretations of a theme first articulated by Peter Knoppert, the ill-fated pet owner in "The Snail Watcher," who proclaims,"'You can't stop nature.'" Repeatedly in these tales, intelligent and respectable people find themselves in unusual situations that provoke them to irrational, beastly behavior. "The Dream of the *Emma C*" tells of a fishing smack that rescues an exhausted young woman swimming in the waters two miles off the coast of Cape Cod. Immediately, the crew of six men, who hitherto have gotten along on the ship, begin squabbling among themselves. The men are attracted almost instinctively to the woman, and as each tries to ingratiate himself with her fights break out, leading to the accidental bludgeoning death of one by the story's end.

Sexuality and violence are similarly conjoined in the title story, about an abandoned house in a small working-class town in upstate New York. The house is reputedly haunted, and many of the older men in town boast of enjoying their first sexual conquests there. Timothy Porter, a young educated man, decides to explore the house and finds it completely empty, making it unlikely to have played a role in any of the tales told about it in the local bar. When Tim mentions this at the bar, the previously friendly patrons take it as a challenge to the personal and social mythology they have constructed about the house. Tim is called outside to fight and is beaten to death.

There is no brutality in "The Terrors of Basket-Weaving," only the disturbing expression of an inexplicable, seemingly innate talent. While scavenging on the beach one day, a sophisticated modern woman finds an old wicker basket with a hole in it and repairs it without thinking. She is so unnerved by her near-instinctive grasp of the primitive craft of basket-weaving that she can only reclaim peace of mind by destroying the basket.

Responsibility and guilt--feelings that separate the civilized from the savage--are constantly complicated and compromised in Highsmith's stories. In "Something the Cat Dragged In," a perfectly ordinary afternoon tea is interrupted when the house cat pulls a severed human hand through the cat door. The guests' immediate feelings of shock and disgust are mitigated when it is discovered the hand belonged to an unscrupulous man who was murdered and dismembered with just cause by a local farmer. The guests decide not to report the murder, concluding that any guilt over its concealment is the farmer's to feel.

In "Under a Dark Angel's Eye," a man discovers that his family's insurance agent has swindled him out of money under the pretense that it went to the care of his mother in a nursing home. His mother actually died five years earlier, and the money was diverted to the care of the agent's dissolute son. Shortly afterward, the agent's son dies in a car wreck, and the agent and nursing-home manager who conspired with him commit suicide. The man interprets events as a working out of the biblical axiom "an eye for an eye" and assuages feelings of guilt he felt for his own vengeful thoughts by burning his copy of the Old Testament.

In "Not One of Us," a clique of successful and fashionable people ostracize one of their own and, through devious acts of seeming friendship, drive him to suicide. At his funeral, when it is discovered that each member of the group did something secretly to ruin the man, the ringleader thinks, "Anyone might have said 'We killed him, you know' but no one did." Typical of Highsmith's characters, women express mild surprise but virtually no remorse at their personal capacity for evil.

MERMAIDS ON THE GOLF COURSE, AND OTHER STORIES

Mermaids on the Golf Course, and Other Stories, like *Slowly, Slowly in the Wind*, is a set of disparate tales rather than a medley with coherent themes. "The Romantic" is a New York story about a young secretary who discovers that she would rather live a safe fantasy life of romance fiction and imaginary dates than take her chances on the singles scene. Another such tale depicts the private emotions of Roland, the father of a child with Down syndrome. Tortured by the unfairness of the child's suffering from Down syndrome and driven to fury by the effects the condition has had on him and his wife, Roland murders a man on the street for no visible reason. The murder is cathartic, somehow balancing with his son's bad luck and giving Roland a sense of control that he lacked before. "Where the Action Is" is an ironic look at fate and fame. A young, barely professional news photographer in a small Wyoming town misses the climax of a bus hijacking because he has to visit the restroom but casually takes a grab shot of one of the victims, a young woman who may or may not have been raped. His chance photograph captures the poignancy of the victim and also fits in with various "crime in the streets" themes being exploited in the press, and his photograph wins the notice of *The New York Times* and then a Pulitzer Prize. Craig, the photographer, finds his career is made, as he parlays his lucky break into a lecture series and then an apologetic book about the invasion of his subject's privacy, though she too seems to have a private agenda. The story neatly depicts how fame can feed on itself, "creating facts" out of chance events.

"Not in This Life, Maybe the Next" presents another situation in which a woman suffering psychic pain begins to notice a small creature around the house, in this case a very stocky, two-foot-tall "man" of enormous strength. As in the other stories of this type, no rational explanation is offered for this manifestation of emotional states. "The Stuff of Madness" is wonderfully mordant, as Christopher and Penny clash over publicity about her hobby of stuffing her dead pets and installing them in the garden, where they rot and mold. Before the news photographers come, Christopher rigs a department store mannequin in the garden to look like one of his past mistresses, triggering a heart attack in Penny and a fitting end for himself. Perhaps the most haunting story is "A Shot from Nowhere," a situation like that of Julio Cortázar's "Blow-Up," in which Andrew, a young painter, witnesses a murder in a small Mexican town. No one is willing to pursue the crime or the criminals, and Andrew himself is blamed. The story ends with Andrew free but the situation unresolved.

TALES OF NATURAL AND UNNATURAL CATASTROPHES

Highsmith's collection *Tales of Natural and Unnatural Catastrophes* is among her best, with lively stories mostly taking a definite turn toward political and social satire. "Operation Balsam: Or, Touch-Me-Not" is a scathing indictment of the morality of nuclear regulators, in this case of a bureaucrat who finds a suitably secret storage place for deadly waste under a football stadium on a university campus and who sacrifices a friend and colleague to a horrible end in order to maintain this secrecy. "Nabuti: Warm Welcome to a UN Committee" is a devastating send-up of a newly independent African country, corrupt and incompetent, attempting to cover up its malfeasance with United Nations money and instead covering up the investigating committee itself. "Sweet Freedom! And a Picnic on the White House Lawn" addresses the policies that have spilled the lunatic, but supposedly benign, out onto the streets of the United States; in this version, the homeless wreak their revenge in a variety of fashions.

"Rent-a-Womb vs. the Mighty Right" satirizes conservative attacks on the surrogate mother phenomenon, while "Sixtus VI, Pope of the Red Slipper" postulates a pope who publicly reverses all significant Vatican policies toward women and procreation. "President Buck Jones Rallies and Waves the Flag" is a heavy-handed satire in the tradition of Stanley Kubrick's film *Dr. Strangelove* (1964), amusing for its outrageousness.

Four stories return to traditional Highsmith concerns. "Moby Dick II: Or, The Missile Whale" is told from the whale's point of view, as in the stories in *The Animal-Lover's Book of Beastly Murder*; like the great white whale, this cetacean does not take kindly to being hunted but has a modern weapon. "Trouble at the Jade Towers" is not an animal revenge story in the earlier pattern but does feature a cockroach occupation of a prestigious Manhattan address. "No End in Sight" and "The Mysterious Cemetery" invoke again the mood and tone of earlier Highsmith, the first about an old lady in a nursing home who refuses to die decently and save everyone a lot of trouble, and the second a spooky tale of human cancer experiments which, when buried in the graveyard, grow enormous, mushroomlike simulacrums of human bodies. Thus, Highsmith, late in her career, moved into more political and satiric writing but also kept her touch for her traditional approaches.

OTHER MAJOR WORKS

LONG FICTION: *Strangers on a Train*, 1950; *The Price of Salt*, 1952 (originally under pseudonym Claire Morgan; also published as *Carol*); *The Blunderer*, 1954 (also as *Lament for a Lover*, 1956); *The Talented Mr. Ripley*, 1955; *Deep Water*, 1957; *A Game for the Living*, 1958; *This Sweet Sickness*, 1960; *The Cry of the Owl*, 1962; *The Glass Cell*, 1964; *The Two Faces of January*, 1964; *The Story-Teller*, 1965 (also as *A Suspension of Mercy*, 2001); *Those Who Walk Away*, 1967; *The Tremor of Forgery*, 1969; *Ripley Under Ground*, 1970; *A Dog's Ransom*, 1972; *Ripley's Game*, 1974; *Edith's Diary*, 1977; *The Boy Who Followed Ripley*, 1980; *People Who Knock on the Door*, 1983; *The Mysterious Mr. Ripley*, 1985 (contains *The Talented Mr. Ripley*, *Ripley Under Ground*, and *Ripley's Game*); *Found in the Street*, 1986; *Ripley Under Water*, 1991; *Small g: A Summer Idyll*, 1995; *The Complete Ripley Novels*, 2008.

NONFICTION: *Plotting and Writing Suspense Fiction*, 1966.

CHILDREN'S LITERATURE: *Miranda the Panda Is on the Veranda*, 1958 (with Doris Sanders).

BIBLIOGRAPHY

Bloom, Harold, ed. "Patricia Highsmith." In *Lesbian and Bisexual Fiction Writers*. Philadelphia: Chelsea House, 1997. Highsmith is discussed by several scholars of gay and lesbian studies, who contextualize her work in terms of that discipline. Bibliographic references.

Chin, Paula. "Through a Mind, Darkly." *People Weekly* 39 (January 11, 1993): 93-94. A biographical sketch of Highsmith's eccentric, reclusive, and forbiddingly private life. Discusses her popularity in Europe and her cult status in America; lists her many honors.

Coburn, Marcia Froelke. "And the Enemy Is Us: Patricia Highsmith." *Film Comment* 20 (September/October, 1984): 44-45. Argues that Highsmith is something of an anomaly among writers of hard-boiled mystery, since she concentrates on the criminals' point of view and often allows them to avoid being caught. Notes Highsmith's focus on the inescapable effects of thought in which consideration of sin is as bad as sinning and often leads inextricably to a forbidden act.

Dubose, Martha Hailey, with Margaret Caldwell Thomas. *Women of Mystery: The Lives and Works of Notable Women Crime Novelists*. New York: St. Martin's Minotaur, 2000. Highsmith's works and life experiences are compared to those of Margery Allingham and Dorothy L. Sayers, among other writers. Includes bibliographic references and index.

Harrison, Russell. *Patricia Highsmith*. New York: Twayne, 1997. This first book-length study of Highsmith in English explores the aesthetic, philosophical, and sociopolitical dimensions of her writing. The study of her short fiction is limited to discussion of *Slowly, Slowly in the Wind* and *The Black House*, which represent, in Harrison's opinion, her strongest collections.

Highsmith, Patricia. "Not Thinking with the Dishes." *Writer's Digest* 62 (October, 1983): 26. Highsmith says she follows no set rules for story writing. She begins with a theme, an unusual circumstance or a situation of surprise or coincidence, and she creates the narrative around it. Her focus is on subjective attitudes, what is happening in the minds of her protagonists. Her settings are always ones she knows personally.

Lindsay, Elizabeth Blakesley, ed. "Patricia Highsmith." In *Great Women Mystery Writers*. 2d ed. Westport, Conn.: Greenwood Press, 2007. Includes an essay containing biographical detail, as well as analysis of Highsmith's works.

Mawer, Noel. *A Critical Study of the Fiction of Patricia Highsmith--from the Psychological to the Political*. Lewiston, N.Y.: Edwin Mellen Press, 2004. Critical analysis of Highsmith's works, including the short stories, which places her writings in the context of her life and the wider culture. Includes an extensive bibliography.

Schenkar, Joan. *The Talented Miss Highsmith: The Secret Life and Serious Art of Patricia Highsmith.* New York: St. Martin's Press, 2009. A comprehensive Highsmith biography, more than seven hundred pages long.

Summers, Claude J., ed. *Gay and Lesbian Literary Heritage.* New York: H. Holt, 1995. Includes an excellent essay by Gina Macdonald on Highsmith's life work to the time of her death in 1995.

Sutcliffe, Thomas. "Graphs of Innocence and Guilt." *The Times Literary Supplement*, no. 4696 (October 2, 1981): 1118. Sutcliffe argues that the uneasy, disquieting force of Highsmith's works comes from her depiction of reason persisting in inappropriate conditions. Her focus on "what it is like to remain sane" while committing horrendous deeds blurs complacent distinctions. At their best, her short stories are brilliant studies of "fear and loathing, moral absolution and culpability"-- "the fragility of . . . untested moral structures."

Symons, Julian. *Mortal Consequences: A History from the Detective Story to the Crime Novel.* New York: Harper & Row, 1972. Symons calls Highsmith "the most important crime novelist at present," more appreciated in Europe than in the United States, but a fine writer, whose tricky plot devices are merely starting points "for profound and subtle character studies," particularly of likable figures attracted by crime and violence. It is her imaginative power that gives her criminal heroes a "terrifying reality" amid carefully chosen settings. She is at her best describing subtle, deadly games of pursuit.

Wilson, Andrew. *Beautiful Shadow: A Life of Patricia Highsmith.* New York: Bloomsbury, 2004. A detailed examination of Highsmith's troubled life and devotion to her work. Discusses her impact on crime fiction and on gay and lesbian fiction.

Andrew F. Macdonald

CHESTER HIMES

Born: Jefferson City, Missouri; July 29, 1909
Died: Moraira, Spain; November 12, 1984

PRINCIPAL SHORT FICTION

> *Black on Black: "Baby Sister" and Selected Writings,* 1973
> *The Collected Stories of Chester Himes,* 1990

OTHER LITERARY FORMS

Chester Himes wrote many novels, including *If He Hollers Let Him Go* (1945), newspaper articles, and two autobiographies. His crime novels set in Harlem were the first of his books to bring him international fame.

ACHIEVEMENTS

Best known for the series of detective stories called the Harlem Domestic, Chester Himes wrote in many genres and with an impressive variety of techniques and themes. Because throughout his career, even after he had immigrated abroad, he confronted without flinching the wrenching effects of racism in the United States, he is sometimes categorized into the group of protest writers. What distinguishes him is his humor, often necessarily grotesque in the grimmest of circumstances.

Upon the posthumous publication of *The Collected Stories of Chester Himes*, a brief review in the magazine *Essence* recommended his stories, written over a forty-year span, because he showed African Americans to themselves as they really are, in all facets of their lives. Such relevance suggests that he captured an essence of African American life, one that is often tragic and violent but also passionate, tender, and sensual. He was awarded the Rosenwald Fellowship in 1944 and the Grand Prix de Littérature Policière in 1958.

BIOGRAPHY

Born on July 29, 1909, in Jefferson City, Missouri, to middle-class black parents, Chester Bomar Himes had an emotionally traumatic home life. Estelle Bomar Himes, his light-skinned mother, and Joseph Sandy Himes, his much darker-skinned father, lived perpetually at war with each other. The racial tension within the family affected the three brown-skinned sons and led to the decline of the family's lifestyle. His father, a professor of metal trades and African American history at southern black colleges, had to keep taking more and more menial jobs because his wife's contempt for his colleagues forced the family to keep moving.

After living in several places in the South, the Himeses finally settled in Ohio. Himes entered Ohio State University at seventeen. Crippled by a fall into an open elevator shaft and then angered by the racial segregation on campus, Himes did not adapt well to academic life. He failed all his courses the first semester and had to withdraw the next. His subsequent life as a juvenile delinquent came to an abrupt end when, in 1928, he was arrested, badly beaten at the police station, tried and convicted of armed robbery, and sentenced to twenty years.

Oddly enough, the incarceration may have given Himes the time and the calm away from his tense family life to discover his talent. His first stories were published by the vitally important black magazine *The Crisis*. By the time he was released from prison in 1936, he was twenty-six and a writer. A year later, he married Jean Johnson, a woman he had known before his imprisonment.

Himes continued to write as he explored the United States for work. During World War II, he was a shipfitter and riveter in California. The bitter racial experiences in Los Angeles led to the novel *If He Hollers Let Him Go*. In 1954, as so many American writers, including frustrated black writers, have done before him, Himes left the United States and traveled through Europe. The French admired his life, particularly appreciating the satire of *Pinktoes* (1961), a ribald novel proposing the solution to racial tensions through indiscriminate sexual relationships. It was his French editor who encouraged Himes to write the detective novels set in Harlem, featuring Grave Digger Jones and Coffin Ed Johnson. Himes wrote these in a hurry, desperate for the money, but they turned out to be the perfect match of form and content. Increasingly pessimistic about the violence of his native country, Himes wrote more and more about the radical solution to the racial problem--violence. The Harlem of his detectives, the detectives themselves, and the people among whom they move are all caught up, trapped in a cycle of violent behavior from which they cannot escape.

With so much pain, personal and cultural, from the beginning of his life, Himes did what talented artists do: He confronted it, fashioned it into a personal vision, and, living fully, even found the love and humor in it. He died in Spain, in 1984, of Parkinson's disease, without returning to the homeland that he had described so vividly.

ANALYSIS

Chester Himes's short stories, he believed, served as his apprenticeship as a writer. They were the first of his writings to be published, and he continued working in the genre intermittently for more than forty years. When an anthology of his short fiction was proposed in 1954, he revealed in his autobiography that he could not feel proud of it. The anthology finally published in 1973, *Black on Black: "Baby Sister" and Selected Writings*, was highly selective, concentrating on the stories of the first two decades of his career. A 1990 edition, *The Collected Stories of Chester Himes*, contains sixty-one pieces, ranging from 1933 to 1978, with nine updated. Many are prison stories, and not all are of even quality, but as a whole they demonstrate Himes's remarkably versatile range of techniques and the ongoing themes and preoccupations of his longer pieces.

"HIS LAST DAY"

Prison life, horrible as it was, gave Himes the subject of several short stories. "His Last Day," about a condemned man's last few hours before the electric chair, already shows some of Himes's trademarks. Spats, a hardened, ruthless criminal who is condemned to death for killing a police officer, reflects wryly that he would not have been identified if the one person left alive during his robbery of a club had not recognized his fawn-colored spats. Even when he manages to hide out for a few days, he is finally trapped--by his past and by a woman. An old sweetheart whom he had abandoned in her pregnancy shoots the man who had provided Spats with refuge, thus attracting the police. Rivetingly grim, this early effort is marred by the dated slang, but even so, Himes's characteristic grisly humor comes through.

"Her Whole Existence"

James Baldwinwrote of Himes that he was the only black writer to describe male-female relationships in terms other than violence. One of Himes's earliest love stories, "Her Whole Existence: A Story of True Love," verges on parody in its clichéd language but also shows Himes's imaginative skill. Written from the point of view of Mabel Miles, the beautiful daughter of a successful African American politician, the story leaps suddenly from the romanticism of Mabel's attraction for Richard Riley, an ambitious, successful, and handsome criminal, to an analysis of class conflict. Trapped between the respect for law instilled by her family and her own passion, Mabel first betrays Richard and then helps him to escape. It is the first of Himes's portrayals of unpredictable but strong women.

"A Nigger"

"A Nigger," with its shockingly simple denouement, suggests Himes's bitter observations about the sexual relationship between blacks and whites. Mr. Shelton, a rich old white man, drops in unexpectedly on Fay, a black prostitute who lives with a light-skinned common-law husband and who is currently involved with another black man, Joe Wolf. Taken by surprise, Fay shoves Joe into the closet to receive her white lover. Joe hears her cajole and flatter Mr. Shelton out of two hundred dollars and, crouched in the dark, recalls other tired, unattractive white men he has known who have turned to black women not in appreciation but in exhaustion. Such men have convinced themselves, he thinks, that it is only black flesh they touch, animal flesh that has no mind or power to judge. When he is ready to leave, Mr. Shelton opens the door of the closet by mistake, looks in, turns away, and leaves. While Fay is jubilant that Joe was not detected, Joe is so furious that he tries to strangle her. He knows that the white man saw him and simply refused to recognize his existence. Back in his own tiny room, he reflects bitterly that he must count himself a "nigger" for allowing his poverty and dependence on a prostitute to rob him of his manhood.

"Headwaiter"

Though many of Himes's stories--and novels--emphasize the pain of being black in the United States, other works portray individuals who can carve a dignified niche in the limited ways available to them. "Headwaiter" presents Dick Small, an African American man in charge of an old-fashioned dining room patronized by a regular white clientele. Imperturbable in this familiar atmosphere, Dick watches over everyone in his care, remembering the personal details of individual customers, waiters, and busboys. In his small way, he does what he can for the less fortunate. When the diners are horrified to learn that one of the best waiters is a former convict, Dick stands firmly by his decision to give the man a second chance, and his polite firmness quells the furor. He is unable, however, to save another waiter who acts drunk; when he has to dismiss him, he does so with sympathy and compassion.

Chester Himes (Library of Congress)

"LUNCHING AT THE RITZMORE"

The complementary story "Lunching at the Ritzmore" differs in tone. A satiric view of the laws that required separate public establishments for blacks and whites, this story suggests, lightheartedly, what Himes was seriously to advocate later: the power that lies in a large crowd to hurl down racist barriers. In "the mecca of the motley" in Pershing Square, Los Angeles, a young college student from Vermont argues that there is no discrimination against Negroes. A drifter in the crowd bets him the price of dinner that a young brown-skinned Negro, an unemployed mechanic, will be refused service if the three eat at a restaurant. As the three set off in search of a suitably challenging place to eat, the crowd around them grows and grows because people think that a free giveaway must be the goal of such a gathering. A policeman follows them, wanting to arrest them but not able to think of a good reason to do so. Finally, an enormous crowd stops outside the very fancy Ritzmore Hotel; there, the debate shifts slightly from race to class, as none of the three is dressed well enough. The diners, the waiters, and the cooks, however, are so stunned by the crowd that the three men are immediately served the only item that they can read on the French menu--ironically enough, it is apple pie. The student wins his bet but has to pay because the drifter is broke.

"ALL HE NEEDS IS FEET"

Few other stories exhibit such lighthearted irony in the face of racial discrimination. "All He Needs Is Feet" is ironic, in the horrifying, brutal way that shocks the reader into realizing why Himes later saw violence as the only solution for African Americans, because they are mistreated so violently by a violent society. Ward, a black man, walking down the sidewalk in Rome, Georgia, steps off to let a white woman and two white men pass. One white man bumps into Ward anyway and provokes him to fight. A crowd that gathers, thinking a lynching is too severe, pours gasoline on Ward's feet and sets him on fire. In jail for assault with a deadly weapon, Ward has his feet amputated. He goes to Chicago with money sent by his family and learns to use crutches and knee pads to work at shining shoes, saving enough money to buy war bonds. In a theater, his crutches tucked out of everyone's way under the seats, Ward cannot stand up for the national anthem at the end of the film. A big, burly man from Arkansas hits him for disrespect to the flag. The ultimate cruelty of the story comes as a punch line, when a policeman arrests the white man: The man from Arkansas blubbers that he could not stand a "nigger" sitting through the national anthem, even if he did not have feet.

The issue of patriotism became very complex for African Americans during World War II, especially for those who fought for democracy against Adolf Hitler and his blatantly racist and fascist goals of a super-race and then had to reflect on the racism in their own democracy. Several of Himes's war stories, such as "Two Soldiers," reveal a man struggling to remain patriotic and optimistic. The most effective of these, "So Softly Smiling," springs from the war atmosphere but is really a beautiful love story. Roy Jonny Squires, a lieutenant in the U.S. Army, returns to Harlem for thirty days. Exhausted by the warfare in North Africa, he heads for a bar late at night and meets Mona Morrison, a successful poet. Her "tawny skin like an African veld at sunset" exactly fulfills the ache for love that fiery raids at dawn have brought upon him. This delicate love story is punctuated throughout with dramatic reminders that the lovers' time together is very short, and their courtship and married life proceed at breakneck speed. It is in this story that Himes touches on the race issue during war, lightly and positively; Roy says that he finally enlisted because he heard someone say that the United States belonged to the Negro as much as it did to anyone.

"TANG"

More than two decades later, Himes seemed to have lost such patriotic optimism. In "Tang," a tired, hungry couple sit watching television in their cold-water slum flat in Harlem, when a long cardboard box with a florist's label is delivered to them. They discover inside it an M-14 army gun and a typewritten sheet warning them to learn how to use this weapon and wait for instructions, for freedom is near. The man, T-bone Smith, who had used such a weapon in the Korean War, is absolutely terrified and wants to report the gun to the police. The woman, Tang, once a beautiful, softly rounded woman who has become hard and angular from her life as a poor prostitute, is ecstatic. She hugs the gun as if it were a lover and cherishes the thought that the gun could chop up a white policeman. She is ready to fight for freedom, even pointing the gun at T-bone to stop him from calling the police. Her defiance enrages him; he whips out a spring-blade knife and slashes her to death, crying that he might not be free of whitey, but he is now free of her.

Writing twenty years before Himes's death, the critic Edward Margolies noted that Himes's characters tend to be reflective, interested in ideas and in intellectualizing the predicaments in which they find themselves. As such, they are quite different from such characters as Bigger Thomas, with whom Richard Wright shocked the United States in his *Native Son* (1940). Wright's success trapped other African American writers whom the literary establishment then automatically described as, or expected to be, "protest" writers. Certainly, the range of Himes's short fiction is so vast that it includes stories of strong protest. However, he wrote stories of individuals caught up in a web of many circumstances. Race is clearly an issue in his fiction, but so are love, sex, poverty, class, war, prison, violence, success, failure, and humor. His short fiction is not only a prelude to his better known novels but also a rewarding world in itself.

OTHER MAJOR WORKS

LONG FICTION: *If He Hollers Let Him Go*, 1945; *Lonely Crusade*, 1947; *Cast the First Stone*, 1952 (unexpurgated edition pb. as *Yesterday Will Make You Cry*, 1998); *The Third Generation*, 1954; *The Primitive*, 1955 (unexpurgated edition pb. as *The End of a Primitive*, 1997); *For Love of Imabelle*, 1957 (revised as *A Rage in Harlem*, 1965); *Il pluet des coups durs*, 1958 (*The Real Cool Killers*, 1959); *Couché dans le pain*, 1959 (*The Crazy Kill*, 1959); *Dare-dare*, 1959 (*Run Man Run*, 1966); *Tout pour plaire*, 1959 (*The Big Gold Dream*, 1960); *Imbroglio negro*, 1960 (*All Shot Up*, 1960); *Ne nous énervons pas!*, 1961 (*The Heat's On*, 1966; also pb. as *Come Back Charleston Blue*, 1974); *Pinktoes*, 1961; *Une affaire de viol*, 1963 (*A Case of Rape*, 1980); *Retour en Afrique*, 1964 (*Cotton Comes to Harlem*, 1965); *Blind Man with a Pistol*, 1969 (also pb. as *Hot Day, Hot Night*, 1970); *Plan B*, 1983 (English translation, 1993).

NONFICTION: *The Quality of Hurt: The Autobiography of Chester Himes, Volume I*, 1972; *My Life of Absurdity: The Autobiography of Chester Himes, Volume II*, 1976; *Conversations with Chester Himes*, 1995 (Michel Fabre and Robert E. Skinner, editors); *Dear Chester, Dear John: Letters Between Chester Himes and John A. Williams*, 2008 (John A. Williams and Lori Williams, editors).

BIBLIOGRAPHY

Cochran, David. "So Much Nonsense Must Make Sense: The Black Vision of Chester Himes." *The Midwest Quarterly* 38 (Autumn, 1996): 1-30. Examines Himes's creation of the hard-boiled cop figure as a reflection of his own experience in Harlem. Argues that he presents Harlem as the underside of American capitalism.

Crooks, Robert. "From the Far Side of the Urban Frontier: The Detective Fiction of Chester Himes and Walter Mosley." *College Literature* 22 (October, 1995): 68-90. Analyzes the emergence of African American detective fiction in the works of Himes and Mosley. Shows how Himes develops a strategy for disrupting the frontier narrative in a way that lays it bare.

Dinerstein, Joel. "'Uncle Tom Is Dead!': Wright, Himes, and Ellison Lay a Mask to Rest." *African American Review* 43, no. 1 (Spring, 2009): 83-98. Analyzes Himes's story "Heaven Has Changed," *Invisible Man*, by Ralph Ellison, and the short-story collection *Uncle Tom's Children*, by Richard Wright, to demonstrates how these works critique the "cultural legacy" of the nineteenth century novel *Uncle Tom's Cabin*. Argues that the object of these authors' criticism is not the literary character of Uncle Tom himself but the cultural practice of masking, through which black people seek the acceptance of white people.

Eburne, Jonathan. "The Transatlantic Mysteries of Paris: Chester Himes, Surrealism, and the Série Noire." *PMLA* 120, no. 3 (May, 2005): 806-815. Charts Himes's transformation from a writer of African American protest fiction to a French writer of crime fiction set in Harlem. Analyzes the black humor and other elements of surrealism in his works.

Fabre, Michel, Robert E. Skinner, and Lester Sullivan, comps. *Chester Himes: An Annotated Primary and Secondary Bibliography*. Westport, Conn.: Greenwood Press, 1992. A comprehensive annotated bibliography of writings by and about Himes.

Himes, Chester. *Conversations with Chester Himes*. Edited by Michel Fabre and Robert Skinner. Jackson: University Press of Mississippi, 1995. A collection of interviews with Himes in which he discusses his life and work.

Lundquist, James. *Chester Himes*. New York: Frederick Ungar, 1976. An introduction to Himes's life and works, with chapters on the war novels, confessional novels, and detective novels. The first chapter, "November, 1928," contains a detailed description of the armed robbery for which Himes was arrested and subsequently tried and imprisoned. Includes chronology, notes, bibliography of primary and secondary sources, and index.

Margolies, Edward, and Michel Fabre. *The Several Lives of Chester Himes*. Jackson: University Press of Mississippi, 1997. Margolies and Fabre spent fifteen years conducting research for this biography. Their book portrays Himes as a creative, highly complex man, and it recounts his rocky relationship with his parents, his skirmishes with the law, his life in Europe, and his efforts to become a serious writer. Includes references to the short stories, which are listed in the index.

Milliken, Stephen F. *Chester Himes: A Critical Appraisal*. Columbia: University of Missouri Press, 1976. Contains an excellent chapter, "Take a Giant Step," on Himes's short stories. Provides sections on the protest, autobiographical, and detective novels. Includes a chronology, bibliography of primary sources, and annotated bibliography of secondary sources.

Muller, Gilbert. *Chester Himes*. Boston: Twayne, 1989. An excellent introduction to Himes's life and works. Traces the evolution of Himes's grotesque, revolutionary view of African American life in the United States, which he expressed in several literary modes, culminating in his detective fiction. Includes chronology, appendix, index, and annotated bibliographies of primary and secondary works.

Rosen, Steven J. "African American Anti-Semitism and Himes's Lonely Crusade." *MELUS* 20 (Summer, 1995): 47-68. Discusses an anti-Semitic streak that runs through Himes's work alongside an anxiety to assert masculinity. Shows how Himes used Jewish characters or formulated Jewish traits as a foil to black American masculinity.

Rosenblatt, Roger. "The Hero Vanishes." In *Black Fiction*. Cambridge, Mass.: Harvard University Press, 1974. Briefly compares one of Himes's heroes to the protagonist in Richard Wright's *Native Son*. The introduction is particularly interesting, providing a broad-ranging discussion of the relationship of black literature to American literature as a whole. Includes index and bibliography.

Sallis, James. *Chester Himes: A Life*. New York: Walker & Co., 2001. Critically lauded biography, in which Sallis, a novelist and literary critic, explores Himes's writing and his life. Details Himes's triple marginalization as a literary realist in the 1940's, a crime novelist, and an African American writer.

Silet, Charles L. P., ed. *The Critical Response to Chester Himes*. Westport, Conn.: Greenwood Press, 1999. Compilation of essays reading Himes through the lens of various schools of literary criticism. Includes bibliographical references and an index.

Williams, John A., and Lori Williams, eds and comps. *Dear Chester, Dear John: Letters Between Chester Himes and John A. Williams*. Detroit: Wayne State University Press, 2008. Himes met Williams, a writer sixteen years his junior, in 1961, and the two remained friends for more than two decades. This book reprints their correspondence during that period, providing information on their personal lives, professional challenges, and their observations of what is was like to be an African American in the United States and Europe.

Shakuntala Jayaswal

Edward D. Hoch

Born: Rochester, New York; February 22, 1930
Died: Rochester, New York; January 17, 2008
Also known as: Ellery Queen, Matthew Prize, R. L.
  Stevens, Mr. X, Pat McMahon, Stephen Dentinger,
  Anthony Circus, Irwin Booth, Lisa Drake, R. T.
  Edwards, R. E. Porter

PRINCIPAL SHORT FICTION

City of Brass, and Other Simon Ark Stories, 1971
The Judges of Hades, and Other Simon Ark Stories,
  1971
The Spy and the Thief, 1971
The Theft of the Persian Slipper, 1978
The Thefts of Nick Velvet, 1978
The Quests of Simon Ark, 1984
Leopold's Way, 1985
Tales of Espionage, 1989 (fifteen stories by Hoch
  and sixteen by other writers, Eleanor Sullivan and
  Chris Dorbandt, editors)
The Spy Who Read Latin, and Other Stories, 1990
The People of the Peacock, 1991
*The Night, My Friend: Stories of Crime and Sus-
  pense,* 1992
*Diagnosis: Impossible--The Problems of Dr. Sam
  Hawthorne,* 1996
The Ripper of Storyville, and Other Ben Snow Tales,
  1997
The Velvet Touch, 2000
The Night People, and Other Stories, 2001
The Old Spies Club, and Other Intrigues of Rand,
  2001
The Iron Angel, and Other Tales of the Gypsy Sleuth,
  2003
*More Things Impossible: The Second Casebook of
  Dr. Sam Hawthorne,* 2006

OTHER LITERARY FORMS

Edward D. Hoch (hohk), in addition to his own short-story collections, published hundreds of uncollected stories, which appeared in periodicals and books. (He wrote these under his own name and the pseudonyms Anthony Circus, Stephen Dentinger, R. L. Stevens, Pat McMahon, Ellery Queen, and Irwin Booth.) Hoch was a well-known editor of short-story anthologies and, in 1976, began editing the annual collection of the year's best mysteries. He also wrote several novels. From August, 1980, through March, 1985, under the pseudonym R. E. Porter, he wrote "Crime Beat," a column of mystery news, for *Ellery Queen's Mystery Magazine* (*EQMM*). Hoch was also a frequent contributor of mystery articles to magazines and reference books in the genre. Many of his stories have been dramatized on television for *The Alfred Hitchcock Hour*, *Night Gallery*, *McMillan and Wife*, *Tales of the Unexpected*, and other series.

ACHIEVEMENTS

By the mid-1980's, it was generally accepted that Edward D. Hoch, almost single-handedly, was keeping alive the tradition of the classic detective puzzle invented by Edgar Allan Poe in his Dupin stories. With great success, at least once each month from 1973 to 2008, he presented intricate mysteries and seemingly impossible crimes solved through the mental prowess of his detective. Clues are invariably fairly presented, so that the reader may match intelligence with the story's protagonist.

In addition to being the most prolific short-story writer in the mystery field (having written nearly a thousand stories by his death), Hoch was highly regarded by fans and his peers for the quality of his work. His story "The Oblong Room" (in *The Saint Magazine*, June, 1967) won the Mystery Writers of America annual Edgar Allan Poe Award, being selected in a year in which a story by John le Carré was also nominated. A later story, "The Most Dangerous Man Alive," was nominated for an Edgar Allan Poe Award. Hoch was elected president of the Mystery Writers of America in 1982. At the twenty-second annual Anthony Boucher Memorial Mystery Convention (Bouchercon), in 1991, Hoch was the guest of honor, in recognition of his long and distinguished writing career. In 2001, the Mystery Writers of America bestowed the title of Grand Master, a rare honor for a short-story specialist. *EQMM* named an award after him, the Edward D. Hoch Memorial Golden Derringer for Lifetime Achievement.

BIOGRAPHY

As a nine-year-old in Rochester, New York, Edward Dentinger Hoch began a lifelong love affair with the mystery story, starting with the works written under the omnibus pseudonym Ellery Queen, generally considered classic detective puzzles. Hoch continued to read widely in the field and eventually, as a teenager, began writing mystery fiction. In 1949, though still unpublished, he was given affiliate membership in the Mystery Writers of America.

For eight years, he wrote whenever he could while attending school, serving in the U.S. Army (1950 to 1952), and working at various jobs, but all the stories that he submitted were rejected. Finally, a story, "Village of the Dead," was published in the December, 1955, issue of *Famous Detective Stories*, one of the last of the "pulp" magazines. Hoch began to be published with increasing frequency, though at first most of his sales were to ephemeral pulp and digest-sized magazines with such titles as *Keyhole Detective Stories* and *Two-Fisted Detective Stories*. From 1954 until 1968, he worked full time as a public relations writer for a Rochester advertising agency and wrote fiction in his spare time. Gradually, he broke into the more prestigious, better-paying mystery periodicals, such as *EQMM* and *Alfred Hitchcock's Mystery Magazine*. In 1965, he sold one of his stories to television, for *The Alfred Hitchcock Hour*. With a contract for his first novel in 1968, he was able to leave his job and become a full-time writer.

Despite writing several novels, Hoch was known for his short stories. Starting in May, 1973, and for many years thereafter, at least one of his stories appeared in every issue of *EQMM*, the leading magazine in the genre. Realizing that the short story was his métier, he abandoned novels after 1975. Hoch remained active in the Mystery Writers of America and became a trustee of the Rochester Public Library, where, as a student, he once had worked as a research assistant. He settled in Rochester, with his wife, the former Patricia McMahon, whom he married in 1957. Hoch and his wife continued to live in Rochester until his death from a heart attack on January 17, 2008.

ANALYSIS

From the outset, Edward D. Hoch's writing followed two tracks, though they frequently merged. In his debut story, he created the first of his more than twenty series detectives, Simon Ark, and provided him with a bizarre, seemingly impossible crime to solve. It is the first of hundreds of stories by Hoch in which he shows his endless inventiveness in

Edward D. Hoch (Getty Images)

presenting perplexing problems and their resolutions, without repeating himself. However, in the same story, there is a plot that reflects Hoch's Catholic roots and the influence, which he acknowledged, of G. K. Chesterton and Graham Greene. As a writer who found his audience in magazines of mystery fiction, Hoch realized that his primary "product" was providing escape, through brainteasing mysteries, and he knew that in mystery short stories, there is insufficient length for deep characterization. One need not read too far between Hoch's lines, however, to see important issues also being treated.

THE QUESTS OF SIMON ARK

Simon Ark, the series detective introduced in "Village of the Dead," owes much to the pulp tradition of the infallible superhero, though he resolves his cases by ratiocination, not physical strength or firepower. He claims to have been a Coptic priest in Egypt, two thousand years earlier, and he presently investigates strange happenings, while he searches for and tries to eradicate evil. Ark is introduced as he arrives in the remote western United States village of Gidaz (a deliberate reversal of Voltaire's Zadig) after hearing of the mass suicide of the entire population. Seventy-three people leaped to their deaths from a hundred-foot cliff. A strong religious leader, calling himself Axidus, had come to town and had great influence on its inhabitants. He is Ark's leading suspect, though he denies responsibility for the deaths. The story's basis is a North African cult, the Circumcellions, part of the Donatist schism from the Catholic Church.

Despite the religious trappings and potential for supernaturalism, Hoch established in this story his practice of resolving all cases rationally and through evidence that he makes as available to the reader as to his detective. The Ark stories--the early ones, in particular--are enlivened by mystical elements that add the suggestion of the supernatural to their characteristically complex puzzles. Just as Ark himself purports to be immortal, so does he consider the criminals whom he brings to justice avatars or incarnations of the "Ultimate Evil" he seeks. "The Man from Nowhere" is based on the true mystery of Kaspar Hauser, a nineteenth century celebrity whose bizarre murder was never solved. In this story, Ark must discover how a

pair of false mystics have staged a stabbing death by an apparently invisible entity, patterned on Hauser's death. "Sword for a Sinner" concerns a murder among a radical sect of Catholic penitents who endure mock crucifixions as part of their purification ritual. Hoch occasionally adds a believable element of pathos to the stories by way of Ark's "Watson," the nameless New York publisher who narrates all the stories and whose fallible character represents the human weakness that gives evil its foothold in the world.

In "The Vicar of Hell," Ark fights a historical order of Satanists as his sidekick fights to resist temptations of the flesh offered by the cult's nubile quarry. "The Judges of Hades" involves the murder of the narrator's father and sister and an inquiry into his family's background complicated by his estrangement from them.

"I'D KNOW YOU ANYWHERE"

Though best known for series detectives, in his early years Hoch wrote many stories without continuing characters. Some of the best of these deal with good and evil on a global level, using the Cold War as metaphor. "I'd Know You Anywhere" starts during World War II with the first encounter between the protagonist, Contrell, and Willoughby Grove, a soldier with no qualms about killing enemy soldiers after they have surrendered. They meet again in the Korean War, and again Grove has disdain for any rules, preferring to kill the people he calls "gooks." At a third meeting in Berlin, shortly after the East Germans erected the Wall in 1961, Grove would shoot communist border guards, even if that might start World War III. Finally, the story flashes to the future, 1969, with Grove an army general. To the concern of Contrell, the president of the United States promises free rein to this man who loves to kill.

THE SPY AND THE THIEF

Though the titles of Hoch's spy stories about Jeffrey (sometimes, Jeffery) Rand, head of Britain's Department of Concealed Communications, are reminiscent of le Carré's first best seller, the stories are far different. Though Rand is fully aware that spying is a dirty business, much of the cynicism and angst of le Carré's characters is missing, replaced by taut action and neat, often ironic, resolutions of cases.

In early stories, such as "The Spy Who Came to the End of the Road" and "The Spy Who Came out of the Night," Rand is pitted against Russian agents, such as his counterpart in Russian intelligence, Taz. Though Rand accepts counterintelligence activities, such as reading Russian or Chinese messages and capturing their spies, he is troubled when he must share the responsibility for assassinating enemy agents. He refuses to accept all the conventional wisdom about espionage and believes that there are decent men. He even comes to share a close kinship with Taz, an implicit recognition that even spying can be a profession that goes beyond boundaries and ideologies.

THE OLD SPIES CLUB

For the stories in *The Old Spies Club, and Other Intrigues of Rand*, Taz is retired, and Rand reaches the end of his career, if not his adventures and their international settings. A subplot runs through many of the stories: exotic romance. In the first, "The Spy and the Nile Mermaid," Rand meets Leila Gaad, a young archeologist who is half Scottish and half Egyptian. Initially suspecting her of trying to have him killed, he later drafts her into helping him solve a mystery. Even though the romance flickers through the following few stories, the pair never looks back. Hoch describes their growing love fleetingly and chastely, for instance, providing the barest of hints that they have slept together before they marry and leaving the wedding itself unmentioned. After Leila moves to England with Rand, she accompanies him on several adventures, but by the end of the book she is a background figure, often impatient with his reentries into the world of spying. By "The Spy and the Cats of Rome" Rand has retired and is called in only on sensitive cases that involve former British agents. The early plots hinge upon codes that, deciphered by Rand, reveal culprits. After Rand's retirement, Hoch largely drops codes from the plots, and Rand works like traditional detectives in his use of contextual clues.

The title story, "The Old Spies Club," sees Rand afforded the honor of joining the most prestigious club for retired intelligence agents. He immediately takes it upon himself to investigate a matter that is alarming many of the members: exposure of a double agent among their ranks. Involved are the papers and belongings of a recently dead journalist that are to be sold at auction. These help Rand discover the double agent, who is about to kill Rand when another shady club member, a former assassin, saves Rand. This theme of "old school" spies runs through the final stories. Hoch makes it clear that, whether from Western democracies or the Eastern bloc, the old spies followed well-understood procedures during the Cold War. With the fall of Communist governments, Rand finds that the old norms are gone, spies are more venal, and it is not clear whom he can trust. The final story, "The War That Never Was," best illustrates the complexities of the post-communism age. Rand sets out to help a desperate former mercenary who fought in the Ayers Rock War, a fifty-hour conflict to subdue rebelling Australian aborigines. The man fears that the same British source who employed the man wants to kill him to keep him quiet. Although he is in fact killed, Rand finds the man responsible, a former friend and bureaucrat in the Ministry of Trade, who even tries to have Rand killed. A lightning-fast war, mercenary warriors, secret operations by nonspy agencies, assassins killing to prevent exposure of government officials, treacherous colleagues, smuggling under cover of espionage--all these elements imbue the collection's final stories with a nostalgia for simpler times.

"SACAJAWEA'S GOLD"

Hoch created two amateur detectives whose cases reflect the United States' past. One of them, Ben Snow, roams the frontier in the late nineteenth and early twentieth centuries, and though he seems law-abiding, a legend has grown that he is actually Billy the Kid. Snow is the character through whom Hoch introduces historical events into his stories, and often it is Native Americans and their mistreatment that come under scrutiny. In "Sacajawea's Gold," Ben is traveling through Yellowstone Park during the 1890's, shortly after the battle at Wounded Knee, when he helps Floating Cloud, a lovely Shoshone, by capturing her runaway pinto. She is seeking her missing father and also a leather pouch of gold coins reputedly given to Sacajawea, guide to Lewis and Clark, by the explorers. Ben decides to help her but finds that there is a third aspect to the investigation: the murder of a half-breed. As often happens, his reputation has preceded him, and an army officer, Captain Grant, assumes that Ben is a gunfighter. Ben finds that his interest in Floating Cloud and in solving the mystery causes conflict with her proud brother, Swift Eagle.

DIAGNOSIS: IMPOSSIBLE

Hoch's tales of Sam Hawthorne, a small-town New England doctor, are concerned with later history. Though the first story appeared in 1974, the series tells of events beginning in the 1920's and moves gradually through the Great Depression. (In one story, Ben, then a very old man, combines with Hawthorne to solve a mystery involving an Indian tepee.) Changes in American lifestyle and medicine are subtly used as background. Hoch has made Northmont the impossible crime capital of the world, and his Hawthorne series is probably his most ingenious. The stories are classic locked-room mysteries, which call for the solution of seemingly impossible crimes committed under circumstances where it would be impossible for anyone to have been at the scene of the crime or to have left it unnoticed. Among dozens of cases, Hawthorne has solved the mystery of a horse and carriage that disappeared after entering a covered New England bridge, the murder of a victim who was alone in a voting booth, and the murder of an escape artist locked by himself in a shack in front of witnesses. The Hawthorne stories are frequently complicated by clues that implicate an "innocent" bystander as the perpetrator.

In "The Problem of the General Store," Madge Murphy, a former suffragist and an early advocate of job opportunities for women, has settled in Northmont in 1928. Many men appear alienated by her equal rights advocacy. Madge is suspected of the shotgun slaying of Max Harkner, proprietor of the general store, because she was found near his body. Hawthorne wonders why, if she committed the murder, she was unconscious at the scene of the crime. He also explores whether her outspokenness earned her an enemy willing to frame her. Hoch gives the mysteries added credibility through references to period history and plot twists that hinge on an appreciation of small-town life and prejudices in times past. "The Problem of the Little Red Schoolhouse," in which Hawthorne must solve the kidnapping of a young boy, deliberately evokes the Leopold and Loeb and Lindbergh kidnapping cases. In "The

Problem of the Haunted Bandstand," the criminal exploits the town's memory of a racially motivated lynching decades earlier. In "The Problem of the Old Gristmill," a key clue to an otherwise insoluble murder is an understanding of how icehouses work. In "The Problem of the Lobster Shack," the motive for murder proves to be the then-unspeakable shame of a homosexual relationship. Hawthorne's convoluted "problems" continue in the fifteen stories of *More Things Impossible: The Second Casebook of Dr. Sam Hawthorne* (2006).

"THE THEFT OF THE GENERAL'S TRASH"

A long-standing tradition in mystery fiction is the rogue, such as Arsène Lupin, or the saint, who, like Robin Hood, robs those who "deserve" it but helps those in need. Hoch's Nick Velvet provides an interesting variation on that theme. When the series began in 1966, Velvet was making a surprisingly good living by stealing only objects of little value yet charging a minimum of twenty thousand dollars per theft. Though suspension of disbelief helps, Hoch has made it plausible that Velvet would be hired to steal, variously, the water from a swimming pool, the remaining tickets for a Broadway show that has closed, a last-place baseball team, a toy mouse, some exposed film, a used tea bag, and an overdue library book.

Velvet is being paid by newspaper columnist Sam Simon to steal that epitome of worthless items, a bag of garbage, in "The Theft of the General's Trash." The general, however, is Norman Spangler, the president's adviser on foreign affairs. Velvet is reluctant at first (it is shortly after the Watergate political scandal), and he agrees only after he ascertains that no military secrets will be involved. Velvet learns that Simon is really trying to track down the missing Carter Malone, a Watergate figure who jumped bail and disappeared rather than go to prison. As happens throughout the Velvet series, a more serious crime (usually murder) occurs while Velvet is stealing the insignificant object. Typically, he must find the killer, sometimes to help an innocent person but often to keep from being arrested himself.

LEOPOLD'S WAY

Captain Jules Leopold of the police department in a large Northeastern city is arguably the most famous soldier in Hoch's small army of detectives. He also has been the subject of more stories than any of Hoch's other sleuths. Hoch's "The Oblong Room" features Leopold and is typical of the early stories in the series in that the policeman's compassion and insight into character are as important as his deductive abilities. In "The Oblong Room," which evokes the 1960's, a college student is suspected of killing his roommate. He is found standing over the victim, with whom he has been alone for the twenty hours after death. In the room are found six sugar cubes saturated with the hallucinogenic drug lysergic acid diethylamide (LSD). Leopold enters a world alien to him, one in which college students experiment freely with drugs and sex, looking for what they claim are religious experiences. The murder room is analogized to a Poe story, "The Oblong Box." Though Leopold never loses his humanity, in later stories, especially beginning in the 1980's, Hoch had him solve very complex, impossible crimes. In one story, a bride disappears just as she is about to walk down the aisle to be married.

"The Sweating Statue"

Hoch made no secret of his Catholicism and interest in the Church; he even edited, with Martin H. Greenberg, a collection of mystery stories in which the Catholic religion is important to each story. One of his lesser-known detectives is Father David Noone, who appeared a few times. By far the most interesting Noone story is "The Sweating Statue," a story suggested by an incident in Central America related by Graham Greene in *Getting to Know the General* (1984). Noone is parish priest at Holy Trinity, a poor inner-city church. After the report that a statue of the Blessed Virgin has repeatedly been seen sweating, people descend on the church and its contributions soar. The cardinal sends Monsignor Thomas Xavier to help Noone investigate, though the woman who discovered this phenomenon asks why the church is reluctant to accept a miracle when the world needs one so badly. With the murder of a church employee, Noone and Xavier have two mysteries to solve.

"The Gypsy Delegate"

One of Hoch's later series, begun in 1985, had to keep up with changing conditions in Eastern Europe. The series character is Michael Vlado, a Romanian Gypsy, created for an anthology about ethnic detectives. In the early stories in the series, Vlado helps Captain Segar, an honest police officer, solve crimes. Events occur in the context of a dictatorship, one supported in Moscow, in which the Gypsy people, as a minority group, are subjected to discrimination, as they were in the Nazi era.

"The Gypsy Delegate" takes place after the December, 1989, uprising. Segar is part of the new government, though, when Vlado congratulates him, he confesses that his goal is getting through the first month without being shot. Vlado, as king of a tribe of Gypsies, is one of five Romanian delegates sent on the Orient Express to Switzerland to meet with King Michael, Romania's exiled ruler. One of the delegates, a famous educator, is murdered on the train, and the weapon, a dagger, is termed "a gypsy weapon," so Vlado, a suspect, is determined to solve the case.

The Iron Angel

The Iron Angel, and Other Tales of the Gypsy Sleuth collects stories from the first year of the series until 2000. They continue to track the changing political conditions in Romania and the European Union, especially the racial backlash against Gypsies. In the early stories, Vlado is an influential but average member of his tribe; Captain Segar is still a police officer and Vlado's virtual sidekick. Romania is socialist, but forces of Western culture soon intrude, changing everything. In "Murder of a Gypsy King," a young American wanderer, Jennifer Beatty, reaches Gravita, Vlado's village, on a stolen motorcycle after fleeing her boyfriend. Vlado befriends Beatty, who has no money, and gives her shelter. When the tribe's king, Carranza, is found murdered on his porch, Vlado tracks down a West German, also found dead, as the suspect. Beatty's boyfriend Peter shows up to reclaim her, but the suspicious Vlado discovers that Peter is Carranza's true murderer. Vlado succeeds to the kingship, and Beatty leaves to return to the United States.

Vlado is not finished with her, however, as Beatty turns up again in the title story, "The Iron Angel." This time she has a drug addict for a boyfriend. A Gypsy is found dead in Bucharest, and Segar, a bureaucrat in the transitional government after the fall of the socialist regime, calls on Vlado to investigate. He finds Beatty impoverished and an addict but still feels protective of her. When her boyfriend is murdered in the same area as the Gypsy, Vlado intensifies his investigation and uncovers a gambling parlor based on an antique slot machine in the form of an iron angel. Vlado reveals its owner, an antiques dealer, to be the murderer, but the climax of the story comes when Beatty, distraught over her lover's death, stabs herself to death. Vlado's involvement with her is symbolic on two related levels. It reflects Vlado's broadening but uneasy acquaintance with the world beyond Romania, and it underscores the ambiguous, turbulent influence of Western culture as Romania transforms into a democracy. In subsequent stories, Vlado becomes more an international figure, solving some crimes as an investigator for the European Roma Rights Centre.

The persecution of Gypsies, which is an undercurrent in early stories, provides the main focus for the last two in the volume, "The Starkworthy Atrocity" and "A Wall Too High." In the first, Vlado, on behalf of the European Union, looks into the mass murder by gassing of fifty-three Gypsies in an English refugee facility. The murderer, Vlado learns, was not actually after the Gypsies but sought vengeance against his mother, who worked at the facility; still, the murderer thought nothing of killing the Gypsies in the process. Likewise, "A Wall Too High" concerns the attempt by a police commander in a Czech city to frame Gypsies with the murder of one of his officers, so that he can launch a pogrom against them. The Gypsies' refugee status, the mistrust and disregard of them, and the overtones of conspiracy reveal the grim, dehumanizing effect of racism.

"THE CHRISTMAS CLIENT"

Hoch's mastery of the puzzle story led inevitably to contributions to anthologies of new stories featuring Sherlock Holmes. Hoch's various pastiches of Arthur Conan Doyle were all respectful and informed extensions of the Holmes canon and come near to making Holmes a minor series character of Hoch's own. "The Return of the Speckled Band," written for *The New Adventures of Sherlock Holmes: Original Stories* (1987), gives a new twist to events modeled on one of the original Holmes stories. Both "The Manor House Case," in *Resurrected Holmes: New Cases from the Notes of*

John H. Watson, M.D. (1996), and "The Adventure of Vittoria the Circus Belle," in *The Mammoth Book of New Sherlock Holmes Adventures* (1997), challenge the master sleuth to unravel mysteries involving concealed identities and wild animal killings. "The Adventure of the Dying Ship," from *The Confidential Casebook of Sherlock Holmes* (1998), pits the aging Holmes against a sham spiritualist aboard the *Titanic*.

One of Hoch's intriguing Holmes tales is "The Christmas Client," written for *Holmes for the Holidays* (1996). Holmes is sought out by Charles Dodgson, best known for his Alice in Wonderland books written under the pseudonym Lewis Carroll. Dodgson is being blackmailed by Holmes's nemesis, Professor Moriarty, with some amateur photographs that Dodgson fears will be considered scandalous. Holmes rightly intuits that the extortion is a subterfuge to distract authorities from an even graver crime Moriarity plans to commit. Clues vital to stopping Moriarity must be deduced from a bit of nonsense verse the criminal has composed in Carrollian style and passed to Dodgson. The story is a showcase for Hoch's research of history and period detail and also an ingenious mystery that has Victorian England's master of logical detection grappling with intrigue grounded in Carroll's special brand of literary illogic.

"THE DETECTIVE'S WIFE"

In a nonseries 1990 story, "The Detective's Wife," Roger and Jenny seem to be an ideally suited couple. Roger works as a police detective, and Jenny works for an advertising agency. Early in their marriage, they often discuss his cases, and Jenny tries to help solve them through use of deduction. His reference to her as "Watson" is an affectionate inside joke between them. Long hours and his frustration at the volume of drug-related crime cause Roger to become depressed and then paranoically jealous of Jenny. In hopes of saving their marriage, she tries to help him with a criminal, a serial killer, who has eluded him. Detection is important to this story, yet it also explores the effect of urban crime on those who must try to cope with it.

When his "streak" in *EQMM* began in 1973, Hoch started to concentrate mainly on stories of puzzle and detection involving his many series detectives. This was especially true in the 1980's. "The Detective's

Wife" appeared in a nongenre magazine, the California literary quarterly *Crosscurrents*. It, along with other evidence, was an indication of Hoch returning to more varied mysteries and, without abandoning his famous puzzle stories, exploring larger issues in society.

OTHER MAJOR WORKS

LONG FICTION: *The Shattered Raven*, 1969; *The Transvection Machine*, 1971; *The Blue Movie Murders*, 1972 (as Ellery Queen; edited and supervised by Frederic Dannay); *The Fellowship of the Hand*, 1973; *The Frankenstein Factory*, 1975; *Medical Center Murders*, 1984 (as Lisa Drake); *Prize Meets Murder*, 1984 (as R. T. Edwards); *This Prize Is Dangerous*, 1985 (as Matthew Prize).

CHILDREN'S LITERATURE: *The Monkey's Clue, and the Stolen Sapphire*, 1978.

EDITED TEXTS: *Dear Dead Days*, 1972; *Best Detective Stories of the Year*, 1976-1981; *All but Impossible! An Anthology of Locked Room and Impossible Crime Stories*, 1981; *The Year's Best Mystery and Suspense Stories*, 1982-1995; *Great British Detectives*, 1987 (with Martin H. Greenberg); *Women Write Murder*, 1987 (with Martin H. Greenberg); *Murder Most Sacred: Great Catholic Tales of Mystery and Suspense*, 1989 (with Martin H. Greenberg).

BIBLIOGRAPHY

Adey, Robert. *Locked Room Murders*. 2d ed. Minneapolis, Minn.: Crossover Press, 1991. Adey analyzes eighty-one of Hoch's impossible crime stories. Each entry has a brief description of the impossible problem (usually, but not limited to, a locked-room murder) presented and, in an appendix at the end of the book, how the crime was solved.

Davis, J. Madison. "The Last Good Man: Edward D. Hoch and the World of the Short Story." *World Literature Today* 82 (July/August, 2008): 9-11. An obituary, retrospective of Hoch's writing career, and lament about the declining publishing opportunities for other short-story writers.

"Edward D. Hoch: Grand Master, MWA." *Ellery Queen Mystery Magazine* 117 (June, 2001): 15. Announcement of the honor to Hoch and a short appreciation of his contributions to the field of mystery fiction.

Hoch, Edward D. "Shortcut to Murder: An Interview with Edward D. Hoch." Interview by John Kovaleski. *The Armchair Detective* 23 (Spring, 1990): 152-169. A thorough interview with the author contains detailed descriptions of many aspects of his career, including his early writing, his writing habits and methods, and the origin of his major series characters. Hoch frankly discusses the reasons for his preference for the short story over the novel. He admits that characterization is often the weak point in his work, a function of the limitations imposed by short-story length.

Lewis, Steve L. "Interview with Edward Hoch." *Mystery*File: The Crime Fiction Research Journal* 45 (August, 2004): 37-40. Hoch reflects on his use of international settings to help keep his stories fresh, on his background research, and on his preference for types of detectives and plots.

Moffatt, June M., and Francis M. Nevins, Jr. *Edward Hoch Bibliography (1955-2004)*. 13th ed. Downey, Calif.: Moffatt House, 2004. A complete listing of the writings of Hoch, with publishing information, including reprints, identification of those stories about continuing characters, and adaptations to other media.

_____. *Twentieth Century Crime and Mystery Writers*, edited by Lesley Henderson. 4th ed. London: St. James Press, 1998. In addition to brief biographical information and an extensive bibliography of Hoch's work, this volume contains an analysis of Hoch's work and place in the genre. Nevins finds the Roman Catholic viewpoint of the early Hoch obtrusive but notes the writer's growth and the stimulating concepts behind many of his plots. Hoch's stories are described as perfect miniatures of the novels of such detective-story giants as Ellery Queen and John Dickson Carr.

Spoto, Mary Theresa. "Needing Burial: Horror and Reconciliation in Edward D. Hoch's 'The Faceless Thing.'" *Studies in Weird Fiction* 20 (Winter, 1997): 13-17. A close reading of Hoch's short horror story "The Faceless Thing," which Spoto praises for an ending different from traditional horror-story endings that reestablish the natural order. Instead, Hoch offers an alternative type of reconciliation that is consistent with the psychology of its characters and provides a closure "that is in harmony with the dis-

harmony of a universe of horror."

Marvin Lachman; Stefan Dziemianowicz
Updated by Roger Smith

A. M. HOMES

Born: Washington, D.C.; December 18, 1961

PRINCIPAL SHORT FICTION
The Safety of Objects, 1990
Things You Should Know: A Collection of Stories,
   2002

OTHER LITERARY FORMS

A. M. Homes is best known for her fiction, including six novels and two collections of short stories; however, she also has produced a travel memoir focusing on Los Angeles and a personal memoir of meeting her birth parents, a screenplay, episodes of a television drama series, and numerous reviews, interviews, and essays. The essays have appeared in a variety of periodicals, including *Art Forum, Blind Spot, Bomb, Granta, Harper's, McSweeney's, The New York Times, The New Yorker, Vanity Fair*, and *Zoetrope*. One of her novels, *The End of Alice* (1996), is particularly well known because of its inflammatory focus on child molestation, and *Jack* (1989), her first novel, is frequently taught in high schools as a coming-of-age story.

ACHIEVEMENTS

Known for her distinctly dark and daring fiction, Homes brings a unique, offbeat wit to her disturbing vision of American life. Over two decades, she has published six novels and two collections of short fiction, in addition to producing in other genres, including the memoir, essay, and screenplay. Active in the New York writing community, Homes has taught fiction writing at the New School and New York University and in the writing program at Columbia University. Her works have been translated into eighteen languages.

Homes is the recipient of numerous awards, including the Benjamin Franklin Award and the *Deutscher Jugendliteraturpreis* (German Youth Literature Prize). She has received fellowships from the John Simon Guggenheim Foundation, the National Endowment for the Arts, the New York Foundation for the Arts, and the Dorothy and Lewis B. Cullman Center for Scholars and Writers at the New York Public Library. Additionally, she has served on the boards of directors of Yaddo, the Fine Arts Work Center in Provincetown, the Writers Room, PEN, and the President's Council for Poets and Writers.

BIOGRAPHY

Amy Michael Homes was born in Washington, D.C., on December 18, 1961, and grew up in Chevy Chase, Maryland. Her adoptive father was a painter, and he instilled in her an early and lasting love of art. Homes did not meet her birth parents until she was thirty-one, and she recorded the difficult initial encounters with them in an essay first published in *The New Yorker* in 2004 as "The Mistress's Daughter" and later wrote a memoir by the same title in 2007.

She earned her B.A. from Sarah Lawrence College in 1985 and her M.F.A. from the prestigious University of Iowa Writers' Workshop in 1988. Homes moved with her young daughter to New York City, where she has published in a variety of genres and has taught creative writing at Columbia University.

Jack, Homes's first novel, was written when she was only nineteen, growing out of a class assignment, and the book was later published to critical acclaim and received an award from the American Library Association. The coming-of-age novel spoke to both youth and adults, with its frank look at families and sexuality. This debut work examines a teenage protagonist's efforts to come to terms with his father's homosexuality and his parents' divorce.

Her subsequent novels and short stories have been characterized as haunting, disturbing, and controversial, yet strangely original and darkly funny. *In a Country of Mothers* appeared in 1993, and its exploration of the complicated relationship between a therapist and her patient considers the thin lines separating reality from madness and compassion from obsession.

Homes followed this work with the two novels that have received the most critical attention: *The End of Alice*, which deals shockingly with madness, murder, and molestation, and *Music for Torching* (1999), which takes a cynical and perverse look at suburban boredom and disappointment. *The End of Alice* chronicles the descent into complete insanity of a convicted child molester. The inmate corresponds from prison with a female college student, who is interested in a twelve-year-old boy. *Music for Torching* expands on characters Paul and Elaine, first introduced in Homes's short-story collection, *The Safety of Objects*. They experiment with crack cocaine and sexual escapades and burn down their home on impulse before taking the children out for steak and ice cream. Her long fiction *This Book Will Save Your Life* appeared in 2006.

In a 2008 "Author Chat" at the New York Public Library, Homes identified John Cheever and Richard Yates as inspirations for her writing, and she is sometimes compared to Vladimir Nabokov and J. D. Salinger. She has mentioned the following teachers and writers as "mentors": Grace Paley, Doris Grumbach, Allan Gurganus, Edward Albee, Harold Pinter, Arthur Miller, and Joseph Heller. In addition to fiction, Homes has published reviews of art and books, interviews of writers and artists, literary essays, and introductions to other works of literature.

ANALYSIS

In her provocative, daring, and darkly comic tales, A. M. Homes is revealed as a deeply moral chronicler of contemporary America's soiled and ripped social fabric. She examines desires and their consequences, loss, and alienation. Wandering within a nightmarish emotional landscape filled with anxiety and despair, her characters yearn for a true human connection.

In her short fiction, Homes's writing style is characterized by the grotesque, the extreme, and the surreal, mingled with the mundane and ordinary. Her descriptive passages of key moments from lives of quiet desperation and dysfunction are coupled with fascinating, train-wreck characters who are often sexually deviant, generally disconnected from the most important people in their lives, and searching for identity, meaning, and self-worth. The reader cannot look away from the quiet horror of the suburban-hell existence that Homes details.

Her adults are often withdrawn emotionally and have become cold and scarred individuals. Other characters are living on the edge of a mental breakdown, while behaving antisocially and dangerously, if not criminally. Many have a notion of false entitlement, believing they should be able to attain their image of the American dream. Most of Homes's characters lead two lives: one seemingly conventional and the other existing in an alternate, surreal universe.

While Homes's grown-ups are somewhat fragile, dependent on their relationships, work, and other circumstances for a sense of self, the young characters are tough, resilient, and imaginative. An example of the latter is the teenage girl in "Chunky in Heat" from *The Safety of Objects*. The story focuses on an overweight adolescent girl, who fantasizes about her massive weight. Sitting in a lawn chair in her backyard, she masturbates, imagining herself as "pure sex."

In her stories, Homes peers closely at marriages and families, her favorite subjects, especially middle-class suburbanites and the anxieties within their relationships. However, unlike other American writers who chronicle contemporary America, Homes adds a dark humor and surreal perspective to these character studies. With rigid expectations and striving for a level of perfection in self and in relationships that does not exist, many of her characters are paralyzed at the possibility of failure, obsessed with success, and not interested in learning from their mistakes. Frequently, her characters are stuck on a particular course because of their rigidity. Change for them is possible but not likely.

In interviews, Homes has commented on her writing process and said that, in imagining a story, she chooses a theme or motif from issues she sees within American culture and experience. She notes that she is particularly interested in revealing contemporary morality and sexuality and how they relate to American culture. Sexual acting out is often portrayed as an attempt to escape from problems and from self.

A typical theme centers on the pain of being human, with a focus on a pervading sense of disconnection, hopelessness, and isolation. In each life, there is a missing emotional element, a deep feeling of loss, or something missing from one's world. In addition, there is an emphasis on vigilance or being prepared for the worst, a sense of disaster looming, and a desire to feel in control in the midst of a chaotic and fragmented life.

THE SAFETY OF OBJECTS

The stories in the collection *The Safety of Objects* reflect how people use objects as sources of comfort and reassurance and how people objectify others in their lives. All ten of the tales are set in suburbia and examine the seemingly ordinary lives of individuals, couples, and families. However, beneath the surface banality, the reader finds bizarre situations and a mixture of realism and surrealism, as the characters search for identity and comfort.

For example, "Adults Alone" deals with identity, relationships, and comfort-seeking behavior. Suburbanites Paul and Elaine expect to be alone for more than a week without their children, who have been packed off to their grandmother's house in Florida for a "vacation." Feeling freed from parenthood and mutually unhappy in their relationship, they decide to have some fun, and they experiment with marijuana, play video games, and indulge in comfort foods, alcohol, and pornography. They then progress to smoking crack cocaine, an experience that is exciting and fulfilling for both. When their children decide they want to come home early, Paul and Elaine are not happy at their loss of freedom, but they put the house back in order and prepare to return to their normal lives. This couple's story is expanded in more detail in the novel *Music for Torching*, in which they continue their search for self and fulfillment.

In another story that deals with identity and disconnected relationships at home, title character Jim Train is so obsessed with his work and caught up in his routines that when his law firm shuts down for a few days because of a bomb threat, he does not have any idea how to cope. His already shaky hold on reality gives way to anxiety attacks and fantasies of worst-case scenarios. His family does not want his company, and he feels lost and anxious. He determines to go into his office on the third day, whether it is open or not, because that is the only place where he feels he belongs.

In "Looking for Johnny," a boy with little energy and low self-esteem is kidnapped by a child molester. The boy's mother is an overwhelmed single parent, raising a mentally challenged daughter, and the relationship with her son is not strong. The boy is taken to the man's house, but the boy does not live up to his captor's expectations. The nine-year-old sits around, complaining about wanting to watch television. Disappointed in the boy, the kidnapper returns the boy to his home.

The final story, "A Real Doll," is possibly the most disturbing, with its matter-of-fact presentation of a teenage boy's sexual obsession with his sister's Barbie doll. In this absurd tale, Barbie speaks with erotic frankness to the young man, and he laces her Diet Cokes with his parents' Valium. As their relationship builds, he masturbates with her and later with the Ken doll. Once he starts interacting with her, he becomes obsessed with seeking her out and cannot stop until the doll is physically ruined by his little sister, who carves off Barbie's breasts. A collection of surreal yet strangely believable stories, *The Safety of Objects* was adapted into a film by director Rose Troche and debuted in 2001.

THINGS YOU SHOULD KNOW

The majority of the stories in *Things You Should Know* are told from a male perspective, but Homes has said that her characterizations have less to do with a specific gender than with the "truth" of that particular character. In her stories, she tries to inhabit the main character fully, to imagine the person's history, experiences, feelings, and point of view, and she often chooses characters who are very different from who she is, including young males, as in "Rockets Round the Moon" and "The Whiz Kids."

Further, the main characters in these stories often have a deep-seated sense of something amiss or out of reach in their lives, but they usually cannot identify the true source of their discomfort. They may feel isolated or disconnected from others, but they do not know how to correct the situation, so they reach blindly for a simple and inadequate fix.

An example of this behavior is illustrated in "Georgica," in which a disillusioned woman believes her life will improve if only she can have a baby, so she attempts to impregnate herself with leftover sperm from condoms abandoned on the beach. She is not interested in becoming involved with a man, for she has been traumatized by a car wreck and the loss of her beloved grandmother, and she is disgusted by the boorish, impotent, and overweight men whom she has dated since the accident. Instead, she stalks the young lifeguards who have sex on the beach late at night and steals their discarded sperm in a pathetic attempt to inseminate herself with hope and new life.

In "The Chinese Lesson," Susan, an Asian American woman, feels alienated from her family and her culture. Alternately, Geordie, her husband, tries to understand his wife and his ailing, wandering mother-in-law. He has a microchip implanted in her back, and he tracks her on her walks, but he is the one who feels lost, searching for a true connection with her, his wife, their daughter, and their mixture of cultures. An absurdly strange story, it resonates with truth.

Another story that examines disconnected lives is "Raft in Water, Floating." There is a profound sadness and alienation between the parents and their anorexic daughter in the story. The parents lead separate lives within their marriage, symbolized by their bed with its dual controls, allowing them to sleep together yet apart. Their daughter has all but disappeared from their lives, as she wastes away from her disease and their neglect. Passive and barely alive, the girl floats like a raft in the pool, seeing visions of a shape-shifting visitor and allowing a boy to molest her, while accepting her parents' disinterest in her pain and suffering.

The parents in "Rockets Round the Moon" are similarly self-absorbed with their healthy, dull lifestyle, and their twelve-year-old son feels distinctly unloved and ignored. As a result, he learns to be a people pleaser and to look elsewhere for recognition and a sense of identity. He idealizes his friend Henry's home life, until two tragedies befall that family and his friend attempts suicide on an amusement park ride, causing the boy to rethink the concepts of home and belonging.

Other characters share this profound feeling of alienation, including the prodigal daughter in "Remedy," who comes home to find she has been replaced in her family's affections by a stranger, and the character styled on Nancy Reagan, dealing with a husband suffering from Alzheimer's disease in "The Former First Lady and the Football Hero." She realizes they will not be able to overcome his illness as they have previous challenges they faced together, and she will have to suffer through his final days stoically, with grace, and alone.

OTHER MAJOR WORKS

LONG FICTION: *Jack*, 1989; *In a Country of Mothers*, 1993; *The End of Alice*, 1996; *Appendix A: An Elaboration on the Novel "The End of Alice,"* 1996; *Music for Torching*, 1999; *This Book Will Save Your Life*, 2006.

SCREENPLAY: *Jack*, 2004 (adaptation of her novel).

TELEPLAYS: *The L Word*, 2004-2005 (season 2).

NONFICTION: *Los Angeles: People, Places, and the Castle on the Hill*, 2002; *The Mistress's Daughter*, 2007.

BIBLIOGRAPHY

Eder, Richard. "Oddness of the Heart." *The New York Times Book Review*, September 29, 2002, p. 16. Argues that bad things happen to Homes's characters in her stories and provides an overview of her short fiction in the collection *Things You Should Know*.

Gottlieb, Stacey. "*Things You Should Know*." *Review of Contemporary Fiction* 23, no. 1 (Spring, 2003): 149. Offers an overview and analysis of the short-fiction collection *Things You Should Know*, emphasizing the literary characteristics for which Homes is known.

Levi, Jonathan. "Tales Through Dark Glasses." *Los Angeles Times Book Review*, December 29, 2002, p. 4. Discusses and evaluates Homes's short-story collection *Things You Should Know*.

Piafsky, Michael, et al. "Interview with A. M. Homes." *The Missouri Review* 28, no. 3 (Winter, 2005): 100-120. Discusses Homes's growth as a writer, her topics, her themes, and her influences.

Smith, Ali. "Fertile Ground." *The Guardian*, May 31, 2003. Analyzes the short-fiction collection *Things You Should Know*; suggests that Homes provides the postmodern, surreal response to F. Scott Fitzgerald's American Dream.

Donna B. Nalley

PAM HOUSTON

Born: New Jersey; 1962

PRINCIPAL SHORT FICTION

Cowboys Are My Weakness: Stories, 1992
Waltzing the Cat, 1998

OTHER LITERARY FORMS

Pam Houston (HEW-ston) began her writing career by contributing nonfiction and short stories to numerous popular and literary periodicals, such as *Vogue*, *The New York Times*, *Quarterly West*, and *The Gettysburg Review*. Some of these stories later appeared in her 1992 collection *Cowboys Are My Weakness* and her 1998 collection *Waltzing the Cat*. Her first novel, *Sight Hound*, was published in 2005. Houston also edited *Women on Hunting: Essays, Fiction, and Poetry* (1995) and has had her stories selected for many works, such as *The Best American Short Stories 1990* and *Prize Stories: The O. Henry Awards* in 1999. Her autobiography, *A Little More About Me*, was published in 1999.

ACHIEVEMENTS

Pam Houston's collection, *Cowboys Are My Weakness: Stories*, was a *New York Times* Notable Book in 1992 and won the 1993 Western States Book Award. In 1999, *Waltzing the Cat* won the first Willa Literary Awards (named after Pulitzer Prize-winning author Willa Cather) for best contemporary fiction.

BIOGRAPHY

Described by many critics as "a modern Annie Oakley," Pam Houston was born in New Jersey but spent much of her childhood in Bethlehem, Pennsylvania. The only child of an actress and unsuccessful businessman, her childhood was filled with parental alcoholism, physical abuse, and unmet expectations. Her father wanted her to become a tennis star; her mother wanted her to be thin and perfectly made-up. Houston wanted to be neither.

When Houston was two and a half years old, her baby-sitter encouraged her to learn to read and write. This became a means of escape from a childhood often fraught with great danger, including sixteen car accidents (once with each of her parents) in as many years of age. Houston graduated second in her class with a degree in English from Denison University in Granville, Ohio. In 1992, she married a South African safari guide, Mike Elkington, but the two later divorced. She later received a Ph.D. from the University of Utah.

Because she spent much of her childhood afraid for her personal safety, Houston claims her attraction to dangerous white-water rafting and emotionally withdrawn cowboy types was a response to feelings of fear and lack of control as a child and a way of returning to an unfortunate but familiar lifestyle. Her work as a hunting and rafting guide in the American West and Alaska forms the basis for most of her literary work.

ANALYSIS

Relying on her outdoor adventures, Pam Houston has carved out her unique niche as a female author writing about topics normally associated with male writers like Ernest Hemingway or Edward Abbey:

exotic landscapes, wanderlust, and struggles against unpredictable natural elements, such as mother grizzlies and deep river currents.

Influenced by D. H. Lawrence and other modernists, Houston's short stories have an autobiographical flavor to them. They are infused with what the *East Bay Express* describes as "an embedded irony in . . . that the tough, outdoorsy heroines could navigate dangerous rapids with expertise, but couldn't quite get a handle on their love lives--especially in relationships with terse men of the west." However, Houston's female characters know that they are responsible for their own lives, truths, and desires for love.

Houston explores these themes of self-reliance and love by mixing personal experience with metaphor in an attempt to discover the real truth behind not only her wilderness experiences but also her relationships with parents, friends, and lovers. Instead of planning out her narrative before she sits down to write, Houston first tries to write out as much as she can remember about a place to keep herself from consciously controlling the meaning of the story because, she explains, "When I'm looking the other direction, that's when the truth emerges."

WALTZING THE CAT

Houston's second book of short stories, *Waltzing the Cat*, is a collection of eleven linked stories about the life of Lucy, a photographer, whose adventures with nature and relationships seem to be metaphors for much of Houston's own life. Leaving the Rockies for Oakland, California, Lucy experiences all kinds of emotional and physical turmoil--hurricanes, rafting accidents, and parents and lovers who are distant and self-obsessed--in what has been described as "a vigorous, often lyrical rendition of a young woman's quiet but intense search for herself."

For example, in "The Best Girlfriend You Never Had," Lucy and her friend Leo recount stories about people they have known, including themselves, who "have their hearts all wrapped around someone who won't ever love them back." In this story, Leo and Lucy, whose relationship parallels that of the story's title, are reading poetry about love aloud while watching various weddings take place in the gardens of the Palace of the Fine Arts in San Francisco. As Lucy

Pam Houston (AP Photo/)

takes photographs of the couples, we learn how Leo, an architect, is in love with Guinevere, a Buddhist weaver, who "seems not to know Leo is alive." From Lucy we learn of her involvement with Gordon, a college professor with an angry, possessive streak who, after dragging Lucy's self-confidence down to his own level, begins stalking her. It is in this story that the reader is introduced to Lucy's parents. Their biting comments about her in front of a traffic cop cause the officer to decide not to give her a ticket for her numerous violations because, as he puts it, "there's nothing I could do to you that's going to feel like punishment."

In the title story "Waltzing the Cat," Lucy must face her mother's death and her father's retreat from reality. The narrator tells the story of the family cat that has become a waddling, overstuffed storehouse for her parent's unexpressed emotions and expectations for each other and their daughter. As Lucy tells the reader, "For as long as I can remember, my parents have eaten vicariously through the cat. Roast chicken, amaretto cheese spread, rum raisin ice cream" was fed to the cat while she was offered "carrots and celery, cauliflower and radishes." At the end of the story, Lucy's hopes for becoming the focus of her father's affections are quickly dashed when, upon hearing her father say "I love you so much," she turns around to find him talking to the cat.

In subsequent stories, Lucy plunges into adventure after adventure as a means of finding some kind of emotional fulfillment. Then in "Moving from One Body of Water to Another," the narrator has a chance encounter with anthropologist and author Carlos Castanada which leads her to finally understand that the spiritual reality and emotional balance that she has been seeking is much closer to home than she realizes. In later stories, Lucy returns to the Rockies and her grandmother's old ranch house to live, concluding a collection of stories that one critic has described as a "consistent pattern of seeking, discovery, loss and compromise." It is in the epilogue that the narrator understands that to find her emotional balance she does not need to try to fulfill parental expectations or find a man. Instead of mastering dangerous rivers and currents, she needs only be brave enough to seek out her true self.

OTHER MAJOR WORKS

LONG FICTION: *Sight Hound*, 2005.

NONFICTION: *Men Before Ten A.M.*, 1996 (photographs by Veronique Vial); *A Little More About Me*, 1999.

EDITED TEXT: *Women on Hunting: Essays, Fiction, and Poetry*, 1995.

BIBLIOGRAPHY

Fanselow, Julie. "The Emotional Truth: Writings of Author Pam Houston." *Writer's Digest* 76, no. 10 (October, 1996): 6. Describes how Houston's first collection of stories *Cowboys Are My Weakness* continues to sell well since its publication in 1992. Houston feels that stories always change in the retelling.

Gilbert, Elizabeth. "Risky Business." Review of *A Little More About Me*, by Pam Houston. *The New York Times Book Review*, September 12, 1999, 25.

Review of Houston's autobiography, which also discusses her numerous adventures and the path that her autobiographical stories take.

Houlihan, Mary. "Wild World of Words; Her Tales Mix Love, Adventure." *Chicago Sun-Times*, October 10, 1999, p. G17. Interview with Houston in which she discusses her early family history, mentors, teaching, and future adventures.

Houston, Pam. "On the River with Pam Houston: Adventure, a Cure for Bad-Love Blues." Interview by Molly O'Neill. *The New York Times*, July 15, 1992, p. C1. Interviewer goes on a three-day river trip with the author while they discuss Houston's childhood, men, and her first book, *Cowboys Are My Weakness: Stories*.

_____. "The Perfect Equality of Our Separate Chosen Paths: Becoming a Mother, or Not." In *The Bitch in the House: Twenty-Six Women Tell the Truth About Sex, Solitude, Work, Motherhood, and Marriage*, edited by Cathi Hanauer. New York: William Morrow, 2002. Houston and the other women included in this collection describe their inner anger, rage, and frustration over various aspects of their lives and relationships.

_____. "Truth and Dare: Pam Houston's Greatest Adventure Is Within Herself." Interview by Lori Tobias. *Denver Rocky Mountain News*, September 12, 1999, p. 1E. Houston discusses her early childhood and autobiography; she also addresses her use of personal experiences in her short stories.

Reynolds, Susan Salter. "I Love Lucy: *Waltzing the Cat*, by Pam Houston." *The Los Angeles Times Book Review*, November 15, 1998, 12. Reviews her second book with a special emphasis on the author's use of personal experience and metaphor as writing strategies.

See, Carolyn. "Running Life's Rapids." *The Washington Post*, October 30, 1998, p. D02. Discusses the issues of concern to Lucy, the main character in *Waltzing the Cat*, such as men, her parents, and risking her life.

Lisa-Anne Culp

WILLIAM DEAN HOWELLS

Born: Martinsville (now Martins Ferry), Ohio;
   March 1, 1837
Died: New York, New York; May 11, 1920

PRINCIPAL SHORT FICTION

A Fearful Responsibility, and Other Stories, 1881
Selected Short Stories of William Dean Howells,
   1997

OTHER LITERARY FORMS

William Dean Howells is known primarily as a novelist, especially for his two acknowledged masterpieces, *The Rise of Silas Lapham* (1885) and *A Hazard of New Fortunes* (1889). He was also a distinguished journalist and editor who presided for years over the "Editor's Easy Chair" column for *Harper's Monthly*. In *Criticism and Fiction* (1891) and *My Literary Passions* (1895) Howells expounded the principles that made him known as a champion of literary realism.

ACHIEVEMENTS

Besides his enormous output in several literary genres, from 1866 until 1881 William Dean Howells was an editor for *The Atlantic*. Beginning in 1886, he was for many years an editorial columnist for *Harper's Monthly*. Howells received an honorary degree from Oxford University in 1904 and was elected the first president of the American Academy of Arts and Letters in 1908.

BIOGRAPHY

William Dean Howells was born in Martinsville (now Martins Ferry), Ohio, on March 1, 1837, and he received much of his early education in the Hamilton printing office of his father's *Intelligencer* before working on the *Ohio State Journal* from 1858 to 1861. His campaign biography of President Abraham

Lincoln earned him an appointment as United States consul in Venice (1861-1865). In 1861, he married Elinor Mead, and they had three children, Winifred (born 1863), John (1868), and Mildred (1872). After his return from Venice, Howells moved to Boston, where he lived until 1888, when he moved to New York City.

Howells was one of the most distinguished men of letters in his day and a close friend of other notables, such as Henry James and Mark Twain, many of whom he wrote about in *Literary Friends and Acquaintances* (1900) and *My Mark Twain* (1910). In his criticism, he championed a realistic approach to fiction but a realism too genteel for some critics, like the naturalistic novelist Frank Norris. The high esteem of the world of letters was reflected in a seventy-fifth birthday gala held for him, with President William Howard Taft attending.

Howells consistently displayed a social conscience. He angered a great many influential people by his vigorous defense of the Haymarket anarchists in 1887, and he helped found the National Association for the Advancement of Colored People (NAACP) in 1909.

ANALYSIS

William Dean Howells is best remembered in literary history for two things: He wrote more than thirty novels, and he tirelessly defended realism over Romanticism. Howells's earliest short stories are weak and imitative, often more sketch than story, and not until 1868 in "Tonelli's Marriage" does he achieve a convincing story by focusing on European social customs as he observed them as consul in Venice.

The death of Howells's daughter Winifred in 1889 may have prompted him to write several stories treating the subject of immortality, including the so-called Turkish Room tales, a series of "psychic romances" named for a small group who gather at a private club in New York City to explore supernatural themes. The narrator of the stories is a novelist, Acton, who, amid the club's exotic Indian and Middle Eastern furnishings, reports the conversations that loosely shape the narratives. As a champion of literary realism, Howells justifies these tales by a distinction between romance and Romanticism:

> Romance [good], as in Hawthorne, seeks the effect of reality in visionary conditions; romanticism [bad], as in Dickens, tries for a visionary effect in actual conditions.

This scheme suggests the famous complementary intentions of Samuel Taylor Coleridge, by Howells's definition a romancer, and William Wordsworth (a Romanticist) in their *Lyrical Ballads* (1798).

Other groupings of Howells's stories include the Dulldale tales, inspired by small towns like Jefferson, Ohio; several children's stories; and the pair of stories about Basil and Isabel March, "A Circle in the Water" and "A Pair of Patient Lovers." Only the March narratives have prompted much significant critical attention.

"THE MAGIC OF A VOICE"

"The Magic of a Voice" is a love story. Stephen Langbourne is awakened one night in his New Hampshire hotel by the voices of two young women in the room next to him. When he falls in love at first sound with one of the girls, Barbara Simpson, he contrives to get her name and address and even to initiate a winter-long correspondence with her from New York City. Barbara even sends him a photograph of herself. Come spring, Langbourne journeys to New Hampshire and boldly arrives at the home of the two girls, Barbara and her friend from the hotel, Juliet Bingham. Langbourne is dismayed to find Barbara not as attractive as he had imagined, for, as a joke, she had sent Juliet's photograph instead. Eventually, once Langbourne gets to know both girls, he discovers, after all the misunderstandings are played out, that it is really plain Barbara whom he loves, and they brace themselves to live happily ever after. Although critics have sneered at this story--when condescending to notice it--it has elements that deserve attention, such as the implications of Langbourne's aural voyeurism. More interesting, however, for gender critics are Howells's remarks about Barbara--that "there was something almost mannish in

her essential honesty," that "her companionship would be as easy and reasonable as a man's, while it had the charm of a woman's," and that "the [hotel register] entry was in a good, simple hand, which was like a man's in its firmness and clarity."

"A DIFFICULT CASE"

"A Difficult Case" is one of Howells's finest stories, a probing of the questions about immortality that had troubled Howells since his daughter's death. A middle-aged minister, Clarence Ewbert, takes a position in a church in a small university community, but his wife's hopes for social success are frustrated when the university members fail to join the small congregation. One faithful parishioner, the aging Ransom Hilbrook, lives alone on a crumbling farm and becomes Ewbert's "difficult case." When Hilbrook makes frequent, long evening visits to the Ewberts' to pursue tortuous arguments about immortality, the Reverend Ewbert reveals a kind interest in the lonely eccentric, but Mrs. Ewbert judges him a socially inconsequential nuisance who is exhausting her husband. Hilbrook's war experiences and the deaths of his wife and child have soured him on life,

William Dean Howells (Library of Congress)

and he prays not for immortality but for an annihilation that will guarantee he never wakes up in his "old identity, with the potentiality of new experiences in new conditions." Ewbert's task becomes, then, to argue for a satisfying immortality, but the process of winning over Hilbrook saps both his health and his own faith. Mrs. Ewbert then turns Hilbrook away one evening and takes Ewbert for a seaside holiday, from which he returns refreshed and gratified by a university congregation. Hilbrook, though, apparently crushed by Mrs. Ewbert, retires to his bed and dies of loss of interest in life. The appeal of this story lies not in the observations on immortality, which are trivial, but in the contrast between Ewbert, a caring man, and his hard wife, and in this respect it reveals the influence on Howells of a writer he greatly admired, Nathaniel Hawthorne, who regarded a lack of charity as an unpardonable sin.

"THE ANGEL OF THE LORD"

The first of Howells's nine Turkish Room stories is "The Angel of the Lord." The rambling narrative of a psychologist, Wanhope, is reported by the first-person narrator, Acton, a novelist. Minver, an artist, and Rulledge, an idler of no apparent occupation, listen and contribute ad libitum. The subjects of Wanhope's tale are a now-dead couple, the Ormonds, and the history of the husband's debilitating obsession with death. When the Ormonds bought an old home in the Connecticut countryside, Ormond (the husband) had found in its library the works of the eighteenth century English poets known as the Graveyard School,

> like Gray and Collins and Young . . . who personified nearly everything from Contemplation to Indigestion, through the whole range of the Vices, Virtues, Passions, Propensities, Attributes, and Qualities, and gave them each a dignified capital letter to wear.

Ormond somehow finds in personification "the reason of things," and the revelation transforms his life as he enjoys perfect tranquillity in his new freedom from his old obsession. In his Bible reading, he fixes on the epithet "The Angel of the Lord," which so consumes his imagination that a passing tramp assumes a holy mission in Ormond's mind, and he bounds joyfully into the woods after the vagrant and falls to his death. This odd story should be seen in the context of its time, when psychologists like Wanhope were

investigating psychic phenomena and the Society for Psychical Research flourished. Howells himself pronounced that visions, whether natural or supernatural, were "precious."

"EDITHA"

When Editha Balcom becomes excited by the prospect of an impending war--presumably the Spanish-American War--she urges her fiancé, George Gearson, to enlist. However, George, much more sensible and realistic than the romantic Editha, reveals a coolness to the idea, which briefly lowers their mutual ardor. Editha magnifies this rift to dramatic proportions: "It all interested her intensely; she was undergoing a tremendous experience, and she was being equal to it." She then composes a naïve letter to George expressing a shallow patriotism, which makes it clear that he must enlist if he wishes to marry her. Before she can send her ultimatum, George appears with the news that he has been commissioned a captain and will lead his own company into battle, and with that news Editha gives him the letter to read "sometime" and experiences a near swoon of desire. Editha prays for George's safety, speaking to God with "the implication of a mutual understanding," but the inevitable happens, and George dies in his first skirmish. Editha and her father then travel from upstate New York to visit George's mother in Iowa. The old lady has received Editha's letter among George's things, and she reproves Editha bitterly:

> You thought it would be all right for my George, *your* George, to kill the sons of those miserable mothers and the husbands of those girls that you would never see the faces of.

With that, Mrs. Gearson orders Editha to remove her mourning black: "Take it off, take it off, before I tear it from your back." Editha is left to revel in her tragedy, consoled by her judgment of Mrs. Gearson as vulgar. "Editha" has been much anthologized and is usually praised for its dramatic clash between the realistic and the romantic temperaments.

OTHER MAJOR WORKS

LONG FICTION: *Their Wedding Journey*, 1872; *A Chance Acquaintance*, 1873; *A Foregone Conclusion*, 1875; *The Lady of the Aroostook*, 1879; *The*

Undiscovered Country, 1880; *Doctor Breen's Practice*, 1881; *A Modern Instance*, 1882; *A Woman's Reason*, 1883; *The Rise of Silas Lapham*, 1885; *Indian Summer*, 1886; *April Hopes*, 1887; *The Minister's Charge: Or, The Apprenticeship of Lemuel Barker*, 1887; *Annie Kilburn*, 1888; *A Hazard of New Fortunes*, 1889; *The Shadow of a Dream*, 1890; *An Imperative Duty*, 1891; *The Quality of Mercy*, 1892; *The Coast of Bohemia*, 1893; *The World of Chance*, 1893; *A Traveler from Altruria*, 1894; *A Parting and a Meeting*, 1896; *The Day of Their Wedding*, 1896; *An Open-Eyed Conspiracy: An Idyl of Saratoga*, 1897; *The Landlord at Lion's Head*, 1897; *The Story of a Play*, 1898; *Ragged Lady*, 1899; *Their Silver Wedding Journey*, 1899; *The Kentons*, 1902; *The Son of Royal Langbirth*, 1904; *Miss Bellard's Inspiration*, 1905; *Through the Eye of the Needle*, 1907; *Fennel and Rue*, 1908; *New Leaf Mills*, 1913; *The Leatherwood God*, 1916; *The Vacation of the Kelwyns*, 1920; *Mrs. Farrell*, 1921.

PLAYS: *The Parlor Car*, pb. 1876; *A Counterfeit Presentment*, pb. 1877; *Out of the Question*, pb. 1877; *The Register*, pb. 1884; *A Sea-Change*, pb. 1887; *The Mouse-Trap, and Other Farces*, pb. 1889; *A Letter of Introduction*, pb. 1892; *The Albany Depot*, pb. 1892; *The Unexpected Guests*, pb. 1893; *A Previous Engagement*, pb. 1897; *An Indian Giver*, pb. 1900; *Room Forty-Five*, pb. 1900; *The Smoking Car*, pb. 1900; *Parting Friends*, pb. 1911; *The Complete Plays of W. D. Howells*, pb. 1960 (Walter J. Meserve, editor).

POETRY: *Poems of Two Friends*, 1860 (with John J. Piatt); *Poems*, 1873; *Samson*, 1874; *Priscilla: A Comedy*, 1882; *A Sea Change: Or, Love's Stowaway*, 1884; *Poems*, 1886; *Stops of Various Quills*, 1895; *The Mother and the Father*, 1909; *Pebbles, Monochromes, and Other Modern Poems, 1891-1916*, 2000 (Edwin H. Cady, editor).

NONFICTION: *Lives and Speeches of Abraham Lincoln and Hannibal Hamlin*, 1860 (with others); *Venetian Life*, 1866; *Italian Journeys*, 1867; *Tuscan Cities*, 1885; *Modern Italian Poets*, 1887; *A Boy's Town*, 1890; *Criticism and Fiction*, 1891; *My Year in a Log Cabin*, 1893; *My Literary Passions*, 1895; *Impressions and Experiences*, 1896; *Stories of Ohio*, 1897; *Literary Friends and Acquaintances*, 1900; *Heroines of Fiction*, 1901; *Literature and Life*, 1902; *Letters Home*, 1903;

London Films, 1905; *Certain Delightful English Towns*, 1906; *Roman Holidays*, 1908; *Seven English Cities*, 1909; *Imaginary Interviews*, 1910; *My Mark Twain*, 1910; *Familiar Spanish Travels*, 1913; *Years of My Youth*, 1916; *Eighty Years and After*, 1921; *The Life and Letters of William Dean Howells*, 1928 (M. Howells, editor); *A Realist in the American Theatre: Selected Drama Criticism of William Dean Howells*, 1992 (Brenda Murphy, editor); *Selected Literary Criticism*, 1993 (3 volumes); *Letters, Fictions, Lives: Henry James and William Dean Howells*, 1997 (Michael Anesko, editor).

CHILDREN'S LITERATURE: *Christmas Every Day, and Other Stories Told for Children*, 1893.

BIBLIOGRAPHY

Abeln, Paul. *William Dean Howells and the Ends of Realism*. New York: Routledge, 2005. Analysis of Howell's late works, including his short story "The Critical Bookstore." Places him in the context of American literary realism, including the writings of his contemporaries Mark Twain and Henry James.

Cady, Edwin H. *The Road to Realism: The Early Years, 1837-1885, of William Dean Howells*. Syracuse, N.Y.: Syracuse University Press, 1956.

_____. *The Realist at War: The Mature Years, 1885-1920, of William Dean Howells*. Syracuse, N.Y.: Syracuse University Press, 1958. Cady's two biographical volumes are classic resources for information on Howells's life and the evolution of his literary theories.

Carter, Everett. *Howells and the Age of Realism*. Philadelphia: J. B. Lippincott, 1954. Howells has always been identified with the critical dicta of realism, and this book establishes the historical context well.

Claybaugh, Amanda. "The Autobiography of a Substitute: Trauma, History, Howells." *Yale Journal of Criticism* 18, no. 1 (Spring, 2005): 45-65. Describes how in "A Fearful Responsibility" and some of his other works Howells sought to reconcile the divisions in American society after the Civil War. Explores how his attempts failed, and how both his life and his fiction epitomize the individual traumas that marked the war's aftermath.

Eble, Kenneth E. *William Dean Howells*. 2d ed. Boston: Twayne, 1982. An excellent introduction to Howells in the Twayne series, although devoted almost entirely to the major novels.

Goodman, Susan, and Carl Dawson. *William Dean Howells: A Writer's Life*. Berkeley: University of California Press, 2005. Critically acclaimed biography that offers a comprehensive account of Howell's life. Describes his complex personality and discusses his significance to American literature. Includes illustrations and bibliography.

Howells, William Dean. *Selected Short Stories of William Dean Howells*. Edited by Ruth Bardon. Athens: Ohio University Press, 1997. Meticulously edited collection of thirteen stories plus generous annotations of thirty-three others. The introduction, the notes, and the works cited list make this a valuable work for Howells scholars.

Klinkowitz, Jerome. "Ethic and Aesthetic: The Basil and Isabel March Stories of William Dean Howells." *Modern Fiction Studies* 16 (Autumn, 1970): 303-322. A good analysis, and one of the few periodical essays devoted to Howells's short fiction.

Lamb, Robert Paul, and G. R. Thompson, eds. *A Companion to American Fiction, 1865-1914*. Malden, Mass.: Blackwell, 2005. Collection of essays about American fiction published after the Civil War and before the start of World War II that help place Howells in the context of his contemporaries and the literary movements of the period. Howells's short fiction is mentioned in an essay by J. Gerald Kennedy; a broader overview and more detailed analysis of his work is provided in Michael Anesko's essay "William Dean Howells and the Bourgeois Quotidian: Affection, Skepticism, Disillusion."

Lynn, Kenneth S. *William Dean Howells: An American Life*. New York: Harcourt Brace Jovanovich, 1970. Excellent critical and biographical study.

Stratman, Gregory J. *Speaking for Howells: Charting the Dean's Career Through the Language of His Characters*. Lanham, Md.: University Press of America, 2001. Analyzes the use of dialogue in Howells's work. Includes bibliographical references and an index.

Frank Day

LANGSTON HUGHES

Born: Joplin, Missouri; February 1, 1902
Died: New York, New York; May 22, 1967

PRINCIPAL SHORT FICTION
The Ways of White Folks, 1934
Simple Speaks His Mind, 1950
Laughing to Keep from Crying, 1952
Simple Takes a Wife, 1953
Simple Stakes a Claim, 1957
The Best of Simple, 1961
Something in Common, and Other Stories, 1963
Simple's Uncle Sam, 1965
The Return of Simple, 1994
Short Stories, 1996

OTHER LITERARY FORMS

Although perhaps best known for his poetry, Langston Hughes explored almost every literary genre. His prose includes novels; humorous books; historical, biographical, autobiographical, and cultural works; translations; and lyrics, librettos, plays, and scripts. His total output includes more than seventy volumes, as well as numerous articles, poems, and stories that have not yet been collected.

ACHIEVEMENTS

Langston Hughes has been acknowledged both before and after his death as the most influential African American writer in the English-speaking world. As a leader of the Harlem Renaissance, he not only wrote in a variety of genres but also edited and encouraged the literary, dramatic, and musical productions of other people of color. Recognition came during his lifetime as early as 1925, when he won the Poetry Prize given by *Opportunity* magazine and the Spingarn prizes of *Crisis* magazine for both poetry and essay writing. His novel *Not Without Laughter* (1930) won the Harmon Gold Medal in 1931. That year he received his first Rosenwald Fellowship, an award repeated in 1941. His receipt of the John Simon Guggenheim Memorial Foundation Fellowship in 1935, the National Academy of Arts and Letters Award for Literature in 1946, and the Ainsfield-Wolf Award in 1953 continued to keep him in the forefront of the literary community, particularly in New York, throughout his life. His alma mater, Lincoln University, awarded him an honorary doctorate in 1943, and he received others from Howard University and Case Western Reserve University in 1963 and 1964, respectively.

BIOGRAPHY

James Mercer Langston Hughes came from an educated family whose energies were spent primarily in entrepreneurial efforts to combat poverty and institutionalized racism in order to survive. His life repeats a well-known pattern of early twentieth century African American families: a resourceful mother who rented out their home to boarders, a father who had to leave home to find work, a grandmother who cared for him during his early years, and a stepfather. He grew up in the Midwest--Kansas, Illinois, and Ohio--and participated in athletics, as well as in literary activities in high school.

Graduating from Central High School in Lincoln, Illinois, in 1920, Hughes attended Columbia University before shipping out on liners bound for Africa and the Netherlands. He also traveled extensively in Europe before returning to the United States in 1925. Then, in 1929, he received a B.A. from Lincoln University in Pennsylvania. Hughes at first subsisted with the help of patrons, but gradually he began to earn a living on the proceeds from his writings and his poetry readings. Although mainly basing himself in Harlem in New York City, Hughes continued to travel extensively. He won numerous prizes, grants, and fellowships for his literary achievements before his death in 1967.

ANALYSIS

Langston Hughes records in *The Big Sea: An Autobiography* (1940) his feelings upon first seeing Africa: " . . . when I saw the dust-green hills in the sunlight, something took hold of me inside. My Africa, Motherland of the Negro peoples! And me a Negro! The real thing!" The trip to Africa confirmed what he already knew--that the subject matter of his writings would reflect his desire "to write seriously and as well as I knew how about the Negro people." Most of Hughes's short stories concern themselves with black people presented from many different perspectives and in both tragic and comic dimensions. Even when a white is the protagonist of a story, as in "Little Dog," the gentle black man to whom Miss Briggs is attracted is given special focus. Hughes, however, is not racist in his presentation. People, regardless of their racial background, are people first participating in a common humanity before they are individuals distorted by prejudice based on ignorance, by fear, or by social conditions which create a spiritual and psychological malaise, sometimes crippling in its effect.

"LITTLE DOG"

"Little Dog" tells the story of a white and gaunt middle-aged woman, head bookkeeper of a coal and coke firm for twenty-one years, who, because of her own sense of prudence, responsibility, and concern, sublimates her own desires to care for her mother, and then, after her mother's death, is left alone and lonely. Although she keeps busy, is comfortably situated, and does not think too much of what she may be missing, she occasionally wonders why she knows no one whom she can appreciate as a friend. One day she inexplicably stops the taxicab in which she is riding in front of a pet shop featuring in its window "fuzzy little white dogs," and she purchases for herself a puppy at a very steep price. She arranges with the janitor of her apartment building, "a tow-headed young Swede," to provide food for her dog, which she names Flips, and soon her life revolves around activities centering on Flips.

One day the janitor does not show up to feed the dog; several days pass until Miss Briggs decides she needs to go down to the basement to search out the janitor. With her dog by her side, she knocks at a door behind which she hears sounds of "happy laughter, and kids squalling, and people moving." The door is opened by a small black boy and soon Miss Briggs discovers that the "tall broad-shouldered Negro" standing amidst the children is the new janitor.

The image patterns and juxtapositions in the story now begin to form meaningful patterns. The white woman, living "upstairs" with the "fuzzy white dog," is contrasted with the black man and his "pretty little brown-black" children who live "downstairs." The gentle and kind black man begins to service Miss Briggs's needs, bringing more food than is good for the dog because he believes the woman desires it and because he is being paid for it; Miss Briggs, however, never tells him that meat every few days is sufficient. Soon Miss Briggs finds herself hurrying home, never realizing that it is no longer the dog but rather the nightly visits of the janitor that compel her to hurry. One evening her words inadvertently reveal her subconscious needs. The black janitor has just left after delivering Flips's food and she can hear him humming as he returns to his family. Suddenly Miss Briggs says to Flips: "Oh, Flips . . . I'm so hungry."

Langston Hughes (Library of Congress)

Now, although she never consciously knows why, Miss Briggs decides she needs to move; ". . . she could not bear to have this janitor come upstairs with a package of bones for Flips again. . . . Let him stay in the basement, where he belonged." The accumulation of references to bones, meat, and services provides for the reader, if not for Miss Briggs, a moment of epiphany: "He almost keeps me broke buying bones," Miss Briggs says to the tall and broad-shouldered black janitor. "True," the janitor answers her. The sustenance the black man provides for the dog is no sustenance for the gaunt and bony woman, nor is the dog, like children, sufficient to keep memory of the departed alive. Miss Briggs moves and shortly is completely forgotten by the people in the neighborhood in which she had lived.

"THANK YOU M'AM"

If Miss Briggs seems a portrait of a woman dead before she is buried, Mrs. Luella Bates Washington Jones of "Thank You M'am" is a picture of a middle-aged woman still vital and vigorous, although she, too, lives alone; and although it appears she has no children of her own, she is still potent, giving new life to a young black boy who attempts to mug her. The child is no match for the woman, who is identified with her purse so large "that it had everything in it but a hammer and nails." She drags him home with her, sees that he washes, and shares with him her frugal meal. Her presence is so overpowering that the boy is more fearful of trying to get away than of staying, but she breaks down his resistance when she speaks to him of common problems. "I was young once and I wanted things I could not get." The boy waits expecting the "but" to follow. The woman anticipates:

> You thought I was going to say, *but I didn't snatch people's pocketbooks.* Well, I wasn't going to say that. . . . I have done things, too, which I would not tell you, son. . . . Everybody's got something in common.

The woman's actions, however, tell the boy more than her words do, and at the end of the story the boy is unable to use words, although his lips try to phrase more than "Thank you M'am."

"PROFESSOR"

One of Hughes's most frequently praised stories is "Professor." Focused through the point of view of its protagonist Dr. T. Walton Brown (*T* for Tom, as in Uncle Tom?), the story examines how a black professor of sociology "bows" and "bobs" like a puppet on a string to members of the wealthy white establishment, doing only those things of which they approve, saying what they want to hear, and, although at times he knows the lies diminish him, still allowing his own needs to determine his behavior patterns.

Bitterly ironic in tone, the story begins with the juxtaposition of Brown in dinner dress against the lobby of a run-down segregated hotel and Brown cared for by a white chauffeur who tucks the professor carefully into the luxury of a limousine to carry him through the black ghetto to a private house as large as a hotel. Brown's posture and attire are carefully contrasted with the "two or three ash-colored children" who run across the street in front of the limousine, "their skinny legs and poor clothes plain in the glare of the headlights." The streets and buildings are similarly contrasted-- "the Negro streets": "pig's knuckle joints, pawnshops, beer parlors--and houses of vice, no doubt--save that these latter, at least, did not hang out their signs" with the "wide lawns and fine homes that lined the beautiful well-lighted boulevard where white people lived."

Brown has bought entry into the white establishment by prostituting himself, by accepting the degradation of the constant diminishing of his selfhood and his negritude. He listens to his white counterpart say, "Why, at our city college here we've been conducting some fine interracial experiments. I have had some colored ministers and high school teachers visit my classes. We found them most intelligent." Although at times Brown is moved to make slight and subtle protest, in the end he agrees with the biased white people, saying, "You are right."

Brown's behavior is dictated by his desire for the money the white people offer him as long as he conforms to their expectations. Money will buy Brown prestige, will enable his college to survive, and will further his career. Money will also "take his family to South America in the summer where for three months they wouldn't feel like Negroes." Thus, he dances to the "tune of Jim Crow education," diminishing both himself and his race. Although carefully constructed, the story offers no subtleties beyond the ironies present; image patterns are at a minimum, complex symbolism nonexistent. Characterization, too, is sparse. The reader learns only enough about the professor to make his behavior immediately credible, but a traditional plotline moves with careful pacing to a climax and pointed resolution, and the theme overshadows technique.

"FINE ACCOMMODATIONS"

Similar in theme and technique to "Professor" is "Fine Accommodations." In this story, a young black porter learns that Dr. Jenkins, booked into sleeping car accommodations, is not the leader of his race and the "fine man" the naïve porter expects but rather another Uncle Tom who keeps on "being a big man" by "bowing to Southern white customs," by helping to keep poor black people just where they have always been "all the time--poor and black." At the end, the porter makes the point of the story: "The last Negro passenger I had in that drawing room was a pimp from Birmingham. Now I got a professor. I guess both of them have to have ways of paying for such fine accommodations."

"BIG MEETING"

From the perspective of complexity, subtlety, and power, "Big Meeting" is a considerably better story. Told in the first person by a young black boy who, with a companion, is observing a church revival meeting held in the woods, the story recounts the boy's moment of epiphany when he realizes, if only subconsciously, that as a cynical observer rather than a participant in the ritual he is more akin to the white folks gathered to watch than to his own people. Making use of dialect and gospel songs, Hughes builds the story to a powerful sermon where the preacher recounts the betrayal of Christ to the accompaniment of echoing refrains and then moves the sermon to the cadences of poetry:

> They brought four long nails
> And put one in the palm of His left hand.
> The hammer said . . . Bam!
> They put one in the palm of His right hand.
> The hammer said . . . Bam!
> They put one through His left foot . . . Bam!

And one through His right foot . . . Bam!
. . . "Don't drive it!" a woman screamed. "Don't drive them nails! For Christ's sake! Oh! Don't drive 'em!"

In the woods observing the action, the narrator and his companion are near enough to a car full of white people to overhear what they are saying as they comment in ways showing their biases, limitations, and prejudices. As the narrator hears these comments, he begins to respond, but not enough to cause him to identify with the participants in the service. Rather, both he and his companion seem more concerned with the behavior of their mothers who are taking part in the church rituals.

At the climax of the story, the narrator hears his mother's voice: "Were you there when they crucified my Lord?/ Were you there when they nailed Him to the tree?" At the same time as the mother cries out the questions, the preacher opens his arms wide against the white canvas tent, and his body reflects a crosslike shadow. As the mother asks the question again, the white people in the car suddenly drive away creating a swirl of dust, and the narrator cries after them, "Don't go. . . . They're about to call for sinners. . . . Don't go!"

The boy's cry to the white people reflects his understanding of the parallel setup between the white people and the betrayers of Christ. Hughes goes further than this, however, and provides in the last sentence of the story an epiphanic moment: "I didn't realize I was crying until I tasted my tears in my mouth." The epiphany projects a revelation dimly understood by the narrator but clearly present--that as bad as the white people's behavior seemed, his own rejection of his people and heritage was worse.

OTHER MAJOR WORKS

LONG FICTION: *Not Without Laughter*, 1930; *Tambourines to Glory*, 1958.

PLAYS: *Little Ham*, pr. 1935; *Mulatto*, pb. 1935; *Troubled Island*, pr. 1935 (opera libretto); *Don't You Want to Be Free?*, pb. 1938; *Freedom's Plow*, pb. 1943; *Street Scene*, pr., pb. 1947 (lyrics; music by Kurt Weill and Elmer Rice); *Simply Heavenly*, pr. 1957 (opera libretto); *Black Nativity*, pr. 1961; *Five Plays*, pb. 1963 (Walter Smalley, editor); *Tambourines to Glory*, pr., pb. 1963; *Jerico-Jim Crow*, pr. 1964; *The Prodigal Son*, pr. 1965.

SCREENPLAY: *Way Down South*, 1939 (with Clarence Muse).

POETRY: *The Weary Blues*, 1926; *Fine Clothes to the Jew*, 1927; *Dear Lovely Death*, 1931; *The Negro Mother and Other Dramatic Recitations*, 1931; *Scottsboro Limited: Four Poems and a Play in Verse*, 1932; *The Dream Keeper, and Other Poems*, 1932; *A New Song*, 1938; *Shakespeare in Harlem*, 1942; *Jim Crow's Last Stand*, 1943; *Lament for Dark Peoples*, 1944; *Fields of Wonder*, 1947; *One Way Ticket*, 1949; *Montage of a Dream Deferred*, 1951; *Selected Poems of Langston Hughes*, 1959; *Ask Your Mama: Or, Twelve Moods for Jazz*, 1961; *The Panther and the Lash: Or, Poems of Our Times*, 1967; *The Poems, 1921-1940*, 2001 (volume 1 of *The Collected Works of Langston Hughes*; Dolan Hubbard, editor); *The Poems, 1941-1950*, 2001 (volume 2 of *The Collected Works of Langston Hughes*; Hubbard, editor); *The Poems, 1951-1967*, 2001 (volume 3 of *The Collected Works of Langston Hughes*; Hubbard, editor).

NONFICTION: *The Big Sea: An Autobiography*, 1940; *Famous American Negroes*, 1954; *Famous Negro Music Makers*, 1955; *The Sweet Flypaper of Life*, 1955 (photographs by Roy De Carava); *A Pictorial History of the Negro in America*, 1956 (with Milton Meltzer); *I Wonder as I Wander: An Autobiographical Journey*, 1956; *Famous Negro Heroes of America*, 1958; *Fight for Freedom: The Story of the NAACP*, 1962; *Black Magic: A Pictorial History of the Negro in American Entertainment*, 1967 (with Meltzer); *Black Misery*, 1969 (illustrations by Arouni); *Arna Bontemps---Langston Hughes Letters: 1925-1967*, 1980; *Remember Me to Harlem: The Letters of Langston Hughes and Carl Van Vechten, 1925-1964*, 2001 (Emily Bernard, editor).

TRANSLATIONS: *Masters of the Dew*, 1947 (of Jacques Roumain; with Mercer Cook); *Cuba Libre*, 1948 (of Nicolás Guillén; with Ben Carruthers); *Gypsy Ballads*, 1951 (of Federico García Lorca); *Selected Poems of Gabriela Mistral*, 1957.

CHILDREN'S LITERATURE: *Popo and Fijina: Children of Haiti*, 1932 (story; with Arna Bontemps); *The First Book of Negroes*, 1952; *The First Book of Rhythms*, 1954; *The First Book of Jazz*, 1955; *The First Book of the West Indies*, 1955; *The First Book of Africa*, 1960.

EDITED TEXTS: *The Poetry of the Negro, 1746-1949*, 1949 (with Arna Bontemps); *The Book of Negro Folklore*, 1959 (with Bontemps); *New Negro Poets: U.S.A.*, 1964; *The Book of Negro Humor*, 1966; *The Best Short Stories by Negro Writers: An Anthology from 1899 to the Present*, 1967.

MISCELLANEOUS: *The Langston Hughes Reader*, 1958; *The Collected Works of Langston Hughes*, 2001-2004 (16 volumes).

BIBLIOGRAPHY

Borden, Anne. "Heroic 'Hussies' and 'Brilliant Queers': Genderracial Resistance in the Works of Langston Hughes." *African American Review* 28 (Fall, 1994): 333-345. Discusses Hughes's focus on the interrelationship between gender and racial issues, as well as his treatment of gender issues within the black community--particularly the ways in which gender affects the struggle to maintain community in a racist society.

Dickinson, Donald C. *A Bio-bibliography of Langston Hughes, 1902-1967*. 2d ed. Hamden, Conn.: Archon Books, 1972. Following its preface by Arna Bontemps, a major scholar and critic of the Harlem Renaissance and a contemporary of Hughes, the book provides both older and updated assessments of Hughes's achievement. Part 1 is a biography, which incorporates information throughout Hughes's life; part 2 includes all his work through 1965, except short newspaper articles, song lyrics, and phonograph records.

Emanuel, James A. *Langston Hughes*. New York: Twayne, 1967. This survey of Hughes's work as a poet and fiction writer emphasizes the reflection of African American speech patterns, rhythms, and idiomatic expressions in his work, as well as the folk culture behind these elements, which he turned into literary devices. Points out pan-African themes in the writings and the peculiar struggle of a writer with Hughes's background in both the sociological and literary contexts.

Gelfant, Blanche H., ed. *The Columbia Companion to the Twentieth-Century American Short Story*. New York: Columbia University Press, 2000. Includes a chapter in which Hughes's short stories are analyzed.

Harper, Donna Akiba Sullivan. "Langston's Simple Genius." *New Crisis* 109, no. 1 (January/February, 2002): 32. Focuses on Simple, the fictional character featured in many of Hughes's short stories. Details the character's appearance in Hughes's column in the Chicago Defendernewspaper and in his subsequent collections of short stories. This issue of the periodical also reprints Hughes's story "Simple and the NAACP."

_____. *Not So Simple: The "Simple" Stories by Langston Hughes*. Columbia: University of Missouri Press, 1995. Traces the evolution of Hughes's character Jesse B. Semple, better known as Simple, from his first appearance in Hughes's column for the *Chicago Defender* to six books of short stories and a play about the character. Analyzes the short stories, compares Hughes's work to other writers, and recounts Hughes's experiences working for the newspaper.

Hokanson, Robert O'Brien. "Jazzing It Up: The Be-Bop Modernism of Langston Hughes." *Mosaic* 31 (December, 1998): 61-82. Examines how Hughes uses be-bop jazz to challenge both the boundaries between music and poetry and the distinctions between popular and high culture. Argues that Hughes's work constitutes a distinctively "popular" modernism that uses jazz to ground its poetic experimentation in the vernacular tradition of African American culture.

Leach, Laurie F. *Langston Hughes: A Biography*. Westport, Conn.: Greenwood Press, 2004. An overview of Hughes's life and development as a playwright, poet, and journalist.

Miller, R. Baxter. *The Art and Imagination of Langston Hughes*. Lexington: University Press of Kentucky, 2006. Argues that readers often miss the complexity in Hughes's work because it appears so accessible. Demonstrates the existence of a "constant symbiotic bond" between the lyrical and the historical in Hughes's works.

Rager, Cheryl R., and John Edgar Tidwell, eds. *Montage of a Dream: The Art and Life of Langston Hughes*. Columbia: University of Missouri Press, 2007. Most of the essays here are previously unpublished and all offer interesting ways of looking at Hughes's writing. Two of the essays focus on his short-story collection *The Ways of White Folks*, and there are numerous references to the short stories that are listed in the index. Some of the other essays discuss many of his lesser-known works, including his autobiographies and translations.

Rampersad, Arnold. *The Life of Langston Hughes*. 2 vols. New York: Oxford University Press, 1986-1988. This major critical biography illustrates not only the triumphs but also the struggles of the man and the writer. The importance of Hughes in the Harlem Renaissance and his symbolic significance in the developing artistic and imaginative consciousness of African American writers come alive in concrete examples in volume 1, *I, Too, Sing America*, and volume 2, *I Dream a World*. These titles, drawn from Hughes's poetry, reveal the themes illustrating the writer's life and detail his own characterization of his struggle.

Tracy, Steven C, ed. *Langston Hughes and the Blues*. Urbana: University of Illinois Press, 1988. Uses the folk traditions of African and African American culture as background but concentrates primarily on the blues tradition within that culture as a way of interpreting Hughes's work. The intellectualizing of this tradition and the deliberate incorporation of the blues dimension in imaginative literature is a major emphasis, along with the oral tradition in African culture. This historical survey of the blues as an art form and its application in criticism seeks to counteract the dismissal of some of Hughes's more popular works by critics such as Donald C. Dickinson (above).

_____. *A Historical Guide to Langston Hughes*. New York: Oxford University Press, 2004. Collection of essays that include discussions of Hughes in the twenty-first century, his use of place and of African American music in his works, and his handling of gender and racial issues. Includes a brief biography and bibliographical essay.

Mary Rohrberger
Updated by Emma Coburn Norris

WILLIAM HUMPHREY

Born: Clarksville, Texas; June 18, 1924
Died: Hudson, New York; August 20, 1997

PRINCIPAL SHORT FICTION
The Last Husband, and Other Stories, 1953
A Time and a Place, 1968
The Collected Stories of William Humphrey, 1985
September Song, 1992

OTHER LITERARY FORMS

Novelist William Humphrey (HUHM-free) began his literary career in the late 1940's as a short-story writer, contributing to a number of the United States' better magazines--*The New Yorker*, *Accent*, *Esquire*, and *The Atlantic*--and publishing a collection of stories before his first novel appeared. His stories have attracted favorable critical comment, but most commentators rate his novels above his stories. Of his novels, the best known are *Home from the Hill* (1958) and *The Ordways* (1965); he also wrote *Proud Flesh* (1973), *Hostages to Fortune* (1984), and *No Resting Place* (1989). Many critics think Humphrey's best piece of writing is *Farther Off from Heaven* (1977), a memoir of the first thirteen years of his life. In addition to his fiction, Humphrey authored several hunting and fishing stories first published in magazines and later reprinted as small books: *The Spawning Run* (1970), *My Moby Dick* (1978), and *Open Season: Sporting Adventures* (1986).

ACHIEVEMENTS

The publisher Alfred A. Knopf called William Humphrey's *Home from the Hill* the best novel to come out of Texas. The book earned for Humphrey the Carr P. Collins Award of the Texas Institute of Letters for best book of fiction by a Texas author in 1958, and it was a finalist for the National Book Award. The success of Humphrey's first novel, which was made into a popular motion picture in 1960, led to his winning a grant from the National Institute of Arts and Letters, which aided him in the writing of his second novel, *The Ordways*, which was selected by the Literary Guild, enjoyed six printings in its first year, and won for Humphrey a second Texas Institute of Letters prize. In 1995. Humphrey also received the Lon Tinkle Award from the Texas Institute of Letters for excellence sustained throughout a career.

BIOGRAPHY

William Humphrey was very secretive about his life, saying once that he considered it bragging to fill out forms sent by *Who's Who* and other dictionaries of biography. Therefore, the entries about Humphrey in such publications are limited to the kind of material found on dust jackets. In later years, he was slightly more forthcoming in interviews and published a memoir that covers the first thirteen years of his life, the years he spent in his native Clarksville, Texas. From notes, hints, and "slips" by the author, it is possible to reconstruct some parts of his life. He was the son of working-class parents (his father was an auto mechanic), and he suffered an affliction as a child that required braces for his legs. He and his mother left Clarksville, never to return, after his father was killed in a car wreck in 1937. Humphrey and his mother moved to Dallas, Texas. He attended Southern Methodist University and the University of Texas at Austin, apparently never receiving a degree. He mentioned in an interview published in 1988 that he left Texas in 1943 during his last semester of college. He decided to leave while sitting in the middle of a German class, so he stood up and walked out, telling the professor that he was headed for Chicago. Where he went is not clear, but for most of the rest of his life he lived in the state of New York, residing in the city of Hudson beginning in the early 1960's. Humphrey, apparently without benefit of a degree, lectured at several colleges, but for most of his life he supported himself, his wife Dorothy, and his daughter Antonia by his writing.

Humphrey told interviewer Ashby Bland Crowder that he studied art between the ages of thirteen and eighteen. Then he found, when he tried to join the Navy during World War II, that he was color-blind. He gave up art and turned to writing, going to New York with a five-act play about Benjamin Franklin. The play was never produced, and Humphrey turned to the writing of fiction. The short-story writer he most admired was fellow Texan Katherine Anne Porter. She wrote her nephew, after reading two of Humphrey's stories in *Accent*, that the young writer had taken two of her stories, "The Cracked Looking-Glass" and "A Day's Work," and turned them into his own. The Humphrey stories, "In Sickness and in Health" and "Man with a Family," do indeed bear remarkable resemblances to Porter's stories. Later, in a letter cited in Joan Givner's *Katherine Ann Porter: A Life* (1982), Humphrey admitted to Porter that he had stolen his first published story from "A Day's Work" and that he always wrote with her stories open to the paragraphs that he most admired. There is no question that Humphrey's stories owe a great debt to Porter's works, especially in their irony and emphasis on place.

Humphrey, whose interest in hunting and fishing can be traced to his father, devoted much of his writing in later years to nonfiction stories about outdoor sports, though his interest in the out-of-doors did not produce a large body of work. The same can be said of his fictional output. In more than forty years, he produced five novels and more than twenty stories.

Humphrey's best work is about Red River County, Texas, but after 1977, the year he published his memoir *Farther Off from Heaven*, about his childhood there, he wrote a number of novels about life in other places. *Hostages to Fortune* is set in Hudson, New York, and describes the effects of a young person's suicide on his parents; *No Resting Place* is about the Cherokees' being uprooted from the South and marched to Texas along the "Trail of Tears" in the 1830's.

In April, 1997, Humphrey was diagnosed with cancer of the larynx. Despite his illness, Humphrey continued to write almost until the end. He died on August 20, 1997, at the age of seventy-three.

William Humphrey (Library of Congress)

ANALYSIS

Most of William Humphrey's stories are set in and around his native Red River County, Texas, which is located in the far northeastern corner of the state. The county borders the state of Oklahoma, and many of the stories take place across the Red River in "the Little Dixie" section of Oklahoma. Northeastern Texas and southeastern Oklahoma were settled by southerners who came west before and after the Civil War, Indians driven west when the South was being cleared of Native Americans during the rapid expansion of the 1820's and 1830's, and slaves--later freed--brought in by both whites and Indians.

THE LAST HUSBAND, AND OTHER STORIES

Humphrey's ancestors came into his part of Texas following the Civil War, and it is this part of the world that Humphrey always understood best, even though he left Clarksville for good in 1937. His best stories and novels are about the people and places he knew when he was a boy growing up in Clarksville. His first book of stories, *The Last Husband, and Other Stories*, shows clearly how much Humphrey is dependent on his homeland for the success of his work. The six best stories in the volume are Texas-based. Five take place in and around Clarksville, and one is about a transplanted Texan isolated in a northern city and longing for home. The four stories set in the East, where Humphrey lived during his writing apprenticeship, lack the life found in his Clarksville stories. It is not that the themes are deficient or that the style suffers in his eastern stories. There are excellent scenes, and some of the characters are as well developed as those in his regional works. Something is missing, however, and it is very clear that it is a sense of time and place that Humphrey must have in order to tell his stories and develop his points. He understands the people of Red River County and can make them speak a language that is real. When he shifts to New York, his "other" setting, place becomes unreal for him. The sense of kinship with the people who speak his language and share his customs disappears. The stories and novels suffer. Even his later works--produced after a lifetime as a fiction writer--lack the immediacy of his earlier works, his works about Clarksville.

The non-Texas stories, written while he was still in his Katherine Anne Porter phase, are technically correct and usually well written. They are typical of the pieces published in highbrow magazines in the years immediately following World War II. The people are modern and sophisticated, and their lives in the suburbs are as hollow as up-to-date social critics and old-fashioned moralists would like one to believe they are. Furthermore, following the modern mode of fiction, the stories are ironic and ultimately depressing.

The book's title story is about a man named Edward Gavin who has a series of mistresses in a desperate attempt to get his wife, an unsuccessful artist with a successful sister, to pay attention to him and live the kind of life that married people are traditionally supposed to live. Edward, whom the reader knows only through a narrator, loses his battle with his wife of two decades, proving that his infidelities netted him nothing. His wife's winning gets her nothing either. They are as dead as people in a wasteland always are.

"The Last Husband" is not a bad story until one begins to compare it to Humphrey's best regional work. His early story "The Hardys" makes a nice contrast to "The Last Husband." The Hardys are an old couple closing their home to move in with their children. Mr. Hardy was widowed before he met his present wife, and Mrs. Hardy has spent years being jealous. The reader learns, in this story, told first from one point of view, and then from another, that Mr. Hardy has long since forgotten his first wife and that Mrs. Hardy has no need to be jealous. (Interestingly, Edward Gavin summarizes "The Hardys" for the narrator when the two are riding the train home from Grand Central Station one night.) "The Hardys" is filled with the homey regional details and carefully rendered speech that make for excellent fiction.

"Quail for Mr. Forester" is a typical Humphrey story in that the reader sees the changing ways of the South through the eyes of a young boy--a method Humphrey uses again and again. Mr. Forester's family once made up the local aristocracy, but in recent years the Foresters have come down in the world. The narrator's father, a top-notch hunter, kills some excellent quail and invites Mr. Forester to dine. The dinner conversation is all about the decline of the Old South, which, ironically, is felt much more keenly by the narrator's family of working-class people than by Mr. Forester. At the end of an evening talking about the glory days before the Civil War, the boy, still awed, muses, "I felt that there was no hope for me in these mean times I had been born into."

The mean times of the North also trouble the southern woman in "A Fresh Snow." She married a man from outside her region and is now sitting sadly in her room watching the flakes fall and thinking how far she is from home and how different the customs are. When her young son comes home and speaks in the harsh dialect of the industrial East, "she sat him on her lap and rocked him softly, his head against her breast, while she told him all about the South, where he was born."

A TIME AND A PLACE

The stories in William Humphrey's second volume *A Time and a Place* are all set in Depression-era Texas and Oklahoma. Heavily ironic, as most of his stories are, these narratives depict the harshness of life during the years of the Dust Bowl, the oil strikes, and the closing years of the Old South in Texas and Oklahoma, a world eradicated by World War II. There are a number of good stories among the ten in this volume. One of the best and most often discussed is "A Voice from the Woods," which flashes back from the undefined present to the time when the outlaws Bonnie and Clyde and Pretty Boy Floyd were heroes to the poor people of Texas and Oklahoma. The narrator, who grew up in Clarksville, lives in the East. His mother is visiting him and his eastern wife, and as they sit drinking beer, they hear the cooing of a mourning dove. The sound recalls to the mother the time that a man she once loved and considered marrying robbed the bank in Clarksville and was killed in a gunfight on the street. She and the son, a very small boy at the time, witnessed the death of the robber. She sits thinking how different her life might have been had she married Travis Winfield, who died in the arms of his latest love, a redheaded woman. The mother recalls how she had a good life with a good husband, but she says, "And yet, thinking of that red-headed woman . . . I felt, well, I don't know what else to call it if not jealousy."

There is a certain sentimentality to the story, but Humphrey evokes the time and the place and the attitude of the people as well as anyone writing about Texas in the 1930's ever has. An equally effective story at evoking the era is "Mouth of Brass," about a brief friendship between a small boy and a black tamale vendor. The vendor travels all over town during the week, but on Saturdays he sets up his tamale boxes in the town square, where "the population doubled--in ginning season tripled--as country folks poured in. . . ." One Saturday, Finus, the vendor, sells a dozen tamales to a little boy who is buying them for his family waiting just off the square. When the boy wolfs down five of the tamales on the way back to the family, the father thinks Finus took advantage of the child's age to cheat him, becomes enraged, and confronts the vendor. One thing leads to another, and the man knifes Finus. Naturally, in the Deep South of the 1930's, it is determined that the white man was provoked, and he is let off on self-defense. The little boy, who was once allowed to make his rounds with Finus, experiences an epiphany about race relations and will never be the same.

These stories and many others in Humphrey's collections paint vivid pictures of the South as it was when Humphrey was a boy and was learning about the injustices of life. His works are filled with the ironies to be encountered in a merciless universe devoid of justice and quick to plunge human beings into misery. His stories are often bleak and hopeless: Men are forced into crime by circumstances and then are punished unmercifully; the underclass is beaten down by the rich; children are jerked suddenly into adulthood by death and destruction. Bad as it is, however, there is a richness to the life found in northeast Texas. Traditions and stories and customs are passed down from generation to generation by word of mouth. Moments of unsurpassed joy balance--at least partially--the violence and cruelty found there and are well described in the writings of William Humphrey.

SEPTEMBER SONG

This collection of twenty stories was also Humphrey's final published book, appearing in 1992, five years before he died. These stories revolve around themes of aging, from the frustrations of dealing with one's declining physical capacities to the need to attach meaning and purpose to one's life. Their quality is uneven, but included here is some of Humphrey's best writing.

Not surprisingly, the stories assume a somber, sad tone, yet they are also full of humor. In "The Dead Languages," for example, hearing loss is both amusing--as the protagonist, a retired reporter, confuses words, such as "cows" with "clouds"--and poignantly tragic in the accuracy and detail with which both the physical loss and other people's reactions to the reporter are described. In the opening story, "Portrait of the Artist as an Old Man" (a reference to the novel by James Joyce, who enjoys other allusions in Humphrey's work), an aging Texas-born writer fabricates wild stories about his life during an interview with the young journalist who has been asked to prepare the writer's obituary.

Human beings' ultimate lack of control over the outcome of life, despite best-laid plans, is a recurring theme, perhaps best developed in the longest story of the collection, "The Apple of Discord." Here, an apple farmer hopes to be able to pass his land to one of three daughters but instead is compelled to sell the land to a developer. The farmer then attempts to give the money to his daughters and follows that with a suicide attempt to spite his girls. One daughter, however, upsets his plan.

The collection's title story is one of Humphrey's best, featuring a seventy-six-year-old protagonist who decides to divorce her husband and reunite with a former lover. The very decline in her husband that has partially prompted the decision is what forces her, in the end, to stay, as she realizes that "he could not look after himself."

Molly Giles, reviewing the book in the *Los Angeles Times* and observing that some of the male characters could easily be "the same boys in Mr. Humphrey's Texas novels, grown up," noted that their older counterparts serve to remind readers that "there isn't such a long long time between May and September." Jonathan Yardley, in a review of the collection appearing in *The Washington Post*, summed up not only *September Song* but also Humphrey's work in general when he described the stories as "interesting and admirable" achievements in serious fiction rather than commercial success and "fashionable glitz."

OTHER MAJOR WORKS

LONG FICTION: *Home from the Hill*, 1958; *The Ordways*, 1965; *Proud Flesh*, 1973; *Hostages to Fortune*, 1984; *No Resting Place*, 1989.

NONFICTION: *The Spawning Run*, 1970; *Ah, Wilderness: The Frontier in American Literature*, 1977; *Farther Off from Heaven*, 1977; *My Moby Dick*, 1978; *Open Season: Sporting Adventures*, 1986; *Far from Home: Selected Letters of William Humphrey*, 2007 (Ashby Bland Crowder, editor).

BIBLIOGRAPHY

Almon, Bert. *William Humphrey: Destroyer of Myths*. Denton: University of North Texas Press, 1998. A comprehensive critical study of Humphrey's fiction, including a discussion of the role of Texas as a setting in his work. Includes a bibliography and an index.

Crowder, Ashby Bland. *Wakeful Anguish: A Literary Biography of William Humphrey*. Baton Rouge: Louisiana State University Press, 2004. Incorporating personal interviews and correspondence, Crowder's biography sheds light on the man and his work. Three of the chapters are devoted to the short-story collections *The Last Husband, and Other Stories*, *A Time and a Place*, and *September Song*.

Givner, Joan. "Katherine Anne Porter: The Old Order and the New." In *The Texas Literary Tradition*, edited by Don Graham, et al. Austin: University of Texas Press, 1983. Givner argues that Humphrey and fellow Texan William Goyen were greatly under the influence of Porter. Here and in the biography that she wrote on Porter, Givner traces Porter's influence on the two younger writers and says that they were eager to imitate Porter and win her favor with letters and flowery dedications. The essay is also interesting because it describes the treatment Porter received in the male-dominated Texas literary establishment of the 1930's and 1940's.

Graham, Don. "Regionalism on the Ramparts: The Texas Literary Tradition." *USA Today* 115 (July, 1986): 74-76. Discusses five distinct literary regions in Texas: East Texas, West Texas, the Gulf Coast, the Border Valley, and Urban Texas. Notes how the southern culture of Texas was depicted by George Sessions Perry during the 1940's and by three East Texans--William Goyen, William Humphrey, and William A. Owens--during the 1950's and 1960's.

Grider, Sylvia, and Elizabeth Tebeaux. "Blessings into Curses: Sardonic Humor and Irony in 'A Job of the Plains.'" *Studies in Short Fiction* 23 (1986): 297-306. Grider and Tebeaux focus on Humphrey's short story "A Job of the Plains," an ironic retelling of the Book of Job as it might have happened in the Dust Bowl of Oklahoma during the Great Depression of the 1930's. Humphrey's story, according to the article's authors, delves into the meaninglessness of life, the cruelty of God's universe, and the pointlessness of human suffering. The theme becomes "the controlling theme for the remaining stories in the collection [*A Time and a Place*]. In every story, Humphrey weaves a similar naturalism into the Dust Bowl/Depression worldview." Grider and Tebeaux compare *A Time and a Place* to Sherwood Anderson's *Winesburg, Ohio* (1919).

Humphrey, William. Interview by Jose Yglesias. *Publishers Weekly* 235 (June 2, 1989): 64-65. A brief discussion of Humphrey's life and career, noting the regional background of some of his best-known fiction. In the interview section of this piece, Humphrey discusses his writing habits, his disdain for the literary establishment, and his relationships with editors, publishers, and other literary figures.

_____. "William Humphrey: Defining Southern Literature." Interview by Ashby Bland Crowder. *Mississippi Quarterly* 41 (1988): 529-540. Humphrey reveals some hitherto unknown facts about his life and hints about his method of working. The interviewer is at great pains to fix Humphrey in the canon of southern literature and to question the author closely on his relationship to William Faulkner and other authors. The persistent attempts to direct the flow of the interview to "southernness" often interrupts Humphrey's commentary on his general attitudes and his view of his place in American literature.

Lee, James Ward. *William Humphrey*. Austin, Tex.: Steck-Vaughn, 1967. One of the volumes in the Southwest Writers series, this sixty-page pamphlet was written when Humphrey had only two novels, a volume of stories, and four uncollected stories in print. The first twenty pages discuss his fourteen stories, while the rest of the study analyzes his novels *Home from the Hill* and *The Ordways*. One of the major emphases is on Humphrey's use of regional materials--the folklore, the naturalistic descriptions, and the customs of northeast Texas.

_____. "William Humphrey." In *American Novelists Since World War II*, 2d series, edited by James E. Kilber, Jr. Detroit: Gale Research, 1980. A six-page essay in which Lee updates the pamphlet he wrote in 1967, placing more emphasis on the novels, the sporting stories, and the memoir *Farther Off from Heaven*. Lee predicts that *Farther Off from Heaven* may be Humphrey's farewell to Red River County and the Clarksville of his boyhood.

Tebeaux, Elizabeth. "Irony as Art: The Short Fiction of William Humphrey." *Studies in Short Fiction* 26 (Summer, 1989): 323-334. Maintains that Humphrey's complex irony is the defining characteristic of his work. His nonheroic, dirt farmer protagonists often make errors of judgment that lead to an ironic reversal that deepens their dilemmas. Analyzes a number of stories to illustrate Humphrey's irony and parody of the tragic.

Winchell, Mark Royde. "The Achievement of William Humphrey." In *Reinventing the South: Versions of a Literary Region*. Columbia: University of Missouri Press, 2006. Analyzes Humphrey's work, including some of the short stories, to discuss his literary depiction of East Texas and other aspects of his writings. Provides biographical information.

_____. *William Humphrey*. Boise, Idaho: Boise State University, 1992. A brief pamphlet that provides a short biographical sketch and introduction to Humphrey's fiction. Suggests that the stories are best when describing a place or exploring the psychological subtleties of human relations. Discusses "The Hardys," "Quail for Mr. Forester," and "The Ballad of Jesse Neighbours" as representative of Humphrey's thematic concerns and technical skill. Analyzes "Mouth of Brass" and "The Human Fly" and appraises them as two of his best stories.

James Ward Lee

ZORA NEALE HURSTON

Born: Notasulga, Alabama; January 7, 1891
Died: Fort Pierce, Florida; January 28, 1960

PRINCIPAL SHORT FICTION

Spunk: The Selected Short Stories of Zora Neale Hurston, 1985
The Complete Stories, 1995

OTHER LITERARY FORMS

Though best known for her novels, especially *Their Eyes Were Watching God* (1937), Zora Neale Hurston (HUR-stuhn) wrote in most major genres during her forty-year career. In addition to two posthumously published collections of short stories, she wrote a few early poems, several short plays, folklore collections, essays, reportage, and an autobiography.

ACHIEVEMENTS

Zora Neale Hurston is best known as a major writer of the Harlem Renaissance literature of the 1920's. Not only was she a major contributor to this literary movement, but also she did much to characterize the style and temperament of the period; indeed, she is often referred to as the most colorful figure of the Harlem Renaissance. Though the short stories and short plays that she generated during the 1920's are fine works in their own right, they are nevertheless apprentice works when compared to her most productive period, the 1930's. During the 1930's, Hurston produced three novels, all telling examples of her creative genius, as well as two collections of folklore, the fruits of her training in anthropology and her many years of fieldwork. It is Hurston's interest in preserving the culture of the black South that remains among her most valuable contributions. Not only did she collect and preserve folklore outright, but she also used folklore, native drama, and the black idiom and dialect in most of her fiction.

Although Hurston's popularity declined during the 1940's and 1950's, and although she died in relative obscurity in 1960, scholars and critics sparked a Hurston revival during the mid-1970's. Hurston's popularity has never been greater, as her works are considered mainstays in any number of canons, among them African American literature, folklore, southern literature, feminist studies, and anthropology.

BIOGRAPHY

Zora Neale Hurston was born in 1891 in Notasulga, Alabama, the youngest daughter and the seventh of eight children born to John and Lucy Hurston. While she was a toddler, the family moved to the all-black town of Eatonville, Florida, near Orlando. Her father was a minister and local government official who wrote many of Eatonville's laws upon its incorporation and served several terms as mayor. Her mother was a homemaker who cared not only for her children but also for an extended family that included, at various times, her own mother and her brother Jim. By all accounts, Hurston's childhood was happy, almost idyllic, free from the poverty and racism that characterized much of the black experience in the South. Indeed, this wholesome upbringing informed much of Hurston's later work and earned for her the designation as an early black cultural nationalist.

Whatever idyllic aspects Hurston's childhood possessed were shattered when Hurston was about nine. The death of Hurston's beloved mother, who encouraged the young Zora to "jump at the sun," precipitated a change. This event was followed by her father's remarriage to a woman who had no interest in the children and the subsequent dismantling of the relative happiness of the Hurston household. The next several years of Hurston's life found her much displaced, living variously with older siblings and receiving only sporadic schooling.

Although exact dates are difficult to place in Hurston's early chronology because she frequently lied about her age, various sources reveal that Hurston joined a Gilbert and Sullivan traveling show when she was about fourteen as a wardrobe maid to one of the show's stars. Hurston worked for this show for several years, traveling throughout the South, sometimes without pay. It was with this show, however, that Hurston's talents as raconteur were first noticed, as she often entertained the company with stories, anecdotes, and tales from the black South, told with their own humor, mimicry, and dialect.

Hurston left her job with the Gilbert and Sullivan show in Baltimore, and, out of an intense desire to complete her education, she enrolled in the high school department of the Morgan Academy (now Morgan State University) in that city, completing the high school program in 1919. From Morgan, Hurston entered Howard University, at that time known as "the Negro Harvard," in Washington, D.C. At Howard, Hurston soon came to the attention of Alain Locke, adviser to the Howard Literary Society and later a principal critic of the New Negro movement. Locke invited Hurston to join the literary society, and she soon began publishing in *Stylus*, the Howard University literary magazine. Her first published short story, "John Redding Goes to Sea," appeared in *Stylus* in 1921.

Hurston's talent soon came to the attention of Charles S. Johnson, founder and editor of the National Urban League's magazine *Opportunity*, which held annual contests for young writers. Johnson encouraged Hurston to submit her works to *Opportunity*, which she did; "Drenched in Light" appeared in December, 1924, and "Spunk" in June, 1925. Both "Spunk" and a short play, "Color Struck," were second-place prize-winners in their respective divisions in *Opportunity*'s 1925 contest, and another short story, "Black Death," won honorable mention.

Hurston traveled to New York to attend the 1925 contest awards banquet and found herself in the midst of the Harlem Renaissance, the great outpouring of artistic expression revolving around Harlem. She became an active member of the Harlem literati and soon became the Harlem Renaissance's most colorful figure. In the fall of 1925, Hurston entered Barnard College,

the women's college of Columbia University, on a scholarship arranged by Annie Nathan Meyer. There, she studied anthropology under Franz Boas and received her degree in 1928.

Beginning in 1927, Hurston traveled throughout the South, collecting folklore, first under the sponsorship of the Association for the Study of Negro Life and History and later through various fellowships, including a Guggenheim, and the private sponsorship of Charlotte Osgood Mason, a wealthy white patron of Harlem Renaissance writers, including Langston Hughes and Alain Locke.

In 1930, Hurston and Hughes collaborated on a black folk play, *Mule Bone* (pb. 1931, pr. 1991), an undertaking that severed the personal and professional relationship between the two writers; the break was never mended and kept the play from being staged until 1991, long after the deaths of both authors. The dispute, precipitated by the question of principal authorship, while certainly unfortunate, nevertheless illustrates the fiercely independent temperament that Hurston maintained throughout her lifetime.

Zora Neale Hurston (Library of Congress)

Though the 1930's got off to a rough start with the controversy with Hughes, the decade proved to be Hurston's most productive. Hurston published her first novel, *Jonah's Gourd Vine*, in 1934, followed in rapid succession by the folklore collection *Mules and Men* in 1935; another novel, the now classic *Their Eyes Were Watching God* in 1937; another folklore collection, *Tell My Horse*, in 1938; and another novel, *Moses, Man of the Mountain*, in 1939. In addition, Hurston wrote several short stories and several essays, notably those on black culture, published in Nancy Cunard's massive collection, *Negro*, in 1934.

In 1942, Hurston published her autobiography, *Dust Tracks on a Road*. While the book won the *Saturday Review*'s Ainsfield-Wolf Award for race relations, it proved to be the last significant work of Hurston's career, although she did publish another novel, *Seraph on the Suwanee*, in 1948. There are several reasons for the decline in Hurston's popularity, the most important among them being that her folk-based literature did not fit into protest literature, the dominant literary trend of the 1940's, coupled with Hurston's growing conservatism. In addition, in September, 1948, shortly before the publication of *Seraph on the Suwanee*, Hurston was falsely charged with seducing a minor, but before the charges could be dismissed as unfounded, the black press, in particular the *Baltimore Afro-American*, had spread the story to its readers and had severely, almost irreparably, damaged Hurston's reputation. Disillusioned and outraged at her treatment by the court and the black press, Hurston moved back to the South, where she lived for the remainder of her life.

The 1950's was a tragic decade for Hurston. Her career was stagnant, and although she kept writing, she received rejection after rejection. She did, however, do some reporting for the *Pittsburgh Courier*, a black newspaper with a national circulation; published several essays; and accepted several speaking engagements. She supported herself with occasional work, including substitute teaching and writing freelance articles for various papers.

Toward the end of the 1950's, Hurston's health became increasingly fragile. She suffered from obesity, hypertension, poor diet, gallbladder trouble, ulcers, and various stomach ailments. In 1959, she suffered a stroke, and in October of that year was placed in the Saint Lucie County welfare home, where, alone and penniless, she died on January 28, 1960. She was buried by subscription a week later in a segregated cemetery, the Garden of the Heavenly Rest, in Fort Pierce, Florida.

ANALYSIS

The bulk of Zora Neale Hurston's short fiction is set in her native Florida, as are most of her novels. Even when the setting is not Florida, however, the stories are informed by the life, habits, beliefs, and idioms of the people whom Hurston knew so well, the inhabitants of Eatonville primarily. One criticism often leveled at Hurston was that she frequently masqueraded folklore as fiction, or, in other cases, imposed folklore on the fictive narrative. Whatever the merits of such criticism may be, Hurston's short stories abound with an energy and zest for life that Hurston considered instructive for her readers.

"JOHN REDDING GOES TO SEA"

Hurston's first published short story was entitled "John Redding Goes to Sea." It was published in the May, 1921, issue of *Stylus*, the literary magazine of Howard University, and was reprinted in the January, 1926, issue of *Opportunity*. While the story is obviously the work of a novice writer, with its highly contrived plot, excessive sentimentality, and shallow characterizations, its strengths are many, and Hurston would continue to draw upon and develop these strengths throughout her career.

The plot is a simple one: Young John Redding, the titular character, wants to leave his hometown to see and explore parts and things unknown. Several circumstances conspire, however, to keep him from realizing his dream. First, John's mother, the pitifully possessive, obsessive, and superstitious Matty Redding, is determined not to let John pursue his ambitions; in fact, she pleads illness and threatens to disown him if he leaves. Second, John's marriage to Stella Kanty seems to tie him permanently to his surroundings, as his new wife joins forces with his mother to discourage John's desire to travel. In addition, his mother's tantrums keep John from even joining the Navy when that opportunity comes his way. Later, when John is killed in a tempest while working with a crew to build a bridge on the St. John's River, his father forbids his body to be retrieved from the river as it floats toward the ocean. At last, John will get his wish to travel and see the world, although in death.

If the plot seems overdone and the sentimentality overwhelming, "John Redding Goes to Sea" does provide the reader with the first of many glimpses of life among black Floridians--their habits, superstitions, strengths, and shortcomings. For example, one of the more telling aspects of the story is that Matty believes that her son was cursed with "travel dust" at his birth; thus, John's desire to travel is Matty's punishment for having married his father away from a rival suitor. Hurston suspends judgment on Matty's beliefs; rather, she shows that these and other beliefs are integral parts of the life of the folk.

Another strength that is easily discernible in Hurston's first short story is her detailed rendering of setting. Hurston has a keen eye for detail, and nowhere is this more evident than in her descriptions of the lushness of Florida. This adeptness is especially present in "John Redding Goes to Sea" and in most of Hurston's other work.

By far the most important aspect of "John Redding Goes to Sea" is its theme that people must be free to develop and pursue their own dreams, a recurring theme in the Hurston canon. John Redding is deprived of self-expression and self-determination because the wishes and interpretations of others are imposed upon him. Hurston clearly has no sympathy with those who would deprive another of freedom and independence; indeed, she would adamantly oppose all such restrictive efforts throughout her career as a writer and folklorist.

"SPUNK"

Another early short story that treats a variation of this theme is "Spunk," published in the June, 1925, issue of *Opportunity*. The central character, Spunk Banks, has the spunk to live his life as he chooses, which includes taking another man's wife and parading openly around town with her. While Hurston passes no moral judgment on Banks, she makes it clear that she appreciates and admires his brassiness and his will to live his life according to his own terms.

When the story opens, Spunk Banks and Lena Kanty are openly flaunting their affair in front of the Eatonville townspeople, including Lena's husband, Joe Kanty. The other town residents make fun of Joe's weakness, his refusal to confront Spunk Banks. Later, when Joe desperately attacks Spunk with a razor, Spunk shoots and kills him. Spunk is tried and acquitted but is killed in a work-related accident, cut to death by a circle saw.

Again, superstition plays an important role here, for Spunk claims that he has been haunted by Joe Kanty's ghost. In fact, Spunk is convinced that Joe's ghost pushed him into the circle saw, and at least one other townsman agrees. As is customary in Hurston's stories, however, she makes no judgment of the rightness or wrongness of such beliefs but points out that these beliefs are very much a part of the cultural milieu of Eatonville.

"SWEAT"

Another early Eatonville story is "Sweat," published in 1926 in the only issue of the ill-fated literary magazine *Fire!*, founded by Hurston, Hughes, and Wallace Thurman. "Sweat" shows Hurston's power as a fiction writer and as a master of the short-story form. Again, the story line is a simple one. Delia Jones is a hardworking, temperate Christian woman being tormented by her arrogant, mean-spirited, and cruel husband of fifteen years, Sykes Jones, who has become tired of her and desires a new wife. Rather than simply leaving her, though, he wants to drive her away by making her life miserable. At stake is the house for which Delia's "sweat" has paid: Sykes wants it for his new mistress, but Delia refuses to leave the fruit of her labor.

Sykes uses both physical and mental cruelty to antagonize Delia, the most far-reaching of which is Delia's intense fear of snakes. When Delia's fear of the caged rattlesnake that Sykes places outside her back door subsides, Sykes places the rattlesnake in the dirty clothes hamper, hoping that it will bite and kill Delia. In an ironic twist, however, Delia escapes, and the rattlesnake bites Sykes as he fumbles for a match in the dark house. Delia listens and watches as Sykes dies a painful, agonizing death.

While "Sweat" makes use of the same superstitious beliefs as Hurston's other stories, a more complex characterization and an elaborate system of symbols are central to the story's development. In Delia, for example, readers are presented with an essentially good Christian woman who is capable of great compassion and long suffering and who discovers the capacity to hate as intensely as she loves; in Sykes, readers are shown unadulterated evil reduced to one at once pitiful and horrible in his suffering. In addition, the Christian symbolism, including the snake and the beast of burden, adds considerable interest and texture to the story. It is this texture that makes "Sweat" Hurston's most rewarding work of short fiction, for it shows her at her best as literary artist and cultural articulator.

"THE GILDED SIX-BITS"

Although Hurston turned to the longer narrative as the preferred genre during the 1930's, she continued writing short stories throughout the remainder of her career. One such story is "The Gilded Six-Bits," published in 1933, which also examines relationships between men and women. In this story, the marriage bed of a happy couple, Joe and Missie May Banks, is defiled by a city slicker, Otis D. Slemmons. Missie May has been attracted by Slemmons's gold money, which she desires to get for her husband. The gold pieces, however, turn out to be gold-plated. Hurston's message is nearly cliché-- "all that glitters is not gold"--but she goes a step further to establish the idea that true love transcends all things. Joe and Missie May are reconciled at the end of the story.

"COCK ROBIN, BEALE STREET"

Hurston's last stories are fables that seem to have only comic value but do, however, advance serious thoughts, such as the ridiculousness of the idea of race purity in "Cock Robin, Beale Street," or the equal ridiculousness of the idea that the North was better for blacks in "Story in Harlem Slang." While these stories are not artistic achievements, they do provide interesting aspects of the Hurston canon.

In many ways, Hurston's short stories are apprentice works to her novels. In these stories, she introduced most of the themes, character types, settings, techniques, and concerns upon which she later elaborated during her most productive and artistic period, the

1930's. This observation, however, does not suggest that her short stories are inferior works. On the contrary, much of the best of Hurston can be found in these early stories.

OTHER MAJOR WORKS

LONG FICTION: *Jonah's Gourd Vine*, 1934; *Their Eyes Were Watching God*, 1937; *Moses, Man of the Mountain*, 1939; *Seraph on the Suwanee*, 1948.

PLAYS: *Color Struck*, pb. 1926; *The First One*, pb. 1927; *Mule Bone*, pb. 1931 (with Langston Hughes); *Polk County*, pb. 1944, pr. 2002.

NONFICTION: *Mules and Men*, 1935; *Tell My Horse*, 1938; *Dust Tracks on a Road*, 1942; *The Sanctified Church*, 1981; *Folklore, Memoirs, and Other Writings*, 1995; *Go Gator and Muddy the Water: Writings*, 1999 (Pamela Bordelon, editor); *Every Tongue Got to Confess: Negro Folk-tales from the Gulf States*, 2001; *Zora Neale Hurston: A Life in Letters*, 2002 (Carla Kaplan, editor).

MISCELLANEOUS: *I Love Myself When I Am Laughing . . . and Then Again When I Am Looking Mean and Impressive: A Zora Neale Hurston Reader*, 1979 (Alice Walker, editor).

BIBLIOGRAPHY

Campbell, Josie P. *Student Companion to Zora Neale Hurston*. Westport, Conn.: Greenwood Press, 2001. Introductory overview of Hurston's life and work, with a chapter devoted to her short fiction.

Chinn, Nancy, and Elizabeth E. Dunn. "'The Ring of Singing Metal on Wood': Zora Neale Hurston's Artistry in 'The Gilded Six-Bits.'" *The Mississippi Quarterly* 49 (Fall, 1996): 775-790. Discusses how Hurston uses setting, ritual, dialect, and the nature of human relationships in the story. Argues that the story provides a solution to the problem of reconciling her rural Florida childhood with her liberal arts education and training.

Cobb-Moore, Geneva. "Zora Neale Hurston as Local Colorist." *The Southern Literary Journal* 26 (Spring, 1994): 25-34. Discusses how Hurston's creation of folk characters enlarges the meaning of local color literature. Shows how Hurston proves that while physical bodies can be restricted, the imagination is always free.

Cooper, Jan. "Zora Neale Hurston Was Always a Southerner Too." In *The Female Tradition in Southern Literature*, edited by Carol S. Manning. Urbana: University of Illinois Press, 1993. Examines the hitherto neglected role that Hurston played in the Southern Renaissance between 1920 and 1950. Argues that Hurston's fiction is informed by a modern southern agrarian sense of community. Suggests that the Southern Renaissance was a transracial, cross-cultural product of the South..

Donlon, Jocelyn Hazelwood. "Porches, Stories, Power: Spatial and Racial Intersections in Faulkner and Hurston." *Journal of American Culture* 19 (Winter, 1996): 95-110. Comments on the role of the porch in Faulkner and Hurston's fiction as a transitional space between the public and the private where the individual can negotiate an identity by telling stories.

Gelfant, Blanche H., ed. *The Columbia Companion to the Twentieth-Century American Short Story*. New York: Columbia University Press, 2000. Includes a chapter in which Hurston's short stories are analyzed.

Glassman, Steve, and Kathryn Lee Siedel, eds. *Zora in Florida*. Orlando: University of Central Florida Press, 1991. This collection of essays by seventeen Hurston scholars explores the overall presence and influence of Florida in and on her works. This collection originated at a Hurston symposium held in Daytona Beach, Florida, in November, 1989, and includes an excellent introduction to the importance of Florida in the study of Hurston.

Hemenway, Robert E. *Zora Neale Hurston: A Literary Biography*. Urbana: University of Illinois Press, 1977. Perhaps the best extant work on Hurston. Hemenway's painstakingly researched study of Hurston's life and literary career was crucial in rescuing Hurston from neglect and establishing her as a major American writer. Although some of the facts of Hurston's chronology have been corrected by later scholarship, Hemenway's study is the most valuable introduction to Hurston's work available. Includes a bibliography of published and unpublished works by Hurston.

Hill, Lynda Marion. *Social Rituals and the Verbal Art of Zora Neale Hurston*. Washington, D.C.: Howard University Press, 1996. Contains chapters on Hurston's treatment of everyday life, science and humanism, folklore, and color, race, and class. Hill also considers dramatic reenactments of Hurston's writing. Includes notes, bibliography, and an appendix on "characteristics of Negro expression."

Howard, Lillie P. *Zora Neale Hurston*. Boston: Twayne, 1980. A good general introduction to the life and works of Hurston. Contains valuable plot summaries and commentaries on Hurston's works. Supplemented by a chronology and a bibliography.

Hurston, Lucy Anne. *Speak, So You Can Speak Again: The Life of Zora Neale Hurston*. New York: Doubleday, 2004. A brief biography written by Hurston's niece. Most notable for the inclusion of rare photographs, writings, and other multimedia personal artifacts. Also contains an audio compact disc of Hurston reading and singing.

Jones, Sharon L. "'How It Feels to Be Colored Me': Social Protest in the Fiction of Zora Neal Hurston." In *Rereading the Harlem Renaissance: Race, Class, and Gender in the Fiction of Jessie Fauset, Zora Neale Hurston, and Dorothy West*. Westport, Conn.: Greenwood Press, 2002. Examines how Hurston and the two other African American women writers sought to challenge oppression in their works. The chapter devoted to Hurston analyzes some of the short fiction in addition to her novels.

King, Lovalerie. *The Cambridge Introduction to Zora Neale Hurston*. New York: Cambridge University Press, 2008. Devotes several pages to an overview of Hurston's short fiction, as well as providing information about her life, the context in which her works were created, and her critical reception.

Newsom, Adele S. *Zora Neale Hurston: A Reference Guide*. Boston: G. K. Hall, 1987. A catalog of Hurston criticism spanning the years 1931-1986, arranged chronologically with annotations. This source is an invaluable aid to serious scholars of Hurston and an especially useful resource for all inquiries. Also contains an introduction to the criticism of Hurston's writings.

Plant, Deborah G. *Zora Neale Hurston: A Biography of the Spirit*. Westport, Conn.: Praeger, 2007. A biography of Hurston that focuses on her strength and tenacity of spirit.Draws on Hurston's 1942 autobiography, *Dust Tracks on a Road*, as well as newly discovered sources.

_____, ed. *"The Inside Light": New Critical Essays on Zora Neale Hurston*. Santa Barbara, Calif.: Praeger, 2010. Collection of twenty newly commissioned essays that apply the latest research and analytical techniques to examine Hurston's writings.

Includes discussions of Hurston in the twenty-first century, Hurston as a pioneering social scientist, masculinity in her texts, and environmental elements in her works.

West, Margaret Genevieve. *Zora Neale Hurston and American Literary Culture*. Gainesville: University Press of Florida, 2005. A chronicle of Hurston's literary career and an examination of why her writing did not gain popularity until long after her death.

Warren J. Carson

I

WASHINGTON IRVING

Born: New York, New York; April 3, 1783
Died: Tarrytown, New York; November 28, 1859
Also known as: Jonathan Oldstyle, Geoffrey Crayon

PRINCIPAL SHORT FICTION

The Sketch Book of Geoffrey Crayon, Gent.,
    1819-1820
Bracebridge Hall, 1822
Tales of a Traveller, 1824
The Alhambra, 1832
Legends of the Conquest of Spain, 1835
The Complete Tales of Washington Irving, 1975,
    reprint 1998 (Charles Neider, editor)

OTHER LITERARY FORMS

Washington Irving distinguished himself in a variety of genres. His finest and most typical book, *The Sketch Book of Geoffrey Crayon, Gent.*, blends essay, sketch, history, travel, humor, and short story; his first best seller was a satire, *A History of New York from the Beginning of the World to the End of the Dutch Dynasties* (1809); he coauthored a successful play, *Charles the Second: Or, The Merry Monarch* (pr. 1824); but he devoted the latter and most prolific part of his career to books of travel and especially of history.

ACHIEVEMENTS

Washington Irving was America's first internationally recognized author. While he achieved national notoriety with his satiric *A History of New York*, his fame abroad was made with *The Sketch Book of Geoffrey Crayon, Gent.* Irving was a prolific writer throughout his life, from his first collaborations with his brother William and friend James Kirke Paulding, to his many biographies of well-known historical figures, including George Washington. Among his most successful works were his collections of sketches and tales, a distinction then made between realistic and imaginative types of fiction. His sketches often make use of historical sources, while the tales usually derive from traditional folktales. His best-known stories, "Rip Van Winkle" and "The Legend of Sleepy Hollow," although largely copied from German folktales, still maintain an originality through their American settings and Irving's own gently humorous style.

BIOGRAPHY

The eleventh and last child of a successful merchant, Washington Irving, somewhat frail and indulged as he was growing up, was the favorite child of his Anglican mother and Presbyterian minister father. As a young man, Irving studied law in the office of Josiah Ogden Hoffman, to whose daughter he was attracted, and enjoyed the social and cultural advantages of New York City as something of a gentleman-playboy. At this time, he dabbled in satirical writing in serial publications. He gained a certain amount of cosmopolitan sophistication with a tour of Europe in 1804-1806, during which time he kept a journal.

Irving was admitted to the New York bar at the age of twenty-three and nominally began to work as a lawyer on Wall Street, although he practiced little. Instead, he wrote serial essays with his brother and James Kirke Paulding for a periodical they called *Salmagundi*, modeled on Joseph Addison's *Spectator*, "to instruct the young, reform the old, correct the town, and castigate the age." This amounted to making light fun of fashion and social mores in high society, although occasionally they made jabs at Thomas Jefferson's "logocratic" democracy.

"Diedrich Knickerbocker's" *A History of New York* followed in 1809; originally intended as a parody of a pretentious New York guidebook, it had become instead a comic history of the Dutch in New York. When

Matilda Hoffman died in the same year, Irving, distraught, stopped writing for a time. He moved in 1811 to Washington, D.C., to lobby for the Irving brothers' importing firm. Still affected by Matilda's death, he drifted into several different occupations, lost the brothers' firm to bankruptcy, yet benefited from his literary contacts to the point where he began to pursue writing with renewed effort. By the time he published *The Sketch Book of Geoffrey Crayon, Gent.* in 1819, he was on his way to supporting himself through his writing. In order to find original materials for his sketches, he made various trips through Europe and America, including a ministry to Spain; he returned to New York finally in 1832. His long absence, reminiscent of Rip Van Winkle's, provided him with a new perspective on the United States, whose the western frontier was beginning to open; he packed again, this time for the West, and wrote many of his books out of the experience. He finally returned home to the Hudson, ensconced in family and friends, where he died in 1859.

ANALYSIS

Washington Irving's masterpiece, *The Sketch Book of Geoffrey Crayon, Gent.*, has a historical importance few American books can match. No previous American book achieved a really significant popular and critical success in England, the only arena of opinion which then mattered; but Irving demonstrated that an American could write not only well but also brilliantly even by British standards. In fact, throughout the century English as well as American schoolboys studied Irving's book as a model of graceful prose.

Irving had achieved some popularity in his own country well before the British triumphs. In 1807-1808, Irving, his brother William, and James Kirke Paulding collaborated on the independently published periodical series, *Salmagundi*. Since the project was a true collaboration, scholars are in doubt as to precisely who deserves credit for precisely what, but two pieces deserve particular notice. "Sketches from Nature" sentimentally sketches two old bachelors, one of whom restores the spirits of the other by leading him through scenes reminiscent of their youth. "The Little Man in Black" is supposedly a traditional story passed through

generations of a single family. Irving here introduces another old bachelor, who wanders into the village a stranger to all and sets up housekeeping in a decrepit house rumored to be haunted. First ostracized by the adults, then tormented by the local children, ultimately he dies by starvation, in his last moments forgiving all, a true but misunderstood Christian.

Both pieces display Irving's graceful style, his prevalent sentimentality, and his wholehearted commitment to charming, pleasing, and entertaining his audience. Both feature an old bachelor stereotype that he inherited from the Addisonian tradition and continued to exploit in later works. The pieces differ in their formal focus, however, and aptly illustrate the two poles of Irving's fictional nature. The second shows his fondness for the tale tradition: He cites a source in family folklore; the narrative hangs on striking incident; and he flavors the atmosphere with a suggestion of the supernatural. The first features virtues of the periodical essay: evocation of character divorced from dramatic incident; a style dominated by smoothness and by descriptions strong on concrete detail; and an

Washington Irving (Library of Congress)

essentially realistic atmosphere. Irving's unique genius led him to combine the best of both traditions in his finest fiction and thereby to create the modern short story in America.

Irving's early career coincided with the rise of Romanticism, and the movement strongly influenced his greatest book, *The Sketch Book of Geoffrey Crayon, Gent.* Here he capitalized on the element that strongly marks his most successful stories: imagination. Consistently, Irving's most successful characters, and stories, are those which most successfully exploit the imagination.

"THE SPECTRE BRIDEGROOM"

In "The Spectre Bridegroom," the title character triumphs not through strength, physical skills, or intelligence, but rather through manipulating the imaginations of those who would oppose his aims. The story's first section humorously describes a bellicose old widower, the Baron Von Landshort, who has gathered a vast audience, consisting mostly of poor relatives properly cognizant of his high status, to celebrate his only daughter's marriage to a young count whom none of them has ever seen. In the story's second part, the reader learns that as the count and his friend Herman Von Starkenfaust journey to the castle, they are beset by bandits; the outlaws mortally wound the count who, with his last breath, begs Von Starkenfaust to relay his excuses to the wedding party. The story's third part returns to the castle where the long-delayed wedding party finally welcomes a pale, melancholy young man. The silent stranger hears the garrulous Baron speak on, among other matters, his family's long-standing feud with the Von Starkenfaust family; meanwhile the young man wins the daughter's heart. He shortly leaves, declaring he must be buried at the cathedral. The next night the daughter's two guardian aunts tell ghost stories until they are terrified by spying the Spectre Bridegroom outside the window; the daughter sleeps apart from her aunts for three nights, encouraging their fears all the while, and finally absconds. When she returns with her husband, Von Starkenfaust, who had pretended to be the Spectre, they both are reconciled with the Baron and live happily ever after.

By becoming in one sense artists themselves, Herman and his bride both manipulate the imaginations of the Baron, the aunts, and the entire wedding party to make their courtship and elopement possible; here, happily, the "dupees" lose nothing and share the ultimate happiness of the dupers. There are at least three dimensions to "The Spectre Bridegroom": As it is read, one can imaginatively identify with the duped family and believe the Spectre genuine, or alternately identify with the young couple innocently manipulating their elders. A third dimension enters when the reader recalls the personality of the frame's Swiss taleteller, occasionally interrupting himself with "a roguish leer and a sly joke for the buxom kitchen maid" and himself responsible (it is surely not the modest and proper Geoffrey Crayon or Washington Irving) for the suggestive antlers above the prospective bridegroom's head at the feast.

"RIP VAN WINKLE"

The narrative perspectives informing Irving's single greatest achievement, "Rip Van Winkle," radiate even greater complexities. At the simplest level the core experience is that of Rip himself, a good-natured idler married to a termagant who drives him from the house with her temper. While hunting in the woods, Rip pauses to assist a curious little man hefting a keg; in a natural amphitheater he discovers dwarfish sailors in archaic dress playing at ninepins. Rip drinks, falls asleep, and awakens the next morning alone on the mountainside. In a subtle, profound, and eerily effective sequence, Irving details Rip's progressive disorientation and complete loss of identity. The disintegration begins mildly enough--Rip notices the decayed gun (a thief's substitute he thinks), his dog's absence, some stiffness in his own body--each clue is emotionally more significant than the last, but each may be easily explained. Rip next notices changes in nature--a dry gully has become a raging stream, a ravine has been closed by a rockslide; these are more dramatic alterations, but still explainable after a long night's sleep.

Upon entering the village, he discovers no one but strangers and all in strange dress; he finds his house has decayed, his wife and children have disappeared; buildings have changed, as well as the political situation and even the very manner and behavior of the people. In a terrible climax, when Irving for once declines to mute the genuine horror, Rip profoundly questions his own identity. When he desperately asks if anyone knows poor Rip Van Winkle, fingers point to another ragged idler at the fringe, the very image of Rip himself as he had ascended the mountain. Even Poe or Franz Kafka never painted a loss of identity more absolute, more profound, more credible, more terrible. After a moment of horror, Irving's sentimental good humor immediately reasserts itself. Rip's now-adult daughter appears and recognizes him; the ragged idler turns out to be his son, Rip, Jr. Rip himself hesitates for a moment, but, upon learning that his wife has died "but a short time since," declares his identity and commences reintegrating himself in the community, eventually to become an honored patriarch, renowned for recounting his marvelous experience.

Thus is the nature of the core narrative, which is almost all most people ever read. The reader values the story for its profound mythic reverberations; after all, throughout Western civilization Irving's Rip has become an archetype of time lost. The reader may also appreciate Irving's amoral toying with lifestyles, although the Yankee/Benjamin Franklin lifestyle Rip's wife advocates and which leads to her death (she bursts a blood vessel while haggling) fails to trap Rip; he triumphs by championing the relatively unambitious, self-indulgent lifestyle Irving identifies with the Dutch. Still, many people feel tempted to reject the piece as a simplistic fairy tale dependent on supernatural machinery for its appeal and effect. This is a mistake.

Those who read the full story as Irving wrote it will discover, in the headnote, that Irving chose to relate the story not from the point of view of an omniscient narrator but from that of Diedrich Knickerbocker, the dunderheaded comic persona to whom years earlier he had ascribed the burlesque *A History of New York*. The presence of such a narrator--and Irving went to some trouble to introduce him--authorizes readers to reject the supernatural elements and believe, as many of Rip's auditors believed, that in actuality Rip simply tired of his wife, ran away for twenty years, and concocted a cock-and-bull story to justify his absence. Looking closer, the reader discovers copious hints that this is precisely what happened: Rip's reluctance to

become Rip again until he is sure his wife is dead; the fact that when his neighbors hear the story they "wink at each other and put their tongues in their cheeks"; and the fact that, until he finally established a satisfactory version of the events, he was observed "to vary on some points every time he told it." In the concluding footnote, even dim Diedrich Knickerbocker acknowledges the story's doubtfulness but provides as evidence of its truth the fact that he has heard even stranger supernatural stories of the Catskills, and that to authenticate his story Rip signed a certificate in the presence of a justice of the peace. "The story, therefore, is beyond the possibility of doubt." Irving clearly intends to convince his closest readers that Rip, like the couple in "The Spectre Bridegroom," triumphed over circumstances by a creative manipulation of imagination.

"THE LEGEND OF SLEEPY HOLLOW"

In "The Legend of Sleepy Hollow" the source is again Diedrich Knickerbocker, and again, creatively manipulating the imaginations of others proves the key to success. The pleasant little Dutch community of Sleepy Hollow has imported a tall, grotesquely lanky Yankee as schoolmaster, Ichabod Crane. Although he is prey to the schoolboys' endless pranks, he himself ravenously and endlessly preys on the foodstuffs of the boys' parents. Ichabod finally determines to set his cap for the pretty daughter of a wealthy farmer, but Brom Bones, the handsome, Herculean local hero, has likewise determined to court the girl. The climax comes when the principals gather with the entire community at a dance, feast, and "quilting frolic" held at Katrina Van Tassel's home. Brom fills the timorous and credulous Ichabod full of tales of a horrible specter, the ghost of a Hessian soldier beheaded by a cannonball, who inhabits the region through which Ichabod must ride that night to return home. As he makes his lonely journey back, Ichabod encounters the dark figure who carries his head under his arm rather than on his neck and who runs him a frightful race to a bridge. At the climax the figure hurls his head and strikes Ichabod, who disappears, never to be seen in the village again. Brom marries Katrina, and years later the locals discover that Ichabod turned lawyer, politician, and newspaperman, and finally became a "justice of the Ten Pound Court."

Again it is the character who creatively manipulates the imagination who carries the day; the manipulatee wins only the consolation prize. Again the Dutch spirit triumphs over the Yankee. In this story there is something quite new, however; for the first time in American literature there is, in the characterization of Brom Bones, the figure of the frontiersman so important to American literature and American popular culture: physically imposing, self-confident, rough and ready, untutored but endowed with great natural virtues, gifted with a rude sense of chivalry, at home on the fringes of civilization, and incorporating in his own being the finer virtues of both the wilderness and the settlements. Irving here brilliantly anticipated both the essence of southwestern humor and of James Fenimore Cooper's seminal Westerns.

Irving wrote a great many other stories, including several romantic tales set in Spain, most of them flawed by superficiality and sentimentality; he also produced a number of gothic stories, some of which are still read with pleasure, among them "The Adventure of the German Student" and "The Devil and Tom Walker." Irving, however, reached his highest point in his first published short story, "Rip Van Winkle." He never equaled it in any subsequent story--but then, only a tiny handful of writers ever have.

OTHER MAJOR WORKS

PLAY: *Charles the Second: Or, The Merry Monarch*, pb. 1824 (with John Howard Payne).

NONFICTION: *A History of New York from the Beginning of the World to the End of the Dutch Dynasties*, 1809; *Biography of James Lawrence*, 1813; *A History of the Life and Voyages of Christopher Columbus*, 1828; *A Chronicle of the Conquest of Granada*, 1829; *Voyages and Discoveries of the Companions of Columbus*, 1831; *A Tour of the Prairies*, 1835; *Astoria*, 1836; *The Adventures of Captain Bonneville*, 1837; *The Life of Oliver Goldsmith*, 1849; *The Life of George Washington*, 1855-1859 (5 volumes).

MISCELLANEOUS: *The Complete Works of Washington Irving*, 1969-1989 (30 volumes).

BIBLIOGRAPHY

Aderman, Ralph M., ed. *Critical Essays on Washington Irving*. Boston: G. K. Hall, 1990. A collection of essays from both the nineteenth and twentieth centuries. Includes discussions of Irving's art and literary debts, the relationship of his stories to his culture, and his generic heritage.

Antelyes, Peter. *Tales of Adventurous Enterprise: Washington Irving and the Poetics of Western Expansion*. New York: Columbia University Press, 1990. Explores the theme of the western frontier in Irving's works.

Bowden, Mary Weatherspoon. *Washington Irving*. Boston: Twayne, 1981. Bowden's general study of Irving discusses the major works in chronological order of composition. While her focus is literary, Bowden begins each chapter with useful biographical information about Irving at the time. The section dealing with *The Sketch Book of Geoffrey Crayon, Gent.* is particularly successful in describing Irving's attitudes toward England and how these are revealed in the sketches.

Bradley, Elizabeth L. *Knickerbocker: The Myth Behind New York*. New Brunswick, N.J.: Rivergate Books, 2009. Examines how Irving's character Diedrich Knickerbocker, the narrator of *A History of New York* and some of the short stories, shaped the identity of New York City. Bradley argues that Knickerbocker inspired New Yorkers to "assert their own idiosyncratic relationship to the city, and to its history."

Hiller, Alice. "'An Avenue to Some Degree of Profit and Reputation': *The Sketch Book* as Washington Irving's Entree and Undoing." *Journal of American Studies* 31 (August, 1997): 275-293. Claims that some of Irving's personal correspondence reveals that *The Sketch Book of Geoffrey Crayon, Gent.* may have been pitched deliberately at the British market, resulting in a paralysis of Irving's ability to write.

Jones, Brian Jay. *Washington Irving: An American Original*. New York: Arcade, 2008. Jones's biography focuses on Irving's private life. Irving's personality is brought to life as Jones delves into his likes and dislikes, and his relationships with friends and lovers.

Killick, Tim. "Washington Irving: Geoffrey Crayon and the Market for Short Fiction." In *British Short Fiction in the Early Nineteenth Century: The Rise of the Tale*. Burlington, Vt.: Ashgate, 2008. Assesses the influence of Irving's short stories on British publishing. The popularity of Irving's short-story collections led British writers and publishers to present short fiction in book-length volumes in order to compete with the novel, and in the process they elevated the short story to a legitimate and respectable literary genre.

McFarland, Philip. *Sojourners*. New York: Atheneum, 1979. While not a conventional biography, this study of Irving's life situates the writer in his various geographic, historic, and literary contexts. Mc-Farland explores in detail the life of Irving, interweaving his biography with those of other important Americans of the time, among them Aaron Burr, the abolitionist John Brown, and businessman John Jacob Astor.

Myers, Andrew B., ed. *A Century of Commentary on the Works of Washington Irving*. Tarrytown, N.Y.: Sleepy Hollow Restorations, 1976. This collection, divided into four chronologically ordered sections, offers a wide range of interpretations of Washington Irving. Part 1 includes essays by contemporaries of Irving, such as William Cullen Bryant and Henry Wadsworth Longfellow; part 2 covers evaluations from the beginning of the nineteenth century. Early twentieth century scholars of American literature, such as Fred Lewis Pattee, Vernon Louis Parrington, and Van Wyck Brooks, are represented in part 3, and part 4 covers the period 1945 to 1975. The collection gives an excellent overview of the development of Irving criticism and provides a point of departure for further investigations.

Piacentino, Ed. "'Sleepy Hollow' Comes South: Washington Irving's Influence on Old Southwestern Humor." *The Southern Literary Journal* 30 (Fall, 1997): 27-42. Examines how nineteenth century southern backwoods humorists adapted Irving's "The Legend of Sleepy Hollow" to a southern setting. Discusses a number of works with clear parallels to Irving's story.

Plummer, Laura, and Michael Nelson. "'Girls Can Take Care of Themselves': Gender and Storytelling in Washington Irving's 'The Legend of Sleepy Hollow.'" *Studies in Short Fiction* 30 (Spring, 1993): 175-184. Argues that Sleepy Hollow is female-centered place. The tales that circulate in the region focus on emasculated, headless spirits and serve to drive out masculine interlopers like Ichabod Crane, thus preserving the old Dutch domesticity based on wives' tales.

Rubin-Dorsky, Jeffrey. *Adrift in the Old World: The Psychological Pilgrimage of Washington Irving*. Chicago: University of Chicago Press, 1988. In this study of Irving's short fiction, Rubin-Dorsky sets out to establish Irving's Americanness, thus reversing a critical tradition that marked him as primarily imitative of British prose style. By placing Irving within his historical context, Rubin-Dorsky underscores his central position in early American letters.

Scofield, Martin. "The Short Story as Ironic Myth: Washington Irving and William Austin." In *The Cambridge Introduction to the American Short Story*. New York: Cambridge University Press, 2006. Describes how Washington's short fiction, including "Rip Van Winkle" and "The Legend of Sleepy Hollow," laid the foundations for a uniquely American genre that would be used to greater achievement by Nathaniel Hawthorne.

Tuttleton, James W., ed. *Washington Irving: The Critical Reaction*. New York: AMS Press, 1993. Contains essays providing critical interpretations of Irving's works.

Wagenknecht, Edward. *Washington Irving: Moderation Displayed*. New York: Oxford University Press, 1962. Wagenknecht has divided his study of Irving into three parts: the life, the man, and the work. "The Man" is by far the largest section and provides an engaging portrait of Irving's personal life and development as a writer. Wagenknecht's biography offers a more streamlined alternative to Stanley T. Williams's two-volume work (below).

Williams, Stanley T. *The Life of Washington Irving*. 2 vols. New York: Oxford University Press, 1935. This very thorough biography of "the first American man of letters" provides a wealth of biographical and literary detail about Irving. Volume 1 is most useful for those interested in Irving's short fiction, as it covers his life and work up to *The Alhambra*. The chapters are organized according to Irving's places of travel or the titles of his works, an arrangement which highlights the various contexts in which Irving wrote.

Walter Evans
Updated by Ann A. Merrill